STRENGTHENING THE DSM®

AF584576

Anne Petrovich, PhD, LCSW, is a professor emerita at California State University, Fresno, Department of Social Work Education, where she has taught foundation generalist and multisystems social work practice; advanced social work practice with individuals, couples and families; and advanced elective courses focused on elders, sexuality, and trauma. She is the author of several journal articles related to multicultural practice, elders, and performance anxiety and a recipient of awards for excellence in teaching and clinical practice. Dr. Petrovich is licensed in both clinical social work and psychology. She has an extensive background in community, hospital, and mental health settings as a clinician, supervisor, and administrator and maintains a small private practice.

Betty Garcia, PhD, LCSW, is a professor at California State University, Fresno, Department of Social Work Education she is also a licensed clinical social worker. She has chaired the Council on Social Work Education (CSWE) Track on Cultural Competence, the National Association of Social Workers (NASW) National Committee on Racial and Ethnic Diversity (NCORED), and sat on the NASW and CSWE boards of directors. She is the coauthor of texts on teaching diversity content and has authored several publications on culturally congruent practice, social justice, substance abuse, and immigration. Dr. Garcia has practiced in various community-based mental and forensic mental health settings; she teaches courses on public mental health, group work, practice with couples and families, and interprofessional collaboration.

STRENGTHENING THE DSM®
Incorporating Resilience and Cultural Competence

SECOND EDITION

Anne Petrovich, PhD, LCSW

Betty Garcia, PhD, LCSW

SPRINGER PUBLISHING COMPANY
NEW YORK

Copyright © 2016 Springer Publishing Company, LLC

All rights reserved.

No part of this publication may be reproduced, stored in a retrieval system, or transmitted in any form or by any means, electronic, mechanical, photocopying, recording, or otherwise, without the prior permission of Springer Publishing Company, LLC, or authorization through payment of the appropriate fees to the Copyright Clearance Center, Inc., 222 Rosewood Drive, Danvers, MA 01923, 978-750-8400, fax 978-646-8600, info@copyright.com or on the Web at www.copyright.com.

Springer Publishing Company, LLC
11 West 42nd Street
New York, NY 10036
www.springerpub.com

Acquisitions Editor: Stephanie Drew
Production Editor: Michael O'Connor
Composition: diacriTech

ISBN: 978-0-8261-2662-7
E-book ISBN: 978-0-8261-2663-4

15 16 17 18 19 / 5 4 3 2 1

Publisher's Acknowledgments

Springer Publishing Company recognizes that the *DSM*® is a registered service mark of American Psychiatric Association (APA) and has applied this service mark to the first mention of the manual in each of the chapters in the book and on its cover.

The author and the publisher of this Work have made every effort to use sources believed to be reliable to provide information that is accurate and compatible with the standards generally accepted at the time of publication. The author and publisher shall not be liable for any special, consequential, or exemplary damages resulting, in whole or in part, from the readers' use of, or reliance on, the information contained in this book. The publisher has no responsibility for the persistence or accuracy of URLs for external or third-party Internet websites referred to in this publication and does not guarantee that any content on such websites is, or will remain, accurate or appropriate.

Library of Congress Cataloging-in-Publication Data
Petrovich, Anne.
Strengthening the DSM® : incorporating resilience and cultural competence / Anne Petrovich, PhD, LCSW, Betty Garcia, PhD, LCSW. — 2nd edition.
pages cm
Revision of: Strengthening the DSM / Betty Garcia, Anne Petrovich.
Includes index.
ISBN 978-0-8261-2662-7 — ISBN 978-0-8261-2663-4 (e-book)
1. Mental illness—Diagnosis. 2. Psychiatric rating scales. 3. Cultural pluralism. I. Garcia, Betty. II. Title.
RC473.P78G37 2015
616.89—dc23
2015014347

Special discounts on bulk quantities of our books are available to corporations, professional associations, pharmaceutical companies, health care organizations, and other qualifying groups. If you are interested in a custom book, including chapters from more than one of our titles, we can provide that service as well.
For details, please contact:
Special Sales Department, Springer Publishing Company, LLC
11 West 42nd Street, 15th Floor, New York, NY 10036-8002
Phone: 877-687-7476 or 212-431-4370; Fax: 212-941-7842
E-mail: sales@springerpub.com

Printed in the United States of America by Gasch Printing.

We dedicate this book to the individuals and their families who, through their actions, demonstrate the power of hope in managing and living with a mental disorder.

Contents

Foreword

The *DSM-III* multiaxial system was an important step forward in the official recognition of the importance of nondiagnostic factors for treatment formulation. This system included separate axes for psychosocial factors and global functioning, with the recognition that accurate and thorough assessment is necessary (although not sufficient) for effective treatment. The text of *DSM-III* also provided epidemiologic information in categories such as age at onset, course, prevalence, gender distribution, predisposing factors, and familial pattern.

As much of a step forward as *DSM-III* was in offering mental health practitioners a language with which to communicate, however, its focus remained on psychopathology—what was wrong with the organism. *DSM-III* and its followers, *DSM-III-R* and *DSM-IV*, did not discuss the other side of the coin—how to recognize and utilize diversity and an individual's resilience in the assessment and treatment of his or her mental disorder. With the first edition of this book, Drs. Garcia and Petrovich provided an important missing piece for our quiver of assessment tools. Now that *DSM-5* has eliminated the multiaxial system, Drs. Petrovich and Garcia have reformulated their assessment and treatment strategies to focus on diversity and resilience, two components that may be more likely to be overlooked without the structure of separate axes. The text of *DSM-5* still includes comments about culture-related diagnostic issues, and risk and prognostic factors, but the basic focus remains on psychopathology.

This new edition emphasizes the need for practitioners to take a broader view in our approach to assessment and treatment formulation and to understand and appreciate the diversity of our clients, and how their different cultures and life circumstances affect their needs today. This more panoramic view encourages us to keep in mind the whole person within a particular environment, from her or his own internal strengths to her or his family factors and other social supports, and even the political context of her or his world. Numerous case examples illustrate the benefits of taking into account our clients' cultural backgrounds and how these affect their patterns of behavior and the resources they can draw upon to deal with or recover from their mental illness.

The first chapter of this book introduces the important role of culture and how it affects our experience of and expression of stress, as well as how it affects our help-seeking behavior. An appreciation of these factors is necessary to understand the boundary between psychopathology and normality. This leads the reader to a multicultural perspective on mental health, acknowledging the complexity of factors that make up our social identities and contribute to personal resilience. The second chapter, illustrated with compelling case examples, reviews the development of the *DSM*® and adds a new model for assessing sources of resiliency and understanding the importance of diversity.

The chapters that follow focus on different major sections of the *DSM-5* classification. Each chapter begins with a comprehensive description of the disorder(s) being covered, and how the diagnostic criteria have changed from *DSM-IV* to *DSM-5*. Current thinking about the etiology and course of the disorder of focus is then reviewed, followed by a section on evidence-informed practice that lays out leading therapeutic approaches to treating these disorders (for mood disorders, for example, this includes psychopharmacological and psychosocial interventions and the importance of matching the intervention to the patient).

A discussion of equity and diversity issues is followed by a description of strength-based contributions to the diagnosis and treatment of these disorders. Each chapter concludes with a case study of one of the major diagnostic categories covered in the chapter that is discussed with and without a diversity and resiliency formulation. Many of the chapters end with a list of suggested discussion questions and activities, and all chapters end with an extensive list of references. Throughout, many case illustrations are provided, and bulleted key points are highlighted in summary boxes to reinforce the main takeaways.

The authors don't shy away from biological hypotheses about etiology and treatment, as many non-medical texts do. It is important for mental health professionals to have a full appreciation of the range of factors that affect mental health, including biological ones, so this content is particularly appreciated.

Drs. Petrovich and Garcia bring rich multidisciplinary backgrounds as clinical social workers and psychologists who practice as well as teach, and they have written a book as useful for practitioners as for teachers. With rich case examples and dozens of teaching aids, this comprehensive book will help all mental health practitioners to think beyond the strict framework included in the *DSM*, and evaluate and treat our clients with the whole person in mind.

Janet B. W. Williams, DSW
Text Editor, *DSM-III* and *DSM-III-R*
Member, Task Force on *DSM-IV*
Chair, Multiaxial Issues Work Group, *DSM-IV*

Professor Emerita
Departments of Psychiatry and Neurology
College of Physicians and Surgeons
Columbia University

Preface

The *DSM-5* signifies a major change in the diagnostic framework. The multiaxial system, introduced in the *DSM-III* and continued through the *DSM-IV-TR*, has been eliminated. The *DSM-III* was an important step forward because its multiaxial format promoted a view of individuals in the context of their lived experience and encouraged the exploration of important nondiagnostic factors relevant to effective treatment A major challenge with the utilization of the *DSM-5* is to introduce diagnostic protocols that focus on what has been lost with the elimination of the multiaxial system. In addition, the challenge for the clinician or educator is to find assessment formulations that address the whole person in her real-life contexts, which offer diverse sources of strength and resiliency to counterbalance sources of stress.

We were inspired to write the first edition of this book due to an interest in addressing the long-standing discontent with the ability of the *DSM*® to offer a diagnostic formulation that takes into account the rich diversity of life contexts and provides a coherent taxonomy as a guide to treatment decisions. The introduction of the *DSM-5* now raises even more challenges to provide a realistic assessment that is functional and has relevance for all populations regardless of history, culture, and life conditions. We strongly believe that effective diagnosis requires a transactional perspective that views individuals in their biopsychosocial, cultural, and spiritual totality, in the context of their history and in relation to strengths originating in personal, family, community, and cultural sources.

The first edition focused on the need for culturally attuned clinical practice that recognizes disparities in mental health service delivery and treatment and greater integration of the individual's strengths and resources, both internal and external, into the clinical formulation. The introduction of the *DSM-5* has sharpened the focus of this second edition in several ways. The exclusion of an individual's psychological, interpersonal, community, cultural, and spiritual sources of strength and resiliency from the current diagnostic classification system and diagnostic process results in the omission of rich and complex sources of information essential for a competent diagnosis (Alegria et al., 2008). This exclusion also undermines identification of vital social support and empowerment. As a consequence, an accurate understanding of the individual in context is compromised, and much of what is needed for effective engagement, diagnosis, and formulation for treatment is lost. Our proposed diversity/resiliency formulation addresses contextual and individual factors related to diversity, equity, and resiliency, comprising internal and external resources that are essential to explore, recognize, and understand for effective clinical practice with the whole person. This, we believe, is an essential counterpoint to an exclusive focus on pathology and on related stress as found in the current structure of the *DSM-5*.

We continue to believe that social justice, the empowerment of oppressed groups, the participation of consumers in service delivery, and a family and community focus are undervalued in diagnostic formulations, research questions, treatment methodologies, policy formation, and program funding. We assert that these are increasingly important in the design of programs and interventions in the 21st century, in order to enhance the ability to utilize emerging research findings in genetics, neurobiology, psychopharmacology, and other biologically based treatments in an effective, culturally competent manner that helps our patients not only reduce their symptoms, but also go on to thrive and flourish.

Although it is a difficult goal to accomplish and often involves a delicate balancing act, we have decided not to limit our book to a discussion of the *DSM-5* but to emphasize how engaging in truly significant assessment of the whole person leads to meaningful and relevant treatment. Thus, we have retained and attempted to strengthen the dual focus of the first edition: helping the reader use the *DSM* in a strength-based manner, and highlighting relevant resiliency- and diversity-based research conducive to effective intervention. In order to accomplish this, we have selected certain disorders, or groups of disorders, to discuss in greater depth, as it was impossible to do justice to the entire taxonomy of the *DSM-5*. We hope the reader will consider the wider application of our diversity/resiliency formulation in responding to any of the *DSM-5* diagnoses!

We are appreciative of the clinical lessons derived from the region where we practice and teach, for it has one of the most diverse profiles in the nation. This context, our commitment to culturally competent practice, and the lively discussion introduced by our students regarding serving diverse populations in a creative, empowering manner, continues to challenge us to ongoing exploration and learning. We are also appreciative of the support given by our colleagues in taking time to review our work and provide incisive and thought-provoking feedback on our manuscript. We value the insight from colleagues in medicine, psychology, nursing, counseling, education, and social work. In addition, we want to emphasize strongly that we intend this book to have widespread applicability for clinicians and educators across the multidisciplinary spectrum of mental health practitioners, as well as for physicians in general practice (i.e., any setting in which the *DSM* is taught and/or utilized).

TERMINOLOGY

We note a few considerations in relation to the terminology used in this book. There are several distinctions about our use of terms that bear clarification, due to the assumption that although some terms are thought to mean the same thing to everyone, in reality there may be many interpretations of any one term or concept. Those that we feel merit explanation as to our usage include:

- The terms *client, patient*, and *consumer* are used interchangeably, consistent with multidisciplinary language.
- Masculine and feminine pronouns are used alternatively throughout the text with the intention of avoiding gender bias in our language.
- *Race, ethnicity*, and *culture* are used interchangeably to refer to what have been called "racial minorities" and/or to socially based class or group differences relevant to our diverse society. Our references to race are made in a context of recognition that race is a social construction rather than an indicator of real differences based on phenotype and other characteristics. *Culture*, however, may refer to occupational or other broad ranges of identities that are sources of meaning to individuals.
- *Diversity*, a broader term, refers to the multitude of complexities within and outside of our clients. This can include gender, social class, immigrant status, age, spirituality, as well as other relevant contexts.
- *Resiliency* refers to both inner, psychological sources of positive functioning as well as to external interpersonal, familial, cultural, and societal sources of support and strength.

HOW THE BOOK IS ORGANIZED

In Chapter 1, we address the importance of professional values that respect difference; we appreciate the role of culture in shaping attitudes (i.e., beliefs, feelings, and behavior) of individuals, families, and communities; and view culture as a source of resiliency and strength, considerations introduced by clinical practice on a global level and the systematic use of the *International Statistical Classification of Diseases and Related Health Problems (ICD-10;* World Health Organization, 1992). Chapter 2 addresses the development of the *DSM* as a context for our current focus on *DSM-5*, summarizes its strengths and weaknesses, and addresses the main controversies in current psychiatric diagnosis. As a corrective to mental health diagnosis based solely on pathology, we propose a model in Chapter 2 for assessing internal and external sources of resiliency and strength and conclude with contrasting case studies illustrating diagnosis with and without the use of the model. Each subsequent chapter is then organized by a discussion of the disorder(s), a case study that demonstrates a presenting problem related to the disorder, a summary of relevant research, and suggestions for multidisciplinary mental health clinicians and educators.

Chapters 3 through 9 deal with specific illnesses, including mood and anxiety disorders, severe mental illness, oppositional and conduct disorders, disorders co-occurring with substance abuse, and Alzheimer's disease. Consistent with its position as its own separate chapter in the *DSM-5*, we have added a new chapter on "Trauma and Stressor-Related Disorders." In selecting these particular disorders, we recognized the impossibility of reviewing the entire spectrum of disorders described in the *DSM*; instead, we chose to highlight diagnoses that challenge all the mental health disciplines, appear continuously in mental health clinics, and offer powerful ways to illustrate the utility of adding our proposed Axis VI to the *DSM* taxonomy. Chapter 10, "Future Directions," identifies challenges that we propose lie ahead in the ongoing development of intelligent and compassionate mental health practice.

The organization of each chapter in this edition includes:

1. An *introduction* to a category of disorder
2. *DSM* diagnostic criteria (includes summary of changes from *DSM-IV-TR*, rationale and implications for treatment)
3. Current understanding of *etiology and course of disorder* and the role of biological, genetic, and psychosocial factors, incidence, review of developmental issues and *co-occurring disorders*, current thinking about risk and protective factors
4. *Evidence based practice* (EBP) that builds on neurobiological and psychosocial findings is identified; updated research findings on best practices are included.
5. An updated review of *equity and diversity–disparities research findings* is included. Disparities research addresses the differences between identified population needs and access of those populations to services. The concept of *equity* has emerged more recently in recognition that it is not sufficient for all populations to have access to standardized services and that services in fact, based on diversity and uniqueness, must be individualized and responsive to individuals' lived experience in order to be effective. Factors related to disempowerment issues associated with socioeconomic class, ethnicity, gender, age, and disability *in relation to disorders* are explored
6. Examples of empowering, resiliency-based diagnosis and intervention
7. Presentation of a *case study*, including diagnostic formulation and treatment planning
8. A contrasting diagnostic assessment of the case study that compares a traditional *DSM-5* diagnosis with and without the addition of the proposed diversity/resiliency formulation for addressing resources of strength and empowerment; all case studies have been constructed from true client experiences, or are composites of several client experiences, with identifying information and contextual clues altered for the purpose of protecting client confidentiality
9. **Summary**
10. **Discussion questions and suggested activities for clinicians, supervisors, and educators**

Ethnographic, narrative, and consumer-driven approaches to communication between clinicians and clients are integrated in our approach to the assessment and diagnostic process. Each chapter includes references to web-based resources that are relevant to research, assessment, and interviewing skills, such as assessment and interviewing protocols and research publications and documents. Inserts address core chapter concepts, discussion points, experiential exercises, and assignments. The updated assignments reflect strength-based multisystems practice and focus on assessment and interventions with individuals, families, and communities. Readers will be challenged to understand and incorporate the social construction of meaning in clients' lives—based on cultural diversity, class, age, gender, life experiences, and other factors—and to view these complexities as sources of resiliency and strength as well as stress.

It is our hope that this text will embolden mental health professionals, educators, and students by clarifying the potential for *DSM-5* to go beyond a focus on the presence of pathological symptoms and environmental stressors to address sources of resiliency, that is, to encounter the whole person. We present both traditional and innovative clinical diagnostic and assessment considerations from a strength-based theoretical perspective in the context of multicultural awareness and competence. We encourage an approach to diagnosis that has the potential to reduce the disempowering, stigmatizing effects of diagnosis by promoting strength and contributing to the possibility of clients' flourishing. Our intention in this second edition is to promote critical thinking, based on an understanding of diagnostic systems, their essential components, and their relationship to the historical and cultural contexts of the individuals whom we serve. The *DSM-5* introduces new possibilities for enhanced diagnosis, but it also contains a significant risk of reinforcing iatrogenic effects of the assessment and intervention processes. It is thus even more essential to recognize the limitations of the diagnostic systems we use to guide our professional practice. We believe it is our ethical and professional responsibility to promote dialogue that challenges these limitations and promotes the enhancement of effective understanding and intervention.

It is our intent that this text be applicable and have utility for all mental health professionals in social work, psychiatry, family medicine, psychology, rehabilitation counseling, marriage and family therapy, and nursing. We are deeply indebted to those consumers of mental health services who have shared their stories and inspired us with their resourcefulness and courage. They deserve the best we have to offer. We hope that the concepts put forth in this book will contribute not only to the enhancement of accurate and relevant clinical diagnosis but also to our commitment to the future in a more caring, compassionate society.

REFERENCES

Alegria, M., Nakash, O., Lapatin, S., Oddo, V., Gao, S., Lin, J., & Normand, S. (2008). How missing information in diagnosis can lead to disparities in the clinical encounter. *Journal of Public Health Management and Practice*, *14*(Suppl.), S26–S35.

American Psychiatric Association. (1980). *Diagnostic and statistical manual of mental disorders* (3rd ed.). Washington, DC: Author.

American Psychiatric Association. (2000). *Diagnostic and statistical manual of mental disorders* (4th ed., text rev.). Washington, DC: Author.

American Psychiatric Association. (2013). *Diagnostic and statistical manual of mental disorders* (5th ed.). Arlington, VA: American Psychiatric Press.

World Health Organization. (1992). *The ICD-10 classification of mental and behavioral disorders: Clinical descriptions and diagnostic guidelines. 10th Revision (ICD-10)*. Geneva, Switzerland: Author.

Acknowledgments

First, we'd like to acknowledge the individuals and activities that led to the inception and growth of this work. The first edition of this book was possible through the development of a course syllabus by Betty Garcia and Richard Salsgiver on a multicultural approach to clinical practice. We are grateful to Steve Rose for recognizing the potential of that syllabus to become a full-fledged text and for his encouraging words suggesting we pursue that goal. We missed Richard's participation in the first text; and respected his decision not to subject himself to the stress of adding another project to his other publication activities. Anne's involvement as coauthor led to the focus on the sixth axis, which highlights diversity and resiliency. Our collaboration toward the second edition led us to reverse the order of authorship for several reasons. For one, this has been a joint endeavor throughout, and we both believe that involves sharing the wealth of authorship. Although we both have engaged in learning about the *DSM-5*, Anne has presented workshops on the *DSM-5*; her insights into the *DSM* are invaluable and add a layer ol depth to the presentation of this content. She is informed by years of practice wisdom, joyful teaching experience, and active involvement in her community. Betty's perspective is enriched by teaching, writing, and activities related to diversity/oppression, clinical practice, public mental health, wellness, and recovery.

This work, like any other meaningful, complex endeavor, is the result of a multitude of contributions at different stages of its evolution. We are indebted to the California State University, Fresno College of Health and Human Services, for past and current faculty development grants, which provided lease time that allowed us to breathe life into the project. We are grateful to our graduate students, Meagan Munson and Rosio Azua Valdez, who helped us update our research for the second edition. We continue to learn through our ongoing dialogues with mental health directors, field instructors, students, clients, peer support specialists, and colleagues. We are humbled by the experiences of clients described in the case studies; their voices are powerful, and their willingness to share their experiences allowed the chapter concepts to become real and alive. We have altered identifying context and details for the purpose of maintaining confidentiality. We could not have mustered the focus and energy needed for this work without all of the generosity, presence, and support of family and friends. Your enthusiasm and warmth have sustained us. Betty appreciates the enduring support and patience of her family and friends, both close and afar, and extends a special thank you to Bill, whose love and support, in the beginning, made it possible for her to discover and do what she loves doing, as in this work. Anne extends a special thank you to her colleagues, friends, and family, especially to Mike and Sarah for their love and patience.

We are also very grateful to Jennifer Perillo, formerly at Springer, whose thoughtful guidance made the first edition possible. We are indebted to Stephanie Drew and Alina Yurova at Springer Publishing Company for their belief in what we were trying to accomplish. Their support, follow-through, and vision regarding this work have been invaluable.

ONE

A Conceptual Framework for the Diversity/Resiliency Formulation

An accurate diagnosis comes from a collaborative effort with a patient. It is both a product of a good relationship and one of the best ways of promoting it. The focus, first and foremost, should be on the patient's need to be heard and understood. This must trump all else. Done well, psychiatric diagnosis leads to appropriate treatment and a good chance for cure or at least substantial improvement. Done poorly, psychiatric diagnosis leads to a nightmare of harmful treatments, unnecessary stigma, missed opportunities, and negative, self-fulfilling prophesies.

—A. Frances

Diagnosis is a critically important process that sets the stage for treatment and also establishes the groundwork for long-term consequences that bear on quality of life and social identity. Mental health professionals learn quickly that any individual you meet is more complex than his or her diagnostic label, and a central aim is to keep the whole person in perspective as one participates in assigning a categorical label to a person. The purpose of the *Diagnostic and Statistical Manual of Mental Disorders* (*DSM*®) is to provide a guide to clinical diagnosis through the identification of clearly articulated descriptive diagnostic criteria based on agreed-on symptoms of pathology for each disorder. As a taxonomy, the *DSM* provides the basis for unambiguous communication among professionals on symptoms associated with disorders. Knowledge of the *DSM* is required not only of all mental health clinicians but also of practitioners who provide a variety of other services to individuals, because mental health clients often receive a variety of services in settings such as schools, hospitals, and social agencies.

Discussion on a litany of limitations in the *DSM* has been ongoing in the literature and has called attention to potential changes that could lead to a strengthened diagnostic taxonomy (Kupfer, First, & Regier, 2002). Publication of the *DSM-5* (American Psychiatric Association [APA], 2013), in principle, represents an advancement over the *DSM-IV-TR*'s (2000) capacity for accurate and effective diagnostics. However, as discussed in this text, substantial discussion continues regarding the assumptions underlying the structural changes and the effectiveness of the new diagnostic format and categories. We address the extensive changes in diagnostic categories and criteria/specifiers relevant to a discrete set of disorders. More important, we address the implications of deletion of the multiaxial format and introduction of a singular diagnosis that is complemented by narrative and outcome measures. One overriding concern is that the new format presumes that clinicians will, of their own accord, invoke use of *DSM-5* codes that address "Other Conditions That May Be a Focus of Clinical Attention" (APA, 2013, p. 715). These "Conditions" reflect content previously addressed in axis IV that were required as part of a complete diagnostic. Most disconcerting is the loss of the multiaxial diagnostic format that mandated examination and documentation on mental illness and personality disorder, if relevant. Responses to the *DSM-5* changes raise concern about potential harm in utilizing only one diagnostic label at the risk of losing the individual and his context.

Implications of the *DSM-5* will be elaborated on in Chapter 2 as well as in relation to the seven diagnostic categories addressed in this text. The purpose of this book is to address changes in the *DSM-5* and highlight diagnostic considerations that need to continue to be addressed in the process of increasing the accuracy, relevance, and effectiveness of the mental health diagnostic process. We hope to accomplish this via two main proposals. Our aim is to (a) balance the assessment of pathology with an appreciation of internal and external strengths and resources in order to understand more accurately the interaction of stressors and resources in the client's life, and (b) identify domains—to be explored in assessment—that illuminate the client's cultural, familial, and socioeconomic contexts and enhance diagnostic information.

We propose that attending to the client's cultural contexts and sources of resiliency must be a formal part of the diagnostic process, in order to understand the client more comprehensively and to develop a treatment plan that incorporates the client's complex contextual world. In this chapter we review issues that continue to challenge the development of a more effective application of the *DSM*. Specifically, there is a need for a more thorough diagnostic process comprising diverse populations and for the incorporation of sources of strength and resiliency in the diagnostic process. This chapter addresses culture and mental health by focusing on updated theoretical and research literature that has explored the meaning of the diverse contexts of our clients and the complex interactions among constructs such as culture, social class, ethnicity, gender, and race. It summarizes the relationship between these contexts and the experience of seeking and receiving help for a diagnosed mental illness and concludes with a rationale for our proposed diagnostic template/format presented in Chapter 2. Chapter 2 presents the diagnostic protocol proposed in this text to enhance a culturally relevant diagnostic process that incorporates internal and external sources of client resiliency.

A major challenge in conducting effective diagnosis is to factor in the totality of the individual in relation to his or her context. Inclusion of the cultural contexts within which individuals live strengthens the clinical formulation, so that it captures the subtleties and substance of experiences and worldviews.

This will enhance the clinician's understanding of mental disorders through the lens of multifaceted cultural and socioeconomic contexts.

The changing demographics of American society, evidenced by the skyrocketing growth of ethnically diverse groups, contribute to the urgency for the *DSM* to provide a framework for accurate diagnosis with all individuals, regardless of such diverse factors as national origin, ethnic identity, religious/spiritual beliefs, socioeconomic position, and gender identity. A relevant mental health workforce is one that is prepared for the heterogeneity in the populations served. An estimated one out of three Americans is a member of a historically underrepresented group (HUG); and as the growth rate of diverse groups increases, immigrant communities are expanding to all corners of the United States. These facts present an immediate challenge to all mental health providers. The Hispanic population alone is projected to almost triple between 2008 and 2050, which means that Hispanics will represent almost one in three residents in the United States (Bernstein & Edwards, 2008). These changes present opportunities for mental health professional communities to evaluate their diagnostic strategies, treatment approaches, and interventions. This increased diversity demands an examination of the assumptions we make about the efficacy of our work when the complexity of clients' lives is taken into account. It also requires attending to the emergent voices of consumer advocates and an effort to make consumers active partners in the diagnostic and treatment process. It is increasingly essential that clinicians understand the need to practice in a culturally congruent manner.

KEY POINTS

1. As the client population becomes ever more diverse, the need for cultural competence in the diagnostic process is crucial.
2. Accurate diagnosis should include the assessment of internal and external sources of resiliency and strength, particularly as these relate to socioeconomic and cultural contexts.
3. Relevant assessment requires a mutual process of collaborative partnership with the consumers of mental and behavioral health services.

CULTURAL COMPETENCE: STATUS OR PROCESS? INTERPERSONAL OR MULTILEVEL LENS?

Surprisingly, the misconception remains alive and well in mental health and other services that *cultural competence* is a status to be achieved in the realm of interpersonal ability. Perhaps the confusion is contained in the term *competence*. This concept suggests to many clinicians that it is possible to achieve a final state of cultural competence by taking a class or securing a certificate, when in reality all learning activities are but points on a lifelong process of ongoing heightened awareness. The concept of culturally competent practice has evolved to include an emphasis on one's actions and behaviors, not just what one feels or one's level of awareness. This focus highlights the identification of measurable behaviors and outcomes that can confirm or disconfirm effectiveness. This approach goes beyond the mere intention of implementing empathic interventions based on awareness and sensitivity. We can assume that all clinicians have the *intention* of conveying empathy. Culturally competent interventions are observable behaviors associated with successful outcomes in relational terms (i.e., engagement, consumer adherence, and commitment to treatment) and are the consequence of the development of personal and interpersonal awareness.

The current focus on cross-culturally effective practice has returned to the earlier notions of cultural sensitivity and humility as gold standards of practice. The intent of this recent shift to the concept of *humility* is to highlight a focus on awareness of the limits of one's understanding, and the reality that the development of cross-cultural clinical skills is a lifelong endeavor. **It is a *process*, not a status** that is influenced by the institutional/organizational context and evolves in relation to changing cultures and practice demands. A process approach to the interpersonal level of cultural competence presumes that we can never entirely achieve full effectiveness in a culture different from our own. However, this does not preclude practice with the intention of meeting the ethical demands associated with the responsibility of having a basic understanding of and motivation to learn about our client's cultural context(s). Such an understanding allows the clinician to size up a client's uniqueness, distinct from stereotypes the clinician may hold (S. Sue, 1998), in relation to her own life experiences and social identifications.

The interpersonal process approach to cultural competence can also obscure the importance of defining cultural competence on multiple levels that lend themselves to ongoing education, research, and organizational proficiency. Clinical relational efficacy, ongoing professional development, and culturally relevant programming are only as strong as organizational policy and leadership that identify with and promote culturally relevant practices applying to all populations—for example, in relation to ethnicity, gender, socioeconomic class, and religion (APA, 2004; APA, 2003; National Association of Social Workers [NASW], 2007; see also the website for the National Center for Cultural Competence at Georgetown University, www11.georgetown.edu/research/gucchd/nccc). Our text focuses on the concept of competence—that is, on what clinicians *do*, with sensitivity, in a *welcoming way* with their clients/consumers of all backgrounds.

Conceptual frameworks that provide guides for effective practice with diverse populations also need to integrate factors—such as social power differences related to socioeconomic status and social standing—between clinician and client. It is invaluable for clinicians to attend to the implications of differences in privilege and social power between themselves and their clients. Foremost, the client's needs lead our engagement efforts; however, it is helpful for clinicians to be attuned to differences between themselves and the client that, if relevant, can benefit from acknowledgment. A clinical perspective that recognizes that there is greater heterogeneity within any group than between groups provides a basis to inquire about factors such as level of acculturation, religion, national origin, and socioeconomic class.

The concept of ***intersectionality*** assists in grasping the complexity of heterogeneity within groups by highlighting the intersecting and interacting elements of gender, socioeconomic class, ethnicity, religion, and other factors that combine in dynamic and changing ways depending on the experiences of an individual. The intersections of various factors related to culture and potentially to marginalized status—such as low socioeconomic status, gender, and disability—introduce unique subjective perspectives. A married, third-generation Latino female with a master's or law degree will have different life experiences with privilege and marginalization than will a second-generation, single Latino female with a high school degree, even though they have the same working-class background. Not to address these complexities is to limit and distort one's understanding of the client's experience and worldview. Differences within groups belie stereotypes and evoke probing that reveals the client's uniqueness and is premised on skilled and genuine inquiry. Clinicians must ask:

- What do I need to do to establish credibility with the population(s) that I serve?
- What conditions must I understand in this client's culture in order to proceed in the diagnostic task?
- What is important to appreciate in the diagnostic process in relation to this person's age, gender, or position in his or her culture?
- What approach will work best with this person in this situation—for example, in order to secure permission to inquire into sensitive areas? (D. W. Sue & Sue, 2008)

Conceptualization of effective culturally competent practice has further advanced, in line with social justice assumptions, to reframe culturally relevant practice as ***transformative*** for all levels of practice (i.e., practitioner, client, organization, institution)—that is, a process that promotes ***equity***. ***Transformational change*** is change that leads to alterations in perception and meaning made by modifying one's assumptions and expectations (Jones, 2010), resulting in behavior that is more "inclusive, discriminating, open, reflective" and emotionally open to change (Mezirow, 2003, p. 59). A multilevel approach to transformation presumes that clients, clinicians, organizations, and institutions change as a result of open exchange and professional growth, where previously unrecognized options and choices come to the fore in the process of greater culturally relevant skills and policy development. The new focus on equity in culturally relevant practice highlights the role of social justice in promoting clinical exchange and mental health services that are *individualized* and pertinent to clients and their families. This perspective represents progress beyond the concept of disparities; it is aimed at providing access to relevant services, and elevates the discussion to quality of services, individualized services, and goodness of fit of the clinical approach to the client's needs.

KEY POINTS

1. Cultural competence is a process, not a status that is achieved and assumed.
2. Cultural competence is never fully attained, because we can never fully experience the diverse worlds of our clients.
3. Cultural competence is adequately evaluated only by examining behaviors and their outcomes in the lives of clients, utilizing the concepts of transactionality and intersectionality to embrace the complexity of an individual's unique experiences.
4. Effective cultural competence is transformative at individual, interpersonal, and institutional levels, thus promoting social justice at all of these levels.

PROBLEM AREAS AND BEST PRACTICES FOR MENTAL HEALTH

Considerable conceptual and empirical work addresses the basis for advancing efforts to increase effectiveness in engagement with clients of all backgrounds. Much of this writing delineates significant clinical issues associated with contextual factors such as culture and socioeconomic class. There are several streams of literature in this regard; these bear on the *DSM* as a social construct, the consequences of bias in the diagnostic process, and proposals for improved competency in diagnosis and assessment. Marsella and Yamada's (2000) review of the literature on culture and psychopathology observes that although the role of culture in influencing the "onset, expression, course, and outcome of psychopathology" is understood, still there remains a need to recognize the assumptions based on Western culture that underlie the *DSM* conceptualization of health and illness (p. 801). Snowden's (2003) discussion on the nature of bias and the need to know more about when and how it operates addresses the stark consequences of the overdiagnosis of schizophrenia in African Americans (Baker & Bell, 1999), the dilemma of clinicians' overpathologizing ethnic individuals by misinterpreting normative behavior as indicative of a mental disorder (Lopez, 1989), and, however inadvertent, the potential for bias to undermine the ever-important therapeutic alliance (Hovarth, 1994).

In their study of 129 mental health intakes, Alegria et al. (2008) data on missing information and bias in the clinical encounter found that clinicians rely more on client report than on *DSM* criteria. This is particularly interesting in that it seems to counter a lot of critics who feel that diagnosis is based too much on criteria, defined as the *DSM* identification of symptoms that may or may not fit the individual's experience. In practice, clinicians may be compensating for the weaknesses of the *DSM* in the diagnostic process. Alegria et al. (2008) propose that the clinical information gathered in the diagnostic assessment and the values that underlie how that information is used in clinical decisions can compromise the accuracy of the diagnosis. Yamada and Brekke's (2008) review of the literature on the need for integrating sociocultural issues into the assessment process concluded with the proposal of an assessment protocol that explores changes in environment, stressors, support, life-control concerns, status of literacy and communication, reference group/network, and expectations about treatment. Moreover, they suggest that the clinician's inquiry and demonstration of curiosity has the additional benefit of communicating interest in the uniqueness of the client and facilitates engagement, thus strengthening the therapeutic alliance.

In response to the need for culturally informed services and equity, all mental health professions have taken steps to address these issues in various ways. Some of these efforts include the development of cultural competence standards and the establishment of commissions for the purpose of developing guidelines for practice and research and/or policy statements (APA, 2004; APA, 2003; NASW, 2007).

KEY POINTS

1. Inadvertent bias in the *DSM* has resulted in the overpathologizing of certain groups by ignoring key strengths and aspects of culture.
2. Culture impacts the way psychopathology is understood and expressed.
3. All the mental health professions have taken steps to address cultural factors in diagnosis.
4. In practice, clinicians unintentionally may go beyond the symptom checklist structure of the *DSM* when they are engaged in diagnosis.
5. Expressing curiosity in the assessment process facilitates effective engagement with the client, which, in turn, enhances the accuracy of diagnosis.

CREATING A CULTURALLY RELEVANT, RESILIENCY-BASED DIAGNOSIS

The proposals put forth in this book are premised on a culturally competent mental health workforce comprising interdisciplinary professionals; this includes psychiatrists, primary care physicians, social workers, psychologists, psychiatric nurses, marriage and family therapists, licensed professional counselors, and pastoral counselors. The collaborative effort among professionals is challenging from many perspectives and strengthening it has become even more important due to the Patient Protection and Affordable Care Act. Health care and behavioral health providers will increasingly need to be skilled in working together in collaborative teams and in a variety of multidisciplinary contexts that include colocations, health care organizations, and other formal and informal networks. Skills in interprofessional collaboration will be increasingly required as a basis of effective communication across disciplines and organizations. Various disciplines approach mental health practice from a variety of missions, purposes, professional identities, theoretical perspectives, ethical standards, and role definitions, with varying degrees of relative power and status. When these professional differences are taken into consideration, the concept of cultural diversity and competence becomes even more complex, as each discipline has its own culture, influencing the clinician's sense of self and role with respect to the client.

Moreover, mental health consumers are rightfully demanding a place at the table through the efforts of organizations such as the National Alliance for Mental Health and the advance of the Recovery Model. The future will bring an even greater need for professionals in all fields to work collaboratively, both with one another and particularly with mental health patients, families, and communities. For one, diversity in the mental health workforce will increase as consumers, in the role of peer support, take their place on interdisciplinary teams. It is hoped that more collaboration, it is to be hoped, will increasingly enhance communication between clinician and client in the diagnostic process.

A multicultural perspective in mental health recognizes the value of and appreciation for the complexity of factors that make up social identity and contribute to personal resilience. This perspective assumes that resilience is promoted by several factors related to culture, including the client's values and beliefs, family ties, and social network resources. When this approach is incorporated into the structure of the *DSM* diagnostics, the diagnosis can become more grounded in a strengths perspective that examines and assesses clients' abilities to cope with and rebound from the challenges of living with a mental disorder. This perspective also explores culturally relevant options that help promote greater knowledge about an individual's mental disorder and acceptance of it. It is based on the view that culture and other client contexts are sources of resiliency and all too often are examined only from the perspective of finding pathology. We propose an empowering perspective that counterbalances an exclusive focus on pathology. This positions culture where it belongs, at the core of diagnosis, rather than as an afterthought or impediment relegated to a *DSM* appendix or romanticized as a consequence of a reductionist approach. All too often Culture 101 is thought of as learning about cultural practices (e.g., food, music, family traditions) at the cost of inquiring about the specifics of the individual client's perceptions and meanings concerning her own life. The discussion on the status and application of cultural content in the diagnostic process draws from the empowerment perspective and Recovery Model principles.

Our emphasis on a multicultural perspective with respect to resiliency and strengths takes into consideration several aspects of the experience of ethnic (e.g., African American, Latino, Asian,[1] Native American) diversity and the heterogeneity within each of these populations. Although we address HUGs in the United States, we recognize that the complex issues faced by these groups are confronted by many populations that deserve unique attention. On a national level, clearly there are many U.S. populations, such as South Pacific, Islamic, and Eastern European, that require increased attention in relation to behavioral health issues. Moreover, there is much to be gained as we expand our awareness of behavioral health issues to include the global, international context and its implications for consumers' lived experience. Regrettably, dominant American culture has all too often marginalized these communities into the "other." To a large degree, the post-9/11 epoch has promoted and increased our recognition

---

[1] In this work we refer to Americans of Latino and Asian descent as Latino and Asian.

of the richness and contributions of other cultures in general, their perspectives on behavioral health, and relevant approaches to effective interventions.

Particular attention is given to the roles of social power, discrimination, racism, and the effects of social marginalization (e.g., invisibility, devaluation) in the lives of individuals with mental disorders. The presence of low-income status and low levels of formal education associated with many, but not all, ethnically diverse individuals suggests that meaningful efforts to comprehend and work with such individuals must be carried out within the context of their socioeconomic and cultural worldviews. This attention to the intersection between ethnicity and socioeconomic class will focus clinicians' attention on clients' experiences with access, efficacy, and social privilege and penalty. Equally important, an awareness by the clinician of the contribution of culture to client sources of internal and external support and resilience is critical to accurate diagnosis and effective intervention.

KEY POINTS

1. Culturally competent, resiliency-enhanced diagnosis requires greater collaboration among mental health professionals and between professionals and consumers.
2. In the diagnostic process, clients must be understood in the contexts of socioeconomic and cultural factors.
3. These factors contribute sources of resiliency as well as stress.

PSYCHOPATHOLOGY, CULTURE, AND MENTAL HEALTH

Culture has a powerful role in the psychological life of individuals. It plays a vital role not only in forming social identity and thus the shaping of preferences, interests, and needs but also in defining distress. Clinicians are challenged to learn many nuances across different cultures. These nuances include attending to the following questions: What is a normative part of life experience? What is not normative? What are culturally relevant ways of coping? What are one's sources for help-seeking? Contextual considerations, such as whether the cultures one identifies with value collectivistic or individualistic behaviors, have significant impacts on the options that consumers seek out once they recognize a need to address psychosocial distress. Although a traditional culture might lead an individual to seek out community-recognized elders, an Euro American[2] working-class individual might first turn to religious sources, and a middle or upper class professional might seek out psychotherapy. Culture influences how a mental disorder is experienced; it determines how it is expressed and how symptoms are interpreted. It also identifies acceptable means of coping, determines how the disorder is viewed socially, and identifies relevant sources of help (Alarcon, Westermeyer, Foulks, & Ruiz, 1999; Kirmayer & Young, 1999; Nichter, 1981).

[2] This text will use Euro American, ethnic White, and European American interchangeably to describe individuals whose social identify reflects a European background.

Eshun and Gurung's (2009) discussion of health seeking and coping highlights cultural variations in explanations of precipitants of mental disorders, which can be viewed as supernatural factors or personal deficits in social functioning.

Not to be underestimated is the decisive influence that one's cultural context has on where one first seeks help. Rogler and Cortes's (1993) discussion on help-seeking pathways describes how culture and worldview influence what can be construed as a trusted source with whom one can disclose sensitive experiences for the purpose of securing help. It is critical to understand these culturally shaped behaviors in regard to early intervention and collaborative efforts with other health care professionals, including indigenous healers. These help-seeking pathways vary based on ethnicity, socioeconomic status, and/or religion/spirituality.

As a contextual worldview related to ethnicity, religion, and other factors, culture influences individual behaviors such as cognition, perception, beliefs, values, interpersonal interactions, customs, and institutions developed by social groups (Cross, Bazron, Dennis, & Isaacs, 1989). As a social construct, culture is not static; it changes over time in response to an individual's experiences and the understandings that evolve from this; as such, culture is instrumental in the development of the labels individuals place on their experiences (Lu, Lim, & Mezzrich, 2008). Thoughtful exploration means listening for idioms of distress and explanatory models of mental illness that are derived from client's cultural identifications. One cannot make assumptions about ethnic identity based on an individual's phenotype (i.e., physical appearance, such as skin color, hair texture, facial features), an individual's values, or even the meaning of terminology. It is important for clinicians to develop effective engagement skills that facilitate explorations of the client's subjective experiences. Stories abound in clinical settings, for example, of using Spanish language from one national origin to speak with a Spanish-speaking client from a different national origin, only to discover that one has inadvertently offended the client. For example, a clinician of Mexican heritage once described, when a Dominican client shared a photo of her son and the clinician called him *guapo* (i.e., good-looking), the client was startled, because that term means "angry appearing" in the Dominican culture!

Concepts such as *explanatory models* and *idioms of distress* assist in listening to clients' narratives with the intent of learning from clients how they understand their condition and the manifestation (i.e., symptoms) of what they are coping with. The concept of explanatory models refers to the constructs used by individuals to explain how they understand their symptoms and their current situation, their timing, the types of symptoms that appeared at onset (e.g., lack of motivation, hallucinations), physical sensations associated with a mental health illness, and their beliefs about what is helpful for their condition (Helman, 1990). Lu et al. (2008) suggest that *explanatory models* can be explored by questioning clients about, for example, what they think has happened; what they believe are the reasons for their reactions (i.e., symptoms)—that is, why they developed; and why they think these reactions occurred now. These theorists also suggest inquiring about possible consequences if nothing is done, how others might be affected, and ultimately what clients think needs to be done that can be helpful. Probes into clients' understanding and perceptions of their symptoms can lead to narratives that illuminate how persons experience and express distress as well as how they manage their feelings about their difficulties (Nichter, 1981). Nichter (1981) suggests that these aspects, *idioms of distress*, are derived from cultural values, norms, perceptions of health issues, and cultural suppositions. The *DSM*'s "Glossary of Culture-Bound Syndromes" presents an extensive list of idioms of distress from various cultures, such as *ataque de nervios*, which is a culturally normative means of expressing distress and grief by agitated behavior and raised voice—for example, in response to an overwhelming personal loss.

A Spanish-speaking clinician once reported communicating in a prison setting with a monolingual Spanish-speaking client who had been stripped to paper clothes and placed in an observational cell by a well-intentioned monolingual English-speaking staff member. The client was thought to be in the midst of a psychotic episode following the death of her infant daughter and was talking to her daughter as if the daughter were alive. The clinician found the woman to be lucid and clearly aware that the infant had died; however, she expressed in Spanish that the grief felt unbearable.

Gurung and Roethel-Wendorf (2009) broaden the discussion of culture's role in shaping perceptions and beliefs to suggest, from a *stress vulnerability perspective*, that stressors introduced by acculturation and/or cultural conflict wrought by tensions among traditional first-generation and second- or third-generation offspring descendants deserve special attention. This perspective opens up questions regarding the mental health implications of stress in life experiences associated with one's social identity, ethnicity, social class, or other variables that can generate stress.

The concept of *microaggressions* (Pierce, Carew, Pierce-Gonzalez, & Willis, 1978) was developed in relation to personal violations that are experienced in relation to ethnicity and refers to everyday experiences of not feeling respected or valued. Awareness of microaggressions brings attention to the social consequences of having a severe mental illness that can evoke negative stereotypes and thus stigma. The perspective on microaggressions by D. W. Sue et al. (2007) offers insightful points on often neglected aspects of life experiences resulting from stigma, discrimination, and marginalization by highlighting how microaggression interactions are normative, embedded in daily experiences, and characterized by rudeness, negation, and exclusion. Common examples include being watched and/or followed in department store settings or students feeling that their professor has low expectations of their academic work. These experiences take their toll on the individual. The authors suggest that these realities in the lives of consumers have implications for clinical practice, specifically practice with individuals who are marginalized as a function of negative stereotypes and/or stigma. This places increased responsibility on clinicians to build an effective, attuned therapeutic working relationship.

The experience of microaggressions may arguably also permeate the context in which a variety of clinicians work, an area neglected in the research, which has focused almost exclusively on the client. For example, in the hierarchy of status, power, and financial remuneration among mental health professionals and peer support staff, those "low on the totem pole" may often feel marginalized or ignored in the work setting. This could be compounded if the low-status clinician is also a member of a marginalized cultural group in the community at large. Her special insights and useful contributions to the diagnostic, assessment, and treatment process may go unexpressed or be discounted, to the detriment of the client and effective treatment planning and intervention.

Accurate diagnosis requires several capabilities that build on clear and knowledgeable clinical skill. In diverse settings, the ability to recognize the stereotypes and expectations that one brings to the clinical encounter is essential. With respect to ethnic populations, bias in assessment has been found to be a pattern in clinical settings rather than an isolated event. Snowden (2003) proposes that bias represents clinical judgments made about people of color, based on perceptions related to race or ethnicity rather than on discerning probes that delve into understanding the presenting symptoms from the perspective of the individual.

KEY POINTS

1. Culture defines how one experiences stress, what is considered normal, and how one seeks help.
2. Accurate diagnosis is impossible without attending to cultural idioms of distress and client explanatory models.
3. Many mental health consumers experience microaggressions on a daily basis; this requires special attention and sensitive attunement on the part of the clinician. Some clinicians, too, may experience microaggressions in the workplace.
4. Accurate diagnosis requires attunement not only to the client's experiences but also to the clinician's own sources of bias.

THE *DSM* AND CULTURE

Historically the *DSM* work groups have made attempts to address the cultural components of diagnosis in various ways. The *DSM-IV-TR* (APA, 2000) included a section titled "Outline for Cultural Formulation and Glossary of Culture Bound Syndromes" at the end of the text, and the *DSM-5* has expanded this passage to include cultural formulation interview (CFI) questions. Although these additions have provided a valuable resource, there is much left to do, as evident in our review of the literature in the preceding sections.

The addition of the "Outline for Cultural Formulation and Glossary of Culture Bound Syndromes" (APA, 2000) was a significant step toward enhancing the responsiveness of the *DSM* format in addressing diverse cultures and their role in understanding mental illness. The idea for the cultural formulation was developed by the National Institute of Mental Health (NIMH) Group on Culture and Diagnosis in 1991, with the intent to "enhance the cultural validity and suitability of the *DSM-IV*" (Mezzich, 2008). This committee's work on the review of existing literature identified four key areas to integrate into practice with diverse clients: the consumer's cultural identity, cultural factors in the consumer's disorder, cultural context and functioning, and cultural elements in the clinician–consumer interaction and relationship. Many complexities of social identity have become more clear over time, such as the reality that individuals may have several cultural identifications, not just one, and that such identifications are not either/or but rather degrees of identification with perhaps both dominant and traditional culture (Phinney, 2003).

The phases of the work group's efforts (Lewis-Fernandez, 2008) are instructive for the challenges faced by mental health professionals practicing within frameworks and approaches that facilitate interaction with the whole person in the context of his or her lived experience.[3] Initially the work group proposed adding a sixth axis with the intent of providing a structure for grasping the subjective experience of individuals and their reference groups (Good & Good, 1986). However, the idea was abandoned when it appeared that such a device potentially could lead to a reductionist, decontextualized approach that would further obscure the individual as a function of the protocol. Lewis-Fernandez (2008) makes several observations regarding the intent. Foremost, the intent was to provide a guide composed of principles that affect "the way clinicians view all five axes ... [and] to render visible the socially constructed context" that influences a consumer presentation and course of illness (p. 95). He added it was aimed at emphasizing the complex range of cultural factors—such as attributions of causality and patterns of help-seeking—such as clinician contextual, institutional factors. A need to recognize that "culture affects every aspect of the clinical encounter" was recognized. As such, it was hoped that the cultural formulation would promote the use of a "mini-ethnographic narrative assessment" that captured the individual's context sufficiently. It was also intended to highlight how cultural factors influence the manifestation of the clinical features (Lewis-Fernandez, 2008, p. 96).

The *DSM-5* moved parts of the *DSM-IV-TR* Appendix I "Outline for Cultural Formulation and Glossary of Culture-Bound Syndromes" to Section III "Emerging Measures and Models" and to the "Appendix." Section III includes expanded narrative on understanding the cultural context and revision of the "Outline for Cultural Formulation" to include more subtleties related to conceptualizations of distress, psychosocial stressors, and cultural features of vulnerability and resilience. Section III also includes the newly developed CFI, CFI–Informant Version (i.e., for collateral data gathering), and narrative on the "Cultural Concepts of Distress" (i.e., syndromes, idioms, and explanations). However, the narrative on examples of concepts of distress was moved to the Appendix (p. 833). Several changes were made consistent with the *DSM-5* authors' aim to emphasize that "clinically important differences often involve explanations or experiences of distress rather than culturally distinctive configurations of symptoms" (i.e., syndromes). For one, several culture-bound syndromes and idioms identified in the *DSM-IV-TR* were eliminated. However, the Appendix narrative on select

[3] We refer to "lived experience" in order to utilize wellness and recovery concepts that highlight consumer's experiences with mental illness.

"Concepts of Distress" is more extensive and addresses differential diagnostic concerns in relation to diverse cultural contexts and *DSM-5* conditions.

Placement of the CFI in Section III and relegation of the distress examples to the Appendix has several implications. For one, this continues the *DSM-IV-TR* pattern of marginalized status of diversity and culturally relevant diagnostic content. In so doing, it places responsibility on clinicians to seek out this content and incorporate it in their diagnostic endeavors. Absent is the structure and direction that challenges clinicians to systematically explore and incorporate strength-based and diversity-sensitive information to view the individual in his totality.

The intent of our work is to advance the development of diagnostic strategies that give primacy to recognition of the person's uniqueness rather than to the diagnostic label in order to facilitate accurate diagnosis. An underlying assumption is that the cultural strengths and resiliency that all individuals have, regardless of ethnicity or culture, deserve more attention in the service of greater accuracy. Much work remains to be done in the development of a comprehensive diagnostic protocol that fosters accurate diagnosis in multicultural settings and that encourages the formulation of an ethnographic narrative. As a social construct, the *DSM* is founded on culturally grounded values of the medical model and thus potentially has limited application across diverse cultural settings. In addition, practice is frequently driven by organizational factors that stress rapid responses to the highest numbers of patients and place a premium on the use of psychopharmacology as a response to the complex worlds of clients. Redesign of the *DSM-5* diagnostic format to one diagnosis, rather than using multiaxial domains, suggests organizational and psychopharmacological expediencies will continue to override individualization of the patient. The unexamined use of a culturally based protocol across diverse cultures raises questions regarding unintended consequences that could lead to harm rather than healing.

An effective *DSM* should minimally address the following: (a) the role of culture and ethnic identity in the individual's biopsychosocial makeup, functioning, perceptions of mental illness and coping methods; and (b) cultural and individual factors that are a basis of strength, resiliency, and resources. An effective *DSM* can lead the way to systematic assessment of multicultural realities that have a role in producing mental health disorders. These realities would encompass enduring, stressful events, and microaggressions (D. W. Sue et al., 2007) related to low-income status, marginalization, and low social power faced by individuals of all backgrounds, including immigrants and people with disabilities. Similarly, the role of important nonmaterial sources of strength and resiliency, such as spirituality and social support, can become a routine part of diagnosis and assessment.

In principle, the *DSM-5* contains the flexibility and complexity to address the unique mental health concerns of all populations, regardless of ethnicity, gender, age, socioeconomic status, or national origin in a manner that encompasses the individual's strengths and capabilities as well as pathologies. In so doing, the individual's culture, spirituality, social support, and other unique sources of strength and resiliency could possibly become as integral a part of the diagnostic process as are symptoms of pathology and disrupted functioning.

Ideally, diagnostic accuracy will be aided by application of the new *DSM-5* format and promote more rigorous understandings of individuals' complexity and ultimately more effective treatment and intervention outcomes. The ideal, however, is unlikely to be realized in the complex, time-pressured world of mental health treatment. With the former axes system, the clinician was expected to attend at least to stressors in the client's world and encouraged to add a cultural formulation. With the elimination of the multiaxial format, attending to cultural factors and dynamics becomes a more obscure possibility, dependent on a highly motivated, culturally competent clinician.

KEY POINTS

1. The *DSM-5* modifications give recognition to inadequacies in the current taxonomy with regard to client contexts, including culture.
2. The culture of medicine, with its emphasis on pathology and the time pressures on its practitioners, reinforces ignoring client culture and sources of resiliency, thus reducing the accuracy of diagnosis.
3. Corrective changes in the *DSM-5* did not promote a more accurate understanding of the uniqueness of the individual beyond the pathological label.

CULTURALLY COMPETENT MENTAL HEALTH: FROM DISPARITIES TO EQUITY

Mental health disparities research addresses the discrepancy between a population's identified need for mental health services and its access to services (Alarcon et al., 2002; Alegria et al., 2008; U.S. Department of Health and Human Services, 1999; Vega, Kolody, Aguilar-Gaxiola, & Catalano, 1999). Yamada and Brekke's (2008) review of research on how sociocultural factors influence access to services identifies factors related to clinician, programming, and organizational factors that can affect bias in the diagnostic process. This research highlights the necessity of providing quality, access, and continuity of services, with particular attention to patterns of diagnostic outcomes that might vary among populations (i.e., between White populations and other ethnic groups; Snowden, 2003).

Most significant, this body of research represents a shift in thinking about the underutilization of services to a transactional perspective that examines the contribution of organizational and consumer behavior factors that result in barriers to services or a lack of access to services, continuity of services, and individualized treatment. In addressing environmental factors that impact health status and quality of care (Aguilar-Gaxiola & Breslau, 2007), attention is given to outreach, culturally competent policy, and service delivery patterns. Factors such as program development, organizational mission and leadership, staffing, and other elements can pose barriers to effective multicultural service delivery and require attention in regard to consumer help-seeking pathways (Rogler & Cortes, 1993). Inquiry into the factors that contribute to disparities in services have identified bias in the form of the overpathologizing of ethnic individuals' behavior and minimization of their identified concerns (Lopez, 1989; Snowden, 2003) ethnic underrepresention in outpatient settings and overrepresention in inpatient and emergency care settings (Chow, Jaffee, & Snowden, 2003; Garyali, 1999; Mukherjee, Shukla, Woodle, Rosen, & Olarte, 1983; Strakowski, Shelton, & Kolbrener, 1993) as well as greater physical and mental disability resulting from lack of health care (U.S. Department of Health and Human Services, 2001). African Americans and Latinos with affective disorders have been found to be misdiagnosed more frequently with schizophrenia (Corrigan, 2014; Metzl, 2009; Mukherjee et al., 1983; Neighbors, Trierweiler, Ford, & Muroff, 2003; Trierweiler et al., 2000), and African Americans have significantly less outpatient psychiatric contact (Kales, Blow, Bingham, Copeland, & Mellow, 2000) compared with other groups.

CASE STUDY 1

A Young Adult and a Mental Health Emergency

A young adult African American male was found wandering the streets of a large American city gesticulating wildly and uttering obscenities. He was 6 feet, 3 inches tall, with a dark complexion and unkempt appearance; his hair was worn in short dreadlocks. He was brought in by police officers to the emergency room of a large inner-city hospital where differential diagnostic considerations included an assumption of homelessness, drug abuse, and/or schizophrenia. He was kept overnight for observation and released within 24 hours with a prescription for Haldol and a follow-up appointment with a public mental health psychiatrist and a substance abuse counselor. He failed to keep his follow-up appointments. During the assessment, he informed the psychiatrist on call that he was a PhD student in physics—a statement that was assumed to illustrate the presence of psychotic delusions; this information, however, was factual. He was suffering from bipolar disorder, not schizophrenia or drug abuse. He fit the prevailing stereotype of a young, inner-city African American male, and thus his strengths were left unrecognized and, in fact, were falsely interpreted as evidence of psychosis. Ashamed and bewildered by his own symptoms, the young man gave the hospital staff a false name. He did not return for the follow-up appointment and ultimately committed suicide.

- What led to this young man's becoming a casualty of an overburdened mental health system?
- What led to the cultural bias that made his individualized needs invisible?

Attention to the fit between services and the specific needs of diverse populations—based on ethnicity, gender, age and other factors—has promoted increased focus on what constitutes culturally competent organizations, policy, and clinical practice (Cross et al., 1989). The underlying assumption of social justice in mental health service provision has now shifted from the term *disparities* to the concept of *equity*. Assurance of access to quality and individualized services now drives change efforts for more effective services. It became clear that access to traditional services for all populations was not meeting the complex and changing needs of diverse groups. Passage of the Patient Protection and Affordable Care Act in 2010, and implementation in 2013, generated significant data on disparities in the American population regarding the privilege of health care insurance. It is alarming that children, the chronically mentally ill, and the aged, who are vulnerable segments of the population, often bear the brunt of the unequal distribution of health care services.

The concept of *health equity* puts forth disparity reduction goals, supports participatory processes that in the past were in the domain of the professional as expert, and identifies needed changes in policy and service delivery. Moreover, efforts are directed at risk reduction, prevention, reducing barriers to access, and supporting the development of a diverse professional workforce (see the website of the Massachusetts Office of Health Equity: www.mass.gov/dph/healthequity).

Implications of Diversity Demographics

The concept of multiculturalism gives recognition to the variety and significance of ethnic and class culture in the lives of individuals, families, and communities. *Multicultural diversity* has wide-ranging variation in definition and uses of the concept. In principle, it refers to the notion that "a variety of cultural identities can be lived out in the same society" (Van Soest, 1995, p. 56); moreover, it has become a lightning rod because it bears on the sensitive topic of "the meaning of America"—that is, who we have been, who we are, and what we as a nation wish to become (Hunter, 1991, p. 50). The complexity of individuals' lives, arising from their multifaceted social identity, suggests that a multicultural perspective is essential. In addition, accurate evaluation of mental health functioning in the context of culture and diversity must include socioeconomic factors that intersect with culture. Diversity considerations need to address various types of difference, for example, in relation to socioeconomic class, ethnicity, gender, disability, and LGBTQ considerations. The individual's social power or lack of it, and how this factor bears on coping with mental illness, is essential to understand.

The absence of a systematic way to examine contextual factors—such as socioeconomic status, immigration, poverty, discrimination, and stigma in the development and maintenance of mental disorders—risks vulnerability of the client/consumer to distortion, by mental health providers, of their lived experience and perceptions of that experience. Intersectionality addresses the importance of recognizing all facets of an individual's life experiences and how these various elements interact. Context helps us understand the contribution of a vast array of factors arising from situational, life course, family system, physical environment (e.g., poverty, neighborhoods, schools, justice system), and societal sources (e.g., racism, oppression, negative stereotyping). Understanding an individual's social identity, historical legacy, and social power alerts the clinician to the powerful influence on the individual of a reference group's view of a mental disorder. The identification of a disorder, the meaning it has in the individual's personal and social life, the diagnostic process, and the identification of interventions are all affected by these factors. In particular, the individual's capacity for hope and openness to change has a tremendous influence on how a disorder is managed.

CASE STUDY 2

A Suicidal Woman

A middle-aged mother of two daughters had struggled all her life with posttraumatic stress disorder and depression, compounded by intense shame and feelings of failure related to her perceived inability to be a good mother to her children because of her mental illness. Her childhood had been filled with severe physical, emotional, and sexual abuse and neglect. From late adolescence on, she had been repeatedly hospitalized in inpatient psychiatric units owing to her intense suicidality.

After approximately 20 years of inpatient and outpatient treatment by a variety of mental health professionals, she entered treatment with a psychiatrist who reduced her medication and encouraged her to give vent to her intense inner rage and grief, offering his office during their sessions as a safe refuge in which she could express her anguish and confusion. His therapeutic stance differed from that of previous therapists in that he refused to collude in agreeing with her self-identity as a chronic mental patient and challenged her to excavate her demons and replace her self-loathing with an acknowledgment of her intelligence, creativity, and ability to function successfully as a mother, grandmother, and citizen. The client sometimes referred to this process as "undergoing surgery without an anesthetic," but she viewed it as lifesaving. She continues to take medication and to see her therapist regularly. She is currently active in her religious community and a leader in statewide and local community groups related to mental health. She has embraced the creative pursuits of gardening and community theater, is an active practitioner of meditation, expresses a delightful, long dormant sense of humor, and reads widely in theology and inspirational literature. In recent years, she has explored her Celtic identity and has become a much sought after speaker in graduate school classrooms, where she eloquently describes her journey into mental health and psychological flourishing. She states that when she became truly aware of "how we are all connected," she began to heal.

- What processes and elements of this client's experience with the psychiatrist were healing?
- If you were to implement this therapist's strategies, what concepts would guide your practice interventions?
- What strengths do you see in the client that enabled her to empower herself and engage in transformative changes?
- How does our current system of mental health care work against this kind of effective treatment?

A small but significant literature on social justice and clinical practice points to concerns about how the diagnostic process is influenced by socioeconomic status (Rose, 2006) and power relations (Parker, 2003; Swenson, 1998). Rose (2006) emphasizes that life course events are cumulative and impact health; health status reflects an "embodiment of prior living circumstances" and has psychosocial dimensions. When low socioeconomic status is involved, these dimensions can promote "low self-efficacy, low self esteem, and low intrinsic locus of control" (pp. 4 5). Parker incisively raises questions about clinicians' capacity for inclusiveness by asking if they primarily view the world from their own perspective, with attention only on those with more power than they, as opposed to mindfulness about their own privileges with respect to the realities of persons who are less privileged. For example, McIntosh proposes White privilege as referring to unearned assets that can be utilized on a daily basis, "but about which I was 'meant' to remain oblivious" (McIntosh, 2013, p. 187). On the other hand, target status perceptions are influenced by experiences with marginalization, devaluation, and invisibility. The concept of intersectionality highlights that most individual have some aspects of privilege and target status; some individuals have more of one than the other. Poland and Caplan (2004) suggest that there are several sources of bias in the diagnostic process arising from factors related to the clinician, professional values, and the context of the diagnostic process. Clinician-related qualities include attitudes about diverse groups, capacity for perspective taking (i.e., empathy), critical self-reflection, information processing biases, and inferences about medications. Factors related to professional values include terminology associated with particular professions, views of clients as passive recipients of care versus self-advocates, and economic requirements. Bias in contextual factors includes, in part, resource availability, requirements of funding sources, and organization of authority. These authors propose several changes that encompass the development of new, alternative diagnostic protocols, based on a strength-based critical-thinking approach, clinician awareness of the context of behavior, a multidimensional perspective, and a constructivist model framework (Corcoran & Walsh, 2006; Gray & Zide, 2005; McAulliffe, Eriksen, & Kress, 2005).

Diversity and Mental Health

Culturally competent practice is premised on culturally relevant organizational settings that provide the context for effective clinical practice. Although a thorough review of the relevant literature is beyond the scope of this book, we nonetheless assert the necessity of not falling into a monolithic, myopic vision that disembodies clinical practice from its context. We proceed to focus on the interpersonal, interactional skill that provides the foundation for effective practice. Both content and process clinical skills are vitally important in conducting an accurate diagnosis within the context of the individual's culture and life experiences. In the larger context of agreement regarding the importance of being informed about diverse cultural values, beliefs, and practices (i.e., content), much discussion continues about process issues, described as the clinician's awareness of the significant role of clinician bias, countertransference, and oppression (Dean, 2001). *Diversity* in this text refers to the ubiquity of culture. All individuals live in the context of a culture based on ethnic, socioeconomic, religious identifications; however, there are many other identifications and communities, such as gender identity/orientation and physical/mental ability that are important to acknowledge. As complex beings, most of us identify with various communities as sources of meaning that represent an asset. It is essential to discover the various sociocultural connections individuals experience that provide a context for their experiences. Those cultural connections and affiliations constitute sources of strength that can have a healing role in treatment planning and interventions.

Diagnosis with diverse populations places greater importance on the knowledge of the cultural meaning of behavioral expression and on information about culturally relevant means for managing psychological states. This requires awareness and/or information gathering on the meaning of the symptoms within a culture and the contextual factors that influence the interpretation of the behavior. The roles of diversity and social power in the lives of clients necessitate mindful attention to sorting out to what degree the problem behavior is a function of a psychological disorder or represents survival in an oppressive situation (D. W. Sue & Sue, 2008). Regardless of one's theoretical approach, comprehensive data gathering is needed in this area and should be reflected in the formulation. It is also essential that the clinician have heightened self-awareness, attunement to others, and relational skills that enable connecting with diverse others for the purpose of creating a working alliance (American Psychological Association, 2003). It is also vital that attention is paid to the organizational and professional cultures that may be sources of hidden institutionalized bias within professional groups and between organizations and their clients.

PROMISING THEORETICAL AND APPLIED CLINICAL ORIENTATIONS

Strength-Based Practice

The core philosophy of strength-based and empowerment practice is increasingly embraced by social workers and other mental health practitioners (Glicken, 2004; Lee, 2001; Poulin, 2005; Saleebey, 2002). Collaborative relationships with clients are promoted and clients are viewed as possessing resources as well as problems. Research in health psychology, in particular, supports strength-based, resiliency-focused attitudes and practices. Enhanced self-efficacy is consistently a powerful predictor, sometimes the most powerful, of the ability to sustain commitment to a goal in the context of uncertain outcome and complex struggle in both organizational, community, and clinical contexts, and in a variety of life-enhancing endeavors, such as the ability to follow through on health-promoting behaviors, or to meet educational and other life-enhancing personal goals (Bandura, 1997). Some self-efficacy research has demonstrated that people sometimes improve their behavior more successfully when given feedback with their errors omitted entirely, focusing only on what they are doing correctly (Bandura, 1997). The groundswell of emphasis on resiliency, expressed as positive personal strengths as well as interpersonal and community support in order to buffer stress and enhance coping with problems, is scientifically impressive and is striking a responsive chord with the public at large.

Resiliency

Practice that is premised on a value of wellness (Cowen, 1991) rather than pathology validates culture as a source of resiliency (Bonanno, 2004; Masten, 2001) and as a protective factor, it examines resources related to individual (attitude, social identity, coping), family (structure, communication, coping), and community (network, roles, support) sources. Assumptions about cultural patterns of behavior and preferences need to be suspended in favor of placing the individual in the foreground and disorder categorization in the background for the purpose of capacity building of individuals and their support systems. Physicians and the specific mental health disciplines of psychiatry, psychology, social work, and nursing ignore resiliency factors at a great cost to the client.

Positive Psychology

A growing body of literature asserts the philosophical position of positive psychology, which represents a paradigm shift in which the science of psychological health and well-being are studied as having equal and perhaps greater significance in relation to recovery from emotional problems than the focus on pathology (Linley & Joseph, 2004). Psychologists are paying systematic attention to the enhancement of personal and environmental strengths and positive coping skills, in the process of diagnosing and treating both mental disorders and related relationship problems (Bandura, 1997; Goleman, 2005; Gottman, Murray, Swanson, Tyrson, & Swanson, 2002; Gottman, Gottman, & Declaire, 2006; Peterson, 2006; Seligman, 2004; Seligman, Steen, Park, & Peterson, 2005). Linley and Joseph (2004) explore values and choices involved in self-regulation and the good life, healthy lifestyle practices, teaching strategies for the promotion of wisdom, the application of positive psychology in clinical practice, and the relationships among individual well-being, community, and social policy. Keyes and Haidt (2003) lament the narrowing of the field of psychology based on a disease model and call strongly for a new model of mental health that can encompass two dimensions, the mental health continuum and the mental illness continuum, as essential to accurate and useful diagnosis. Lopez et al. (2006) endorse this point of view and apply these concepts to their suggested alterations in the *DSM*, including their own concept of adding an additional axis to the diagnostic structure.

Wellness/Recovery Approach Model

Social work, in particular, is premised on the person–environment interaction and biopsychosocial approaches, and frames practice within resiliency and cultural diversity perspectives (Appleby, Colon, & Hamilton, 2007; Cohen,

Tran, & Rhee, 2007; Lum, 2011). These perspectives are increasingly recognized in all mental health professions. Corcoran and Walsh's (2006) observation—that the lack of a systematic diagnostic mechanism for addressing resilience, strength, and positive extra-individual contexts in the individual's life is lacking—summarizes a major theme in many writings. These authors go on to suggest that the "*DSM* makes no provisions for recording client strengths ... [and] could allocate one or more axes to strengths" (p. 23). Noteworthy is that, in line with our first edition, the *DSM-5* (APA, 2013) Cultural Formulation, the *DSM-5* encourages identification of "psychosocial stressors and cultural features of vulnerability and resilience" (p. 750). Unfortunately, comments such as the aforementioned are buried in small print in Section III of the *DSM-5* and are likely to be unnoticed. They underscore, however, the need to emphasize context and resiliency as the *DSM-5* format risks losing sight of these factors in the diagnostic process.

The Recovery Model identified in the President's New Freedom Commission on Mental Health Report (see the website for the President's New Freedom Commission on Mental Health [2002], www.mentalhealthcommission.gov) assumes the capacity for resiliency in all individuals with mental health disorders. It shifts the medical model focus on symptom reduction and mental illness as disease to diagnosis and healing, meaning a focus on living *with* mental illness. This focus emphasizes the "recovery of functional abilities, [the ability to live] independently, to work productively, to have social relationships, and to participate in community life" (Spaulding, Sullivan, Poland, & Ritchie, 2010, p. 328).

Recognition of the significance of the consumer's role in the recovery process promotes consumer agency in the diagnostic process, reframes the role of the professional as expert, and moves the consumer from the margin to the center. The idea of living with the illness as a central goal promotes the notion that the key aim of effective mental health services is for the consumer to "live with" mental illness and rebuild a life (Ralph & Corrigan, 2005) based on client self-determination. The role of the clinician in supporting exploration of consumers' desires, abilities, and needs in the service of promoting a full life stands in sharp contrast to the traditional emphasis on symptom reduction. Noteworthy is the existence of a consumer/survivor movement, which has received increasing traction over the decades. Everett (1994) proposes the consumer/survivor movement as a fourth movement, following the asylum, mental hygiene, and deinstitutionalization movements. Further, she suggests that the consumer/survivor movement is split between advocacy and nonpsychiatric services-based recovery. At the heart of the movement is choice to determine one's own way of living with one's mental illness and integration into one's community. Substantial attention is given to the presence of stigma, both personal and public (Corrigan, 2014; Frese & Davis, 1997).

SUMMARY

An approach that values diversity and culture and embraces a strengths perspective explores questions that all too often are not on the radar when diagnosis and treatment planning are based on standardized, traditional approaches or when treatment is limited to medication. For instance, the use of bilingual, bicultural translators requires specific skills on the part of the clinician as well as the utilization of probes that tap into the client's perceptions of his or her experience.

In this book, attention is given to the instrumental role of formulation in conceptualizing the etiology of client's problems via historical and cultural context and behavioral information (i.e., symptoms) and its importance in pulling together clinical understanding of sources that are internal and external. Our discussion particularly focuses on the development and application of a strength-based formulation that draws from several domains of an individual's life and attends to resiliency in the person as well as in his or her network, family, and culture.

Much of the current theoretical discussion and empirical research concerning multicultural issues, however, is largely presented within a framework of pathology and/or ethnic/cultural explanations of mental disorders. The *DSM-5* provides some contextualization via the V/Z codes; however, they are not systematically invoked via a *DSM* diagnostic format. The adaptive emphasis that we propose in this book examines cultural, intrapsychic, and contextual factors in terms of their *contributions* to an individual's strengths and resiliency. The proposed "Formulation Diagnostic Model" in Chapter 2 addresses the empowering aspects of the individual's functioning and recognizes culture as an important variable in order to promote a more realistic diagnostic formulation that can provide a pragmatic link to treatment planning and intervention. We hope to strengthen the bridge between disparities and equity research and evidence-informed mental health practice with diverse populations in order to increase the relevance and accuracy of diagnosis and facilitate positive treatment outcomes for underserved populations. The *DSM*, we argue, needs to continue expansion that accounts for the client's culture, multiple life contexts, and internal and external sources of strength, resiliency, and support.

DISCUSSION QUESTIONS AND ACTIVITIES

1. Describe the difference between pathology-based and strength-based approaches to understanding an individual.
2. Without censoring yourself, write down three adjectives that immediately come to mind when you think of the following: an old man, an old woman, an African American male, a Mexican farm worker, an anorexic female, an Asian American, a lesbian, a homosexual male, a homeless person, and a Euro American entrepreneur. Examine your adjectives for themes that might arise.
3. Describe the difference between culture as language and customs versus culture as personal identity. How do you think this would affect your ability to diagnose a client's mental illness?
4. Think of your professional context (for example, school, clinic, private practice). What are the values of the professional culture? Do these values clash with the ethnically diverse cultures of clients? What enhancements or barriers to accurate diagnosis and treatment may exist?

5. Are there invisible cultures in your community? Think about this from an ethnic, social class, professional, gender, racial, and age perspective. If you can't think of examples, ask this question of colleagues, friends, and a variety of community members until you hear some stimulating answers!
6. Find a colleague who is a member of a culture different from yours. Interview the colleague, using the structured interview format presented here. Then reverse roles and ask the colleague to interview you. Having completed this exercise, what were you able to learn about yourself and your partner? Write a paragraph about your experience.
   a. How is someone greeted in your culture? Is there someone who should be greeted first (e.g., father, recognized leader, male)? What body gestures are used (handshakes or bows, for example)? Is eye contact encouraged or avoided? How is respect shown?
   b. How should someone enter your home? If someone is invited for a visit, what is expected or appreciated (i.e., a gift, flowers, food)?
   c. Who in your family takes responsibility for things like the following, and what would he or she do about them?
      i. Preparing meals
      ii. Making sure children get to school and get their homework done
      iii. Helping with an important and serious problem or crisis
      iv. Taking care of a sick child or adult
      v. Taking care of elderly family members
      vi. Handling a marital problem or other family conflict
      vii. Managing a teenager in trouble with the law
      viii. Managing money
   d. Would your family seek help outside of the immediate family? From whom? What kinds of concerns would prompt you or your family members to seek outside help?
   e. If someone not of your culture were to try to help you with any of the problems in item "c", what would be most helpful? How would it be different with someone of your own race/ethnicity/culture?
   f. What would definitely *not* be helpful, would be a big mistake, or would be harmful? How would this apply to someone of your own ethnicity/race/culture?
   g. What do you most treasure about your culture/ethnicity/racial identity? Are there ways in which you have chosen to reject or change aspects of your cultural heritage? If so, how and why?
   h. When have you felt most comfortable, most understood by someone of your own or another culture? What was special about this experience? When have you felt least understood, stereotyped, or treated without respect, and what stands out about this experience?
   i. What would be the most important thing you'd want your partner to know about your family and your culture/ethnicity/race?
7. Imagine that you had just been diagnosed with schizophrenia and/or Alzheimer's disease. What would you want the mental health professional to know about you?

8. When you consider your worldview, what brings hope to your life? What factors contribute to your experience of hope?
9. Consider what "wellness" means to you. What comes to mind? What role do physical and/or psychosocial factors have? What role does your daily mood (e.g., energy, active) and/or life satisfaction have?

WEB RESOURCES

www11.georgetown.edu/research/gucchd/nccc
www.mass.gov/dph/healthequity

REFERENCES

Aguilar-Gaxiola, S., & Breslau, J. (2007, June). *Disparities in mental health: What are (some of) the questions to ask and what does (some of) the data tell us?* Presentation at Prevalence of Mental Illness in California: Estimating Disparities and Need. California Department of Mental Health & California Institute for Mental Health Conference, Sacramento, CA.

Alarcon, R., Alegria, M., Bell, C., Boyce, C., Kirmayer, L., Lin, K. M., ... Wisner, K.L. (2002). *Beyond the funhouse mirrors: Research agenda on culture and psychiatric diagnosis.* In D. Kupfer, M. First, & D. Regier (Eds.). A research agenda for *DSM-V*. (pp. 219–282). Washington, DC: American Psychiatric Press.

Alarcon, R. D., Westermeyer, J., Foulks, E. F., & Ruiz, P. (1999). Clinical relevance of contemporary cultural psychiatry. *Journal of Nervous Mental Disorders, 187*, 465–471.

Alegria, M., Nakash, O., Lapatin, Sh., Oddo., V., Gao, S., Lin, J., & Normand, S. (2008). How missing information in diagnosis can lead to disparities in the clinical encounter. *Journal of Public Health Management and Practice, 14*(Suppl.), S26–S35.

American Psychiatric Association. (2000). *Diagnostic and statistical manual of mental disorders* (4th ed., text rev.). Washington, DC: Author.

American Psychiatric Association. (2004). *Reducing mental health disparities for racial and ethnic minorities: A plan of action.* Arlington, VA: Author.

American Psychiatric Association. (2013). *Diagnostic and statistical manual of mental disorders* (5th ed.). Arlington, VA: American Psychiatric Press.

American Psychological Association. (2003). Guidelines on multicultural education, training, research, practice, and organizational change. *American Psychologist, 58*, 377–402.

Appleby, G. A., Colon, E. A., & Hamilton, A. (2007). *Diversity, oppression, and social functioning: Person-in-environment assessment and intervention* (2nd ed.). Boston, MA: Pearson.

Baker, F. M., & Bell, C. (1999). African Americans: Treatment concerns. *Psychiatric Services, 50*, 362–368.

Bandura, A. (1997). *Self-efficacy: The exercise of control.* New York, NY: W. H. Freeman.

Bernstein, R., & Edwards, T. (2008). *An older and more diverse nation by midcentury.* U.S. Department of Commerce, U.S. Census Bureau News. Retrieved from www.census.gov/newsroom/releases/archives/population/ cb08-123.html.

Bonanno, G. A. (2004). Loss, trauma, and human resilience. *American Psychologist, 59*(1), 20–28.

Chow, J., Jaffee, K., & Snowden, L. (2003). Racial/ethnic disparities in the use of mental health services in poverty areas. *American Journal of Public Health, 93*(5), 792–797.

Cohen, N. A., Tran, T. V., & Rhee, S. Y. (2007). *Multicultural approaches in caring for children, youth and their families.* Boston, MA: Pearson Education.

Corcoran, J., & Walsh, J. (2006). *Clinical assessment and diagnosis in social work practice.* New York, NY: Oxford University Press.

Corrigan, P. W (Ed.) (2014). *The stigma of disease and disability.* Washington, DC: American Psychological Association.

Cowen, E. (1991). In pursuit of wellness. *American Psychologist, 46*(4), 404–408.

Cross, T., Bazron, B. J., Dennis, K. W., & Isaacs, M. R. (1989). *Towards a culturally competent service of care* (Vol. 1). Washington, DC: Georgetown University Center for Child and Human Development.

Dean, R. (2001). The myth of cross cultural competence. *Families in Society, 82*(6), 623–630.
Eshun, S., & Gurung, R. A. R. (Eds.). (2009). *Culture and mental health*. Malden, MA: Wiley-Blackwell.
Everett, B. (1994). Something is happening: The contemporary consumer and psychiatric survivor movement in historical context. *Journal of Mind and Behavior, 15*(1–2), 55–70.
Frese, F. J., & Davis, W. W. (1997). The consumer-survivor movement, recovery, and consumer professionals. *Professional Psychology: Research and Practice*, 28, 243–245.
Frances, A. (2013). *Essentials of Psychiatric Diagnosis: Responding to the Challenge of DSM-5*. New York, NY: Guilford Press.
Garyali, V. (1999). The color of suspicion: Race profiling or racism? *Journal of American Academy of Psychiatry & Law, 27*, 630–632.
Glicken, M. D. (2004). *Using the strengths perspective in social work practice*. Boston, MA: Pearson, Allyn & Bacon.
Goleman, D. (2005). *Emotional intelligence*. New York, NY: Bantam Books.
Good, B. J., & Good, M. D. (1986). The cultural context of diagnosis and therapy: A view from medical anthropology. In J. E. Mezzich & G. Caracci (Eds.), *Cultural formulation: A reader for psychiatric diagnosis* (pp. 27–50). Lanham, MD: Jason Aronson.
Gottman, J., Murray, J., Swanson, C., Tyrson, R., & Swanson, K. (2002). *The mathematics of marriage: Dynamic nonlinear models*. Cambridge, MA: MIT Press.
Gottman, J. M., Gottman, J. S., & Declaire, J. (2006). *Ten lessons to transform your marriage: America's love lab experts share their strategies for strengthening your relationship*. New York, NY: Crown.
Gray, S., & Zide, M. (2005). *Psychopathology: A competency based treatment model for social workers*. Belmont, CA: Thomson Brooks/Cole.
Gurung, R. A. R., & Roethel-Wendorf, A. (2009). Stress and mental health. In S. Eshun & R. A. R. Gurung (Eds.), *Culture and mental health* (pp. 35–53). Malden, MA: Wiley-Blackwell.
Helman, C. G. (1990). *Culture, health and illness* (2nd ed.). Oxford, UK: Butterworth-Heinemann.
Hovarth, A. (1994). Reliance on the alliance. In A. Hovarth & I. Greenberg (Eds.), *The working alliance: Theory, research, and practice* (pp. 121–155). New York, NY: John Wiley & Sons.
Hunter, J. D. (1991). *Culture wars: The struggle to define America*. New York, NY: Basic Books.
Jones, P. (2010). Responding to the ecological crisis: Transformative pathways for social work education. *Journal of Social Work Education, 46*(1), 67–84.
Kales, H., Blow, F., Bingham, C., Copeland, L., & Mellow, A. (2000). Race and inpatient psychiatric diagnosis among elderly veterans. *Psychiatric Services, 51*, 795–800.
Keyes, C. L. M., & Haidt, J. (Eds.). (2003). *Flourishing: Positive psychology and the live well-lived*. Washington, DC: American Psychological Association.
Kirmayer, L. J., & Young, A. (1999). Culture and context in the evolutionary concept of mental disorder. *Journal of Abnormal Psychology, 108*, 446–452.
Kupfer, D. J., First, M. B., & Regier, D. A. (Eds.). (2002). *A research agenda for the DSMV*. Washington, DC: American Psychiatric Association.
Lee, J. A. B. (2001). *The empowerment approach to social work practice: Building the beloved community* (2nd ed.). New York, NY: Columbia University Press.
Lewis-Fernandez, R. (2008). Cultural formulation of psychiatric diagnosis. In J. E. Mezzich & G. Caracci (Eds.), *Cultural formulation: A reader for psychiatric diagnosis* (pp. 93–103). Lanham, MD: Jason Aronson.
Linley, P. A., & Joseph, S. (Eds.). (2004). *Positive psychology in practice*. Hoboken, NJ: John Wiley & Sons.
Lopez, S. (1989). Patient variable biases in clinical judgment: Conceptual overview and methodological considerations. *Psychological Bulletin, 106*, 184–203.
Lopez, S. J., Edwards, L., Pedrotti, J. T., Prosser, E. C., LaRue, S., Spalitto, S. V., & Ulven, J. C. (2006). Beyond the *DSM-IV*: Assumptions, alternatives, and alterations. *Journal of Counseling and Development, 84*(3), 259–267.
Lu, R. G., Lim, R. F., & Mezzrich, J. E. (2008). Issues in the assessment and diagnosis of culturally diverse individuals. In J. E. Mezzich & G. Caracci (Eds.), *Cultural formulation: A reader for psychiatric diagnosis* (pp. 115–148). Lanham, MD: Jason Aronson.

Lum, D. (Ed.) (2011). *Culturally competent practice.* (4th ed.). Belmont, CA: Brooks/Cole.

Marsella, A. J., & Yamada, A. M. (2000). Culture and psychopathology: Foundations, issues and directions. In I. Cuellar & F. Paniagua (Eds.), *Handbook of multicultural mental health* (pp. 3–24). San Diego, CA: Academic Press.

Masten, A. S. (2001). Ordinary magic: Resilience processes in development. *American Psychologist, 56*(3), 227–238.

McAulliffe, K., Eriksen, K., & Kress, V. (2005). A developmental, constructivist model for ethical assessment. In K. Eriksen & V. E. Kress (Eds.), *Beyond the DSM story* (pp. 187–205). Thousand Oaks, CA: Sage.

McIntosh, P. (2013). White privilege: Unpacking the invisible knapsack. In Fiske-Rusciano (Ed.), *Experiencing race, class, and gender in the United States* (6th ed., pp. 187–190). New York, NY: McGraw-Hill.

Metzl, J. M. (2009). *The protest psychosis: How schizophrenia became a black disease.* Boston, MA: Beacon Press.

Mezirow, J. (2003). Transformative learning as discourse. *Journal of Transformative Education, 1*(1), 58–63.

Mezzich, J. E. (2008). Cultural formulation: Development and critical review. In J. E. Mezzich & G. Caracci (Eds.), *Cultural formulation: A reader for psychiatric diagnosis* (pp. 87–92). Lanham, MD: Jason Aronson.

Mukherjee, S., Shukla, S., Woodle, J., Rosen, A. M., & Olarte, S. (1983). Misdiagnosis of schizophrenia in bipolar patients: A multiethnic comparison. *American Journal of Psychiatry, 140*, 1571–1574.

National Association of Social Workers. (2007). *Indicators for the achievement of the NASW standards for cultural competence in social work practice* (National Committee on Racial and Ethnic Diversity [NCORED]). Washington, DC: Author.

Neighbors, H. W., Trierweiler, St. J., Ford, B. C., & Muroff, J. R. (2003). Racial differences in *DSM* diagnosis using a semistructured instrument: The importance of clinical judgment in the diagnosis of African Americans. *Journal of Health and Social Behavior, 43*, 237–256.

Nichter, M. (1981). Idioms of distress: Alternatives in the expression of psychosocial distress. *Culture, Medicine & Psychiatry, 5*, 379–408.

Parker, L. (2003). A social justice model for clinical social work practice. *Affilia, 18*(3), 272–288.

Peterson, C. (2006). *A primer in positive psychology.* New York, NY: Oxford University Press.

Phinney, J. S. (2003). Ethnic identity and acculturation. In K. M. Chun, P. B. Organista, & G. Marin (Eds.), *Acculturation: Advances in theory, measurement, and applied research* (pp. 63–81). Washington, DC: American Psychological Association.

Pierce, C., Carew, J., Pierce-Gonzalez, D., & Willis, D. (1978). An experiment in racism: TV commercials. In C. Pierce (Ed.), *Television and education* (pp. 62–88). Beverly Hills, CA: Sage.

Poland, J., & Caplan, P. J. (2004). The deep structure of bias in psychiatric diagnosis. In P. J. Caplan & L. Cosgrove (Eds.), *Bias in psychiatric diagnosis* (pp. 9–24). Lanham, MD: Jason Aronson.

Poulin, J. (2005). *Strengths-based generalist practice: A collaborative approach* (2nd ed.). Belmonct, CA: Thompson/Brooks/Cole.

Ralph, R., & Corrigan, P. (Eds.). (2005). *Recovery in mental illness: Broadening our understanding of wellness.* Washington, DC: American Psychological Association.

Rogler, L. H. & Cortes, D. E. (1993). Help-seeking pathways: A unifying concept in mental health care. *The American Journal of Psychiatry, 150*(4), 554–561.

Rose, S. M. (2006, February). *Embodied inequalities: A social work perspective on class and health.* Paper presented at the Council on Social Work Education Annual Program Meeting, Chicago, IL.

Saleebey, D. (2002). *The strengths perspective in social work practice* (3rd ed.). Boston, MA: Allyn and Bacon.

Seligman, M. E. P. (2004). Can happiness be taught? *Daedalus, 133*(2), 80–87.

Seligman, M. E. P., Steen, T. A., Park, N., & Peterson, C. (2005). Positive psychology progress: Empirical validation of interventions. *American Psychologist, 60*, 410–421.

Snowden, L. (2003). Bias in mental health assessment and intervention: Theory and evidence. *American Journal of Public Health, 93*(2), 239–243.

Spaulding, W. D., Sullivan, M. E., Poland, J. S., & Ritchie, A. J. (2010). State psychiatric institutions and the left-behinds of mental health reform. *American Journal of Orthopsychiatry*, *80*(3), 327–333.

Strakowski, S. M., Shelton, R. C., & Kolbrener, M. L. (1993). The effects of race and comorbidity on clinical diagnosis in patients with psychosis. *Journal of Clinical Psychiatry*, *54*(3), 96–102.

Sue, D. W., Capodilupo, C. M., Torino, G. C., Bucceri, J. M., Holder, A. M. B., Nadal, K. L., & Esquilin, M. (2007). Racial microaggressions in everyday life. *American Psychologist*, *62*(4), 271–286.

Sue, D. W., & Sue, D. (2008). *Counseling the culturally diverse* (5th ed.). New York, NY: John Wiley & Sons.

Sue, S. (1998). In search of cultural competence in psychotherapy and counseling. *American Psychologist*, *53*(4), 440–448.

Swenson, C. (1998). Clinical social work's contribution to a social justice perspective. *Social Work*, *43*(6), 527–537.

Trierweiler, S. J., Neighbors, H., Munday, C., Thompson, E., Binion, V., & Gomez, J. P. (2000). Clinician attributions associated with the diagnosis of schizo-phrenia in African American and non-African American patients. *Journal of Consulting and Clinical Psychology*, *68*(1), 171–175.

U.S. Department of Health and Human Services. (1999). *Mental health: A report of the Surgeon General* (U.S. Department of Health and Human Services, Substance Abuse and Mental Health Services Administration, Center for Mental Health Services, National Institutes of Health, National Institute of Mental Health). Washington, DC: U.S. Government Printing Office.

U.S. Department of Health and Human Services. (2001). *Mental health: Culture, race, and ethnicity—A supplement to Mental health: A report of the surgeon general* (U.S. Department of Health and Human Services, Public Health Service, Office of the Surgeon General). Washington, DC: U.S. Government Printing Office.

Van Soest, D. (1995). Multiculturalism and social work education: The non-debate about competing perspectives. *Journal of Social Work Education*, *31*(1), 55–66.

Vega, W., Kolody, B., Aguilar-Gaxiola, S., & Catalano, R. (1999). Gaps in service utilization by Mexican Americans with mental health problems. *American Journal of Psychiatry*, *156*(6), 928–934.

Yamada, A. M., & Brekke, J. S. (2008). Addressing mental health disparities through clinical competence not just cultural competence: The need for assessment of sociocultural issues in the delivery of evidence-based psychosocial rehabilitation services. *Clinical Psychology Review*, *28*, 1386–1399.

TWO

Adding Diversity and Resiliency to the Diagnostic Process: A Formulation

What a piece of work is a man!
How noble in reason! How infinite in faculty!
In form and moving how express and admirable!
In action how like an angel! In apprehension how like a god!
The beauty of the world! The paragon of animals!
And yet, to me, what is this quintessence of dust?
—William Shakespeare, *Hamlet* (Act II, Scene 2)

We humans are, above all, complicated beings, capable of infinite creativity and imagination, accomplishment, joy, and fulfillment, on the one hand, and beset by self-doubt, anxiety, and a bewildering variety of mental ills on the other. Shakespeare's *Hamlet* struggles classically with paranoia, obsessive thinking, paralyzing self-doubt, ambivalence, suicidality, and existential angst, questioning the very nature of what it means to be human in the familiar quotation at the start of the chapter. Great literature, in fact, often captures the experience of mental illness and emotional suffering more eloquently than do academic textbooks by portraying the complexity of the human experience in language that reveals and alludes to the unspoken mysteries of emotional anguish and healing.

The language used to describe the mental and emotional challenges of persons from all walks of life can serve to strengthen or further demoralize them. Diagnostic systems and broader assessment protocols have traditionally focused narrowly on signs of pathology, most often described as located within the individual, while largely ignoring the individual's context. As a result, the conceptualization of diagnosis, treatment, and recovery has often remained too narrow, confined to the remediation of pathology, with the typical goal of symptom removal and/or adequate coping. In the previous chapter, we have seen how the voices of clients of diverse backgrounds who are labeled with a mental or emotional disorder are all too often trivialized, and that those clients are more likely to be members of groups demonstrated in the mental health disparities literature to lack equal access to effective mental health services, diagnosis, and treatment. These clients may suffer exacerbated stigmatization due to double jeopardy (i.e., ethnicity and mental disorder) related to psychiatric labeling. When the consumer's uniquely complex internal and external contexts are taken into consideration as sources of resiliency as well as stress, however, the aim of diagnosis, assessment, and intervention includes the integration of difficult life experiences into a more empowering sense of self, transcending the limited focus on symptom removal and coping.

THE COMPLEXITIES OF DIAGNOSIS AND ASSESSMENT

The term *diagnosis* derives from medicine and historically focuses on signs and symptoms descriptive of illness—presumed to have one or more causes—for which effective treatment is sought; diagnosis focuses on pathology located within the individual, conceptualized as mental illness. The term *assessment*, often used interchangeably with *diagnosis*, is usually broader in meaning and employed to describe many facets of patient functioning, which may include the patient's relationship with larger systems such as the family, workplace, and community. Assessment can thus be conceptualized to include both pathology and strength.

The need for more comprehensive assessment, which incorporates biopsychosocial and, more recently, cultural and spiritual aspects of an individual's functioning, is increasingly recognized and even systematized in the multidisciplinary world of mental health treatment. The social work profession developed and officially endorsed the person-in-environment (PIE) approach (Karls & Wandrei, 1994) and has historically taken the lead in recognizing the complexity of the individual's world and the multidirectional interactions between the environment and the individual. Recent social work texts and auxiliary training manuals, noted in Chapter 1, emphasize competency, resilience, diversity, and empowerment (Anderson & Carter, 2003; Cooper & Lesser, 2005; Corcoran & Walsh, 2006; Delgado, Jones, & Rohani, 2005; Dworkin, 2005; Gambrill, 2006; Gray & Zide, 2008; Mackelprang & Salsgiver, 2009). Nurses use care plan models that not only explore signs and symptoms of pathology but also attend to patient strengths, coping behaviors, and family support in recognition of the powerful role of social support. Counselors rely on a combination of diagnosis and assessment, emphasizing an ongoing process in which the client collaborates with the counselor, forming hypotheses about the client's concerns. Subdivisions of the American Psychological Association have proliferated in recent years, increasingly recognizing the role of complexity in the lives of persons seeking treatment for mental and emotional problems; these include divisions related to cultural diversity, community psychology, trauma, refugee mental health, gender, spirituality, and positive psychology (see the website www.apa.org). Additionally, those who train physicians in general practice have come to recognize the importance of relationship building, cultural competence, and the connections between access to and barriers to care and outcome.

Psychiatry and the *Diagnostic and Statistical Manual of Mental Disorders*

Rcognizing the multidimensional nature of individual functioning and the need for a diagnostic system that incorporates the complex factors involved in mental and emotional disorders, psychiatry developed the *Diagnostic and Statistical Manual of Mental Disorders (DSM®)*. First published in 1952, as a variant of the World Health Organization's (WHO, 1952) *ICD-6*, the *DSM-I* (American Psychiatric Association [APA], 1952) focused on descriptions of diagnostic categories of mental disorders for the purpose of clinical utility and reflected a view of mental disorders as reactive to psychological, social, and biological factors. The term, *reaction*, was eliminated from the *DSM-II* (APA, 1968), which in other respects, remained similar to the *DSM-I*. *DSM-III*, published in 1980, introduced the multiaxial system with explicit diagnostic criteria and a descriptive, atheoretical focus. The multiaxial system recognized the effects of external environmental stressors on the individual and the need to assess overall functioning. Both *DSM-IV* (APA, 1994) and *DSM-IV-TR* (APA, 2000) valued and retained the multiaxial system. The revisions introduced in the *DSM-IV* resulted from a careful review of the growing empirical literature and the requirement of a more explicit rationale for diagnostic categories. The *DSM-IV-TR* attempted to correct any factual errors in *DSM-IV*, to update *ICD-9* (WHO, 2009) codes developed since the publication of the *DSM-IV*, to reflect new information available, and to strengthen the use of the *DSM* as an educational tool (American Psychiatric Association [APA], 2000).

DSM-IV-TR to *DSM-5*: A Summary of Changes

The publication of the *DSM-5*, in May 2013 (APA, 2013), however, eliminated the multiaxial system described previously. In an effort to make the diagnostic process in psychiatry more consistent with other medical specialties, the APA now requires mental health practitioners to use only one diagnosis (formerly Axis I or II). Contextual patient features, such as external stressors or descriptions of overall functioning, formerly described by Axes IV and V are no longer required and are expected to be voluntarily included using V or Z Codes for contextual conditions that affect the mental disorder. Exhibit 2.1 depicts major changes in the *DSM-5*. The reader is referred to the Preface of the *DSM-5* for a more complete description of these changes (APA, 2013, pp. xli–xliv).

We summarize changes from *DSM-IV-TR* to *DSM-5* as they apply to each disorder we focused on in the chapters to follow. For a snapshot summary of the criteria and name changes from the former to the current *DSM* manual, see the Appendix at the end of this chapter. Significant for the purpose of this text, however, is the removal of the multiaxial system. An acknowledgment of patient contexts, in the form of life stressors and a descriptor of adaptive functioning, will no longer be standard practice unless the clinician has the time and is highly motivated to create one in the form of a paragraph added to the single diagnostic label. The *DSM-5*, like its predecessors, remains focused exclusively on pathology and ignores patient strengths, even as it acknowledges environmental stressors in its V/Z codes. Thus it maintains the focus on internal pathology and on negative but not positive patient contexts.

EXHIBIT 2.1 Summary of Innovations, *DSM-5*

1. An emphasis on human development

   Chapter organization reflects a life-span approach, beginning with disorders of infancy and ending with disorders of old age. The concept of internalizing (experienced as body sensation, cognition, and emotion) versus externalizing disorders (expressed in behavior directed outward) influences the groupings of disorders. Descriptors are added to explain how each disorder may change across the life span. Age-related factors, specific to the diagnosis, are also added. When applicable, culture and gender issues are integrated into text descriptions.

2. From categorical toward dimensional classification

   Specifiers of symptom severity have been added for use across diagnostic categories to encourage the recognition of dimensionality in diagnosis. Cross-cutting assessment measures are presented for the clinician to use, in recognition of common symptoms or disturbances of functioning that appear across diagnostic categories.

3. Recent research influences changes in diagnostic groupings and descriptors

   Diagnostic formulations are responsive to recent neuroscience research and emerging genetic linkages among diagnostic groups. Genetic and physiological risk factors, prognostic indicators, and diagnostic markers, when available, are highlighted. The enhanced ability to identify diagnosis based on neurocircuitry, genetic vulnerability, and environmental exposures is noted.

4. An alternative way to conceptualize personality disorders is offered for consideration, and the clinician is referred to web-based sources for expanded assessment tools and access to current research.

5. All *DSM-5* codes are consistent with current and future *ICD* WHO codes for global consistency in mental health diagnosis. This was true in the past but is emphasized more clearly in *DSM-5*. Especially notable is the addition of *ICD* V/Z Codes in the *DSM-5*; these are considerably more extensive than in past *DSM*s.

Diagnosis, the Clinical Relationship, and Treatment Outcome

Increased complexity in diagnostic and assessment systems has followed from the recent proliferation of psychotherapy outcome research, with consistent findings related to factors such as extra-therapeutic relationships; placebo, hope, and expectancy effects; and model or technique. Client characteristics, qualities of the relationship, and shared interactive aspects of the alliance, rather than theoretical orientation or technique, have emerged as the most powerful predictors of positive therapeutic outcome regardless of diagnosis (Kivlighan, 2007; Linley & Joseph, 2004). As a result, research focused on the essential qualities of the effective therapeutic relationship (Hubble, Duncan, & Miller, 1999) is receiving more attention and respect. Current research controversies critically analyze the meaning of the term *evidence-based practice* (Norcross, Beutler, & Levant, 2006); focus on the place of psychotherapy in the managed care arena; and struggle with whether research should focus on characteristics of the effective client–practitioner relationship, the development of treatment protocols for specific disorders, or both.

Research funding often focuses narrowly on the development of psychopharmacological and other biological treatments, owing to the influence of pharmaceutical companies on research funding and public awareness (Gambrill, 2006; Norcross et al., 2006). It is impossible to watch prime-time television on any given evening without being bombarded with anxiety-producing commercials, suggesting signs and symptoms of depression, insomnia, erectile dysfunction, and dementia to the viewer and offering relief in the form of the latest medications. The impetus for a toolkit approach to mental health intervention, mandating specific treatment protocols for specific diagnoses, is further strengthened by the mandates of insurance companies for managed care, utilizing brief treatment. Thus what is assessed, funded, and promoted may bear little resemblance to the reality-based, complex worlds of the client (Kirk & Kutchins, 1992) or to what has been demonstrated to predict treatment outcome. The elimination of the axis system from *DSM-5* may exacerbate this disconnection.

In the often-heated controversies concerning mental health diagnosis and treatment, few professionals disagree with the need for diagnosis itself in order to communicate with other professionals, qualify for insurance reimbursement, or use a diagnostic label for the purpose of helping the client understand his or her condition. The critical issue, however, relates to whether diagnosis is utilized in a helpful, constructive, empowering way rather than in a stigmatizing manner (Gambrill, 2006; Lee, 2001; Preston, 1998). Most researchers and practitioners concur that a diagnostic system is crucial in order to identify, understand, and classify emotional and mental health problems, speak a common language, and work effectively in a multidisciplinary context. Preston (1998) asserts that "diagnostic maps" enable the clinician to be guided by a concept of the nature of the patient's problem, which can lead to appropriate strategies for treatment and contribute to the client's feeling understood, which is crucial to developing an effective relationship. Notably, Preston asserts that an understanding of the client's resiliency, defined as her ability to face stress and resist impairment by virtue of her strengths, is an essential component in diagnosis (Preston, 1998).

KEY POINTS

1. The term *diagnosis* traditionally focuses on symptoms of illness located within the individual, congruent with the medical model.
2. The broader term *assessment* focuses on both symptoms within the individual and the individual's functioning with respect to external systems, such as family, community, workplace, and culture, congruent with biopsychosocial/spiritual models.
3. The former multiaxial structure of the *DSM-IV-TR* (APA, 2000) incorporated both diagnosis and aspects of assessment, including environmental stressors and a global assessment of functioning. The elimination of the multiaxial structure in *DSM-5* runs the risk of making patient contexts more invisible

unless V(Z) codes are voluntarily used to identify stressors and the clinician makes use of suggested assessment instruments in the Section III of the *DSM-5* (APA, 2013) manual.

4. The processes and languages of diagnosis and assessment can be used to pathologize and disempower persons, or conversely to facilitate their empowering themselves.
5. All of the mental health professions increasingly emphasize the role of individual strengths, resiliency, culture, and other relevant external contexts in predicting positive treatment outcomes; yet the *DSM-5* diagnostic system continues to ignore these factors.

DSM: STRENGTHS AND WEAKNESSES

When the *DSM* is considered in light of the issues of diagnosis and assessment described previously, some notable strengths and weaknesses emerge. The *DSM III* (APA, 1980) through *IV-TR* (APA, 2000) succeeded in creating a descriptive taxonomy of symptoms separate from the theoretical controversies that have historically raged regarding etiology, allowed for co-occurring conditions to be recognized, and incorporated domains of relevant information, including medical diagnoses, external sources of stress, and the general level of functioning. As we have seen, the *DSM-5* eliminated the multiaxis typology while strengthening the relationship between diagnostic categories and research findings, made the diagnostic system more consistent with other medical specialties, and stressed the alignment of the *DSM*'s coding with the WHO's *ICD* classification system. The move toward dimensionality and away from discrete categories and the addition of severity and other specifiers relevant to particular diagnoses represent a greater recognition of interactive complexity in symptom presentation in the *DSM-5*. Despite these obvious strengths, however, the *DSM-5* continues to focus exclusively on pathology, ignore sources of resilience and support and trivialize the role of culture, by retaining its position in the back of the manual. There is no clear relationship among etiology, symptom checklists, diagnostic label, and treatment.

Strengths

Standardization Promotes Communication

The *DSM* provides a standard taxonomy that fosters communication among all mental health professionals, now more than ever on a global level. In the plethora of classification and assessment systems used among the mental health disciplines, the *DSM* is universally recognized and used in professional education, training, research, and treatment institutions in the United States. The WHO's (2010) *International Statistical Classification of Diseases and Related Health Problems* (*ICD-10*) represents the international taxonomy system and includes physical as well as mental disorders. Initially the plan was for a shift of the *ICD-9* codes to *ICD-10* codes in October 2014; plans are underway to introduce the *ICD-11* in 2015. Once implemented, the use of these codes will be mandatory for all international members of the WHO (Goodheart, 2014). The education, training, and licensure requirements of all the mental health disciplines aim to ensure that new professionals understand and utilize the *DSM* effectively. With greater emphasis on awareness that *DSM* codes are the same as *ICD* codes, mental health practitioners and researchers in our increasingly interactive global world will be more likely to be speaking the same language when they discuss mental disorders.

The DSM *Promotes Pragmatic Conceptualization for Research Design*

The standardization of terms and their descriptions provided by the *DSM* can facilitate the formulation of ongoing research and the general search for new knowledge. Standardization can aid in the precision with which mental disorders are conceptualized, discriminated from one another, and discussed. The formulation of research hypotheses, using *DSM/ICD* language ideally promotes lively discussion about what these diagnostic terms mean across cultures and geographies, allows for tests of reliability and validity of the terms, and facilitates refinement of their meaning over time.

The DSM *Is not Confined to Specific Theoretical Concepts*

The *DSM* has been deliberately designed to be atheoretical in nature in order to promote a common language that transcends ideological and philosophical commitments to concepts of etiology (APA, 2000). This descriptive taxonomy was designed to facilitate more constructive communication among treatment professionals who may adhere to differing schools of thought but have a common interest in the effective diagnosis and treatment of mental disorders.

The DSM *Has Been Responsive to Emerging Research and Societal Change*

The *DSM* is viewed as a flexible instrument that has responded to newly emerging research and cultural change. Beginning in the mid-1950s, the *DSM* has gone through several revisions reflective of emerging social movements, notably, feminism, lesbian and gay rights, survivors of war trauma, and groups advocating cultural diversity competency. As in the broader assessment systems previously mentioned, the historical evolution of the *DSM* illustrates the increased recognition of the complex sources of mental and emotional functioning. Originally beginning with three axes, it focused on psychiatric symptoms, pathological functioning, and medical complications (Axes I through III). In later revisions, Axes IV and V were added and acknowledged the contributions of environmental stressors and the need to determine the patient's overall level of functioning when reaching a diagnosis. Although Axes IV and V were more subjective and considered less reliable and valid in research, the need to understand the general content of these axes in making an adequate patient diagnosis was largely accepted. In their introduction to the classification system, the writers of the *DSM-IV-TR* acknowledged that diagnosis is only the beginning of a comprehensive assessment (APA, 2000). The elimination of the multiaxial system in

DSM-5, arguably weakens the recognition of complexity while focusing more on the neurobiological and genetic bases of mental disorders.

Several changes or additions to diagnoses in *DSM-5* illustrate its continued responsiveness to research, and the reader is again referred to the *DSM-5*'s preface and corresponding texts for each diagnosis to understand this in detail. Highlights include the addition of gambling disorder, which emphasizes addictive behaviors that cause great impairment and are related to disordered behaviors. Similarly, additional criteria for the diagnosis of trauma in children recognize increased awareness of the nonverbal ways children express traumatic mental injury. In recognition of a more precise and less stigmatizing categorization of dysphoria around one's gender identity as separate from a sexual dysfunction, gender dysphoria is presented separately from sexual disorders in the *DSM-5*. This change clarifies that a transgender identity is not a mental disorder in itself. Greater awareness of the experiences of transgendered children and adults has facilitated these changes. Other changes, including the elimination of the bereavement exclusion in mood disorder, the addition of a temper dysregulation disorder in children, and the addition of a minor impairment category in the cognitive disorders section, are extremely controversial and are regarded by some as weaknesses, not strengths, of the *DSM-5* (Frances, 2013).

A recent study by social work educators explored perceptions of the usefulness of the *DSM* and concluded that professional social workers increasingly view it as necessary to their work and important in social work education (Newman, Dannenfelser, & Clemmons, 2007). The *DSM-5* illustrates the pace of neurobiological research, our increasing global interconnectedness, and promotes an ongoing link to emerging knowledge through the Internet in our information age.

Weaknesses

The aforementioned strengths, however, must be considered in the context of larger problematic concerns and are thus weakly realized assets of the *DSM-5*. When considered in the light of the most recent research on resiliency, the role of culture, the reality of mental health disparities, and past and present environmental conditions on an individual's functioning, described in Chapter 1, the official diagnostic classification system (the *DSM*) leaves much to be desired. There is great concern about the potential for the *DSM-5* to pathologize normal human suffering, and in so doing, to reinforce what many feel is an unethical relationship between the drug industry and psychiatry (Frances, 2013). The increased emphasis on the neurobiological bases of mental disorders continues to obscure the complexity of the whole person in the diagnostic process. We summarize the weaknesses in *DSM-5* as follows:

Minimal Multidisciplinary Input in the DSM *Formulation and Decision-Making Process*

The ongoing task forces that shape the criteria for diagnoses in the *DSM* are composed predominantly of physicians, a few PhD psychologists, and, rarely, a social worker. Perhaps, as a result, the focus is more on the signs and symptoms of pathology with an implicit assumption of exclusive etiology based in neurobiology—that is, on what is problematic or missing—than on indicators of, or forces contributing to well-being. The medical model has proven to be important but insufficient when applied to the complexity of human problems. This becomes obvious when one notes the many alterations to the evolving structure of the *DSM* over time. The process of decision making has been strongly criticized as secretive and extremely political (Frances, 2013). Although the *DSM-5* task force announced its intention to invite input from practitioners, consumers of mental health services, and the general public by opening a web page inviting responses to proposed changes, the web page closed suddenly and without notice in spring 2013. Deliberations about diagnosis were held behind closed doors, and field trials were abruptly halted in order to publish the manual by May 2013. To learn more about the decision-making process and the politics of the *DSM*, the reader is referred to *Saving Normal* (Frances, 2013).

Limiting the formation and conceptualization of the diagnostic manual to one profession—psychiatry—when other mental health professions encounter mentally ill persons far more frequently and in a greater a variety of real-life settings makes no sense to us. Both overtly stated and covertly implied motives have influenced the structure of the *DSM-5* that has resulted from this closely guarded, political progress. Requiring only one diagnostic label and eliminating the multiaxial system makes psychiatric diagnoses look more like those of the rest of medicine. This change promotes surface consistency within medicine and at the same time responds to the desire of psychiatry to gain more respect from other medical specialists by appearing more "scientific." The change to a single required diagnostic label may also be related to what some critics consider the undue influence of the psychopharmaceutical industry on how research questions are formulated and resulting studies are designed, reinforcing a focus on the neurobiology of mental illness at the expense of psychosocial factors (Frances, 2013). The diagnostic labels that result end up largely as lists of symptoms indicating dysfunction unrelated to etiology or to indicators for interventions.

Considerable concern remains about the possible harmful effects of pathological labeling, and many researchers have called for greater social work and consumer involvement on the *DSM* task forces (Newman et al., 2007). We concur with these authors' recommendations, advocating for greater participation in the design and alteration of diagnostic classification processes by a profession that focuses its efforts on the interactions between individuals and their contexts and maintains an ethical commitment to social justice and to eliminating mental health disparities. Each of the mental health professions encounters persons with mental disorders in a different way; each conducts research and has important insights to offer the diagnostic classification process; thus each should have a presence in the decision-making process. Unfortunately, with the partial exception of psychology, the other mental health professions were left out of the development of the *DSM-5*.

Powerful Predictors of Successful Treatment Outcome Are Ignored

The *DSM* ignores precisely those client characteristics that most powerfully predict the outcome of mental health treatment, namely, those factors that can enable clients to adhere to the medication and evidenced-informed treatment protocols their practitioners can offer. These are referred to in outcome research as the "common factors" or "common psychosocial factors" (Hubble et al., 1999). The qualities of the practitioner–patient relationship, along with personality characteristics the patient brings to the relationship, combined with external events in the patient's life and his or her subjective interpretations of the diagnostic and treatment experience, profoundly influence how clients and consumers respond to mental health treatment. These factors are better predictors of both positive outcome in psychotherapy and of adherence to medically recommended psychopharmacology interventions than particular techniques, theoretical orientations, or practitioner training.

The invisibility of these characteristics is promoted by several factors related to the structure of the *DSM*. The elimination of the multiaxial system in *DSM-5*, with its exclusive focus on one diagnostic label, does not encourage the clinician to pay attention to the complex contextual world of the patient. The time pressures faced especially by physicians mitigate against inquiring about the patient's life and reinforce an exclusive focus on symptoms and the prescription of medication as the primary intervention. This problem is reinforced by the current practice of many agencies, in this technological era, to use a computerized list of symptoms, in boxes to be checked off on the form, when interviewing a client. Focusing on the form rather than the patient runs the risk of damaging the very relationship qualities that promote an effective response to the diagnostic and treatment process. Any expectation that clinicians will change their approach to practice with the complex, diverse clients they serve needs to be supported by professional frameworks and tools, such as the *DSM*, along with an organizational climate that will promote such change. The elimination of the multiaxial system in *DSM-5* arguably weakens support to the clinician to address the whole person. It is our hope that the recent passage of the Patient Protection and Affordable Care Act in March 2010, with its emphasis on integrated interdisciplinary health care, may encourage and reinforce attention to the patient characteristics, relationship qualities, and external contexts that best predict outcome in mental health diagnosis and treatment.

We believe that the role of personal strengths and talents, social and community support, and culture—which the individual client brings to the relationship with the professional—cannot be left to chance or to the special province of one or two disciplines through a subsequent assessment process. On the contrary, because these internal and external resources make the difference in whether the client can respond to the treatment offered or even form an effective relationship in which interventions can be discussed, the *DSM* must formally integrate them in order to diagnose the complex world of the client accurately and set the stage for an effective response.

Pathology Is Emphasized, Strengths and Resources Are Ignored

Assessment tools that mental health professionals use to complement the *DSM* have increasingly incorporated client strengths (Jordan & Franklin, 2011; Linley & Joseph, 2004; Lopez & Snyder, 2003), but literature reviews of collections of assessments/diagnostic and measurement tools reveal very little that is not exclusively pathology focused (Gambrill, 2005). Pathology remains a consistent theme in all of the *DSMs* versions. Changes in the *DSM-5* do not appear to correct these challenges. Consistent with earlier predictions, the *DSM-5* added dimensional considerations and more precise conceptualizations of symptoms, but the underlying value on an exclusive emphasis on pathology remains. Even in the V/Z codes, itemizing many sources of stress in the environment that affect the clinician–patient encounter, internal or external sources of strength and support are ignored. To make matters worse, the V/Z codes are likely to be ignored because they are not required to be noted. Fewer than 10% of those using the *DSM* used V codes in the past, which became an argument for their elimination in the *DSM-5*. Patient contexts, unique and varied sources of stress and support, are rendered even more invisible.

Physicians and the specific mental health disciplines of psychiatry, psychology, social work, and nursing ignore the combination of internal and external sources of resiliency at great cost to the client. Saleebey (2002) summarizes the debilitating consequences of a diagnostic classification of symptoms based solely in pathology. To begin with, the person is viewed as synonymous with the problem or pathology named:

> Once labeled … other elements of a person's character, experiences, knowledge, aspirations, slowly recede into the background, replaced by the language of symptom and syndrome. Inevitably, conversation about the person becomes dominated by the imagery of disease, and relationships with the ailing person re-form around such representations. To the extent that these labels take hold, the individual, through a process of surrender and increasing dependence, becomes the once alien identification. (Saleebey, 2002, p. 4)

In the process of pathological identity formulation described in the preceding quotation, self-stigmatization is reinforced (Corrigan, 2014), and it becomes ever harder for a human being so labeled either to hold on to a positive self-image or to fight against the negative public stereotypes of the mentally ill. It is difficult to exaggerate the consequences, evident in changing public policy over the past 50 years, in attitudes toward and treatment of persons with mental illness, most of whom are now responded to more in the criminal justice system or in homeless shelters than in mental health clinics (Torrey, 2014). As citizens with mental illness become ever more invisible, or visible only in disturbing ways, our ability even to notice their strengths, sources of resiliency, or cultural uniqueness is weakened. The *DSM-5* appears to exacerbate, not correct, this problem.

Professional Cynicism Is Facilitated

The language of pessimism, deficiency, and doubt leads to professional cynicism, a process that Andrew Weil, MD, calls "medical hexing" (Weil, 1995), in which the ability of patients to cope with the challenges of life and engage in processes of natural healing is ignored. The relationship between helper and helped is characterized by distance, power inequality, and control. If the client disagrees with the helper, he or she can be labeled resistant. The diagnostic classification system of the *DSM*, composed of lists of symptoms and stresses, reinforces the view of the client as defective and the mental health professional as an all-knowing and expert judge. Persons with mental illness have been found to receive fewer medical services than those without diagnostic labels or in treatment with mental health professionals, thus an exclusive focus on pathology can unwittingly contribute to stigmatization (Corrigan, 2014).

The cynicism and defensive distancing from persons with mental illness become clearer and more poignant when viewed from the perspectives of the patients and their families. In his poignant and highly praised memoir, *Imagining Robert*, Jay Neugeboren (1997/2003), the brother of a man with schizophrenia, describes his repeated encounters with psychiatrists, psychologists, social workers, and other personnel in both inpatient and outpatient settings. All too often, mental health professionals forgot important details about his brother's treatment or condition, ignored his individuality, failed to return phone calls, avoided answering questions, and engaged in a process that the author considers demeaning and dehumanizing. We have heard similar sentiments expressed by peer support specialists regarding the way they feel they are treated by professional colleagues.

The elimination of the multiaxial system, previously in the *DSM-IV-TR*, runs the risk of making a bad situation worse. The structure of the *DSM-IV-TR* at least suggested that the mental health professional consider that the patient lives in the midst of occupational, financial, familial, and community contexts and assess whether these contexts are creating stress that worsens the patient's symptoms. Frances (2013) wisely and repeatedly emphasizes the need to listen to the patient, to regard the diagnostic process as a team effort, and to take time without rushing to judgment because doing otherwise can risk iatrogenic harm through hasty labeling of the patient. The multiaxial system of the *DSM-IV-TR* implied the importance of the listening encounter with its structure of domains of functioning. With the axes eliminated from *DSM-5*, the tendency of the mental health professional to relate to her patients in a distant, aloof manner, limited to the discussion of a diagnostic label, the problem of cynicism is likely to be reinforced.

Decontextualizing Prevents Recognition of Potential Sources of Healing

Problem-based diagnoses ignore the clients' complex contexts by encouraging an individualistic rather than an ecological understanding of clients:

> When we transform persons into cases, we often see only them in terms of how well they fit in a category. In this way, we miss important elements of a

> person's life—cultural, social, political, ethnic, spiritual, and economic—and how they contribute to, sustain, and shape a person's misery or struggles or mistakes. The irony here is that, in making a case we really do not individualize. Information about context not considered relevant to an assessment scheme, might indicate important resources for help and transformation as well as problem-solving. (Saleebey, 2002, p. 5)

If the patient's contexts are ignored, we believe accurate diagnosis becomes impossible. In its current form, the *DSM* cannot do justice to the complexity of a patient's problems. Because it is limited to labels based in pathology, the *DSM* becomes reductionistic, focused only on what is problematic in the feelings or behavior of the client. Its use of diagnostic labels often lacks parsimony, ignores the client's context, and fails to take into account the strengths and sources of resilience that are crucial to an accurate fit between diagnosis and treatment (Gambrill, 2006; Linley & Joseph, 2004), thus offering a view of the client that violates logic and distorts reality. We illustrate this process in each chapter as we apply our recommended Diversity/Resiliency Formulation to a variety of clinical vignettes illustrating diagnostic categories.

The DSM *Is Subject to Bias, Affecting Reliability and Validity*

Diagnostic labels assigned to clients or patients vary with the age and theoretical orientation of the clinician, the client's race, and the environmental context in which the case history is presented (Pottick, Kirk, Hsieh, & Tian, 2007). We have known for years that in some studies nonprofessionals and patient peers are more reliable in their diagnoses than professionals (Rosenhan, 1973)! In reflecting on the Rosenhan study in his discussion of the lack of reliability and validity and the misuses of diagnosis, Whitaker (2002, p. 170) writes:

> Rosenhan's study was akin to proving that American psychiatry had no clothes. It was evidence that American psychiatry was diagnosing schizophrenia in a willy-nilly frivolous manner. As if that weren't threatening enough, a number of studies showed that American doctors were preferentially applying the label to people with black skin and the poor.

The shameful history of mental health disparities in the diagnosis and treatment in African Americans is carefully documented by Metzl (2009), who presents an excellent description of the interaction among race, class, culture, history, and stigma in psychiatric diagnosis.

Diagnostic categories are rarely discreet, and clients, more often than not, have coexisting conditions. With its section on cross-cutting measures and the addition of dimensional ratings of severity, the *DSM-5* has attempted to acknowledge the reality of coexisting conditions and to encourage the practitioner to remain abreast of current research through its emphasis on updated reports on its web page. But, despite the hope for scientific certainty, mental illness remains a complex interplay of nature and nurture. The diagnostic endeavor as a process is subjective, often unclear, and subject to change.

> There are no biological tests in psychiatry, and (with the exception of tests for dementia), none are in the pipeline for at least the next decade. Psychiatric diagnosis depends completely on subjective judgments that are necessarily fallible, should always be tentative, and must constantly be tested as you know the patient better. (Francis, 2013, p. 11)

Creating the one-label *DSM-5* system, designed to make psychiatry appear as "scientific" as the rest of medicine, does not correct the essential reality of complexity in mental health diagnosis and may ultimately make the problem worse by obscuring this issue.

Links Among Cause, Disease, and Cure Are Unclear and May Be Inaccurate

In assuming disease through a diagnosis based exclusively on pathology, one can also assume a cause for the disorder that leads logically to a solution. In the complexity of human problems, however, there often is no clear-cut link among cause, disease, and cure. The "supposition of disease also takes out of the hands of the person, family and friends, the neighborhood—the daily life of all involved—the capacity and resources for change" (Saleebey, 2002, p. 6). In so doing, these linkages—as perceived by the patient, family, and friends, which have their own meanings and related validities—are usually ignored. Thus links that may not be present may be assumed while empowering and useful connections may be ignored.

As it currently exists, the *DSM* does not offer a logical connection between diagnosis and useful interventions, despite the current emphasis on "evidence-based treatment," and the debate about its meaning and validity. The problem of transferring manualized treatments, designed and tested in the research setting, to the complicated worlds of the clinician diagnostician has led to healthy debate about what is meant by "evidence" and "treatment" (Norcross et al., 2006; Wachtel, 2010).

A useful link between diagnosis and treatment planning incorporates the genuine complexity of human beings, including strengths and assets, problems and pathology, and what is known about the predictive features of treatment outcome—namely, client and relationship characteristics (Linley & Joseph, 2004).

The relative absence of a logical connection between diagnostic label and choice of intervention is widely acknowledged throughout the mental health professions and may become even more obscure in *DSM-5*, with the elimination of the multiaxial system. One notable attempt to correct this imbalance is the recent publication of the *Psychodynamic Diagnostic Manual* (*PDM* Task Force, 2006), a collaborative effort of psychiatrists, psychologists, and clinical social workers seeking to address the need to take the whole person, with his or her complexity, into systematic account in the process of diagnosis. The authors argue for a diagnostic system that goes beyond a descriptive list of symptom patterns to embrace methodologies comprising a better fit for the phenomenon being analyzed—the intricate multifaceted nature of human mental health and illness. This, we believe, is an impressive effort in the right direction. Despite the merits of the *PDM*, which we would recommend for all mental health professionals as an extremely useful complement to the *DSM*, this psychoanalytically based, multidisciplinary volume does not address patient strengths, the contributions of positive psychology, or personal and cultural resilience. The *PDM* also ignores the effects of the larger social contexts, such as homelessness, correctional settings, marginal existences categorized by poverty and environmental vulnerability that are so prominent in the lives of much of the seriously mentally ill in our society. Although the *PDM* task force is to be commended for addressing complexity, discussing current research findings, and modeling interdisciplinary collaboration, the emphasis on pathology remains intact.

An additional problem with diagnostic conceptualizations, such as the *PDM* and the PIE models of social work, is that they are largely unknown and unused outside of a particular profession or treatment community and thus lack the ability to influence the structure of the *DSM*. Although potentially more relevant to the real world of patients, with greater acknowledgment of the relationship between diagnosis and treatment and of resiliency as well as pathology, these alternative structures remain largely invisible.

KEY POINTS

1. *Mental health practitioners generally agree that the DSM is an important diagnostic tool, essential to professional training and practice.*
2. The *DSM* provides a common, now global, language, transcends theoretical wars, and promotes efficient interdisciplinary communication.
3. Despite its usefulness, the *DSM* has serious flaws in its emphasis on description at the expense of etiology, its potential for reinforcing the stigma associated with a mental illness label, its uncertain reliability and validity, its lack of fruitful connection between the diagnostic label and a treatment plan, and its almost complete lack of attention to individual strengths, sources of resiliency, and diversity contexts.
4. The *DSM-5* has arguably made the situation worse.

RESEARCH AND DIAGNOSIS

There is strong support in the literature for recognition of the need to view the client presenting with mental or emotional concerns as a whole person, composed of strengths as well as weaknesses and possessed of internal and external resources as well as stresses. It would be unthinkable today in the field of medicine to treat heart disease simply with medicine or surgical procedures without also formally inquiring about psychological stress and lifestyle practices, such as smoking, diet, and exercise. These are necessary to address in order to mobilize positive coping behaviors of the patient. Neither would morbid obesity be treated with surgery alone, without first encouraging the patient to utilize available nutritional resources exercise programs and support groups, and then assessing the patient's psychological suitability for surgery. Likewise one would not refer a patient with Alzheimer's disease to a skilled nursing facility without attempting at the same time to utilize and strengthen her family support system. Andrew Weil, the eclectically trained and Harvard-educated physician, recognizes and endorses the equal importance of health-promoting practices and remediating interventions and calls physicians to task for focusing too exclusively on symptoms of illness while minimizing opportunities to enhance wellness and failing to notice the effects of relationship factors on their patients (Weil, 1995). In medical practice there is newer respect for approaches that strengthen the immune system and promote patient self-determination and well-being such as herbal medicine, acupuncture, physical therapy, massage, tai chi, and mindfulness meditation. These are all gaining in respectability and widespread acceptance. In other words, the process of medical diagnosis, to be relevant and realistic, needs to incorporate the broader processes of assessment.

Positive Psychology, Mindfulness, and Happiness

Many prominent psychologists (Bandura,1995; Keyes & Haidt, 2003; Linley & Joseph, 2004; Lopez & Snyder, 2003) stress the importance of systematic attention to and enhancement of personal and environmental strengths and positive coping skills in the process of diagnosing and treating mental disorders and related relationship problems. Others advocate for the importance of knowing what makes us happy, in order to understand and make use of how our brains work and to increase our experience of pleasure versus pain (Gilbert, 2007).

Research in health psychology, in particular, supports strength-based, resiliency-focused attitudes and practices. Enhanced self-efficacy is consistently a powerful predictor, sometimes the most powerful, of the ability to sustain commitment to a goal in the context of uncertain outcome and complex struggle (Bandura, 1997). When the focus is behavior change, some self-efficacy research has demonstrated that people improve their behavior more successfully when they are given feedback with their errors omitted entirely, focusing only on what they are doing correctly (Bandura, 1997).

Using forms of the relaxation response to enhance the mind–body connection in order to cope with stress, mental and emotional problems, physical pain, and illness is the focus of an esteemed clinic at the University of Massachusetts, and research generated there has been respected and widely utilized by physicians and allied health professionals (Kabat-Zinn, 1990). Clinical research on the process of forgiveness as a core issue in resolving anger, depression, and anxiety helps us think about and illuminate connections between spiritual and psychological well-being (Enright & Fitzgibbons, 2000). The call for research in areas of positive psychology, spirituality, and cultural competence is echoing in both professional and nonprofessional worlds. The reader is encouraged to explore the explosion of books and journal articles in these areas.

Social Work and Strength-Based, Empowerment Practice

Social workers increasingly embrace a core philosophy of strength-based and empowerment practice (Anderson & Carter, 2003; Glicken, 2004; Lum, 2007; Saleebey, 2002)—an attitude that promotes collaborative, culturally competent relationships with clients, who are viewed as possessing resources as well as having problems. Contemporary practitioners emphasize resiliency as a conceptual framework for effective assessment and intervention (Fraser, Richman, & Galinsky, 1999; Goldstein & Brooks, 2005). As a useful perspective in practice, the concept of resiliency leads the practitioner to design interventions that promote competence and to recognize the need for multifaceted approaches that take into consideration varied sources of risk and protective factors and are sensitive to the client's context (Yates & Masten as cited in Linley & Joseph, 2004).

Neurobiology and Attachment

Recent biological research on attachment and other brain–behavior connections (Schore, 1994/2003; Siegel & Hartzell, 2003) provides neurological evidence of the attuned relationship between mother and infant and between therapist and client as powerful predictors of therapeutic outcomes by giving increased credibility to the focus on qualities of the relationship. Patterns of brain functioning in attuned relationships between infants and mothers are paralleled by attuned brain functioning in the positive therapist–patient relationship (Siegel, 2010). Similarly, changes in levels of brain neurotransmitters have resulted from both psychotherapy and antidepressants, indicating that the therapeutic relationship can have some of the same neurological effects as prescribed medication. Therapeutic interventions that continue after the treatment of acute depression with antidepressants can contribute to improvement in the long-term prognosis of patients and, for some, may be preferred as an alternative to maintenance pharmacological treatment. Talk therapy appears to target symptoms related to guilt, hopelessness, negativity, and low self-esteem—residual symptoms largely untouched by antidepressant medications—and to alter brain metabolism in ways that both parallel and enhance the effects of antidepressants.

Protective Factors

The definition and function of protective factors is little understood. Protective factors cannot be assumed to be the opposite of risk factors. For example, although low intelligence may be a risk factor, high intelligence may not necessarily be a protective factor. Similarly, positive, warm, and consistent parenting may not be sufficient, in the context of a highly stressful environment and antisocial peers, to overcome the daily accumulation of risk factors. Protective factors may buffer the effects of risk factors, but how this works remains obscure. It is generally considered important to focus on multiple rather than single domains and as much on the enhancement of protective factors as on the reduction of risk factors (Allen-Meares & Fraser, 2004; Goldstein & Brooks, 2005).

Resiliency

The groundswell of emphasis on resiliency based to a large degree on the Werner and Smith (1982) research—expressed as positive personal strengths, interpersonal, and community-supporting in order to buffer stress and enhance coping with problems—is striking a responsive chord with the public at large. Consider these popular titles, to name only a few: *The Survivor Personality: Why Some People Are Stronger, Smarter, and More Skillful at Handling Life's Difficulties, and How You Can Be Too* (Siebert, 1996); *The Resilience Factor: 7 Keys to Finding Your Inner Strength and Overcoming Life's Hurdles* (Reivich & Shatte, 2002); and *Resilience at Work: How to Succeed No Matter What Life Throws at You* (Maddi & Khoshaba, 2005). Pop psychology favorites, these and similar titles are attracting attention in a highly stressed society. The need to go beyond identification of diagnosis, taking medication, and focusing on problems to embrace one's strengths and enhance one's sources of self-efficacy has perhaps never been greater.

A paradigm shift is occurring in the worldview of medical and mental health professions, embracing Eastern and Western philosophies, acknowledging the core importance of meaning construction to human beings, and embracing the importance of spirituality in the process of recovery from mental and emotional problems. The goal, then, of effective diagnosis and intervention must include a focus on strengths, resiliency, and ultimately the integration of positive and negative experience into a more empowered identity; that is, it requires an assessment of the mental health as well as mental illness dimension.

KEY POINTS

1. Recent research trends in mental health diagnosis and treatment focus on factors outside of the client, including sources of strength, spirituality, a blend of Eastern and Western thought, the nature of the client–practitioner relationship, and extra-therapeutic factors that predict outcome.
2. Constructs receiving theoretical and empirical attention include positive psychology, resiliency, cultural competency, social support, resiliency, and the idea of a health or wellness continuum as well as an illness continuum for diagnosis and treatment.
3. These trends, occurring in interdisciplinary fields and not limited to psychiatry within medicine, are not in opposition to an understanding of the neurobiological bases of mental illness; rather, they support approaches to diagnosis and intervention that go beyond medication to mobilize inner and external sources of resiliency.

THE NEED FOR A DIVERSITY/RESILIENCY FORMULATION

The evidence for the incorporation of resiliency and strengths—related to personal, cultural, spiritual, family, interpersonal, and community resources—should be assessed and added to the diagnostic classification system utilized by all mental health professions and taught in all training programs. The positive side of the equation cannot be left to chance, referred for later consideration by others, or relegated only to the subsequent assessment process. For the sake of scientific accuracy, realistic diagnosis, reflective of the complexity of human beings in their contexts and logically related to effective treatment interventions, must be required as integral to the diagnostic process.

This is a not a new idea. Lopez et al. (2006) similarly criticized the *DSM-IV-TR*'s focus on pathology and categorical thinking and suggested alternatives for broadening the former Axis IV and/or adding an Axis VI to assess psychosocial and environmental resources and the client's capacity for flourishing. Saleebey (2002) noted that the idea for a sixth axis was suggested, tongue in cheek, by his students during academic seminars. The former *DSM-IV-TR* included a Global Assessment of Relational Functioning (GARF) as well as a Social and Occupational Functioning Assessment Scale (SOFAS) in its appendix, describing areas needed for further study (APA, 2000). These changes were needed before the advent of *DSM-5*, and they are still needed now. In our first edition, we proposed the Diversity/Resiliency Axis VI as a necessary corrective to the currently skewed diagnostic classification system. Strengths and resources unique to the individual, we asserted, must be added to the *DSM* so that attention can focus on the whole person in context whenever anyone who uses the *DSM* encounters a client. With the publication of the *DSM-5* and the elimination of the axis system, we have altered our proposed Axis VI, and are advocating for the suggested, Diversity/Resiliency Formulation instead.

We chose the designation "Diversity/Resiliency" because, in our view, it best represents the combination of intrapersonal, interpersonal, environmental resources, and diverse identifications available to the individual as he or she mobilizes to face emotional and mental challenges, stressors, or disorders. Examination of the diverse meanings and resources (e.g., ethnic, spiritual, community) available to individuals places symptoms in the context of the world in which the individual lives.

As illustrated in Chapter 1, diversity issues greatly impact both the way individuals are responded to by mental health professionals as well as the way individuals experience and communicate about their symptoms. Further, culture, social class, occupational identification, spirituality, and other factors, we believe, are vital components of the resiliency a client brings to the encounter with the mental health clinician. The client cannot accurately be diagnosed or understood by the clinician without attending to these issues of diversity and resiliency.

Previously conceptualized as internal to the individual and largely inborn, resiliency is currently understood as composed of traits or abilities within the person combined with the minimization of risk factors and the maximization of protective factors external to the person via the availability of interpersonal, family, community, spiritual, cultural support (Yates & Masten as cited in Linley & Joseph, 2004). Formally legitimizing the assessment of these internal and external resources in the diagnostic classification system would go a long way toward rebalancing the skewed view of the patient in terms of his or her deficiencies and pathology and would consequently lead more directly to effective intervention planning, already begun by the mental health professions at the conceptual stage but inadequately financed and researched. One recent publication focuses on resiliency enhancement as an important theoretical framework for social work practice, emphasizing its relevance for strengths-building interventions with populations at risk (Norman, 2007). We support this approach but believe that resiliency deserves a formal place in the *DSM* system in order to give the sources of internal and external client support the status and legitimacy they deserve in the assessment and intervention processes. Strengthening resiliency may not only relieve symptoms but also promote more effective coping and ultimately empower the client to integrate difficult life experiences into a transformed sense of meaning and identity.

It should be noted that our concept of diversity, as defined in this text, is both different from and goes beyond the Cultural Formulation of both the *DSM-IV-TR* and the *DSM-5*. Attention to cultural idioms of distress, cultural explanations for symptoms, culturally influenced help-seeking behaviors, cultural identification, and cultural differences between clinicians and patients is extremely important, and we remain concerned that the *DSM's* section on culture remains relegated to Section III in the *DSM-5*. Our suggested Diversity/Resiliency Formulation, however, addresses factors ignored in the Cultural Formulation, namely, both internal and external sources of social support and resiliency, unique talents, strengths, and abilities, and broader issues of diversity important to the patient and family. These factors include social class, gender identification, spiritual understandings and practices, occupational cultures, and unique characteristics of neighborhood and community. We believe these broader sources of support and strength can illuminate the meaning of diagnosis, make the process of assessment more accurate, and promote useful links between diagnosis and effective treatment.

THE DIVERSITY/RESILIENCY FORMULATION DEFINED

In our first edition, we proposed that logically, Axis VI should be the counterpoint to Axis IV. Where there are stressors, there are also corollary strengths, talents, and resources. In place of a formal axis structure, we now urge that the mental health practitioner, regardless of discipline, be trained to create a Diversity/Resiliency Formulation as an essential part of the diagnostic process. The Diversity/Resiliency Formulation can be presented in outline form, delineating content areas, or in a paragraph summary, to complement the *DSM-5* diagnostic label addressing the following domains:

- **A.** *Intrapersonal:* Strengths, capabilities, interests, and talents; educational/occupational attainment, past successes and effective coping experiences, physical and emotional wellness practices such as exercise, healthy diet, and altruistic behaviors.
- **B.** *Interpersonal:* Availability of support from family members, friendships, social life, and community network.
- **C.** *Community:* Affiliation with and/or access to supportive, prosocial informal and formal networks and organizations.
- **D.** *Spiritual:* Identification with spiritual beliefs/practices and/or formal religious organizations, spiritual leaders, and/or spiritual practices; perception of and ability to utilize support from these sources. The meaning-making aspect of spirituality is associated with beliefs, faith, and practices that provide a basis for ever significant hope. What hope is present and where does the person draw from for hope or a sense of wellness? What does he or she hope for?

E. *Diversity:* Positive sources of self-definition and meaning as well as emotional and social support via diverse identifications (i.e., beliefs, values, and practices) and memberships. Depending on the cultural identification, there may be cultural leaders and healers as resources. All cultures have culture-specific definitions of strength and well-being and a framework for understanding symptoms and their expression. Occupational and other identity cultures (e.g., membership in the deaf community, participation in social action or community service networks or causes) can provide rich sources of personal and social empowerment to the individual.

As in the previous use of Axis IV and now considered via the use of V and Z codes to describe stressors and special environmental conditions that may interfere with treatment, the mental health practitioner utilizing the Diversity/Resiliency Formulation needs to inquire into and note the client's resources in each domain listed previously. Special attention should be paid to unique talents and sources of support and to meanings and interpretations unique to the client's view of her uniquely diverse sources of support. The practitioner needs to consider the assessment of these resiliency sources to be equal in importance to signs and symptoms of pathology and stress. The Diversity/Resiliency Formulation can be incorporated as an essential component of training and to the application of mental and emotional diagnosis, patient–practitioner and interdisciplinary communication and collaboration, treatment planning, intervention, and the evaluation of clinical outcomes. To illustrate how the Diversity/Resiliency Formulation could enhance the accuracy and completeness of diagnosis, consider the following case study.

CASE STUDY

The Diversity/Resiliency Formulation Applied: The Case of Mrs. M.

Mrs. M., a 34-year-old married mother of three young children, comes to a primary care physician with the following presenting complaints of a few months' duration: fatigue, tearfulness, pessimism, loneliness, self-doubt about her abilities as a mother, social isolation, and resentment about the amount of time her husband devotes to his job. A complete physical exam reveals no medical abnormalities. Mrs. M. is a Latina, a college graduate, who received her BA in secondary education and hopes to return to work when her youngest child is in kindergarten. She and Mr. M. relocated from California to the Midwest 3 months earlier because of a job offer Mr. M. received after being recommended highly to his present firm by a former professor. Mrs. M.'s husband, a recent law school graduate, works long hours in an attempt to advance at his firm and puts in additional hours at home studying for the bar exam in the couple's new state. Mrs. M. misses her former community, her parents, and especially her sisters. Formerly an active softball player and amateur dancer, she is currently immersed in caring for her children alone at home in a new community. Raised Roman Catholic in a Mexican American community in California centered around the neighborhood parish, Mrs. M. is bilingual in Spanish and English but feels increasingly cut off from her cultural roots. She presents without a past history of depression; her pregnancies and deliveries have been uneventful.

*Using the **DSM-5**, Mrs. M.'s diagnosis might be:*

309.0 Adjustment Disorder with depressed mood
V62.89 Other Problem Related to Psychosocial Circumstances

If the mental health practitioner were to add a Cultural Formulation, it might be as follows:

Mrs. M. identifies as a Latina and a Roman Catholic. As a member of a strong, extended Mexican American family, ties with parents, siblings, aunts, uncles, and cousins are important to her, and the loss of daily contact with family members, due to her move, has significantly impacted her. In her female gender role in the family, she views herself as responsible for the emotional well-being of her husband and children. Although fluent in both English and Spanish, she may be more comfortable and spontaneous in expressing the complexities of her emotional feelings in Spanish and thus might prefer a Spanish-speaking physician or mental health professional. The extent to which she feels a part of her new, predominantly Anglo Midwestern community would be an important issue to explore.

(*Note*: In most medical and/or mental health settings, it is very unlikely that the V codes or Cultural Formulations used here would be a part of the diagnosis.)

Attending to Mrs. M.'s symptoms of adjustment disorder, her primary care physician might offer reassurance and encouragement and perhaps suggest the temporary use of an antidepressant. Recognizing the increased stress and loss of important support, it is hoped her physician would also refer Mrs. M. to a mental health counselor; on the other hand, he or she might take a wait-and-see attitude, assuming that Mrs. M's symptoms are temporary and reactive to stress. Mrs. M.'s physician may or may not bring up for discussion the contexts of Mrs. M.'s depressive symptoms. Her alert physician would inquire into a past history of depression in Mrs. M. or her family and would assess for suicidality, attending to whether more severe pathology was present.

Adding the Diversity/Resiliency Formulation to Diagnosis

Consider how Mrs. M. might be understood and responded to differently if the Diversity/Resiliency Formulation were added to the diagnosis:

DSM-5 diagnosis:

309.0 Adjustment Disorder with depressed mood
V62.89 Other Problem Related to Psychosocial Circumstances

Adding the Diversity/Resiliency Formulation

In outline form:

Intrapersonal: College graduate, former softball player and amateur dancer
Interpersonal: Close relationships with siblings, parents
Community: Close relationships with former neighbors

Spiritual: Roman Catholic, formerly active in her church
Cultural: Mexican American cultural identity, bilingual

Or in paragraph form:

Mrs. M. is married and the mother of three young children, is a college graduate with a BA in secondary education and was active in campus leadership. She is a former softball player and amateur dancer. She is close to siblings and parents in CA and valued former neighbors. She is Roman Catholic and was formerly active in her church, where she taught children and sang in the choir. She is proud of her Mexican American identity, her bilingual abilities, and her educational achievements.

The *DSM-5* diagnostic labels alone, which would be the normative presentation of identified concerns, give the clinician only a sense of depressive symptoms (fatigue, pessimism, self-doubt, tearfulness, loneliness) related to the stress of her move and suggest that they may be related to her psychosocial environment in some way. The Cultural Formulation helps by adding important data about Mrs. M's ethnic identity and how this might affect her assessment of her gender roles, contribute to her sense of loneliness and loss, and limit or enhance her relationship with her physician or other clinician. The Diversity/Resiliency Formulation, however, adds, in very few words, a more complete picture of Mrs. M. by highlighting special talents, achievements, sources of pride and resiliency. What begins to emerge for the clinician is the picture of a whole, unique person who is much more than the collection of her symptoms. In this brief format, the clinician, we believe, is encouraged to be more curious about the interesting multifaceted client whom he or she is encountering. This glimpse of Mrs. M. beyond her pathology could and should enhance a more effective engagement and the creation of an ongoing relationship that promotes a good treatment outcome. We believe that if the *DSM* were to *require* the practitioner, regardless of professional identification and training, to consider sources of support and resiliency, described as the Diversity/Resiliency Formulation, Mrs. M. would more likely be viewed as the unique person she is, affected by complex systems, possessing strengths as well as problems, and enjoying membership in ethnic, spiritual, and other diverse communities. In sum, Mrs. M. would be viewed more realistically through a wider lens. An appreciation of her symptoms and external stressors would be balanced with an appreciation of her talents, strengths, and internal/external sources of support in her unique family, community, and diversity contexts. As a result, useful directions for effective intervention would more immediately be apparent, and the practitioner would approach her from a more diversity-competent strengths perspective.

Implications for Interventions

First, Mrs. M.'s therapist might use tools, such as the community genogram (Rigazio-DiGilio, Ivey, Kunkler-Peck, & Grady, 2005), in order to assess and plan to utilize Mrs. M.'s current links with sources of both stress and support in her environment. For example, Mrs. M. might be encouraged to become involved in her neighborhood parish, and the practitioner could focus on a supportive community spiritual link. Her bilingual abilities would be recognized as a significant strength, and she might be encouraged to connect with other Latinas in her new community and/or to do volunteer work in which she could use her Spanish. Referrals to sports and/or dance organizations might immediately be considered. The loneliness and estrangement from her husband, linked to the demands of his profession and the loss of contact with her cultural roots, could be normalized and reframed as opportunities to work toward greater relationship empathy and connectedness in order to enhance the marriage. Such an approach would ideally be cost-effective in that Mrs. M.'s first contact with her primary care physician might result in immediate attention to some of these areas of resiliency, reinforcing Mrs. M.'s view of herself as competent and balancing a problem focus, based on pathological symptoms, with an empowerment focus based on strengths. In the context of the Diversity/Resiliency Formulation, psychopharmacological and other pathology-based interventions, we believe, would have a greater chance of lasting success.

In time, a thoughtful mental health practitioner to whom Mrs. M. might be referred by her physician would of course most likely explore all of the previously outlined areas with Mrs. M. Whether this would occur, however, is left much more to chance without the inclusion of resiliency resources as an official part of the diagnostic process. We believe that interventions linked to diagnosis have a greater chance of success in a context that enhances Mrs. M's resources for using a collaborative helping relationship. Such a process is much more likely to occur, we believe, if resiliency factors are attended to from the first contact with a professional, whether this is a family physician or psychiatrist, a nurse practitioner, a social worker, or a psychologist.

Evaluating the Effectiveness of the Diversity/Resiliency Formulation

Although the Diversity/Resiliency Formulation is a proposed addition to the *DSM* diagnostic process, we have noted in this chapter its logical connection to critical thinking and outcome research on diagnostic validity and predictors of successful treatment of mental disorders. We suggest that its usefulness can be measured with respect to the degree with which both diversity and resiliency factors are identified in the diagnostic process. Resulting clinical formulations identify not only signs and symptoms of pathology but also the presence of factors that contribute to the development of a meaningful life.

The use of the Diversity/Resiliency Formulation can further be evaluated with respect to the meaningful connection between a diagnosis that includes diversity/resiliency, the development of a treatment/intervention plan that incorporates diversity/resiliency contexts, and clinical outcome research that measures the contributions of the formulation to the reduction of clinical symptoms. Existing depression and anxiety scales, psychiatric rating inventories, and similar instruments would be useful in evaluating change in measures of pathology, while additional instruments evaluating client satisfaction and the adequacy of communication between practitioner and client need development. Assessment measures for well-being, happiness, self-efficacy, and other constructs of positive psychology are already available to the clinician (Lopez & Snyder, 2003). The use of the Diversity/Resiliency Formulation would address neglected areas of cultural language, protective factors, individual and interpersonal strengths, spirituality, and community support. In so doing, it would contribute to a neglected area of research in all diagnostic categories.

Clinician inquiry and observation as well as client satisfaction measures would help the clinician assess whether systematic attention to resiliency and diversity issues are experienced as helpful to the client. Just as the clinician can note whether stressors in the client's world, noted in V/Z codes we hope, have declined, the clinician can also note whether the client has increased in his or her ability to use internal and external sources of strength and resiliency. In time, if the Diversity/Resiliency Formulation is increasingly utilized by practitioners, more systematic evaluation tools would be developed in order to strengthen and validate attending to resiliency and diversity as core to the diagnostic process.

The following chapters illustrate the use of the Diversity/Resiliency Formulation in the diagnosis and related intervention planning for a variety of disorders and problems: major depressive and bipolar disorder, anxiety disorder, schizophrenia, conduct and oppositional defiant disorders, substance abuse disorders, trauma and stressor-related disorders, and Alzheimer's disease. Research has explored disparities issues in many of the disorders identified previously and highlighted the need for social support, attention to lifestyle issues, and sources of strength. As authors, we made a decision not to attempt to apply the Diversity/Resiliency Formulation to every diagnosis in the *DSM-5* in this book as the process would have been exhausting and ultimately too superficial. The categories of mental disorders addressed in the following chapters were chosen for their relevance in illustrating the usefulness of adding the Diversity/Resiliency Formulation to the *DSM* diagnostic process and for their ability to showcase creative, diversity-competent interventions that attempt to overcome mental health disparities and support the rich resources available both within clients and in their natural environments.

KEY POINTS

1. The Diversity/Resiliency Formulation adds the dimensions of strengths, resiliency, and diversity to the *DSM* formulation, elements missing in the current structure of the *DSM*.
2. As a result, the client can be encountered as a whole person, with strengths as well as problems, existing in complex interpersonal and societal contexts.
3. Relating to the patient as a whole person can foster a more authentic encounter, leading to more accurate information gathering, a relationship that is more therapeutic, and the promise of effective interventions related both to the diagnosis and to the client's real worlds.
4. The use of the Diversity/Resiliency Formulation should not be left to chance but should be part of the essential training of physicians, social workers, psychologists, counselors, and spiritual advisors. This will not occur unless it becomes an official part of the diagnostic process, utilized in the training of mental health professionals and incorporated routinely in clinical practice.

SUMMARY

The diagnosis and assessment of mental health concerns is a complex process, traditionally focusing on signs and symptoms of pathology. Although mental health professionals embrace broad assessment protocols, which attempt to incorporate biopsychosocial, and, more recently, the cultural and spiritual identities of the individual, attention is rarely given to the individual's unique internal and external sources of strength and support. The limitations of traditional medical model diagnosis, particularly in the form of the *DSM* classification system, have been noted by many researchers and practitioners. At the same time, research has focused on predictive factors in treatment outcome, both in terms of client characteristics and in the utility of evidence-based treatment protocols applied to specific mental disorders. The cumulative themes in contemporary discussions of diagnostic systems and effective treatments, logically related to diagnosis, suggest the need for an additional core component of the diagnostic system, for which the authors advocate the Diversity/Resiliency Formulation.

DISCUSSION QUESTIONS AND ACTIVITIES

1. Define the terms *diagnosis* and *assessment*. How are they similar and different? Should they always occur together? Why or why not?
2. How should the diagnosis/assessment process ideally occur in an integrated care setting? How do you think each discipline (e.g., medicine, nursing, psychology, social work, pastoral care) should contribute to the process? How would you include the client and his or her family members in the process?
3. Why is a diagnostic system needed and what should it accomplish?
4. Is recent research focused on evidence-informed practice and psychotherapy outcome relevant to diagnosis? Explain.
5. Why is it important to factor in diversity considerations in order to understand the presenting symptoms of an individual? How do you define the terms *culture* and *diversity*? How do you recognize them when you see them?
6. What does the term *resiliency* mean, and what do the authors mean by a Diversity/Resiliency Formulation?
7. Create a diagnosis for two clients at your internship or place of work first using the *DSM-5* alone and then adding the Diversity/Resiliency Formulation for each. Did your viewpoint about your client change? How? Do you think *DSM-5* was an improvement over *DSM-IV-TR?* Why or why not?
8. Use a community genogram (see Ivey, D'Andrea, Ivey, & Simek-Morgan, 2002) to assess the contexts in which one of your client's lives. The community genogram expands individual and family genograms to help professionals understand clients within their broader social contexts of

community and culture. This concept is directly relevant to our proposed Diversity/Resiliency Formulation because it serves to identify strengths and resources that the client can draw on for support. Specific directions and templates for the use of a community genogram can be found on the Internet by entering the keywords *community genogram*. How did the construction of the community genogram help you to understand diversity/resiliency factors in the life of your client?

WEB RESOURCES

www.apa.org
www.dsm5.org
www.mentalhealthnews.org
www.nasw.org
www.positivepsychology.net
www.ppc.sas.upenn.edu
www.psych.org
www.psychologytoday.com/basics/positive-psychology

REFERENCES

Allen-Meares, P., & Fraser, M. W. (2004). *Interventions with children and adolescents: An interdisciplinary approach*. Boston, MA: Pearson Education.

American Psychiatric Association. (1952). *Diagnostic and statistical manual of mental disorders*. Washington, DC: Author.

American Psychiatric Association. (1968). *Diagnostic and statistical manual of mental disorders* (2nd ed.). Washington, DC: Author.

American Psychiatric Association. (1980). *Diagnostic and statistical manual of mental disorders* (3rd ed.). Washington, DC: Author.

American Psychiatric Association. (1994). *Diagnostic and statistical manual of mental disorders* (4th ed.). Washington, DC: Author.

American Psychiatric Association. (2000). *Diagnostic and statistical manual of mental disorders* (4th ed., text rev.). Washington, DC: Author.

American Psychiatric Association. (2013). *Diagnostic and statistical manual of mental disorders:* (5th ed.). Arlington, VA: American Psychiatric Press.

Anderson, J., & Carter, R. W. (2003). *Diversity perspectives in social work practice*. Boston, MA: Allyn & Bacon.

Bandura, A. (1995). *Self-efficacy in changing societies*. Cambridge, UK: Cambridge University Press.

Bandura, A. (1997). *Self-efficacy: The exercise of control*. New York, NY: H. H. Freeman.

Cooper, M., & Lesser, J. G. (2005). *Clinical social work practice: An integrated approach* (2nd ed.). Boston, MA: Pearson.

Corcoran, J., & Walsh, J. (2006). *Clinical assessment and diagnosis in social work practice*. New York, NY: Oxford University Press.

Corrigan, P. (Ed.). (2014). *The stigma of disease and disability: Understanding causes and overcoming injustices*. Washington, DC: American Psychological Association.

Delgado, M., Johnes, K., & Rohani, M. (2005). *Social work practice with refugee and immigrant youth in the United States*. Boston, MA: Allyn & Bacon.

DiGiuseppe, R., & Tafrate, R. C. (2007). *Understanding anger disorders*. New York, NY: Oxford University Press.

Dworkin, J. (2005). *Advanced social work practice: An integrative, multilevel approach*. Boston, MA: Allyn & Bacon.

Enright, D., & Fitzgibbons, R. (2000). *Helping clients forgive: An empirical guide for resolving anger and restoring hope*. Washington, DC: American Psychological Association.

Frances, A. (2013). Opening Pandora's box: The 19 worst suggestions for DSM5. *Psychiatric Times COMMENTARY*. Retrieved from www.psychiatrictimes.com/ display/article/10168/1522341?CID=rss&verify=0

Fraser, M. W., Richman, J. M., & Galinsky, M. J. (1999). Risk, protection, and resilience: Toward a conceptual framework for social work practice. *Social Work Research*, 23(3), 131–143.

Gambrill, E. (2005). *Critical thinking in clinical practice: Improving the quality of judgments and decisions* (2nd ed.). Hoboken, NJ: John Wiley & Sons.

Gambrill, E. (2006). *Social work practice: A critical thinker's guide* (2nd ed.). New York, NY: Oxford University Press.

Gilbert, D. (2007). *Stumbling upon happiness*. New York, NY: Alfred A. Knopf.

Glicken, M. D. (2004). *Using the strengths perspective in social work practice: A positive approach for the helping professions*. Boston, MA: Allyn & Bacon.

Goldstein, S., & Brooks, R. B. (Eds.). (2005). *Handbook of resilience in children*. New York, NY: Springer Science and Business Media.

Goodheart, C. D. (2014). *A primer for ICD-10-CM users: Psychological and behavioral conditions*. Washington, DC: American Psychological Association.

Gray, S. W., & Zide, M. R. (2008). *Psychopathology: A competency-based assessment model for social workers*. Belmont, CA: Brooks/Cole.

Hubble, M. L., Duncan, B. L., & Miller, S. D. (Eds.). (1999). *The heart and soul of change: What works in therapy*. Washington, DC: American Psychological Association.

Ivey, A. E., D'Andrea, M., Ivey, M. B., & Simek-Morgan, L. (2002). *Theories of counseling and psychotherapy: A multicultural perspective* (5th ed.). Boston, MA: Allyn & Bacon.

Jordan, C., & Franklin, C. (2011). *Clinical assessment for social workers: Quantitative and qualitative methods*. Chicago, IL: Lyceum Books.

Kabat-Zinn, J. (1990). *Full catastrophe living: Using the wisdom of your body and mind to face stress, pain, and illness*. New York, NY: Dell.

Karls, J. M., & Wandrei, K. E. (1994). *Person-in-environment system: The PIE classification system for social functioning problems*. Washington, DC: NASW Press.

Keyes, C. L., & Haidt, J. (2003). *Flourishing: Positive psychology and the life well-lived*. Washington, DC: American Psychological Association.

Kirk, S. A., & Kutchins, H. (1992). *The selling of the DSM: The rhetoric of science in psychiatry*. New York, NY: Aldine de Gruyter.

Kivlighan, D. M. (2007). Where is the relationship in research on the alliance? Two methods for analyzing dyadic data. *Journal of Counseling Psychology*, 54(4), 423–433.

Lee, J. (2001). *The empowerment approach to social work practice: Building the beloved community*. New York, NY: Columbia University Press.

Linley, A. P., & Joseph, S. (Eds.). (2004). *Positive psychology in practice*. Hoboken, NJ: John Wiley & Sons.

Lopez, S. J., Edwards, L., Pedrotti, J. T., Prosser, E. C., LaRue, S., Spalitto, S. V., & Ulven, J. C. (2006). Beyond the DSM-IV: Assumptions, alternatives, and alterations. *Journal of Counseling and Development*, 84(3), 259–267.

Lopez, S. J., & Snyder, C. R. (2003). *Positive psychological assessment: A handbook of models and measures*. Washington, DC: American Psychological Association.

Lum, D. (2007). *Culturally competent practice: A framework for understanding diverse groups and justice issues* (3rd ed.). Pacific Grove, CA: Brooks/Cole.

Mackelprang, R., & Salsgiver, R. (2009). *Disability: A diversity model approach in human service practice*. Chicago, IL: Brooks Cole.

Maddi, S. R., & Khoshaba, D. M. (2005). *Resilience at work: How to succeed no matter what life throws at you.* New York, NY: AMACOM.

Metzl, J. C. (2009). *The protest psychosis: how schizophrenia became a black disease.* Boston, MA: Beacon Press.

Neugeboren, J. (2003). *Imagining Robert, a memoir: My brother, madness, and survival.* New Brunswick, NJ: Rutgers University Press. (Original work published 1997)

Newman, B. S., Dannenfelser, P. L., & Clemmons, V. (2007). The *diagnostic and statistical manual of mental disorders* in graduate social work education: Then and now. *Journal of Social Work Education, 43*(2), 297–307.

Norcross, J. C., Beutler, L., & Levant, R. (Eds.). (2006). *Evidence-based practices in mental health: Debate and dialogue on the fundamental questions.* Washington, DC: American Psychological Association.

Norman, E. (Ed.). (2007). *Resiliency enhancement: Putting the strengths perspective into social work practice.* New York, NY: Columbia University Press.

PDM Task Force. (2006). *Psychodynamic diagnostic manual.* Silver Spring, MD: Alliance of Psychoanalytic Organizations.

Petrovich, A. (2013, September 7) *The DSM-5: Context and clinical applications.* Presentation to California Society for Clinical Social Work. Fresno, CA: California State University.

Pottick, K. J., Kirk, S. A., Hsieh, D. K., & Tian, X. (2007). Judging mental disorder in youths: Effects of client, clinician, and contextual differences. *Journal of Consulting and Clinical Psychology, 75*(1), 1–8.

Preston, J. (1998). *Integrative brief therapy: Cognitive, psychodynamic, humanistic and neurobehavioral approaches.* San Luis Obispo, CA: Impact.

Reivich, K., & Shatte, A. (2002). *The resilience factor: 7 keys to finding your inner strength and overcoming life's hurdles.* New York, NY: Broadway Books.

Rigazio-DiGilio, S. A., Ivey, A. E., Kunkler-Peck, K. P., & Grady, L. T. (2005). *Community genograms using individual, family, and cultural narratives with clients.* New York, NY: Teachers College Press.

Rosehan, D. (1973). On being sane in insane places. *Science, 179,* 250–258.

Saleebey, D. (2002). *The strengths perspective in social work practice* (3rd ed.). New York, NY: Allyn & Bacon.

Satel, S. (2007, September 13). Mind over manual. *The New York Times,* p. A13.

Schore, A. (1994). *Affect regulation and the origin of the self: The neurobiology of emotional attachment.* Hillsdale, NJ: Lawrence Erlbaum Associates.

Schore, A. (2003). *Affect regulation and the repair of the self.* New York, NY: W.W. Norton.

Siebert, A. (1996). *The survivor personality: Why some people are stronger, smarter, and more skillful at handing life's difficulties, and how you can be too.* New York, NY: Berkeley.

Siegel, D. (2010). *The mindful therapist: A clinician's guide to mindsight and neural integration.* New York, NY: W.W. Norton.

Siegel, D., & Hartzell, M. (2003). *Parenting from the inside out.* New York, NY: Penguin Press.

Torrey, E. F. (2014). *American psychosis: How the federal government destroyed the mental illness treatment system.* New York, NY: Oxford University Press.

Wachtel, P. (2010). Beyond "ESTs": Problematic assumptions in the pursuit of evidence-based practice. *Psychoanalytic Psychology, 27*(3), 251–272.

Weil, A. (1995). *Spontaneous healing: How to discover and embrace your body's natural ability to heal itself.* New York, NY: Ballantine.

Werner, E., & Smith, R. (1982). *Vulnerable but invincible: A study of resilient children.* New York, NY: McGraw-Hill.

Whitaker, R. (2002). *Mad in America.* New York, NY: Basic Books.

World Health Organization. (2010). *International statistics classification of diseases and related health problems (ICD-10)* (2nd ed.). Geneva, Switzerland: Author.

APPENDIX: CHANGES FROM *DSM-IV-TR* TO *DSM-5*

DSM-IV-TR	*DSM-5*
NEUROCOGNITIVE DISORDERS	
Intellectual Disabilities Mental retardation replaced by .... Assessment by IQ	Intellectual Disability (Intellectual Developmental Disorder) Assessment by both IQ and adaptive functioning required. Adaptive functioning determines severity
Communication Disorders Expressive and Mixed-Receptive Language Disorder combined and replaced by .... Phonologic disorder replaced by............................. Stuttering replaced by	Language Disorder Speech Sound Disorder Childhood Onset Fluency Disorder Added—Childhood (pragmatic) Communication Disorder
Autism Spectrum Disorder Asperger's, autistic disorder, Rett's disorder, childhood disintegrative disorder, and Pervasive Developmental Disorder, Not Otherwise Specified - (PDD-NOS) replaced by................	Autism Spectrum Disorder New criteria for application across life span
Attention-Deficit Hyperactivity Disorder (ADHD) Some symptoms before age 7 changed to...... Subtypes replaced....by	Several present prior to age 12 Specifiers matched to previous subtypes New—Comorbid diagnosis with Autism Spectrum Disorder allowed Symptoms threshold change for adults—five; for younger persons, six
Reading Disorder, Mathematics Disorder, Disorder of Written Expression, and Learning Disorder NOS combined to.......................................	**Specific learning disorder** (area of disorder listed as specifier)
Motor Disorders	No change in names. Tic criteria standardized for all disorders.
SCHIZOPHRENIA SPECTRUM AND OTHER PSYCHOTIC DISORDERS	
Schizophrenia **Changes to Criterion A** Special attribution of Schneiderian first-rank hallucinations (two voices conversing) eliminated... Subtypes eliminated...	Two Criterion A symptoms now required; one must be delusions, hallucinations, or disorganized speech Dimensional ratings (Section III) for core symptom type and severity
Schizoaffective Disorder....................................	Major mood episode must be present for majority of duration of disorder after Criterion A met
Delusional Disorder.. Delusions must be nonbizarre	Delusions no longer need to be nonbizarre; bizarre delusions added as specifier
Catatonia as subtype of Schizophrenia eliminated	Uniform criteria described throughout *DSM-5*; may be specifier for Depressive Disorder, Bipolar Disorder, Schizophrenia, context of a medical condition, or specified diagnosis
BIPOLAR AND RELATED DISORDERS	
	Criteria now include changes in both mood and activity, energy levels
Bipolar I, Mixed Episode replaced with...................	Specifier, *with mixed features*

(*continued*)

APPENDIX: CHANGES FROM *DSM-IV-TR* TO *DSM-5* (*continued*)

DSM-IV-TR	*DSM-5*
	Other Specified Bipolar and Related Disorders (ex-past history of Major Depressive Disorder [MDD] with all criteria for hypomania met except duration, or too few symptoms to meet criteria for hypomania but adequate duration—4 days) *Anxious distressed* specifier added
DEPRESSIVE DISORDERS In Appendix B in *DSM-IV*.................................... **Dysthymia eliminated—now**....................................	**Disruptive mood dysregulation disorder** added (children up to 18, irritability and emotional dysregulation) **Premenstrual Dysphoric Disorder** **Persistent Depressive Disorder** **Specifier** with mixed features, added for coexistence of major depressive episode with at least three manic features insufficient to meet criteria for manic episode **Bereavement exclusion eliminated**—can now diagnose if major depressive symptoms exist after loss for less than 2 months **Specifier** with mixed symptoms added to both Bipolar Disorder and MDDs
ANXIETY DISORDERS **Obsessive-Compulsive Disorder (OCD) moved to new section of its own** **Social Phobia replaced with**.................................. **Social Anxiety and Specific Phobia requirement** that individuals over 18 must recognize fear as unrealistic, and excessive **Panic disorder and agoraphobia linked** *Generalized* specifier for social anxiety disorder replaced with.. **Onset of Separation anxiety must be before age 18**	**Social Anxiety Disorder** **Changed criteria for social anxiety and specific phobia:** no longer requires recognition that fear is unrealistic; 6 months duration extended to all ages; fear must simply outweigh danger or threat **Panic disorder and agoraphobia separate disorders** *Performance only* specifier **Added as anxiety disorders—separation anxiety and selective mutism**; wording added to criteria to represent separation anxiety in adulthood **Onset requirement eliminated; duration statement** *typically lasting for 6 months or more* **added** to avoid overdiagnosis of transient fears
OBSESSIVE-COMPULSIVE AND RELATED DISORDERS Trichotillomania formerly in impulse control disorders in *DSM-IV* now... *Poor insight* specifier for OCD changed.................	**NEW DIAGNOSES: Hoarding Disorder, Excoriation (skin-picking) Disorder, Substance/Medication-Induced Obsessive-Compulsive and Related Disorder, Obsessive-Compulsive and Related Disorder Due to Another Medical Condition.** **Trichotillolomania (hair-pulling disorder)** **Now** *with good or fair insight, poor insight, or absent insight/delusional* (analogous specifiers added for Body Dysmorphic Disorder) *Tic-related* specifier added for OCD

(*continued*)

APPENDIX: CHANGES FROM *DSM-IV-TR* TO *DSM-5* (*continued*)

DSM-IV-TR	*DSM-5*
	Muscle Dysmorphia specifier added for Body Dysmorphic Disorder
Delusional variant of Body Dysmorphic Disorder double coded as Delusional Disorder.........................	No longer double coded. Designated as Body Dysmorphic Disorder with *absent insight/ delusional* specifier. Additional possible diagnoses: **Other Specified Obsessive-Compulsive and related disorder** (includes body-focused repetitive behavior and obsessional jealousy) and **Unspecified Obsessive-Compulsive and Related Disorder**.
TRAUMA AND STRESSOR-RELATED DISORDERS	**NEW CHAPTER IN *DSM-5*** **Explicit terms for how trauma is experienced**
Criterion A2 Subjective reaction of horror, so on	**Criterion A2 eliminated** **Adjustment disorders placed in this section and reconceptualized as reactive stress syndromes** **Changes in Posttraumatic Stress Disorder (PTSD) criteria:** Explicit terms added re-events qualifying as trauma (A1); A2 eliminated
PTSD 3 symptom clusters (re-experiencing, avoidance/ numbing and arousal) **changed to......**	**Four symptom clusters:** Avoidance and numbing separate criteria. Numbing now defined as persistent negative emotional states. Irritable behavior, or angry outbursts and reckless or self-destructive behavior now added to definition of arousal. PTSD now more developmentally sensitive. Lowered thresholds for adolescents and children. Separate criteria for children 6 and under.
Reactive attachment disorder has two subtypes: emotionally withdrawn/inhibited and indiscriminately social/disinhibted	**Reactive attachment disorder** now placed in Trauma Disorders section. Subtypes now exist as separate disorders**: Reactive Attachment Disorder and Disinhibited Social Engagement Disorder**.
DISSOCIATIVE DISORDERS	
Depersonalization Disorder now..............................	**Depersonalization/derealization disorder**
Dissociative Fugue becomes................................	**A specifier for new disorder, dissociative amnesia** **Dissociative Identity Disorder criteria changes:** **1.** Disruptions of identity may be observed as well as reported **2.** Gaps in recall may occur for ordinary as well as traumatic events **3.** Experiences of pathological possession in some cultures added to description of identity disruption

(*continued*)

APPENDIX: CHANGES FROM *DSM-IV-TR* TO *DSM-5* (*continued*)

DSM-IV-TR	*DSM-5*
SOMATIC SYMPTOM AND RELATED DISORDERS	
Somatoform Disorders now called...........................	**Somatic Symptom and Related Disorders** Reduced # and subcategories of disorders
Somatization, Hypochondriasis, Pain Disorder..............	Eliminated
Hypochondriasis...	Persons previously diagnosed with somatization disorder must now have maladaptive thoughts, feelings, and behaviors, as well as somatic symptoms **Now illness Anxiety Disorder** if high anxiety and no somatic symptoms
Psychological factors affecting medical condition moved from Other Conditions That May Be a Focus of Clinical Attention moved to..................................	**NEW DIAGNOSIS psychological factors affecting medical condition**. Placed in this section with **factitious disorder** because psychological factors are predominant focus and encountered most in medical settings
Conversion Disorder criteria (formerly emphasizing psychological criteria) changed to......................	**Conversion Disorder (Functional Neurological Symptom Disorder)** to emphasize essential importance of neurological examination. Psychological factors may not be present at time of diagnosis **Other Specified Somatic Symptom and Related Disorder:** contains only Other Specified Somatic Symptom Disorder, Other Specified Illness Anxiety Disorder, and Pseudocyesis
FEEDING AND EATING DISORDERS	
Chapter "Disorders Usually First Diagnosed During Infancy"..	**Eliminated in *DSM-5*. Pica and rumination Disorder now in this section.**
Feeding Disorder of Infancy or Early Childhood.........	**Renamed Avoidant/Restrictive Food Intake Disorder**—criteria expanded;
Anorexia Nervosa..	Amenorrhea criterion eliminated. Added wording to assist in judging whether individual is significantly below expected body weight (Criterion A) Criterion B—adds *persistent behavior that interferes with weight gain* to overtly expressed fear of weight gain
Bulimia Nervosa	Frequency criteria for binge eating and inappropriate compensatory behavior reduced from twice to once a week.
Preliminary in Appendix B.....................................	**NEW DIAGNOSIS Binge-Eating Disorder**—minimum average frequency once a week vs. previously 2 days a week over 6 months
ELIMINATION DISORDERS	
Placed in chapter, "Disorders Usually First Diagnosed During Infancy, Childhood, or Adolescence"	**No changes in diagnostic criteria** Now an independent classification in *DSM-5*

(*continued*)

APPENDIX: CHANGES FROM *DSM-IV-TR* TO *DSM-5* (*continued*)

DSM-IV-TR	*DSM-5*
SLEEP–WAKE DISORDERS	
Sleep Disorder Related to Other Medical Disorder..........	**Eliminated**
	Greater specification of other coexisting disorders for each sleep–wake disorder
Primary Insomnia renamed.......................................	**Insomnia Disorder**
	Narcolepsy distinguished from Hypersomnolence disorder
	Pediatric and developmental information integrated in text
Breathing Regulated Sleep Disorders divided into...	**Obstructive Sleep Apnea**
	Hypopnea
	Central sleep Apnea
Subtypes of Circadian Rhythm Sleep Disorders expanded to...	**Sleep-Related Hypoventilation**
	Advanced Sleep Phase
	Irregular Sleep–Wake Type
Jet lag type..	**Eliminated**
SEXUAL DYSFUNCTIONS	
	Gender-specific sexual dysfunctions added
For females, sexual desire and arousal disorders....	Combined into **female sexual interest/arousal disorder**
	Minimum duration 6 months required for all disorders except substance/medication-induced sexual dysfunction; more precise severity criteria added
Vaginismus and Dyspareunia combined into.............	**Genito-Pelvic Pain/Penetration Disorder**
Sexual Aversion Disorder.......................................	**Eliminated**
	Only two subtypes, all disorder: lifelong vs. acquired and generalized vs. situational
	Associated features added to text for all disorders: Partner, relationship, individual vulnerability, cultural or religious, and medical factors
GENDER DYSPHORIA	**NEW CLASSIFICATION IN *DSM-5***
	Concept of gender incongruence vs. cross-gender identification identity; term *gender* replaces term *sex*
For adolescents/adults, previous Criterion A (cross-gender identification) and B (aversion toward one's gender)	**Separate criteria sets for children, adolescents-adults**
	Merged in *DSM-5*
Repeatedly stated desire to be other sex.................	**Replaced by strong desire to be of the other gender; this now required but insufficient to make diagnosis (more restrictive, conservative criteria)**
Subtyping of sexual orientation.............................	**Eliminated**
	Posttransition specifier added and differentiated in meaning from term remission

(*continued*)

APPENDIX: CHANGES FROM *DSM-IV-TR* TO *DSM-5* (*continued*)

DSM-IV-TR	*DSM-5*
DISRUPTIVE, IMPULSE CONTROL, AND CONDUCT DISORDERS Required physical aggression	Verbal aggression and noninjurious physical aggression allowed. Additional specificity re-frequency, nature, and consequences (resulting relationship, financial, occupational impairment) of aggression and minimum age of 6 or equivalent developmental level added.
SUBSTANCE-RELATED AND ADDICTIVE DISORDERS	**Gambling disorder = new in *DSM-5***
Abuse and Dependence = separate disorders	**Abuse and Dependence combined to = Substance Use Disorders** Criteria for intoxication, withdrawal, substance-induced disorders, unspecified substance-related disorders, where relevant
Substance-related legal problems...........................	Eliminated
Threshold criteria for diagnosis 1 for abuse, 3 for dependence	**New criteria**—Strong desire or craving or urge Threshold criteria = 2
Caffeine withdrawal under study in Appendix B	Severity based on # of criteria endorsed **New disorders: Cannabis Withdrawal and caffeine Withdrawal**
Specifier for physiological subtype; Diagnosis of polysubstance dependence	**Both eliminated in *DSM-5***
	Early remission = 3 but less than 12 months (except craving) **Sustained remission =** at least 12 months (except craving) **Additional specifiers =** *in a controlled environment* and *on maintenance therapy*
NEUROCOGNITIVE DISORDERS **Dementia and Amnestic Disorders** replaced by..........	**Major Neurocognitive Disorder (NCD)** **May use term** *dementia* where this is standard **New term Mild NCD**
Alzheimer's, Vascular, and Substance-Induced Dementias are separate diagnoses	**Major or Mild Alzheimer's and Vascular Dementia retained**
Others are Dementias Due to Another Medical Condition (specified as head trauma, HIV, Parkinson's, Pick's, Creutzfeldt–Jakob diseases, and Other Medical Conditions)	**Now separate criteria (diagnoses) for:** **Major or Mild Frontotemporal NCD** **NCD with Lewy Bodies** **NCD Due to Traumatic Brain Injury** **NCD Due to Substance/Medication** **NCD Due to HIV Infection** **NCD Due to Prion Disease** **NCD Due to Parkinson's Disease** **NCD Due to Huntington's Disease** **NCD Due to Another Medical Condition** **NCD Due to Multiple Etiologies** **Unspecified NCD also a diagnosis**

(*continued*)

APPENDIX: CHANGES FROM *DSM-IV-TR* TO *DSM-5* (*continued*)

DSM-IV-TR	*DSM-5*
PERSONALITY DISORDERS **No changes in disorders or criteria**	**Alternative model for assessment placed for future study and research in Section III.**
PARAPHILIC DISORDERS	**New specifiers—all disorders–in a controlled environment and in remission** Paraphilic Disorders not ipso facto Mental Disorders Paraphilia (urges) = Criterion A = not a disorder Paraphilic disorders = Criterion A and B Criterion B = causing distress or impairment to individual or satisfaction of paraphilia causes harm or risk of harm to others

THREE

Mood Disorders and the Diversity/Resiliency Formulation

I measure every grief I meet
With analytic eyes:
I wonder if it weighs like mine,
Or has an easier size.
I wonder if they bore it long,
Or did it just begin?
I could not tell the date of mine,
It feels so old a pain.
I wonder if it hurts to live,
And if they have to try,
And whether, could they choose between,
They would not rather die.

—EMILY DICKINSON, I MEASURE EVERY GRIEF I MEET

Depression is often considered the "bread and butter" of psychiatry, the essential source of business and income for psychiatrists. Depression is the second leading cause of disability after heart disease (Nemeroff & Owens, 2002). In the United States, depression has sometimes been described as the most prevalent lifetime disorder, experienced by up to 16.6% (Kessler et al., 2003) of the population, with a lifetime risk of 20% to 25% in women and 7% to 12% in men. Furthermore, these rates increased five times between the 1950s and the 1990s (Corcoran & Walsh, 2006). The relative space allotted to disturbances of mood in the *DSM*® tripled in the *DSM-IV-TR* (American Psychiatric Association [APA], 2000) in comparison with past editions (Corcoran & Walsh, 2006), and their relative importance continues in the *DSM-5* (APA, 2013), where mood disorders are now divided into two chapters. The reasons for the prominence of mood disorders in the *DSM* are widely debated, and there is concern that depression rates are inflated in response to psychiatry's relationship with the pharmaceutical industry (Kutchins & Kirk, 1997; Shorter, 2009; Whitaker, 2010). For the purposes of reviewing current issues in diagnosis, etiology, and treatment, we have chosen in this chapter to focus in greater detail on two specific mood disorders: Major Depressive Disorder (MDD) and Bipolar I, despite their placement in two separate chapters in the *DSM-5*, as much of the research on effective, strength-based treatment is overlapping and applicable to both. We illustrate the application of the Diversity/Resiliency Formulation to a case vignette and conclude with recommendations for teaching, learning, and practice across the mental health disciplines.

DSM DIAGNOSTIC CRITERIA: CHANGES, *DSM IV-TR* TO *DSM-5*

Mood Disorders are combined in *DSM-IV-TR* and are divided into two separate chapters in the *DSM-5*: Bipolar and Related Disorders and Depressive Disorders. The *DSM-5* retains the descriptions of depressive, manic, and hypomanic, but the episodes are not separate diagnoses per se; rather, they are symptom patterns that are building blocks of the bipolar or depressive disorders.

Bipolar and Related Disorders

In the *DSM-5*, the placement of Bipolar and Related Disorders between the schizophrenic spectrum and depressive disorders reflects their conceptualization as a bridge between these diagnostic classes in terms of their symptomatology, family history, and genetics. Bipolar disorders (BPDs) are divided into several diagnostic categories related to the order and severity of symptom presentations. Bipolar I requires the presence of manic or mixed or both manic and depressive episodes. In a manic episode, the individual displays a distinctly abnormal and persistently elevated, expansive, or irritable mood, along with increased goal-directed behavior or energy for at least 1 week almost all the time. If hospitalization is needed, there is no duration criterion. Three of more of the following symptoms are required for the diagnosis: grandiosity/inflated self-esteem, less need for sleep, pressured talking, racing thoughts or a flight of ideas, distractibility, agitation, and increased goal-directed activity, and excessive involvement in the type of activity that can bring about painful consequences, often sexual or financial. Psychotic symptoms may be present, and hospitalization to protect the individual from harm to self or others may be required. A hypomanic episode has many of the same features, but the impairment is less serious and does not require hospitalization. A major depressive episode has a 2-week duration period in which there is a decline from previous functioning and either a depressed mood or a loss of pleasure or interest. There may be significant weight loss or gain, fatigue, and sleep problems. Suicidal ideation or plans are common, along with feelings of worthlessness and inappropriate guilt. This disorder is related to the former manic–depressive disorder, but in the modern understanding of BPD, neither a psychotic episode or an experience of a major depressive episode is a requirement for the diagnosis. Bipolar I is coded with mild, moderate, or severe specifiers, with psychotic features, if present, and with a list of other unique specifiers: with anxious distress, mixed features, rapid cycling, melancholic features, atypical features, mood-congruent psychotic features, mood-incongruent psychotic features, catatonia, peripartum onset, and seasonal pattern (American Psychiatric Association [APA], 2013).

In the *DSM-5*, bipolar II requires a lifetime experience of at least one episode of major depression and at least one hypomanic episode (less severe in presentation than a manic episode and without psychotic features). Significantly, in *DSM-5*, bipolar II is no longer considered a less severe form of bipolar I because individuals with Bipolar II suffer from extensive bouts of depression, unstable moods, and related serious occupational and social impairment. Adults with Cyclothymic Disorder suffer for at least 2 years from both hypomanic and depressive symptoms without meeting full criteria for mania, hypomania, or major depression; in children, the required duration is 1 year. Additional diagnoses in this section are related to bipolar and related disorders associated with substance abuse, prescribed medication, and medical conditions. An additional category of Other Specified Bipolar Disorder in the *DSM-5* recognizes that children and adolescents can experience bipolar-like symptoms without meeting full criteria for bipolar I, II, or cyclothymia. In the future, a short-duration hypomania diagnosis may be added to this section; for now, this disorder has been placed in Section III of the *DSM-5* manual to encourage further research. The reader is referred to the *DSM-5* for an extensive description of bipolar and related disorder symptoms presentations (APA, 2013).

Depressive Disorders

Depressive disorders are complex. They are still poorly understood and there is considerable overlap among categories. For some patients, episodes of depression last at least 2 years, much longer than the reported median duration of about 20 weeks, with resulting devastating effects on quality of life and health. Depressive Disorders in the *DSM-5* have in common sad, empty, or irritable mood, along with somatic and cognitive changes that create impairment in functioning. They differ in terms of timing, duration, and presumed etiology. MDD is the classic diagnosis in this category, characterized by at least 2 weeks' duration of changes in affect, cognition, and neurovegetative functions, with interepisode remissions. Usually this disorder is a recurrent one, and episodes typically last much longer than 2 weeks. The depressive symptoms are identical to those of a depressive episode in BPDs: weight loss or gain, insomnia or hypersomnia, psychomotor agitation or retardation, loss of energy and fatigue, feelings of worthlessness or excessive guilt, diminished ability to concentrate, and thoughts of death or suicide (APA, 2013).

The *DSM-IV-TR* had a bereavement exclusion; major depression could not be diagnosed in the wake of a significant interpersonal loss. In a controversial change, the *DSM-5* allows major depression to be diagnosed when an individual is grieving a loss, but cautions the clinician to delineate carefully the presence of normal sadness and grief from a major depressive episode. The justification for this change is that bereavement-related depression occurs in persons vulnerable to depressive disorders, the symptoms and related impairment are more severe, and the prognosis is poorer. The former diagnoses of Dysthymia and Chronic Major Depression in *DSM-IV-TR* are combined in the *DSM-5* into Persistent Depressive Disorder. This is a chronic, low level of mood disturbance that continues for at least 2 years in adults and 1 year in children, and is characterized by depressive symptoms that include changes in appetite, sleep, energy, self-esteem, concentration, and hope. The dysthymia label is retained in parenthesis.

Other changes from *DSM-IV-TR* to *DSM-5* include the additions of two new diagnoses: Disruptive Mood Dysregulation Disorder and Premenstrual Dysphoric Disorder. Disruptive Mood Dysregulation Disorder may be diagnosed in children who display persistent irritability and episodes of extreme behavioral dyscontrol. The justification for this controversial change is based on the recognition that children who display this symptom pattern typically develop a unipolar depression or an anxiety disorder in adulthood. This disorder was also added to avoid the overdiagnosis of BPD in children but at the same time to give children with this symptom pattern the help they need. The evidence for establishing the validity of Disruptive Mood Dysregulation Disorder and providing guidelines for its differential diagnosis from other disorders has increasingly emerged (Eme & Mouritson, 2013). Critics, however, argue that this addition will result in the overpathologizing and overmedication of large numbers of children who are simply displaying a range of normal temperamental human behavior or reacting to environmental conditions that need addressing (Frances, 2013).

Premenstrual Dysphoric Disorder was moved from its previous location in the appendix of the *DSM-IV-TR*, where it was placed pending further study, to the main Section II of the *DSM-5*. The justification for its new status as a bona fide diagnosis is evidence based. According to the *DSM-5* authors, 20 years of research have confirmed that this is a specific treatment-responsive form of depressive disorder in women, beginning shortly after ovulation, markedly impairing functioning, and remitting after menses begins. As in the chapter on Bipolar and Related Disorders, the *DSM-5* recognizes diagnoses of Substance/Medication-Induced Depressive Disorders and Depressive Disorder Related to Another Medical Condition (APA, 2013).

Issues in Differential Diagnosis

Bipolar Disorder I

Bipolar I Disorder must be distinguished from an MDD, other BPDs, anxiety disorders, attention-deficit hyperactivity disorder (ADHD), and bipolar or depressive disorders due to a medical condition or substance abuse. Personality disorders, and other disorders with prominent irritability, need to be considered and ruled out. BPD often co-occurs with an anxiety disorder. Presentations of BPD are often confusing at best, complicated by substance abuse and psychotic symptoms that may initially be difficult to distinguish from schizophrenia or schizoaffective disorders (APA, 2000, 2013).

CASE STUDY 1

The Phenomenology of BPD

> At first, everything seemed so easy. I raced about like a crazed weasel, bubbling with plans and enthusiasm.... I felt I could do anything, that no task was too difficult. My mind seemed clear, fabulously focused.... (My friends) were less than transfixed by my insights ... although considerably impressed by how exhausting it was to be around my enthusiastic ramblings.... Then the bottom began to fall out of my life and mind. My thinking, far from being clearer than a crystal, was tortuous.... I was used to my mind being my best friend.... Now, all of a sudden, my mind had turned on me: it mocked me for my vapid enthusiasms; it laughed at all of my foolish plans; it no longer found anything interesting, enjoyable, or worthwhile. It was incapable of concentrated thought and turned time and again to the subject of death: I was going to die, what difference did anything make? Life's run was only a short and meaningless one, why live? I was totally exhausted and could scarcely pull myself out of bed in the mornings. It took me twice as long to walk anywhere as it normally did, and I wore the same clothes over and over again, as it was otherwise too much of an effort to make a decision about what to put on. I dreaded having to talk with people, avoided my friends whenever possible.... Each day I awoke deeply tired.... Then, a gray, bleak preoccupation with death, dying, decaying, that everything was born but to die, best to die now, and save the pain while waiting. (Jamison, 1995, pp. 36–39)

1. What symptoms of BPD are evident in this personal account?
2. How do you imagine the author's friends' reactions to her behavior?
3. What crisis issues do you note, both in the manic and depressed phases?

Major Depressive Disorder

The diagnostic process requires that MDD be differentiated from depressive symptoms related to a general medical condition, such as hypothyroidism, cancer, dementia, myocardial infarction, or diabetes. However, MDD can co-occur with any of the previously described medical conditions. Many patients can and do become depressed in reaction to the reality of coping with a difficult medical condition. Conversely, depressive symptoms can manifest as panic attacks, obsessive worry, complaints of bodily pain, or sexual dysfunction. Job and relationship difficulties can either cause or be the result of a mood disorder. In children, separation anxiety may signal depression; in adolescents or children, anger or behavioral problems may be the most prominent symptoms of depression. Psychosocial stressors—such as divorce, geographical relocations, childbirth, or the death of a loved one—can trigger a major depressive episode. Notably suicide (ideation, attempts, or completion) is a prominent feature of mood disorders.

More than 75% of patients with a persistent depressive disorder experience what is described in the literature as double depression (persistent depressive disorder and MDD) from time to time, and 25% of patients with a major depressive episode experience persistent depressive disorder. Some researchers feel that persistent depressive disorder causes more cognitive symptoms, such as difficulty concentrating, low self-esteem, and feelings of hopelessness, whereas major depression is characterized by more vegetative symptoms, such as poor sleeping and eating, sleep disturbance, and reduced energy (Gelenberg, Kocsis, McCullough, Ninan, & Thase, 2006; Harvey, Tilkey, Kornstein, & Clary, 2007; Klein et al., 2009; Torpey & Klein, 2008). Individuals with persistent depressive disorder are at higher risk for substance use and anxiety disorders than individuals with MDD (APA, 2013). Finally, all individuals will experience periods of sadness from time to time, especially when they lose a loved one. Kay Jamison, noted author, psychologist, expert on and sufferer from BPD, has wryly and aptly distinguished bereavement from depression, noting that bereavement is caused by death, whereas depression causes death (Jamison, 2009).

Specific diagnoses that should be considered and ruled out in assessing for MDD include the following: mood disorder due to another medical condition, substance/medication-induced depressive or BPD, ADHD, adjustment disorder with depressed mood, and ordinary sadness. MDD often co-occurs with substance-related disorders, panic disorder, obsessive-compulsive disorder (OCD), anorexia nervosa, bulimia nervosa, and borderline personality disorder (APA, 2013).

CASE STUDY 2

The Phenomenology of MDD

My life had come to a sudden stop. I was able to breathe, to eat, to drink, to sleep. I could not, indeed, help doing so; but there was no real life in me. I had not a single wish to strive for the fulfillment of what I could feel to be reasonable. If I wished for anything, I knew beforehand that, were I to satisfy the wish, nothing would come of it, I should still be dissatisfied. Had a fairy appeared and offered me all I desired, I would not have known what to say. If I seemed to have, at a given moment of excitement, not a wish, but a mood resulting from the tendencies of former wishes, at a calmer moment I knew that it was a delusion that I really wished for nothing. I could not even wish to know the truth, because I guessed what the truth was. The truth lay in this, that life had no meaning for me. Every day of life, every step in it, brought me nearer the edge of a precipice, whence I saw clearly the final ruin before me. To stop, to go back, were alike impossible; nor could I shut my eyes so as not to see the suffering that alone awaited me, the death of all in me, even to annihilation. Thus I, a healthy and a happy man, was brought to feel that I could live no longer, that an irresistible force was dragging me down into the grave. (Tolstoy, 1887, as cited in LeCroy & Holschuh, 2012)

1. What is your immediate, gut-level reaction to this personal account?
2. Did it impact you to realize that one of the most beloved novelists of all time could have suffered so deeply from depression?
3. How would you respond to hearing about this from a friend or loved one?

Although this experience was described over 127 years ago, it remains an eloquent description of the emotional paralysis and existential despair of a major depression that overtook the famous Russian novelist Leo Tolstoy in the prime of his life and success.

The issue of differential diagnosis in these disorders is complex and multifaceted. Many persons who are depressed are also highly anxious, and highly anxious persons are often depressed about being anxious. During periods of high stress, many people coping with the vicissitudes of daily life temporarily feel overwhelmed or under par in their ability to function. For example, at rates reported up to 25%, patients admitted to one mood disorder clinic were misdiagnosed (Busko, 2008a). Out of 100 patients with a primary diagnosis of BPD, only 60% actually had it; 26% of this cohort had an anxiety disorder, a thought disorder, or a personality disorder. The researcher concludes that BPD is often misdiagnosed, when the previously mentioned diagnoses are the real culprits. Close attention to the patient and the administration of screening tests are recommended. In addition, Busko (2008b) stresses that not everyone needs medication, that not every presentation of human suffering is a mental disorder, and that often talk therapy is sufficient to offer patients relief. Errors of diagnosis lead to errors of treatment, especially when psychopharmacology is employed; thus accurate diagnosis is very important.

A controversial area related to this is the diagnosis of BPD in children. A recent review of the literature concludes that in approximately 33% of persons with BPD, the symptoms first appear in childhood or adolescence, at a rate of one in 200 persons (Harvard Medical School, 2007). Others feel that the diagnosis is overused in children, with the result that drugs are prescribed too freely, sometimes with iatrogenic results, and that clinicians fail to attend to social and psychological issues, such as abuse and trauma, family conflict, or inadequate parenting (Whitaker, 2010).

KEY POINTS

1. Rule out medical illnesses or substance abuse as causation.
2. Evaluate for suicidality (thoughts, plans, intent, means, and history) and take steps to keep the patient safe.
3. Antidepressant use should be avoided when symptoms of mania are present; evaluate for Bipolar Disorder. Nonmedical professionals should work closely with physicians in this process of diagnosis.
4. A mixed presentation of anxiety and depression is common.

5. **Listen for sadness and confusion in response to the stress of being human; respond with empathy and support.**

CURRENT THINKING ABOUT THE ETIOLOGY AND COURSE OF MDD AND BPD

A complex mixture of heredity and environment appears to be implicated in the onset of MDD, but there is stronger evidence for a genetic and biological etiology in the case of BPD. The symptoms of many medical illnesses also masquerade as depression, and experiences of stress and loss in the life cycle potentiate depressive reactions.

Genetic Heritability

Consistent differences between the genetic profiles of persons with and without mood disorders have not been found; however, a recent meta-analysis that examined the results of studies of both BPD and MDD (Johnston, 2010, p. 21) found that individuals with either disorder carry a specific allele on the same gene (most significantly, marker rs2251219 on chromosome 3). This is the first study to demonstrate genetic overlap between depression and BPD and to show a relationship between a specific chromosome and a psychiatric disorder. However, the authors note that the findings do not explain why some individuals with the particular allele develop MDD or BPD and others do not; this supports the validity of a stress–diathesis model of mental illness regardless of genetic predisposition.

Twin studies and family history research support the clustering of BPD and MDD in families. First-degree relatives (siblings and parents) are up to 24% more likely to be diagnosed with either disorder as well as to experience earlier onset. In both identical and fraternal twins, concordance rates have been reported at 85% for BPD and up to 42% for major depression (Corcoran & Walsh, 2006). Inquiry into the patient's family history during the diagnostic process is important, perhaps using traditional therapeutic tools, such as the genogram (McGoldrick, Gerson, & Petry, 2008).

Neurobiological Factors

No consistent diagnostic laboratory markers have been found for either MDD or BPD (APA, 2000). Some laboratory findings have been more abnormal in groups of individuals with a major depressive episode compared with control subjects and in individuals with severe symptoms that include melancholic or psychotic features. Most abnormalities vary with the presence or absence of depressive symptoms, but some may precede the onset of the episode or persist after its remission. Sleep EEG abnormalities are evident in 40% to 60% of outpatients and in 90% of patients with a major depressive episode. Alterations in cerebral blood flow are evident in the limbic, paralimbic, and lateral prefrontal cortex regions of the brain in some individuals, and late-life depression has been associated with periventricular vascular brain changes. Other depressed individuals show hormonal disturbances, including elevated glucocorticoid secretion, blunted growth hormone, alterations in thyroid-stimulating hormone, and abnormal prolactin levels in response to various challenge tests. However, none of these changes are present in all patients with major depression, nor has any one of these changes proven to be a specific marker for depression. Similarly, although no consistent laboratory findings have been discovered to be diagnostic markers for BPD, the *DSM* reports some observed differences between bipolar patients and controls, including polysomnographic abnormalities, increased cortisol secretion, and possible abnormalities in norepinephrine, serotonin, acetylcholine, dopamine, or gamma–aminobutyric acid neurotransmitter systems (APA, 2000).

Chemical imbalance theories of depression have been developed from experience with the effects of antidepressant medications on neurotransmitter levels in the limbic regions of the brain. Most antidepressants affect norepinephrine or serotonin levels or both. A recent study in mice, conducted by researchers at Columbia University Medical Center (Richardson-Jones et al., 2010), demonstrated that increasing receptor levels in raphe neurons reduce antidepressant response and, conversely, that decreasing these receptors can restore the effectiveness of antidepressant drugs. Persons resistant to antidepressant medication have been found to have a genotype associated with higher levels of 5-HT(1A) autoreceptors. Exploring the effects of this genetic variation in mice demonstrated that increasing the serotonin in mice with higher levels of 5-HT(1A) reduces serotonin production by setting in motion a negative feedback loop, such that the more the selective serotonin reuptake inhibitor (SSRI) medications attempt to increase serotonin, the less serotonin the neurons produce. Individuals with even subtle changes in the serotonin receptor are thus more vulnerable to depression and unresponsive to SSRIs. Researchers hope that reducing the number of 5-HT(1A) autoreceptors, and/or blocking their activity might help treatment-resistant individuals; therefore they are seeking to confirm that surplus serotonin autoreceptors play a similar role in humans (Kelly, 2010).

Theories based on brain chemistry have been criticized as being too reductionistic because medications focusing on one or two transmitters actually affect many neurological systems at a level of complexity that is poorly understood and because psychosocial events also affect neurotransmitter levels (Valenstein, 1998). Psychosocial stress, such as interpersonal loss or environmental problems, may create changes in neurotransmitter levels rather than the reverse. Thus correlation becomes confused with causality (Andreasen, 2001) in that clinicians and researchers may assume that inherited biological differences in brain chemistry create the depressive symptoms, rather than interpreting differences in brain chemistry as the result of interpersonal or other environmental stress. Both the development of the neurotransmitter theories and the consensus-based *DSM* decision-making process have been challenged by critics who assert that the politics of diagnosis, along with the power of the pharmaceutical lobbies, obscure the differences between truly biologically based melancholia and psychologically driven human suffering (Breggin, 1994; Shorter, 2009). In the rush to produce newer drugs in a regulatory context requiring, for Food and Drug Administration (FDA) approval, a minimal level of demonstrated effectiveness that is only better than placebo, psychiatry, they argue, fails to attend carefully to the individual patient, minimizes the demoralizing and sometimes toxic side effects of medication, and creates labels for illnesses that do not exist. Shorter (2009) asserts:

> Most of the antidepressants today don't work very well.... Similarly, many of the diagnoses of mood disorder today really don't make a lot of sense. New drugs are needed with fewer side effects and more effectiveness than the industry standards now possess. New diagnoses are required ... for which drugs of the future will have a powerful and highly specific effect....Psychiatry is floundering in an ivory-tower-spun web of diagnoses that jumble different diseases together, in a mesh of patent-protected remedies that represent, if anything, a loss of knowledge rather than a gain. This is not progress. (pp. 213–214)

The point of view expressed in this quotation, which highlights the conflation of diagnosis with the aggressive pharmaceutical promotion of medications, is supported in part by a recent meta-analysis of antidepressant drug effects related to depression severity (Fournier et al., 2010), which found that medication versus placebo effects varied substantially as a function of baseline severity of symptoms. The authors conclude that antidepressant medication remains the most effective intervention for severe depression but may have minimal to no real efficacy in patients with mild or moderate symptoms. The latter may benefit more from careful attention to the unique combination of internal and external stressors that are producing their symptoms and from nonpharmaceutical intervention rather than being given an antidepressant as a first-line treatment. These issues are elaborated on later in this chapter.

Many researchers have described difficulties with the diagnostic categories of anxiety and mood disorders in general, noting overlap in symptoms and in medication effects in various mood and anxiety categories. Brown, Chorpita, and Barlow (1998) discuss the lack of dimensionality in mood and anxiety diagnostic criteria in the former *DSM-IV* (APA, 1994) as well as the tendency to increase the number of diagnoses as the years go by. In real life, the symptom criteria are rarely wholly present or absent but vary by degree and kind from individual to individual. To correct for this problem, the *DSM-5* directs the clinician to a specific mild, moderate, or severe level of severity, accounting for dimensionality.

The creation of more and more categories of diagnosis may be due to greater refinement of the mental condition being described; on the other hand, this proliferation of diagnostic labels may ignore underlying traits that would better predict and explain symptoms. Diagnosing mood disorders in isolation belies the strong relationship and overlap in the domains of anxiety and depression; in reality, these domains may not be empirically distinct. Brown et al. (1998) support the concepts proposed earlier by Clark, Watson, and Mineka (1994), suggesting an underlying tripartite structure for anxiety and/or depression. Affect or general distress is considered to be shared by both anxiety and mood disorders, physiological arousal is more characteristic of anxiety, and the absence of positive affect is more characteristic of depressive disorders. A mixed anxiety–depressive disorder was considered as an addition to the *DSM-5* but ultimately not adopted.

In BPD, the search for a neurobiological basis of the disorder has been conducted by comparing siblings with and without diagnosed BPD. Kruger et al. (2006) induced a state of emotional sadness in both groups and measured differences in cerebral blood flow while the subjects were experiencing dysphoric emotions. Siblings with and without BPD had similar changes in the anterior cingulate area of the brain, but only in the bipolar group was there a decrease in blood flow to the medial frontal cortex. In the healthy sibling, blood flow to the medial frontal cortex, where cognitive processing of emotions and altered emotional perspective taking can take place, was similar to that of persons without bipolar illness. This differential response was interpreted to indicate evidence of neurological mediating of resiliency versus vulnerability in siblings contrasted with their bipolar family member.

Controversy surrounds the etiological paradigms of mood disorders. There are no consistent biological markers of either unipolar or bipolar depression, but stronger evidence exists for a genetic predisposition for bipolar illness and severe depression with melancholic features. Depressive and anxiety symptoms present a complex diagnostic picture more often than not. Biological and neurological research fails to explain why some individuals with a family history of either bipolar or unipolar illness do not have manic or major depressive episodes. Although there is a growing trend to view depression as a biological illness, the data are mixed.

A strong argument exists for viewing mild to moderate depression more in terms of a psychosocial condition, different in etiology from the more inherited, biologically based severe forms of either bipolar or unipolar mood illnesses. Gupta (2009) describes major depression as a medical illness with objective and fairly consistent physical signs that correlate positively with the severity of the illness. These symptoms include slowed movement; diminished gestures and expressions; fatigue; self-absorption and loss of interest in one's surroundings; anxiety as an integral element of the affective state; the presence of wringing hands, moaning, and repetitive verbalization of misery; tachycardia; dry mouth; sweaty palms; clammy skin; pallor; dilated pupils; tremor; and fluctuations in blood pressure with wide pulse pressure. The author believes that because the *DSM* does not include these physical signs as an integral part of the clinical picture of depression, the diagnosis of major depression becomes subjective and imprecise, perhaps explaining the large placebo response to treatment in clinical drug trials.

The perceived causes of depression can impact both depressed persons and societal attitudes toward them. The National Alliance for the Mentally Ill (NAMI) argues for a biological model of mental illness in general and of depression in particular in an effort to reduce stigma toward persons with mental illness. Patients diagnosed with depression have been found to prefer to view their illness as biologically based, but this attribution can reduce the belief in the ability to help oneself. Patients subscribing to a psychosocial model of depression have been found to be more proactive in seeking treatment, but a negative consequence of a belief in psychosocial causation may be a tendency to blame the victim, either the patient or his family (Gammell & Stoppard, 1999). A review of the state of current knowledge about causation argues for the acknowledgment of the strong role of heredity and biology in the etiology of severe unipolar and bipolar illness, supporting the efficacy of medication and other biologically based interventions, while implying a stronger basis for complex person–environment causation in the case of mild to moderate depression. Both more severe and milder illnesses contain psychosocial risk and protective factors, causes, and effects. This reality underlines the importance of effective intervention that goes beyond the use of medication, reduces stigma and blame, and empowers patients and their family members to be proactive in the treatment and management of mood disorders.

KEY POINTS

1. Causation remains complex and controversial, with both biological and psychosocial components that vary from person to person.
2. Severe unipolar and BPDs are considered to be biologically based and more likely to run in families.
3. For patients, a biological view of causation may reduce stigma, but a psychosocial model may enhance empowerment.

EVIDENCE-INFORMED PRACTICE

Depression remains a prevalent, debilitating reality in the lives of many individuals and families. Callahan and Berrios (2005) review the history of the treatment of depression in primary care over the past half century, concluding that although new strategies for treatment have evolved, the overall societal burden of depression has not decreased. Arguing for a public health perspective focused on understanding the epidemiology of depression in society and efforts at prevention, these authors assert that the prevailing etiologic models, described in the preceding section, fail to take into account the role of society and culture in depression and that a public health perspective is needed. The scientifically and socially invented model of depression, controlled by the cultures of medicine and pharmacology, defines who is sick and who gets treated, with the result that most patients receive antidepressant medication in the context of primary care, despite repeated evidence that a high percentage of patients do not respond to antidepressants and that the placebo effect is large in outcome studies. Psychiatric practices may or may not be similar to nonspecific primary care approaches. Considered in contexts broader than the consulting room, the process of diagnosis extends to the need to understand the relationship between the individual and his family, community, and society.

Psychopharmacology

Since the approval of fluoxetine (Prozac) by the U.S. FDA in 1987, the rate of disability due to mental illness has doubled; psychopharmacology has become the first-line treatment of choice for depression (Whitaker, 2010). The influence of pharmaceutical companies has dominated the research agenda for depression for years and is widely criticized for its influence on psychiatry (Kutchins & Kirk, 1997; Shorter, 2009; Whitaker, 2010). The proliferation of drugs for MDD and BPD is well known, and the pros and cons of the use of medication should be a part of any assessment and treatment planning process. Research related to the effectiveness of medications is ongoing and is summarized in the following sections.

Major Depression

Heterocyclics (HCAs) and monoamine oxidase inhibitors (MAOIs) have been used for several decades in the treatment of unipolar depression. These medications increase the levels of norepinephrine in the brain either directly, in the case of HCAs, or indirectly, by inhibiting the main enzyme that breaks down norephinephrine, in the case of the MAOIs. Most antidepressants must be taken for several weeks before efficacy can be determined. HCAs cause troubling side effects (constipation, urinary retention, impaired sexual functioning, blurred vision, dry mouth, drowsiness, and increased heart rate), which vary from person to person. Side effects are usually experienced prior to beneficial effects, causing many patients to stop taking medication before beneficial effects are experienced. Because MAOIs impair the ability to break down tyramine, persons taking MAOIs must avoid foods such as aged cheeses, beer and red wine, aged meat, chocolate, some fish, and other foods high in tyramine. MAOIs can also interact with cough medications to cause dangerously high levels of blood pressure (Gray & Zide, 2005, 2007).

SSRIs act to increase serotonin levels in the brain and have been increasingly used in the treatment of depression in the past few decades, in part because they produce fewer side effects than other medications. Many patients, however, still complain of side effects; the chief complaint relating to a significant loss of libido. Selective serotonin–norepinephrine reuptake inhibitors (SNRIs) combine the serotonergic and norepinprehinergic effects of the SSRIs and HCAs. No particular drug has been found to be more effective than another. In a meta-analysis of outcome studies after 6 to 12 weeks of treatment, 45% to 55% responded positively as defined by a 50% reduction in symptoms measured by Hamilton Depression Scale (Klein et al., 2009). Only 25% of persons with chronic depression, however, achieved remission from the first drug. Persons with chronic depression may need longer treatment and long-term maintenance therapy (Klein et al., 2009). When a return to a premorbid nondepressed level of functioning was assessed, results were even less impressive; after 6 to 8 weeks, only 35% to 40% were free of significant depressive symptoms, and the reason for their improvement was unclear (Nemeroff & Owens, 2002).

Bipolar Disorder

Lithium, a naturally occurring salt in the body, remains the gold standard in the treatment of BPD; it is the most studied medication and is most effective in the treatment of mania. Stabilization of mood usually occurs within 14 days. Significant improvement is attained in 70% of patients; 20% are symptom free after 2 weeks; and manic symptoms are reduced by half in 50% of patients after 3 weeks. Relapse levels remain high, however; symptom-free functioning declines from 85% after 1 year to 37% after 5 years, and reported relapse rates vary from 55% to 73% in 3 to 4 years (Corcoran & Walsh, 2006).

To avoid toxic side effects, lithium levels must be monitored via blood tests. Adolescents may require higher levels of lithium to achieve a therapeutic effect, whereas older persons metabolize drugs less efficiently and may be vulnerable to toxic effects. Side effects may include thirst, weight gain, hand tremor, fatigue, and confusion; more seriously, such effects may include severe diarrhea, dizziness, nausea, slurred speech, and spasticity. As in unipolar disorder, many patients cease taking their medication owing to its side effects—a decision that can be dangerous in patients on lithium, which should be tapered gradually to avoid a rebound of manic symptoms. Other commonly used medications in the treatment of BPD include anticonvulsants (e.g., valproate, carbamazepine, and lamotrigine), which take effect more quickly, in 2 to 5 days, compared with lithium. The use of lithium and anticonvulsants is contraindicated in pregnant women and nursing mothers. Anticonvulsant medications are increasingly used as an initial treatment strategy and have comparable effectiveness to lithium in the treatment of acute mania (Corcoran & Walsh, 2006; Gray & Zide, 2005, 2007).

BPD, Medication, and the Timeliness of Diagnosis

The diagnosis of BPD is considered one of the most daunting challenges for the medical profession and mental health practitioners. Differential diagnosis of manic behavior involves assessing for substance intoxication, withdrawal syndromes, anxiety disorders, personality disorders, schizophrenia, and delirium. Inflated mannerisms, talkativeness, breakdown in clarity, and focus of speech and grandiosity are considered special clues to the presence of mania. Failure to recognize the disorder delays appropriate management, and misdiagnosis can affect the course of the disease negatively. Although mood stabilizers, described previously, are the classic treatment, newer atypical antipsychotics are also used. The use of antidepressants in the treatment of the depressive phase of BPD is controversial, as this may aggravate the illness over time, potentiating a manic episode. Growing evidence consistently demonstrates that adjunctive psychosocial interventions improve the patient's long-term functioning; thus multidisciplinary collaboration is vitally important in the diagnostic process and in the establishment of a medication regimen (Culver, Arnow, & Ketter, 2007; Cusack, 2002; Sussman, 2007).

Accurate and timely diagnosis of BPD is of central importance in that the failure of timely diagnosis is common and can have devastating effects. In one study of claims from a large U.S. health plan (Stensland & Schultz, 2008), more than 25% of individuals diagnosed with BPD had a subsequent depression misdiagnosis during a follow-up period, resulting in increases in psychiatric hospitalization and emergency room visits, often because of a relapse into manic symptoms potentiated by the effects of antidepressants prescribed for the erroneous diagnosis of unipolar depression.

Providers and patients have different priorities with respect to the diagnosis and treatment of BPD. In a study comparing provider and patient viewpoints about diagnosis and treatment of BPD, Lewis (2005) found that providers emphasize consistent diagnostic systems and tools, awareness of symptoms and treatment options, appropriate referrals, adequate insurance coverage, and fewer demands on their professional schedules. Patients, on the other hand, emphasize reduction in stigma, quicker-acting medications that are effective while producing fewer side effects, and adequate access to medication. Patients want to be active partners, not only in diagnosis and treatment but also in the design of research; they value the opportunity to share their experience of the disorder and their viewpoints about effective treatment. Few patients had been asked important targeted questions by their physicians, such as "How many hours are you sleeping?" versus "How are you feeling?" More than one third had waited more than 10 years for an accurate diagnosis after consulting an average of four physicians. Less than one third had been referred to support groups, even though support groups improve treatment adherence by 86% and reduce the need for inpatient hospitalization (Lewis, 2005). Barriers to effective diagnosis and treatment revolved around physicians' lack of understanding of patient needs and inadequate communication between patients and physicians.

Stigma represents another barrier to timely diagnosis and treatment. The National Depressive and Manic-Depressive Association is concerned with the role of stigma in hindering the organization's educational outreach efforts because of the widespread belief that mood disorders are not real but represent personality flaws. Consumers and family members who visit the website for information about their diagnosis and for peer support are linked to a variety of studies supporting the usefulness of psychosocial interventions for consumers and family members (see www.ndmda.org). Ongoing problems have been reported with the underdiagnosis of BPD, underfunding of research, and lack of consumer satisfaction with treatment (Landino, Roy, & Buckley, 2009).

The Growing Reliance on Polypharmacy

A cross-sectional study tracked national trends in the way American psychiatrists prescribed psychotropic drugs between 1998 and 2007 (Marcus & Olfson, 2010). The findings show that the use of two or more medications increased from 42.6% to 59.8% over the time period, and the use of three medications per patient increased even more, from 16.9% to 33.2%. Similarly, the median number of psychotropic medications increased from one in 1996–1997 to two in 2005–2006, representing a 40.1% mean increase. Patients diagnosed with major depression were significantly more likely to be prescribed two or more antidepressant drugs, but those with BPD were less likely to be prescribed two or more mood stabilizers. The researchers express concern that, despite clinical trials that support some of the prescribed combinations, others are of unproven efficacy and may put patients at heightened risk for drug interactions.

Psychosocial Interventions

Prior to the emergence of the previously described mood stabilizers and antidepressants in the 1950s, severely depressed patients were treated with a variety of drugs, including alkaloids, alcohol, opium, cannabis, barbiturates, and amphetamines, often with reported beneficial results, or they were sent to spas for rest and "water cures" (Shorter, 2009). The advances in pharmaceutical treatment that followed in the second half of the last century, however, have had their limitations. Effectiveness in the reduction of symptoms, such as insomnia or melancholia, does not automatically translate into improved relationships with others, optimism, self-efficacy, or productivity, and medication compliance is contingent on culturally competent communication in the context of a positive therapeutic relationship. A variety of psychosocial interventions has been tested; the interventions described here have been applied to the treatment of MDD and BPD.

Depression

Cognitive behavioral therapy (CBT) and interpersonal therapy have been compared with psychopharmacology in the treatment of MDD with respect to their short- and long-term ability to reduce or eliminate the symptoms of the disorder (Harvard Medical School, 2009a). CBT targets self-defeating cognitions linked to depressed mood, whereas interpersonal therapy focuses on impaired relationships or on the effects of relationship loss. CBT employs practical self-monitoring techniques to help patients understand the relationship between thoughts, mood, and behavior. Patients are taught to track changes in mood and accompanying thought patterns during a series of time periods, identify distortions in thinking that focus on negative evaluations of experience, and replace negative cognitions with more hopeful, empowering ones. The relationships between negative thoughts, mood, and behavior, which lead to withdrawal and social isolation, are examined. Patients are taught and encouraged to practice assertive social skills, such as conflict resolution and social problem solving, and to manage their anxiety through the use of techniques such as mindfulness meditation or relaxation training. The therapist's role is active and often directive, modeling behavior, assigning homework between sessions, and encouraging the structuring of mood-enhancing activities in daily life. Outcome studies have produced generally positive results, with a reduction of symptoms for as long as 2 years (Cuijpers, 1998; Reinecke, Ryan, & Dubois, 1998). CBT is more effective than medication in reducing or eliminating depressive symptoms (Sanderson & McGinn, 2001) and in preventing relapse (Greenberg & Fisher, 1997); it is equally effective and less costly when delivered in the setting of group therapy rather than individually (McDermutt, Miller, & Brown, 2001).

Other studies, however, have not demonstrated that CBT surpasses the effectiveness of other approaches, such as family therapy or supportive individual therapy, after 2 years (Birmaher et al., 2000). Relationship therapy, based in CBT theory, has succeeded in reducing depressive symptoms, especially when the relationship is viewed as a core contributor to the depression (Beach & Jones, 2002), and reminiscence therapy has had strong effects in reducing depression in elders (Bohlmeijer, Smit, & Cuipers, 2003).

Interpersonal therapy focuses on relationships as important sources of depression, in which the goal of the therapist is to help the patient repair conflicts and resolve interpersonal deficits (Weissman, Markowitz, & Klerman, 2000). This model is considered "user friendly" for practitioners, as psychotherapy training in general focuses heavily on relationship. In pre–post test studies, 80% to 90% of clients recovered, maintaining gains for at least a year (Mufson & Fairbanks, 1996; Mufson et al., 1994; Santor & Kusumakar, 2001). Interpersonal therapy has been compared in effectiveness with CBT, attaining comparable results in symptom remission (Rosello & Bernal, 1999).

Severe, Chronic, and Recurrent Depression

One type of therapy designed especially for this population is the cognitive behavioral analysis system of psychotherapy (CBASP; McCullough, 2003). Based on the assumptions that chronically depressed patients think, behave, and communicate in ways that make traditional therapy difficult, CBASP confronts and challenges these perceptions and behaviors. Targeted cognitions and behaviors include focusing on oneself, being uncooperative, having difficulty controlling one's emotions, and interpreting current situations in terms of past negative events or as signs of a similarly negative future. In a randomized controlled study comparing drug treatment with CBASP in 662 patients, 48% responded equally to either treatment; however, combining drug with CBASP treatment boosted the response rate to 73%. Following active treatment, monthly CBASP sessions helped prevent a recurrence in a subset of these patients. Studies of standard CBT and interpersonal therapy with chronically depressed patients indicate that the therapy needs to be more intensive and longer.

Drug treatment may be more effective for patients with a strong family history of mood disorders, in contrast to patients with an overly active stress response originating in early childhood abuse or maltreatment, who benefit more from CBT (Klein et al., 2009). Hormones may also be implicated in response to treatment of chronic depression. One study found that menstruating women responded better to drug treatment than menopausal women and older men, and another reported improvement in middle-aged dysthymic men who received testosterone injections. It is theorized that late-onset depression may be related to age-related hormonal changes (Harvey et al., 2007; Seidman et al., 2009).

Relapse prevention is gaining ground as an important component of psychosocial treatments for severe, recurrent depression. A recent longitudinal follow-up study in the Netherlands demonstrated positive outcomes for long-term preventive effects for at least 5.5 years in patients with recurrent MDD (Bockting, Spinhoven, Wouters, Koeter, & Schene, 2009). Patients with a history of four or more previous episodes were assigned either to a Treatment As Usual (TAU) condition (individual monitoring and medication) versus treatment augmented with brief group CBT. The addition of the augmented cognitive group therapy reduced relapse rates from 95% to 75%, a medium effect size. The authors stress the need for systematic attention to relapse prevention in the continuing care of patients with recurrent depression.

Treatment-Resistant Depression and Electroconvulsive Therapy

Despite the extensive research on pharmacological and nonmedical therapies, many individuals continue to struggle with depression with little sustained relief. The Sequenced Treatment Alternatives to Relieve Depression study (STAR*D, www.nimh.nih.gov; 2008) concluded that only one third of patients achieved remission of symptoms, even after trying four different medication strategies. Relapse rates in this group were thought to be even worse than in the total group because relapse was a significant problem at every level. At the study's end, 50% of patients who were able to achieve remission only after their fourth treatment relapsed on average after only 2.5 months. One expert estimated that only 43% of STAR*D participants were able to sustain their recovery. Thus interest remains in nonpharmacological interventions, including electroconvulsive therapy (ECT), vagus nerve stimulation (VNS), and transcranial magnetic stimulation (TMS). Insurers are more willing to pay for ECT than for VNS or TMS; the former is no more beneficial than ECT, whereas the latter is too new and untested. Thus ECT is the most available and practical of these alternatives, particularly as it is covered by health insurance. ECT is currently considered a viable option for the following groups: (a) those whose depression has not been relieved after trying three or more medications, (b) individuals considered at high risk for suicide, (c) pregnant women or those who have just given birth and do not want to take antidepressants, and (d) older patients who do not respond as well to drugs or have become more sensitive to side effects. ECT has not been well studied in children and adolescents; the research has focused almost exclusively on adults. Guidelines for its use, according to the American Academy of Child and Adolescent Psychiatry, are limited to children and adolescents who have shown no response to two or more medications and to situations in which fast treatment is necessary because symptoms are so severe (Harvard Medical School, 2009b).

The Consortium for Research in ECT (CORE) and the Columbia University Consortium (CUC) have demonstrated that remission rates with ECT were between 86% and 55%, respectively, higher than with medication. An analysis of 18 studies showed ECT to be more effective than drugs. Limitations may be that drug dosages may not have been optimal, and studies in university-based research may achieve more impressive-looking results because of their more restrictive selection criteria. One study of seven community hospitals showed remission rates of only 30% to 47% after ECT. Relapse after ECT may be reduced by tapering gradually once remission is achieved. Researchers conclude that ECT is not perfect (subsequent memory and thinking problems are usually temporary but very bothersome to some) but that it may be the best alternative for patients with disabling symptoms (Harvard Medical School, 2009b).

Children and Adolescents

Sonawalla and Fava's (2010), review of best practices with children and adolescents noted that a combination of biological, psychological, and social factors (related to duration of the illness before treatment, severity, the modality and dosage used, and the duration and compliance to treatment) combine to predict outcome. In their review of outcome research, the authors note that TCAs and SSRIs have equivalent efficacy and that atypical antipsychotics have shown some benefit. An SSRI–TCA combination, although controversial, may reduce severe symptoms more rapidly, and CBT, although inadequately studied with respect to severe depression, might be considered, especially when patients refuse medication or do not respond well to it.

Treatment-Resistant Depression and Transcranial Magnetic Brain Stimulation

In October 2008, the FDA approved TMS for a limited group of patients with depression who have not benefited from multiple drugs. TMS is a technique for stimulating neurons in the cerebral cortex through the scalp. The procedure is considered to be safe and to elicit little to no discomfort. Single-pulse and repetitive stimulation have been tested, and competing theories have been advanced as to the mechanisms of action. A growing body of evidence from meta-analyses of recent studies, reported in Wasserman and Zimmerman (2012), have found that TMS improves mood to a somewhat greater extent in patients not on antidepressant medication and that seizures or other adverse effects did not occur, but significant effects may not last longer than 2 weeks after treatment. Economic barriers may prevent the widespread clinical use of TMS.

TMS is now being tested in adolescents with treatment-resistant MDD in response to estimates that 30% to 40% of the teen population fails to benefit from antidepressant medication. In a recent small study of 18 male and female adolescents, results were similar to those in adults. Results included substantial declines in depression severity, statistically significant improvements in memory and delayed verbal recall, and no impairment in neurocognitive function over the course of 30 treatments (Wall et al., 2013). Follow-up effects post-treatment, however, were not reported, and more controlled investigations are needed.

Matching Patient With Treatment: Medication and/or Psychotherapy

When depressed patients are asked what treatments they feel have been most helpful to them, they strongly favor the combination of medication and talk therapy. The National Survey on Drug Use and Health (2008) summary of treatment for major depressive episode in adults during 2005 and 2006 reported that individuals who had talked with a professional and also used medication were more likely than those who did not use medication to describe the professional as being extremely helpful or helping a lot. These findings support the importance of listening carefully to how the consumers experience treatment interventions and of combining biological with psychosocial intervention.

Evidence-based treatment research, which has historically focused on comparative outcomes, confirms the experience of consumers, indicating that a combination of drug and talk therapy leads to the best results, measured in terms of symptom reduction or remission. Different theoretical approaches may vary in their usefulness, depending on client characteristics. Sotsky et al. (2006) factored in patient characteristics as predictors of response to psychotherapy and pharmacotherapy. Six patient characteristics, in addition to severity of symptoms, were found to predict outcome and were important in relation to the type of intervention, as follows: (a) low social dysfunction predicted superior response to interpersonal psychotherapy, (b) low cognitive dysfunction predicted superior response to CBT and imipramine, (c) high work dysfunction predicted superior response to imipramine, (d) high depression severity and impairment of function predicted superior response to imipramine and interpersonal psychotherapy. Attention to the matching of patient to selected alternative treatments may be important and deserves continued study.

Bipolar Disorder

S. L. Johnson and Leahy (2004) describe the use of CBT to address automatic thoughts and beliefs fueling suicidal behavior. Like many other professionals, they stress the need for comprehensive, integrated multiple sources of intervention, promoting an awareness of early prodromal signs of the BPD, the perception of the illness as treatable, effective problem solving by patient and family, and proven strategies to promote medication adherence.

Lam, Hones, Hayward, and Bright (1999) present one of the clearest available descriptions of the application of CBT to the treatment of BPD in their guidebook for therapists. Treatment of CBT occurs in phases. First, a psychoeducational presentation of a diathesis–stress model of etiology is taught. Next, patients learn cognitive and behavioral skills that enable them to discover, monitor, and challenge the links among mood, thought, and behavior relating to bipolar symptoms. Other components of treatment include the identification of early warning signs of a manic episode, stabilization of biological patterns of sleep and self-care, moderation of excessively driven achievement and self-expressive behavior, and relapse prevention.

Recognizing that CBT is well established as an effective nonpharmacological intervention in ongoing courses of BPD and in preventing relapse, Jones and Burrell-Hodgson (2008) applied the CBT treatment formulations of Lam et al. (1999) over a 6-month period of 14 to 18 therapy sessions to persons newly diagnosed with BPD. The results identified improvement in the reduction of reported depressed mood, increased hope and self-control behaviors, greater stabilization of sleep and activity patterns, and the ability of patients to recognize and cope with early warning signs of relapse. The authors emphasize that the techniques taught were most successful in the context of a collaborative relationship with the patient and when they were formulated in terms of the patients' own accounts of their experiences with the illness. Emphasis on the patient–therapist relationship and attention to the patient's subjective experience underline the importance of individualized approaches based on the perceptions and meanings the patient brings to the therapeutic exchange (i.e., the tailoring of the model to the patient rather than forcing the patient to conform to the model).

Clinician awareness of bipolar symptoms is critical, as bipolar illness can have a variable course, accurate diagnosis is often delayed, and relapse is common. Most undiagnosed patients seek treatment first within the primary care setting; thus it is extremely important that primary care providers and allied health professionals become expert in recognizing the condition (Miller, 2006). In addition, from the perspectives of the patients themselves, at least one study found that when factors associated with hospital readmission rates for schizophrenia are compared with those for BPD, denial of the reality of the illness is predictive of schizophrenia relapse, whereas discomfort with the side effects of medication is more correlated with readmission for patients with BPD (Saenz, 2001). Motivational interviewing has been successfully used to address the ambivalence of patients with BPD concerning their disorder and to improve their adherence to medication regimens (Laakso, 2012).

BPD is very stressful for families. It is evident that practitioners need to communicate with patients and family members on an ongoing basis regarding their patients' responses to medication in order to reduce susceptibility to relapse. Family members are able to cope better and feel less burdened when they understand that their relative's behavior is caused by an illness rather than by a character defect or a deliberate need to disrupt family communication. Effective family treatment avoids blaming either the patient or family members for the bipolar symptoms. A review of outcome literature on family interventions related to BPD emphasizes the following commonalities in family approaches to managing the disease: (a) the active collaboration between therapist and family; (b) psychoeducation about the illness and available treatments; (c) improved problem-solving and communication skills; (d) decreasing the level of criticism in the family; (e) recognizing prodromal and residual symptoms; (f) developing strategies for relapse; and (g) the provision of support for coping with the disturbing, fluctuation course of the illness (Keitner, Ryan, & Heru, 2005).

KEY POINTS

1. Biologically based mood disorders—such as severe major depression, double and/or treatment-resistant depression, and BPD—respond best to a combination of medication and individual, group, or family therapy.
2. Severe, recurrent, treatment-resistant unipolar depression may respond best to ECT; TMS is increasingly used with promising short-term results.
3. Nonmedical psychotherapeutic interventions are important in fostering better communication with physicians, improving medication compliance, providing coping skills to patients, and preventing relapse.
4. The growing reliance on psychopharmacology, especially polypharmacy, is unsupported with respect to mild to moderate depression and may be contraindicated owing to uncomfortable side effects and drug interactions.

EQUITY AND DIVERSITY ISSUES

Nowhere is attention to cultural competence and accessibility to care more important than with respect to mood disorders. Cultures attach meaning to the experience of sadness, alienation, and loss and they vary in their receptivity to the many theories and treatments offered to persons with BPD and MDD.

In the following section, we introduce the reader to examples of culture and diversity issues as they apply to the diagnosis and treatment of mood disorders. Because culture is ever changing and evolving and our world is becoming ever more diverse, the following studies and their conclusions should be taken as examples of fluctuation and developing realities in the processes of culture and acculturation. Furthermore, generalizations about culture and diversity issues can never be applied to a single patient, who must always be prized by the clinician as the unique individual he or she is.

Depression

The under- or overdiagnosis of depression often results from a lack of attention to the influence of culture on the definition of the illness by the consumer, to the subjective experience of the disorder, and to the communication of symptoms of depression to others. Culture shapes the experience, perceptions, and communication of clinicians, patients, and family members about the meaning of major depression, the attitude toward approaches to treatment and healing, and the management of symptoms (Loue, 2007). In some cultures, depression is experienced largely in somatic terms—for example, as "nerves" or headaches in Latino and Mediterranean cultures; weakness, tiredness, and "imbalance" in Chinese and Asian cultures; problems of the "heart" in Middle Eastern cultures; or feeling "heartbroken" in Hopi culture. Cultures may differ with respect to the seriousness with which symptoms, such as irritability, sadness, or withdrawal, are regarded socially. Culturally distinctive experiences, such as a fear of being hexed or bewitched, feelings of "heat in the head," crawling sensations of worms or ants, or vivid feelings of being visited by those who have died, must be distinguished from hallucinations or delusions that are part of an MDD. It is also imperative that the clinician not routinely dismiss a symptom merely because it is viewed as the "norm" for a culture (APA, 2000, 2013).

No relationship has been found between any culturally specific diagnosis, symptom cluster, or syndrome and the *DSM* or the World Health Organization (WHO) diagnostic system known as the *International Classification of Diseases* (*ICD-10*; WHO, 2010). This represents a significant issue that needs more careful investigation in order to avoid either the overpathologizing of culturally expressed symptoms or the minimization of culturally unique expressions as indicative of suffering needing an effective, empathic response. Cultural syndromes such as *ataques de nervios*, neurasthenia, and *susto* have been associated to some extent with depression and anxiety, but the relationship between psychiatric diagnoses of mood disorder and cultural expressions of distress has been little researched. Guarnaccia and Pincay (2008) review these issues extensively and recommend strongly that cultural syndromes be included in future versions of the *DSM* and *ICD* diagnostic manuals, citing numerous links between cultural factors and mood disorders in the Pennsylvania Amish, Chinese Americans, and Mexican Americans.

Children and adolescents are known to express depression in the form of somatic complaints, irritability, and/or withdrawal; their depressive symptoms are often observed in conjunction with other mental disorders, such as disruptive behavior disorder, ADHD, eating disorders, and substance-related disorders.

The presentation of depression is also complex in older adults; depressive symptoms are often mixed with cognitive impairment and the biological challenges of chronic illness. Women, especially in studies in the United States and Europe, are considered to be at significantly greater risk of a major depressive episode; their increased risk emerges during adolescence and may coincide with the onset of puberty. Women are consistently diagnosed with a major depressive episode at a rate twice as high as that found in men, and they make more suicide attempts than men, although men complete suicide more often than women (APA, 2000, 2013).

The aged are neglected in outcome research on late-life major depression, even though depression is known to interact with and exacerbate cognitive impairment, disability, and medical illnesses in this population, and even though older White males are the highest risk group for suicide. One review of the effectiveness of psychosocial interventions (Kiosses, Leon, & Arean, 2011) found none that met criteria to be efficacious acute treatment of MDD, three that were probably efficacious, and two that showed inconclusive results. Baseline anxiety and stress, personality disorders, endogenous depression, and reduced self-rated health were associated with worse treatment outcomes. Notably, the role of cognitive impairment in response to therapy was not addressed in spite of the fact that up to 30% of older adults have mild cognitive impairment, and many more have cognitive complaints. This illustrates a gap in the research for this vulnerable group, as many psychosocial therapies, such as CBT, rely on intact cognitive processes to be effective. In addition, the researchers note that the studies they reviewed were highly selective, comprised for the most part of the young-old, healthy, cognitively intact, educated, White participants. There has been virtually no focus on ethnic minorities, persons older than 80 years, or those with cognitive impairment and low education. The researchers call for the development of novel psychosocial interventions in nontraditional settings, including both patient homes and institutions, focused on the patient's ecosystems with the goal of environmental modifications to help improve their functioning.

Gender and culture may interact to affect the diagnosis of depression. Mellsop and Smith (2007) discuss the common assumption that gender differences in the diagnosis of depression necessarily reflect epidemiological reality, noting that higher rates of diagnosed schizophrenia—along with lower rates of depression and higher rates of violence and aggression— have been observed in minority groups such as African Americans in the United States and the Maori population in New Zealand. In their study comparing clinician diagnoses of depression versus psychological problems related to aggression/overactivity in Maori and non-Maori men and women, these researchers describe a pattern of diagnosis in which Maori men are diagnosed with problematic aggression/overactivity at significantly higher rates than Maori females or non-Maori persons of either gender, and non-Maori subjects and females were diagnosed with depression at much higher rates than Maori males. At the same time, Maori males had a high rate of completed suicides, consistent with unrecognized depression. The authors note similarities to patterns involving African Americans and discuss the role of gender expectations that reinforce the display of aggressive masculinity, supported by high levels of competitiveness and the "entertainment value" of violence in New Zealand culture. These findings suggest that current diagnostic systems are flawed in that they do not account for the experience of depression across cultures and genders.

Anthropologists have noted that the experience of depression in Chinese immigrants is experienced as physical rather than psychological. Culture affects not only the diagnosis and management of depression in these individuals but also help seeking, patient–practitioner communication, and the role of risk versus social support factors that contribute to the development of depression in the first place (Kleinman, 2004). Accurate diagnosis must include an evaluation of the culturally relevant sources of support in the lives of these patients, avoid stereotyping on the basis of culture, and recognize that culture is a process, not a fixed entity. The lack of research into the phenomenology of depression in non-Western cultures is underscored by Lee, Kleinman, and Kleinman (2007) in their ethnographic study of how Chinese individuals experience depressed affect. These Asian subjects expressed their depressed symptoms in the form of bodily complaints, indigenous affective terms, social disharmony, pain that could not be put into words, implicit sadness that was experienced but not expressed, and a core struggle with sleeplessness. The researchers conclude that the psychiatric symptoms recognized by Western psychiatry apply to the Chinese but that the experiences and verbal expressions between East and West diverge when the embodied language and experience of depression as described by Chinese individuals, particularly focused on the heart, are taken into account. The Western construct of embodied emotional expression as metaphorical, idiomatic, or evidence of somatization does not capture the Chinese person's experience and in fact may suggest that the experience is not literally genuine. With respect to contemporary psychiatric nomenclature and diagnostic symptoms, the *DSM* describes depression more accurately in the West than in China. The authors describe how the diagnostic process ignores the Chinese individual's personal experience and context:

> In sharp contrast to the somato-emotional experiences that were actively reported, we found that sadness and depressed mood were often communicated and understood contextually without explicit verbal articulation. Chinese who complain of the body in the clinic will talk more directly of feelings at home with family members. Human language is far from ideal in representing the self through ordinary terms. Until the necessary vocabularies are invented, some private emotional experiences will remain prelinguistic and indescribable. (Lee et al., 2007, p. 5)

Aguilar-Gaxiola and Gullotta (2008) identified depression in Hispanic immigrants and their American-born children as a significant mental health problem that is experienced differently among these people than in any other cultural group, owing to the heterogeneity of this subculture, differential acculturation across generations, and the prevalent American stereotype of the "illegal immigrant." These authors emphasize the context of depression for Latinos in the United States, the widespread co-occurrence of depression and substance abuse in this population, and special features in the diagnosis of mood disorder in Latino children, adolescents, and adults. These realities underscore the importance of community-based interventions that go beyond pharmacological treatment. Stigma has been found to be an important concern of Latinos receiving antidepressants. Stigma accompanies the diagnosis of depression, causing negative social consequences and undermining adherence to treatment (Interian, Martinez, Guarnaccia, Vega, & Escobar, 2007).

The subjective experience of mood symptoms as well as the manner in which they are expressed not only differ among cultures but are also affected by the stresses of acculturation. Western measures of depression may bias diagnosis and fail to take into account these interrelationships. In one sample of 177 Koreans and Korean Americans, 49% were diagnosed as depressed as measured by several scales, but scale scores were best predicted by the amount of acculturation and acculturation stress experienced by the subjects (Ji & Duan, 2006). A conventional response to these individuals, on the basis of diagnosis alone, would ignore their unique cultural challenges.

One cross-cultural qualitative study in a Slovakian sample proposes a model of depression as the outcome of a dialectical relationship between culture and biology, exploring the connections between culture, history, and depression. The ever-evolving relationship between culture and history challenges the notion of a universal diagnosis of depressive disorder. The author found that there was a dramatic shift from somatic to psychological explanations of depressive symptoms after the fall of Communism and the integration of Slovakia into the European Union. The very definition and treatment of depression mirrored a historical shift toward capitalism, modernism, and a more individualistic concept of self (Husarova, 2009).

Manson (1995) addressed the role of culture in the diagnosis of mood disorders through the use of case examples that challenge assumptions underlying the *DSM* approach to the diagnosis of depression. Mental health professionals need a better understanding of the phenomenology of major depression across varied cultural settings, a consideration of social contexts, an awareness of cultural forces that give meaning to relationships, life events, and the manner in which individuals express their emotions. The traditional boundaries of culture are changing with the processes of industrialization and urbanization and the influence of the media. Bhugra's (2004) review of the effects of the globalization on depression across cultures concludes that somatic symptoms are common across the world but that psychological symptoms are found with effective probing and that feelings of guilt and suicide rates may be underdiagnosed across cultures.

Bipolar Disorder

The *DSM-5* notes the importance of attending to culture in the diagnosis of bipolar as well as unipolar illness. Adolescents are likely to present with psychotic features as well as complicated associated problems, such as school truancy and/or failure, antisocial behavior, and substance abuse, and many teens have a history of long-standing behavior problems that may precede the onset of a manic episode (APA, 2000, 2013). There is no reported differential incidence of bipolar I disorder based on race or ethnicity, but there is some evidence that clinicians may have a tendency to favor a diagnosis of schizophrenia rather than BPD in some ethnic groups and younger individuals as compared with Whites in general. BPD is equally common in men and women. In males, the first episode is more likely to be manic; in women, it is more likely to be depressive (APA, 2000).

In the past, BPD was diagnosed more frequently in African Americans than non-Hispanic Whites; however, more recent studies report similar rates in these groups (Loue, 2008a). Consistent lifetime rates of approximately 1% have been reported across many countries and in findings from family and molecular genetic studies. Loue (2008a) discusses the possible association between BPD and higher socioeconomic status, which may involve a diagnostic bias. Symptoms of mania and hypomania are similar to characteristics associated with success, such as high energy and productivity (Loue, 2008a). African Americans, however, are more likely to be codiagnosed with schizophrenia, leading to an unstable course of treatment; they are also less likely to have access to effective treatment and to remain in it (Kilbourne, 2008). Cultural groups may interpret the effects of medication differently, influencing their response to treatment. Language barriers and issues of stigma may prevent members of certain cultural groups from understanding their diagnosis or treatment issues and may prevent them from obtaining equal access to participation in research (Loue, 2008b). Martin (2007) reminds the mental health diagnostician to attend to the phenomenology and complex contextual worlds of the individual with mood disorder. Living with BPD must be understood as a part of the human condition in a process that has a cultural life beyond the confines of diagnostic symptoms and is part of the everyday rational and irrational practices that define human communities.

The Culture of Medicine

Ironic, disturbing, and little researched are the sources of disparity within the mental health professions themselves. A medical study group exploring this issue reported a consensus statement in the *Journal of the American Medical Association* (Center et al., 2003), calling for a transformation in the culture of medicine in order to encourage physicians to seek help. The statement acknowledges that the culture of medicine, in which physicians are discouraged from displaying dependency needs or uncertainty, ignores physician mental health despite evidence of untreated mood disorders and high suicide rates in the medical profession. It also points out punitive barriers to help-seeking behavior, including discrimination in licensing, hospital privileges, and career advancement. In a study of 370 British psychiatrists, most reported that they would be reluctant to disclose that they suffered from a mental illness despite the well-known high rates of suicide among members of their own profession. If they had personally suffered from a mental illness, they were significantly less likely to discuss their problems with anyone and were more likely to cite stigma as the reason. These physicians were concerned about injury to their careers and threats to their professional integrity. Citing many similar findings by other researchers, the authors assert strongly that in the concern for disparities in access to mental health care, too little attention has been paid to the mental health professionals who are the healers (White, Shiralkar, Hassan, Galbraith, & Callaghan, 2006).

The ripple effects of undiagnosed depression, often culminating in suicide, can be devastating, not only for the patients of physicians but also for their colleagues. The following is an excerpt from the anguished response of a physician to the suicide of a colleague:

> Today I learned that you died, and nothing will ever be the same again. I refused to believe the words I heard, that you committed suicide. Only terribly depressed people kill themselves. You weren't terribly depressed … but then I learned that, yes, secretly you had been. How could I not know, not realize? … Why didn't you ask your physician colleagues for help? Why did you hide your depression from us? Did I, as your colleague and friend, fail you? These questions circle relentlessly through my mind. I need to understand, need somehow for this all to make sense. (Middleton, 2008, p. 268)

Suicide is a significant risk for patients diagnosed with depressive or BPDs (Gray & Zide, 2005, 2007). In a recent study of psychiatric patients with BPDs, 80% had either suicidal ideation or ideation and attempts. Key indicators of risk included depression and hopelessness, co-occurring personality disorders, and previous suicide attempts (Valtonen et al., 2005). A cross-cultural discussion of suicide risk is beyond the scope of this book, but the point must be underscored that suicide crosses all barriers of ethnicity, race, age, income status, and gender, and assessment for suicidality must be part of the diagnostic process. Hopelessness and despair may coexist in professional helpers and their patients, underscoring the need for social support and attention to resiliency and strength on both sides.

Essential Components of Cultural Competence and Mood Disorders

Carpenter-Song, Schwallie, and Longhofer (2008) recommend the following attitudes and behaviors with respect to the development of cultural competence in the diagnosis and treatment of mood disorders: (a) practitioners must move beyond a critique of current practice to suggesting clinically relevant recommendations; (b) critical reviewers, researchers, academics, and other observers need to recognize that the demands of time and economic constraints work against the ability to apply the findings of diversity; (c) it is vital to listen to the patient's nuanced story, even when doing so is challenging in the institutional mental health world; (d) practitioners must avoid the uncritical and casual use of psychiatric labels as is common in the popular culture and marketed to consumers via the direct advertising of psychopharmaceuticals; (e) professionals should focus on models of cultural competence as something *to be ready for* rather than on *something to know*; (f) the culture of medicine must be altered so that it focuses on the whole individual ("How are you feeling?") rather than on a collection of symptoms ("Where does it hurt?"); that is, the focus should be on understanding diagnosis as an interplay between biology and culture, not simply as an underlying disease within the person; (g) the clinical encounter should be regarded as a two-way learning process in which the clinician is open to new information and willing to seek clarification. To this end, clinical training should involve the teaching of anthropological techniques, such as miniethnography, brief life history, and the elicitation and negotiation of the patient's explanatory model.

KEY POINTS

1. Stigma, present in most cultures for different reasons, may prevent members of some cultures from seeking treatment, depending on the context.
2. Adverse impact results from language barriers, a devaluing of culturally normative expressions of symptoms, and a failure to understand the patient's phenomenological experience of mood disorder.
3. Culture, acculturation stress, income, and social class interact to affect access to accurate diagnosis and high-quality treatment.
4. The presence of depression may be missed in children and adolescents if the main symptom presentation is irritability and behavior problems and in men when aggressiveness is the outward expression of a mood disorder. Depression in elders often remains overlooked and undiagnosed.
5. Professionals must care for themselves as well as others, allowing themselves to ask for help when they themselves struggle with mood disorder symptoms.
6. The culture of the workplace should be assessed and not overlooked, as it may either contribute to a mood disorder or enhance personal functioning.
7. The patient's personal experience should always be honored; the patient should never be stereotyped in terms of group racial, ethnic, cultural, or gender stereotypes.

STRENGTH-BASED CONTRIBUTIONS TO DIAGNOSIS AND TREATMENT

Diversity-competent and strength-promoting approaches to the diagnosis and treatment of depression and BPD emphasize multifaceted approaches that go beyond an exclusive reliance on psychopharmacology to combine the use of medication with a variety of psychotherapies and lifestyle behaviors. These approaches include an awareness of the need for personal empowerment in order to combat helplessness, social support, the promotion of a positive cultural and racial identity, and mind–body wellness. In these studies, intervention—in the context of case finding, accessibility, and prevention efforts—is understood to occur even before a diagnosis is made. Strength-based approaches thus include culturally competent outreach to diverse communities, the identification of individuals and populations at risk, education and case finding, and easy, ongoing accessibility to support and treatment. The diagnostic process is designed to be inclusive and relevant enough to the whole person to include those aspects of individual functioning that lie outside the assessment of pathological symptoms in order to connect the diagnosis to the individual's contexts and thus to ensure effective intervention. A sampling of strength-based approaches is presented in the following sections.

Feminist Approaches

Clinical applications of feminist theory to mood disorders have historically emphasized the social construction of power and gender, emphasized the validity of subjective experience, and addressed the situational contexts in which mood disorders occur or worsen. Feminist critiques of traditional psychotherapy have focused on the unconscious absorption of patriarchal social norms by the therapist as well as the client; the connections between anger, depression and female roles of dependency, self-sacrifice, female work inhibition, and guilt; and a challenge to mother-blaming in psychoanalytic theory and practice (Caplan, 1989; Lerner, 1988).

Studies of women's responses to the diagnosis and treatment of depression have suggested that the medicalization of depression treatment, with an exclusive reliance on psychopharmacology as the treatment of choice, is incompatible with empowerment. Gammell and Stoppard's (1999) findings document how participants who had accepted a biomedical explanation of their symptoms and perceived antidepressant medication as beneficial in reducing distress later experienced disempowering life changes. The authors suggest that the negative impact of medicalized explanations of and treatment for depression could be mitigated by offering women a greater range of choices in available types of treatment. These options could include referrals to nonmedical professionals for the purpose of CBT or client-focused insight therapies that foster a phenomenological understanding of experience.

Goodman et al. (2007) examined Reaching Out About Depression (ROAD), a multilevel empowerment intervention for low-income women with depression, which includes peer support and community advocacy and is based on the assumption that mental health is directly linked to peer support and political action and should not be limited to intrapsychic exploration. Social isolation, feelings of helplessness, and lack of agency are viewed as preventing communities from organizing to support their members. This approach combines attention to the individual's contexts, which include family relationships, social supports, and membership in community organizations in combination with psychological and pharmacological treatment. In addition to engaging in individual actions to reduce symptoms of mood disorder, participants are encouraged to engage in social and political action. The aim is to increase both psychological and political empowerment without sacrificing either.

A Family Prevention Model

Depression is known for its ripple effects on all family members. The results of a longitudinal family-based prevention program highlight the benefits of being mindful of opportunities to promote resilience from the moment of diagnosis (Beardslee, Gladstone, Wright, & Cooper, 2003). Clinical discussions with the children of a depressed parent immediately after diagnosis proved superior to a psychoeducational lecture format in preventing the emergence of depression in the children of a parent with a mood disorder at 2½-year follow-up. Both parent and child understood the diagnosis better, and the children did not blame themselves for their parent's depression. Depressed parents in this study were able to remain engaged with their children and to encourage their development with the use of supportive friends and relatives and activities outside the family. Finally, the parents themselves changed their behaviors with their children in a positive direction and demonstrated better understanding of their own mental disorder. This study highlights the importance of prevention and the efficacy of attending to sources of support as well as to pathology. The focus on relating to all family members rather than only to the identified patient empowers both patient and family and mitigates the transmission of depression to the next generation.

Culture-Specific Models

The Adolescent Depression Empowerment Project (ADEPT) successfully addressed depression in low-income African American adolescents from an empowerment perspective (McClure, Connell, & Zucker, 2005). Designed as a psychosocial intervention, this approach to depression in African American adolescents acknowledged the effects of racial discrimination and poverty in the lives of African American teens as well as the strengths inherent in African American families and communities. ADEPT's treatment approach contains components of CBT, interpersonal therapy for adolescents, and family systems interventions designed to strengthen the quality and quantity of social support available to these adolescents.

Coconstructed narratives have been used to reframe elements of the clinical process in a culturally resonant manner with Chinese Americans who have been diagnosed with MDD (Yeung & Kam, 2008). The authors thoughtfully critique the limitations of the *DSM* and advocate for systematic attention to the patient's familial, community, and cultural sources of support in the diagnostic process. They suggest the following steps in discussing a depressive diagnosis with a Chinese American patient: (a) elicit the patient's illness beliefs, (b) understand and acknowledge multiple explanatory models, (c) contextualize depressive symptoms with respect to the relationship between the patient's physical health and social systems, (d) introduce Western psychiatric theories in ways that reflect assumptions shared by traditional Chinese medicine (TCM), (e) involve patients' families whenever possible, and (f) use terminology that avoids unintended stigma.

Kupfer et al. (2009) altered their approach to at-risk patients with BPD in response to client cultural considerations. Middle-aged urban patients were more accustomed to diagnostic and referral processes, had access to better transportation to appointments, could better afford copays, and were more able to accommodate to clinic hours. Recognizing that adolescents, older persons, African Americans, and rural residents with BPD were less likely than middle-aged White urban patients to be adequately diagnosed and treated, to remain in treatment, and to have positive outcomes, the Bipolar Disorder Center for Pennsylvanians (BDCP) altered its recruitment and screening methods to address these disparities. Persistent and varied outreach, using the media and community-based organizations, was used to recruit at-risk populations, with a special focus on African Americans. Treatment protocols involved interventions that included extensive psychoeducation for patients and family members about BPD, medication compliance and side effects, ongoing support, relapse prevention, financial assistance with barriers such as parking and copayment, and follow-up within 36 hours with any problems of concern to patients and their families. The location and hours of their services were made more varied, and clinicians received specialized training for identifying and treating at-risk patients. These findings highlight the need to engage in rigorous recruitment and assessment procedures in order to overcome the disparity of access to treatment and ensure appropriate care.

These researchers also found that socioeconomic status and comorbid anxiety were stronger predictors than race of whether or not patients were taking psychotropic medication at the time of entry into the study; these were also stronger predictors of suicide attempts. This suggested that the interaction among class, race, and co-occurring disorders, economic status, and anxiety influence poorer outcomes among African Americans than race itself (Kupfer et al., 2009).

Another study focused on the relationship between resilience and depressive symptoms in African American women in a community-based primary health care center (Holden, Bradford, Hall, & Belton, 2013). Depressive symptoms were experienced by 49% of these 290 women, and 10% had a history of suicidal ideation. Depressive symptoms were strongly predicted by previous diagnoses of a mental health condition, the presence of at least one chronic disease, and unemployment. These women had experienced a multitude of psychosocial and economic stresses in an environmental context in which many disparities existed with respect to the access to and quality of mental health care available to them. Women possessing the most resilience saw themselves as strong and able to take on life's challenges, trusted in their own instincts, had a positive ability to accept change, felt secure about their relationships and their control over their lives, and had a stronger spirituality.

Mendenhall, Keller, Baird, and Doherty (2008) describe the experience of a female Hmong refugee from Thailand who came to a family medicine clinic with symptoms understood by Western medicine as characterizing depression. The diagnosis of depression was insufficient to describe this woman's cultural challenges. Active participation of the patient in her treatment over time was achieved only by integrating conventional therapies with active collaboration with cultural brokers. An important aspect of the patient's recovery was her involvement in community activism, helping the agency provide culturally competent services to other members of the Hmong community. This illustrates the importance of viewing culture as a source of empowerment and of actively incorporating this perspective in the diagnostic and treatment process.

Oquendo and Graver (2008) report a case study involving the treatment by a Latina therapist of an Indian woman with a diagnosis of major depression. The therapist's ability to learn about her client's culture and to create a psychologically safe environment for the exploration of cultural issues proved central to accurate diagnosis and positive therapeutic outcome. Ambivalence about acculturation and the ability to sort out family from environmental issues related to racism were essential issues in the patient's ability to understand and recover from depression. This therapy involved the integration of psychopharmacological, psychodynamic, and cultural interventions that empowered this patient to make important decisions for herself.

Lozano-Vranich and Petit (2003) present an intervention designed for traditional-culture Latino women that focuses on a balance of medical guidance and traditional wisdom through the use of cultural traditions. Structured around seven beliefs, which form a guide to self-efficacy, this step-by-step guide encourages empowerment by supporting Latinas to utilize Hispanic cultural traditions and mutual support and to understand and confront everyday challenges and depressive symptoms in an assertive way. Personal narratives from patients in recovery and an emphasis on spirituality characterize this psychosocial approach, which supports the use of medication within an empowering personal and cultural context. The centrality of cultural wisdom and identity in this treatment approach promotes resiliency by incorporating culture as a source of support and strength rather than as a barrier to be overcome.

Rural and other geographically isolated patients often lack access to treatment for depression. Telephone conferencing and a web-based discussion format have been used to deliver group psychotherapy to a pilot group of patients diagnosed with epilepsy and depression (Busko, 2008b). The CBT and mindfulness techniques utilized in this distance-learning approach were found to be very helpful. It is probable that the use of technology to bring help to geographically isolated patients will continue to expand.

Empowerment and Strength-Based Models

An attributional style has been found to predict recovery from depression for psychiatric inpatients (J. G. Johnson, Han, Douglas, Johannet, & Russell, 1998). Psychiatric inpatients on antidepressant medication who attributed positive events to causes they viewed as stable, such as the reliable accessibility of social support, expressed less hopelessness independent of antidepressant medication. Decreases in hopelessness mediated an association between global attributions for positive events and decreases in depressive symptoms. These findings suggest that clinicians should focus on the promotion of enhancing cognitions and increased hopefulness. This is consistent with previous research reporting greater benefit from combined antidepressant and CBT than from antidepressant treatment alone (Fava, Grandi, Qielezny, Rafanelli, & Canestrari, 1996).

The way in which client empowerment emerges in the course of process-experiential (PE) psychotherapy for depression in reaction to the diagnosis and intervention process has been explored qualitatively by Timulak and Elliott (2003), using comparisons of client and therapist responses to taped therapy sessions. The researchers delineate five types of empowerment in the therapeutic process. These are (a) *poignant:* the client experiences sadness about attachment issues in the context of therapist empathy, (b) *emergent:* the client expresses the intention to act in the direction of coping with relationship problems while valuing the self, (c) *decisional:* the client uses a two-chair task to explore feelings and needs and moves toward resolution, (d) *determination:* the client plans to use personal agency to pursue resolution, and (e) *accomplishment:* the client describes actions taken or planned in the context of validation and support from the therapist. These researchers relate the concept of empowerment to client changes in intrapsychic experience and self-understanding in the course of psychotherapy.

Dion (1992) proposes an interdisciplinary rehabilitation model of treatment for BPD that uses a combination of cognitive, psychoeducational, behavioral, and environmental interventions in the context of an empathic relationship. Clients are taught about the illness and its course; they learn ways to manage their symptoms, actively practice cognitive and behavioral skills, and create specific environmental goals that are meaningful to them. The central goal of treatment is the empowerment of the individual to change the course of his or her life.

Participants in a wilderness-based treatment reported not feeling depressed during the wilderness experience and maintained a stable, positive mood for 3 months after completing the program; they also reported an improvement in school problems, substance abuse, and family conflict (Norton, 2007). The study suggests the importance of holistic interventions with depressed adolescents focused on psychosocial health. Essential therapeutic elements were defined as a positive group experience, positive communication with parents, being in nature, challenge and adventure, and contemplation. Creative interventions like this arguably deserve more attention in the research, including replication with varied socioeconomic populations and longer follow-up studies of comparative effectiveness as compared to more traditional interventions. The elements of an empowering community along with bodily and mental mastery over environmental challenges appear important in combating the pessimism, helplessness, and negative self-assessment characteristic of depression.

Recent reviews and clinical models of treatment of BPD emphasize the inadequacy of an approach to treatment that relies exclusively on psychopharmacology (Lawson, 2005). Psychotherapy is strongly recommended as important in the management of bipolar illness, along with strength-based and empowering self-management assessment and monitoring tools based on CBT concepts. Moreover, the clinical examples offered are applied to patients from a variety of cultures.

Creativity and social support/sense of community were perceived as important protective factors in coping with bipolar illness and depression in a sample of 49 community mental health outpatients (Barber, 2008). The researcher recommends that creative outlets, as well as the encouragement of clients to build a sense of community in their daily lives, be included in the diagnostic and treatment-planning process. Similarly, social connectedness, problem-solving confidence, and locus of control were determined to be significant protective factors in a recent study of young adults who had made medically serious suicide attempts, especially when high levels of depressive symptomatology were present (Donald, Dower, Correa-Velez, & Jones, 2006). Mindfulness meditation, now a mainstream coping skill in psychology, is being applied to the treatment of BPD and depression and is considered a creative application of CBT techniques (Ball, Corry, & Mitchell, 2007; La Torre, 2001).

Exercise

Exercise is increasingly emphasized as equally or more effective than antidepressant medication in individuals with mild to moderate depression. One meta-analysis of 11 treatment outcome studies on the use of exercise for the treatment of affective disorders demonstrated a substantial benefit of exercise over control conditions; the authors strongly encourage clinicians to integrate adjunctive exercise interventions into their clinical practice with depressed clients (Stathopoulou, Powers, Betty, Smits, & Otto, 2006). Craft (2005) compared women who exercised with nonexercising controls; the former had lower depression scores and higher self-efficacy. The researcher hypothesized that exercise may offer an experience of mastery that contributes to greater confidence about coping with depression. The combination of exercise with other interventions, such as CBT and light therapy, has also been suggested for the management of major depression following the failure of depressed patients to respond to medication—a reality reported in up to one third of depressed patients (Shelton, 2006). Exercise can also serve as a protective factor for individuals repeatedly exposed to emotional stressors involving negative affect and thus prevent relapse in individuals who have recovered from major depression (Mata, Hogan, Joorman, Waugh, & Gotlib, 2013). Walking as a promising treatment for depression is also being investigated in primary care settings as a safe and inexpensive intervention, devoid of the side effects of antidepressant medication, and researchers suggest that future studies investigate factors that enhance patients' adherence to walking programs (Robertson, Roberston, Jepson, & Maxwell, 2012).

The investigation of the neuroimmune effects of physical activity on depression is a rapidly growing area of research. Recent findings suggest that physical activity enhances the beneficial and reduces the detrimental effects of the neuroimmune system by reducing inflammation and visceral fat and increasing T cells, along with a host of other biological changes (Eyre, Papps, & Baune, 2013). The researchers assert that biological factors may become useful biomarkers for the treatment of MDD with physical activity, and the neurobiological effects of physical activity may lead to future therapeutic interventions.

The experience of depression is characterized by cognitive, somatic, and emotional symptoms that add up to the subjective experience of hopelessness. These studies suggest that practices that get the body moving, such as exercise, along with active attempts to alter negative cognitions and emotions via CBT or meditation, combat the phenomenology of hopelessness and helplessness, resulting in greater self-efficacy and a more empowered client.

Mindfulness

Mindfulness practice is receiving increased attention on many medical and psychological fronts. Mindfulness-based practices have been combined with mindfulness-based cognitive behavioral therapy (MBCT) and mindfulness-based stress reduction (MBSR) techniques, resulting in significantly reduced symptoms of treatment-resistant depression, improved overall psychological functioning, indicators of increased psychological well-being, and reduced relapse (Hofmann, Sawyer, Witt, & Oh, 2010; Piet & Hougaard, 2011; Segal et al., 2010). A closer examination of effective components of these interventions indicated that formal—but not informal—mindfulness practice was associated with decreased rumination, which in turn facilitated symptom alleviation (Hawley et al., 2014). Formal practice took place in groups or individually; both MBCT and MBSR techniques involve psychoeducational material and guidance by therapists. Results correlating frequency of practice with outcomes were mixed. The researchers stress that informal practice, although not demonstrated to be effective, should not be discounted, as mindfulness skills may start to generalize during this unstructured practice and lead to better adaptation to stressful events. They recommend that precise measures of informal practice be developed.

Sleep Patterns, Assessment, and Prevention

Sleep problems increase the risk of developing depression. It is striking that 65% to 90% of adults and 90% of children with major depression experience sleep problems, most often insomnia. Patients who report insomnia are four times more likely to develop major depression 4 years later (Cho, Lavretsky, Olmstead, Levin, & Oxman, 2008). Sleep problems affect depression, in that people with insomnia are less likely to respond to treatment, are more susceptible to relapse, and are at higher risk of suicide. It has been found that 69% to 99% of patients with BPD experience insomnia or report less need for sleep during a manic episode, whereas 23% to 78% of those experiencing bipolar depression sleep excessively (hypersomnia). Insomnia worsens before an episode of mania or depression, and lack of sleep can trigger mania, adversely affect mood, and contribute to relapse. SSRIs may cause or worsen insomnia. Some physicians combine a sleep medication with an antidepressant. Drugs most often prescribed for insomnia in bipolar patients are newer benzodiazepine-like agents (Sonata) or anticonvulsants (Neurontin, Gabitril). Tricyclic antidepressants, often prescribed for sedating effects, can trigger mania in bipolar patients (Cho et al., 2008).

Adolescents with late bedtimes versus earlier bedtimes mandated by parents have been found to have higher rates of depression and suicidal ideation (Harrison & Martin, 2010). Adolescents whose parents mandated a bedtime of 10 p.m. or earlier averaged 33 minutes more of sleep per night than those with a bedtime after 11 p.m. Adolescents with 5 or fewer hours of sleep per night were 71% more likely to be depressed and 48% more likely to think about committing suicide than adolescents with 8 hours of sleep per night. These and similar studies highlight the need, in the diagnostic process, to attend not just to sleep patterns but also to the relationship context in which they occur. These studies further imply important opportunities to empower family members to intervene constructively in ways that support physiological resilience. The reasons for bedtime patterns and their relationship to parental control are undoubtedly complicated and may relate to socioeconomic status, cultural norms, and to other undefined factors in family and community life.

Empowerment and Self-Care

Depression increases the risk of heart disease and vice versa; unhealthy behaviors—such as social withdrawal, unhealthy eating, and lack of exercise—contribute to the demonstrated link between depression and heart disease. Medication, psychotherapy, and exercise all help to reduce these risks. Researchers exploring the relationships between healthy and unhealthy behaviors, heart disease, and depression recommend an assessment of self-care behaviors as part of the diagnostic process (Grippo & Johnson, 2009; Hoen et al., 2008; Lichtman & Bigger, 2008). This is consistent with the recommended addition of the Diversity/Resiliency Formulation, which would mandate that the clinician conducting the diagnosis ask specific questions about the presence of social support, exercise, and diet as part of the assessment for a mood disorder.

One assessment of chronically ill patients with co-occurring depression and anxiety focused on encouraging self-management for patients frequently seen in the emergency room of an Australian acute-care hospital. Comorbid depression was considered to be underdiagnosed in patients who struggled with chronic illnesses, such as cancer, stroke, asthma, and heart disease, with the result that their symptoms were often exacerbated, and they frequently returned to the emergency room for treatment. The researchers recommend that screening tools for depression and anxiety become a routine part of assessment, with results and related recommendations noted in written action care plans. They further recommend that emergency room (ER) staff collaborate with patients to identify triggers and risks of relapse, provide strategies for preventing and/or acting on symptoms before their condition deteriorates, and make action plans available to community service providers, with the patients' permission. Simply noticing these patients' needs for extra support, guidance, and motivation is considered very important. Training of ER staff in motivational interviewing, goal setting, and focused problem solving was recommended in order to identify patients' readiness for change and encourage preventive patient self-care (Hill, Litt, Epstein, & Epstein, 2013).

A meta-analysis of self-help interventions for patients with physical illnesses and co-occurring depression and anxiety concluded that written self-help materials, if based on a theoretical model such as CBT, resulted in modest symptomatic improvement. Providing information alone, however, was ineffective but not harmful. The researchers caution that considerable methodological and theoretical limitations were found in the research and that robust conclusions cannot be made without higher quality evidence (Matcham et al., 2014).

Telehealth interventions have also been tested for their ability to improve the self-management of illness for individuals with serious psychiatric and medical disorders. In one study, 70 adult consumers at a community mental health center with diagnoses that included psychiatric disorders, such as major depressive and BPD, along with serious medical diseases, were selected for their instability and frequency of emergency room visits. These participants were provided with an automated telehealth device with a liquid crystal display (LCD) screen connected to their home telephone lines. Daily telehealth sessions assessed their health behaviors, self-management knowledge, and symptom levels, along with answering questions, providing feedback, and offering extra help to those at special risk. If participants were not taking their medications, they were asked why, and given information related to their specific concerns. Each telehealth session ended on an upbeat note with a trivia question or fun fact designed to enhance engagement and motivation. These patients' self-efficacy for managing their depression, BPD, and medical condition improved significantly, and there were reductions in their visits to urgent care and primary care (Pratt et al., 2013).

Diagnosis and related interventions that are empowering are linked to the patient's cultural identity, the promotion of positive healthy behaviors, supportive bonds with family and community, and increased self-efficacy. Clinicians and institutions that attend to these issues focus on creative ways to ensure accessibility, reach out to potential patients in their own environment, identify and reduce barriers to treatment, and provide education about diagnosis and treatment. The stance of the clinicians and the organizations is reciprocal; clinicians listen and learn from potential and actual patients and their families as well as vice versa.

Hope

Recently developed strength-based models for the treatment of MDD emphasize improvement in quality of life by increasing hope and positive expectations for the future. A new intervention, future-directed therapy (FDT), was compared with CBT, utilizing a group format (Vilhauer et al., 2013). Both treatments improved depression, hopelessness, and positive future anticipation, but those treated with FDT demonstrated significant improvements in quality of life, whereas those in the CBT group did not. In addition, the magnitude of change in the main variables (quality of life, depressive symptoms, and hopelessness) was significantly larger in the FDT group. The variables of hopelessness and change in positive anticipation also predicted change in quality of life in the FDT group but not in the CBT group. A core emphasis in this new therapy was on teaching participants how to close the gap between where they are in life and where they want to be, along with strengthening their perceived ability to close the gap (their self-efficacy). Closing this gap builds hope and is asserted to be the main therapeutic goal for depressed patients. Quality of life (QOL) is referred to as the core outcome to be measured in assessing interventions for MDD. This focus on wellness and a greater ability to thrive in life is consistent with the ideas of the recovery model of mental illness and the positive psychology movement.

KEY POINTS

1. Strength-based, empowering diagnosis and interventions are multisystemic.
2. Diagnosis involves systematic inquiry into resiliency-promoting behavior and contexts, such as healthy eating, exercise, social support, cultural identity, and levels of self-efficacy.

3. Accurate diagnosis is impossible without cultural competence and an environment that encourages participation and accurate information gathering; hence the need for case finding in the patient's natural environment, psychoeducation that reduces stigma, and the reduction of barriers to help-seeking behavior.
4. Empowering interventions are culturally specific, framed around the client's subjective experience and verbal expression, involve mind–body self-care, often including exercise, meditation, and other active mastery practices, and engender hope and self-efficacy.

CASE STUDY WITH AND WITHOUT THE DIVERSITY/RESILIENCY FORMULATION

Bipolar Disorder

The following vignette describes one individual's struggle with an emerging BPD in the context of higher education, African American racial identity, and cultural disparities. The diagnostic process and its relationship to treatment is discussed with and without the use of the authors' proposed Diversity/Resiliency Formulation.

Henry was an 18-year-old African American college freshman at a prestigious university in a southwestern state. The pride and joy of his parents, Henry had always excelled academically and demonstrated considerable theatrical and musical ability, playing the violin in his high school orchestra and acting in numerous school and community theater productions. Described as an intense, excitable child, Henry was subject to fits of irritability in adolescence, which sometimes deepened into outbursts of rage, especially at his father, and when his parents attempted to confront him about neglected household chores. His family's involvement in their local neighborhood church, a conservative Christian largely African American congregation, provided support and structure for both Henry and the family during these years, as his pastor was more than once called to the house to help settle intense and often confusing family disputes. His parents' expectations concerning "Godly behavior" involved consistent bedtimes and an atmosphere free of alcohol or drug use during high school, despite Henry's sometimes angry reactions to the rigidity of his parents' rules. Encouraged by his school counselor, Henry applied for and was accepted in an accelerated academic program at a university several hours from his home; he was awarded a scholarship that required the maintenance of a specified grade point average. In November of his first term at the university, Henry's parents received a call from the student counseling center of the university stating that Henry was failing his courses, had stopped attending class, and had been admitted to a local emergency psychiatric inpatient unit after the police had been called to a dormitory brawl involving drunkenness, vandalism, and verbal threats to other residents. Henry had apparently not slept in days, was disheveled in appearance, and was expressing outrage that his captors did not appreciate that he had been ordered by God to "drive the money changers out of the temple." Henry's dormitory room was discovered to be littered with empty beer bottles, and he had completely depleted the money his father had deposited in a local bank account for his daily expenses. His dormitory mates had increasingly distanced themselves from him because he was "acting weird" and drinking heavily. Henry had also been dating Cassandra, a coed, who had expressed alarm at his behavior, told him he needed help, and called off their relationship when she felt frightened of his insistent and intense sexual overtures. A brief family history, taken over the phone, revealed that Henry's father had been subject to intense mood swings as a younger man but had overcome them "with the help of prayer." A paternal uncle had committed suicide at the age of 30; and a paternal grandfather had been discharged from military service for psychiatric reasons.

Diagnostic Impression and Clinical Response Using *DSM-5*

Presenting symptoms, former functioning, and family history, led to the following working *DSM-5* diagnosis:

> 296.43 Bipolar I Disorder, Current or most recent episode manic, Severe, with Alcohol Abuse

Henry was started on a trial of lithium medication with good results. Although frightened and overwhelmed by his diagnosis, Henry denied suicidal ideation or intent. His mood stabilized within 10 days, and he was discharged from the hospital to the care of his parents with a referral to a local psychiatrist in his hometown. Henry was granted a medical leave from the university and allowed to return at the beginning of the second semester. With letters of support from his psychiatrist, he did not lose his scholarship. Henry's parents drove to the hospital and attended a family session with Henry. They were also given information about BPD and the importance of Henry's taking his medication and keeping regular appointments with his psychiatrist. However, upon returning home, Henry became depressed and withdrawn. His religious denomination subscribed to strict beliefs in the power of prayer and did not encourage the use of mental health professionals or reliance on psychotropic medication. Although Henry had been referred to Alcoholics Anonymous and had expressed a desire to attend while in the hospital, he did not follow through at home. His entire family, but especially his parents, were shocked at Henry's behavior and felt stigmatized by the label of mental illness, which was perceived in their religious community as a sign that the family and especially Henry had strayed from their faith. They were also dismayed and disgusted by the appearance of alcohol use in Henry's dormitory room. Henry was encouraged by his pastor to attend church regularly and to pray diligently. Henry retreated to his room and did not respond to calls from former high school friends. He did not respond to a follow-up call from the university counseling center. Henry's father became increasingly frustrated with Henry, and there were intense quarrels between them, with his mother attempting to soothe both Henry and his father, to no avail. Henry did not return to the university for the spring semester. Approximately a year later, Henry committed suicide with a gun borrowed from a neighbor. Journal writings found in his room expressed intense guilt and confusion related to his inability to reconcile his religious upbringing with his emerging sense of self and the incorporation of the view that his illness represented personal moral and spiritual failure.

Adding Diversity/Resiliency Formulation

Attending to Henry's strengths and sources of resiliency, in addition to the presenting symptoms of BPD and alcohol abuse, the hospital psychiatrist inquired with interest into Henry's musical and theater experiences. She learned that he had been planning to audition for the upcoming university production of Shakespeare's *Othello*, had been excelling until recently in his music theory course, and was hoping to major in African American studies and theater. An idealistic young man, Henry had dreams of going to graduate school after college and developing an African American theater program in his home community. His psychiatrist further learned that Henry was intensely interested in religion and philosophy and conflicted about the discrepancies he had been encountering between his college courses and his religious upbringing. In a family session, she explained the diagnosis of BPD in detail to both Henry and his parents, with special emphasis on the artistic and intellectual abilities that often accompany the disease and the connection between medication and the ability to maintain and use one's strengths. As Henry's thinking cleared, he was encouraged to read the memoir *An Unquiet Mind* (Jamison, 1995), as well as other memoir writings by African Americans recovering from mental disorders.

If a mental health professional were to attend systematically to Henry's strengths, diversity issues, and sources of resiliency, the following would be added to the *DSM-5* diagnostic label applied previously:

Henry's Diversity/Resiliency Formulation

In outline form:

Intrapersonal: Superior intelligence, accomplished violinist; some acting experience; interests in African American history and drama.
Interpersonal: Former high school friends interested and willing to be supportive; supportive parents; university counseling center with student support group. Close-knit, intact immediate and extended family.
Cultural: Connected to African American historical roots and current church community; interested in cultural self-expression, especially in music and theater.
Community: Supportive university community with services available upon return to campus; well regarded in home community, with ties to local theater and musical organizations.
Spiritual: Strong, conservative Christian faith in family; religious views of patient in process of reexamination and change.

In paragraph form:

Henry is a college student of superior intelligence, an accomplished violinist with some acting experience and special interests in African American history and drama. Former high school friends have expressed interest in his well-being. He is a member of a close-knit, immediate and extended family. Henry is a student in a supportive university community with services available to him on his return to campus. He is well regarded in his home community with ties to local theater and musical organizations. Henry is a member of a strong, conservative African American religious congregation.

A careful assessment of Henry's sources of resiliency might include a stronger attempt to enable him to remain in the university environment, if possible, in order to minimize his experience of isolation and defeat. Henry might be referred to a social worker for ongoing case management and support. In a family session, the strengths of persons with BPD would be emphasized, and the family would be referred to a bipolar family support group in their local community and actively connected with an African American representative of the support group before their return home. Henry and his family would actively discuss alternatives related to the diagnosis and his recovery. If Henry could remain at the university on the condition that he remain in treatment and take his medication, he would be enrolled in a local support group, connected with Alcoholics Anonymous and a sponsor, and encouraged to play his violin in the university symphony for the rest of the semester while being permitted to take a greatly reduced class load until he felt confident enough to return. He would meet regularly with a therapist at the university counseling center, discuss his reactions to his medication, and be encouraged to express his opinions about his diagnosis and treatment. Together with his therapist, he would develop and monitor a personal relapse plan.

Alternatively, Henry might choose to return home. If this second alternative were deemed preferable, Henry would be connected with an African American therapist in his hometown who could act as a cultural broker between the mental health community and his local family and church communities, possibly actively involving Henry's pastor in a psychoeducational and relapse prevention process. The issue of stigma, with its attendant religious connotation of spiritual failure, would be addressed respectfully, using the decision-tree algorithm of cross-cultural care presented in item 6 in the following "Discussion Questions and Activities." The local clinician would attempt to work with Henry's pastor, if Henry chose, to negotiate and frame the language of diagnosis and treatment in a manner acceptable to his family and spiritual community. The concept of BPD as a moral flaw versus a biological disease would be discussed openly with Henry, his family, and his pastor. Every attempt would be made to maintain and reinforce Henry's sources of resiliency while reducing and reframing the conflicts between his religious community and his diagnosis, using psychoeducation, support, and an ethnographic approach to negotiate a working therapeutic alliance with Henry, his family, and his pastor.

The description of Henry's experience, should not imply that the diagnosis and treatment of BPD would be a smooth process if only the Diversity/Resiliency Formulation were added. Nevertheless, the routine attention to and addition of this information in the patient's record at the time of diagnosis would call attention to Henry's complexities as a whole person and to his relationship to both internal and external strengths and contexts. With this information, intervention plans have a greater chance of relevance to the subjective worlds of this patient, reducing his isolation as well as the shock that accompanies the onset of a major mental illness. With the addition of the Diversity/Resiliency Formulation, we would also be more likely to get to know and appreciate Henry as a whole person.

SUMMARY

Mood disorders are among the greatest challenges to mental well-being and are diagnosed in increasing numbers despite advances in research and treatment. Although genetic, neurological, and biological factors are increasingly understood, the complex admixture of these etiological causes with psychosocial stress presents an ongoing challenge to the medical and mental health professions. The preponderance of the evidence suggests that BPDs and severe unipolar depression have strong biological hereditary origins and benefit from psychopharmacological intervention as well as other medical treatments such as ECT. The best results, however, involve a combination of medical and psychosocial treatments; in mild to moderate depression, the efficacy of CBT and interpersonal therapies is proven beyond that of medication. Moreover, strength-based interventions—such as exercise, meditation, healthy eating, and sleeping habits, and a lifestyle with strong interpersonal social support that encompasses culture, ethnicity, neighborhood, and community—may be the most powerful form of protection and prevention. The addition of the Diversity/Resiliency Formulation to the *DSM* diagnostic system, with its attention to internal and external sources of resiliency, ensures that attention is systematically paid to the patient's unique identity and his salient personal contexts.

DISCUSSION QUESTIONS AND ACTIVITIES

1. Read two memoirs (see the following "Personal Accounts/Memoirs" section), describing personal experiences with bipolar illness and with severe depression. Reflect on their personal impact on you and on your professional role.
2. Consider your own family, religious, and cultural upbringing. What do you and/or the members of your cultural group say when they describe feeling depressed? How is this experienced in terms of bodily sensations? How is this experience viewed, judged, and responded to in your cultural world? Would you be reluctant to share your depression with your family? Your neighbors? Your coworkers? Your church group? Explain why. Then complete an ethnographic interview with someone from a different culture, asking the same questions in relation to his or her perceptions of how these experiences are perceived within his or her cultural groups.
3. Interview an adolescent or child who often seems angry but whom you would not necessarily describe as depressed. Seek to understand the phenomenological experience of anger for this individual without attempting to reframe his or experience, give advice, or help. Examine the response and determine whether you think depression or loneliness lies beneath the anger.

4. Visit a practitioner of Chinese medicine. Ask about how he helps individuals with depression, how he describes this experience, what language he uses, and what his alternative treatments consist of.
5. Assume that Henry, the patient in the case vignette in this chapter, was a gay male. What do you know about the incidence of depression and suicide in lesbian, gay, or transgendered (LGBT) persons? What cultural characteristics and societal attitudes pertaining to the LGBT community would you need to take into account in responding effectively to the diagnosis and treatment of Henry if he were gay?
6. Apply the following model of integrated patient–clinical diagnosis, offered by Yeung and Kam (2008), to a client whose culture is different from yours and who presents with a mixture of physical, anxiety, and depressive complaints that you feel indicate the presence of a mood disorder:

Clinician–Patient System Decision Tree Algorithm for Cross-Cultural Care

Explore the patient's/family's explanatory models by creating open-ended and follow-up questions to begin the listening process. Then …

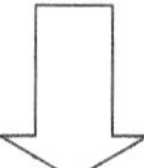

Validate the patient's/family's explanatory model. Then introduce your additional, alternative explanatory model. Next …

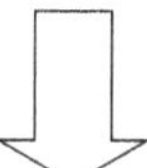

Obtain information from patient/family regarding culturally relevant folk theories, indigenous healers, and preferred care modalities. Then present alternative psychiatric, medical, or psychosocial treatments that are likely to be beneficial (Yeung & Kam, 2008).

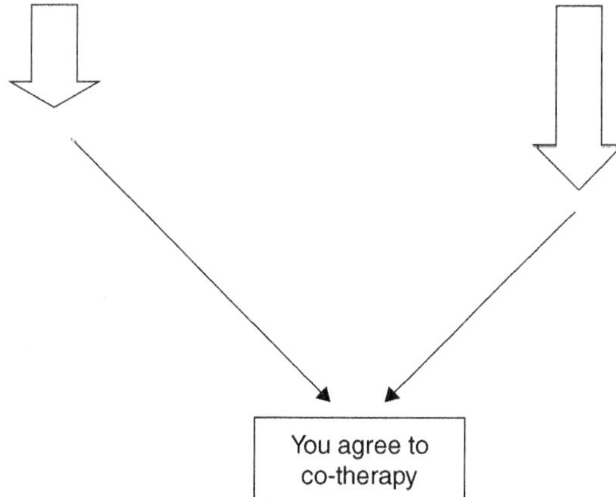

Apply The Diversity/Resiliency Formulation to a client or patient whom you have diagnosed as depressed or to a clinical teaching vignette. Plan a related intervention applying research findings from the empowerment and strength-based models described in this chapter and/or other models you have researched.

7. Visit an online support group or chat room for depressed or bipolar persons. See if you can identify the three most salient concerns of the chat room participants. Note references to sources of strength and resiliency.
8. Design an outreach program to a subcultural group in your community that lacks access to mental health treatment because of income, language or cultural barriers, or sources of disparity. Determine relevant natural community organizations and institutions where you could reach out in the form of educational presentations, information, media presentations, or other activities. How would you involve indigenous leaders in this process? Plan a program in detail, complete with components of needs assessment, community-engaged interventions, evaluations, and a timetable for completion.
9. The culture of the workplace is real but often hidden, unconsciously absorbed, and unacknowledged. Think about the atmosphere in a variety of occupational settings, such as law, education, construction work, service industries, business, the clergy, sales, and so on. How would you go about identifying hidden norms about the acceptability of acknowledging the existence of a mood disorder and asking for help? What could you do to facilitate constructive change in occupational norms in the direction of a mentally healthy culture?
10. The implication of a clinical diagnosis of depression for the reorganization of the self is discussed by Hermans (2003) in the description of a client who appeared to be "enslaved" to his diagnosis of depression, having incorporated it as a central element of his identity. Sources of internal support, based on past experiences viewed by the client as empowering, were utilized in his treatment. First, the memory of contact with a former teacher was used to bolster a "protected area" in the client's sense of self. Next the emerging self-concept as a "fighter" was strengthened in opposition to the client's sense of self-concept as a "depressed" person. The author stresses the importance of understanding the account of self as an ever-changing dynamic multiplicity of parts in a personality system capable of reorganizing itself. Apply these concepts to your own life or to the life of a client. How might you substitute positive for negative past experiences in order to generate alterations in self-concept that are more hopeful and empowering?
11. Ponder the role of hope in the diagnosis and treatment of persons with bipolar or MDD. How would you address this with a client in the context of encouraging movement toward a hoped-for envisioned future?

PERSONAL ACCOUNTS/MEMOIRS

Casey, N. (Ed.). (2002). *Unholy ghost: Writers on depression*. New York, NY: HarperCollins.

Duke, P., & Hochma, G. (1992). *A brilliant madness: Living with manic depression*. New York, NY: Random House.

Hinshaw, S. P. (2002). *The years of silence are past: My father's life with bipolar disorder*. New York, NY: Cambridge University Press.
Jamison, K. R. (1995). *An unquiet mind: A memoir of moods and madness*. New York, NY: Alfred A. Knopf.
Styron, W. (1992). *Darkness visible: A memoir of madness*. New York, NY: Random House.
Thompson, T. (1996). *The beast: A journey through depression*. Middlesex, UK: Penguin Books.

WEB RESOURCES

Numerous web sources exist for mental disorder diagnoses. Note that although these sites contain useful information, many also serve as major advertising venues for pharmaceutical companies.
www.healthline.com
www.mayoclinic.com
www.nimh.nih.gov
www.nlm.nih.gov/medlineplus

REFERENCES

Aguilar-Gaxiola, S. A., & Gullotta, T. P. (Eds.). (2008). *Depression in Latinos: Assessment, treatment and prevention: Issues in children's and families' lives*. New York, NY: Springer Science and Business Media.
American Psychiatric Association. (2000). *Diagnostic and statistical manual of mental disorders* (4th ed., text rev.). Washington, DC: Author.
American Psychiatric Association. (2013). *Diagnostic and statistical manual of mental disorders* (5th ed.). Washington, DC: Author.
Andreasen, N. C. (2001). *Brave new brain: Conquering mental illness in the era of the genome*. New York, NY: Oxford University Press.
Ball, J, Corry, J., & Mitchell, P. (2007). Mindfulness meditation and bipolar disorder. In D. A. Einstein (Ed.), *Innovations and advances in cognitive behaviour therapy* (pp. 37–41). Bowen Hills, QLD, Australia: Australian Academic Press.
Barber, C. L. (2008). Identification of risk and protective factors among adults with bipolar disorder with major depressive disorder comparison group. *Dissertation Abstracts international: Section B: The Sciences and Engineering*, 69(2-B), 1314.
Beach, S., & Jones, D. (2002). Marital and family therapy for depression in adults. In I. H. Gotlib & C. L. Hammen (Eds.), *Handbook of depression* (pp. 422–440). New York, NY: Guilford Press.
Beardslee, W. R., Gladstone, T. R., Wright, E. J., & Cooper, A. B. (2003). A family-based approach to the prevention of depressive symptoms in children at risk: Evidence of parental and child change. *Pediatrics*, *112*(2), 3119–3193.
Bhugra, D. (2004). Globalisation and mental disorders: Overview with relation to depression. *British Journal of Psychiatry*, *184*(1), 10–20.
Birmaher, B., Brent, D. A., Kolko, D., Baugher, M. A., Bridge, B. S., & Holder, D. (2000). Clinical outcome after short-term psychotherapy for adolescents with major depressive disorder. *Archives of General Psychiatry*, *57*(1), 29–36.
Bockting, C. L., Spinhoven, P., Wouters, L. F., Koeter, M. W., & Schene, A. H. (2009). Long-term effects of preventive cognitive therapy in recurrent depression: A 5.5 year-year follow-up study. *Journal of Clinical Psychiatry*, *70*(12), 1621–1628.
Bohlmeijer, E., Smit, F., & Cuipers, P. (2003). Effects of reminiscence and life review on late-life depression: A meta-analysis. *International Journal of Geriatric Psychiatry*, *18*, 1088–1094.
Breggin, P. R. (1994). *Talking back to Prozac: What doctors aren't telling you about today's most controversial drug*. New York, NY: Saint Martin's Press.
Brown, T., Chorpita, B., & Barlow, D. (1998). Structured relationships among dimensions of the *DSM-IV* anxiety and mood disorders and dimensions of negative affect, positive affect, and autonomic arousal. *Journal of Abnormal Psychology*, *107*(2), 179–192.

Busko, M. (2008a, October 3). One in 4 adults admitted to a mood-disorder clinic are misdiagnosed. *MedscapeMedical News*. Poster 85 presented at American Psychiatric Association 60th Institute on Psychiatric Services Meeting, Honolulu, Hawaii.
Busko, M. (2008b, October 3). Patients welcome telepsychiatry approach to depression treatment. *Medscape Medical News*. Presented at the American Psychiatric Association 60th Institute on Psychiatric Services Meeting, Honolulu, Hawaii.
Callahan, C. M., & Berrios, G. E. (2005). *Reinventing depression: A history of the treatment of depression in primary care, 1940–2004*. New York, NY: Oxford University Press.
Caplan, P. J. (1989). *Don't blame mother: Mending the mother–daughter relationship*. New York, NY: Harper and Row.
Carpenter-Song, E., Schwallie, M. N., & Longhofer, J. L. (2008). Using care with culture. In S. Loue & J. Sajatovic (Eds.), *Diversity issues in the diagnosis, treatment, and research of mood disorders* (pp. 3–17). New York, NY: Oxford University Press.
Center, C., Davis, M., Detre, T., Ford, D., Hansbrough, W., Henolin, H., ... Silverman, M. (2003). Confronting depression and suicide in physicians: A consensus statement. *Journal of the American Medical Association, 289*, 3161–3166.
Cho, H. J., Lavretsky, H., Olmstead, R., Levin, M. J., & Oxman, M. N. (2008). Sleep disturbance and depression recurrence in community-dwelling older adults: A prospective study. *American Journal of Psychiatry, 165*(12), 1543–1550.
Clark, L. A., Watson, D., & Mineka, S. (1994). Temperament, personality, and the mood and anxiety disorders. *Journal of Abnormal Psychology, 103*, 103–116.
Corcoran, J., & Walsh, W. (2006). *Clinical assessment and diagnosis in social work practice*. New York, NY: Oxford University Press.
Craft, L. L. (2005). Exercise and clinical depression: Examining two psychological mechanisms. *Psychology of Sport and Exercise, 6*, 151–171.
Cuijpers, P. (1998). A psychoeducational approach to the treatment of depression: A meta-analysis of Lewinsohn's "Coping with Depression" course. *Behavior Therapy, 29*, 521–533.
Culver, J. L., Arnow, B. A., & Ketter, T. A. (2007). Bipolar disorder: Improving diagnosis and optimizing integrated care. *Journal of Clinical Psychology, 63*(1), 73–92.
Cusack, J. R. (2002). Challenges in the diagnosis and treatment of bipolar disorder. *Drug Benefit Trends, 14*(10), 34–38.
Dickinson, Emily. (n.d.). *I measure every grief I meet*. Retrieved from https://en.wikisource.org/wiki/I_measure_every_Grief_I_meet
Dion, G. L. (1992). A renabilitation model for persons with bipolar disorder. *Comprehensive Mental Health Care, 2*(2), 87–102.
Donald, M., Dower, J., Correa-Velez, I., & Jones, J. (2006). Risk and protective factors for medically serious suicide attempts: A comparison of hospital-based with population based samples of young adults. *Australian and New Zealand Journal of Psychiatry, 40*(1), 87–96.
Eme, R., & Mouritson, J. (2013). The addition of disruptive mood dysregulation disorder to *DSM-5*: Differential diagnosis and case examples. *The Practitioner Scholar: Journal of Counseling and Professional Psychology*, 2, 84–94.
Fava, G. A., Grandi, S., Qielezny, M., Rafanelli, C., & Canestrari, R. (1996). Four-year outcome for cognitive behavioral treatment of residual symptoms in major depression. *American Journal of Psychiatry, 153*, 945–947.
Fournier, J. C., DeRuseis, R. J., Hollon, S. D., Dimidjian, S., Amsterdam, J. D., Shelton, R. C., & Fawcett, J. (2010). Antidepressant drug effects and depression severity. *Journal of the American Medical Association, 303*(1), 47–53.
Frances, A. (2013). *Saving normal: An insider's revolt against out-of-control psychiatric diagnosis, DSM-5, big pharma, and the medicalization of ordinary life*. New York, NY: Harper Collins.
Gammell, D. J., & Stoppard, J. M. (1999). Women's experiences of treatment of depression: Medicalization or empowerment? *Canadian Psychology, 40*(2), 112–128.
Gelenberg, A. J., Kocsis, J. G., McCullough J. P. Jr., Ninan P. T., & Thase M. E. (2006). The state of knowledge of chronic depression. *Primary Care Companion to Journal of Clinical Psychiatry, 68*(2): 60–65.

Goodman, L. A., Litwin, A., Bohlig, A., Weintraub, S., Green, A., Walker, J., ... Ryan, N. (2007). Applying feminist theory to community practice: A multilevel empowerment intervention for low-income women and depression. In E. Aldarondo (Ed.), *Advancing social justice through clinical practice. Social justice through clinical empowerment* (pp. 265–290). Mahwah, NJ: Lawrence Erlbaum.

Gray, S. M., & Zide, M. R. (2005). *Psychopathology: A competency-based treatment model for social workers*. Belmont, CA: Thomson, Brooks/Cole.

Gray, S. M., & Zide, M. R. (2007). *Psychopathology: A competency-based assessment model for social workers* (2nd ed.). Belmont, CA: Thomson, Brooks/Cole.

Greenberg, R., & Fisher, S. (1997). Mood-mending medicines: Probing drug, psychotherapy and placebo solutions. In S. Fisher & R. Greenberg (Eds.), *From placebo to panacea: Putting psychiatric drugs to the test* (pp. 115–172). New York, NY: John Wiley & Sons.

Grippo, A. J., & Johnson, A. K. (2009). Stress, depression, and cardiovascular dysregulation: A review of neurobiological mechanisms and the integration of research from preclinical disease models. *Stress*, *12*(9), 1–21.

Guarnaccia, P., & Pincay, I. M. (2008). Culture-specific diagnoses and their relationship to mood disorders. In S. Loue & M. Sajatovic (Ed.), *Diversity issues in the diagnosis, treatment, and research of mood disorders* (pp. 32–53). New York, NY: Oxford University Press.

Gupta, R. K. (2009). Major depression: An illness with objective physical signs. *World Journal of Biological Psychiatry*, *10*(3), 196–201.

Harrison, P., & Martin, B. N. (2010). Depression, suicidal ideation more likely in adolescents with late vs. earlier set bedtimes. *Medscape Clinical Briefs*. Retrieved from http://cme.medscape.com/viewarticle/715049?src=cmemp&uac=117792MK

Harvard Medical School. (2007, May). Bipolar disorder in children: Difficult to diagnosis, important to treat. *Harvard Mental Health Letter*, *23*(11), 1–3.

Harvard Medical School. (2009a, December). Managing chronic depression: Long-term treatment increases chances of response and remission. *Harvard Mental Health Letter*, *26*(6), 1–3.

Harvard Medical School. (2009b, January). Options for treatment-resistant depression. *Harvard Mental Health Letter*, *25*(7), 1–3.

Harvey, A. T., Tilkey, S. B., Kornstein, S. G., & Clary, G. M. (2007). Acute worsening of chronic depression during a double-blind randomized clinical trial of antidepressant efficacy: Differences by sex and menopausal status. *Journal of Clinical Psychiatry*, *68*(6), 951–958.

Hawley, L. L., Schwartz, D., Bieling, P. J., Irging, J., Corcoran, K., Farb, N. A., ... Segal, Z. V. (2014). Mindfulness practice, rumination and clinical outcome in mindfulness-based treatment. *Cognitive Therapy Research*, *38*, 1–9.

Hermans, H. J. M. (2003). Clinical diagnosis as a multiplicity of self-positions: Challenging social representations theory. *Culture and Psychology*, *9*(4), 407–414.

Hill, N., Litt, L., Epstein, P., & Epstein, I. (2013). Encouraging self-management in chronically ill patients with co-morbid symptoms of depression and anxiety: An emergency department study and response. *Social Work in Health Care*, *52*(2–3), 207–221.

Hoen, P., Whooley, M., Martins, E., Na, B., Van Melle, J. D., &. deJonge, P. M. A. (2008). Depressive symptoms, health behaviors, and risk of cardiovascular events in patients with coronary heart disease. *Journal of the American Medical Association*, *300*(20), 2379–2388.

Hofmann, S. G., Sawyer, A. T., Witt, A. A., & Oh, D. (2010). The effect of mindfulness-based therapy on anxiety and depression: A meta-analytic review. *Journal of Consulting and Clinical Psychology*, *78*, 169–183.

Holden, K. B., Bradford, L. D., Hall, S. P., & Belton, A. S. (2003). Prevalence and correlates of depressive symptoms and resiliency among African American women in a community-based primary health care center. *Journal of Health Care for the Poor and Underserved*, *24*(4 Suppl), 79–93.

Husarova, D. (2009). The dialectic relationship among culture, history and depressive phenomena: A cultural study of Slovakia. *Dissertation Abstracts International: Section B. Sciences and Engineering*, *69*(7-B), 4424.

Interian, A., Martinez, I. E., Guarnaccia, P. J., Vega, W. A., & Escobar, J. I. (2007). A qualitative analysis of the perception of stigma among Latinos receiving antidepressants. *Psychiatric Services*, *58*(12), 1591–1594.

Jamison, K. R. (1995). *An unquiet mind: A memoir of moods and madness*. New York, NY: Alfred A. Knopf.

Jamison, K. R. (2009). *Nothing was the same*. New York, NY: Alfred A. Knopf.

Ji, P., & Duan, C. (2006). The relationship among acculturation, acculturation stress, and depression for a Korean and a Korean-American sample. *Asian Journal of Counseling, 13*(2), 235–270.

Johnson, J. G., Han, Y-S., Douglas, C. J., Johannet, C. M., & Russell, T. (1998). Attributions for positive life events predict recovery from depression among psychiatric inpatients: An investigation of the Needles and Abramson model of recovery from depression. *Journal of Consulting and Clinical Psychology, 66*(2), 369–376.

Johnson, S. L., & Leahy, R. L. (2004). *Psychological treatment of bipolar disorder*. New York, NY: Guilford Press.

Johnston, C. (2010). Analysis shows genetic link between major mood disorders. *Nature*. Retrieved from http://arstechnica.com/science/news/2010/01

Jones, S. H., & Burrell-Hodgson, G. (2008). Cognitive-behavioural treatment of first diagnosis bipolar disorder. *Clinical Psychology and Psychotherapy, 15*, 367–377.

Keitner, G., Ryan, C., & Heru, A. (2005). Families of people with bipolar disorder. In J. Leff, J. J. Lopez-Ibor, M. Mario, & A. S. Okasha (Ed.), *Families and mental disorders: From burden to empowerment* (pp. 69–85). New York, NY: John Wiley & Sons.

Kelly, J. C. (2010). *Surplus of serotonin receptors may explain failure of antidepressants in some patients*. Retrieved from www.medscape.com/viewarticle/715337?sssdmh=dm1.582085&src=nldne&uac=1

Kessler, R. C., Berglund, P., Demler, O., Jin, R., Koretz, D., Merikangas, K., ... Wang, P. S. (2003). The epidemiology of major depressive disorder: Results from the national comorbidity survey replication (NCS-R). *Journal of the American Medical Association, 289*, 3095–3105.

Kilbourne, A. M. (2008). Models for the delivery of care. In S. Loue & M. Sajatovic (Eds.), *Diversity issues in the diagnosis, treatment and research of mood disorders* (pp. 178–195). New York, NY: Oxford University Press.

Kiosses, D., Leon, A., & Arean, P. (2011). Psychosocial interventions for late-life major depression: Evidence-based treatments, predictors of treatment outcomes, and moderators of treatment effects. *Psychiatric Clinics of North America, 34*:377–401.

Klein, D. N., Arnow, B. A., Barkin, J. L., Dowling, F., Kocsis, J. H., & Leon, A. C. (2009). Early adversity in chronic depression: Clinical correlates and response to pharmacotherapy. *Depression and Anxiety, 26*(8), 701–710.

Kleinman, A. (2004). Culture and depression. *New England Journal of Medicine, 351*(10), 951–953.

Kruger, S., Alda, M., Young, L. T., Goldapple, K., Parikh, S., & Mayberg, H. (2006). Risk and markers in bipolar disorder: Brain response to emotional challenges in bipolar patients and their healthy siblings. *American Journal of Psychiatry, 163*(2), 257–264.

Kupfer, D. J., Axelson, D. A., Birmaher, B., Brown, C., Fagiolini, A., Frank, E., ... Whyte, E. (2009). Bipolar Disorder Center for Pennsylvanians: Implementing an effectiveness trial to improve treatment for at-risk patients. *Psychiatric Services, 60*(7), 888–897.

Kutchins, H. K., & Kirk, S. A. (Eds.). (1997). *Making us crazy: DSM, the psychiatric bible and the creation of mental disorders*. New York, NY: Free Press.

Laakso, L. (2012). Motivational interviewing: Addressing ambivalence to improve medication adherence in patients with bipolar disorder. *Issues in Mental Health Nursing, 33*:8–14.

Lam, D., Hones, S. H., Hayward, P., & Bright, J. (1999). *Cognitive therapy for bipolar disorder: A therapist's guide to concepts, methods, and practice*. Hoboken, NJ: John Wiley & Sons.

Landino, J. M., Roy, J. M., & Buckley, J. M. (2009, June). *Stigma of mental illness continues to impede early diagnosis and treatment of affective illness in the US*. Priory Lodge Education, Ltd. Retrieved from http://priory.com/-psychiatry/Stigma_Mental_Disorder.htm

La Torre, M. A. (2001). Meditation and psychotherapy: An effective combination. *Perspectives in Psychiatric Care, 37*(3), 103–106.

Lawson, W. B. (2005). Bipolar disorder in African-Americans. In A. M. Georgiopoulos & J. M. Rosenbaum (Eds.), *Perspectives in cross cultural psychiatry* (pp. 135–142). Philadelphia, PA: Lippincott Williams & Wilkins.

LeCroy, C. & Holschuh, C, Eds. (2013). *First person accounts of mental illness and recovery*. Hoboken, NJ: John Wiley & Sons.

Lee, D. T., Kleinman, J., & Kleinman, A. (2007). Rethinking depression: An ethnographic study of the experiences of depression among Chinese. *Harvard Review of Psychiatry, 15*, 1–8.

Lerner, H. G. (1988). *Women in therapy*. Northvale, NJ: Jason Aronson.

Lewis, L. (2005). Patient perspectives on the diagnosis, treatment, and management of bipolar disorder. *Bipolar Disorders*, 7(Suppl. 1), 33–37.

Lichtman, J., & Bigger, J. T. (2008). Depression and coronary heart disease: Recommendations for screening, referral, and treatment. A science advisory from the American Heart Association Prevention Committee of the Council on Cardiovascular Nursing, Council on Clinical Cardiology, Council on Epidemiology and Prevention, and Interdisciplinary Council on Quality of Care and Outcomes Research: Endorsed by the American Psychiatric Association. *Circulation, 118*(17), 1768–1775.

Loue, S. (2007). Cultural issues in the diagnosis and treatment of bipolar disorder. In M. Sajatovic & F. C. Blow (Eds.), *Bipolar disorder in later life* (pp. 182–192). Baltimore, MD: Johns Hopkins University Press.

Loue, S. (2008a). The epidemiology of mood disorders among U.S. minority populations. In S. Loue & M. Sajatovic (Eds.), *Diversity issues in the diagnosis, treatment and research of mood disorders* (pp. 54–68). New York, NY: Oxford University Press.

Loue, S. (2008b). Legal and ethical issues in research relating to mood disorders. In S. Loue & M. Sajatovic (Eds.), *Diversity issues in the diagnosis, treatment and research of mood disorders* (pp. 231–249). New York, NY: Oxford University Press.

Loue, S., & Sajatovic, M. (2008). *Diversity issues in the diagnosis, treatment, and research of mood disorders*. New York, NY: Oxford University Press.

Lozano-Vranich, B., & Petit, J. (2003). *The seven beliefs: A step-by-step guide to help Latinas recognize and overcome depression*. New York, NY: Rayo.

Manson, S. M. (1995). Culture and major depression: Current challenges in the diagnosis of mood disorders. *Psychiatric Clinics of North America, 18*(3), 487–501.

Marcus, S. C., & Olfson, M. (2010). National trends in the treatment for depression from 1998 to 2007. *Archives of General Psychiatry*, 67(12), 1265–1273.

Martin, E. (2007). *Bipolar expeditions: Mania and depression in American culture*. Princeton, NJ: Princeton University Press.

Mata, J., Hogan, C. L., Joorman, J., Waugh, C. E., & Gotlib, I. H. (2013). Acute exercise attenuates negative affect following repeated sad mood inductions in persons who have recovered from depression. *Journal of Abnormal Psychology, 122* (1), 45–50.

Matcham, F, Rayner, L., Hutton, J., Monk, A., Steel, C., & Hotopf, M. (2014). Self-help interventions for symptoms of depression, anxiety, and psychological distress in patients with physical illness: A systematic review and meta-analysis. *Clinical Psychology Review, 34*, 141–157.

McClure, E. B., Connell, A. M., & Zucker, M. (2005). The Adolescent Depression Empowerment Project (ADEPT): A culturally sensitive family treatment for depressed African American girls. In E. D. Hibbs & P. S. Jensen (Eds.), *Psychosocial treatments for child and adolescent disorders: Empirically based strategies for clinical practice* (2nd ed., pp. 149–164). Washington, DC: American Psychological Association.

McCullough, J. P. (2003). Treatment for chronic depression using cognitive behavioral analysis system of psychotherapy (CBASP). *Journal of Clinical Psychology*, 59(8), 833–846.

McDermutt, W., Miller, I., & Brown, R. (2001). The efficacy of group psychotherapy for depression: A meta-analysis and review of the empirical research. *Clinical Psychology: Science and Practice, 8*, 98–116.

McGoldrick, M., Gerson, R., & Petry, S. (2008). *Genograms: Assessment and intervention* (3rd ed.). New York, NY: W.W. Norton.

Mellsop, G., & Smith, B. (2007). Reflections on masculinity, culture, and the diagnosis of depression. *Australian and New Zealand Journal of Psychiatry, 41*, 850–853.

Mendenhall, T. J., Keller, M. T., Baird, M. A., & Doherty, W. J. (2008). Overcoming depression in a strange land: A Hmong woman's journey in the world of Western medicine. In R. Kessler & D. Stafford (Eds.), *Collaborative medicine case studies: Evidence in practice* (pp. 326–340). New York, NY: Stringer Science and Business Media.

Middleton, J. L. (2008). Today I'm grieving a physician suicide. *Annals of Family Medicine, 6*, 267–269.

Miller, K. (2006). Bipolar disorder: Etiology, diagnosis, and management. *Journal of the American Academy of Nurse Practitioners, 18*(8), 368–373.

Mufson, L., & Fairbanks, G. (1996). Interpersonal psychotherapy for depressed adolescents: A one-year naturalistic follow-up study. *Journal of the American Academy of Child and Adolescent Psychiatry, 35*, 1145–1155.

Mufson, L., Moreau, D., Weissman, M., Wickramaratne, P., Martin, J., & Samilov, A. (1994). Modification of interpersonal psychotherapy with depressed adolescents (IPT-A): Phase I and II studies. *Journal of the American Academy of Child and Adolescent Psychiatry, 33*, 695–705.

National Survey on Drug Use and Health. (2008, January 3). *The NSDUH Report: Treatment for past year depression among adults*. Washington, DC: SAMHSA, Office of Applied Studies. Retrieved from http://oas.Samhsa.gov/2k8/depressionTX.htm

Nemeroff, C. B., & Owens, M. J. (2002). Treatment of mood disorders. *Nature Neuroscience Supplement, 5*, 1068–1070.

Norton, C. L. (2007). Understanding the impact of wilderness therapy on adolescent depression and psychosocial development. *Dissertation Abstracts International: Section A. Humanities and Social Sciences, 68*(4-A), 1661.

Oquendo, M. A., & Graver, R. (2008). Treatment of an Indian woman with major depression by a Latina therapist: A cultural formulation. In J. E. Mezzich & B. Caracci (Eds.), *Cultural formulation: A reader for psychiatric diagnosis* (pp. 237–247). Lanham, MD: Jason Aronson.

Piet, J., & Hougaard, E. (2011). The effect of mindfulness-based cognitive therapy for prevention of relapse in recurrent major depressive disorder: A systematic review and meta-analysis. *Clinical Psychology Review, 31*, 1032–1040.

Pratt, S., Bartels, S., Mueser, K., Naslund, J., Wolfe, R., Pixley, H., & Josephson, L. (2013). Feasibility and effectiveness of an automated telehealth intervention to improve illness self-management in people with serious psychiatric and medical disorders. *Psychiatric Rehabilitation Journal, 36*(4), 297–305.

Reinecke, M., Ryan, N., & Dubois, D. (1998). Cognitive-behavioral therapy of depression and depressive symptoms during adolescence: A review and meta-analysis. *Journal of the American Academy of Child and Adolescent Psychiatry, 37*, 26–34.

Richardson-Jones, J. W., Craige, C. P., Guiard, B. P., Stephen, A., Metzger, K. L., Kung H. F., ... Leonardo E. D. (2010). 5-HT(1A) autoreceptor levels determine vulnerability to stress and response to antidepressants. *Neuron, 65*(2), 40–52.

Robertson, R., Robertson, A., Jepson, R., & Maxwell, M. (2012). Walking for depression or depressive symptoms: A systematic review and meta-analysis. *Mental Health and Physical Activity. 5*, 66–75.

Rosello, J., & Bernal, G. (1999). The efficacy of cognitive-behavioral and interpersonal treatments for depression in Puerto Rican adolescents. *Journal of Consulting and Clinical Psychology, 67*, 734–745.

Saenz, D. (2001). A retrospective study of the correlation between diagnosis of schizophrenia or bipolar disorder and medication noncompliance. *Dissertation Abstracts International: Section B. Sciences and Engineering, 61*(10-B), 5580.

Sanderson, W. C., & McGinn, L. K. (2001). Cognitive-behavioral therapy of depression. In M. M. Weissman (Ed.), *Treatment of depression: Bridging the 21st century* (pp. 249–279). Washington, DC: American Psychiatric Publishing.

Santor, D., & Kusumakar, V. (2001). Open trial of interpersonal therapy in adolescents with moderate to severe major depression: Effectiveness of novice IPT therapists. *Journal of the American Academy of Child and Adolescent Psychiatry, 40*(2), 236–240.

Seidman, S. N., Orr, G., Raviv, G., Levi, R., Roose, S., Kravitz, E., … Weiser, M. (2009). Effects of testosterone replacement in middle-aged men with dysthymia: A randomized, placebo-controlled clinical trial. *Journal of Clinical Psychopharmacology*, *29*(3), 216–221.

Segal, Z. V., Bieling, P. J., Young, T., MacQueen, G., Cooke, R., Martin, L., … Levitan, RD. (2010). Antidepressant monotherapy versus sequential pharmacotherapy and mindfulness-based cognitive therapy, or placebo, for relapse prophylaxis in recurrent depression. *Archives of General Psychiatry*, *67*, 1256–1264.

Shelton, R. C. (2006). Management of major depressive disorder following failure of first antidepressant treatment. *Primary Psychiatry*, *13*(4), 73–82.

Shorter, E. (2009). *Before Prozac: The troubled history of mood disorders in psychiatry*. New York, NY: Oxford University Press.

Sonawalla, S. B., & Fava, M. (2010). Severe depression: Is there a best approach? *CNS Drugs*, *15*(10), 765–776.

Sotsky, S. M., Glass, D. R., Shea, T., Pilkonis, P. A., Collins, F., Elkin, I., … Oliveri, E. (2006). Patient predictors of response to psychotherapy and psychopharmacotherapy: Findings in the NIMH Treatment of Depression Collaborative Research Program. *Focus*, *4*, 278–290.

Stathopoulou, G., Powers, M. B., Betty, A. C., Smits, J. A., & Otto, M. W. (2006). Exercise interventions for mental health: A quantitative and qualitative review. *Clinical Psychology: Science and Practice*, *13*(2), 179–193.

Stensland, M. D., & Schultz, J. F. (2008). Diagnosis of unipolar depression following initial identification of bipolar disorder: A common and costly misdiagnosis. *Journal of Clinical Psychiatry*, *69*(5), 749–758.

Sussman, N. (2007). Bipolar disorder: Changing patterns of diagnosis and treatment. *Primary Psychiatry*, *14*(10), 15–16.

Timulak, L., & Elliott, R. (2003). Empowerment events in process-experiential psychotherapy of depression: An exploratory qualitative analysis. *Psychotherapy Research*, *13*(4), 443–460.

Torpey, D. & Klein, D. (2008). Chronic depression: Update on classification and treatment. *Current Psychiatric Reports*, *10*(6): 458–464.

Valenstein, E. (1998). *Blaming the brain: The truth about drugs and mental health*. New York, NY: Free Press.

Valtonen, H., Suominen, K., Mantere, O., Leppamaki, S., Arvilommi, P., & Isometsa, E. (2005). Suicidal ideation and attempts in Bipolar I and II. *Journal of Clinical Psychiatry*, *66*, 1456–1462.

Vilhauer, J. S., Cortes, J., Moali, N., Chung, S., Mirocha, J., & Ishak, W. W. (2013). Improving quality of life for patients with major depressive disorder by increasing hope and positive expectations with future directed therapy (FDT). *Innovations in Clinical Neuroscience*, *10*(3), 12–22.

Wall, C., Croarkin, P., McClintock, S., Mursphy, L., Bandel, L., Sim, L., & Sampson, S. (2013). Neurocognitive effects of repetitive transcranial magnetic stimulation in adolescents with major depressive disorder. *Frontiers in Psychiatry*, *12*(4), 1–8.

Wasserman, E, & Zimmerman, T. (2012). Transcranial magnetic brain stimulation: Therapeutic promises and scientific gaps. *Pharmacology and Therapeutics*, *133*, 98–107.

Weissman, M. M., Markowitz, J. C., & Klerman, G. L. (2000). *Comprehensive guide to interpersonal therapy*. New York, NY: Basic Books.

Whitaker, R. (2010). *Anatomy of an epidemic: Magic bullets, psychiatric drugs, and the astonishing rise of mental illness in America*. New York, NY: Crown.

White, A., Shiralkar, P., Hassan, R., Galbraith, T., & Callaghan, R. (2006). Barriers to mental health care for psychiatrists. *Psychiatric Bulletin: The Royal College of Psychiatrists*, *30*, 382–384.

Yeung, A., & Kam, R. (2008). Ethical and cultural considerations in delivering psychiatric diagnosis: Reconciling the gap using MDD diagnosis delivery in less-acculturated Chinese patients. *Transcultural Psychiatry*, *45*, 531–552.

FOUR

Anxiety Disorders and the Diversity/Resiliency Formulation

You may laugh if you like. It is terrible and I cannot get over it. I am afraid of the walls, of the furniture, of the familiar objects, which are animated, as far as I am concerned, by a kind of animal life. Above all, I am afraid of my own dreadful thoughts of my reason, which seems as if it were about to leave me, driven away by a mysterious and invisible agony.

—De Maupassant

Anxiety is a predictable part of life experience, most often related to stress, and has become a familiar theme in popular culture, as evidenced by the increase of articles in the popular press on understanding anxiety and on how to manage it. It is common and probable for someone to experience anxiety on feeling heightened anticipation about an upcoming event, regardless of whether the perception of the event is positive or negative. It can be particularly anxiety arousing if an anticipated situation is perceived as having the potential for significant consequences for the individual. Uncertainty and ambiguity are difficult to manage and can lead to anxiety; some would posit that this occurs because we are not "wired" to tolerate ambiguity for very long. Clearly, during periods of major social, political, and/or economic unsteadiness, where hardship abounds, feeling troubled and uneasy about one's situation and the future well-being of one's family brings anxiety as one considers one's responsibilities and significant roles (e.g., parent, provider, professional). There are a multitude of sources of anxiety that, regardless of individual differences, affect most people. Some responses are internal, related to how we function; other sources are external and related to the environment that we all share.

As uncomfortable as anxiety might feel, it also serves a highly adaptive function. Although anxiety creates feelings of discomfort and uneasiness, a manageable amount assists us in particular situations that require additional energy or effort. Novel circumstances may feel like they throw us off; however, the edge that one feels in such situations produces that extra effort needed to give such situations our best try. Anticipation of events is helpful for coping because it promotes that keenness, focus, and motivation, which are so essential in order to rise to those special occasions that feel important, such as presentations, interviews, or meeting new people. Anxiety becomes dysfunctional when safe situations are interpreted as unsafe and/or "activated for extended periods of time" (Schmidt, Norr, & Korte, 2013, p. 57).

Anxiety disorders vary in their presenting symptoms, whose range includes physiological, emotional, and cognitive behaviors. Physiological responses include heightened physiological arousal, such as accelerated heart rate as well as heightened respiratory reactions that can create chest pain, palpitations, difficulty breathing, or sensations of choking or smothering. The range of emotional responses includes intense fear, worry, distress, apprehension, terror, and a fear of "going crazy" or losing control (American Psychiatric Association [APA], 2000, 2013). The cognitive symptoms intricately related to the development of the anxiety disorders are more related to processing difficulties—for example, making distorted attributions and having unrealistic anticipation of future events—than to difficulties with maladaptive cognitions (Hofmann, Alpers, & Pauli, 2009). Many of these responses reflect a fight, flight, or freeze response associated with extreme apprehension and fear.

Findings on the functioning of emotions in relation to the brain are instructive in elucidating the dynamics of anxiety. Greater clarity has emerged on the decades-long discussion of whether individuals first experience an emotion such as fear and subsequently become cognitively conscious of the feeling, or if the perception of threat precedes the affective and physiological response associated with anxiety. We know more of the amygdala's central role in "appraisal of meaning, processing social signals and activation of emotion" (Siegel, 2012, p. AI-2) based on its capacity to receive signals from all the senses (i.e., visual, hearing, tactile, olfactory, and gustatory; Debiec & LeDoux, 2009). Based on the information from the senses, the amygdala swiftly sends signals to the hypothalamus and brainstem, which then trigger the release of the hormone cortisol, often before cognitive appraisal can occur. Misappraisals of sensory information can mistakenly set off a series of physiological responses that are the basis of an anxiety reaction. Knowledge about the role of the amygdala in orchestrating responses from several parts of the brain in reaction to experience, and the sequences that occur, is invaluable in understanding anxiety responses, particularly in relation to the identification of treatment approaches. Recognition of the coexistence of fear and anxiety in an individual's responses in some anxiety disorders constitutes one of the diagnostic advantages in the *Diagnostic and Statistical Manual of Mental Disorders* (*DSM*®).

Prevalence of Anxiety Disorders

Anxiety disorders represent the most common incapacitating mental health disorders. They are often diagnosed along with other disorders, such as mood disorders and substance abuse, and are often accompanied by somatic conditions. Specific phobia is the most prevalent, with a 6% to 12% range of lifetime prevalence (Kessler, Ruscio, Shear, & Wittchen, 2009). The prevalence of the early onset of anxiety disorders and their presence prior to the onset of many depressive or substance abuse disorders highlight the importance of treating anxiety to limit the development of the other disorders (Onate, Xiong, & McCarren, 2009). The fact that anxiety disorders can pose a significant risk for suicide is all too often underestimated.

Lifetime prevalence rates for anxiety disorders range from 8% to 29% (Kessler et al., 2005) in mental health settings; they are potentially higher in primary care settings (Chavira, Stein, & Roy-Byrne, 2009). The greater presence of interdisciplinary teams in primary care settings associated with the implementation of the Patient Protection and Affordable Care Act (ACA) could potentially increase effectiveness in making treatment more accessible. Anxiety rates are higher than those of mood disorders, which have a prevalence rate of 20.8%; impulse control disorders, with a 24.8% rate; and substance abuse disorders, with a 14.6% rate (Kessler et al., 2005). There is some indication that generalized anxiety and panic disorders are the most often diagnosed. Prior to the publication of the *DSM-5* (APA, 2013), there was concern that the new criteria would result in an increase of prevalence rates (Kessler et al., 2009).

DSM-5 DIAGNOSTIC CRITERIA

The *DSM-5* changes signal shifts in assumptions regarding the nature of anxiety. The heightened attention to the role of both fear and avoidance in the experience of anxiety and the specific inclusion of fear as criteria for anxiety, broadens our understanding of anxiety. This broadened view supports the perspective of the role of physical arousal associated with the subjective experiences of fear and anxiety, and how physical experience can be now seen as preceding the cognitive awareness of anxiety.

The changes in anxiety disorders include features aimed at addressing a wider range of factors that can assist in individualizing a client's condition. These factors can have a role in the development of the disorder and increase our understanding of how the person experiences her disorder. For example, the interaction between genetic and environmental factors and cultural context is essential to understand in the development of a disorder. An individual's explanation of his condition and how it developed is critical for clinicians to explore. Broadening diagnostic criteria to address the diverse meanings of behavior related to cultural context are essential in order for the DSM to serve its basic functions.

The shift in the *DSM-5* from a categorical to a dimensional diagnostic data-gathering process affords greater, expanded scope of flexibility in the identification of behaviors associated with specific criterion, and in inclusion of a client's cultural context. The move away from a bifurcation (in which the symptoms is either present or absent) format used in the *DSM-IV-TR* (APA, 2000) promotes exploration of a wider scope of behaviors and assists in illuminating psychosocial complexities in individuals' lives. Emmelkamp and Power's (2009) review of research on phobias and panic points out the possible "genetic architecture" of anxiety disorders and also how dimensional assessment can be helpful with the classification of anxiety disorders in particular (p. 49).

The anxiety disorder cluster in the *DSM-5* reflects a major reorganization of this disorder group. Several disorders have been removed from this classification and placed into their own new discrete criteria sets or chapter. Disorders that had previously been in another criteria set have been moved into the anxiety disorder grouping. In addition, newly developed disorders are included in this classification. Posttraumatic Stress Disorder is now in its own separate chapter, "Trauma- and Stressor-Related Disorders," which includes Acute Stress Disorder. Also, Obsessive-Compulsive Disorder is now in the Obsessive-Compulsive and Related Disorders classification. Newly included in the trauma criteria set are Separation Anxiety Disorder and Selective Mutism, which were formerly in the Other Disorders of Infancy, Childhood, or Adolescence. The following will identify specific changes of disorders in this classification group and review their current criteria.

The *DSM-5* "Anxiety Disorders" include the following: Separation Anxiety Disorder, Selective Mutism, Specific Phobia, Social Anxiety Disorder (Social Phobia), Panic Disorder, Panic Attack Specifier, Agoraphobia, Generalized Anxiety Disorder, Substance/Medication-Induced Anxiety Disorder, Anxiety Disorder Due to Another Medical Condition, Other Specified Anxiety Disorder and Unspecified Anxiety Disorder.

In line with the *DSM-5* framework, formulations of disorders and clustering of disorders aim to highlight internalizing and externalizing factors, and sequence disorders in relation to a developmental continuum. Thus, "Anxiety Disorders" begin with Separation Anxiety and Selective Mutism. Although there is variation on the presence of specifiers and criteria, all disorders include specifiers on duration and level of impairment.

Separation Anxiety Disorder

In the *DSM-5*, Separation Anxiety Disorder was moved into the "Anxiety Disorders" chapter. The move from Disorders Usually First Diagnosed in Infancy, Childhood, or Adolescence in the *DSM-IV-TR* into the *DSM-5* anxiety classification broadens this diagnosis to include adults, and modifies onset to include ages older than 18. Eight criteria are identified and at least three must be met. The eight criteria address symptoms, such as worry about attachment figures' well-being, loss of that person, accidents that could separate the anxious individual from that person, reluctance to go out alone, or to go to sleep when separated from the attachment figure. In instances in which criteria are met, severity and course of the disorder must be identified. Two other criteria address *duration* (i.e., at least 4 weeks in children and adolescents, and more than 6 months in adults), and *level of distress or impairment*. The last criteria, D, addresses the relevance of alternate diagnoses. In instances in which criteria are not met, and a clinician believes the core disorder is separation anxiety but does not observe sufficient symptoms, the diagnostic narrative can read "Unspecified Separation Anxiety Disorder."

Selective Mutism

The move of Selective Mutism, formerly in "Other Disorders of Infancy, Childhood, or Adolescence," to "Anxiety Disorders" is based on evidence that many minors with selective mutism display anxiety. The criteria remain basically the same in the *DSM-5* as in the *DSM-IV-TR*; the criteria address failure to speak in particular social situations, even though speaking occurs in other situations. Other criteria address level of functioning, for example, when there is interference with educational or occupational achievement or with social communication; and required duration is at least 1 month. Criteria address differential diagnosis in relation to two areas. For one, there is assessment of external factors that could explain the behavior, such as limited knowledge of the expected language; and second, there is exploration of other disorders that could explain the communication problem, such as a communication-based disorder, an autism spectrum disorder, or a psychotic disorder.

Specific Phobia

Similar to the *DSM-IV-TR*, the *DSM-5* identifies the main aspects of Specific Phobia as fear or anxiety that is related to a particular situation or object. The major change in the *DSM-5* is the deletion of the prior age requirement of 18 years or younger. Narrative in the *DSM-5* identifies increased incidence of phobias with an aging population, tendency of phobias to occur with medical concerns, and their increased presence as quality of life declines as the rationale for the basis of inclusion of all ages. The minimum of a 6-month duration remains the same in the *DSM-5*.

Specific Phobia is a marked or persistent fear of specific objects or situations in which mere exposure to situations perceived as threatening provokes anxiety to the degree that situations are avoided or endured with great apprehension (APA, 2013). Specific phobia is one of the most common anxiety disorders, estimated to have a lifetime prevalence rate of 12.5% (Kessler et al., 2005). The types of fear or avoidance identified in the *DSM-5* (i.e., animal, natural environment, blood-injection-injury, situational, and other) remain in the *DSM-5* as specifiers. The animal and natural environment subtypes often have a childhood onset. The blood-injection subtype is further differentiated by *International Classification of Disease* (*ICD*)-based criteria regarding whether the fear arises from fear of blood, fear of injections and transfusions, other medical care, or injury.

Criteria also address severity, such as phobic objects or situations that consistently provoke fear or anxiety, avoidance, or an excessive response that is persistent and often lasts 6 months or more. Level of impairment and differential diagnosis are also conducted by assessing functioning in social, occupational and other domains, and differential diagnosis.

Social Anxiety Disorder (Social Phobia)

Social Anxiety Disorder (SAD) was formerly called Social Phobia in the *DSM-IV-TR*. Changes include removing a criterion for individuals over 18; now there is no age requirement. Criteria include excessive fear or anxiety, and a

6-month requirement for symptom duration. The "generalized anxiety" specifier in the *DSM-IV-TR* has been replaced with a *performance*-only specifier, meaning the fear is related specifically to public speaking or performance. The signature qualities of Social Anxiety Disorder are an intense fear or anxiety in social situations in which an individual may be appraised by others and fears negative appraisal. The anxiety extends to a fear of demonstrating any anxious feelings or putting others off.

The fear of social situations and magnitude of fear and anxiety that can precede events sets this disorder apart from common anticipatory anxiety. The fear of embarrassment in social situations can lead to sufficient stress that individuals will avoid the feared situation rather than experience intense distress. Other criteria focus assessment on the level of distress or impairment and on distinguishing the behavior from other possible disorders or connection to substance use or medication. Koyuncu et al. (2014) found that "about ninety percent of the SAD patients have at least one comorbid disorder ... the most frequent comorbidity was major depression" (p. 368).

Panic Disorder

In the *DSM-5*, Panic Disorder was changed to delete the *DSM-IV-TR* qualifiers related to Agoraphobia. Thus, Panic Disorder and Agoraphobia are now distinct from each other. This move was based on evidence that many individuals with Agoraphobia do not present with panic symptoms. The *DSM-5* criteria focus on noting whether the panic attacks are recurrent, their physical symptoms, duration of the concern and worry, and possible compromised functioning (i.e., change in behavior). Consistent with other *DSM-5* diagnoses, criteria focus on exploration of other possible explanations (i.e., differential diagnosis) for the panic attack, such as substance use or a medical condition, and the possibility that another mental disorder best explains these symptoms.

The *DSM-5* defines a panic disorder as repeated unexpected attacks that are characterized by abrupt and intense fear or discomfort that peaks within minutes. Panic Disorder no longer includes panic attack as a specifer; panic attacks are now assumed to be a symptom. Expected panic attacks can be evoked by predictable triggers, meaning the individual is aware of the capacity of a situation to incite a panic attack. In the *DSM-5*, panic attack specifiers are no longer confined to Panic Disorder. Panic attack specifiers promote the clinician's gathering information on severity, course, and comorbidity both with Panic Disorder and with *all* other DSM disorders. However, consistent with the *DSM-IV-T-R*, the specifiers include a broad range of physiologically and psychologically distressing symptoms, such as pounding heart, sweating, trembling, nausea, and fear of dying or losing control. The move in the *DSM-5* to distinguish Panic Disorder as distinct from Agoraphobia, shifts the attention to the attack symptoms, their predictability, severity, and differential diagnosis. Severity is noted by criteria related to continued worry about other panic attacks or effects of the worry, for a month following the attack. This can lead to unusual and maladaptive efforts to avoid future panic attacks.

Findings on individuals who present with panic disorder support the new focus in the *DSM-5* on the term *heat sensations* rather than *hot flushes* for the purpose of greater cultural relevance and clinical accuracy (Craske et al., 2010). There is evidence that onset of panic disorder most frequently occurs between the ages 20 and 24, but it can also occur in childhood or after the age of 45 (APA, 2013). Risk and prognostic factors are known to include temperament, environmental triggers, and genetic and physiological factors (APA, 2013). Discussion in the *DSM-5* highlights potential culturally based explanatory models that individuals utilize to understand their responses, such as "nervios" for Latinos and emphasizes the necessity of comprehending an individual's fears and anxieties within the context of her culture.

Panic Attack *Specifier*

The *DSM-5* identifies panic attack symptoms as a specifier to all disorders rather than confining them only to panic disorder. Panic attacks vary in quality in relation to physical and psychological responses. They may include limited attack symptoms, unexpected or "uncued" attacks, and situationally predisposed attacks. These distinctions address features of the panic attack that deal with the number of symptoms present, panic attacks that occur in locations that are presumed to be safe, attacks evoked by known feared sources, and attacks often but not always associated with specific situations (Antony, Federici, & Stein, 2009).

Panic attacks can awaken one out of sleep, can occur in calm states, and have a capacity to peak within minutes. Attacks are distinguished by the onset of intense discomfort and fear that can rapidly peak in intensity, and have a significant role in differential diagnosis. The *DSM-5* identifies two areas of risk and prognostic factors. For one, temperament characterized by "proneness to experiencing negative emotions" and tendency "to believe that symptoms of anxiety are harmful" is viewed as a risk factor. Second, environmental factors, such as smoking, interpersonal stressors, or stressors related to physical well-being, are associated as risk and prognostic factors.

Cognitive and behavioral models of panic attacks differ in their explanations of the dynamics of attacks. Although the cognitive model views panic attacks as a function of a "catastrophic misinterpretation" of physical and psychological reactions (e.g., chest pains mean a heart attack), behavioral models view the panic attack as a conditioned reaction to physical responses (Hoffart, Sexton, Hedley, & Martinsen, 2008). The former views individuals as learning to become afraid of bodily sensations following a panic attack, based on a misappraisal of their responses as connected to catastrophic outcomes (Nazarian & Craske, 2008); and the latter views panic as aroused by a conditioned response to body changes (i.e., assessment focuses on cognitions or bodily sensations). These various perspectives are significant in that they form the basis for determining different approaches to treatment. A focus on perceptions by the cognitive model leads to interventions that aim to change the interpretations of body responses, whereas a focus on panic as a conditioned response leads to treatment aimed at behavioral change, using desensitization processes to decondition the panic response.

Agoraphobia

In the *DSM-5*, Agoraphobia is no longer linked as a specifier to Panic Disorder. The *DSM-5* inclusion of Agoraphobia as a codable disorder is based on evidence that many individuals who experience agoraphobia, do not experience panic symptoms (APA, 2013). Overall, the criteria in the *DSM-5* are similar to those in the *DSM-IV-TR* with a few minor changes. There is a greater focus in the *DSM-5* on the presence of fear or anxiety in specific types of situations, severity of impairment, duration, presence of a medical condition, and differential diagnosis.

Behavioral features associated with agoraphobia include an intense fear or anxiety engendered by exposure or anticipated exposure to a range of situations including public venues, open spaces, confined spaces, crowds, or being away from home alone. The discomfort can arise from fear that individuals cannot leave or get help if they become overwhelmed and/or feel incapacitated by panic-like symptoms. The excessive magnitude of the symptoms in relation to a situation distinguishes this response from a response that can be construed as sensible. This focus encourages greater exploration of an individual's perceptions of his experience, particularly in relation to the sociocultural context of the episodes.

The *DSM-5* change to a new classification for Agoraphobia represents efforts to improve diagnostic effectiveness. This change places greater attention on avoidance behaviors and exploration of behaviors other than those associated with the panic attacks.

Generalized Anxiety Disorder

The *DSM-5* Generalized Anxiety Disorder criteria are similar to the *DSM-IV-TR* criteria. The few changes are minor. There is greater attention to the symptoms' relationships to several domains of one's life (e.g., work and social), elimination of the possibility that symptoms are related to physiological origins, and differential diagnosis. In addition, the *DSM-5* does not contain Overanxious Disorder of Childhood. Described as incessant worry and anxiety about normal life events, generalized anxiety disorder (GAD) is characterized by excessive apprehension about areas of one's life, such as family, health, finances, and school or work difficulties. GAD is the most common anxiety disorder and one of the most difficult to treat (Robichaud & Dugas, 2009). It is considered a chronic state that cycles in and out of symptomatic behavior. The intensive apprehension persists for several months, creates an edgy feeling and/or muscular tension, and leads to avoidance of situations that cause worry, inordinate amounts of time in preparation for situations one worries about, procrastination, and/or a constant need for reassurance from others. The worries associated with the disorder are notable for being excessively difficult to control, and are overreactions to feared events and outcomes (Antony et al., 2009, p. 7).

Co-Occurring Disorders

Chavira et al.'s (2009) review of the research on the comorbidity of anxiety disorders points out that more than half of individuals have an anxiety disorder.

KEY POINTS

1. Anxiety disorders are the most common mental disorders.
2. Anxiety may be related to internal or external stimuli and varies in intensity from person to person. The *DSM-5* aims to support greater distinction between internalizing and externalizing responses and emphasizes a dimensional versus a categorical approach to assessing symptoms.
3. Anxiety disorders are characterized by a combination of excessive arousal of fear and avoidance of the feared object or situation.
4. All anxiety disorders have physiological, cognitive, and behavioral components.
5. An anxiety disorder often co-occurs with depression and/or substance use; thus, early identification is important.
6. It is always essential to assess for suicide risk.
7. Agoraphobia is a diagnosis with a distinct set of criteria, separate from Panic Disorder.
8. Greater attention is focused on the individual's capacity for insight regarding anxiety symptoms.
9. Descriptive terms need to be culturally relevant, and the clinician needs to inquire into the client's unique cultural perspective on anxiety symptoms.

Substance/Medication-Induced Anxiety Disorder

The *DSM-5* (APA, 2013) Substance/Medication-Induced Anxiety Disorder is similar to the *DSM-IV-TR* Substance-Induced Anxiety Disorder, in that the focus remains on determining that the symptoms of panic or anxiety are outcomes of the effects of a substance resulting from drug abuse, medication, or exposure to a toxin. New language explicitly specifies symptoms developing during or soon after substance use withdrawal, or following exposure to medication and the capacity of the substance to produce the identified symptoms (APA, 2013). In addition, there is more precise narrative on alternate explanations for the symptoms and a caveat regarding not to utilize a substance intoxication diagnosis when panic attacks and anxiety symptoms are prominent. *ICD-9-CM* (World Health Organization, 1976) and *ICD-10-CM* codes, respectively, require identification of type of substance and level of severity. Key points are that panic or anxiety can occur in relation to intoxication or withdrawal depending on the type of substance. Differential diagnosis assessment promotes exploring substance intoxication and withdrawal, however, it also focuses on anxiety disorder, delirium, and anxiety disorder due to another medical condition, and the medical condition's diagnostic criteria. These criteria highlight the presence of panic attacks or anxiety, and symptoms that result from another medical condition.

In line with the elimination of Not Otherwise Specified (NOS) from the *DSM-5*, the new Other Specified Anxiety Disorder includes specifiers. Likewise, Unspecified Anxiety Disorder refers to symptom presentation that does not meet full criteria and the clinician chooses not to specify why criteria are not met but includes a description of presenting symptoms (APA, 2013, p. 233).

DSM-5 changes collapse several criteria for the purpose of creating more consistency across anxiety disorders and improving clinical assessment by inclusion of the fear response and emphasis on active avoidance or endurance of symptoms. Narrative also was changed to highlight how both fear and anxiety can be out of proportion to the perceived danger and that individuals may not recognize their symptoms. The *DSM-5* changes are clearly extensive. The challenges to reflect the complexity and prevalence of anxiety reactions across the globe and in various cultures are essential to explore.

CURRENT THINKING ABOUT THE ETIOLOGY, COURSE OF DISORDERS, AND COMORBIDITY

There is substantial research on factors that cause or predispose individuals to an anxiety disorder and on factors that affect the health and illness of specific populations. Significantly, because anxiety disorders—as compared with mood disorders—are known to have an onset early in life, they co-occur with other mental disorders as the primary diagnosis and are rarely recognized and responded to quickly. However, it is important that anxiety disorders be treated early to forestall the possible development of other disorders (Kessler et al., 2005, 2009). For example, the finding that many adolescents who are diagnosed with an anxiety disorder also present with substance abuse issues (Zimmermann et al., 2003) highlights the importance of early intervention to prevent the development of disorders that could have lifelong consequences (Kendall & Kessler, 2002). Specific phobias are diagnosed more often in children, adolescents, and young adults (Emmelkamp & Wittchen, 2009). Findings of motor functioning impairment scores for children with anxiety disorders also suggest greater attention to effective assessment and treatment planning (Skirbekk, Hansen, Oerbeck, Wentzal-Larsen, & Kristensen, 2012). Mohr and Schneider (2013) propose that the *DSM-5* organizational shift to highlighting the developmental sequence of disorders requires assessment protocols that are sensitive to developmental pathways.

There is insufficient evidence that would point to a single etiological factor accountable for the development of the complexity and diversity that abounds in anxiety disorders (Antony et al., 2009). Contemporary thinking is building on prior knowledge about the role of physiological factors (e.g., genetics) and the environment (e.g., learning, physical, and social environment) by exploring more biopsychosocial factors, including the environment and behavior (cognition, affect).

The majority of behavioral health professions now utilize diagnostic approaches that emphasize a biopsychosocial perspective (Antony et al., 2009) directing clinicians to review biological (e.g., genetics, health status, and brain function), psychological (e.g., cognitive, affective, and behavioral), and social (physical and social environmental) factors. This perspective is premised on a person–environment interaction perspective that emphasizes contributions by the individual (choices), environmental factors, and the interaction between the two. This approach suggests that greater attention be given to factors arising from the individual's environment that may be highly influential in shaping the personal perception of self, options available to the individual, and/or decision making. For example, it is increasingly clear that factors, such as poverty and abuse, introduce formative influences that can constrict and limit individual perceptions, choices, and functioning.

Generalized Anxiety Disorder

Several factors are recognized as having a role in the development of GAD, including genetic predisposition, histories of trauma early in life, and/or poor attachment (Borkovec, Alcaine, & Behar, 2004; Bowlby, 1982). Poor interpersonal skills have been proposed to have a role in persistence of the disorder (Sibrava & Borkovec, 2006). However, it is also recognized that there is insufficient research on the development of the disorder than is needed for the advancement of more effective treatment (Robichaud & Dugas, 2009).

Kessler et al. (2009) propose that the course of illness "has been less well studied in epidemiological studies of anxiety disorders than either prevalence or age of onset" (p. 21). Kessler and colleagues proceed to point out that available data infer that anxiety disorders can be equally "persistent throughout the life course" (p. 22) and that variation in the intensity of the disorder might be related to the specific co-occurring anxiety disorders that present. Niles, Lebeau, Liao, Glenn, and Craske (2012) tout the *DSM-5* changes that emphasize dimensionality measures and use of measures regarding self-report on percentage of the day individuals worry and number of identified worry domains as effective measures for severity of symptoms.

Co-Occurring Disorders

Chavira et al.'s (2009) review of the research on the comorbidity of anxiety disorders points out that more than half of individuals with an anxiety disorder are diagnosed with an additional disorder. Approximately 33% to 76% of individuals with anxiety disorders are diagnosed with multiple anxiety disorders (Rodriguez et al., 2004); about the same proportion are also diagnosed with a depressive disorder (Nisenson, Pepper, Schwenk, & Coyne, 1998; Olfson et al., 2000; Roy-Byrne et al., 1999), and approximately 15% are also diagnosed with substance abuse disorders (Grant et al., 2004; Rodriguez et al., 2004). Marmorstein (2012) found that substance use disorders were preceded by social phobia or panic disorder, onsets of agoraphobia could occur prior to some substance use, and generalized anxiety disorder could follow the development of substance use disorders.

Risk and Protective Factors

Each anxiety disorder is associated with a unique set of risk factors. Taylor's (2006) review concluded that although the cause of panic disorder is not known, genetic factors and fear oversensitivity, exposure to trauma, and substance abuse could have a role.

KEY POINTS

1. Early exposure to trauma, antisocial behavior, and socioeconomic stress increases the vulnerability to an anxiety disorder.
2. Genetic factors make some individuals more physiologically reactive than others.
3. The course of anxiety through the life span is less well known than onset, and the etiology is complex and varied.
4. Substance abuse and anxiety disorders have a complicated inter-relationship, in that anxiety symptoms can be caused by substance abuse, and individuals can abuse substances to cope with anxiety symptoms.

EVIDENCE-INFORMED PRACTICE

Psychopharmacology and Anxiety

Medications target the physiological experience of anxiety (Bentley & Walsh, 2006/2014): motor tension (shaking, feeling restless and/or exhausted, and tensing one's muscles), autonomic nervous system hyperactivity (racing heart, sweating, clamminess, shortness of breath, frequent urination, and nausea), and hypervigilance (startle response, feeling edgy, irritability, and sleep disturbance). Medications in current use are benzodiazepines, beta-blockers, and buspirone. Antidepressants are also often used in conjunction with anti anxiety medication as the biological causes of anxiety and depression are often thought to overlap. Benzodiazepines (e.g., Xanax, Librium, Klonopin, Tranxene, Valium, and Atavan, among others) act quickly (within 30 min) to block central nervous system stimulation related to emotions. The clinician should be aware that these medications can become addicting over time; the development of tolerance to dosage and effect varies among individuals. Common side effects include dizziness, drowsiness, confusion, headache, irritability, and sometimes impaired muscle coordination. Some clients complain of impaired task performance and transient amnesia; less commonly, clients report diminished sexual drive and impaired vision.

Buspisone (Busbar) is a newer medication acting to balance serotonin levels. This medication is often favored for patients who have experienced negative side effects after benzodiazepine use, especially elders, as Busbar is not addictive and does not produce psychomotor, withdrawal, or cardiac problems. Some patients complain of dizziness shortly after taking Busbar; headache, nausea, nervousness, and insomnia are reported less often. Busbar is not yet available in generic form and, as a result, is expensive.

Beta-blockers (atenolol, metoprolol, nadolol, and propranolol), originally developed and widely used in the treatment of hypertension, are prescribed, at lower doses, in the treatment of anticipatory anxiety. These medications reduce the physical sensations associated with anxiety, such as rapid heartbeat, shaking hands, and dry mouth, without causing confusion. They are not addicting, but are prescribed less often than other anxiety drugs because their effectiveness lasts only a few hours. Beta-blockers are contraindicated for persons with cardiac problems or asthma.

Although antianxiety drugs may help restore biological balance by promoting better sleep and reducing the intensity of symptoms, they run the risk of creating psychological dependency on medication if used exclusively. Psychological interventions that promote coping skills to manage anxiety are important, in conjunction with medication, to promote the client's sense of self-efficacy and empowerment.

Psychological Treatments

Exposure and response prevention therapy has gained recognition in treating anxiety disorders. This approach emphasizes the creation of a hierarchy of fears, subscribes to the view that anxiety is a thought as well as a behavioral problem, and addresses avoidance as well as assurance-seeking behaviors. The client is helped to face the feared situation at increasing levels of intensity while preventing himself from responding with avoidance. Other treatments known to be effective include interoceptive exposure for Panic Disorder and Agoraphobia, Social Phobia, and Specific Phobias, as well as for Posttraumatic Stress Disorder and Obsessive-Compulsive Disorder (Parsons & Rizzo, 2008). Activities are also utilized to address the management of symptoms. Interoceptive interventions are exercises that initiate and recreate the physiological changes aroused by the disorder; however, this is done within a treatment context that paces the exposure and provides the needed support. For example, with panic disorder, individuals can be directed to regulate breathing, hyperventilate, or run in place. For agoraphobia, individuals can be encouraged to go to particular places alone and/or to locations that can cause psychological and emotional discomfort. On the other hand, individuals with social phobia can be directed to initiate interactions with others; for a specific phobia, treatment focuses on graded exposure to the specific fear, such as particular animals or heights.

The perspective proposed by Foa and Kozak (1986) is that fear associated with a memory is adaptive when the threat is real, in that fear leads to efforts to escape. However, when the cues are not realistic, fears can be evoked in harmless situations and are easily triggered; when this occurs, the reactive behavior becomes maladaptive. The treatment aim is to activate the maladaptive response and provides new information that is integrated with the fear response and is evoked when fear is experienced. The aim is to help individuals "confront safe but anxiety-evoking situations to overcome their excessive fear and anxiety" (Foa, Hembree, & Rothbaum, 2007, p. 1). Interventions include normalizing the reactions, education about what to expect, breathing exercises, repeated in vivo exposure to situations and/or objects the person may be avoiding, and prolonged exposure via imagery to the trauma memory. Effective use of this treatment involves clinical knowledge of when and with whom to use this approach. Interestingly, virtual reality is gaining some recognition as building on the imaging intervention and is described as more effective than exposure via imagination (DeAngelis, 2009).

There is increasing discussion on the effectiveness of mindfulness training for various anxiety disorders. Vollestad, Nielsen, and Nielson's (2012) review of the literature points out that mindfulness and acceptance-based interventions' (MABI) focus on observation and acceptance of one's behavior has the advantage of providing an "emphasis on strategies that alter an individual's relationship to his or her internal experience," in contrast with modifying the cognition alone, as is done with CBT (p. 252). There is also a beginning exploration of repetitive transcranial magnetic stimulation (rTMS) with anxiety disorders, to reduce withdrawal-related feelings and enhance approach-related feelings (Machado et al., 2012).

Earlier, we discussed how treatments for panic and other anxiety disorders often focus on misappraisals of uncomfortable body sensations and the individual's level of discomfort tolerance. Clinical observations on how discomfort intolerance can result in increased reactivity (i.e., the development of symptoms) underscore the importance of exploring these misappraisals in the diagnostic process (Schmidt, Anthony, Cromer, & Buckner, 2007). Treatment for panic disorder focuses on specific fears and the generalized chronic anxiety that often accompanies the disorder by making aversive events more predictable and thus manageable. One effective strategy is to aim for lessening the conditioned response to a particular context or situation by recognizing cues that lead to symptoms (Fonteyne, Vervliet, Hermans, Baeyens, & Vansteenwegen, 2009). Virtual-reality interventions have shown effectiveness with posttraumatic stress disorder and are becoming a common, effective treatment for anxiety and specific phobias (Parsons & Rizzo, 2008).

The chronic, excessive worry, and associated levels of distress and impairment experienced by individuals with GAD are the focus of research and clinical interventions. Five models of GAD that are helpful in understanding the disorder and identifying relevant treatment and intervention plans include the Avoidance Model of Worry and GAD (AMW), the Intolerance of Uncertainty Model(IUM), the Metacognitive Model (MCM), the Emotion Dysregulation Model (EDM), and Acceptance-Based Model of Generalized Anxiety Disorder (ABM; Behar, DiMarco, Hekler, Mohlman, & Staples, 2009). These five models integrate and acknowledge various gradations of worry and deal with difficulties in the self-monitoring of responses to various experiences, emotional processing, the stressfulness of ambiguity, negative attributions about worrying, coping with intense emotions triggered by the anxiety, and negative reactions to subjective experiences.

Behar et al. (2009) suggest that a wide variety of strategies are relevant as treatment goals for GAD, including self-monitoring of personal experience and behaviors, relaxation, desensitization, education, and assessment of negative beliefs. Introduction to alternative ways of coping, other than worrying, and strengthening emotional regulation are valuable. Hozel et al. (2013) describe how mindfulness-based stress reduction (MBSR) can lead to fronto-limbic changes that assist in managing emotion and thus assist in symptom reduction. Lee and Orsillo (2014) suggest that mindfulness can enhance cognitive flexibility with this population.

Empirical findings guide us in learning and understanding more about a disorder; likewise, issues related to diversity expand our diagnostic process to understand the worldview of the individual and its role in the development and treatment of his or her disorder.

KEY POINTS

1. Treatment interventions variously target the ability to manage the physiological fear response, confront avoided situations, and alter negative cognitions.
2. Key issues include the ability to tolerate discomfort and ambiguity.
3. All interventions involve a form of exposure.
4. The internal experience and interpretation of anxiety symptoms are important to understand in the context of the client's culture.

EQUITY AND DIVERSITY ISSUES

Several issues are identified in the discussion of the need for greater knowledge about the role of culture in the development and maintenance of anxiety disorders. Antony et al. (2009) point out that although research on the effects of culture are in a preliminary stage, there is strong support for the view that "religious beliefs, norms, gender expectations, and illness perceptions" of culture influence the presentation of symptoms (p. 10). As a worldview that embodies values regarding what is good, what is bad, and how to live, culture influences the meanings that individuals ascribe to the psychological and somatic responses that the *DSM* defines as anxiety symptoms.

Asmal and Stein's (2009) review of research on anxiety disorders in different cultures proposes that there are universal psychobiological factors that influence the development of anxiety disorders; however, it is essential to understand the role of gender, ethnicity, and social factors in the manifestation of anxiety disorders. Research on how culture influences the development and expression of anxiety disorders has led to findings that anxiety disorders appear across cultures, and that expression in various cultures is remarkably different (Antony et al., 2009). For example, Hinton and Good (2009) propose that cultures vary in the meanings ascribed to sensations related to panic disorders; cultures also differ regarding which sensations are feared and to what degree fear is aroused.

The role of culture, ethnicity, and other factors (e.g., socioeconomic and marginalization) bears closer examination in light of research on health outcomes of members of traditional cultures who immigrate to developed nations. Findings demonstrate that there is a shift toward the development of problems with nutrition, mental health, and substance abuse for some immigrants (Alegria et al., 2008; Borges et al., 2009; Grant et al., 2004; Vega et al., 1998). Alegria et al. (2008) found that U.S.-born Latinos had higher rates of many psychiatric disorders, such as anxiety and both mood and substance disorders, compared with Mexican immigrants.

In relation to gender differences, women have a significantly higher risk for anxiety disorders than men (Asmal & Stein, 2009; Kessler et al., 2005). A meta-analysis by Bekker and van Mens-Verhuist (2007) found that women are four times more likely than men to develop agoraphobia and twice as likely to develop panic disorder. Moreover, women were three times more likely to develop both panic disorder and agoraphobia.

To address cultural and diversity issues, the following presents some questions to use as prompts in diverse settings; additional information is contained in the Cultural Formulation interview:

1. In what ways can anxiety or nervousness pose problems for you? Please describe how these feelings of anxiety or nervousness affect you on an everyday basis.
2. What do you understand to trigger your feelings of anxiety?
3. What do you feel makes your anxiety get better (Onate et al., 2009)?

KEY POINTS

1. Women are at higher risk for anxiety disorders than men.
2. Culture influences the meaning individuals give to their anxiety symptoms, what sensations are feared, and how intensely they are experienced.
3. The partnering of traditional mental health professionals with cultural healers can promote true recovery, which involves the individual's reconnection with her community.

Empowering, Resiliency-Based Diagnosis and Interventions

There is much room for the introduction of strength-based approaches to the treatment of anxiety disorders. Most research on treatment is based on data from adults in Western cultures and focuses on generalized anxiety disorder; there is little data on effective treatments with children or elders, or on best treatments for co-occurring disorders (Antony et al., 2009). In addition, there is insufficient research on agoraphobia, panic disorders, and panic attacks (Schmidt et al., 2013). Relevant research methodology must incorporate contextual and diversity factors for effective individualized diagnosis. A strength-based approach recognizes the unique needs of specific populations based, at the least on ethnicity, gender, ability, and age.

Attention to gender-based anxiety disorder issues related to rape, domestic violence, and abuse have broadened the recognition of healing factors to include a wider range of interventions. The interventions, as singular activities or in combination, include insight-oriented therapy, peer support, and self-advocacy activities, such as self-defense training. Many of these reflect an empowerment practice approach. The reader is referred to Johnson (2009) for an excellent summary of these integrative, empowering interventions.

KEY POINTS

1. Strength-based approaches are characterized by empowering interventions, including body work, self-care/defense, and peer support. Moreover, the focus on wellness and recovery highlights the significant role of self-care in coping with anxiety.
2. Little research exists on effective, strength-based approaches with elders or on co-occurring anxiety and substance use.

CASE STUDY WITH AND WITHOUT THE DIVERSITY/RESILIENCY FORMULATION

James was a 39-year-old software designer working on the West Coast for a large aeronautics company. He had been employed there in research and development ever since grad school (about 10 years), had received positive mentoring from his supervisor, the vice president of a large company division, and earned consistently positive performance evaluations. About a year prior to his referral to a clinical social worker, James's supervisor had urged him to apply for an opening in middle management, which would require him to supervise a research team of engineers and other scientists. James had declined the promotion offer, but his supervisor persisted and encouraged him to apply again when a similar position opened up. Flattered by his supervisors' faith in him, James applied for and received the promotion.

Immediately upon assuming the new management position, however, James experienced insomnia, recurring nightmares with themes of helplessness and disaster, fatigue, and a feeling of dread upon wakening and having to go to work. He broke into a cold sweat in anticipation of leading a management meeting and felt even worse (as if he was going to faint and/or urinate in public) when he had to make a presentation to other departments in the corporation or to potential funding sources. He became noticeably more irritable with his wife and three children at home and began to drink a few beers at night to calm his nerves. Although there was no outward corroboration that he was failing in his new position, inwardly James felt fraudulent, doubting his competence, and inwardly preoccupied with thoughts that he was making a fool of himself. He rebuffed his wife's attempts to explore what was wrong and increasingly felt he was failing his family, as they had celebrated his promotion with great excitement. Overwhelmed by anxiety and shame, James withdrew from social gatherings, except to attend his children's parent–teacher conferences and school performances, and seemed to retreat into a shell at home alone in his den, reading books or watching TV. Exasperated and worried, James's wife, Martha, insisted that he see a mental health professional and, when he refused, made an appointment for him with a highly respected clinical social worker, and insisted that he keep it. She had waited patiently for over 6 months and worried that things were getting worse, not better, with time.

In the intake interview, the social worker learned that James had been considered a shy, anxious child. He had trouble adjusting to kindergarten, preferring to sit alone by himself and suck his thumb, and his parents had briefly consulted a psychologist in order to cope with his refusal to leave home in the morning to attend school. James was nevertheless very bright and well liked by his teachers throughout all of his educational experiences, due to his conscientiousness and quiet curiosity. He had been raised on the East Coast in a boisterous Irish Catholic family, the third of four brothers, with a younger sister. His lively extended family loved sports; holidays were filled with laughter and raucous games of touch football and sarcastic but loving humor and warmth.

Although he had felt loved by his parents, James experienced himself as a disappointment to them, especially with respect to his father, a police officer, who had obviously been proud of James's athletically gifted brothers but less able to connect easily with this introverted, sensitive, mathematically gifted son. During his elementary years, James often missed school due to "an upset stomach" until the school nurse advised his parents to make him come to school and allowed him to "rest" in her office if he felt unwell. James preferred to read a book by himself rather than to go outside to play during recess and did not volunteer for leadership roles in school, but did excellent academic work and received accolades, especially for math and science. In high school, he participated in robotics, science, and chess clubs, at the encouragement of his teachers, where he made a few, similarly shy friends. He continued to avoid large social gatherings, and remained a "loner" in college and grad school, considered by peers to be a "brain" and respected for his intellect. James met Martha in a college class and responded to her warm attempts to draw him out and her genuine respect for his honesty and intelligence. James and Martha married after grad school and had three children. James's circle of friends and activities had always been limited to situations in which he felt comfortable and psychologically safe until his recent promotion. Martha considered James to be a "worry wart" who tended to ruminate about his health, family finances, and the welfare of his wife and children, but the couple had managed over the years to tolerate and adapt to each other's personalities.

DSM-5 Diagnosis

300.22 Generalized Anxiety Disorder

James worries excessively about a number of things (finances, work, his health, his wife, and his children) and has been unable to control his worries (Criteria A and B). He has exhibited several of the symptoms listed in Criterion C in the *DSM*—fatigue, sleep disturbance, irritability—and is experiencing a great deal of distress. This diagnosis offers no specifiers or severity indicators. James appears to have a highly sensitive temperament and to be an introvert by nature. He has struggled with anxiety symptoms for years, beginning in early childhood, without severe enough impairment to warrant treatment, except for his parents' brief encounter with a psychologist when James was in kindergarten. From the information given, it appears unlikely his current anxiety symptoms are caused by substance abuse or a medical condition, as he has been in good health and has no history of substance abuse. He may be at risk for the latter, however, as he is coping with anxiety by "drinking a few beers" in the evening.

Some clinicians might give James a secondary diagnosis of social anxiety disorder (300.23), perhaps with the added specifier of "performance only," but the social anxiety he displays appears to be triggered by an exacerbation of underlying chronic anxiety symptoms, which are more characteristic of GAD, which is thought to be related to an inborn sensitive temperament. The specific symptoms related to work performance, however, would need to be addressed in treatment regardless of what diagnostic label is applied to James.

Intervention Without the Diversity/Resiliency Formulation

The social worker explains her diagnostic thinking to James, reassures him about how common anxiety symptoms are, and gives him information about both generalized anxiety disorder and social anxiety disorder. She carefully assesses for symptoms of depression, suicidality, and substance abuse. She refers James to a psychiatrist for a medication evaluation and for help in ruling out any medical problem that may be causing his symptoms. The psychiatrist may suggest the use of an anxiety medication, such as Xanax, which may or may not be helpful to James, as it might leave him feeling tired and depressed. Depending on the severity of James's anxiety at work, he may be given a brief medical leave and/or encouraged to request his old job back. If James were willing, the social worker would help him utilize cognitive behavioral therapy to identify the connection between his physiological responses and accompanying thoughts (predicting disaster and humiliation) and to engage in practices, such as relaxation techniques, to remain on the job and calm himself. Over time, it is hoped that James would be better able to control his symptoms and either remain on the job or transfer to one better suited to his temperament.

Adding the Diversity/Resiliency Formulation to James's Diagnosis and Treatment

Intrapersonal: James has a superior IQ, is an honest, conscientious person of integrity, who values taking responsibility. His personal performance in academic and work settings has been of a high quality throughout his life. He has always been interested in science and activities such as chess and reading.

Interpersonal: James has maintained a small circle of friends with whom he feels comfortable due to common interests. He is devoted to his wife and children. His socializing is valued by others, who consistently respect his integrity and intelligence.

Community: Despite his shy nature, James is a thoughtful and helpful neighbor in his community and is viewed as a "family man."

Spiritual: A Roman Catholic, James attends mass regularly with his family. His participation in the church is minimal, unlike Martha, who is active on several church committees.

Cultural: James has an ambivalent relationship with his Irish Catholic extended family. On the one hand, he is proud of his Celtic roots; on the other, he associates his Irish identity with lively parties, heavy drinking, and sports bars, which make him uncomfortable.

Would Treatment Planning Change If the Diversity/Resiliency Formulation Were Incorporated?

Because James is such an introverted fellow whose life appears largely circumscribed by work and family, the Diversity/Resiliency Formulation might at first glance appear less useful than in more dramatic or varied case presentations. Thinking about the diversity/resiliency factors from a position of strength and empowerment, however, encourages the clinician to be creative, to "think outside the box." For example, in the case of *intrapersonal* characteristics, James could be encouraged to value, rather than disparage, his thoughtful, introverted nature and to reframe his quieter leadership style as an asset to his employer. His social worker could recommend reading, such as the recent bestseller *Quiet* (Cain, 2012), which could be an empowering experience for him. James could combine traditional relaxation and CBT techniques with a genuine empowering view of his personal style as useful and necessary in a world of extroverts. To break his social isolation, James could also be encouraged to re-engage in his former pursuits of chess and robotics with a few interested friends on a regular basis. His social worker could refer James to a Toastmaster's chapter for help in leading meetings and making public presentations. By participating in this group, James would feel less alone and less stigmatized. These activities might nudge James effectively toward better functioning in the *interpersonal* realm. It is unlikely that James will suddenly shift in his participation in church activities. But, *spiritually*, James could be encouraged to take a more forgiving, accepting attitude toward himself and his struggles. Rather than to view himself as pathologically defective, he could consider himself with compassion as a member of an imperfect and marvelously varied human community. In the *cultural* arena, James could be encouraged to explore his Irish Celtic identity in an intricate way, to encounter famous Irish poets who were shy and introverted, and to study the meaning of hospitality in Celtic identity, which goes beyond boisterous partying to a deeper sense of fellow feeling with all of humanity, an attitude which leaves plenty of room for anxious personalities like James's. (*Authors' note:* James is a composite of several psychotherapy clients who responded well to these empowering interventions and were ultimately able to thrive on the job.)

The Diversity/Resiliency Formulation is not meant to perform miracles and is often subtle in its relevance and effects. What is does offer, especially for clients like James, is a shift in perspective from one in which the focus is pathology and the amelioration of symptoms (a necessary and often lifesaving endeavor) to one that adds an appreciation for and acceptance of oneself, which can reduce the client's sense of shame and empower him to embrace life's challenges from a position of greater personal strength and increased hope. Clients with GAD have usually lived under a cloud of dread and self-doubt much of their lives, and shifts in perspective, though small at first, can nudge them in a more life-affirming direction.

SUMMARY

Anxiety disorders are the most common types of disorders that present in clinical and health care settings. Hill, Joubert, and Epstein (2013) pointed out that the level of comorbidity of chronic health issues and anxiety warrants systematic inquiry into the level of stress and behavioral health concerns as part of emergency room procedures. Some of the subtypes (e.g., phobias and generalized anxiety) share both anxiety and fear responses, which are proposed to receive equivalent attention in the *DSM-5*. A strong theme in the literature is the necessity of early identification of this type of disorder in children and adolescents owing to its frequent occurrence with substance abuse and the development of other disorders later in life. Many changes proposed in current *DSM-5* discussions will sharpen thinking about diagnostic considerations and systematic integration of prompts that will encourage exploration of cultural factors. However, the role of culture in shaping and defining fears and anxieties and the importance of an assessment of client strengths as well as pathological symptoms in the diagnostic process requires further development of diagnostic protocols, as would, for example, be provided with the Diversity/Resiliency Formulation data-gathering efforts.

DISCUSSION QUESTIONS AND ACTIVITIES

1. Assume you are working in a clinic that provides mental health services to all age groups. How would you approach diagnosing a child's fear of spiders?
2. What meaning might the child's culture or level of acculturation contribute to your thinking about this case?
3. What approach would you take in assessment and treatment if the child were of the American dominant culture? If the child were an immigrant? If the parents were immigrants and the child was born in the United States?
4. What questions would you ask to explore the child's strengths in managing this fear?
5. How would you explore how the child's and family's cultural context views this phenomenon, and if there are any culturally based treatments that are viewed as helpful by the family?
6. In your work setting, does the assessment process routinely include questions exploring the presence of substance abuse along with anxiety, with respect to the cause or effect relationship between anxiety and substance use? If not, how might you suggest procedural changes to bring this about?
7. Describe how you would work in a collegial manner with a psychiatrist who is prescribing medication for the treatment of anxiety for one of your clients? How would you engage in a dialog about the differential usefulness of behavioral, culturally relevant, or strength-based approaches in the context of medical/pharmacological treatment?
8. Imagine that you have been asked to develop a support group in an integrated care setting for persons diagnosed with a variety of anxiety disorders and their family members. Make an outline of the psychoeducational information you would want to include. Consider how you would integrate empowering activities that would promote an awareness of diverse cultural perspectives, interject fun, and active behavioral

experiments in the group meetings in a way that would promote self-efficacy and hope.

WEB RESOURCES

http://intl-tmt.sagepub.com
http://isstdheadquarters@isst-d.org
www.adaa.org
www.apa.org/journals/tra
www.nimh.nih.gov/healthinformation/anxietymenu.cfm
www.nimh.nih.gov/health/topics/anxiety-disorders/index.shtml
www.nimh.nih.gov/health/publications/anxiety-disorders-listing.shtml
www.nimh.nih.gov/science-news/science-news-about-anxiety-disorders.shtml
www.nimh.nih.gov/health/publications/anxiety-disorders/index.shtml
www.nimh.nih.gov/health/publications/anxiety-disorders/how-to-get-help-for-anxiety-disorders.shtml
www.nimh.nih.gov/health/publications/mental-health-medications/what-medications-are-used-to-treat-anxiety-disorders.shtml
www.nimh.nih.gov/health/topics/generalized-anxiety-disorder-gad/index.shtml
www.nimh.nih.gov/topics/topic-page-social-anxiety-disorder.shtml
www.nimh.nih.gov/health/publications/social-phobia-social-anxiety-disorder/index.shtml
www.nimh.nih.gov/health/publications/when-fear-overwhelms-panic-disorder/complete.pdf
www.nimh.nih.gov/health/publications/post-traumatic-stress-disorder-ptsd/nimh_ptsd_booklet.pdf
www.nimh.nih.gov/health/topics/coping-with-traumatic-events/index.shtml
www.nimh.nih.gov/health/trials/prevention-of-mental-disorders.shtml
www.search.nimh.nih.gov/?q=Anxiety+Disorders&entqr=0&ud=1&sort=date%3AD%3AL%3Ad1&output=xml_no_dtd&oe=UTF-8&ie=UTF-8&client=internet_frontend&proxystylesheet=internet_frontend&site=internet_collection&btnG.x=15&btnG.y=5

REFERENCES

Alegria, M., Canino, G., Shrout, P., Woo, M., Duan, N., Vila, D., … Meng, X. L. (2008). Prevalence of mental illness in immigrant and non-immigrant U.S. Latino groups. *American Journal of Psychiatry*, *165*, 359–369.

American Psychiatric Association. (2000). *Diagnostic and statistical manual of mental disorders DSM-IV-TR* (4th ed., text rev.). Washington, DC: Author.

American Psychiatric Association. (2013). *Diagnostic and statistical manual of mental disorders DSM-5* (5th ed.). Washington, DC: Author.

Antony, M. M., Federici, A., & Stein, M. B. (2009). Overview and introduction to anxiety disorders. In M. M. Antony & M. B. Stein (Eds.), *Oxford handbook of anxiety and related disorders* (pp. 3–14). New York, NY: Oxford University Press.

Asmal, L., & Stein, D. (2009). Anxiety and culture. In M. M. Antony & M. B. Stein (Eds.), *Oxford handbook of anxiety and related disorders* (pp. 657–677). New York, NY: Oxford University Press.

Behar, E., DiMarco, I. D., Hekler, E. B., Mohlman, J., & Staples, A. M. (2009). Current theoretical models of generalized anxiety disorder (GAD): Conceptual review and treatment implications. *Journal of Anxiety Disorders*, *23*, 1011–1023.

Bekker, M. H. J., & van Mens-Verhuist, J. (2007). Anxiety disorders: Sex differences in prevalence, degree, and background, but gender-neutral treatment. *Journal of Gender Medicine*, *4*(Suppl.), S178–S193.

Bentley, K., & Walsh, J. (2014). *The social worker and psychotropic medication: Toward effective collaboration with clients, families, and providers*. Belmont, CA: Brooks/Cole. (Original work published 2006)

Borges, G., Breslau, J., Su, M., Miller, M., Medina-Mora, M., & Aguilar-Gaxiola, S. (2009). Immigration and suicidal behavior among Mexicans and Mexican Americans. *American Journal of Public Health, 99*(4), 728–733.

Borkovec, T. D., Alcaine, O. M., & Behar, E. (2004). Avoidance theory of worry and generalized anxiety disorder. In R. Heimberg, C. Turk, & D. Mennin (Eds.), *Generalized anxiety disorder: Advances in research and practice* (pp. 77–108). New York, NY: Guilford Press.

Bowlby, J. (1982). *Attachment and loss.* New York, NY: Basic Books.

Cain, S. (2012). *Quiet: The power of introverts in a world that can't stop talking.* New York, NY: Random House.

Chavira, D. A., Stein, M. B., & Roy-Byrne, P. (2009). Managing anxiety in primary care. In M. M. Antony & M. B. Stein (Eds.), *Oxford handbook of anxiety and related disorders* (pp. 512–522). New York, NY: Oxford University Press.

Craske, M. G., Kircanski, K., Epstein, A., Wittchen, H., Pine, D. S., Lewis-Fernandez, R., ... Hinton, D. (2010). Panic disorder: A review of *DSM-IV* panic disorder and proposals for *DSM-V. Depression and Anxiety, 27*(2), 93–112.

DeAngelis, T. (2009). Virtual healing. *Monitor on Psychology, 40*(8), 36–40.

Emmelkamp, P., & Powers, M. (2009). Neo-Kraepelinian diagnosis: Adequacy for phobias and panic. In D. McKay, J. Abramowitz, S. Taylor, & G. Asmundson (Eds.), *Current perspectives on the anxiety disorders: Implications for DSM-V and beyond* (pp. 41–76). New York, NY: Springer Publishing Company.

Emmelkamp, P. M., & Wittchen, H. -U. (2009). Specific phobias. In G. Andrews, D. Charney, P. J. Sirovatka & D. A. Regier (Eds.), *Stress-induced and fear circuitry disorders, specific phobias* (DSM V, Chap. 4, pp. 77–101). Arlington, VA: American Psychiatric Publishing.

Foa, E. B., Hembree, E. A., & Rothbaum, B. O. (2007). *Prolonged exposure therapy for PTSD: Emotional processing of emotional experiences.* New York, NY: Oxford University Press.

Foa, E. B., & Kozak, M. J. (1986). Emotional processing of fear: Exposure to corrective information. *Psychological Bulletin, 99*, 20–35.

Fonteyne, R., Vervliet, B., Hermans, D., Baeyens, F., & Vansteenwegen, D. (2009). Reducing chronic anxiety by making the threatening even predictable: An experimental approach. *Behavior Research and Therapy, 10*, 830–839.

Grant, B., Stinson, F., Dawson, D., Chou, P., Dufour, M., Compton, W., ... Pickering, R. P. (2004). Prevalence and co-occurrence of substance use disorders and independent mood and anxiety disorders: Results from the National Epidemiological Survey on Alcohol and related conditions. *Archives of General Psychiatry, 61*, 807–816.

Hinton, D. E., & Good, B. (2009). *Culture and panic disorder.* Stanford, CA: Stanford University Press.

Hill, N., Joubert, L., & Epstein, I. (2013). Encouraging self-management in chronically ill patients with co-morbid symptoms of depression and anxiety: An emergency department study and response. *Social Work Health Care, 52*(2–3), 207–21. doi: 10.1080/00981389.2012.737900.

Hoffart, A., Sexton, H., Hedley, L. M., & Martinsen, E. W. (2008). Mechanisms of change in cognitive therapy for panic disorder with agoraphobia. *Journal of Behavioral Therapy, 39*, 262–275.

Hofmann, S. G., Alpers, G. W., & Pauli, P. (2009). Phenomenology of panic and phobic disorders. In M. M. Antony & M. B. Stein (Eds.), *Oxford handbook of anxiety and related disorders* (pp. 34–46). New York: Oxford University Press.

Hozel, B. K., Hoge, E. A., Greve, D. N., Gard, T., Creswell, J. D., Brown, K. W., ... Lazar, S.W. (2013). Neural mechanisms of symptom improvements in generalized anxiety disorder following mindfulness training. *NeuroImage: Clinical*, 2, 448–458.

Kendall, P. C., & Kessler, R. C. (2002). The impact of childhood psychopathology interventions on subsequent substance abuse: Policy implications, comments, and recommendations. *Journal of Consulting and Clinical Psychology, 70*, 1303–1306.

Kessler, R. C., Berglund, P., Demler, O., Jin, R., Merikangas, K. R., & Walters, E. E. (2005). Lifetime prevlaence & age of onset distributions of DSMIV Disorders in the National Co-Morbidity Survey replication. *Archives of General Psychiatry, 62*(6), 59–602.

Kessler, R. C., Ruscio, A. M., Shear, K., & Wittchen, H. U. (2009). Epidemiology of anxiety disorders. In M. M. Antony & M. B. Stein (Eds.), *Oxford handbook of anxiety and related disorders* (pp. 19–33). New York: Oxford University Press.

Koyuncu, A., Ertekin, E., Binbay, Z., Ozyildirim, I., Yukesel, C., & Tukel, R. (2014). The clinical impact of mood disorder comorbidity on social anxiety disorder. *Comprehensive Psychiatry*, 55, 363–369.

Lee, J. K., & Orsillo, S. M. (2014). Investigating cognitive flexibility as a potential mechanism of mindfulness in Generalized Anxiety Disorder. *Journal of Behavioral Therapy and Experimental Psychiatry*, 45, 208–216.

Machado, S., Paes, F., Velasques, B., Teixeira, S., Piedade, R., Ribeiro, P., ... Aarias-Carrion, O. (2012). Is rTMS an effective therapeutic strategy that can be used to treat anxiety disorders? *Neuropharmacology*, *62*, 125–134.

Marmorstein, N. (2012). Anxiety disorders and substance use disorders: Different associations by anxiety disorder. *Journal of Anxiety Disorders*, *26*, 88–94.

Mohr, C., & Schneider, S. (2013). Anxiety disorders. *European Child Adolescent Psychiatry*, 22(Suppl. 1): S17–S22.

Nazarian, M., & Craske, M. G. (2008). Panic and agoraphobia. In M. Hersen & J. Rosqvist (Eds.), *Handbook of psychological assessment, case conceptualization, and treatment* (Vol. 1, pp. 171–203). Hoboken, NJ: John Wiley & Sons.

Nisenson, L. G., Pepper, C. M., Schwenk, T. L., & Coyne, J. C. (1998). The nature and prevalence of anxiety disorders in primary care. *General Hospital Psychiatry*, *20*, 21–28.

Niles, A. N, Lebeau, R. T., Liao, B., Glenn, D. E., & Craske, M. G. (2012). Dimensional indicators of generalized anxiety disorder severity for DSM-V. *Journal of Anxiety Disorders*, *26*(2), 279–86. doi: 10.1016/j.janxdis.2011.12.007.

Olfson, M., Shea, S., Feder, A., Fuentes, M., Nomura, Y., Gameroff, M., ... Weissman, M.M. (2000). Prevalence of anxiety, depression, and substance use disorders in an urban general medicine practice. *Annals of Family Medicine*, *9*, 876–883.

Onate, J., Xiong, G. L., & McCarron, R. (2009). The primary care psychiatric interview. In R. McCarron, G. Xiong, & J. A. Bourgeois (Eds.), *Lippincott's primary care psychiatry*. Philadelphia, PA: Lippincott Williams & Wilkins.

Rodriguez, B., Weisberg, R., Pagano, M., Machan, J., Culpepper, L., & Keller, M. (2004). Frequency and patterns of psychiatric co-morbidity in a sample of primary care patients with anxiety disorders. *Comprehensive Psychiatry*, *45*, 129–137.

Roy-Byrne, P., Stein, M. B., Russo, J., Mercier, E., Thomas, R., & McQuaid, J. (1999). Panic disorder in the primary care setting: Comorbidity, disability, service utilization and treatment. *Journal of Clinical Psychiatry*, *60*, 492–499.

Schmidt, N. B., Anthony, R. J., Cromer, K. R., & Buckner, J. D. (2007). Discomfort intolerance: Evaluation of a potential risk factor for anxiety psychopathology. *Behavior Therapy*, *38*(3), 247–255.

Schmidt, N. B., Norr, A. M., & Korte, K. (2013). Panic disorder and agoraphobia: Considerations for *DSM-V*. *Research in Social Work Practice*, *24*(1), 57–66.

Siegel, D. J. (2012). *Pocket guide to interpersonal neurobiology*. New York, NY: W.W. Norton.

Skirbekk, B., Hansen, B. J., Oerbeck, B., Wentzel-Larsen, T., & Kristensen, H. (2012). Motor impairment in children with anxiety disorders. *Psychiatry Research*, *198*, 135–139.

Taylor, C. B. (2006). Panic disorder. *British Medical Journal*, *332*, 951–955.

Vega, W., Kolody, B., Aguilar-Gaxiola, S., Aldrete, E., Catalano, R., & Caraveo-Anduaga, J. (1998). Lifetime prevalence of *DSM-III-R* psychiatric disorders among urban and rural Mexican Americans in California. *Archives of General Psychiatry*, *55*, 771–778.

Vollestad, J., Nielsen, M. B., & Nielsen, G. H. (2012). Mindfulness- and acceptance-based interventions for anxiety disorders: A systematic review and meta-analysis. *British Journal of Clinical Psychology*, *51*, 239–260.

World Health Organization. (1976). *The ICD-9 diagnosis and procedure codes: Abbreviated and full code titles. 9th Revision (ICD-9)*. Geneva, Switzerland: Author.

World Health Organization. (1992). *The ICD-10 classification of mental and behavioral disorders: Clinical descriptions and diagnostic guidelines. 10th Revision (ICD-10)*. Geneva, Switzerland: Author.

Zimmermann, P., Wittchen, H.-U., Hofler, M., Pfister, H., Kessler, R. C., & Lieb, R. (2003). Primary anxiety disorders and the development of subsequent alcohol use disorders: A 4-year community study of adolescents and young adults. *Psychological Medicine*, *33*, 1211–1222.

FIVE

Traumatic- and Stressor-Related Disorders and the Diversity/Resiliency Formulation

I later learned that a hundred or so people die each year in the U.S. while being put or kept in restraints.... Nothing at the [hospital] had horrified me as much as this did. No single hallucination, no threat of demonic forces or impulses I couldn't control had ever held me hostage like this.

—E. Saks

Posttraumatic stress responses have been recognized since the end of the 19th century, as investigated by Charcot in 1887 (as cited in van der Kolk, 2003). Later, in relation to combat veterans, traumatic disorders were called various names such as "traumatic neuroses" "soldier's heart," "shell shock," or "combat fatigue" (Friedman, 2009a; Kardiner, 1941). Although the experience of Vietnam veterans in the 1960s brought much attention to the trauma responses, Courtois and Gold (2009) propose that it was only in the 1970s, when visibility of the problems faced by Vietnam veterans was combined with the feminist movement's attention to rape, domestic violence, and child abuse, that significant consideration was given to trauma. Interestingly, as we will touch on later, the ubiquitousness of symptoms across diverse trauma survivors has evoked openness in thinking about relevant treatments for diverse groups (e.g., vets, sexual abuse, and rape). Basic features of trauma disorders develop following exposure to an actual or potential life-threatening event. The strong affective changes that can occur as part of the symptomology have led to posttraumatic stress disorder (PTSD) be considered a "disorder of reactivity" (Friedman, 2009b, p. 65). It has also been thought of as a disorder of coping and adaptation due to the behavioral processes associated with posttraumatic stress responses.

PTSD first appeared in 1980 in the *DSM-III* (*Diagnostic and Statistical Manual of Mental Disorders*, 3rd ed.; American Psychiatric Association [APA], 1980), has stimulated a significant amount of research, and over the years has undergone revision of its criteria in each edition of the *DSM*® (Schnurr, 2009). The changes in the *DSM-5* (APA, 2013) are not only significantly different from the *DSM-IV-TR* (2000), but some suggestions are the most substantial changes in the *DSM*. Although the interpretation of trauma early in the *DSM-III* lacked clarity regarding the ubiquity of trauma, its pervasiveness and complexity are now clearly recognized. The study of trauma has been integrated into many behavioral sciences curricula (Courtois & Gold, 2009), yet the need for its integration into behavioral health curricula remains a challenge that has gained increasing attention. It is now well known that all treatment and interventions, regardless of disorder, must be *trauma informed* due to the ubiquitousness of trauma in the lives of individuals.

Trauma is experienced by 60.7% and 51.2% of American men and women, respectively (Kessler, Sonnega, Bromet, Hughes, & Nelson, 1995). Lifetime rates of PTSD in the general U.S. population range from approximately 8% to 14% (Breslau, 1998; Breslau, Davis, Andreski, & Peterson, 1991; Kessler et al., 1995), and women are twice as likely as men to develop PTSD (Kessler et al., 1995). Research indicates that most people recover within 3 months (Rothbaum, Foa, Riggs, Murdock, & Walsh, 1992). PTSD is often associated with other disorders, particularly mood disorders and substance abuse disorders. Kessler et al. (1995) suggest that when PTSD persists a year or more after the traumatic event, it is unlikely to resolve without treatment. The importance of addressing the need for treatment is underscored by Schnurr and Green's (2004) finding that trauma survivors report more health problems as compared with individuals who do not have PTSD.

Trauma symptoms develop in relation to a variety of responses, such as fear, helplessness, or dissociation associated with feeling overwhelmed and being flooded with affect. Trauma does not affect all individuals in the same way, and most resolve the effects within a short period. Factors such as support and prior history of trauma are known to play a role in how individuals respond. Clearly, more information is needed on factors that place individuals at high risk for developing PTSD and for the purpose of the development of more effective individualized treatment.

There is greater attention to psychosocial struggles of diverse trauma survivors, such as veterans and individuals who are reared in high-violence neighborhoods, and to understanding the implications for treatment regardless of source of trauma or shared symptomology, for example, irritability, avoidance, hypervigilance, anxiety, nightmares, difficulty sleeping. Findings on how prolonged and continuous violence, such as childhood abuse, have "led to an expanded conceptualization of the long-term effects of prolonged and repeated interpersonal violence" (Mendelsohn et al., 2011, p. 6). Herman (1992a) developed the concept of *complex trauma*, which refers to prolonged and repeated interpersonal violence and involves "a complex combination of frightening, alienating, and demoralizing experiences in the absence of adequate response or protection" (Grasso, Greene, & Ford, 2013, p. 81). Herman (1992a) proposes that assessment of complex trauma requires inquiry into three possible areas of behavior: (a) different types of symptoms such as somatization, dissociation, and emotional dysregulation; (b) behaviors potentially related to personality disorders characterized by difficulties with relational and identity issues; and (c) vulnerability to additional harm by self or from others. Grasso et al.'s (2013) review of the research points out that complex trauma findings arise from different areas of focus, including adverse childhood experiences, polyvictimization, and cumulative trauma; these "multiple adversities [impact] psychological development," and there is no single diagnostic category that can explain the combination of symptoms (p. 81). The reality is that some individuals experience substantial, ongoing interpersonal trauma in the form of abuse, either by being the victim or by being a witness, and/or by loss and separation from caregivers. Consider, for example, children who live with substance abusing or violent parents, and are repeatedly removed from home, placed in foster care, possibly returned home in attempts at family reunification, removed from home again, and placed in a variety of child welfare settings over a period of years. Even in the absence of obviously harmful experiences, such as sexual abuse, these repeated attachment ruptures can leave emotional scars that result in traumatic disorders.

This perspective highlights how trauma can be cumulative and can result in other subsequent instances of victimization, thus making it distinct from trauma related to one event (Herman, 1992a). Van der Kolk, Roth, Pelcovitz, Sunday, and Spinazzola (2005) proposed Disorders of Extreme Stress Not Otherwise Specified (DESNOS) as trauma that can evolve from experiencing chronic interpersonal trauma at a vulnerable age as a minor. Trauma responses include behaviors such as emotional dysregulation, dissociation, somatization, self-stigma, identification with the perpetrator, relationship difficulties, and doubts about a view of a just world (Mendelsohn et al., 2011). Van der Kolk et al. later developed the conceptualization of Developmental Trauma Disorder (DTD) with the aim of concentrating diagnosis and treatment on the complexity of abuse experience and the implications for development and attachment relationships (Wylie, 2010).

Some individuals may have less interest in activities they were interested in before, have difficulty feeling warmth toward others, and may not be able to relate to a future for themselves (e.g., career, committed relationship, becoming parents). Many experience difficulty sleeping, irritability and/or outbursts, difficulty concentrating, hypervigilance, and heightened startle reactions. For example, the aftermath following the Haitian 2010 earthquake continued to overwhelm the mental health system for months with instances of "earthquake shock" (i.e., a persistent sensation that the earth is still shaking), nightmares, memory lapses, sleep disturbance, and loss of appetite (Sontag, 2010).

There is a growing body of research on the dissociative symptoms often present in PTSD, such as numbing, feeling detached from others, being in a daze, and difficulty remembering (Birmes et al., 2001; Bremmer et al., 1992; Brunet et al., 2001). The dissociative response is immediate, as the event occurs, and can create an altered sense of the experience in relation to "self, time, place, and meaning, which confer a sense of unreality to the event as it is occurring" (Marmar, Metzler, & Otte, 2004, p. 146). These acute dissociative responses, referred to as peritraumatic responses, often include a sense of time slowing down or the feeling that one is in a dream instead of living an all too real and terrifying experience. Numbing involves a sense of depersonalization, splitting off of painful feelings and cognitions, and reducing awareness of one's surroundings. Brooks et al. (2009) propose that although these responses are found to correlate with posttraumatic stress symptoms, there remains a lack of clarity regarding the concept of peritraumatic responses.

Bessel van der Kolk (2005) observes that there are many childhood life experiences, such as significant loss and abuse (emotional and physical), that do not meet *DSM* criteria but can have significant consequences in adulthood. The potential for effects on the development of the mind and brain (e.g., internal working models) can be particularly powerful in their capacity to undermine a child's ability to manage aroused emotional states because of the role of the caregiver as the source of distress. Although there was much advocacy to include DTD in the *DSM-5*, this disorder was not adopted. The *DSM-5* gives greater attention to the diversity of responses related to developmentally induced traumatic responses such as externalizing symptoms (e.g., impulsivity, aggression, acting out, substance use, self-harming behaviors), cognitive or interpersonal difficulties, and somatization (Friedman, 2013). Moreover, there is substantial evidence of other effects such as emotional dysregulation and identity (e.g., effects of loss and abandonment on self-image) difficulties (Ford et al., 2013; van der Kolk, 1987). Mullett-Hume, Anshel, Guevara, and Cloitre's (2008) study, with 9/11 World Trade Center (WTC) children survivors, found that a "history of multiple traumas is a significant and potentially more potent risk factor for psychiatric impairment than the severity of exposure" to an event (p. 106.). Clearly, more attention needs to be given to this proposed disorder as a formative factor that, once identified, can lead to significant early interventions in children's lives.

Posttraumatic growth (PTG) refers to positive changes in trauma survivors that result from struggling with trauma that shatters or undermines significant beliefs and worldviews, and where coping involves critical reflection that leads to the creation of new meanings (Tedeschi & Calhoun, 2004; Tedeschi, Park, & Calhoun, 1998). PTG is proposed to differ from resilience in that resilience relates to rebounding from a traumatic experience, whereas PTG regards a "paradigm shift" involved in meaning making and integrating the experience into one's life (Nelson, 2011). Discussion and research highlights how trauma can tear at individuals' assumptions about fairness, and thus affect their perspective on the world they live in; coping is a complex phenomenon that bears on personal as well as external factors (Tedeschi, Calhoun & Cann, 2007; Zoellner & Maercker, 2006). The finding that there is variation in how individuals respond to trauma, based on the context of the trauma and available support, places great significance on effective assessment and intervention planning.

Dsm-5 Diagnostic Criteria Changes

Several major changes are reflected in the *DSM-5* related to trauma and trauma-related disorders that include a new chapter entitled "Trauma- and Stress-Related Disorders," as well as changes in criteria for several disorders. PTSD is no longer considered an anxiety disorder. The change was made based on observations that psychological distress following a traumatic event does not always reflect anxiety or fear, but rather can cause one to exhibit difficulty experiencing pleasure, disagreeable mood, externalizing anger, aggression or dissociative symptoms (APA, 2013). This change is viewed as an opportunity to enhance differential diagnosis by supporting exploration of PTSD specific symptoms and placing less emphasis on symptoms that are often related to other disorders

(Koffel, Polusny, Arbisi, & Erbes, 2012). In line with the *DSM-5* emphasis on highlighting disorders on a developmental continuum, the new trauma chapter begins with Reactive Attachment Disorder (RAD), which in the *DSM-IV-TR* was located in the chapter entitled, "Other Disorders of Infancy, Childhood, or Adolescence." The following discussion is organized in accordance with the sequence of disorders in this new chapter and thus begins with RAD. The discussion will highlight changes and distinctions between the *DSM-IV-TR* and *DSM-5*.

RAD and Disinhibited Social Engagement Disorder

The *DSM-5* determined these two classifications, RAD and Disinhibited Social Engagement Disorder (DSED), to be two different disorders. RAD *DSM-IV-TR* criteria included subtypes that encompassed both of these disorders (i.e., emotionally withdrawn/inhibited and indiscriminately social/disinhibited). The *DSM-5* criteria for both include similar etiology in relation to neglect and deprivation, repeated changes of primary caregivers and rearing in situations that hinder the formation of selective attachments. These experiences deprive the child of having her needs met and undermine attachment processes by not supporting individualized attachments. Such experiences during their formative years put minors with these disorders at risk for developmental delays, for example, related to cognition and speech. RAD criteria focus on emotionally withdrawn behavior such as not seeking comfort when distressed or not allowing caregivers to soothe. RAD behavior is characterized by minimal responsiveness to others, limited positive affect, and unpredictable episodes of irritability, sadness, or fearfulness. Differential diagnosis is important, particularly in relation to the autism spectrum, presence of symptoms prior to 5 years of age, and a developmental age of at least 9 months; the 9-month requirement relates to a child's capacity to form attachments. Duration and current level of severity are also assessed, along with the age requirement and developmental level. In addition, two specifiers address persistence and current level of severity. Severity level examines how many symptoms are present and their level of manifestation. Minors with an RAD diagnosis who receive effective interventions that introduce a consistent holding environment are viewed as having sufficient resilience to change and adapt. The prognosis for minors with DSED is not as optimistic.

DSED is characterized by behavior in which the child does not display reticence in approaching unfamiliar adults, may act overly familiar, doesn't check in with a caregiver after wandering away, and goes off with unknown adults with little if any hesitation. Differential diagnosis is needed in relation to attention-deficit hyperactivity disorder. Children with DSED may continue to demonstrate symptoms, even though the conditions that evoked the symptoms are alleviated.

Posttraumatic Stress Disorder

A major change in the *DSM-5* criteria for posttraumatic stress disorder (PTSD) is greater criteria specificity regarding having direct experience and/or witnessing an event(s), learning of a traumatic event occurring to a close friend or family member, and in cases of actual or threatened death of close ones, learning that the events had been violent precipitated by an accident. The *DSM-5* eliminated the *DSM-IV-TR* criterion regarding experiencing a response that involved intense fear or horror as some persons do not exhibit this symptom and yet are clearly suffering from the effects of trauma (APA, 2000). The *DSM-5* also broadens the symptom criteria to include difficulty feeling positive emotions.

Three symptom clusters in the *DSM-IV-TR* (i.e., reexperiencing, avoidance/numbing, and arousal) have been modified in the *DSM-5 into* four symptom clusters: (a) reexperiencing, (b) avoidance, (c) persistent negative alternations in cognitions and mood, and (d) alterations in arousal and reactivity. Although there was some reorganization of criteria clusters, the key criteria, such as intrusive, dissociative, avoidance, and arousal symptoms remain.

Avoidance was expanded in the *DSM-5* into two-symptom clusters: avoidance and persistent negative alterations in cognitions and mood. The latter keeps much of the numbing aspects but adds symptoms such as persistent negative emotional state. The *DSM-5* notes that "witnessing" does not include media exposure. Specifiers include whether dissociative symptoms (i.e., depersonalization, derealization) are present, and whether there is delayed expression, meaning symptoms are not manifested until 6 months after the event(s).

PTSD is now more developmentally sensitive and can be applied in *DSM-5* to a child of 6 years old or younger. There are separate criteria for children 6 years and younger, thus addressing preverbal-age children. The section for PTSD for Children 6 Years and Younger includes criteria similar to those for adults (e.g., direct experience or witnessing, intrusion symptoms, avoidance, etc.) however, there are more specific criteria, for example, negative alterations in cognitions.

The *DSM-5* expansion of criteria to include learning about life-threatening experiences of a close relative or friend and exposure to repeated aversive facts applies to first responders or professionals who collect meticulous data of atrocious acts. It is well known that the effects of responses to catastrophes and horrific events, such as airline crashes, can emotionally exhaust first responders and lead to trauma. First responders are often trained teams, such as police, fire, and medical emergency staff, who are the first to arrive on site at disasters. Attention to the needs of first responders in situations in which there is often overwhelming injury and possible death highlights the importance of exploring team members' responses, rather than minimizing or dismissing their significance.

Acute Stress Disorder

Acute Stress Disorder (ASD) results from exposure to actual or imagined life-threatening events. ASD shares several symptoms with PTSD in that it occurs after direct or indirect exposure to life-threatening experiences, such as injury or sexual assault, and has a rapid onset. The symptoms occur within 3 days to a month following exposure to a traumatic event; the distinguishing difference from PTSD is duration of symptoms. As with PTSD the symptoms can include numbing, derealization, depersonalization, and dissociation (Antony,

Federici, & Stein, 2009). The *DSM-5* reflects several changes in ASD criteria that were made to refine the disorder and to enhance specificity. Criterion A includes explicitness regarding whether the trauma was experienced directly, by observing others, or if it was experienced indirectly, for example, by learning that close family or friends experienced an accidental or violent event. Second, the *DSM-5* dropped *DSM-IV-TR* criteria of having intense experiences of "fear, helplessness, or horror." The rationale for these changes is the conclusion that *DSM-IV-TR* criteria overemphasized dissociation. Also there is recognition of the importance of acknowledging the diversity and heterogeneity of responses to direct and indirect trauma events.

The *DSM-5* criteria require that individuals meet a minimum of 9 of 14 symptoms that cluster in five sets. These five sets include intrusion symptoms; negative mood; dissociative symptoms; avoidance and arousal symptoms; recurrent, distressing memories and/or dreams; dissociative reactions in which one can't recall significant aspects of the event or reexperiences it to the degree of losing awareness of one's current surroundings or depersonalization. Dissociation refers to "the splitting off of clusters of mental contents from conscious awareness" (Shahrokh & Hales, 2003, p. 63) and can be experienced as psychological or physical numbing, detachment, or absence of feelings and lessened awareness. Flashbacks are distinguished from intrusive memories by the intense affect, which creates a sense of reliving the traumatic experience and being in the traumatic situation again. Disruptive dreams can include images or feelings related to the event associated with the flooding of affect and the sense of feeling overwhelmed that can occur with traumatic events.

Other possible symptoms include difficulty feeling positive emotions, avoiding memories or situations perceived as potential triggers of distressed feelings, and arousal symptoms such as sleep disturbance, hypervigilance, difficulty concentrating, and/or startle responses. *DSM-5* specifiers address duration, level of distress and/or impairment, and differential diagnostic considerations that clarify the symptoms are not due to other medical condition(s).

Adjustment Disorders

In the *DSM-5*, Adjustment Disorders are viewed as distress responses in which there is an identifiable stressor that can be a discrete event or multiple stressors, as in relationship or occupational difficulties; thus the stressors can be recurrent or ongoing. Stressors are broadened to now include lifestage developmental challenges, or grief reactions resulting from a significant loss in which there is excessive grief. However, there is a separate set of criteria for *persistent complex bereavement*. In the *DSM-IV-TR* Adjustment Disorders were diagnosed in association with disorders in which distress was present in reaction to an external stressor, and presenting symptoms did not meet criteria for a specific disorder. Thus the *DSM-5* takes these disorders more seriously as diagnoses in their own right, deserving of attention and helpful intervention.

DSM-5 criteria require development of the symptoms within 3 months of the onset of the stressor, and sufficient distress that there is impairment in social, occupational, or other significant areas of functioning. Additional criteria include differential diagnosis to eliminate the possibility of other disorders or normal bereavement and discontinuation of the symptoms within 6 months. Specifiers relate to identifying depressed mood, anxiety, mixture of anxiety and depressed mood, disturbance of conduct, mixed disturbance of emotions and conduct, and unspecified meaning in which the behavior cannot be categorized. From a cultural perspective, it is essential to explore whether the behavior falls within normative parameters or is maladaptive. *DSM-5* narrative identifies major depressive disorder, PTSD, and personality disorders as alternate disorders to consider in differential diagnosis. Also, it is pointed out that Adjustment Disorders can be associated with any number of other mental or medical disorders, which can occur if there is no connection between the specific behavior and stressor(s). Despite their shorter duration, adjustment disorders can cause real suffering, including suicidality, and should not be minimized by the clinician.

Other Specified Trauma- and Stressor-Related Disorder

This diagnosis in *DSM-5* refers to symptoms of trauma and other stress-related disorders that cause clinically significant impairment but do not reach the levels of severity required for the diagnosis of a trauma or stress-related disorder. Examples are provided that include delayed onset after 3 months, prolonged duration of more than 6 months, cultural syndrome-based behaviors, and persistent complex bereavement disorder. See the *DSM-5* Section III on Persistent Complex Bereavement Disorder for fuller discussion on the need for further study on this disorder (APA, 2013).

The category of Unspecified Trauma- and Stressor-Related Disorder is also utilized in *DSM-5* for instances in which symptoms may be typical of a trauma- and stressor-related disorder, and affect level of functioning, but do not meet criteria. As noted before, the clinician does not need to specify the rationale for criteria not being met.

CURRENT THINKING ABOUT THE ETIOLOGY; COURSE OF DISORDERS AND COMORBIDITY

Evidence shows that a history of prior trauma, the presence of other mental disorders, and a lack of social support leads to vulnerability to the development of a trauma disorder. Because of this, it is essential to conduct a thorough assessment (Caffo & Belaise, 2003) regarding previous and potential trauma (Schlenger, Jordan, Caddell, Ebert, & Fairbank, 2004). Courtois and Ford (2009) suggest that the high comorbidity of PTSD with other disorders, such as anxiety and personality disorders, and physical health issues (e.g., somatization) require rigorous assessment of areas that were formerly structured into the *DSM-IV-TR* multiaxial assessments. In addition, they suggest the potential effects of PTSD on broad levels of functioning and impairment. Kisiel et al. (2014) observe that the *DSM* does not include a diagnosis that captures the "complex constellation of symptoms often exhibited among children exposed to chronic, interpersonal trauma such as aggressive behavior and multiple placements" (p. 3).

Koenen, Moffitt, Poulton, Martin, and Caspi's (2007) study of early childhood factors that can place an adult at risk for trauma exposure and the development of PTSD included externalizing characteristics (e.g., antisocial behavior, hyperactivity), a family history of mental health issues, and a family history of coping with major difficulties. These researchers also found low IQ and chronic stressors, such as low socioeconomic status, to produce a risk for the development of PTSD. It is significant that although a history of trauma creates a vulnerability to the experience of new trauma, the new experience is not viewed as retraumatization; rather, the experience is viewed as an altogether new trauma with implications for unique diagnosis and treatment planning.

Bryant, Friedman, Spiegel, Ursano, and Strain's (2011) review of research found that most individuals who meet *DSM* criteria for ASD are at risk for the development of PTSD, whereas most people who develop PTSD do not have a history of ASD symptoms. The change in the *DSM-5* to expand ASD criteria and move away from overemphasis on dissociative symptoms is supported by evidence that ASD is best considered in relation to severity of acute stress responses (Bryant et al., 2011). The *DSM-5* changes address concern about the *DSM-IV-TR*'s focus on ASD's anxiety symptoms and promotes exploration of other associated symptoms, such as depression, guilt, shame, anger, and somatic responses (Isserlin, Zerach, & Solomon, 2008).

KEY POINTS

1. Early exposure to trauma, antisocial behavior, and socioeconomic stress increase the vulnerability to life-span psychological and medical disorders.
2. Trauma responses can occur from direct or potential life-threatening experiences, and learning of a close friend or family member having that experience.
3. First responders and professionals who deal with detail on horrific events may be at risk for the development of trauma responses.
4. Greater attention is needed to chronic, ongoing abusive experiences during the formative years in relation to their basis for creating trauma.
5. The *DSM-5* recognizes that young children exhibit effects of trauma differently from adults and underscores the importance of acknowledging and addressing these effects.

EVIDENCE-INFORMED PRACTICE

Recognition of the various types of trauma and heterogeneity in responses places significant importance in effective assessment, diagnosis, and treatment planning. Steel, Dunlavy, Stillman, and Pape's (2011) review of PTSD measures concludes that utilization of a structured clinical interview is more effective compared with scales and checklists. Assessment and diagnostic considerations are key in relation to individualized treatment that attends to what treatment, for whom, and for what purpose. As always, careful listening is most important!

The most utilized approaches in treating trauma are cognitive behavioral approaches, exposure therapy, and psychopharmacology. Cognitive behavioral therapy (CBT) focuses on altering behavior by developing insight into maladaptive connections between thoughts and feelings. Exposure therapy engages the individual in repeatedly confronting the distressful memories until they become desensitized, also called habituation. Another somewhat controversial yet popular approach, eye movement desensitization and reprocessing (EMDR), has the individual focus on the traumatic memory while looking at and following the back and forth motion of the therapist's fingers or another repetitive motion or sound (Shapiro, 2001).

Most interesting is van der Kolk's biopsychosocial perspective on trauma, that is, trauma's capacity to effect the brain in ways that limit the capacity to articulate one's experience (e.g., the speech center is compromised). The difficulty, in van der Kolk's view, is that the brain processes activated by trauma (e.g., fight, flight, or freeze response triggered in the amygdala), can leave individuals continuing to produce stress hormones produced by triggers long after the event has passed. This perspective leads to a treatment approach that focuses on working with somatic responses. This approach is premised on the brain's responses to trauma (e.g., effect on speech center and powerful effects on body responses). See van der Kolk's (2014) *The Body Keeps the Score: Brain, Mind & Body in the Healing of Trauma* for an in-depth discussion on the key role of psychobiology in trauma. Understanding how trauma has impacted their bodies can help trauma survivors better understand their physiological responses to triggers, reduce their sense of shame and aloneness, and motivate them to engage in efforts to sooth themselves more effectively. The long-term effects described by van der Kolk of the body's continuous preparation for fight/flight take on a significant role in treatment planning and have implications for addressing symptoms on psychobiological levels.

A major challenge in treating posttraumatic stress is that trauma affects parts of the brain that compromise the ability to talk about the traumatic event and influences the development of heightened awareness and sensations (hypervigilance). This is particularly challenging in that these symptoms restrict the brain's integrative function of bringing together various cognitive and affective processes, which are the foundation for meaning making and decision making. An approach by Mollica (2006) to the treatment of trauma disorders utilizes the phenomenological method by focusing on "discover[ing] the true nature of (individuals' subjective) clinical problem and the best way of helping them cope with their emotional upset … by abandoning … theories, opinions, prejudices and biases" (p. 15). The point for the clinician is not to narrow her inquiry into the client's experience by limiting herself to prior beliefs about the theories of trauma. This approach has led, for example, to increased attention to fatigue reported by individuals and to developing interventions to regain vitality and energy in one's life (R. Mollica, personal communication, May 20, 2014).

Research suggests that practice with minors in foster care must be informed by a developmental trauma framework for the purpose of identifying the complexity of short- and long-term needs (Kisiel et al., 2014), which if untreated can result in psychiatric and physical difficulties in later life (Felitti et al., 1998). The combination of and relationship between attachment processes and complex trauma is essential to explore due to the possible negative effects on development and functioning (Kisiel et al., 2014). Ford et al. (2013) found that clinicians do not perceive most evidence-based PTSD interventions as helpful for DTD, whose symptoms support more effective diagnosis that includes focusing treatment on psychobiological dysregulation proposed by D'Andrea, Ford, Stolbach, Spinazzola, and van der Kolk (2012).

There is unanimity in the professional community regarding the importance of prevention efforts, recognition that initial distress following a traumatic event may be normal, rather than abnormal, and that most individuals cope by utilizing their support networks. From a treatment perspective it is important to assess for the presence of social support, to create safety, and to provide education that builds awareness about the usefulness of treatment (Litz, 2008). The trauma literature identifies many types of interventions at different stages (i.e., immediate, acute, and chronic) following a traumatic event. Herman (1992b) identified three stages that are essential. First it is critical to establish safety, so that, second, "the healing work of remembrance, integration, and mourning" of losses can occur, and third, the individual can regain her connections with others and her community, in newer self-affirming ways. Virtual-reality interventions are showing increasing effectiveness with PTSD and are also becoming a common, effective treatment for anxiety and specific phobias (Parsons & Rizzo, 2008). Creative, strength-based approaches to the treatment of PTSD include body work, martial arts training, art and dance therapy, journal writing, massage, yoga, and meditation.

Five broad foundational and functional competencies related to trauma-focused and trauma-informed knowledge, assessment, interventions, professionalism, and relational and systems levels of practice provide direction on effective practice (Cook & Newman, 2014). These new competencies build on prior work by various groups and aim to "create minimal standards across a diversity of ages and types of trauma survivors, and across theories" (p. 301). These competencies are intended to be cross-cutting, and integrate individualized treatment with cultural and developmental concerns based on shared decision making that enhances recovery.

EQUITY AND DIVERSITY ISSUES

Treatment of PTSD has not given sufficient attention to healing practices that abound in other cultures, and there is recognition that Western approaches are limited in assessing and understanding trauma in relation to diverse cultures (Wilson, 2007). Many dissociative experiences, such as meditative or hypnotic states, are regarded as normal in some cultures. In addition, culture-specific idioms of distress are known to represent culturally based acceptable expressions and represent culturally relevant characterizations of trauma (Kirmayer, 1996). Draguns's (1996) review of ethnocultural considerations in the treatment of PTSD highlights the importance of not applying treatment strategies thoughtlessly without considering, for example, with children, what might be a variety of their unmet needs and unique concerns.

Considerations of context related to ethnicity, gender, religion, and other factors promotes inquiry into the rituals and practices that individuals and communities may have in place, which they have used before and found effective. For example, the Southeast Asian Hmong culture's shamans and tribal leaders provide valuable resources for learning about the Hmong person's experience of trauma and their reliance on these indigenous spiritual healers for help. Some practices may appear not to have a logical basis for effectiveness; however, a truly consumer-based, culturally respectful approach involves being willing to listen to, explore, and learn about what has worked for the client, family, and community. Herman (1992b) highlights the importance of the final stage of healing as one in which the individual rejoins his or her community. It is essential for clinicians to be informed about these resources, both for short-term treatment and long-term purposes.

Zayfert (2008) focuses on process skills by suggesting that clinical effectiveness in understanding posttraumatic stress in a culture other than one's own requires successful engagement with individuals, learning about their ethnocultural sources of avoidance, numbing, and maintenance of the trauma responses. An understanding of the individual client's context—with its unique values, beliefs, and practices—provides insights into the development of the trauma and its treatment.

Diversity considerations also bring us to considerations regarding elders and possible contributions of ageism in creating risk for what is called relocation stress or transfer trauma (Carpenito, 2000; Warchol, n.d.). Transfer trauma is most often seen with elders moving into care facilities where lack of support and preparation for this major transition can lead to anxiety, depression, confusion, or negative affect. The discussion on the severity of possible outcomes is unclear, that is, whether this life threatening. What is clear is that supports are needed for the transition from potentially lifelong residence to a new facility that should include relationship building, possibly psychotropic medications, and considerations to the reality that the elder may have poor judgment regarding his or her abilities (Carpenito, 2000).

Regarding minors, the *DSM-5* points out how essential it is to understand what is known about child attachment within specific cultural contexts. A culturally relevant perspective with culturally congruent practices will explore values and norms about child-rearing practices and options for coping with challenging situations with children.

The following case study illustrates the trauma experience as endured by many who are court involved and have incarceration histories. All too often, this population is invisible, yet their formative and incarceration experiences can have far-reaching effects if not recognized and addressed in treatment.

CASE STUDY WITH THE DIVERSITY/RESILIENCY FORMULATION

Colin, a 34-year-old, is the third of five brothers who grew up in a northeast urban setting. His parents have remained married, however, the relationship and home life has been marked by marital conflict mainly fueled by his father's alcoholism. The father's drinking was in the form of weekend binge drinking.

Although his father was able to hold his union job as an electrician; his return to the home after the drinking episodes often led to arguments with his older sons, who in defense of their mother would argue with their father. As a middle child Colin ended up a target for his father's angry outbursts, and endured physical and emotional abuse from his father, which left him overly sensitive to criticism in some situations. Although the father went into recovery, the troubled and tense relationship continued between his parents until they divorced when Colin was 24. Colin's middle school and high school years were influenced by his older brother's dropping out of high school in his senior year due to drug use and alcoholism. Even though his interest in computer science and sports caught the attention of his teachers, who recognized his talent with computers and love for soccer, Colin's attendance at school was uneven. His part-time job at a sports shop meant being out until 6 p.m., however, his arrival at home after 9 p.m. on school nights left his mother concerned about possible substance use.

Colin was particularly shaken by his older brother's death by asphyxiation when Colin was 20. The traumatic death devastated Colin primarily because he found his brother's body and had to cope with the first responders. For several weeks following the event, he was distracted by memories to the degree that he spent less time with friends, had nightmares about finding his brother, and would feel like he was reliving the event. It was difficult for him to enjoy the company of his girlfriend, felt troubled when he couldn't remember all the details, and avoided his brother's friends even though they all hung out at the same bar. He had difficulty sleeping and often found he was irritable or had difficulty concentrating. These symptoms eventually subsided after a month. Through considerable effort Colin graduated from high school, began working full time at the sports shop, and became more seriously involved with his girlfriend. Although he drank with friends on weekends and began using some cocaine with his surviving older brother's friends, he was able to sustain employment and continue his relationship to the point where he and his girlfriend began to assume they would eventually marry and talked about having children.

At the age of 23 he was out late one weekend night with his bar buddies and was targeted by a neighborhood group of bikers, apparently based on the fact he had previously dated one of the biker's girlfriends. The attack by the biker startled him to the degree that he feared for his life and battered the assailant so forcefully that the assailant was knocked to floor, hit his head on the bar foot rail, was taken to the emergency room (ER) and pronounced dead due to head trauma. Colin was sentenced to 3 years in prison for involuntary manslaughter. At the end of the first year, a fight broke out in the prison mess hall during lunch by a couple of prisoners sitting next to him. The abrupt explosion of yelling and physical violence, plus flashes of weapons that a couple of prisoners had fashioned in their cells, triggered feelings of panic and vulnerability in Colin. Without thinking, he fought back so aggressively that the officers singled him out as a provocateur of the episode. The correctional staff determined that Colin's behavior required sending him into isolation for 45 days. The isolation was one of the most painful experiences that Colin endured during his imprisonment in that he had derived much of his strength in the past from his limited social interaction with other inmates. While in isolation there were occasions when insects appeared in his cell; he was particularly distressed by this when he observed them around meal time. Although he was generally outgoing, he became more guarded and vigilant following the solitary confinement. Increasingly, following this period of isolated confinement, he showed signs of greater withdrawal and less initiative in interacting with prisoners with whom he had created a bond and served as a protective "enclave" for him. His girlfriend continued to visit; however, she was disappointed that he wrote less and didn't utilize the opportunity to call when it was possible to do so.

When he eventually left prison after 3 years of confinement, he moved in with his girlfriend, Kathleeen. Kathleen had steady employment at a hardware store and Colin was hopeful about returning to school to study computer science, restore their relationship, and purchase a home together in anticipation of marriage. Initially, the relationship was challenged by periods of Colin's withdrawal and inclination to prefer staying in on weekend nights rather than going out with mutual friends or to listen to music. In time, Kathleen felt strongly they needed couple's counseling due to Colin's constant sense of worry, tiredness, restless feelings, difficulty in being able to concentrate to the point of forgetting activities they had planned for, and his occasional irritability and difficulty sleeping. Although he drank on occasion with her and with friends, his behavior did not interfere with their relationship or his job. With some reluctance, Colin agreed to go to counseling and "explore" how it could be useful to their goals. Within a few meetings the therapist suggested that the couple engage in individual treatment first, for a few months, for the purpose of clarifying their needs and perceptions of the relationship problems, and regroup within a few months in couple's treatment.

Within a few weeks of the weekly meetings with Colin, he discussed the life-shattering experience of solitary confinement. He explained that throughout the difficulties with his parent's troubled marriage and domestic violence he could always get away to hang out with his friends or play sports. Not having any options for activities to engage in left him restless and agitated. His attachment to his girlfriend and ties with his parents and younger brothers supported his capacity to cope with his circumstances and even to consider what kind of future he might want. The aim of treatment was to refocus on the goals that he had hoped for, process the feelings that solitary confinement had evoked, and explore other unresolved life issues that could undermine his hopes for his future.

Diversity/Resiliency Formulation Additions to Colin's Diagnosis

Intrapersonal: Insightful, commitment to Kathleen, strong identification with his family and motivation to have his own family with Kathleen; interest in computers, strong sense of identification with community; willingness to recognize and explore painful feelings, which can assist in processing any unresolved issues related to his older brother's death and parents' conflicted marriage

Interpersonal: Capacity for open communication, connection with and positive relationship with Kathleen; sense of responsibility for younger siblings; concern regarding effect of his prison experience on his family, not wanting his brothers to go through the same thing; positive relationship with teachers
Community: Love of sports and connection with that network as well as neighborhood connections
Spiritual: Strong identification with family, particularly brothers; motivation to build a family life with Kathleen, values meaningfulness of relationships
Cultural/Diversity: Working-class roots and values; social identity based in neighborhood connections and value of family

Engagement in individual and couple's therapy could provide a "holding environment" for Colin to identify, at his own pace, unresolved feelings related to a tumultuous home life and devastating loss of his brother. He could explore feelings and personal consequences of his father's departure and brother's traumatic death. Colin may not feel that exploration of these type of feelings fits in with his idea of masculinity or cultural values. Only after recognizing his thoughts and feelings about these events, can he begin to recognize how these experiences may have a role in how he copes. Examination of his experiences while incarcerated can assist in normalizing his responses to solitary confinement and the potential value in processing those experiences. Colin's insightfulness and perceptiveness encourage his motivation to pursue these concerns. With a stronger sense of perspective in recognizing and understanding his feelings, Colin could approach couple's counseling from a position of strength with a willingness to explore his own and Kathleen's needs.

1. If you were Colin's therapist how would you broach the topic of the importance of exploring past experience as a basis of having a stronger relationship with Kathleen? What barriers do you expect you could encounter?
2. What are some areas that you would want him to choose to examine?
3. What concerns do you have regarding possible consequences for Colin if he were not to be open to individual and couple's work?
4. Are there any strength-based, wellness or resiliency-focused interventions that you would consider in your work with Colin and/or in couples work?
5. If Colin and Kathleen went into therapy after they had children. What questions might you have regarding family dynamics, children's needs and/or couple dynamics?

Examples of Empowering, Resiliency-Based Diagnosis and Intervention

Creative, strength-based approaches to the treatment of PTSD include body work, martial arts training, art and dance therapy, journal writing, massage, yoga, and meditation. The reader is referred to Johnson (2009) for an excellent summary of these integrative, empowering interventions.

CASE STUDY WITH AND WITHOUT THE DIVERSITY/RESILIENCY FORMULATION

Sophia, age 17, is a Latina who resides with her parents in a remote rural area in California, and is the older of two children; her brother Joseph is 14. She was referred to therapy by a music teacher in spring semester owing to a significant change in her behavior during her senior year of high school. Sophia had become increasingly distracted, detached from herself and others, and was not following through on her studies to the degree that her grades were affected. The teacher was becoming concerned that this could affect Sophia's graduation in spring and her application to college. Although her parents had not gone to college, they supported her decision to pursue study in a health profession, which left her feeling even more committed to pursuing higher education and not disappointing her family. Sophia's behavior and academic problems were disconcerting to the music teacher, who was a mentor to Sophia and had a role in motivating her to consider applying for university study. Through the teacher's efforts, Sophia took a music class and also joined a group of students who met weekly after school to practice for a performance at the school graduation in May. The teacher was dismayed to see that Sophia began to miss practice sessions and occasionally seemed remote and subdued.

In interviewing Sophia, the therapist discovered that early in fall, Sophia began experiencing difficulty concentrating, irritability, and apprehensiveness manifested in her easily being startled. She reported that her sleep had been disrupted since fall by dreams related to a serious car accident that had occurred the previous spring, in which a cousin had died. Sophia and her family members were in the car. Sophia's father had been driving the family home from evening religious services when a car that ran a four-way stop on a dark, unlit road hit them. Her brother was in the front seat with her father; she and her cousin Gabriela, with whom she was very close, were in the back seat. Sophia, her brother, and her father sustained minor injuries and have since recovered, but Gabriela did not survive. Sophia's boyfriend has been a significant source of support for her emotionally and has helped her stay in contact with her friends.

Sophia began a driver's education course in the fall so that she could assist the family in driving the maternal grandmother to medical appointments and church activities. Once she got her license, however, she became unusually cautious in her driving, particularly at night. As the anniversary date of the accident approached in early spring, she found that she began to avoid roads where the scenes evoked recurrent images of the accident. Some of the images were sufficiently powerful that she felt she was back in the accident's aftermath, when the police and ambulance arrived. Most often the recurrent images are distracting and unexpected; they interfere with Sophia's interactions at school and with friends and family as well as in focusing on her studies. Friends and family notice that she is irritable, has outbursts that are inconsistent with her personality, and occasionally appears remote and detached. Fortunately, they respond with patience and empathy, and support her in whatever ways they can.

Sophia's parents migrated from Mexico almost 20 years ago, met in the United States, and married a few years later. Both parents work; however, they remain undocumented. The mother is the youngest of eight children and comes from a family with a history of domestic violence. At the age of 7 she witnessed her father fatally shoot her mother and wound a brother who attempted to intervene and protect his mother. Sophia's father comes from a home with a predominantly absentee, alcoholic father who did not provide for the children's emotional or material needs, leaving the mother to raise him and a younger sister as a single parent. Although reticent to talk in detail about their histories, both parents promoted independence among their children. In the spirit of encouraging a better life for their offspring, they have been open and communicative about the family history and their experiences.

DSM-5 Diagnostic Impression and Treatment Without Diversity/Resiliency Formulation

Sophia was injured in a fatal car accident that killed her cousin. She experiences distressing memories and dreams, some dissociative reactions (flashbacks), and both experiences distress when driving in areas reminiscent of the accident and avoids the area where the accident occurred. Family notices that she gets startled easily, has difficulty concentrating and doesn't sleep well. She has difficulties studying and feels increasingly disconnected from her immediate and extended family and friends. She is failing in academics and in music practice, and worries that she might not fulfill her dream of beginning college in fall. Although the accident was over a year ago, her responses persist. Sophia does not drink nor use substances, legal or prescribed.

Sophia's DSM-5 Diagnosis Would Be:

PTSD 309.81 (F. 43.10)

With

- Depersonalization (Sophia reports feeling detached from reality).
- Delayed expression (Sophia's behavior changes occurred at least 6 months after the accident)

The weekly sessions between Sophia and the clinician, Alice, began with an individual meeting with Sophia during which Sophia discussed her distress at experiencing recurrent images and occasional flashbacks and her confusion about why she would have such powerful reactions. Sophia stated that she felt she was a strong person who could cope with most upsets and that she thought she had dealt with her cousin's death. She shared with Alice her feelings about the accident as she approached the anniversary date and the possible effects of frequent driving, both day and night, now that she has her license. The meeting also gave Sophia an opportunity to disclose physical reactions, such as nausea and stomachaches, that she felt during and after some of the recurring images; she had not shared these symptoms with anyone for fear of unnecessarily worrying her family. Although family support was a valuable source of affirmation for Sophia, the intensity of the trauma event, combined with added effects of intergenerational loss issues, was overwhelming to her. She experienced severe startle reactions with anything that reminded her of the noise of the accident, and nightmares were recurrent.

The problem areas that Sophia and Alice identified in their treatment planning dealt with the flashbacks, distressed responses, isolation from friends, and failing academic performance. The objectives focused on managing the flashbacks and distressed responses, monitoring her feelings and recognizing triggers, returning to social and academic activities (e.g., music practice) in incremental steps, and making a plan for improving her academic work. The treatment planning also included revisiting grief and loss issues that might yet be unresolved, even though Sophia felt she had dealt with her cousin's catastrophic death. Alice began working with Sophia by applying prolonged exposure techniques related to her feelings and sensations as well as exposure to the conditions (e.g., driving at night) that represented triggers. Sophia was referred to an academic advisory office that provided tutorial services so that she could get the support that she needed to develop and carry out plans to improve her academic performance. She was also referred for a psychiatric evaluation to assess whether medication might be helpful in managing her symptoms; the temporary use of an antianxiety medication was recommended for the purpose of restoring normal sleep patterns, and Sophia was given the choice of a trial of an antidepressant with proven effectiveness in managing trauma symptoms.

Diversity/Resiliency Formulation Additions to Sophia's Diagnosis

Attending to the content suggested by the Diversity/Resiliency Formulation, Alice added the following diagnostic impressions to her assessment of Sophia:

> *Intrapersonal*: High intelligence; motivation for learning in music and in a health profession; identification with parental values related to achievement and personal growth
>
> *Interpersonal*: Strong family and friendship ties; positive relationship with boyfriend; supportive relationships with teachers
>
> *Diversity/Cultural*: Strong intergenerational and extended family identification with grandparents; intergenerational support; work ethic related to parental hopes for a better future for the younger generation; family pride in having overcome significant hardships and trauma before, during, and after the challenges of immigration and acculturation
>
> *Community*: Supportive network and Latino cultural context for identity and connection; involvement in musical performing group. Motivation for a future life that reflects her personal interests
>
> *Spiritual*: Strong identification with family and cultural religious and spiritual practices. Diagnostic information gathered via attention to the Resiliency/Diversity Formulation expanded the exploration of the cultural and social word that Sophia lives in by probing further into her identifications and hopes as well as the meanings of these identifications

As Alice explored the range of activities that Sophia was involved in and the relationships in her life, she began to notice several things about Sophia indicating that she was a buoyant, resourceful, adventuresome adolescent on her way to a bright future when this accident occurred. Alice noted that Sophia was a member of a Latino family with strong cultural extended family bonds and a history of triumph over severe past trauma. Alice talked with Sophia about securing an informed consent from her parents and suggested the possibility of involving her parents and her brother in their therapeutic work, particularly because of their experience with the accident and loss of their niece. The clinician felt it might be important from several perspectives to involve Sophia's family. For one, the close family bonds made it helpful for Sophia's healing to have family support that allowed for openness to talk about the tragedy. In addition, the need for other family members to process their feelings could be assessed, and family meetings or individual sessions for other family members could be suggested. Sophia communicated that her parents are bilingual and agreed to ask her parents to meet with Alice the following week. The parents' work schedules required some planning to coordinate schedules; also, Sophia raised concern about implications of her parent's legal status in relation to their receiving services. Alice emphasized the confidential nature of the interventions and the independence of her therapeutic services from any government agency related to immigration status.

With attuned sensitivity, Alice gradually explored the meanings of the losses experienced by Sophia, her parents, and her brother, and Sophia's understanding of the effects on family life and her response to the trauma. Growing up in a traditional immigrant family immersed Sophia in several traditional practices, such as religious observances, a strong family network, and responsibilities as a granddaughter to the older generation. In addition, she was responsive to her teacher's initiative to engage her in a music group and guidance in career planning toward a professional career. Moreover, Sophia's capacity to continue her relationship with her boyfriend, at a time when she was having difficulty interpersonally, survived based on friendship and strong communication between them. Alice validated the effects of the trauma on all family members and demonstrated positive regard for the family's support of Sophia's recovery as well as for their ability to discuss how the trauma had effected everyone and to support one another in the recovery process. Sophia's family elected to come to two more family sessions and to face their fears by going on short automobile trips to favorite scenic spots that contained memories of happy family outings in the past. They were also encouraged to engage in a mentoring program offered by their local Catholic parish, assisting recent immigrants with a variety of challenges related to acculturation in their new community.

In individual sessions, Alice highlighted Sophia's capacity to continue her relationship with her boyfriend at a time when she was having difficulty interpersonally, emphasizing how this relationship had survived based on friendship and strong communication between Sophia and her boyfriend. As treatment progressed, Alice recognized the importance for Sophia of continuing to see herself as an independent female with professional and intellectual interests (e.g., music) who maintained her strong connections and responsibilities to family; these factors were as significant as interventions dealing with her flashbacks. In time, supporting these roles and rebuilding connections with friends took on an equal focus to techniques addressed at managing the trauma symptoms. Alice also actively encouraged Sophia to engage in vigorous physical exercise and to attend self-defense classes offered at her community center. In consultation with a psychiatrist, Alice and Sophia decided to defer the immediate use of medication in favor of individual and family interventions designed to build self-efficacy for the management of anxiety, to build on Sophia's unique cultural and familial strengths, and to use medication only if her anxiety symptoms became debilitating.

Diagnostic information collected via information gathering on her level of functioning expanded the exploration of the cultural and social world that Sophia lives in by probing further into her identifications and hopes as well as the meanings of these identifications. Sophia's identification with family, church, and hoped- for future provided resources of intrapersonal and interpersonal strengths. The diagnostic assessment might have been limited to a few aspects of her life had an assumption been made that her identification was primarily traditional and acculturation was low. However, on exploring more of her perceptions, feelings, and insights, it became evident that Sophia has a strong bicultural identification that expands her sources of support as well as opportunities for coping (i.e., music, variety of friendships, religion). In the course of treatment, it also became clear to Alice that the significance of Sophia's connections and responsibilities as a friend and family member were sufficiently vital to her that treatment for the posttraumatic stress reactions could be effectively dealt with by both reconnecting her with her support network and utilization of prolonged exposure and exposure techniques that focused on desensitization.

Use of the Diversity/Resiliency Formulation would have helped the clinician to know about and utilize Sophia's strengths from the beginning. Treatment could potentially have focused more quickly and been more helpful at an earlier stage.

- If you were Sophia's clinician, would you have involved the family in her treatment? Explain your rationale for your response.
- What are some areas that you would want to explore for possible effects of the trauma that the clinician did not address?
- What concerns do you have, if any, regarding possible long-term consequences for Sophia that need to be explored?
- Are there other strength-based interventions you would have considered?

SUMMARY

Trauma disorders are viewed as developing following exposure to an actual or threatened life threatening event. The *DSM-5* has expanded this disorder to include learning that loved ones, that is, family or close friends, have experienced life-threatening events. Trauma was first recognized in war-related experiences and subsequently expanded to include a broad range of experiences, such as violence (e.g., abuse, interpersonal violence, rape), and direct or vicarious exposure to violent events as experienced by first responders and other professionals such as police and social workers. Not all individuals who experience these events develop trauma; supportive relationships can make a difference, particularly with children. A significant factor related to healing for all forms of trauma is a strong connection with one's family, support network, and more important, community ties.

Remarkably, the wide range of trauma experiences result in similar responses, yet pose challenges in creating individualized treatment. An awareness of how neurological processes are affected by trauma assists in understanding many of the subsequent symptoms such as difficulty in remembering or articulating the trauma experience. The necessity of integrating trauma-informed assessment and interventions into all practice is increasingly acknowledged in behavioral health practice; trauma can be precipitated in many contexts that don't necessarily involve a specific event, but rather could originate in complex trauma (Herman, 1992a) or disorders of extreme stress not otherwise specified, known as DESNOS (van der Kolk et al., 2005). Interventions include a broad range of treatments such as CBT, REM, structured interviewing, medication, and relaxation-focused mindfulness activities that address the fatigue that can ensue.

DISCUSSION QUESTIONS AND ACTIVITIES

1. In connection with a recent major natural catastrophic event (e.g., earthquake, tsunami, torrential storm), identify the range and type of physical destruction and the losses experienced by individuals, families, and communities. Discuss the types of trauma responses you might expect to hear from individuals and families. Reflect on how you would feel as you listened to their stories and witness their overwhelming affect. How would you respond and how would you begin to assess their mental status?
2. Identify a traumatic event experienced by a community that was initiated by human error or intent (e.g., Santa Barbara/Isla Vista, Columbine shooting, West Virginia Tech shooting, Three-Mile Island, 9/11 Twin Towers attack, Oklahoma City bombing). How would you conduct outreach to the affected community and for what purpose? How would you approach survivors, and what would you assess for? What goals would you have?
3. Consider a major natural catastrophe in another country (e.g., earthquake, storms) where there has been tremendous loss and death and families have been separated. Imagine that you are a Red Cross mental health volunteer who arrives to assist as a first responder. What would you want to learn about the culture and its resources in relation to the supportive networks that might be present or coalesce in response to the catastrophe (e.g., with whom would you meet and what would you ask)? How would you want to approach those networks/support systems in a culturally relevant way, and what would be the focus of your assessment process? How would you go about learning about the culturally based resources that individuals would want to turn to at a time of such loss? Reflect on insights this experience might give you in working with that population of immigrants in the United States.

4. Assume you are working in a clinic that provides mental health services to all age groups. How would you approach diagnosing a child's fear of spiders? What meaning might the child's culture or level of acculturation contribute to your thinking about this case? What approach would you take in assessment and treatment if the child were of the American dominant culture? If the child were an immigrant? If the parents were immigrants and the child was born in the United States? What questions would you ask to explore the child's strengths in managing this fear? How would you explore how the child's and family's cultural context views this phenomenon, and whether there are any culturally based treatments that are viewed as helpful by the family?
5. Consider a White, middle-class couple who appear for treatment in a mental health clinic. The couple had a terrifying experience the previous fall when the rural area they live in was evacuated due to extensive, fast-moving fires. In the process of packing some possessions and driving away, the wife began to have difficulty breathing; she also experienced chest pain, sweating, and nausea. Since that event, she experienced several similar episodes when she was in the family car, smelled smoke from local fireplaces, or drove down the escape road at about the same time of day as when they evacuated. The husband had some immediate emotional reactions to the fire and evacuation experience; however, his responses did not escalate, as did his wife's. What would you explore in your assessment to understand their different responses? What would you want to explore with the wife and the husband in relation to a diagnosis and treatment planning? How would the role of culture (e.g., traditional, dominant) influence you in exploring the diagnosis and treatment?
6. Trauma is a ubiquitous and everyday occurrence in the United States. How have the terrorist attacks of 9/11, the numerous and horrifying school shootings, and the very recent controversies involving police officer shootings of young men of color with the resultant civil unrest, affected you personally? How has trauma impacted your own life in other ways? Reflect on how you have responded to daily TV reports of violence and mayhem. How can you use your own personal awareness to deepen your sensitivity to societal and personal trauma?

WEB RESOURCES

http://intl-tmt.sagepub.com; *Traumatology Journal*

http://isstdheadquarters@isst-d.org; International Society for the Study of Trauma & Dissociation

samhsa.gov/product/TIP-57-Trauma-Informed-Care-in-Behavioral-Health-Services/Most-Popular/SMA14-4816?sortBy=4; Trauma Informed Care (SAMHSA)

www.figleyinstitute.com/indexMain.html; Figley Institute

www.nctsnet.org; National Child Traumatic Stress Network

www.nimh.nih.gov/health/publications/when-fear-overwhelms-panic-disorder/complete.pdf; NIMH Health Publications

www.nimh.nih.gov/health/topics/post-traumatic-stress-disorder-ptsd/index.shtml

www.nimh.nih.gov/health/publications/post-traumatic-stress-disorder-ptsd/nimh_ptsd_booklet.pdf; Posttraumatic Stress Disorder booklet

www.nimh.nih.gov/health/topics/coping-with-traumatic-events/index.shtml; NIMH Health Topics
www.nimh.nih.gov/health/trials/prevention-of-mental-disorders.shtml

REFERENCES

American Psychiatric Association. (1980). *Diagnostic and statistical manual of mental disorders* (3rd ed.). Washington, DC: Author.

American Psychiatric Association. (2000). *Diagnostic and statistical manual of mental disorders* (4th ed., text rev.). Washington, DC: Author.

American Psychiatric Association. (2013). *Diagnostic and statistical manual of mental disorders* (5th ed.). Arlington, VA: American Psychiatric Press.

Antony, M. M., Federici, A., & Stein, M. B. (2009). Overview and introduction to anxiety disorders. In M. M. Antony, & M. B. Stein (Eds.), *Oxford handbook of anxiety and related disorders* (pp. 3–14). New York, NY: Oxford University Press.

Birmes, P., Carreras, D., Ducasse, J., Charlet, J., Warner, B., Lauque, D., & Schmitt, L. (2001). Peritraumatic dissociation, acute stress, and early posttraumatic stress disorder in victims of general crime. *Canadian Journal of Psychiatry, 189*, 649–651.

Bremmer, J. D., Southwick, S., Brett, E., Fontana, A., Rosenheck, R., & Charney, D. S. (1992). Dissociation and posttraumatic stress disorder in Vietnam combat veterans. *American Journal of Psychiatry, 149*, 328–332.

Breslau, N. (1998). Epidemiology of trauma and posttraumatic stress disorder. In R. Yehuda (Ed.), *Psychological trauma* (pp. 1–29). Washington, DC: American Psychiatric Press.

Breslau, N., Davis, G. C., Andreski, P., & Peterson, E. (1991). Traumatic events and posttraumatic stress disorder in an urban population of young adults. *Archives of General Psychiatry, 48*, 216–222.

Brooks, R., Bryant, R., Silove, D., Creamer, M., O'Donnell, M., McFarlane, A., & Marmar, C. (2009). The latent structure of peritraumatic dissociative experiences questionnaire. *Journal of Traumatic Stress, 22*(2), 153–157.

Brunet, A., Weiss, D. S., Metzler, T. J., Best, S. R., Neylan, T. C., Rogers, C., ... Marmar, C. R. (2001). The Peritraumatic Distress Inventory: A proposed measure of PTSD criterion A2. *American Journal of Psychiatry, 158*, 1480–1485.

Bryant, R. A., Friedman, M. J., Spiegel, D., Ursano, R., & Strain, J. (2011). A review of acute stress disorder in *DSM-5*. *Depression and Anxiety, 28*, 802–817.

Caffo, E., & Belaise, C. (2003). Psychological aspects of traumatic injury in children and adolescents. *Child and Adolescent Psychiatric Clinics of North America, 12*, 495–535.

Carpenito, L. J. (2000). *Nursing diagnosis: Application to clinical practice* (8th ed.). Philadelphia, PA: Lippincott.

Cook, J. M., & Newman, E. (2014). A consensus statement on trauma mental health: The New Haven competency conference process and major findings. *Psychological Trauma: Theory, Research, Practice, and Policy, 6*(4), 300–307.

Courtois, C., & Ford, J. D. (2009). Treating complex traumatic stress disorders: An evidence-based guide. New York, NY: The Guilford Press

Courtois, C., & Gold, S. (2009). The need for inclusion of psychological trauma in the professional curriculum: A call to action. *Psychological Trauma: Theory, Research, Practice and Policy, 1*(1), 3–23.

D'Andrea, W., Ford, J. D., Stolbach, B., Spinazzola, J., & van der Kolk, B. A. (2012). Understanding interpersonal trauma in children: Why we need a developmentally appropriate trauma diagnosis. *American Journal of Orthopsychiatry, 82*(2), 187–200.

Draguns, J. G. (1996). Ethnocultural considerations in the treatment of PTSD therapy and service delivery. In A. J. Marsella, M. J. Friedman, E. T. Gerrity, & R. M. Scurfield (Eds.), *Ethocultural aspects of posttraumatic stress disorder: Issues, research, and clinical applications*. Washington, DC: American Psychological Association.

Felitti, V. J., Anda, R. F., Nordenberg, D., Williamson, D. F., Spitz, A. M., Edwards, V., … Marks, J. S. (1998). Relationship of childhood abuse and household dysfunction to many of the leading causes of death in adults: The Adverse Childhood Experiences (ACE) Study. *American Journal of Preventive Medicine, 14*(4), 245–258.

Ford, J. D., Grasso, D., Greene, C., Levine, J., Spinazzola, J., & van der Kolk, B. A. (2013). Clinical significance of a proposed developmental trauma disorder diagnosis: Results of an international survey of clinicians. *Journal of Clinical Psychiatry, 74*(8), 841–849.

Friedman, M. J. (2009a). PTSD and other posttraumatic syndromes. In D. McKay, J. S. Abramowitz, S. Taylor, & G. J. Asmundson (Eds.), *Current perspectives on the anxiety disorders: Implications for the DSM-V and beyond* (pp. 377–409). New York, NY: Springer Publishing Company.

Friedman, M. J. (2009b). Phenomenology of posttraumatic stress disorder and acute stress disorder. In M. M. Antony & M. B. Stein (Eds.), *Oxford handbook of anxiety and related disorders* (pp. 65–72). New York, NY: Oxford University Press.

Friedman, M. J. (2013). Finalizing PTSD in *DSM-5*: Getting here from there and where to go next. *Journal of Traumatic Stress, 26*, 548–556.

Grasso, D., Green, C., & Ford, J. D. (2013). Cumulative trauma in childhood. In J. D. Ford & C. A. Courtois (Eds.), *Treating complex traumatic stress disorders in children and adolescents* (pp. 79–99). New York, NY: Guilford Press.

Herman, J. (1992a). Complex PTSD: A syndrome in survivors of prolonged and repeated trauma. *Journal of Traumatic Stress, 3*, 377–391.

Herman, J. (1992b). *Trauma and recovery*. New York, NY: Basic Books.

Johnson, S. (2009). *Therapist's guide to posttraumatic stress disorders intervention*. San Diego, CA: Academic Press.

Kardiner, A. (1941). *The traumatic neuroses of war*. New York, NY: Paul B. Hoeber.

Kessler, R. C., Sonnega, A., Bromet, E., Hughes, M. H., & Nelsen, C. B. (1995). Posttraumatic stress disorder in the National Comorbidity Survey. *Archives of General Psychiatry, 52*, 1048–1060.

Kirmayer, L. J. (1996). Confusion of the senses: Implications of ethnocultural variations in somatoform and dissociative disorders for PTSD. In A. J. Marsella, J. J. Friedman, E. T. Gerrity, & R. M. Scurfield (Eds.), *Ethnocultural aspects of post-traumatic stress disorder: Issues, research, and clinical applications* (pp. 803–838). Washington, DC: American Psychological Association.

Kisiel, C. L., Fehrenbach, T., Torgersen, E., Stolbach, B., McClelland, G., Griffin, G., & Burkman, K. (2014). Constellations of interpersonal trauma and symptoms in child welfare: Implications for a developmental trauma framework. *Journal of Family Violence, 29*, 1–14.

Koenen, K., Moffitt, T. F., Poulton, R., Martin, J., & Caspi, A. (2007). Early childhood factors associated with the development of post-traumatic stress disorder: Results from a longitudinal birth cohort. *Psychological Medicine, 37*, 181–192.

Koffel, E., Polusny, M. A., Arbisi, P. A., & Erbes, C. R. (2012). A preliminary investigation of the new and revised symptoms of posttraumatic stress disorder in *DSM-5*. *Depression and Anxiety, 29*, 731–738.

Litz, B. T. (2008). Early intervention for trauma: Where are we and where do we need to go? A commentary. *Journal of Traumatic Stress, 21*(6), 503–506.

Marmar, C. R., Metzler, T. J., & Otte, C. (2004). The peritraumatic dissociative experiences questionnaire. In J. P. Wilson & T. M. Keane (Eds.), *Assessing psychological trauma and PTSD* (pp. 144–167). New York, NY: Guilford Press.

Mendelsohn, M., Herman, J. L., Schatzow, E., Coco, M., Kallivayalil, D., & Levitan, J. (2011). *The trauma recovery group: A guide for practitioners*. New York, NY: Guilford Press.

Mollica, R. F. (2006). *Healing invisible wounds: Paths to hope and recovery in a violent world*. Nashville, TN: Vanderbilt University Press.

Mullett-Hume, E., Anshel, D., Guevara, V., & Cloitre, M. (2008). Cumulative trauma and posttraumatic stress disorder among children exposed to the 9/11 World Trade Center attack. *American Journal of Orthopsychiatry, 78*(1), 103–108.

Nelson, S. (2011). The posttraumatic growth path: An emerging model for prevention and treatment of trauma-related behavioral health conditions. *Journal of Psychotherapy Integration, 21*(1), 1–42.

Parsons, T. D., & Rizzo, A. A. (2008). Affective outcomes of virtual reality exposure therapy for anxiety and specific phobias: A meta-analysis. *Journal of Behavioral Therapy*, *39*, 250–261.

Rothbaum, B. O., Foa, E. B., Riggs, D. S., Murdock, T. B., & Walsh, W. (1992). A prospective examination of posttraumatic stress disorder in rape victims. *Journal of Traumatic Stress*, *5*, 455–475.

Saks, E. (2007). *The center cannot hold*. New York, NY: Hyperion.

Schlenger, W. E., Jordan, B. K., Caddell, J. M., Ebert, L., & Fairbank, J. A. (2004). Epidemiological methods for assessing trauma and PTSD. In J. P. Wilson & T. M. Keane (Eds.), *Assessing psychological trauma and PTSD* (pp. 226–261). New York, NY: Guilford Press.

Schnurr, P. P. (2009). The changing face of PTSD diagnosis. *Journal of Traumatic Stress*, *22*(1), 1–2.

Schnurr, P. P., & Green, B. L. (Eds.). (2004). *Trauma and health: Physical health consequences of exposure to extreme stress*. Washington, DC: American Psychological Association.

Shahrokh, N., & Hales, R. E. (2003). *American psychiatric glossary* (8th ed.). Washington, DC: American Psychiatric Publishing.

Shapiro, F. (2001). *Eye movement desensitization and reprocessing (EMDR): Basic principles, protocols, and procedures* (2nd ed.). New York, NY: Guilford Press.

Sontag, D. (2010, March 20). Mental care in Haiti goes from bad to horrid. *New York Times*, p. 2.

Steel, J. L., Dunlavy, A. C., Stillman, J., & Pape, H. C. (2011). Measuring depression and PTSD after trauma: Common scales and checklists. *Injury International Journal of the Care of the Injured*, *42*(3), 288–300.

Tedeschi, R. G., & Calhoun, L. G. (2004). Posttraumatic growth: Conceptual foundations and empirical evidence. *Psychological Inquiry*, *15*, 1–18.

Tedeschi, R. G., Calhoun, L. G., & Cann, A. (2007). Evaluating resource gain: Understanding and misunderstanding posttraumatic growth. *Applied Psychology: An International Review*, *56*(3), 396–406.

Tedeschi, R. G., Park, C. L., & Calhoun, L. G. (1998). Posttraumatic growth: Conceptual issues. In R. G. Tedeschi, C. L. Park, & L. G. Calhoun (Eds.), *Posttraumatic growth: Positive changes in the aftermath of crisis* (pp. 1–22). Mahwah, NJ: Erlbaum.

van der Kolk, B. A. (1987). *Psychological trauma*. Washington, DC: American Psychological Press.

van der Kolk, B. A. (2003). Posttraumatic stress disorder and the nature of trauma. In M. F. Solomon & D. J. Siegel (Eds.), *Healing trauma: Attachment, mind, body, and brain* (pp. 168–195). New York, NY: W. W. Norton.

van der Kolk, B. A. (2005). Developmental Trauma Disorder: Toward a rational diagnosis for children with complex trauma histories. *Psychiatric Annals*, *35*(5), 401–408.

van der Kolk, B. A. (2014). *The body keeps the score: Brain, mind & body in the healing of trauma*. New York, NY: Viking Books.

van der Kolk, B. A., Roth, S., Pelcovitz, D., Sunday, S., & Spinazzola, J. (2005). Disorders of extreme stress: The empirical foundation of a complex adaptation to trauma. *Journal of Traumatic Stress*, *18*, 389–399.

Warchol, K. (n.d.). *Transfer trauma—A real issue for many individuals with dementia*. Retrieved from www.crisis/prevention.com/resources

Wilson, J. (2007). Preface. In J. P. Wilson & C. Tang (Eds.), *Cross-cultural assessment of psychological trauma and PTSD* (pp. xii–xvii). New York, NY: Springer.

Wylie, M. S. (2010). The long shadow of trauma. *Psychotherapy Networker*, *34*(2), 20–27, 50–51, 54.

Zayfert, C. (2008). Culturally competent treatment of posttraumatic stress disorder in clinical practice: An ideographic transcultural approach. *Clinical Psychology: Science and Practice*, *15*(1), 68–73.

Zoellner, T., & Maercker, A. (2006). Posttraumatic growth in clinical psychology—a critical review and introduction of a two component model. *Clinical Psychology Review*, *26*, 626–653.

SIX

Oppositional Defiant Disorder, Conduct Disorder, and the Diversity/ Resiliency Formulation

Good luck to them. I tried for the better part of sixteen years to punish Kevin. Nothing I took away mattered to him in the first place. What's the New York State juvenile justice system going to do? Send him to his room? Tried that. He didn't have much use for anything outside his room or in it; what's the difference? And they're hardly going to shame him. You can only subject people to anguish who have a conscience. You can only punish people who have hopes to frustrate or attachments to sever; who worry what you think of them.

—L. Shriver, *We Need to Talk About Kevin*

The "magic years" of childhood are anything but that for many parents. In our fast-paced, competitive society, those who are faced with meeting the developmental needs of children with diagnosed psychiatric disorders face bewildering choices and circumstances. Idealized accounts of the greater wisdom and maturity acquired by living with children with special challenges belie the incredible stress encountered by their parents, siblings, teachers, and peers, not to mention what is experienced by these children themselves! When family discord, poverty, peer influences, and violence-ridden neighborhoods are added to the mix, the complexity of childhood mental disorders can become overwhelming, not only for children and families but also for researchers, clinicians, and educators.

CHANGES, *DSM-IV-TR* TO *DSM-5*

The DSM®-*IV-TR* (*Diagnostic and Statistical Manual of Mental Disorders*, 4th ed., text rev.; American Psychiatric Association [APA], 2000) devoted a substantial number of pages to the section titled, "Disorders First Diagnosed in Infancy, Childhood, or Adolescence" (APA, 2000). The authors noted that the distinction between the three age groups was for the purpose of convenience and was not meant to imply that childhood and adult disorders can be clearly demarcated or even that these disorders are always diagnosed before adulthood. In addition, other disorders, notably depression, in the *DSM-IV-TR* may be present in children or adolescents but were not placed in this section. This heterogeneous grouping of disorders and their symptoms included learning disorders, mental retardation, motor skills disorders, communication disorders, pervasive developmental disorders, attention-deficit and disruptive behavior disorders, feeding and eating disorders, tic disorders, elimination disorders, and a catchall category entitled Disorders of Infancy, Childhood, and Adolescence Not Otherwise Specified (NOS), which essentially embraced any symptom constellations not sufficient to meet the full criteria for existing diagnoses in the *DSM-IV-T-R* (APA, 2000).

Consistent with research that demonstrates differences between externalizing and internalizing disorders, the creators of the *DSM-5* removed several disorders from the former "Disorders First Diagnosed in Infancy, Childhood, or Adolescence" and created a new chapter, "Disruptive, Impulse-Control, and Conduct Disorders." Oppositional Defiant Disorder (ODD), Conduct Disorder (CD), and Specified and Unspecified Disruptive, Impulse-Control, and CDs (formerly grouped as Impulse-Control Disorders NOS in *DSM-IV-TR*) are now located in the new chapter. The new chapter also contains Intermittent Explosive Disorder, Pyromania, and Kleptomania, disorders previously placed in the *DSM-IV-T-R* chapter, "Impulse-Control Disorders Not Elsewhere Classified." Antisocial Personality Disorder (APD) is listed in both this new chapter and in the chapter titled, "Personality Disorders" in the *DSM-5*; in the latter it is described in detail. All of these disorders have been grouped together in the *DSM-5* because they have in common problems in emotional and behavioral self-control (APA, 2013).

The authors of the *DSM-5* delineate three types or symptom presentations of ODD: angry/irritable mood, argumentative/defiant behavior, and vindictiveness (APA, 2013). In addition, the clinician is permitted to diagnose a child or adolescent with both CD and ODD in the *DSM-5*; this change removes the exclusionary criterion for CD in *DSM-IV-TR*, which did not allow both diagnoses at the same time. Although we will not be addressing intermittent explosive disorder in this chapter, we call attention to a primary change in the *DSM-5* in the type of aggressive outbursts that the clinician should note. In the *DSM-IV-TR*, physical aggression was required for the diagnosis, but in the *DSM-5*, nondestructive/noninjurious physical aggression and verbal aggression also meet the criteria for aggressive outbursts; and there are additional clarifications related to frequency, consequences, and age of symptom presentation. Consistent with emerging research, to be described more fully in the pages to follow, an important specifier, *with limited prosocial emotions*, has been added to the CD criteria, to help identify an especially pernicious subtype of CD, described later in this chapter.

For the purpose of illuminating the utility of our Diversity/Resiliency Formulation, we chose a focus that would encourage the reader to "think outside the box" when engaging in the diagnostic process with children and adolescents. We concentrate on ODD and CD because these disruptive behavior disorders pull the mental health professional especially strongly toward a negative focus on pathology and arouse negative reactivity in persons in the child's environment. These two disorders are seen in mental health and community clinics more than any other disorders in minors, are often co-occurring with other psychiatric disorders, and may be complicated by substance abuse and severely delinquent behavior (Loeber, Burke, Lahey, Winters, & Zera, 2000; Steiner & Remsing, 2007). As externalizing disorders, they are visible to the observer and disruptive in the child's environment. In contrast, internalizing disorders—such as anxiety, depression, or learning disabilities—are not as easily observed by others and cause less environmental havoc (S. Goldstein & Rider, 2005). The failure to respond effectively to these disorders can have dire consequences for these children and adolescents when they become adults. For example, CD symptoms constitute a criterion for the adult diagnosis of APD (APA, 2000); and ODD, which often precedes CD, can wreak havoc with school adjustment and family harmony owing to the intensity of anger and resistance to authority that these children exhibit.

A combination of ODD and CD, often co-occurring with attention-deficit hyperactivity disorder (ADHD), greatly reduces a child's opportunity for a normal life adjustment. These disorders often precipitate major adverse outcomes in school, family, health, and vocational functioning, extending into adult life.

DSM DIAGNOSTIC CRITERIA

Oppositional Defiant Disorder

ODD is less severe than CD because the exhibited behavior does not violate the basic rights of others or age-appropriate social norms or rules. Aggressive acting out may not be as noticeable in school or other community settings outside the family. These children are better able to conform their behavior to social norms when away from home. This may hinder accurate and timely diagnosis, however. For example, if teachers, physicians, or mental health professionals do not observe the behavior at first hand, they may minimize or otherwise invalidate parents' concerns, and parents may be less motivated to address behavior that has not come to the attention of external authorities (Hagener, 2005). ODD is similar to CD in its persistent pattern of disobedience and opposition to authority patterns. The symptoms of ODD, leading to its official diagnosis, usually appear 2 to 3 years earlier than CD, emerging in late preschool or the early school years. ODD was first described in 1980 in the *DSM-III*. Subsequent *DSM* revisions have focused on issues of duration, frequency, the number of required symptoms, and on disagreements about the definition of impairment (Angold & Costello, 1996), with the result that the reported prevalence has been reduced (Steiner & Remsing, 2007). Lifetime prevalence of ODD is estimated at 11.2% for males and 9.2% for females (Nock, Kazdin, Hiripi, & Kessler, 2007), and is reported as ranging from 1% to 11% in the *DSM-5*, with more males diagnosed before adolescence (APA, 2013).

Criteria for a diagnosis of ODD are determined by a pattern of angry/irritable mood, argumentative/defiant behavior, or vindictiveness for at least 6 months. At least four of the following symptoms, exhibited in interaction with at least one individual who is not a sibling, are required for the diagnosis: losing one's temper, arguing with adults, actively defying or refusing to comply with adult requests or rules, deliberately annoying people, blaming others for one's own mistakes or misbehavior, being touchy or easily annoyed by others, and evincing anger and resentment and/or spitefulness or vindictiveness. Frequency criteria distinguish behaviors within normal developmental levels from behaviors that are symptomatic, and severity indicators differ in terms of the number of settings in which the behavior is evident.

Children and teenagers diagnosed with ODD are noted for their stubbornness, persistent resistance to directions, and refusal to compromise or negotiate, especially with family members or persons they know well. They may deliberately test the limits by ignoring orders, arguing intensely, and refusing to accept responsibility for their behavior. They appear to be deliberately annoying others but do not experience themselves as oppositional, justifying their behavior as a response to unfair circumstances or unreasonable demands by others (APA, 2000).

Males often have had difficulty being soothed in the preschool years and display a pattern of high motor activity. Self-esteem may be either low or overinflated, and these children may use tobacco, alcohol, or illicit drugs earlier than their peers. Conflict with teachers and peers is frequent, often escalating into a vicious cycle, in which the parents, teachers, and children reinforce each other's negative behavior. Although the disorder is more prevalent in males before puberty, the reported gender rates are equal thereafter; males are found to be more confrontational and their symptoms more persistent. Under discussion is whether these gender differences are adequately understood. Preliminary attempts to assess for measurement bias as a factor contributing to gender differences have not uncovered it. Similar heritability for ADHD and ODD has been found in both boys and girls. The current speculation about the reported differences between girls and boys with ODD is that behavioral expression of the genes is somewhat different with respect to gender (Derks, Dolan, Hudziak, Neale, & Boomsma, 2007). Some researchers feel that more girls may have ODD than is reported, as their aggressive behavior may be more covert, expressed indirectly in the context of relationships, and thus not recognized in relation to the symptoms required for the diagnosis (Connor, 2002; Steiner & Remsing, 2007; Zoccolillo, 1993). Whether or not girls with ODD have more co-occurring symptoms of mental health problems than boys (the gender paradox hypothesis) is debatable, as some studies have found more symptoms in boys (Munkvold, Lundervold, & Manger, 2011).

ODD has been found to be more prevalent in families that have had many different caregivers or in which parenting practices have been harsh or inconsistent. Prevalence rates are reported as 2.6% to 15.6% in community samples and 28% to 65% in clinical samples. This disorder is usually diagnosed between age 8 and early adolescence (Loeber, Burke, & Pardini, 2009). Lifetime ODD is estimated to be 11.2% for males and 9.2% for females. In addition, 92.4%

of those with lifetime ODD meet criteria for at least one other *DSM-IV* (APA, 1994) disorder involving mood, anxiety, impulse control, and substance use (Loeber et al., 2009). ODD often co-occurs with ADHD, learning disorder or communication disorder; along with CD, it has a unique pattern of severity when co-occurring with autism spectrum disorder and ADHD (Guttmann-Steinmetz, Gadow, & DeVincent, 2009). ODD is more common in families characterized by severe marital discord or when one parent has a history of mood disorder, substance-related disorder, APD, or a disruptive behavior disorder (APA, 2000; Steiner & Remsing, 2007). Complexity and heterogeneity characterize this multidetermined disorder, and persons with ODD are at greater risk for later CD, anxiety, and depressive disorders.

Conduct Disorder

This disorder is characterized by serious, persistent, repetitive violation of the rights of others and/or of societal norms (APA, 2013). Children and adolescents with CD may display little empathy or concern for the feelings of others, may bully others, and often misperceive others' behavior as hostile or threatening, thus justifying their aggressive responses. When expressed, remorse may not be genuine but may be displayed to avoid punishment. A posture of toughness is often observed despite inward low self-esteem. Individuals with CD have more accidents and often are restless and irritable. School expulsion, sexually transmitted diseases, unplanned pregnancies, suicidal ideation and/or attempts, legal problems, and the early use of illegal substances and alcohol are frequent complications. Academic achievement, especially in reading and verbal skills, is often low, and an additional diagnosis of a specific learning or communication disorder or of ADHD may be warranted. A diagnosis of CD requires that three or more of the following symptoms be present during the previous year, one of which must occur during the previous 6 months: aggression toward people or animals, destruction of property, deceitfulness or theft, and a serious violation of parental rules or other societal norms, such as running away or truancy. Severity is specified as mild, moderate, or severe. These symptoms must be severe enough to cause impairment in social, academic, or occupational functioning (APA, 2013).

The *DSM-5* identifies three subtypes, based on age of onset, which the clinician is asked to identify: childhood, adolescent, or unspecified onset. Childhood-onset CD is especially pernicious, occurs more often in males, who demonstrate physical aggression, disturbed peer relationships, and often have concurrent ADHD and other neurodevelopmental problems. Symptoms usually meet full criteria before puberty and are likely to persist into adulthood, developing into APD. Females are almost as likely as males to exhibit adolescent-onset CD, and the behaviors of this subtype are less aggressive, with more normative peer relationships.

The specifier, *with limited prosocial emotions*, is an important addition in the *DSM-5* and is more common in childhood-onset CD. To merit this specifier, the individual must display at least two of the following four characteristics in multiple relationships and settings over a minimum of 12 months: lack of remorse or guilt (or remorse only when caught), callous lack of empathy (cold, uncaring, and indifferent to harm caused to others), lack of concern about performance (not putting out effort needed to perform well and unconcerned about the result of poor performance), and shallow or deficient affect (not showing emotion to others, being insincere or superficial, and/or using emotions to intimidate or manipulate others). This pattern of behavior must be typical of interpersonal and emotional functioning, not an occasional occurrence in some situations. To diagnose this trait accurately, the clinician must obtain information not just from the individual, but from other persons, such as parents, peers, and teachers, who have known the person for an extended period of time.

It is important to take into account the individual's social and economic context in the diagnostic process. The CD label should not be applied when the individual is attempting to cope with a threatening, impoverished, or high-crime environment. For example, refugee children from traumatic war-torn environments are often forced to engage in aggressive and violent behavior in order to survive. In the aforementioned settings patterns of disruptive behavior may be viewed as near normative (APA, 2013).

Symptoms of CD usually emerge from middle childhood to adolescence, but can begin during the preschool years. ODD commonly emerges before CD in childhood; CD usually remits by adulthood, and the symptoms rarely emerge for the first time in adults. The severity of behaviors usually worsens with age in conduct-disordered persons. When the more damaging, physically aggressive behaviors occur at an earlier age and callous–unemotional (CU) traits are observed, the prognosis is considered worse; these children are more vulnerable to school failure, involvement with the juvenile justice system, and imprisonment as adults. In less severe cases, constituting the majority of children with CD, the disorder remits by adulthood. Many children with CD bully others, engage in physical fighting, exhibit cruelty to people or animals, destroy property, skip school, join gangs, ignore parental rules, and run away from home. Running away in reaction to physical or sexual abuse, however, is not a symptom of CD in and of itself. Individuals with CD often misperceive others as threatening and respond with what they feel is justifiable aggression. They are often thrill seeking, irritable, easily frustrated, and temperamental. Many engage in substance abuse, especially adolescent females, and have a higher than average suicide rate. The reported prevalence of CD has increased in recent years and is more frequently diagnosed in urban settings. Prevalence rates in community samples vary from 11.8% to 16.0% in boys and from 0.8% to 9.2% in girls (Loeber et al., 2009). This is one of the most frequent diagnoses applied to children in mental health facilities; yet, few children with CD receive treatment (APA, 2013).

Genetic factors are known to play a part in a child's vulnerability to ODD and CD. Children with a biological or adoptive parent with APD or a sibling with CD are at higher risk. Factors that predispose a child to the development of CD include difficult infant temperament, parental rejection or neglect, harsh parental discipline, large family size, frequent changes of caregivers, maternal smoking during pregnancy, peer rejection or a delinquent peer group, and neighborhood exposure to violence (APA, 2013). It is evident from this constellation of factors that this is a complex, multidetermined, heterogeneous disorder. The fact that CD is more frequently diagnosed in urban settings, along with its increased prevalence in recent years, indicates that a stress–diathesis conceptualization, acknowledging the mixture of nature and nurture in etiology and course, is vital to effective diagnosis and treatment.

The term *conduct disorder* is often used interchangeably with *delinquency* and/or *antisocial behavior*; however, *delinquency* is a legal term that refers to court involvement. Three classes of behavior are considered delinquent from a legal perspective: vandalism and theft without personal confrontation of the victim; physical, verbal, or indirect aggression, either predatory or defensive; and status offenses, such as the under-age consumption of alcohol (Tremblay, 2003). Aggression alone does not predict delinquency; but when aggression is combined with social rejection, the child is more vulnerable to later involvement with the justice system (Kellam, Simon, & Ensminger, 1983).

KEY POINTS

1. ODD and CD are complex, heterogeneous, externalizing disorders causing disruption in the child's environment.
2. ODD and CD are related developmentally in that ODD usually occurs first, and the symptoms can worsen over time so that an additional diagnosis of CD is warranted.
3. Issues in the diagnosis of ODD and CD involve distinguishing normal temperamental differences, adolescent rebellion, and coerced antisocial behavior due to circumstance from the mental disorder.
4. In CD, CU traits and earlier onset of symptoms indicate poor prognosis and greater vulnerability for an antisocial lifestyle as an adult; in ODD persons are at greater risk for later anxiety or depressive disorders.
5. Accurate diagnosis involves an understanding of the interaction between internal and external complexity (i.e., nature–nurture issues that characterize these disorders).
6. Gender differences are poorly understood and are under ongoing scrutiny by researchers.

CURRENT THINKING ABOUT THE ETIOLOGY AND COURSE OF CD AND ODD

Earlier, more homogenous conceptualizations of etiology, described as coercion or social interaction models, focused on inept parenting practices as the main cause of CD and ODD. In contrast, more recent models are transactional in nature and emphasize the following: distinctions between reactive and proactive aggression, affect modulation and self-regulation, cognitive skills related to the learned ability to comply with reasonable external authority, internal factors of temperament, the mutual reinforcement of child characteristics and parental response, and co-occurring disorders (Green & Doyle, 1999). A complex interaction of temperament, neuropsychological functioning, intelligence, academic performance, attachment, and social cognition is now understood to predispose individuals to the development of a behavioral disruptive disorder. Both ODD and CD are thought to arise out of a mix of risk and protective factors characterizing the biopsychosocial status of the individual (Steiner & Remsing, 2007). Nature–nurture thinking about etiology is summarized here, followed by a description of the developmental course of the disorders and their relationship to co-occurring disorders.

Neurobiology

Studies of biological factors have explored familial clustering of symptoms, genetic predispositions, temperament, baseline arousal, exposure to pre or postnatal toxins, abnormalities in brain function, disruptions of neurotransmitter functioning, and elevated cortisol or testosterone levels (Steiner & Remsing, 2007). Although a lower IQ is sometimes considered a precursor to a disruptive behavior disorder, the relationship between IQ and a behavior disorder is unclear, as persons with high IQs can have many conduct problems and the pathways among IQ, school achievement, and behavior are complex. As early as age 3, children classified as hyperactive and oppositionally defiant, based on mothers' reports, have shown a greater family history of CD and ODD, suggesting a link to biologically based risk factors (Harvey, Friedman-Wyeneth, Goldstein, & Sherman, 2007). The biological stress response, indicated by elevations in cortisol due to the reactivity of the hypothalamic–pituitary–adrenocortical system, is observed in infants and small children in situations capable of producing negative emotional reactions. It is unclear whether this indicates anxiety or distress; the response may simply be due to the biological cost of adaptive functioning correlated with children's active and appropriate attempts to cope with potentially distressing circumstances (Gunnar, 1992). Higher cortisol reactivity and lower cortisol recovery are related to the experience of shame in early childhood; more frequent in boys, shame experiences, characterized by global negative self-assessment, predict later shame responding and increase the risk of mental health problems (Mills, Imm, Walling, & Weiler, 2008). This may relate to the development of externalizing defenses characteristic of children with ODD and CD. The relationships among cortisol, the modulation of the stress response, and ODD/CD symptoms are undergoing increased scrutiny and remain unclear.

Numerous other researchers have explored the complex relationships between neurological and hormonal functioning and behaviors characteristic of ODD and CD (S. Goldstein & Rider, 2005). Prenatal and early developmental exposure to toxins, especially lead, along with physical damage to brain structures have repeatedly been linked with disruptive behavior disorders in children (Burke, Loeber, & Birmaher, 2002; Needleman, Riess, Tobin, Biesecker, & Greenhouse, 1996). Aggressive preschool children, especially boys, demonstrate impaired inhibition in neuropsychological tasks (Raaijmakers et al., 2008). An increased risk of violent behavior is associated with frontal lobe dysfunction (Pliszka, 1999). Davidson, Putnam, and Larson (2000) discovered a link between impaired amygdalar functioning (site of the flight-or-fight response) and impaired connections between the amygdala and prefrontal lobe regions (sites connected with the ability to plan and choose rational courses of action) with the impaired reading of social cues and the inability of children to suppress negative emotion. Lower serotonin levels in the cerebrospinal fluid of children with CD have been linked with higher rates of aggression (Clark, Murphy, & Constantino, 1999). Physiological underarousal and lower heart rates correlate with disruptive behavior in children and antisocial behavior in adolescents and are predictive of adult criminality (Mezzacappa, Tremblay, & Kindlon, 1997; Pliszka, 1999; Raine, Venables, & Williams, 1990). Passive avoidance of learning, nonresponsiveness to punishment, overprocessing of negatively valent stimuli at the expense of other stimuli, and difficulty with the semantic processing of words are characteristics typical of children with CD and ODD and have been linked with paralimbic brain dysfunction (Blair, 2004; Blair, Peschardt, Budhani, Mitchell, & Pine, 2006a; Kiehl, 2006; Loeber et al., 2009). In children who experience little arousal to others' distress (lack of empathy, callousness), and show decreased physiological arousal to their own distress, low basal cortisol fails to trigger stress activation (Shirtcliff et al., 2009).

Bubier and Drabick (2008) found a relationship between impaired affective decision making and the externalizing behaviors (blaming one's behavior on others, rationalizing) characteristic of male children and adolescents with ADHD and ODD in inner-city Philadelphia youth. The relationship, found in boys but not in girls, was mediated by low sympathetic activation during an emotion-inducing task. The results suggest that boys who do not physiologically experience fear and sadness may be more impulsive because they lack the experience of emotions and the neurological access to executive functioning that are important for guiding and learning socially appropriate behavior. These autonomic markers may be malleable in young children, shaped by alteration in the child's environment through the provision, for example, of an enriched preschool environment as well as by interventions to reduce marital conflict, parental stress, and other contextual disadvantages, such as poverty and other neighborhood characteristics. The findings suggest the usefulness of identifying risk and protective factors in subgroups of children with these biological markers at an early age, evaluation of what environmental factors would increase risk or protection of children from later externalizing problems, and searching for the presence of sensitive periods in the development of pathological traits related to ODD and CD.

The Interaction of Temperament, Family Distress, Heredity, Gender, and Intergenerational Family Transmission

Disruptive behavior disorders are so complex in their origin and development that it is difficult, if not impossible, to separate out the contributions of heredity from environment. Genetic influences on ODD and CD have been suggested by twin studies (Eaves et al., 2000; Tuvblad, Zheng, Raine, & Baker, 2009) and studies of sibling behavior (Pike, McGuire, Hetherington, Reiss, & Plomin, 1996). There is some evidence that heredity is more influential than environment in aggression, whereas environmental factors may be more important in nonaggressive delinquency (Edelbrock, Rends, Plomin, & Thompson, 1995), and adult criminal behavior may be more genetically based than early criminal behavior (Lyons, True, Eisen, Goldberg, & Meyer, 1995). Differences in levels of aggression may be driven primarily by temperament, and adult criminal behavior may be more impervious to prosocial influences than youthful delinquency that is reactive to peer pressure.

More recent research, however, has emphasized the importance of shared environmental influences in adolescent psychopathology, such as that of siblings in family divorce and conflict (Burt, 2009). Disruptive and antisocial behaviors are observable across generations in families, and parental antisocial behavior is correlated with preadolescent onset of CD (Elkins, Iacono, Doyle, & McGue, 1997; Farrington, Joliffe, Loeber, Stouthamer-Loeber, & Kalb, 2001; Frick et al., 1992; Lahey, Loeber, & Quay, 1998). Parental psychological distress is more strongly correlated with antisocial behavior in boys than in girls, and parental depression is linked to earlier onset and persistence of ODD and CD in both genders (Campbell, Pierce, Moore, Marakovitz, & Newby, 1996). As early as age 3, children described as hyperactive and oppositional have been found to experience higher levels of family stressors than nonproblem children on a variety of variables, including intense couple conflict and mental health problems of either or both parents. The families of this subgroup are characterized by more maternal avoidance and verbal aggression during marital conflict than families of nonproblem children (L. H. Goldstein et al., 2007b).

Temperament is an important construct in searching for a biological basis for ODD and for the emergence of the disruptive behaviors of CD. Temper dysregulation in childhood and adolescence has been demonstrated to evoke maladaptive parenting and can facilitate the development of CD. Early displays of negative emotionality, intense and reactive responding, and inflexibility predict externalizing behavior problems in late childhood. The relationship between temperament and attachment patterns to disruptive behavior disorders is mixed and will require further research to predict later problem behaviors from attachment patterns (Burke et al., 2002). A meta-analysis by Fearon, Bakersmans-Kranenburg, VanIJzenboorn, Lapsley, and Roisman (2010) has demonstrated a significant association between early insecure parental attachment and later externalizing behavior, especially in boys. Impulsivity and behavioral inhibition also have a complex relationship with ODD and CD. Behavioral but not cognitive impulsivity has been demonstrated to be related to antisocial behavior (White et al., 1994). In boys, behavioral inhibition decreases the risk of later delinquency, whereas social withdrawal significantly increases it (Kerr, Tremblay, Pagani, & Vitaro, 1997). The hypothesized explanation for these associations is that inhibition is related to anxiety, which can moderate physical aggression, even in boys known for disruptive behavior (Harden, Pihl, Vitaro, Gendreau, & Tremblay, 1995).

Although the relationship between intelligence and behavior disorders is confounded by the impact of school failure and low achievement on conduct, reading disorders are clearly related to CD even when factors of socioeconomic status (SES) and ethnicity are controlled (Maguin, Loeber, & LeMahieu, 1993; Sanson, Prior, & Smart, 1996). In boys, disruptive behavior poses a risk for later reading problems; in girls, early reading problems predict later adolescent disruptive behavior (Maughan, Pickles, Hagell, Rutter, & Yule, 1996; Sanson et al., 1996).

There is overwhelming consensus that childhood-onset, life-course-persistent CD is almost exclusively a male disorder and that biological variables are major influences in this gender difference. Eme (2007) describes a three-level model composed of genetic differences, biological consequences of being male or female (such as differential vulnerability to certain physical hazards), and proximal risk or protective effects (such as the greater vulnerability of males to neuropsychological impairment). The male gender vulnerabilities to CD described by Eme (2007) are summarized in the following list:

1. Estrogen heightens the tend–befriend stress response in females. Testosterone heightens flight-or-fight stress response in males.
2. Owing to sex-specific chromosomal differences, males exhibit greater developmental immaturity, reduced genetic repair mechanisms, and more vulnerability to physical hazards, such as complications in the mother's pregnancy, infections, and malnutrition.
3. Greater male size, strength, and differences in brain function, the result of evolutionary selection, predispose males to aggression.
4. The male disposition for rough-and-tumble play, fearlessness, and response to threat prime males for aggressive responses, risk taking, and less concern for harm to others.
5. Males are more susceptible to ADHD and deficits in cognitive abilities and executive functioning, proximal risks for CD.

Thus the slow, early, and insidious development of CD is influenced by biologically based psychological dispositions that increase the likelihood for males to engage in physical aggression. As a result, the small percentage of males (6%) who evidence a high stable pattern of aggression are most likely to continue in a long-term adolescent and adult course defined as persistent and pathological. In fact, they account for more than 50% of crimes committed in the United States (Moffitt, 2006). These are, in particular, the children with externalizing behavior disorders who most need earlier, consistent intervention—a daunting task, because maintaining compliance with effective treatments over time has proven extremely difficult (Rutter, 2003).

In clinical samples of ODD, boys were more likely to deliberately annoy or blame others and have comorbid ADHD, along with greater impairment in school and community. In contrast, girls were more likely to have higher comorbidity with internalizing disorders, such as depression and anxiety. Thus, attention to gender is important in effective treatment (DeAncos & Ascaso, 2011).

Psychosocial Factors

Attachment

Neurobiological factors in CD and ODD, expressed in temperament and the stress reactions described previously, can affect the quality of maternal–infant bonding and attachment. Some attachment theorists have noted commonalities between anxious–avoidant attachment and behavioral symptoms of ODD. Oppositional behavior in general can be interpreted as an attachment signal to an unresponsive parent. However, empirical findings related to support for attachment disruptions have been inconsistent (Steiner & Remsing, 2007). Fearon et al. (2010) completed a meta-analysis of 53 studies with a total of 5,947 children and found that supportive comforting relationships between parents and children promote social abilities in children and reduce the possibility of aggressiveness, whereas early insecure maternal attachment was linked with higher levels of later emerging negative behaviors, such as noncompliance, aggression, and hostility, especially in boys. Only four of the studies reviewed, however, were based on samples from predominantly ethnic minority communities, and the directionality of the symptoms is unclear (i.e., difficult behaviors or temperaments can elicit problematic parental attachment behavior in otherwise mentally healthy parents).

Interpersonal Competence

Deficits in interpersonal social skills are important factors in disruptive behavior disorders. Boys with ODD and CD have trouble attending to social cues, tend to attribute hostile intentions to other boys, focus on concrete and external qualities in others, have an egocentric bias in describing their peers, select aggressive responses to problems, and feel more confident than others in their ability to be aggressive (Dodge, Pettit, Bates, & Valente, 1995; Matthys, Cuperus, & Van Engeland, 1999; Matthys, Walterbos, Van Engeland, & Koops, 1995; Wong & Cornell, 1999). Both boys and girls with CD are lower in empathy and in the identification of interpersonal cues than those without CD (Cohen & Strayer, 1996). Aggressive children have more trouble generating nonaggressive alternative solutions to problems and anticipate being rewarded for aggressive behavior (Steiner & Remsing, 2007). Cognitive schemas characterized by grandiosity and the justification of violence have been shown to predict aggressive and delinquent behavior in both male and female adolescents for up to 6 months, especially in males, who were also more impulsive (Calvete, 2008). These maladaptive self-cognitions function as self-serving distortions, enabling these adolescents to believe that their own rights and beliefs are so important that they can be indifferent to the rights of others and to view their antisocial behavior as admirable. This schema provides further justification for violence and improves these adolescents' image with aggressive peers. Early experiences that guide this distorted information processing may include permissive or harsh parental discipline (Calvete, 2008).

Although ODD is thought to begin in early childhood and to be a developmental precursor of CD, few studies have attempted to identify antecedents or predictors of symptom emergence. An exception to this dearth of information, one community-based, ethnically diverse study of 128 4- to 8-year-old children found a negative correlation between ODD symptoms and factors of sympathy, the ability to take another's perspective, and moral attributions of behavior (Dinolfo & Malti, 2013). Caregiver expressions of sympathy mediated the strength of the correlations, indicating that early parental response might modify the development of ODD symptoms.

Parenting

Numerous studies emphasize the importance of contextual factors related to the severity of ODD and CD and the necessity of evaluating multiple risks related to parenting, school, and peer/community domains in the assessment process. When 3-year-olds with symptoms of hyperactivity and ODD are compared with normal peers, the parents of the former group were found to be less warm, to show more negative affect, and to be more lax than parents of nonproblem children; the mothers reported more parenting stress, especially in reaction to oppositional behavior (L. H. Goldstein, Harvey, & Friedman-Weieneth, 2007a). ODD and CD children suffer greater exposure to delinquent peers, lowered parental self-efficacy, greater parental hostility, and more stressful life events (Kolko, Dorn, Bukstein, & Burke, 2008). These findings were similar for both boys and girls. The degree of parental involvement with the child, parental conflict management, behavioral monitoring, and harsh, inconsistent discipline have been correlated with disruptive, aggressive, and/or delinquent behaviors (Eddy, Level, & Fagot, 2001; Frick, 1994; Wasserman, Miller, Pinner, & Jaramillo, 1996). Sexual or physical parental abuse significantly increases the risk of CD (Fergusson, Lynsky, & Horwood, 1996). Culture, gender, and the nature of the parent–child relationship have a bearing on the effects of physical parental discipline (Deater-Deckard & Dodge, 1997).

More recent studies emphasize the bidirectional reciprocal association between parenting practices and conduct problems, especially in boys (Pardini, Fite, & Burke, 2008). Previous studies had supported a coercive unidirectional model in which parenting practices were considered a cause rather than an effect of youth conduct problems (McLeod, Kruttschnitt, & Dornfeld, 1994), whereas the influence of conduct problems on parenting behavior had been largely ignored (Crouter & Booth, 2003). In contrast, Pardini et al. (2008) found the influence of conduct problems on changes in parenting practices to be as just as strong if not stronger than the influence that parenting behaviors have on changes in conduct problems. These researchers recommend that treatment interventions be designed to normalize the way in which youth with conduct problems elicit less than optimal parenting practices, so that parents feel supported rather than blamed, thus enhancing their receptivity to suggested changes in response to their child's conduct problems. They further suggest that programs designed to prevent the escalation of negative parent–child exchanges begin during the early elementary school years. Dodge and Pettit (2003) recommend further that interventions target key transition points in children's development, such as moves from elementary to junior high school and the onset of puberty, as well as nonnormative transitions, such as family moves and divorce. In general, studies of parent–child bidirectional influences on the development of externalizing behavior problems have been based on written reports of parents and teachers rather than on direct observation; they have focused mostly on boys and rarely on boys and girls in the same study and have failed to include fathers. The reader is referred to Pettit and Arsiwalla (2008) for an extensive summary of this research.

CASE STUDY

Ian

One typical afternoon, my children came home from school and Ian was visibly upset about something. Abby and I were in the kitchen, and Ian came out in a rage, making demands. I did not understand what had set him off. I knew he needed to calm himself down and quickly. I sent him to his room to cool off. He refused and started to become aggressive. He wanted to engage me in a physical fight. I took him by the arm and physically dragged him down the hallway to his room. With him on the floor in his room, I shut the door and walked back to the kitchen. As I was walking through the kitchen, Abby said, "Mom, watch out! He's right behind you!" I turned around in time to see Ian, pure contempt and rage on his face, lunging at me with both fists clenched. I dragged him again to his room and shut the door. He would not leave the door closed and kept running after me. By this point, Abby was clearly shaken over what she had just witnessed. I could not control my son. I was not strong enough physically or emotionally. Afraid of an 8-year-old boy? You bet (Hagener, 2005, p. 106).

1. Think about and describe this incident from the point of view of the mother, the sister (Abby), and the son (Ian).
2. How do you assess the mother's response to Ian?
3. Does this incident illustrate the concept of bidirectional reciprocal influence with respect to parenting? Why or why not?

Subbarao et al. (2008) found links between parental negativity and antisocial behavior, between mothers' depression and antisocial behavior, and between fathers' negativity and antisocial behavior in adolescents. Parental suggestions about how to cope with stressful situations have been found to be correlated with CD and ODD symptoms (Abaied & Rudolph, 2009). Parents were asked what advice they gave to children about how to deal with stressful situations. Helping girls to engage in problem solving and the regulation of their emotions protected them from the development of externalizing behavior, and this effect increased over time. In boys, the opposite was true. Engagement suggestions made ODD and CD symptoms worse, as boys tended to engage in more aggressive, dominating behavior. Disengagement suggestions (encouragement to avoid, deny, or distract oneself from stress or negative emotions) were more effective under conditions of mild stress. Results also differed in terms of contextual factors, such as the school environment and the nature of the neighborhood.

Peer Relationships

A variety of difficulties with peers characterize disruptive behavior disorders, varying with childhood developmental stages. Peer rejection in childhood is a significant factor in the experience of children with CD (Coie & Dodge, 1998). Associating with delinquent peers is related to delinquent behavior in boys (Coie & Miller-Johnson, 2001; Elliott & Menard, 1996). Peers further reinforce aggressive behavior by acquiescing to it. Peer aggression alone, which could take the form of indirect or interpersonal aggression, predicts serious delinquency in girls, whereas a combination of peer rejection and aggression predicts serious delinquency in boys (Miller-Johnson et al., 1999). Oppositional behavior with one's peers correlates closely with physical aggression and bullying and may be very important in screening for more serious behaviors and designing effective interventions (Taylor, Burns, Rusby, & Foster, 2006).

Exposure to Stress

Stressful environments—such those of public housing or poor, disadvantaged neighborhoods, unemployment, neighborhood violence, low socioeconomic status (SES)—and other exposures to daily stresses related to the environment are all significant factors in the incidence of CD and ODD (S. Goldstein & Rider, 2005). Wikstrom and Loeber (2000) found that the effects of living in public housing countered any and all individual protective factors that were present for boys with disruptive behavior. Socioeconomic disadvantage makes it harder for parents to mediate the effects of stressful environments on problematic behavior (McLloyd, 1998). In general, exposure to daily stressors has been shown to be positively related to disruptive behavior, maladaptive coping, and self-harm (Burke et al., 2002). On the other hand, most studies of psychopathology and SES indicate that the amount of variance explained by SES is less than 1% (Mash & Duzois, 1996; Steiner & Remsing, 2007). This is explored further in the "Equity and Diversity Issues" section in this chapter.

Risk Versus Protective Factors

All of the aforementioned etiological factors may be considered risk factors for CD or ODD. Although risk factors are more predictive of CD than of ODD, it is also true that more research has focused on risk factors, specifically aggressive behavior, for CD than for ODD (Burke et al., 2002). The onset of a behavior-disruptive disorder is considered to be influenced by the accumulation of risk factors rather than the result of one risk factor operating in isolation. Protective factors may buffer the effects of risk factors, but this is poorly understood; and protective factors, such as warm, consistent parenting, may be insufficient to overcome the multitude of risk factors in the context of antisocial peers and/or a highly stressful environment (Burke et al., 2002). In their review of the accumulation of risk versus protective factors, Loeber and Farrington (2001) conclude that it is important to focus on multiple domains and to focus as much on the enhancement of protective factors as on the reduction of risk factors. The risk factors are summarized in Exhibit 6.1.

In an excellent summary of the evidence for a neurobiological model of childhood antisocial behavior (van Goozen, Faichild, Snoek, & Harold, 2007), the complex and multidirectional interaction of the internal and external etiological factors described previously is emphasized. Individual differences in the onset and severity of antisocial behavior in both CD and ODD are partially explained by temperament and differential ability to regulate stress. An intense fight-or-flight response can create the misperception of threat in interpersonal situations. Children who exhibit little fear of punishment and who underreact physiologically to stress may be predisposed to seek out stimulation and to engage in risky behavior, which may help explain their poor socialization and inability to read social cues accurately. These authors propose a theoretical model in which the interplay between neurobiological deficits and cognitive and emotional functioning mediates between early adversity and antisocial behavior problems in childhood. Difficult temperaments are overreactive to poor parenting and community environments; conversely, difficult temperaments elicit negative responses from parents and community members.

EXHIBIT 6.1 Childhood Risk Factors for Conduct Disorder (CD) and Antisocial Personality Disorder (APD)

Intrinsic individual differences	ADHD and impulse-control problems, difficult-to-manage temperament, negative emotionality, aggression evident in preschool related to poor peer relationships, depression and anxiety, academic underachievement, lower IQ and language skills
Related personality traits	Lack of empathy related to harsh standards for others, overestimation of own abilities, poor awareness of social expectations; disrespect for others, desire to dominate resulting in anger; perceived ideal and real self at odds; reduced opportunities for character development
Psychosocial/environmental factors	Rejection of nondeviant peers; attachment to delinquent peer group; inconsistent family supervision combined with harsh discipline; large family size; institutional living early in life; parental rejection; inconsistent parental figures; presence of alcoholic father; parental conflict; single parenthood; maternal depression; low SES; racism, social isolation, family violence, abuse, and neglect
Genetic and nutritional factors	APD and substance abuse in parents; twin studies show 50% heritability of ODD/CD; fetal exposure to alcohol and drugs; mild cognitive impairment attributed to low birth weight, prematurity, and childhood exposure to toxins
Neurochemical factors and CD	Medications that reduce aggression may reduce risk by enhancing dopaminergic function; low serotonin in aggressive boys is a tentative finding
Compoundedness and duration	Earlier onset, longer duration of life stressors, and number of risk factors greatly increase risk

From Holmes, Slaughter, and Kashani (2001); Mack (2004)

Acknowledging and addressing the complex etiology of ODD and CD, described previously, is considered extremely important if effective interventions are to be designed. Van Goozen, Fairchild, Snoek, and Harold (2007) call for longitudinal research that could help to identify and respond to the needs of children who are at risk owing to neurobiology, temperament, and family environment. The goals of intervention would include restoring the stress response to a normal state of activity and intervening in the distorted emotional appraisal and cognitions that correlate with neurobiological factors in especially aggressive and antisocial children. One example of such an effort, a recent report on the effective use of parental emotion coaching to help children regulate their emotions, suggests that maternal emotion coaching is a protective factor for children with ODD, especially for those with high emotional lability (Dunsmore, Booker, & Ollendick, 2013). Longitudinal studies could help to clarify neurobiological markers related to CD and ODD, determine whether these are a cause or consequence of engaging in disruptive behavior, design and prioritize more effective treatment interventions, and develop effective psychopharmacology.

Early interventions could possibly deflect the life course of the persistent offender—an outcome that has consistently eluded treatment professionals. In one study (Scott, Knapp, Henderson, & Maughan, 2001, reviewed in Duggan, 2011) the societal costs of those with childhood CD were compared to those without CD at age 27. Adults with childhood CD were 10 times more costly to society, mostly due to their criminal behavior; yet, the authors point out, there is a dearth of empirical information showing the cost benefits of successful interventions with this CD group. The researchers recommend longitudinal outcome studies of early intervention parent training (PT) programs for young children, of intensive multisystemic family therapies, and of community-wide crime prevention programs as worthwhile attempts to prevent adult APD and its attendant social costs.

KEY POINTS

1. CD and ODD are multidetermined. Heredity contributes to disruptive behavior, especially with respect to temperament, aggression, and response to stress.
2. CD and ODD are sensitive to external stressors, such as poverty, environmental toxins, parental substance abuse, and rigid, punitive parenting.
3. Children with CD and ODD are also sources of stress to those in their school and home environment, creating a downward-spiraling interactive effect. Those who intervene should avoid blaming parents and interventions should begin in the early elementary school years. Parental distress should be normalized to increase parental receptiveness to suggested changes in parenting practices.
4. Risk factors for ODD and CD are cumulative in their effects and are powerful enough to overcome protective factors, which are less well defined and understood.
5. Both the reduction of risk factors and the strengthening of protective factors should be considered in the design of effective interventions that address the complexity of these disorders.

6. Weaknesses noted in research methodologies include a lack of focus on females, on cultural and racial minorities, and on children from low-SES communities; in addition, there are few longitudinal studies that shed light on factors influencing the course of these disorders from childhood to adulthood.

Co-Occurring Disorders and the Developmental Course of ODD and CD

Along with the aforementioned attempts to discover the complex etiology of CD, it is important to understand the relationship of these disruptive behavior disorders to other co-occurring disorders as well as how these disorders manifest and develop over time. ADHD often coexists with or precedes ODD and CD, but ODD and CD are considered to be distinct from ADHD. Children with ADHD, however, are at significantly greater risk for ODD and CD (Yoshimasu et al., 2012). These three disorders co-occur more with each other than with other psychiatric conditions. The association of ADHD with either ODD or CD indicates a poorer prognosis, as these children are generally more aggressive, exhibit a greater range and persistence of problem behaviors, are more severe underachievers, and are more rejected by their peers (Steiner & Remsing, 2007). When severe conduct problems begin in childhood, parenting is more dysfunctional, more CU traits are evident, and affiliation with delinquent peers is more common. CD is significantly more common in boys and increases in prevalence with age, whereas if CD symptoms are not present, ODD declines with age. CD and ODD show high levels of overlap (Maughan, Rose, Messer, Goodman, & Meltzer, 2004).

Adolescent-onset CD is associated with rebellious nonconformity with respect to authority and traditional institutions (Dandreaux & Frick, 2009). Substance abuse is often present, especially in teenagers when the complexity of risk factors has not been addressed and/or when interventions have not worked. Oppositional and antagonistic behaviors are extremely common in adolescents and may be a normal response to the developmental challenges of the teen years. Oppositional behavior may indicate a defensive response to overwhelming demands in the family, the neighborhood, or the school and may present as a part of the diagnostic picture of a pervasive developmental disorder or a language or learning disorder (Steiner & Remsing, 2007).

Numerous researchers have attempted to delineate the developmental course of disruptive behavioral disorders (S. Goldstein & Rider, 2005; Loeber, Green, Lahey, Frick, & McBurnett, 2000). During the preschool years, disruptive oppositional and mildly aggressive symptoms appear to be unidimensional, with the emergence of ADHD as observable by first grade, leading to a debilitating cycle of learning problems, difficulty in acquiring basic foundational academic skills, and social rejection in grade school, followed by a cycle of increased risk for school failure, dropout, underachievement, and risk taking by adolescence and adulthood (Barkley, Fisher, Edelbrock, & Smallish, 1990; Barkley & Gordon, 2002).

There is a general consensus that ODD precedes CD along three developmental and often parallel behavioral pathways defined as overt, covert, and authority conflict. Overt behaviors progress from minor aggression to physical fighting and violence; covert behaviors include stealing from home and sometimes progress to property damage and more serious status and criminal behavior, such as substance abuse violations and fire setting. Authority conflict progresses from stubbornness to defiance and the avoidance of authority by running away or truancy. Early onset of disruptive behaviors, especially overt aggression, is most predictive of significant problems in adulthood (Kelly, Loeber, Keenan, & DeLamatre, 1997). Most but not all youth with CD have a history of ODD, but the reverse is not true (S. Goldstein & Brooks, 2005); most children diagnosed with ODD do not go on to develop CD (Green & Doyle, 1999).

Complicating the developmental picture is the co-occurrence with ADHD, ODD, and CD of other psychiatric disorders, including anxiety, depression, and somatoform disorders. Impulsiveness is thought to act as a catalyst for a variety of disorders and their consequences. As a result of social problems, school failure, and possibly the side effects of medication, the child or adolescent is at greater risk of depression, especially in the context of adverse life events; the link between ODD and depression is a source of increased research scrutiny (Loeber et al., 2009). Somatoform disorders and depression may be more the outcome than the cause of co-occurring disorders (S. Goldstein & Rider, 2005), but the relationship is unclear. ODD is associated with depression and anxiety (internalizing disorders) across childhood and adolescence. The degree of comorbidity varies over time in different groups of children; that is, older youth have more comorbid internalizing disorders; boys experience both comorbid depression and anxiety; and girls with ODD experience more co-occurring anxiety. These patterns need further study, as children with ODD early in life may be at special risk for later anxiety and depressive disorders (Boylan, Vaillancourt, Boyle, & Szatmari, 2007). These debilitating interrelationships become more and more serious in the context of adverse environmental circumstances.

Although gender differences have been observed in the way symptoms are expressed and in their consequences for the child or adolescent, this is an area needing more empirical investigation (Loeber et al., 2000, 2009). Later onset of CD is more common in girls and may not be preceded by ODD; it is also unclear whether more serious CD symptoms, such as stealing, are usually preceded by less serious symptoms, such as lying (Burke et al., 2002).

The developmental course of ODD and CD is often described in relation to the presence or absence of ADHD. In early childhood a disruptive behavior pattern is observed, ultimately labeled ODD, which is sometimes but not always preceded by ADHD. There is a direct trajectory from ODD, CD, and APD in adulthood. ADHD can potentiate and worsen the severity of CD. The directional relationship between anxiety, depression, or somatoform disorders with CD is less clear, with CD and depression being bidirectional but depression more often the result of the consequences of CD or the negative affect component of ODD (Loeber et al., 2009). Substance abuse and depression are bidirectional (Loeber et al., 2000).

The research of Lahey et al. (2009) on the role of inattentive–hyperactive and oppositional behavior as developmental precursors to conduct problems was tested recently in the children of 6,466 women across the United States. Conduct problems at ages 4 to 7 robustly predicted conduct problems at ages 8 to13. More notable, after genetic and environmental influences on conduct problems at 4 to 7 years were taken into account, inattentive–hyperactive and oppositional behavior at 4 to 7 years had little causal influence on conduct problems at 8 to 13 years. This suggests that after early conduct problems are controlled, little is gained by treating early inattentive–hyperactive and oppositional behavior as developmental precursors to later conduct problems. However, the role of psychopathic symptoms—defined by interpersonal features, such as manipulativeness, deceitfulness, superficial charm, and grandiosity, along with affective characteristics, including shallow affect, lack of empathy, lack of guilt or remorse, and failure to accept responsibility—is considered increasingly important in predicting antisocial behavior in adulthood. Factor analysis has illuminated these features as distinct in both boys and girls, and researchers are advocating their inclusion in models of the development of both CD and ODD (Loeber et al., 2009).

KEY POINTS

1. ODD and CD have complex co-occurring relationships with ADHD and, to a lesser and more varied extent, with depression, anxiety, and somatic and learning disorders.
2. The developmental course of these disruptive behavior disorders often begins with symptoms of hyperactivity and oppositional behavior in early childhood, developing into more serious conduct problems often accompanied by substance abuse and culminating in APD in adulthood.
3. Poor prognosis is associated with early onset of CD symptoms, CU traits, and the presence of ADHD.
4. It is important to distinguish ODD and CD from the normal rebelliousness and questioning of authority in adolescent development.

EVIDENCE-INFORMED PRACTICE

It is generally assumed that any successful intervention with either CD or ODD must take into account the heterogeneity and complexity of these disorders, addressing the co-occurrence of ADHD, depression, substance abuse, family dysfunction, and other issues (Burke et al., 2002). CD has been considered extremely difficult to treat and largely resistant to treatment because of its complex determinants, as described previously. Interventions that have focused on multiple needs are reportedly more successful, but those that have proven effective for both prevention and treatment require intensive resources and prolonged active participation by the youth involved as well as their families, making implementation difficult (F. Goldstein, Dawson, Smith, & Grant, 2012). ODD has been similarly difficult to treat, often showing initially promising results that are not maintained in follow-up studies. In general, most outcome studies include only short-term follow-up, outcome measures have been largely limited to assessment of clinical symptoms, and controlled studies do not resemble clinical practice. As a result, a large gap exists between the research base on the one hand and clinical practice in real-life situations on the other (Burns, Hoagwood, & Mrazek, 1999). Many studies do not separate out children and adolescents with CD and/or ODD from children with other disorders. The bulk of the intervention studies have been designed to reduce antisocial behavior in general, to prevent institutionalization in juvenile justice or inpatient mental health facilities, or to improve overall mental health care (Loeber et al., 2009). Those studies that seem most relevant to the diagnoses considered herein are included in the following sections.

Preventive Interventions

The powerful multiplicative effects of risk factors described previously have increased recognition of how essential prevention is to an effective response to CD and ODD. There is some evidence that preschool programs, such as Head Start, have reduced future delinquency rates (Connor, 2002; Greenspan, 1992). A meta-analysis of 55 early family–PT programs indicated that the programs had a small to moderate effect on reducing child behavior problems (Piquero, Farrington, Welsh, Tremblay, & Jennings, 2009). These programs had been designed to strengthen parental competency in the appropriate disciplining and monitoring of child behavior, to increase parental involvement in the child's school, and to improve the child's social and emotional competence. The researchers recommend longitudinal follow-up and ongoing support for large-scale programs to improve parenting skills, especially of new mothers. Programs in the natural environment are considered especially promising. One example of this type of intervention is the Colorado's Nurse Home Visitor Program (NHMP), created in 2000 and founded on an evidence-based home visiting program developed by Olds et al. (1998).

Prevention programs reported in the literature are largely secondary and tertiary in nature. Rather than preventing the emergence of CD and ODD altogether, these programs identify at-risk children who have already exhibited disruptive behavior problems and attempt to prevent the more serious long-term consequences of ODD and CD, such as peer rejection, school failure and dropout, substance abuse, teen pregnancy, and delinquency. Successful prevention programs are delivered in schools, clinics, and family/community sites. Elements considered critical to their success address multiple risk domains, including parent-directed components, social and academic skills training, classroom management, teacher training, and individual or group therapy. Many also target building resistance to substance abuse and creating effective universal interventions, such as community policing, to address environmental stresses (Burke et al., 2002). Comprehensive prevention programs are, in reality,

EXHIBIT 6.2 Interventions for Childhood Disruptive Behavior Disorders

Source	Title and/or Targeted Diagnosis/Problem	Interventions
Eyberg, Boggs, and Algina (1995)	ODD and early behavioral problems	Direct observation of parent–child interaction with covert feedback to parents
Webster-Stratton (1996)	Incredible years—young children with behavior problems	Parent management training
Greenberg, Kusche, Cook, and Quamma (1995)	Promoting Alternative Thinking Strategies (PATHS – c)	Prevention activities in school settings for entire school population
Augimeri, Farrington, Koegl, and Day (2007)	Stop Now And Plan (SNAP program)—behaviors typical of CD, children who come to attention of police	Cognitive behavioral strategies; group format for parents and children; separate models for boys and girls
Lochman and Lenhart (1993)	Anger coping	Interventions targeted to affective features of disruptive behavior

a combination of prevention and forms of treatment designed to halt the progression of ODD and CD to more serious forms of the disorder, such as APD in adulthood. Exhibit 6.2 displays examples, as reported in Loeber et al. (2009).

In addition to the more generic efforts described previously, recent neurobiological research related to the most pernicious traits—callousness and lack of empathy—suggest the importance of developing specific, focused, and intensive interventions that target these traits early on and enable these at-risk children and adolescents to be more responsive to the warmth and rewards of social affiliation (Shirtcliff et al., 2009).

Small-Treatment-Group Interventions

The finding that treatment groups composed of CD peers can have iatrogenic effects highlights the strong influence of deviant peers on delinquent behavior (Dishion, McCord, & Poulin, 1999). To aid the development of prosocial behaviors, community-based group interventions with delinquent boys are encouraged to include prosocial peers and to minimize participation of those who might reinforce antisocial behavior (Burke et al., 2002; Steiner & Remsing, 2007).

Individual Interventions

Individual interventions are considered more effective as a component of broader, more comprehensive treatment programs. These interventions may contain anger control/stress inoculation, assertiveness training and rational-emotional therapy, prosocial communication, problem-solving skills, and moral development; however, the reported outcomes are modest at best (Brestan &

Eyberg, 1998; Burke et al., 2002). Kazdin and Crowley (1997) report the most improvement in antisocial children with better reading achievement and less severe symptoms when skill building was combined with parental observation and facilitation of application at home.

Contextual factors—such as socioeconomic disadvantage, parent dysfunction, and adverse child-rearing practices—were adversely related to treatment outcome. Interestingly, child IQ and a history of antisocial symptoms were not related to outcome; older children and girls had more positive outcomes. Another study compared a collaborative problem solving (CPS), cognitive behavioral model with PT in 47 affectively dysregulated children with ODD. CPS proved equivalent or superior to PT across all domains measured, both at treatment termination and at 4-month follow-up (Greene et al., 2004). This study was noteworthy in constructing interventions that, although guided by a manual, allowed flexibility for individualized application, contained random assignment to treatment condition, and focused on clinically referred, highly comorbid samples; thus it resembled real-world situations to a greater degree than most treatment outcome research. The CU features of ODD and CD have been specifically targeted and effectively reduced in follow-up intervals of 6 months and 3 years, according to parent and teacher reports, in other interventions using cognitive behavioral interventions with 6- to 11-year-old children (Hawes & Dadds, 2007; Kolko et al., 2009). Traditional, psychodynamic child psychotherapy has not proven effective unless parents were actively involved in the treatment; traditional therapy with adolescents alone, without parental involvement, may be somewhat effective (Burns et al., 1999).

One 12-week evidenced-based study of children with ODD and CD and their parents specifically attempted to address issues of comorbidity, complexity, and barriers to treatment (Kazdin & Whitley, 2006). Comorbidity did not affect ultimate treatment outcome, and most complexity was either unrelated or positively related to therapeutic change. Perceived barriers—defined as obstacles to perceived participation in treatment, attitudes toward the therapist, and relevance of approach—were associated with less improvement, but even these children improved significantly. Notable, however, and consistent with other studies, was a dropout rate of 24.1%; these noncompleters were more likely to be of lower SES status, receiving public assistance, and of non-European American origin. These findings highlight the need to attend to perceived barriers to treatment and to focus on the reasons for noncompletion of treatment; complexity, in and of itself, is considered a given and not necessarily problematic in terms of outcome.

Parent and Family Treatment

Effective family treatment strategies have been the predominant focus of empirical research (Steiner & Remsing, 2007); they include variations of PT, problem solving, communication training, reciprocity training, and multisystemic approaches (Reed & Sollie, 1992). Combined PT and individual intervention is more effective than either component alone (Webster-Stratton &

Hammond, 1997). Parent management training (PMT) and parent–child interaction training (PCIT) have proven more effective than problem-solving training alone (Burke et al., 2002). The latter includes nondirective play skills for parents, management strategies to promote compliance, and coaching in a naturalistic setting (Schumann, Foote, Eyeberg, Boggs, & Algina, 1998). Few studies have reported changes of sufficient clinical significance to move a child into the nonclinical range of functioning. Up to 50% of children in some studies are not demonstrating normal functioning at termination. Because more severely impaired children and families drop out of PMT treatment, the effectiveness of PMT in more severe cases is unknown; claims of long-term efficacy of PMT cannot be made without extreme caution (Green & Doyle, 1999).

One approach that has resulted in successful treatment of youth involved in the juvenile justice system is multisystemic therapy (MST). This intervention is intensive in that, if needed, it is administered daily, is time limited, and specifically designed for youth delinquents based on empirically identified risk factors for deviant behavior (Henggeler, 1999). Described as an exemplary approach because of its elaborate training, supervision, and monitoring for treatment adherence, MST works directly with the family, peers, school, and neighborhood to identify and target factors contributing to the youth's problem behaviors.

Home-based services, also known as in-home or family preservation or intensive family services, attempt to prevent out-of-home placement, strengthen family coping, and connect the child or adolescent to an outside support system. Features common to these services, identified by Stroul and Goldman (1990), include the following: the family, rather than the individual child, is considered the client and services are delivered in the home; an ecological perspective emphasizes collaborative work with community agencies and sources of support; family preservation and/or reunification is emphasized unless it is unsafe for the child to remain with the family; service delivery hours are flexible and 24-hour crisis intervention is available; a variety of multifaceted services are offered, including counseling, skill training, and coordination of services, varying in intensity and duration with the needs of the family; small caseloads enable staff to work actively with the family and to establish a close, intense, personal relationship; core values include empowering family members and instilling hope. In a meta-analysis of home-based programs, Fraser, Nelson, and Rivard (1997) found that 75% to 90% of children and adolescents did not subsequently require out-of-home placement and that both verbal and physical aggression had decreased.

Family intervention and family support services emphasize efforts to stop blaming parents for problems in their children; these approaches represent a shift from viewing families as recipients of services to engaging them as partners in the provision of service. Friesen and Koroloff's (1990) findings showed that parents regarded emotional support to them, regardless of its form, as the most helpful intervention in that they benefitted from increased access to information, improved problem-solving skills, and more positive views of their parenting and of their children (Friesen & Koroloff, 1990).

Community Interventions and Case Management

Burke et al. (2002) present a review of community-based interventions that describes mild positive outcomes at best, with little behavioral change and occasionally worsened behavior, especially in the context of group interventions that have reinforced deviant behavior. The literature on community interventions and case management is mixed and noted for its inconsistency and lack of rigorous methodology. Community interventions often involve antibullying programs, tailored curricula, monitoring of playground behavior, and an attempt to alter school philosophy and organization. Some promising community interventions have involved intensive case management, home-based treatment, and therapeutic foster care or group homes, developed largely as alternatives to institutionalized care (Burns et al., 1999). Case management is useful in providing coordination of services and individualized care for children (Paulson, Gratton, Stuntzer-Gibson, & Summers, 1995). A wraparound approach called Family Centered Intensive Case Management (FCICM) utilizes a team system of case management and was successful in reducing behavior problems and improving overall functioning in both the families and children (Evans, Armstrong, & Kuppinger, 1996). Case management programs vary from community to community and consistent standards for models of care are lacking; nevertheless, these programs appear to hold promise in preventing institutionalization and in improving youth and family functioning.

Mentors

Mentors have been used as sources of support and role modeling for at-risk youth by encouraging students to pursue educational goals, get involved in extracurricular activities, and learn problem-solving skills. The process of mentoring is an empowering one for adolescents.

Mentors, who are often community volunteers or paraprofessionals, help to build confidence as well as social and academic skills; they also provide a buffer against association with delinquent peer groups (Burns et al., 1999). Mentored children have been found less likely to begin drug or alcohol use or to hit someone, have improved school attendance and attitudes toward school, and enjoy improved relationships with peers and family members (Tierney, Grossman, & Resch, 1995).

Multimodal Intervention

Comprehensive programs that address multiple risk factors at once show the greatest success in treating CD and ODD and are the most cost-effective (Burke et al., 2002). The use of the Early Risers "Skills for Success" program, targeting serious conduct problems related to ODD and CD symptoms, has demonstrated significantly positive results after 6 years with K–6 students in ODD symptom reduction, improved social skills, and more effective parental discipline (Bernat, August, Hektner, & Bloomquist, 2007). Components of the program included a summer camp program, peer-support children's groups, family skills parent groups, a children's buddy system with prosocial peers, parent communication training, and family program nights. The buddy system, in particular, is valuable in that social skills training alone cannot overcome a peer rejection process. The program had a 3-year intensive phase followed by a 2-year booster phase. Replication in real-world community settings, not as tightly controlled by the researchers, has demonstrated similarly positive results.

One program designed to Link Interestsof Families and Teachers (Project LIFT) carries out multimodal interventions that include PT, classroom social skills, a playground behavior program, and systematic communication between parents and teachers (Reid, Eddy, Fetrow, & Stoolmiller, 1999). Results have included significant reductions in playground aggression and in adverse parenting behaviors; improved classroom/social skills behavior was also seen as compared with control groups of first and fifth graders.

MST provides carefully supervised, flexible interventions at the individual, family, peer, school, and neighborhood levels and is designed to address all the factors for each child that contribute to antisocial behavior, including, but not limited to: parental marital conflict and substance abuse, delinquent peers, academic performance, and communication skills. Especially, notable in this approach is the careful attention to the training of supervisors and ongoing team case reviews (Borduin, 1999).

Burns et al. (1999) summarized 82 studies conducted between 1966 and 1995 involving 5,272 youth treated for conduct problem behavior, applying criteria derived from the American Psychological Association for "well established" and "probably efficacious" treatments. Two studies, involving living with children and the use of videotaped modeling PT, were considered well established. Ten treatments—anger-control training including, stress inoculation, assertiveness training and delinquency prevention, MST, parent–child interaction therapy, PT in problem-solving skills, rational–emotive therapy, and time-out plus signal seat training were deemed "probably efficacious" by these reviewers. Notably, girls and ethnic minority populations were not sufficiently represented in these studies, and it could not be assumed that the identified treatments would work for them.

A more recent review of empirically supported family-based treatments for adolescents with CD and delinquent behavior identified multisystemic family therapy (MFT), functional family therapy, multidimensional treatment in foster care, and, to a lesser extent, brief strategic family therapy as evidence-based treatments that have been widely used in a variety of community settings (Henggeler & Sheidow, 2012). These researchers emphasize the difference between *efficacy* (studies conducted under optimally controlled settings that investigate whether treatments *can* work) and *effectiveness* (whether or not a treatment can be successful when delivered in real-world community clinical settings. The latter entails less supervision, the use of community practitioners, and clients with more co-occurring disorders. Family-based treatments are complex, require extensive training and supervision, and are difficult to transport to real-life settings. These therapies need extensive validation with ethnic minorities, who are disproportionally represented in the mental health, juvenile justice, and social welfare service systems (Huey & Polo, 2010).

Psychopharmacology

Numerous attempts have been made to treat the impulsivity and aggressiveness of CD and ODD with lithium, haloperidol, carbamazepine, risperidone, methyphenidate, and clonidine, with mixed results. However, most studies were based on small samples of aggressive youths (Connor, 2002), and the data analyzed were based only on treatment completers and did not take into account the effects of co-occurring disorders. Atypical antipsychotics were the most commonly prescribed medications for acute and chronic maladaptive aggression. At best the medications were only partially helpful, and effects were improved when combined with psychosocial treatment. Clinicians are encouraged to consider the use of medication for the management of very severe or nonresponding CD. The benefits of drug treatment should be weighed against side effects, which include sedation, secondary cognitive effects, hypotension, extrapyramidal symptoms, tardive dyskinesia, and obesity. Notably, because substance abuse is a high risk with this population, cautions needs to be exercised when prescribing stimulants.

Youth should be carefully assessed for the presence of co-occurring disorders, especially mood disorders. Adherence to treatment is generally poor in youths, especially with CD, and should be monitored carefully (Burke et al., 2002). As an adjunctive treatment, medication is palliative and not curative. It is generally only effective after a strong therapeutic alliance is established and should never be the sole intervention with this population (Steiner & Remsing, 2007).

Treatment Settings and Efficacy

In their comparison of the efficacy of treatment across a variety of clinical settings, the clinical outcomes of Burns et al. (1999) were less positive in real-world settings than in research settings, where the conditions of treatment are more controlled. Day treatment and partial hospitalization programs can offer more flexibility than outpatient settings and can be closely linked with schools and sometimes even located in schools. Day treatment has been found to be more effective after 6 months than traditional outpatient treatment in reducing behavior problems, decreasing symptomatology, and improving family functioning (Grizenko, 1997; Grizenko, Papineau, & Sayegh, 1993; Kutash & Rivera, 1996). Improved functioning did not necessary include better academic functioning, indicating that school-based models should be considered (Grizenko, 1997; Kutash & Rivera, 1996). More than IQ, diagnosis, or other personal characteristics, ecological factors, such as the availability of community support and the effectiveness of the school and family, have been found to predict positive outcomes 6 months after residential treatment (Lewis, 1988).

Inpatient treatment has yielded poor results for children with CD unless family members were active participants (Kutash & Rivera, 1996). Studies of inpatient treatment results rarely include effective follow-up or control or comparison groups. One well-constructed study, comparing inpatient treatment with MST, reported MST as more effective than inpatient treatment in increasing family cohesion and keeping children in school and out of the hospital (Burns et al., 1999).

In an exploratory, qualitative study investigating therapist, parent, and youth perspectives of treatment barriers to family-focused outpatient treatment of youths with disruptive behavior problems, these stakeholders reported widespread dissatisfaction with outpatient mental health services (Baker-Ericzen, Jenkins, & Haine-Schlagel, 2013). Parents felt blamed and unsupported by their child's therapist, which caused discomfort and resistance to participating in the treatment. The youth themselves were dissatisfied with mental health therapy and wanted more active, directive family-focused approaches. Therapists highly endorsed family-focused therapy but were frustrated by the lack of family involvement and overwhelmed by the complexities of the families' needs.

Interventions Targeted to CU Traits

Children who display the CU trait, identified in the *DSM-5* by the specifier, *with limited prosocial emotions*, are particularly resistant to standard behavioral interventions, do not respond well to punishment techniques, such as time-out, and respond unevenly to rewards or combined approaches (Miller et al., 2013). There is also significant overlap among CU, ADHD, and ODD that is not well understood, partially because the CU trait is more variable in the preschool years and becomes more stable over time with more obvious links to specific domains of social impairment, such as bullying, and academic functioning. This suggests the importance of both early intervention during the preschool years as well as developmentally sensitive assessments and interventions targeted at specific problematic behaviors (Brammer & Lee, 2012). The strength of the trait alone predicts a poor response to treatment despite multimodal psychosocial interventions and pharmacotherapy. Suggested recommendations for future interventions that have not been systematically researched include PT intervention in very young (before age 6) children with conduct problems, and intensive treatment (unspecified as to type and amount) of older children and adolescents (Masi et al., 2013).

CU traits in children are linked to more heritable antisocial behavior (Viding, Blair, Moffitt, & Plomin, 2005) and show a more specific neurocognitive profile related to amygdala/orbitofrontal dysfunction, which manifests as insensitivity to punishment and to distress cues (Blair et al., 2006a; Dadds et al., 2006). This profile is similar to that of adult psychopaths (Lynam & Gudonis, 2005) and dissimilar to that of other children with CD, who can be hypersensitive to anger and punishment cues (Blair, Peschardt, Budhani, Mitchell, & Pine, 2006b). This specifier may have important relevance to effective treatment, as children with CU traits do not respond well to typically recommended parental socialization practices (Hawes & Dadds, 2005; Hipwell et al., 2007). In addition, this trait is considered stable over time and predicts poor outcome with respect to later antisocial behavior (Burke, Loeber, & Lahey, 2007). Moffitt et al. (2008) recommend research into girls with this trait, the appearance of the trait in preschool children, and the incorporation of children with this trait in intervention research. Preliminary research for children with CD who exhibit the

CU trait indicates the need for early identification and intervention, with continued multimodal assessment and attention throughout the elementary school years to reduce the risk of later delinquency and adult criminal behavior.

The most current comprehensive review of the research specific to the designation of the CU trait in this subgroup of children and adolescents with severe conduct problems strongly supports the validity of adding this specifier to the *DSM-5* (Frick et al., 2014). These children show decifits in their response to punishment and in their ability to respond to fear and distress in others. They exhibit less anxiety and more thrill-seeking behavior when compared to other antisocial youth. Their traits are more strongly associated with genetic influences, and are less related to hostile and coercive parenting practice compared to children with conduct problems without the CU trait. Summaries of treatment outcomes for children with elevated CU traits did offer some hope for this subgroup, defined as a difficult clinical challenge. Interventions showing significant improvement were very intensive, often combining medication for ADHD, cognitive behavioral treatment, PMT, and crisis management. PT stressed rewards, rather than punishment, targeted the self-interests of adolescents, and taught empathy skills. Stronger responses to intervention were found in the youngest (ages 3–5) children when parents were given intensive training in behavioral management skills as well as emotional and instrumental support. These researchers strongly recommend an emphasis in future research on new and innovative treatments for children and adolescents with elevated levels of CU traits.

KEY POINTS

1. The addition of the "callous and unemotional" specifier for CD in *DSM-5* appears important, as this trait is particularly pernicious and related to poor prognosis. Evidence-based research is needed regarding the etiology of the trait and its effect on the developmental trajectories of the children who have it. Effective treatment appears linked to early and intensive intervention.
2. Gender differences need more research focus. Although CD is reported to be more frequent in males, girls' relationship aggression has proven to be both challenging and treatable.
3. Increased attention is given to distinguishing normal from pathological behavior.

General Recommendations for the Assessment and Treatment of ODD and CD

In their recent review of practice parameters for the assessment and treatment of ODD, Steiner and Remsing (2007) recommend the following steps, which may be equally useful in responding to a diagnosis of CD:

1. Establish therapeutic alliances with both child and family.
2. Consider cultural issues in diagnosis and treatment, especially standards of obedience and parenting in ethnic subgroups.

3. Obtain information not only from the child, but also from parents and other significant persons in the child's environment.
4. Attend to all significant comorbid conditions.
5. Obtain information from multiple sources.
6. Consider using specific questionnaires for assessing and tracking progress.
7. Individualize treatment plans to each child's situation.
8. Use empirically tested parent interventions.
9. Assess the use of medications, but only as an adjunct to treatment, to reduce symptoms and address issues of comorbidity.
10. Evaluate the need for intensive and prolonged treatment if the condition is severe and persistent.
11. Avoid dramatic short-term interventions, such as boot camps or shock incarceration; these are not effective and can sometimes make things worse.

In their review of evidence-based treatment for mental disorders of children and adolescents, Burns et al. (1999) addressed many issues relevant to an effective response to youth with CD and ODD and their families and came to several general conclusions. First, although many services have proliferated in recent years, established evidence-based interventions are minimally available in clinical practice settings, and many services exist whose efficacy has not been established. The most effective services have been designed with known risk factors in mind, are based at home, and are well coordinated with the community, especially the schools. Research findings need to be replicated in and adapted to real-world clinical settings, and interventions without demonstrated effectiveness need to be eliminated. These authors call for the involvement of policy makers, community and professional stakeholders, and family members with clinicians and academics in the construction and design of research; they argue for systematic changes in clinical training programs in the direction of evidence-based interventions.

KEY POINTS

1. Information essential to diagnosis must be obtained from multiple sources.
2. Effective interventions embrace complexity, encompass both prevention and treatment, are multimodal in nature, acknowledge bidirectionality and sensitive developmental transitions. Promising interventions are intensive and multifaceted, delivered in the community, and involve family members and other supportive persons as partners versus patients in an individualized treatment plan. Specialized treatment programs should focus on core traits of psychopathy (CU behavior).
3. By their very nature, CD and ODD involve noncompliance; therefore, effective intervention programs should be designed with components to reward and enhance compliance.
4. Outcome research contains gaps with reference to gender, cultural diversity, and low SES.

5. Community organizations that duplicate service, lack coordination, or do not follow up—along with poorly designed group interventions—can actually produce a worsening of disruptive behaviors.
6. The use of medication can be effective as an adjunctive treatment in more severe cases of disruptive behavior, but only if treatment adherence is carefully monitored and other interventions are in place.
7. Evidence-based treatments demonstrated as effective in research settings do not necessarily transfer to the real world of clients; more observational studies in community clinical and naturalistic settings, such as homes and schools, are needed.

EQUITY AND DIVERSITY ISSUES

Race, Culture, and SES Status

Multicultural responsivity, a term used to define the cultural fairness of assessment instruments, is an issue that transcends specific diagnoses in childhood and adolescence; it is an important consideration because of its potential for adverse impact on disadvantaged and/or minority youth (Harry, Sturges, & Klinger, 2005). Diagnostic tests used by clinicians and teachers to assess adaptive behavior in youth become part of the basis for decisions about eligibility for special classrooms for intellectually challenged or emotionally disturbed children. Numerous studies have documented the overrepresentation of ethnic minority students in special education classes, where, especially if children are African American, they are less likely to receive any instruction in a mainstream classroom, more likely to face harsher discipline than their peers, less likely to graduate from high school, and more likely to be unemployed or arrested for criminal behavior (Harry et al., 2005; Hosp & Reschly, 2004). Inner-city children in mental health clinics have a mean of 3.5 mental disorder diagnoses on admission, yet they are rarely included in empirically validated interventions developed in controlled research settings (Burns et al., 1999). This is unfortunate, as SES and environmental stress are consistently described as significant risk factors in ODD and CD.

In reviewing assessment instruments used in the past 25 years for placement of children in special education classes, Allen-Meares (2008) notes that although these instruments have evolved over time, the element of culture is still not a standard component in these tests, asserting that adequate attention to a child's culture is essential to the prevention of the mislabeling and related misplacement of children. Adequate attention to culture involves attending to how culture affects behavior in micro (i.e., child, teacher, and parent), mezzo (i.e., school) and macro (i.e., societal norms and school policies that affect the school community) systems.

SES, culture, ethnicity, gender, and race may affect who receives the diagnoses of CD and ODD, which, in turn, influences how children are responded to in the school setting. This lends support to the usefulness of the Diversity/Resiliency Formulation in the diagnostic and assessment process. Systematic attention to the resources and support as well as the stressors involved in the child's racial, cultural, and spiritual communities, as would be required by this formulation, would contribute to more accurate assessment of those factors that are known to predict outcome, thus facilitating more balanced attention to risk and protective factors.

Culture, race, and ethnicity may influence how parents discipline and respond to disruptive behaviors. Although past studies have shown that African American parents are more likely to use physical punishment as a disciplinary method, their increased use of physical punishment in response to conduct problems is unclear (Pardini et al., 2008). These researchers conducted a longitudinal exploration of the bidirectional relationship between parenting practices and conduct problems in boys from childhood to adolescence. Physical punishment was more strongly related to teacher-reported conduct problems for African American children than for White youth; otherwise, there were few differences between African American and White families. Previous research had found physical punishment to be unrelated to the development of conduct problems in African American youth or perhaps even protective against such outcomes (Lansford, Deater-Deckhard, Dodge, Bates, & Pettit, 2004). Abusive physical punishment is reported to be more associated with externalizing (oppositional or conduct) problems in African American than in White youth (Lansford et al., 2002). Research in this area has been limited by small African American samples and the difficulty of distinguishing between nonabusive and abusive physical punishment.

Schmitz (2003), comparing African Americans, European Americans, and Hispanics, examined the influence of race, ethnicity, and family environment on the trajectory of child hyperactivity and antisocial behavior symptoms. Child hyperactivity was found to mediate the effects of family environment on child antisocial behavior. The initial level of child hyperactivity symptoms was reduced over time by a more cognitively stimulating and emotionally supportive home environment, which then influenced the level of child antisocial behavior. These effects were strongest for European Americans, and changes in child hyperactivity predicted changes in child antisocial behavior only for Hispanics. Racial differences in the trajectory of child behavior problems almost disappeared after controlling for socioeconomic, family structure, family environment, and discipline practices. The authors conclude that ecological processes are central to understanding the development of child antisocial behavior and that patterns of family interaction need to be assessed as adaptive responses to the environment.

Rates of psychiatric disorders with low-income children in the Netherlands did not differ between native and nonnative children, but the presence of a psychiatric disorder did correlate with parental psychopathology as well as peer and school problems; more boys than girls had diagnosed disorders (Zwirs et al., 2007). Externalizing disorders, such as CD, were more prevalent in boys, especially when ADHD and anxiety disorders were also present, but ODD was distributed equally between the genders. These findings highlight the importance of responding to empirically based risk factors versus making automatic assumptions about pathology based on ethnocultural group differences.

Leung et al. (2008) explored the prevalence of *DSM-IV* disorders in 541 Chinese adolescents. These researchers found overall rates of mental disorders similar to other international studies and somewhat higher rates of ODD and no gender differences in rates of ODD and CD; but they concluded that their findings could not be considered a valid cross-cultural comparison because of methodological dissimilarities and the difficulty assessing the level of impairment required by *DSM-IV* criteria.

Outcome reviews of the effectiveness of treatment programs for ODD and CD (Burke et al., 2002) note that noncompliant behavior is the hallmark of both of these disorders and that, especially for children with more severe CD, parents are usually disadvantaged because of their greater levels of psychosocial and economic stresses. Disruptive behavioral disorders are more embedded in societal issues—such as community crime, poverty, environmental toxins, parental stress, and substance abuse—than any other mental disorder. Moreover, community response to children with CD is fragmented and uncoordinated. Multiple mental health, educational, child welfare, and juvenile justice agencies respond to disruptive child behaviors. In one study (Shamsie, Sykes, & Hamilton, 1994), the severity of antisocial behaviors of children seen in a mental health center actually increased over time; the cause was in large part attributed to the lack of follow-up and coordination by individual agencies. On average, 15 agencies were involved with each child over a 9-year period.

Aneshensel and Sucoff (1996) focused on SES and its relationship to adolescent mental health in their study of 877 adolescents in Los Angeles County. Youth in low-SES neighborhoods perceived their neighborhoods as more hazardous with respect to crime, violence, drug use, and graffiti than youth in high-SES neighborhoods. These perceptions, in turn, influenced symptoms of ODD and CD. CD was most common in low-SES neighborhoods, whereas ODD was more common in middle-class neighborhoods, leading to the view of these disorders as having somewhat different risk factors. The authors argue that an ecological perspective, with a focus on socioeconomic and demographic environment, is essential to an adequate assessment of adolescent mental health disorders, and that diagnosis should not be limited to an individual developmental perspective that focuses too narrowly on physical growth, sexual maturation, and cognitive advancement.

Many factors must be addressed in research designs, including selection bias, social control, trust, institutional resources, and routine neighborhood and community activity patterns. A review of 40 studies between the mid-1990s and 2001 (Sampson, Morenoff, & Gannon-Rowley, 2002) highlights the complexity of assessing neighborhood effects on problem behaviors among adolescents. The researchers recommend continued attention to neighborhood social process through a variety of methodologies, including systematic observation.

The impact of heredity versus environment varies with respect to culture, gender, and reactive versus proactive forms of aggression. One study of over 1,200 twins between 9 and 10 years of age in an ethnically diverse urban area found strong support for a two-factor (proactive–reactive) model of aggression and for gender and ethnic differences. Males scored significantly higher on both proactive and reactive aggression, Asian Americans scored lower than other ethnic groups on reactive aggression but equivalent to Whites on proactive aggression, and African Americans scored higher than other ethnic groups on all measures of aggression except caregiver reports. Genetic influences were more important in boys' proactive (50%) than reactive (38%) aggression, but environmental influences accounted for almost all of the variance in both forms of aggression in girls.

Karriker-Jaffe, Foshee, Ennett, and Suchindran (2008) focused on White and African American youth in rural areas of North Carolina, exploring gender differences in trajectories of physical and social aggression, found significant clustering of physical aggression at a neighborhood level. Males had higher levels of aggression at all ages, but males and females were similar in the shape and magnitude of social aggression. Physical and social aggression increased until adolescence, followed by decreases in physical aggression after age 14.0 and in social aggression after age 13.8. This study used self-reports of aggression rather than teacher or parent ratings and probably included incidents known to students but not reported to authority figures; reported rates were higher than in former studies. Racial differences in the trajectories of aggression were not noted. The design of this study is notable in that information was sought from the youth themselves rather than from external observers, which may have elicited more valid results. This suggests that qualitative, narrative research, in which children with CD and ODD are offered the opportunity to share their own perspectives, might be a useful direction for future research.

Gender

Girls have generally been neglected in the study of disruptive behavior disorders, especially with respect to CD, as CD in girls was presumed to be rare; however, CD in girls is a common diagnosis with stable long-term symptoms and serious consequences. Keenan, Loeber, and Green (1999) noted the increased risk of comorbid conditions in girls, especially internalizing disorders, such as depression and anxiety. Although many risk factors for CD in girls were similar to those in boys, the researchers discovered some significant differences. The possibility of gender-based bias in the diagnostic criteria was noted, as symptoms and subtypes have focused more on bullying and physical aggressiveness more characteristic of boys' behaviors, whereas the developmental course and prognosis for girls may be different. The authors hypothesize that the symptom of impulsivity may be the more important risk factor for girls, as it may elicit more negative responses from teachers. The combination of ODD and ADHD is considered more significant a risk factor for girls, as girls with ODD were reported to be less socially adept, more unhappy, and more disliked by their peers than boys (Carlson, Tamm, & Gaub, 1997). Girls were also more likely to feel guilty about their disruptive behavior's impact on others, making them more vulnerable to depression along with CD. Girls were also noted to engage more in social than physical aggression and to be more vulnerable to its effects.

The differential rates of physical maturation between boys and girls are considered to be so important that maturation may be the most significant factor distinguishing the genders in terms of the development of CD (McGee & Stanton, 1992). For example, it is unclear in the research whether or not the early onset of CD may in fact be more important for girls than for boys; adolescent onset in girls may be more important. Adolescent girls are especially vulnerable to anxiety, depression, and accompanying suicidality and somatization symptoms; the latter predict delinquency in girls but not in boys. Girls who are antisocial in their behavior are also more likely to engage in alcohol or marijuana use than boys; this is especially important, as adolescent girls are more likely to engage in unprotected sex, acquire a sexually transmitted disease, get pregnant, engage in risky behavior during pregnancy, and subject their subsequent children to poor child-rearing practices, thus extending the CD risks to the next generation. Girls also appear to be more sensitive than boys to disruptions in their home and social environment, especially with respect to their father's hostility (McGee & Stanton, 1992). The association with deviant peers, especially for girls with early onset of puberty, is another heightened risk factor (Stattin & Magnussen, 1990).

These gender differences in risk factors and developmental issues suggest the need for more focus on diagnosis and treatment that is gender specific. Ohan and Johnston (2005) demonstrated that *DSM-IV* symptoms of ADHD, ODD, and CD are seen by mothers as more typical of boys, and that girls manifest disruptive behaviors in ways different from symptom descriptions in *DSM-IV*. As a result, girls may not be diagnosed until their oppositional and conduct problems have become serious and more difficult to change. Although these researchers do not recommend separate gender diagnostic categories for the disruptive behavior disorders, they recommend consideration of adding female-sensitive behavioral indicators to the symptom checklists.

Keenan et al. (1999) suggest that treatment for girls may need to focus more on family discord, communication with peers, and emotional experiences in addition to cognitive/behavioral skills. One recent experiment targeted at relational aggression in adolescent girls (Cannon, Hammer, Reicherzer, & Gilliam, 2012) used relational–cultural theory to promote empathy and relational competence in middle school girls who had been both victims and perpetrators of cyberbullying via texting. The ability to express emotions authentically and in person facilitated growth-fostering connections both within and beyond the group.

Diagnostic and treatment models have largely been based on the male gender. The phenomenon of behavioral disruption in girls has been understudied. Future research needs to focus on acutely identifying the developmental precursors of CD in girls, the age of onset, the extent and type of comorbidity, and the interaction of age and gender with respect to risk factors. It is hypothesized that because girls in general appear to be at lower risk for CD, female gender itself may be a protective factor for CD but a risk factor for depression; this needs further exploration, as an understanding gender differences may illuminate causal factors, developmental pathways, and the development of gender-sensitive intervention for both sexes (Keenan et al., 1999). In general, girls and ethnic minorities have not been sufficiently represented in research on effective treatment (Burns et al., 1999).

KEY POINTS

1. Low SES is a significant risk factor, especially for CD; to the extent that racial and ethnic minorities suffer more from the effects of poverty, their children are at higher risk for CD. Assessment instruments may result in the further marginalization of minority children and youth.
2. Marginalized populations, particularly ethnic and racial groups, have not been the focus of controlled outcome research and are more likely to drop out of studies; hence, the barriers to effective treatment are poorly understood.
3. Cultural differences affect the extent and type of aggressive behavior displayed by youth.
4. The bulk of the research on CD has focused on boys. ODD and CD in girls have serious and long-term consequences, and girls are especially susceptible for co-occurring depression. Promising interventions with girls have focused on relational aggression; however, serious gaps in research and intervention remain with respect to the female gender.

STRENGTH-BASED CONTRIBUTIONS TO DIAGNOSIS AND TREATMENT

Protective Factors

The factors that seem to protect children from psychiatric disorders in general are described as likely but not certain to be protective in the case of disruptive behavior disorders; namely, living in an intact household, having parents free of serious psychiatric disorders, living above the poverty level, and having parents whose parenting style is consistent and available. The biological bases of resilience are considered important but unstudied; moreover, resilience receives little attention in the risk-factor literature (S. Goldstein & Brooks, 2005). The authors propose nine clinical guidelines for resiliency enhancement in youth with disruptive behavioral disorders. These include helping them transform scripts (words and behavior that guide daily functioning) from negative to positive, teaching stress-management skills, modeling and instructing effective communication with others, promoting self-acceptance without identifying oneself as inadequate, providing opportunities for positive mentoring of others, promoting a view of one's mistakes as challenges to overcome, promoting areas of competency and success, and developing self-discipline and self-control.

In a highly stressed urban elementary school, a yoga intervention was piloted over a 2-year period in small groups of 37 fourth and fifth graders identified as having emotional and behavioral disorders, including CD and ODD (Steiner et al., 2013). The groups of seven to 10 students met twice per week for an hour for 3½ months. The study was carefully introduced to ensure awareness and buy-in from the school administration, and the groups were carefully scheduled as to avoid interfering with teaching priorities. Teachers reported improved attention in class and adaptive skills and reduced depressive, behavioral, and internalizing symptoms. Students anecdotally described being calmer and able to focus more. Feasibility challenges were noted, however, in that out of 74 children originally identified as having behavioral and emotional disorders,

41 enrolled, and 37 ultimately participated. The biggest challenge to full participation was lack of accessibility and mobility of the families; many had no phone numbers or had moved or did not return forms after initially expressing interest. Satisfaction response rates for those who participated were 100% for teachers, 62% for parents, and 100% for students, who indicated being helped to relax, to focus, and to get into less trouble. The researchers recommend replication with a larger randomized control samples and careful assessment of classroom behavior and academic performance. This is an interesting study indicating creative attention to resiliency sources in an inner-city environment characterized by a multitude of environmental stresses.

A unique attempt to examine adolescent perspectives on how their mental health diagnoses affected their perceived quality of life was recently reported in the *Journal of Culture Medicine and Psychiatry* (Chavez, Mir, & Canino, 2012). Using a grounded theory approach, these Puerto Rican researchers conducted in-depth interviews and focus groups with 60 Puerto Rican male and female teenagers diagnosed with ADHD, CDE, ODD, and depression or generalized anxiety in outpatient mental health clinics. Their purpose was to develop an assessment scale composed of qualitaty-of-life indicators, emphasizing positive, wholistic, health-enhancing aspects of life rather than a negative orientation, in an effort to identify sources of resilience and strategies of coping. An unusual strength of this research was the measurement of mental health outcomes in the context in which they occur (family, school, and community). CD/ODD adolescents in this sample repeatedly emphasized the absence of a parental figure and the need for family activities/bonding in their lives. Of utmost importance to them was the ability to practice sports activities! These teens wanted to get along with family, believe in God, struggle to have a future, stay away from problems and behave well, have a good attitude, be thankful and respect others, to eat healthfully and be happy. They reported that having a mental health diagnosis was disturbing, but expressed relief about being able to receive help and learn how to control specific behaviors and emotions. The researchers are in the process of refining and testing the psychometric properties of their instrument, the Adolescent Quality of Life-Mental Health Scale (AQOL-MHS). This research effort, we believe, is an important step forward. It relates diagnosis directly to desired treatment outcomes, defined in terms of the perceptions of the identified patients, in positive strength-based terms that link the mental health disorder to defined outcomes in a way that provides useful direction in treatment planning and emphasizes hope.

Corcoran and Nichols-Casebolt (2004) advocate for the use of a risk and resilience ecological framework as an assessment and goal-setting tool for social workers, noting that although risk and protective factors have been empirically supported, there is failure to integrate this content systematically in assessment and intervention planning for children. These researchers suggest a system of micro (individual), mezzo (family), and macro (community, institutional, and social policy) levels of systematic assessment, with attention to risk and protective factors at each level. When intervention goals are considered within this framework, the complex biopsychosocial contexts of the child are treated with attention and respect. Because CD and ODD are so powerfully predictive of numerous problems in adulthood, it is clear that biological and environmental sources of resilience need to be identified and strengthened. This is a vital area for future research.

KEY POINTS

1. Even in texts devoted to resiliency-based interventions, the enhancement of protective factors is virtually absent with respect to ODD and CD. This is true despite the awareness that, because of the intransigence and disruptive effects of these disorders, effective interventions should begin in early childhood.
2. Assessment is based on a deficiency model that emphasizes pathology. To study how protective factors can be enhanced, a strength-based model of assessment needs to be established, followed by systematic exploration of related interventions.
3. Effective, strength-building responses must partner mental health professionals with educators, the performing arts community, churches, and other nonmedical sources of support.
4. Protective factors are ignored in the *DSM-5*.

Arguably no other diagnoses contain the multisystem complexities that characterize CD and ODD. As we have illustrated, these externalizing disorders have been demonstrated to be multidetermined and cannot simplistically be ascribed to nature or nurture. Further, they are interactional and multidirectional in nature, with the potential to turn an otherwise supportive family and environment into a negatively reactive one as the child and the parents bring out the worst in each other. That we are abysmally ineffective in our response to children with these disorders is evident in the all too frequent trajectory of school failure, substance abuse, and ultimate incarceration in the criminal justice system. The following case illustrates the hypothesized differences in the diagnostic process, contrasting the current *DSM-5* diagnostic process with the addition of our proposed Diversity/Resiliency Formulation.

CASE STUDY WITH AND WITHOUT THE DIVERSITY/RESILIENCY FORMULATION

Conduct Disorder

Nick Richards, age 8½, is the oldest of three children in a White family living in an upper-middle-class suburb of New York City. His mother, Elizabeth, is a stay-at-home mom. Nick's father, John, an executive in New York City, commutes to work daily and returns home in the early evenings. Nick has two younger siblings: Josh, age 7, and Christy, age 5. His mother describes Nick as having been a very difficult child from infancy on. Elizabeth had trouble breastfeeding Nick, who suffered from colic and "screamed for hours." After several infant formulas were unsuccessfully tried, a soy formula was found to work better for him.

Although Nick's developmental milestones were on schedule, he struggled with peer relationships almost immediately after beginning half days at preschool at age 3. Easily frustrated, Nick reacted with intense anger when asked to take turns or share, often biting and kicking his peers if he was unable to wrest a desired toy away from them. If confronted about negative behavior, Nick would lie about what had occurred, denying his own behavior and blaming the conflict on others ("I didn't do it," "Not my fault," "He took it from me"). If his peers cried in distress, Nick appeared unmoved. Similarly, he did not respond to "time-out" or other disciplinary techniques, such as the withdrawal of privileges or the removal of favorite playthings.

By the time he was enrolled in kindergarten, Nick's peers attempted to avoid him, and he was invited less and less often to birthday parties or on play dates. Unable to enter a group of children on the school playground in a socially acceptable manner, Nick behaved aggressively, grabbing the ball or hitting and kicking when he did not get his way. On the advice of kindergarten personnel, Nick repeated kindergarten in order to give him more time to develop prosocial skills and was placed with a teacher who was noted for her combination of firmness, structure, and emotional warmth. His second year in kindergarten reportedly went somewhat more smoothly, as Nick was given privileges for good behavior and could better hold his own in cognitive learning tasks. At home, however, Nick was increasingly aggressive in his behavior toward his younger siblings and the family pet, an affectionate yellow lab named Spunky. Nick seemed to adore Spunky but became easily frustrated when Spunky wanted to continue playing ball endlessly; occasionally, Nick reacted by kicking Spunky and/or throwing something at him. Elizabeth was increasingly reluctant to trust Nick around either Spunky or his younger siblings.

During first grade, Nick had considerable difficulty with reading and math. When frustrated with classroom tasks, he would scribble angrily on his papers and/or tear them up. Parental attempts to structure his homework time and keep him on task with reminders and rewards met with enough limited success that he was able to pass first grade with marginal-level work. On several occasions, though, Elizabeth and John were called in for parent–teacher conferences because of Nick's fighting on the playground. At least once he was caught stealing lunch money or food from a peer. Sometimes Nick simply grabbed the peer's envied possession after intimidating him with threats. In the spring, Nick's teacher, with his parents' consent, placed him on a referral list for testing by the school psychologist; but owing to a backlog of referrals, this was not accomplished during the first-grade year and was scheduled for the fall of second grade.

During the summer, Nick's peer relationships in his home neighborhood deteriorated significantly. He was viewed by both his neighborhood peers and his younger siblings as mean and untrustworthy. If younger children fell down and got hurt, he would laugh derisively; when confronted about cheating in card and board games, he would either deny it or shrug and say, "So what?" Nick was increasingly excluded from neighborhood birthday parties and play dates after the mother of two preschool girls reported to Elizabeth that Nick had lured her daughters into a garage with promises of seeing a kitten and then asked them to pull down their pants. Family and marital discord increasingly worsened in reaction to Nick, who seemed to be sucking up all the energy in the family. John, who was away when much of the behavior occurred, felt that Nick needed a firmer hand and criticized his wife for being too inconsistent in her responses to Nick. Elizabeth regarded her husband as too punitive and also observed that his punishments of Nick (usually confinement to his room and occasionally an angry spanking) were ineffective. John was not home enough, in her view, to establish a warm, supportive relationship with Nick or even to know what was really going on with him. Both parents felt frustrated, defensive, and confused. Elizabeth talked with the family pediatrician about Nick's behavior and was counseled to be patient, to offer positive reinforcement, to try to keep Nick busy with day camp and church activities, and to await the report in the fall from the school psychologist. Both of the parents began to feel like neighborhood pariahs, and Josh and Christy preferred being out of the house and away from Nick.

In second grade, things got worse. On one occasion Nick threw a kindergarten child against a chain link fence, causing skin abrasions on his arms and a split lip; on another, Nick hit a student who would not lend him a pencil, was sent to the principal's office, and while waiting to see the principal, overturned a table in the school office, shattering a pottery vase and breaking a lamp. After two parent–teacher conferences and several attempts to manage his behavior in the classroom proved futile, Nick's teacher referred him to the school social worker. Large for his age, Nick was becoming more and more of a bully. At home, when Nick taunted her by threatening to pull out the eyes of her favorite doll, Christy burst into tears and told Nick she hated him. Josh attempted to fight back when Nick threatened him but was rewarded by having his arm twisted painfully behind his back until he screamed in pain and gave in. At school, Josh was also in the second grade, as he had not repeated a grade. Josh was an amiable student, popular and athletic, and Christy was a bright young kindergartner who was well liked by her peers and teacher. Nick clearly resented his more popular and successful siblings. It was no longer safe for his parents to leave Nick unsupervised with them, even for 10 minutes.

The school social worker facilitated the completion of psychological testing by the school psychologist, and a school conference was held. Nick was found to have an average IQ but to be below grade level in his academic achievement. The discrepancy between his aptitude and achievement was not enough for Nick to acquire the official label of a learning disability. The school psychologist felt that if Nick's behavioral problems were successfully treated, he could be more successful academically. She recommended that the parents solicit a referral from Nick's pediatrician to a child psychiatrist for the purpose of evaluation for psychotropic medication; she also gave them the names of community clinical psychologists who could do more individualized, comprehensive psychodiagnostic testing. The social worker facilitated the development of a behavioral management plan to be coordinated between home and school.

After a wait of several weeks, Nick was seen by a child psychiatrist. Around the same time, testing was begun with a child psychologist. The psychiatrist's *DSM-5* diagnosis of Nick was as follows:

> 312.81 Conduct Disorder, Childhood Onset Type, with limited prosocial emotions, Severe
> V62.3 Academic Problem
> V61.20 Parent–Child Relational Problem
> V61.8 Sibling Relational Problem

(**Note**: We added V codes here as we feel they are important indicators of needed treatment focus. In the typical time-pressured psychiatrist's office, however, V Codes are unlikely to be added, and only the CD diagnosis noted.)

Differential Diagnosis

Nick clearly meets the criteria for CD. He exhibits aggressive, bullying behavior toward his siblings and school peers, has attempted to exploit neighborhood girls sexually, and has been cruel to both other children and the family pet. Furthermore, Nick displays a callousness and indifference to the effects of this behavior on others that is of special concern, as this trait predicts criminal behavior and eventual incarceration for many; thus, he receives the specifier, *With limited prosocial emotions*. Although he is still a child, he was given the *Severe* specifier, due to the pervasive nature of his destructive behavior in a variety of settings, his sexual exploitation of neighborhood children, his cruelty to the family dog, and his mother's fear of leaving him alone with other children or the family pet. Other diagnoses that were considered and ruled out include bipolar disorder, ODD, major depressive disorder, ADHD, intermittent explosive disorder, and specific learning disorder.

As has been discussed previously in this chapter, ODD and ADHD often precede CD in the developmental sequence of disruptive behavior disorders. ODD is characterized by argumentativeness and rationalization and can create havoc, especially in the family, but is less likely to cause the kind of school problems Nick displays. ODD is not characterized by the destructive physical aggression, sexual manipulation, and cruelty, all of which are evident in Nick's behavior. Similarly, CD and ADHD can coexist, as both are characterized by impulsivity, lack of frustration tolerance, and resistance to tasks requiring sustained attention. However, Nick does not display the impulsivity and distractibility characteristic of ADHD; in fact, much of his negative behavior appears to be premeditated. Because his academic problems will be a focus of intervention, however, Nick was given the diagnosis of academic problem. He is performing below his intellectual ability, but the gap is not large enough for a specific learning disorder diagnosis. After thorough psychodiagnostic testing, repeated at recommended intervals, Nick may in the future qualify for a learning disability diagnosis, which would entitle him to specific educational interventions.

Regardless of what the psychological tests show, Nick's learning problems contribute to his frustration and repeated experiences of failure and must be addressed in his treatment plan. Intermittent explosive disorder does not fit Nick because the prominent issue is not the impulsive display of aggression, but rather the tendency to hurt and violate others combined with indifference to others' pain in response; this is characteristic of CD.

Bipolar disorder and major depressive disorder were considered, because mood symptoms are often expressed through anger and acting-out behavior in children. The pattern of Nick's behavior problems, however, is better explained by CD and differs from BD and MDD owing to the violation of social norms and the callousness with which Nick responds to the pain he causes others. Nick does not appear to internalize his anger and convert it into sadness and hopelessness, as would be the case in a depressive diagnosis. Nevertheless, Nick's rejection by peers and difficulty with siblings may cause great inner turmoil and feelings of sadness that Nick disguises under an "I don't care; big deal" defensive response. Nick should be monitored throughout his treatment for depression. Several V Code diagnoses were added to stress that these issues should be a focus of clinical attention: sibling relational problem, parent–child relational problem, and academic problem. Nick's behavior has certainly exacerbated family and marital conflict, which can, in turn, worsen Nick's symptoms. Finally, the practitioner should refer Nick to a physician in order to rule out any medical conditions that could be contributing to or causing his symptoms.

Discussion: Diagnostic and Treatment Response

Nick is a very vulnerable child. At an age when skill mastery is very important and contributes to a child's self-esteem, Nick is avoiding the slow, frustrating process of interpersonal and academic skill building. He is already being rejected by his peers and his siblings; and his parents are stressed by his behavior, causing increased marital discord. He appears to lack the remorse and empathy needed to evaluate his own behavior, become aware of its effects on others, and make amends. He is impervious to ordinary discipline, especially punishment. The interventions that followed from his *DSM-5* diagnosis included a cognitive behavioral management plan (rewards for compliant behavior earned by Nick and sometimes applied to the entire classroom) as well as weekly meetings with the school social worker, in which Nick was given tools for self-monitoring and role plays of effective social interaction, which included learning to take the perspective of others, to identify his own and others' emotions, to connect his behavior with its consequences, and to express sympathy. When bullying incidents occurred, the social worker involved Nick and the child he bullied, as well as the parents of each, with a focus on taking responsibility for one's behavior, understanding the emotional pain that results from bullying, and developing a plan for conflict resolution. The school principal also instituted an antibullying program, which the district purchased to be implemented in every school. At home, Nick's parents were encouraged to respond positively to Nick whenever possible, to use a system of rewards that were meaningful to Nick (trips to MacDonald's, to major league baseball games, and so on) when Nick earned them by accumulating points for good behavior, and to hire a tutor to help Nick catch up in school. Nick was also seen by a therapist trained in functional family therapy, who coordinated his treatment and maintained regular contact with his tutor, his teacher, the school principal, and the entire family. Nick participated in the development of the behaviorally specific goals toward which progress was consistently monitored by his therapist and all of the players involved.

Adding the Diversity/Resiliency Formulation to Nick's *DSM-5* Diagnosis

Nick's *DSM-5* diagnosis led to a number of multisystemic interventions, described previously. However, as mentioned, CD has proven to be extremely difficult to treat over time; most clinical interventions are not effective enough to result in a change of diagnosis or in changed behavior that falls into the symptom-free range. Children like Nick are avoided by their pro social peers, and this pattern, once set in motion, is extremely difficult to reverse. For children with CD, risk factors are more easily identified than protective factors. In Nick's case, the risk factors include inconsistent parenting and difficult temperament. However, the protective factors of an intact family with the resources to get Nick the help he needs are important to his diagnosis and treatment plan. The literature, summarized earlier in this chapter, emphasizes early intervention as extremely important, along with an individualized, multisystemic response. The response to Nick engendered by his *DSM-5* diagnosis has the potential to help Nick become more successful at school and more accepted by his siblings and peers; however, it leads to interventions designed to control negative behavior rather than to enhance sources of strength. Let us turn now to how the diagnostic and treatment process might be enhanced by adding a Diversity/Resiliency Formulation to Nick's diagnosis, as follows:

Diversity/Resiliency Formulation

In outline form:

> *Intrapersonal*: average intelligence, likes active sports, lack of complete indifference—demonstrates jealousy of siblings; responds to one-on-one tutoring and attention; likes music, especially percussion
> *Interpersonal*: loving, intact family; positive teacher and school setting; parents can afford treatment
> *Community*: upper-middle-class community has many extracurricular activities; few negative community role models, such as gangs
> *Spiritual*: family attends local Presbyterian church
> *Cultural/ethnic*: White family with Scotch-Irish origins

Or in paragraph form:

Nick is in the average range of intelligence and could perform at grade level with the help of tutoring and the effective treatment of his CD. Although lacking in remorse and unresponsive to punishment, he is not indifferent to the disapproval of his siblings and peers and would like to have friends. He is attached to his dog, Spunky. He loves sports, especially football, and displays some musical talent, with a special interest in percussion instruments. The family is connected with a supportive church community, and the immediate neighborhood contains potentially supportive families and a variety of community activities for children. Nick has favorite TV programs and electronic games and will work for rewards connected with his favorite possessions and activities. This is a White family with Scotch-Irish origins.

Considering the *DSM-5* diagnosis alone can reinforce the overwhelmed, exhausted, defeated stance of his parents and probably of Nick, himself. A practitioner using the Diversity/Resiliency Formulation as a routine part of diagnosis would have discovered that Nick loves sports and sincerely wants to be a part of informal neighborhood play. He has his favorite teams and likes to watch them on television. Nick also likes music, especially with a strong beat, and enjoys the aggressive, loud, clashing aspects of percussion instruments! He has a strong sense of rhythm and musicality. Previous to the recent worsening of his symptoms, his little brother regarded Nick with admiration. Although his parents differ with respect to disciplining Nick, they are open to suggestions and have a committed marriage. The local Presbyterian church offers excellent children's programs, and the youth leaders have expressed an interest in Nick. Nick likes the youth leaders ("They are cool") but is wary of social rejection. Nick's ethnic background contains proud and resilient prototypes in the hospitality and pride of Celtic culture. Nick's residential neighborhood is usually a friendly place; families that have previously shunned Nick would be likely to be more welcoming if they witnessed some improvement in Nick's behavior.

Using a diagnostic system that requires taking the aforementioned strengths as well as symptoms of pathology into routine consideration, a mental health professional would learn about what is right as well as wrong with Nick and thus would have discovered from the start some unique interests and potential abilities that could compete with negative acting out for his attention. Attention to the Diversity/Resiliency Formulation would push the practitioner toward more positive engagements and a more individualized and more comprehensive treatment plan. A few risk factors are important in Nick's case—namely, the CU trait and inconsistent parental discipline. On the other hand, Nick is fortunate in that he lives in an intact family, his parents are not abusive, he possesses normal intelligence, and he is not surrounded by an antisocial peer group. A prosocial older peer could be assigned to Nick by the school as a role model for effective social skills. In Nick's case, MST (described in greater detail earlier in the chapter), if implemented, would provide Nick with a variety of supportive relationships and activities specifically designed to increase his empathic capability and promote the use of prosocial skills in his interactions with family and peers. Rather than being responded to largely in terms of his symptoms, Nick would practice new forms of communication and be rewarded in meaningful ways with the genuine approval of peers and siblings. Specifically, Nick would be required to pay attention to the effects of his behavior on others and to make amends, with a genuine display of remorse, to those whom he hurt. Participating in a buddy system, Nick would experience a sustained commitment to his welfare by an older peer, which would render him less susceptible to antisocial influence in the future.

In the spirit of MST, Nick's parents would be supported rather than being blamed for his symptoms and would be able to participate in psychoeducational support groups focused on how to parent a difficult child. Nick's father would be encouraged to arrange to spend more one-on-one time with Nick. Both parents would be encouraged to follow up aggressively on Nick's interests, taking him to ball games and getting him percussion lessons. Nick would also be encouraged to try out for Little League and to exercise regularly. If possible, arrangements would be made to work one on one with a trainer to increase these prosocial skills. Nick would be given percussion lessons to build on an area of motivation and strength. In addition, using the MST approach, a variety of people in Nick's life—including mental health professionals, church personnel, neighbors, and his peer mentor—would meet with Nick and develop a formal plan, each making a commitment to specific behaviors that express the ongoing promise to help Nick. Nick would be included in every part of this process, helping with the design of all the interventions proposed for him. Unless more extensive psychological testing indicates that he has ADHD, the use of medication would be postponed until the effects of the previous approaches could be assessed. Emphasizing self-efficacy, all aspects of the treatment plan described previously would be geared to developing Nick's ability to empower himself to act in prosocial ways, to acquire friends, and to assume his former position of admired big brother in his family.

Assessment Tools

One helpful tool for assessing Nick's relationship with his environment is the eco-map presented by Hartman and Laird (1983). Composed of a series of circles connected by lines, the eco-map illustrates the client's ecological world by depicting the directional flow of energy in relationships, both in and outside of the family, illustrating closeness versus distance, intensity, and conflict. For an example, see Figure 6.1.

The eco-map illustrates how Nick has connections to individuals or systems with whom he has a relationship. This eco-map represents Nick's view of his ecological world at one moment in time. The map does not reflect his parents' or siblings' perceptions of these relationships but rather Nick's point of view only.

Discussion Questions

1. How do you think this map would look from the point of view of Nick's mother?
2. How would you change the distance between the circles and Nick? Which would you bring closer? Which would you make further apart? Explain your rationale.

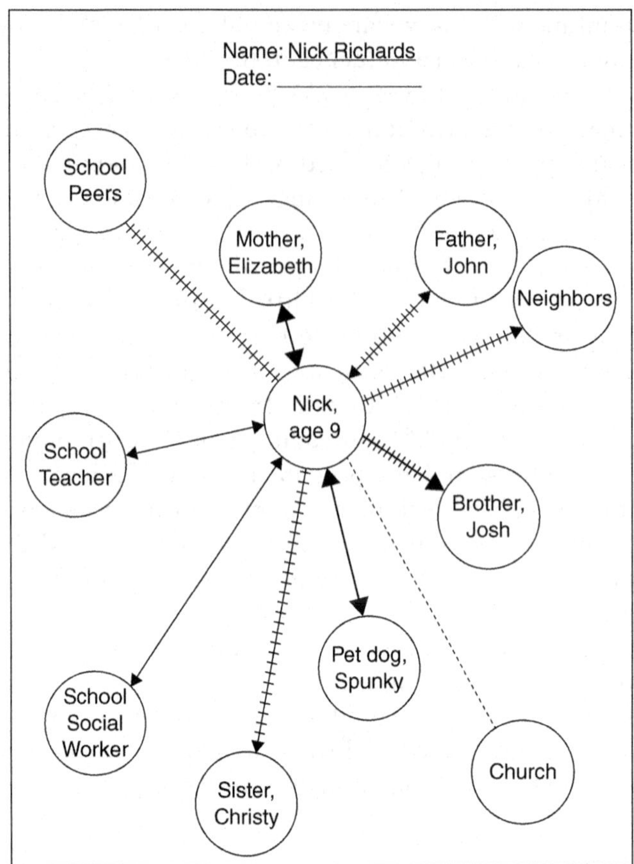

Figure 6.1 Nick's eco-map. Nearness or distance of circles indicates relative importance of relationships. Dark lines = stronger relationships; light lines = more tenuous or fragile relationships. Lines with horizontal crossbars = conflictual relationships. Arrows depict direction of energy.

An analysis of the eco-map in Figure 6.1 indicates that Nick feels closest to his mother and experiences this relationship as mutual, with energy flowing back and forth between them. His dog, Spunky, and his brother, Josh, are next in closeness. Nick experiences his relationship with Spunky as a reciprocal exchange of energy. With respect to his brother, Nick experiences himself as putting energy into this relationship but not receiving energy back. Although he describes his relationship with his father as reciprocal, his father is depicted as more distant than his mother, dog, or brother. That Nick experiences his relationships with his teacher and the school social worker as reciprocal is a good sign, although Nick has not allowed these relationships to be salient to him; they are depicted as somewhat distant. Nick feels that he is directing energy toward neighborhood peers and toward his sister, Christy, but does not feel that he is receiving energy from them. His relationships with the church and with school peers are very tenuous; he does not perceive himself as reaching out to them or vice versa and appears to have given up on these major sources of prosocial learning. In addition, relationships with school peers, siblings, father, and neighbors are all perceived by Nick as conflictual.

The use of the eco-map can be empowering for Nick as he draws it along with the school social worker. In doing so, he can become more aware of strengths in his life and also of relationships he would like to secure. The map can be redrawn from the point of view of the entire family or any of its members, as depicted in the center circle. This simple tool could be used by physicians and any allied mental health professional as a way of diagnosing for both Axis IV and VI and could also be used as a normative evaluation tool to assess changes in Nick over time as an intervention plan is implemented.

The clinician could also use parent/guardian cross-cutting symptom rating scales recommended in the *DSM-5* to check for suicidality, anxiety, somatic and sleep problems, depression, substance abuse, and other symptoms exacerbating the CD symptoms Nick is displaying. Measurements most often reported in the most current surveys of research on CD refer simply to verbal reports on the presence and severity of traits by clinicians, teachers, and parents. We favor the eco-map as especially useful because it elicit's Nick's cooperation, engages his own view of his relational world, and in so doing, validates his perspective and his ability to engage.

In summary, CD is a tenacious, hard to treat, multifaceted disorder. Children with CD elicit repeated negative attention from their environment, and this pattern reinforces Nick's behavior. Any single-factor solutions—such as individual therapy, medication, or support groups at school—are unlikely to bear fruit in terms of sustained success over time. The use of *DSM-5* alone would give the practitioner an understanding of Nick's contextual world in terms of risk factors and negativity, but it would not focus on existing and/or potential strengths. A multisystemic, individualized, long-term approach would involve Nick's family, school personnel, church leaders, tutors, neighborhood parents, and a buddy in making specific substantial and intense commitments to Nick, and Nick would be asked to make a commitment to the activities proposed as well. Progress would be measured continuously, as all the parties would be held accountable. This early, comprehensive response to the complex phenomena of CD stands the best chance of long-term success. Although the intense, multifaceted nature of this approach might be expensive in dollars and person-hours in the short run, it could be a bargain in the long run, preventing many of the costly outcomes of CD, such as accidents and crime related to substance abuse, school failure, and incarceration.

Diversity Considerations

Application of the role of culture in Nick's situation, requires grasping the values, beliefs, practices, and perceptions that are often hidden and not easily discerned. Oftentimes the assumption is put forth that "culture" applies only to ethnic groups; however, the approach proposed here emphasizes understanding an individual's worldview and particularly recognizing the heterogeneity within any culture group. That is, everyone lives within a cultural context. In Nick's situation, his parents have the financial means to get help for him, and there are many prosocial role models in his peer group in the neighborhood, church, and school. In his upper-middle-class largely White environment, Nick is expected to be a high achiever who will go on to college someday. His parents may feel especially stigmatized and labeled as parental failures because of Nick's problems. Their Celtic cultural heritage may be virtually unknown to Nick and not perceived as a source of strength or resiliency. Learning about his culture, along with his parents, might be helpful to Nick's sense of identity and mastery in the future.

AUTHORS' NOTE: We purposely chose to highlight a White middle-class family to illustrate CD with limited prosocial emotions for several reasons. In our clinical experience, the most severely conduct-disordered children, with the CU trait presentation, have not been the stereotypic children of color living in poverty, who may often display antisocial behavior as a result of environmental role models in a neighborhood characterized by violence and chaos, but have often been privileged White children whose busy parents are invested in demanding careers. Conduct-disordered children in this more privileged context may fly under the radar and go unnoticed until they commit a heinous crime, such as a school shooting. When lesser antisocial acts are committed, they are less likely to be referred to the criminal justice system and more likely to be referred instead to traditional psychotherapy, which has proven to be ineffective and to alienate parents from sources of help. If an African American boy in the inner city of Detroit or a Latino boy in the barrios of Los Angeles were to display the same behaviors as Nick, the environmental challenges would be more complicated and the resources more limited. The diagnostic challenge would be to separate out environmental etiology from the presence of the CU personality trait. Intensive intervention, using a multisystemic family focus, would be indicated for these children too and less likely to be available. Sadly, a child of color is at greater risk for a lifetime in the criminal justice system, but may be less dangerous to society than a child like Nick who goes untreated.

SUMMARY

The bulk of the research related to CD and ODD has focused on indicators of pathology, etiology, and risk factors. Intervention research has similarly focused on reducing and/or preventing risk factors or on remediating disruptive behavior and its consequences. Data on long-term outcomes are limited at best, controlled research studies have high dropout rates, and adults formerly diagnosed with CD are well represented in our prison populations. Little to no research has focused on the strengthening of protective factors. Most studies measure the reduction in pathological symptoms in individuals but do not describe interventions designed to identify and make use of individual, family, or community strengths and resilience; that is, they focus on what is wrong and try to correct it rather than balancing this focus with an emphasis on what is right and how to strengthen it.

We believe that this state of affairs is in part due to the medicalization and pathological focus of assessment and treatment of externalizing behavior disorders. Yet the complexity of causation and context for CD and ODD is well known to be a combination of internal neurobiology and environmental stress. Children like Nick upset us, elicit negative attention and a focus on control. Programs that aim to strengthen at-risk youth but lie outside the domain of mental health research and intervention may be a promising arena for future study, especially for their effectiveness in inner-city and multicultural populations. For example, anecdotal accounts of programs focused on the arts (Turnbull, 1995) or on journal writing (Salzman, 2003) provide passionate testimonials about the effects of singing and autobiographical writing on the lives of at-risk youth, some of whom were already incarcerated in juvenile facilities. Effective responses to children with ODD and CD must involve systematic attention to building their strengths in the context of safe and supportive communities. This, we believe, will entail the combined efforts of medical, mental health, and educational personnel working with community leaders and community programs.

DISCUSSION QUESTIONS AND ACTIVITIES

1. Read the article by Corcoran and Nichols-Casebolt (2004) titled "Risk and Resilience Ecological Framework for Assessment and Goal Formulation" (see "References"), and use its concepts to frame your diagnosis of a child or adolescent with CD or ODD, adding the Diversity/Resiliency Formulation to your diagnosis. Although this article was written for a professional social work journal, its concepts are useful for mental health professionals in a variety of roles. Regardless of whether you are a physician, nurse, school counselor, social worker, or in another role with the client, how would your use of these concepts enrich the diagnostic process and influence your treatment/intervention goals?
2. How would the presenting symptoms of the case vignette differ if Nick were a girl? Discuss and apply the Diversity/Resiliency Formulation to a reply.
3. Imagine that a child with the symptoms described in Nick's case vignette is an African American or Latino child living in the ghetto, barrio, or low-income area within a large city. Describe the barriers to mental health care that would exist and the nature of risk and protective factors that might be present. How would you enhance protective factors, reduce risk factors, and address the role of culture as an empowering factor? Discuss in terms of clinical and system-wide interventions.

4. Describe a client who you feel has oppositional or antisocial traits. Create a hypothesized eco-map, referring to the previous material. Then, do an eco-map with a teenager you know in order to assess for the pattern of relationships in his or her life. In the classroom setting, members can role-play the creation of eco-maps without describing the client out loud and then engage in a discussion about how they perceive the client's world as depicted in the eco-map.
5. Visit one of the websites in the "Web Resources" section and apply the material, hypothetically, to Nick.
6. Do you think the concept of bidirectional reciprocity is applicable to how his parents respond to Nick? Discuss this and develop a plan to cope with the effects of Nick's behavior on his parents.
7. How do you think Nick's behavior, if not remediated, will affect Nick's siblings over time? What would you do to prevent this?
8. Nick's case illustrates the ideal response to a child with CD. How would you adapt the systemic model described to your real-world setting? What would be the barriers to applying the comprehensive, multisystemic response to Nick's problems, and how would you reduce or eliminate them?
9. Define the difference between punishment and abuse. What are the different factors that distinguish them from each other? Then imagine that you are working with Nick's family and the issue of spanking comes up. Nick's father believes that he should be spanked more, not less. You disagree. How would you intervene with respect to the issue of discipline while maintaining a good working relationship with both of Nick's parents?
10. Develop a model plan for the prevention of CD and ODD in your community. Evaluate your plan for feasibility, then create a powerpoint presentation for community groups, schools, churches, and community agencies.

WEB RESOURCES

http://cfc.uoregon.edu/atp.htm
http://modelprograms.samhsa.gov
www.colorado.edu/cspv/blueprints
www.conductdisorders.com
www.incredibleyears.com
www.pcit.org

REFERENCES

Abaied, J. L., & Rudolph, K. D. (2009). Mothers as a resource in times of stress: Interactive contributions of socialization of coping and stress to youth psychopathology. *Journal of Abnormal Child Psychology*. Retrieved from www.pubget.com/paper/19908139.

Allen-Meares, P. (2008). Assessing the adaptive behavior of youths: Multicultural responsibility. *Social Work*, *53*(4), 307–316.

American Psychiatric Association. (1980). *Diagnostic and statistical manual of mental disorders* (3d ed.). Washington, DC: Author.

American Psychiatric Association. (1994). *Diagnostic and statistical manual of mental disorders* (4th ed.). Washington, DC: Author.

American Psychiatric Association. (2000). *Diagnostic and statistical manual of mental disorders* (4th ed., text rev.). Washington, DC: Author.

American Psychiatric Association. (2013). *Diagnostic and statistical manual of mental disorders* (5th ed.). Arlington, VA: Author.

Aneshensel, C. S., & Sucoff, C. A. (1996). The neighborhood context of adolescent mental health. *Journal of Health and Social Behavior*, *37*(4), 293–310.

Angold, A., & Costello, J. (1996). Toward establishing an empirical basis for the diagnosis of Oppositional Defiant Disorder. *Journal of the American Academy of Child and Adolescent Psychiatry*, *35*(9), 1205–1212.

Augimeri, L. K., Farrington, D. P., Koegl, C. J., & Day, D. M. (2007). The SNAP under 12 outreach project: Effects of a community based program for children with conduct problems. *Journal of Child and Family Studies*, *16*, 799–807.

Baker-Ericzen, M., Jenkins, M., & Haine-Schlagel. (2013). Therapist, parent, and youth perspectives of treatment barriers to family-focused community outpatient mental health services. *Journal of Child and Family Studies*, 22, 854–868.

Barkley, R. A., Fischer, M., Edelbrock, C. S., & Smallish, L. (1990). The adolescent outcome of hyperactive children diagnosed by research criteria: I. An eight-year prospective follow-up study. *Journal of the American Academy of Child and Adolescent Psychiatry*, *29*, 546–557.

Barkley, R. A., & Gordon, M. (2002). Comorbidity, cognitive impairments, and adaptive functioning in adults with ADHD: A comprehensive approach. In S. Goldstein & S. Teeter Ellison (Eds.), *Clinicians' guide to adult ADHD: Assessment and intervention* (pp. 46–69). New York, NY: Academic Press.

Bernat, D., August, G., Hektner, J. M., & Bloomquist, M. L. (2007). The early riser preventive intervention: Testing for six-year outcomes and meditational processes. *Journal of Abnormal Child Psychology*, *35*, 605–617.

Blair, R. J. (2004). The roles of orbital frontal cortex in the modulation of antisocial behavior. *Brain and Cognition*, *55*, 198–208.

Blair, R. J. R., Peschardt, K. S., Budhani, S., Mitchell, D. G. V., & Pine, D. S. (2006a). The development of psychopathy. *Journal of the American Academy of Child and Adolescent Psychiatry*, *40*, 1418–1425.

Blair, R. J. R., Peschardt, K. S., Budhani, S., Mitchell, D. G. V., & Pine, D. S. (2006b). The development of psychopathology. *Journal of Child Psychology and Psychiatry*, *47*, 262–275.

Borduin, C. M. (1999). Multisystemic treatment of criminality and violence in adolescents. *Journal of the Academy of Child and Adolescent Psychiatry*, *38*, 242–249.

Boylan, K., Vaillancourt, T., Boyle, M., & Szatmari, P. (2007). Comorbidity of internalizing disorders in children with oppositional defiant disorder. *European Child & Adolescent Psychiatry*, *16*(8), 484–494.

Brammer, A., & Lee, S. (2012). Impairment in children with and without ADHD: Contributions from oppositional defiant disorder and callous-unemotional traits. *Journal of Attention Disorders*, *16*, 535.

Bubier, J. H., & Drabick, A. G. (2008). Affective decision-making and externalizing behaviors: The role of autonomic activity. *Journal of Abnormal Child Psychology*, *36*, 941–953.

Burke, J. D., Loeber, R., & Birmaher, B. (2002). Oppositional defiant disorder and conduct disorder: A review of the past 10 years: Part II. *Journal of the American Academy of Child and Adolescent Psychiatry*, *41*, 1275–1293.

Burke, J. D., Loeber, R., & Lahey, B. B. (2007). Adolescent conduct disorder and interpersonal callousness as predictors of psychopathy in young adults. *Journal of Clinical Child and Adolescent Psychology*, *36*, 334–346.

Burns, B. J., Hoagwood, K., & Mrazek, P. F. (1999). Effective treatment for mental disorders in children and adolescents. *Clinical Child and Family Psychology Review*, *2*(4), 199–254.

Burt, S. A. (2009). Rethinking environmental contributions to child and adolescent psychopathology: A meta-analysis of shared environmental influences. *Psychological Bulletin*, *135*(4), 608–637.

Calvete, E. (2008). Justification of violence and grandiosity schemas as predictors of antisocial behavior in adolescents. *Journal of Abnormal Child Psychology*, *36*, 1083–1095.

Campbell, S. B., Pierce, E. W., Moore, G., Marakovitz, S., & Newby, K. (1996). Boys' externalizing problems at elementary school age: Pathways from early behavior problems, maternal control, and family stress. *Developmental Psychopathology*, *8*, 701–719.

Cannon, K., Hammer, T., Reicherzer, S., & Gilliam, B. (2012). Relational-cultural theory: A framework for relational competencies and movement in group work with female adolescents. *Journal of Creativity in Mental Health*, 7, 2–16.

Carlson, C. H., Tamm, L., & Gaub, M. (1997). Gender differences in children with ADHD, ODD, and co-occurring ADHD/ODD identified in a school population. *Journal of the American Academy of Child and Adolescent Psychiatry*, *36*, 1706–1714.

Chavez, L., Mir, K., & Canino, G. (2012). Starting from scratch: The development of the Adolescent Quality of Life-Mental Health Scale (AQOU-MHS). *Journal of Culture Medicine and Psychiatry*, *36*, 465–479.

Clark, R. A., Murphy, D. L., & Constantino, T. N. (1999). Serotonin and externalization behavior in young children. *Psychiatry Research*, *86*, 29–40.

Cohen, D., & Strayer, J. (1996). Empathy in conduct disordered and comparison youth. *Developmental Psychology*, *32*, 988–998.

Coie, J. D., & Dodge, K. A. (1998). Aggression and anti-social behavior. In W. Damon (Series Ed.) & N. Eisenberg (Ed.), *Handbook of child psychology* (5th ed., Vol. 3). *Social, emotional and personality development* (pp. 779–862). New York, NY: John Wiley & Sons.

Coie, J. D., & Miller-Johnson, S. (2001). Peer factors and interventions. In R. Loeber & D. P. Farrington (Eds.), *Child delinquents* (pp. 191–209). Thousand Oaks, CA: Sage.

Connor, D. F. (2002). *Aggression and antisocial behavior; I children and adolescents: Research and treatment*. New York, NY: Guilford Press.

Corcoran, J., & Nichols-Casebolt, A. (2004). Risk and resilience ecological framework for assessment and goal formulation. *Child and Adolescent Social Work Journal*, *21*(3), 211–235.

Crouter, A. C., & Booth, A. (2003). *Children's influence on family dynamics: The neglected side of family relationships*. Mahwah, NJ: Erlbaum.

Dadds, M. R., Perry, Y., Hawes, D. J., Merz, S., Riddell, A. C., Haines, D. J, & Abeygunawardane, A. I. (2006). Attention to the eyes and fear-recognition deficits in child psychopathy. *British Journal of Psychiatry*, *189*, 280–281.

Dandreaux, D. M., & Frick, P. (2009). Developmental pathways to conduct problems: A further test of the childhood and adolescent-onset distinction. *Journal of Abnormal Child Psychology*, *37*, 375–385.

Davidson, R. J., Putnam, K. M., & Larson, C. L. (2000) Dysfunction in the neuro circuitry of emotion regulation as a possible preclude to violence. *Science*, *289*, 591–594.

DeAncos, E., & Ascaso, L. E. (2011). Sex differences in oppositional defiant disorder. *Psicothema*, *23*(4), 666–671.

Deater-Deckard, K., & Dodge, K. A. (1997). Externalizing behavior problems and discipline revisited: Non-linear effects and variation by culture, context, and gender. *Psychology Inquirer*, *8*, 161–175.

Derks, A. M., Dolan, C. V., Hudziak, J. J., Neale, M. C., & Boomsma, D. I. (2007). Assessment and etiology of attention hyperactivity disorder and oppositional defiant disorder in boys and girls. *Behavior Genetics*, *37*, 559–566.

Dishion, T. J., McCord, J., & Poulin, J. (1999). When interventions harm: Peer groups and problem behavior. *American Psychologist*, *54*, 755–764.

Dodge, K. A., & Pettit, G. S. (2003). A biopsychosocial model of the development of chronic conduct problems in adolescence. *Developmental Psychology*, *39*, 349–378.

Dodge, K. A., Pettit, G. S., Bates, J. E., & Valente, E. (1995). Social information processing patterns partially mediate the effect of early physical abuse on later conduct problems. *Journal of Abnormal Psychology*, *104*, 632–643.

Duggan, C. (2011). National Institute for Health and Clinical Excellence antisocial personality disorder guidance in the context of *DSM-5*: Another example of a disconnection syndrome? *Personality and Mental Health*, *5*, 122–131.

Dunsmore, J., Booker, A., & Ollendick, T. (2013). Parental coaching and child emotion regulation as protective factors for children with Oppositional Defiant Disorder. *Social Development*, *22*(3), 444–446.

Eaves, L., Rutter, M., Silberg, J. L., Shillady, L., Mahes, H., & Pickles, A. (2000). Genetic and environmental causes of covariation in interview assessments of disruptive behavior in child and adolescent twins. *Behavioral Genetics*, *30*, 321–334.

Eddy, J. M., Level, L. D., & Fagot, B. I. (2001). Coercive family processes: A replication and extension of Patterson's coercion model. *Aggressive Behavior*, *27*, 14–25.

Edelbrock, C., Rends, R., Plomin, R., & Thompson, L. A. (1995). A twin study of competence and problem behavior in childhood and early adolescence. *Journal of Child Psychology and Psychiatry*, *36*, 775–785.

Elkins, I. J., Iacono, W. G., Doyle, A. E., & McGue, M. (1997). Characteristics associated with the persistence of antisocial behavior: Results from recent longitudinal research. *Aggressive Violent Behavior*, *2*, 101–124.

Elliott, D. S., & Menard, S. (1996). Delinquent friends and delinquent behavior: Temporal and developmental patterns. In J. D. Hawkins (Ed.), *Delinquency and crime: Current theories* (pp. 28–67). New York, NY: Cambridge University Press.

Eme, R. F. (2007). Sex differences in child-onset, life-course-persistent conduct disorder. A review of biological influences. *Clinical Psychology Review*, *27*, 607–627.

Evans, M. E., Armstrong, M., & Kuppinger, A. (1996). Family-centered intensive case management: A step toward understanding individualized care. *Journal of Child and Family Studies*, *5*, 55–65.

Eyberg, S. M., Boggs, S. R., & Algina, J. (1995). Parent–child interaction therapy: A psychosocial model for the treatment of young children with conduct behavior and their families. *Psychopharmacology Bulletin*, *31*, 83–91.

Farrington, D. P., Jolliffe, D., Loeber, R., Stouthamer-Loeber, M., & Kalb, L. M. (2001). The concentration of offenders in families, and family criminality in the prediction of boys' delinquency. *Journal of Adolescence*, *24*, 579–596.

Fearon, R. P., Bakersmans-Kranenburg, M. J., VanIJzenboorn, M. H., Lapsley, A.-M., & Roisman, G. I. (2010). The significance of insecure attachment and disorganization in the development of children's externalizing behavior: A meta-analytic study. *Child Development*, *81*(2), 435–456.

Fergusson, D. M., Lynskey, M. T., & Horwood, J. J. (1996). Factors associated with continuity and change in disruptive behavior patterns between childhood and adolescence. *Journal of Abnormal Child Psychology*, *24*, 553–553.

Fraser, M. W., Nelson, K. E., & Rivard, J. C. (1997). Effectiveness of family preservation services. *Social Work Research*, *21*, 138–153.

Frick, P. J. (1994). Family dysfunction and the disruptive behavior disorders: A review of recent empirical findings. *Advances in Clinical Child Psychology*, *16*, 203–226.

Frick, P. J., Lahey, B. B., Loeber, R., Stouthamer-Loeber, M., Christ, M. A. G., & Hanson, K. (1992). Familial risk factors to oppositional defiant disorder and conduct disorder: Parental psychopathology and maternal parenting. *Journal of Consulting and Clinical Psychology*, *60*, 45–55.

Frick, P. J., Ray, J., Thornton, T., & Kahn, R. (2014). Annual research review: A developmental psychopathology approach to understanding callous-unemotional traits in children and adolescents with serious conduct problems. *Journal of Child Psychology and Psychiatry, 55*(6), 532–548.

Friesen, B. J., & Koroloff, N. M. (1990). Family-centered services: Implications for mental health administration and research. *Journal of Mental Health Administration*, *17*, 13–25.

Goldstein, L. H., Harvey, E. A., & Friedman-Weieneth, J. L. (2007a). Examining subtypes of behavior problems among 3-year-old children. Part III: Investigating differences in parenting practices and parenting stress. *Journal of Abnormal Child Psychology*, *35*, 125–136.

Goldstein, L. H., Harvey, E. A., Friedman-Weieneth, J. L., Pierce, C., Tellert, A., & Sippel, J. C. (2007b). Examining subtypes of behavior problems among 3-year-old children. Part II: Investigating differences in parent psychopathology, couple conflict, and other family stressors. *Journal of Abnormal Child Psychology*, *35*, 111–123.

Goldstein, F., Dawson, D., Smith, S., & Grant, B. (2012). Antisocial behavioral syndromes and 3-year quality-of-life outcomes in United States adults. *Acta Psychiatrica Scandinavica*, *126*, 137–150.

Goldstein, S., & Brooks, R. B. (Eds.). (2005). *Handbook of resilience in children*. New York, NY: Springer Publishing Company.

Goldstein, S., & Rider, R. (2005). Resilience and the disruptive disorders of childhood. In S. Goldstein & R. Brooks (Eds.), *Handbook of resilience in children* (pp. 203–222). New York, NY: Springer Publishing Company.

Green, R. W., & Doyle, A. E. (1999). Toward a transactional conceptualization of oppositional defiant disorder. *Clinical Child and Family Psychology Review*, 2(3), 129–148.

Greenberg, M. T., Kusche, C. A., Cook, E. T., & Quamma, J. P. (1995). Promoting emotional competence in school aged children: The effects of the PATHS curriculum. *Development and Psychopathology*, 7, 117–136.

Greene, R., Ablon, J. S., Goring, J. C., Raezer-Blakely, L., Markey, J., Monuteaux, M. C., ... Rabbitt, S. (2004). Effectiveness of collaborative problem solving in affectively dysregulated children with oppositional defiant disorder: Initial findings. *Journal of Consulting and Clinical Psychology*, 72(6), 1157–1164.

Greenspan, S. I. (1992). *Infancy and early childhood: The practice of clinical assessment and intervention with emotional and developmental challenges*. Madison, CT: International Universities Press.

Grizenko, N. (1997). Outcome of multimodal day treatment for children with severe behavior problems: A five-year follow-up. *Journal of the American Academy of Child and Adolescent Psychiatry*, 36, 989–997.

Grizenko, N., Papineau, D., & Sayegh, L. (1993). Effectiveness of a multimodal day treatment program for children with disruptive behavior problems. *Journal of the American Academy of Child and Adolescent Psychiatry*, 32, 127–134.

Gunnar, M. R. (1992). Reactivity of the hypothalamic-pituitary-adrenocortical system to stressors in normal infants and children. *Pediatrics*, *90*(3), 491–497.

Guttmann-Steinmetz, S., Gadow, K. D., & DeVincent, C. J. (2009). Examining the clinical correlates of autism spectrum. *Journal of Autism and Developmental Disorders*, *39*, 976–985.

Hagener, N. (2005). *The dance of defiance: A mother and son journey with oppositional defiant disorder*. Scottsdale, AZ: Shamrock Books.

Harden, P. W., Pihl, R. O., Vitaro, F., Gendreau, P. L., & Tremblay, R. E. (1995). Stress response in anxious and nonanxious disruptive boys. *Journal of Emotional and Behavioral Disorders*, 3, 183–190.

Harry, B., Sturges, K. M., & Klinger, J. K. (2005). Mapping the process: An exemplar or process and challenge in grounded theory analysis. *Educational Researcher*, 34, 3–13.

Hartman, A., & Laird, J. (1983). *Family-centered social work practice*. New York, NY: The Free Press.

Harvey, E., Friedman-Weieneth, J. L., Goldstein, L. H., & Sherman, A. H. (2007). Examining subtypes of behavior problems among 3-year-old children. Part I: Investigating validity of subtypes and biological risk factors. *Journal of Abnormal Child Psychology*, 35, 97–110.

Hawes, D. J., & Dadds, M. R. (2005). The treatment of conduct problems in children with callous-unemotional traits. *Journal of Consulting and Clinical Psychology*, 73, 737–741.

Hawes, D. J., & Dadds, M. R. (2007). Stability and malleability of callous-unemotional traits during treatment for childhood conduct problems. *Journal of Clinical Adult and Adolescent Psychology*, 36, 347–355.

Henggeler, S. W. (1999). Multisystemic therapy; an overview of clinical procedures. *Child Psychiatry and Psychology*, 4, 2–10.

Henggeler, S. W., & Sheidow, A. S. (2012). Empirically supported family based treatments for conduct disorder, and delinquency in adolescents. *Journal of Marital and Family Therapy*, *38*(1), 30–58.

Hipwell, A. E., Pardini, D. A., Loeber, R., Sembower, M., Keenan, K., & Stouthamar-Loeber, M. (2007). Callous-unemotional behaviors in young girls. Shared and unique effects relative to conduct problem. *Journal of Clinical Child and Adolescent Psychology*, 36, 293–304.

Hosp, J. L., & Reschly, D. J. (2004). Disproportionate representation of minority students in special education: Academic, demographic, and economic predictors. *Exceptional Children*, *70*, 185–189.

Huey, S. J., Jr., & Polo, A. J. (2010). Assessing the effects of evidence-based psychotherapies with ethnic minority youths. In J. R. Weisz & A. E. Kazdin (Eds.), *Evidence-based psychotherapies for children and adolescents* (2nd ed., pp. 451–455). New York, NY: Guilford Press.

Karriker-Jaffe, K., Foshee, V. A., Ennett, S. T., & Suchindran, C. (2008). The development of aggression during adolescence: Sex differences in trajectories of physical and social aggression among youth in rural areas. *Journal of Abnormal Child Psychology*, *36*, 1227–1236.

Kazdin, A. E., & Crowley, M. (1997). Moderators of treatment outcome in cognitively based treatment of antisocial children. *Cognitive Therapy and Research*, *21*(2), 185–207.

Kazdin, A. E., & Whitley, M. K. (2006). Comorbidity, case complexity, and effects of evidence-based treatment for children referred for disruptive behavior. *Journal of Consulting and Clinical Psychology*, *74*(4), 455–467.

Keenan, K., Loeber, R., & Green, S. (1999). Conduct disorder in girls: A review of the literature. *Clinical Child and Family Psychology Review*, *2*(1), 3–19.

Kellam, S. G., Simon, M. B., & Ensminger, M. D. (1983). Antecedents in first grade of teenage substance use and psychological well-being: A ten-year community-wide perspective study. In D. J. Ricks & B. S. Dohrenwend (Eds.), *Origins of psychopathology* (pp. 17–42). Cambridge, MA: Cambridge University Press.

Kelly, B. T., Loeber, R., Keenan, K., & DeLamatre, M. (1997). *Developmental pathways in boys' disruptive and delinquent behavior*. Washington, DC: U.S. Department of Justice, Office of Juvenile Justice and Delinquency Prevention.

Kerr, M., Tremblay, R. E., Pagani, L., & Vitaro, F. (1997). Boys' behavioral inhibition and the risk of later delinquency. *Archives of General Psychiatry*, *54*, 809–816.

Kiehl, K. A. (2006). A cognitive neuroscience perspective on psychopathology: Evidence for paralimbic system dysfunction. *Psychiatry Research*, *142*, 107–128.

Kolko, D. J., Dorn, L. D., Bukstein, O., & Burke, J. D. (2008). Clinically referred ODD children with or without CD and healthy controls: Comparisons across contextual domains. *Journal of Child Family Studies*, *17*, 714–734.

Kolko, D. J., Bukstein, O. G., Dorn, L. D., Pardini, D., Hart, J. A., & Holden, B. A. (2009). Community clinic-based modular treatment of children with early-onset ODD or CD: A clinical trial with three year follow up. *Journal of Abnormal Child Psychology*, *37*, 591–609.

Kutash, K., & Rivera, V. R. (1996). *What works in children's mental health services: Uncovering answers to critical questions*. Baltimore, MD: Paul H. Brookes.

Lahey, B. B., Loeber, R., & Quay, H. C. (1998). Validity of *DSM*-IV subtypes of conduct disorder based on age of onset. *Journal of the American Academy of Child and Adolescent Psychiatry*, *37*, 435–442.

Lahey, B. B., Van Hulle, C. A., Rathouz, P. J., Rodgers, J. L., D'Onofrio, B. M., & Waldman, I. D. (2009). Are oppositional-defiant and hyperactive-inattentive symptoms developmental precursors to conduct problems in late childhood? Genetic and environmental links. *Journal of Abnormal Child Psychology*, *37*, 45–58.

Lansford, J. E., Deater-Deckhard, J., Dodge, K. A., Bates, J. E., & Pettit, G. S. (2004). Ethnic differences in the link between physical discipline and later adolescent externalizing behaviors. *Journal of Child Psychiatry and Psychology*, *45*, 801–812.

Lansford, J. E., Dodge, K. A., Pettit, G. S., Bates, J. E., Crozier, J., & Kaplow, J. (2002). A 12-year prospective study of the long-term effects of early child physical maltreatment on psychological, behavioral, and academic problems in adolescence. *Archives of Pediatrics & Adolescent Medicine*, *156*, 824–830.

Leung, P. W. L., Hung, S., Ho, T., Lee, C., Liu, W., Tang, C., & Kwong, S. (2008). Prevalence of *DSM-IV* disorders in Chinese adolescents and the effects of an impairment criterion: A pilot community study in Hong Kong. *European Journal of Child Adolescent Psychiatry*, *17*, 452–461.

Lewis, W. W. (1988). The role of ecological variables in residential treatment. *Behavioral Disorders*, *13*, 98–107.

Lochman, J. E., & Lenhart, L. A. (1993). Anger coping intervention for aggressive children—Conceptual models and outcome effects. *Clinical Psychology Review*, *13*, 785–805.

Loeber, R., Burke, J. D., Lahey, B. B., Winters, A., & Zera, M. (2000). Oppositional defiant and conduce disorder: A review of the past 10 years, Part I. *Journal of the American Academy of Child and Adolescent Psychiatry*, *39*(10), 1468–1484.

Loeber, R., Burke, J., & Pardini, D. A. (2009). Perspective on oppositional defiant disorder, conduct disorder, and psychopathic features. *Journal of Child Psychology and Psychiatry*, *50*(1–2), 133–142.

Loeber, R., & Farrington, D. P. (Eds.). (2001). *Child delinquents: Development, intervention, and service needs*. Thousand Oaks, CA: Sage.

Loeber, R., Green, S. M., Lahey, B. B., Frick, P. J., & McBurnett, K. (2000). Findings on disruptive behavior disorders from the first decade of the developmental trends study. *Clinical Child and Family Psychology Review*, *3*(1), 117–140.

Lynam, D. R., & Gudonis, L. (2005). The development of psychopathy. *Annual Reviews of Clinical Psychology*, *1*, 381–407.

Lyons, M. J., True, W. R., Eisen, S. A., Goldberg, J., & Meyer, J. M. (1995). Differential heritability of adult and juvenile antisocial traits. *Archives of General Psychiatry*, *52*, 906–915.

Mack, K. 2004. Explanations for conduct disorder. *Child and Youth Care Forum*, *33*(2), 95–112.

Maguin, E., Loeber, R., & LeMahieu, P. (1993). Does the relationship between poor reading and delinquency hold for different age and ethnic groups? *Journal of Emotional Behavior Disorders*, *1*, 88–100.

Mash, E. J., & Duzois, D. J. (1996). Child psychopathology: A developmental-systems perspective. In E. J. Mash & R. A. Barkely (Eds.), *Child psychopathology* (pp. 3–60). New York, NY: Guilford Press.

Masi, G., Muratori, P., Manfredi, A., Lenzi, F., Polidori, L., Ruglioni, L., Milone, A. (2013). Response to treatments in youth with disruptive behavior disorders. *Comprehensive Psychiatry*, *54*, 1009–1015.

Matthys, W., Cuperus, J. M., & Van Engeland, H. (1999). Deficient social problem-solving in boys with ODD/CD, with ADHD, and with both disorders. *Journal of the American Academy of Child and Adolescent Psychiatry*, *38*, 311–321.

Matthys, W., Walterbos, W., Van Engeland, H., & Koops, W. (1995). Conduct-disordered boys' perceptions of their liked peers. *Cognitive Therapy and Research*, *19*, 357–372.

Maughan, B., Pickles, A., Hagell, A., Rutter, M., & Yule, W. (1996). Reading problems and antisocial behavior: Developmental trends in comorbidity. *Journal of Child Psychology and Psychiatry*, *37*, 405–418.

Maughan, B., Rose, R., Messer, J., Goodman, R., & Meltzer, H. (2004). Conduct disorder and oppositional defiant disorder in a national sample: Developmental epidemiology. *Journal of Child Psychology and Psychiatry*, *45*(3), 609–621.

McGee, R., & Stanton, W. R. (1992). Sources of distress among New Zealand adolescents. *Journal of Child Psychology and Psychiatry*, *33*, 999–1010.

McLeod, J. D., Kruttschnitt, C., & Dornfeld, M. (1994). Does parenting explain the effects of structural conditions on children's antisocial behavior? A comparison of blacks and whites. *Social Forces*, *73*, 575–604.

McLloyd, V. C. (1998). Socioeconomic disadvantage and child development. *American Psychologist*, *53*, 185–204.

Mezzacappa, E., Tremblay, R. E., & Kindlon, D. (1997). Anxiety, antisocial behavior, and heart rate regulation in adolescent males. *Journal of Child Psychology and Psychiatry*, *38*, 457–469.

Miller, N., Haas, S., Waschbusch, D., Willoughby, M., Helseth, S., Crum, K., ... Pelham, W. (2013). Behavior therapy and callous-unemotional traits: Effects of a pilot study examining modified behavioral contingencies on child behavior. *Behavior Therapy*. Retrieved from http://dx.do.org/10.1016/j.beth.2013.10.006

Miller-Johnson, S., Winn, D. M., Coie, J., Maumary-Grremaud, A., Lochman, J., & Terry, R. (1999). Motherhood during the teen years: A developmental perspective on risk factors for childrearing. In D. Cicchetti (Ed.), *Development and psychopathology* (pp. 85–100). New York, NY: Cambridge University Press.

Mills, R. S. L., Imm, G. P., Walling, B. R., & Weiler, H. A. (2008). Cortisol reactivity and regulation associated with shame responding in early childhood. *Developmental Psychology*, *44*(5), 1369–1380.

Moffitt, T. (2006). Life-course-persistent versus adolescent-limited antisocial behavior. In D. Cicchetti & D. Cohen (Eds.), *Development psychopathology* (Vol. 3, pp. 570–598). New York, NY: John Wiley & Sons.

Moffitt, T. E., Arseneault, L., Jaffee, S. R., Kim-Cohen, J., Koenen, K. C., Odgers, & Viding, E. (2008). Research review: *DSM-V* conduct disorder: Research needs for an evidence base. *Journal of Child Psychology and Psychiatry*, *49*(1), 3–33.

Munkvold, L., Lundervold, A., & Manger, T. (2011). Oppositional defiant disorder-gender differences in co-occurring symptoms of mental health problems in a general population of children. *Journal of Abnormal Child Psychology*, *39*, 577–587.

Needleman, H. L., Riess, J. A., Tobin, M. J., Biesecker, G. E., & Greenhouse, J. B. (1996). Bone lead levels and delinquent behavior. *Journal of the American Medical Association*, *275*, 363–369.

Nock, M. K., Kazdin, A. E., Hiripi, E., & Kessler, R. D. (2007). Lifetime prevalence, correlates, and persistence of oppositional defiant disorder: Results from the National Comorbidity Survey Replication. *Journal of Child Psychology and Psychiatry*, *48*(7), 703–713.

Ohan, J. L., & Johnston, C. (2005). Gender appropriateness of symptom criteria for attention-deficit/hyperactivity disorder, oppositional defiant disorder, and conduct disorder. *Child Psychiatry and Human Development*, *34*(4), 359–381.

Olds, D., Henderson, C. R., Cole, R., Eckenrode, J., Kitzman, H., Luckey, D., ... Powers, J. (1998). Long-term effects of nurse home visitation on children's criminal and antisocial behavior: 15-year follow-up of a randomized controlled trial. *Journal of the American Medical Association*, *280*, 1238–1244.

Pardini, D. A., Fite, P. J., & Burke, J. D. (2008). Bidirectional associations between parenting practices and conduct problems in boys from childhood to adolescence: The moderating effect of age and African-American ethnicity. *Journal of Abnormal Child Psychology*, *36*, 647–662.

Paulson, R., Gratton, J., Stuntzer-Gibson, D., & Summers, R. (1995, November 19). *Oreson Partners Project: Progress and outcomes report*. Paper presented at the Building on Family Strengths Conference. Portland, OR.

Pettit, G. S., & Arsiwalla, D. D. (2008). Commentary on special section on "Bidirectional parent–child relationships": The continuing evolution of dynamic, transactional models of parenting and youth behavior problems. *Journal of Abnormal Child Psychology*, *36*, 711–718.

Pike, A., McGuire, S., Hetherington, E. M., Reiss, D., & Plomin, R. (1996). Family environment and adolescent depressive symptoms and antisocial behavior: A multivariant genetic analysis. *Developmental Psychology*, *32*, 590–603.

Piquero, A. R., Farrington, D. P., Welsh, B. C., Tremblay, R., & Jennings, W. G. (2009). Effects of early family/parent training programs on antisocial behavior and delinquency. *Journal of Experimental Criminology*, *5*, 83–120.

Pliszka, S. R. (1999). The psychobiological of oppositional defiant disorder and conduct disorder. In H. C. Quay & A. E. Hogan (Eds.), *Handbook of disruptive behavior disorders* (pp. 371–395). New York: Kluwer Academic/Plenum.

Raaijmakers, M. A. J., Smidts, D. P., Sergeant, J. A., Maassen, G. H., Posthumus, J. A., van Engleland, H., & Matthys, W. (2008). Executive functions in preschool children with aggressive behavior: Impairments in inhibitory control. *Journal of Abnormal Child Psychology*, *36*, 1097–1107.

Raine, A., Venables, P. H., & Williams, M. (1990). Relationships between central and autonomic measures of arousal at age 15 years and criminality at age 24 years. *Archives of General Psychiatry*, *47*, 1060–1064.

Reed, R. R., & Sollie, D. (1992). Conduct disordered children: Familial characteristics and family interventions. *Family Relations*, *41*(3), 352–358.

Reid, J. B., Eddy, J. M., Fetrow, R. A., & Stoolmiller, M. (1999). Description and immediate impacts of a preventive intervention for conduct problems. *American Journal of Community Psychology*, *27*, 483–517.

Rutter, M. (2003). Commentary: Causal processes leading to antisocial behavior. *Developmental Psychology*, *39*, 372–378.

Salzman, M. (2003). *True notebooks*. New York, NY: Alfred A. Knopf.

Sampson, R. G., Morenoff, J. D., & Gannon-Rowley, T. (2002). Assessing "neighborhood effects": Social process and new directions in research. *Annual Review of Sociology*, 2(28), 443–478.

Sanson, A., Prior, M., & Smart, D. (1996). Reading disabilities with and without behaviour problems at 7–8 years: Prediction from longitudinal data from infancy to 6 years. *Journal of Child Psychology and Psychiatry*, *37*, 529–541.

Schmitz, M. F. (2003). Influences of race and family environment on child hyperactivity and antisocial behavior. *Journal of Marriage and Family*, *65*, 835–849.

Schumann, E. M., Foote, R. C., Eyberg, S. M., Boggs, S. R., & Algina, J. (1998). Efficacy of parent–child interaction therapy: Interim report of a randomized trial with short-term maintenance. *Journal of Clinical Child Psychology*, *27*, 34–45.

Scott, S., Knapp, M., Henderson, J., & Maughan, B. (2001). Financial cost of social exclusion: Follow up study of antisocial children into adulthood. *British Medical Journal*, *323*, 191–194.

Shamsie, J., Sykes, C., & Hamilton, H. (1994). Continuity of care for conduct disordered youth. *Canadian Journal of Psychiatry*, *39*, 415–420.

Shirtcliff, E. A., Vitacco, M. J., Graf, A. R., Gostisha, A. J., Merz, J. L., & Zahn-Waxler, C. (2009). Neurobiology of empathy and callousness: Implications for the development of antisocial behavior. *Behavioral Sciences and the Law*, *27*, 137–171.

Shriver, L. (2003). *We need to talk about Kevin*. New York, NY: Harper Collins.

Stattin, J., & Magnusson, D. (1990). *Pubertal maturation in female development*. Hillsdale, NJ: Erlbaum.

Steiner, H., & Remsing, L. (2007). Practice parameter for the assessment and treatment of children and adolescents with oppositional defiant disorder. *Journal of the American Academy of Child Adolescent Psychiatry*, *46*(1), 126–141.

Steiner, N., Sidhu, T., Pop, P., Frenette, E., & Perrin, E. (2013). Yoga in an urban school for children with emotional and behavioral disorders: A feasibility study. *Journal of Child and Family Studies, 22*, 815–826.

Stroul, B. A., & Goldman, S. K. (1990). Study of community based services for children and adolescents who are severely emotionally disturbed. *Journal of Mental Health Administration*, *17*, 61–77.

Subbarao, A., Rhee, S. H., Young, S. E., Ehringer, M. A., Corley, R. P., & Hewitt, J. K. (2008). Common genetic and environmental influences on major depressive disorder and conduct disorder. *Journal of Abnormal Child Psychology*, *36*, 433–444.

Taylor, T. K., Burns, G. L., Rusby, J. C., & Foster, E. M. (2006). Oppositional defiant disorder toward adults and oppositional defiant disorder toward peers: Initial evidence for two separate constructs. *Psychological Assessment*, *18*(4), 439–443.

Tierney, J. Grossman, J. B., & Resch, N. L. (1995). *Making a difference: An impact study of big brothers/big sisters*. Philadelphia, PA: Public/Private Ventures.

Tremblay, R. E. (2003). Why socialization fails: The case of the chronic physical aggression. In B. B. Lahey, T. E. Moffit, & A. Caspi (Eds.), *Causes of conduct disorder and juvenile delinquency* (pp. 185–206). New York, NY: Guilford Press.

Turnbull, W. (1995). *Life every voice: Expecting the most and getting the best from all of God's children*. New York, NY: Hyperion.

Tuvblad, C., Zheng, M., Raine, A., & Baker, L. (2009). A common genetic factor explains the covariation among ADHD ODD and CD symptoms in 9–10 year old boys and girls. *Journal of Abnormal Child Psychology*, *3*, 153–167.

Van Goozen, S., Fairchild, G., Snoek, H., & Harold, G. (2007). The evidence for a neurobiological model of childhood antisocial behavior. *Psychological Bulletin*, *133*(1), 149–182.

Viding, E., Blair, R. J. R., Moffitt, T. E., & Plomin, R. (2005). Evidence for substantial genetic risk for psychopathy in 7-year-olds. *Journal of Child Psychology and Psychiatry*, *46*, 592–597.

Wasserman, G. A., Miller, L. S., Piner, E., & Jaramilo, B., (1996). Parenting predictors of early conduct problems in urban, high-risk boys. *Journal of the American Academy of Child and Adolescent Psychiatry*, *35*, 1227–1236.

Webster-Stratton, C. (1996). Early intervention with videotape modeling: Programs for families of children with oppositional defiant disorder or conduct disorder. In E. D. Hibbs & P. Jensen (Eds.), *Psychosocial treatment research of child and adolescent disorders: Empirically based strategies for clinical practice* (pp. 435–474). Washington, DC: American Psychological Association.

Webster-Stratton, C., & Hammond, M. (1997). Treating children with early-onset conduct problems: A comparison of child and parent training interventions. *Journal of Consulting and Clinical Psychology*, *65*, 93–109.

White, J. L., Moffitt, T. E., Caspi, A., Bartusch, D. J., Needles, D. J., & Stouthamer-Loeber, M. (1994). Measuring impulsivity and examining its relationship to delinquency. *Journal of Abnormal Psychology*, *103*, 192–205.

Wikstrom, P. O., & Loeber, R. (2000). Do disadvantaged neighborhoods cause well-adjusted children to become adolescent delinquents? A study of male juvenile serious offending, risk and protective factors, and neighborhood context. *Criminology*, *38*, 1109–1141.

Wong, W., & Cornell, D. G. (1999). PIQ>VIQ discrepancy as a correlate of social problem solving and aggression in delinquent adolescent males. *Journal of Psychoeducational Assessment*, *17*, 104–112.

Yoshimasu, K., Barbaresi, W., Colligan, R., Voigt, R., Killian, J., Weaver, A., & Katusic, S. (2012). Childhood ADHD is strongly associated with a broad range of psychiatric disorders during adolescence: A population-based birth cohort study. *Journal of Child Psychology and Psychiatry*, *53*(10), 1036–1043.

Zoccolillo, M. (1993). Gender and the development of conduct disorder. *Developmental Psychopathology*, *5*, 65–78.

Zwirs, B. W. C., Burger, H., Schulpen, T. W. J., Wiznitzer, M., Fedder, H., & Buitelaar, J. K. (2007). Prevalence of psychiatric disorders among children of different ethnic origin. *Journal of Abnormal Child Psychology*, *35*, 556–566.

SEVEN

Neurocognitive Disorders: Alzheimer's Disease and the Diversity/Resiliency Formulation

I fear I am not in my perfect mind. Methinks I should know you and know this man; Yet, I am doubtful; for I am mainly ignorant. What place this is; and all the skill I have Remembers not these garments; nor I know not Where I did lodge last night. Do not laugh at me.

—William Shakespeare, *King Lear* (Act IV, Scene 7)

Alzheimer's disease (AD) is classified as a neurocognitive disorder in the *DSM®-5* (*Diagnostic and Statistical Manual of Mental Disorders*, 5th edition; American Psychiatric Association [APA], 2013). For the purposes of illustrating the utility of the Diversity/Resiliency Formulation for diagnosis and effective treatment, we highlight this diagnosis in detail along with its major differential diagnostic issues. We have chosen to focus on the most prevalent form of neurocognitive disorder, AD, which occurs predominantly in elders, in confidence that the lessons learned are widely applicable to persons with other neurocognitive disorders regardless of their age or situation. We elaborate on the complex challenges of aging and its relationship to mental health diagnosis because it is high time, we believe, that all of our clients, but especially our elders, be lovingly understood and responded to as more than the sum of their physical and emotional ailments—their "organ recitals," as one of the author's friends likes to say. It is imperative that we look and really see each elder as a unique individual with a rich history. We address this issue, especially in the latter part of the chapter, in applying the Diversity/Resiliency Formulation to a case example.

CHANGES, *DSM-IV-TR* TO *DSM-5*

The chapter titled, "Delirium, Dementia, and Amnestic and Other Cognitive Disorders" in the *DSM-IV-TR* (APA, 2000) is titled, "Neurocognitive Disorders" in the *DSM-5* (APA, 2013). Consistent with the developmental approach of the *DSM-5*, the placement of these disorders has been moved closer to the end of Section II in the *DSM-5*, emphasizing the emergence of most neurocognitive disorders late in life. Due to the proliferation of recent research, dementias that were formerly categorized as specified subtypes of Dementia Due to a General Medical Condition are coded as separate diagnoses with their own criteria. These include the following neurocognitive disorders: frontotemporal, Lewy bodies, traumatic brain injury, substance/medication, HIV infection, prion disease, Parkinson's disease, Huntington's disease, other medical conditions, and multiple etiologies. Unspecified neurocognitive disorder may also be diagnosed. Neurocognitive disorders are described as unique among *DSM-5* categories in that they in that the underlying causes may potentially be determined and detectable though medical tests. Currently, consistently agreed-on biomarkers for mental disorders do not exist.

In the *DSM-5*, dementia and amnestic disorders of the *DSM-IV-TR* are combined under the new term, *major neurocognitive disorder*. New and controversial in the *DSM-5* is the addition of a less severe level of cognitive impairment, termed *mild neurocognitive disorder*. The rationale for this change was to allow for the identification of symptoms that were less disabling but of enough concern to be the focus of attention and treatment. Critics have deplored the addition of this new diagnostic category, arguing that this change will result in the misdiagnosis of hordes of anxious senior citizens and increase the profits of the psychopharmaceutical companies while furthering their undue influence on American psychiatry (Frances, 2013). A recent investigation of the benefits of screening for early or mild cognitive impairment (MCI) in older adults found no evidence that benefits would outweigh the harm of early screening and recommended against routine screening (Moyer, 2014).

All of the mild and major neurocognitive disorders are diagnosed in the *DSM-5* in terms of an assessment of specific cognitive domains: complex attention, executive function, learning and memory, language, perceptual–motor, and social cognition. The authors provide a table for the clinician with a working definition of these key domains, along with examples of symptoms, a description of how everyday activities are affected, and sample assessments. Guidelines are also provided for clinical thresholds; these form the basis for making the diagnosis. Depending on the number of specified criteria met, diagnostic coding is separated into probable versus possible disorders (APA, 2013).

The term *dementia*, although not an official title in the diagnostic categories, may still be used for etiological subtypes of neurocognitive disorders, in recognition of the widespread global use of and familiarity with the term. The rationale for the preferred term, *neurocognitive disorder*, is based on the recognition that dementia usually refers to degenerative cognitive conditions in aging adults, whereas neurocognitive disorder is a broader term that can encompass impairments in younger persons secondary to traumatic brain injuries or HIV infection. Individuals with a decline in just one of the aforementioned domains, for example, those with an amnesic disorder, can now be diagnosed with a major neurocognitive disorder due to another medical condition; the narrower term, *dementia*, would be inappropriate for an amnesic disorder (APA, 2013).

The aforementioned changes in the *DSM-5* still fail to address the repeated concerns about the omission of patient contexts and the emphasis on pathology at the expense of strengths. Culture is ignored, and the medicalization of aging, along with the emphasis on treating this stage of life with medicine rather than with social support, is reinforced. These changes appear to ignore the state of the art in elder care and the voices of the elders themselves.

DSM-5 DIAGNOSTIC CRITERIA

Neurocognitive Disorders

In the *DSM-5*, these disorders are divided into types of delirium and types of major and mild neurocognitive disorders. Diagnosis involves assessment of the domains mentioned previously: complex attention, executive function, learning and memory, language, perceptual motor, and social cognition. Declines in functioning result from a medical condition, the effects of a substance, or multiple etiologies. Elders often present with confusing symptom patterns comprised of elements of delirium, dementia, and depression, often referred to as the 3 Ds of aging. Dementias are characterized by insidious onset and gradual or stepwise progression of impairment, whereas the onset of delirium is more acute, with a changing and brief course.

Delirium

Although not the focus of this chapter, it is important that the clinician know the difference between the types of delirium and the mild or major cognitive disorders, as delirium may be a medical emergency requiring an acute response. The core symptom of delirium is disturbed attention or awareness accompanied by a decline in cognition that cannot be accounted for by a preexisting or developing neurocognitive disorder. The individual may be unable to focus, maintain, or shift attention. Her mind may wander; she may repeat herself or be easily distracted. She may be less oriented to her environment and even to herself. Delirium develops quickly, in a matter of hours, usually lasts about a week and has a fluctuating course. The symptoms, verifiable by history, physical exam, or laboratory findings, are due to an underlying medical condition, substance intoxication or withdrawal, medication, toxin exposure, or some combination thereof. Confusing the diagnostic picture, delirium can occur in the context of an underlying major neurocognitive disorder, as these individuals are more vulnerable to delirium. The sleep–wake cycle is often disturbed, and the individual's emotional states may shift rapidly, accompanied by disturbing behaviors, such as moaning, screaming, or calling out. Delirium is very frequent in elders in nursing homes or post-acute care settings and in the great majority of individuals at the end of life. If the underlying medical cause is undiagnosed and treated, the patient's condition may worsen, and coma, seizure, or death can result. Delirium is discussed further in this chapter in the "Co-Occurring Disorders and Differential Diagnosis: Depression and Delirium" section.

Major and Mild Neurocognitive Disorders

Major Neurocognitive Disorder

Major neurocognitive disorders may look similar based on their symptoms but differ in etiology, and the complex interaction of causation is poorly understood. Major neurocognitive disorder is diagnosed when there is a significant decline from a previous level of performance in one or more of the previously mentioned cognitive domains. Information about the decline comes from the expressed concern of the individual, an informant, or clinician, and/or from substantial impairment in cognitive performance, documented by standardized neuropsychological testing or other quantified clinical assessment. The cognitive deficits must be severe enough to cause impairment in the ability to perform independent living tasks such as paying bills, managing medications, or other instrumental activities. The deficits in functioning are not better explained by another mental disorder; they do not occur only when a delirium is present. The clinician is asked to specify whether the symptoms are due to AD, frontotemporal lobar degeneration, Lewy body disease, vascular disease, traumatic brain injury, substance medication, HIV infection, prion disease, Parkinson's disease, Huntington's disease, another medication, or multiple etiologies. Criteria are specified for all of these. This greater specificity has been supported as an improved ability to cover the variety of entities leading to dementia, reflective of recent research, since prior criteria were essentially based on the typical development of AD (Bajenaru, Tiu, Antochi, & Roceanu, 2012). The clinician also specifies whether or not behavioral disturbances, such as apathy, agitation, psychotic, or depressive symptoms, are present, and whether the disorder is mild, moderate, or severe (APA, 2013).

Mild Neurocognitive Disorder

These disorders, new in the *DSM-5*, require a modest cognitive decline from previous performance in one or more of the aforementioned cognitive domains, based on the concern of the individual, an informant, or clinician, along with modest impairment in cognitive performance, as measured in neuropsychological testing or other quantitative clinical assessment. Although the cognitive deficits do not interfere with the individual's capacity for independence in everyday activities, greater effort is required to perform the complex instrumental activities of daily living (ADLs), and compensatory strategies or accommodations might be required. As in major neurocognitive disorder, mild neurocognitive disorder is not diagnosed when symptoms occur exclusively in the context of a delirium or when they are better explained by another mental disorder, such as depression or schizophrenia. The clinician is asked to specify etiological categories, as in major neurocognitive disorder and to note the presence or absence of behavioral disturbance (APA, 2013).

KEY POINTS

1. In the *DSM-5*, dementias are now called Mild or Major Neurocognitive Disorders, although the term *dementia* may still be used.
2. Specificity of these disorders has been updated as a result of recent research.
3. Critics fear the addition of mild neurocognitive disorders in the *DSM-5* may result in the misdiagnosis and intensified anxiety of many normally aging elders while increasing the profits of the pharmaceutical industry.
4. Changes from *DSM-IV-TR* to *DSM-5* remain focused exclusively in pathology.

Alzheimer's Disease: National and Global Contexts

Alzheimer's Disease (AD) is considered to be the leading cause of dementia. By the year 2030, more than 10 million Americans over 70 years of age will have some form of dementia; of those 85 years of age and older, it is estimated that 50% will have AD (Gravenstein, Franklin, & Davidson, 2003). This represents a huge professional and societal challenge. The percentage of U.S. elders over age 85 will increase from 13% to 24% of the elder population by 2050; elders are also America's fastest growing immigrant group, projected to number 16 million by 2050 (Hooyman & Kiyak, 2008). In California, 33% of seniors are foreign born.

By 2020, for the first time in human history, there will be more people over age 65 than under age 5. The global magnitude of the challenge of meeting the needs of elders has been well documented by numerous experts in many professions (Fos & Clark, 2008; Hooyman & Kiyak, 2008; Novak, 2009). Worldwide, the global age distribution is shifting from a pyramid to a cylinder, with fewer younger persons available to support increasing numbers of older persons. In Italy, the median age will increase from 39 to 52 by the year 2030; in Japan, from 39 to 50; in Mexico, from 23 to 34; and in the United States, from 36 to 39 (Hooyman & Kiyak, 2008). Declining birth rates, increased longevity, differential poverty rates, and the pressures of modernization on traditional cultures have variously rendered elders more vulnerable. By 2050, South Korea, for example, will have the highest percentage of elders, defined as people 65 years of age and older, thus representing the world's fastest transition to a "super-aged society" (Kim, 2008). The ancient Confucian ethic, characterized by the mandate to honor and care for elders, is challenged by the pace of economic growth, with the result that South Korea has the distinction of having the highest elder suicide rate among the world's 30 wealthiest nations (Shinn, 2009). In the United States, older White males have consistently been reported to commit suicide at higher rates than any other age group (Corr, Nabe, & Corr, 2009; Gray & Zide, 2008; Hooyman & Kiyak, 2008; Kennedy, 2000; Novak, 2009). The impact of dementia and the depressive effects of the pileup of losses in old age are staggering.

Alzheimer's Disease: *DSM-5* Criteria

Although the age of onset varies with etiology, Major or Mild Neurocognitive Disorder Due to Alzheimer's Disease usually occurs late in life, most often at age 85 or older; the biggest risk factor for dementia is age. Prevalence figures for AD range from 1.4% to 1.6% for individuals ages 65 to 79 years; the disease is rare before age 65. By age 85, prevalence figures range from 16% to almost 50%, depending on the study, with most predicting that 50% of elders 85 years of age and older will have AD (APA, 2000; Hebert, Scherr, Bienias, Bennett, & Evans, 2003).

As defined in the *DSM-5* (APA, 2013), diagnostic criteria for Alzheimer's specify meeting general criteria for mild or major neurocognitive disorder, described previously, along with an insidious onset and gradual impairment in one or more cognitive domains. Probable major neurocognitive disorder due to Alzheimer's is diagnosed if there is either evidence of genetic mutation from family history or genetic testing, along with a decline in memory or learning and at least one other cognitive domain, steady and progressive decline without extended plateaus, and no evidence of other causes of the cognitive decline. If only one of these factors is present, possible Alzheimer's is diagnosed. For mild neurocognitive disorder, probable AD is diagnosed in the presence of the same symptom picture in the context of mild impairment, as described earlier, and possible AD is diagnosed when there is no evidence of a causative genetic mutation or family history of Alzheimer's.

As AD progresses, gradually increasing deficits in memory are followed by language, motor, and object recognition impairment, along with difficulties in executive function and personality changes, which may include increased irritability and other behavioral changes. Cognitive disturbances include aphasia (language), apraxia (motor function impairment), agnosia (inability to recognize objects), and the inability to plan and carry out activities. Additional specifiers indicate early or late onset (before or after age 65) and require the clinician to assess whether behavioral disturbances, such as agitation or wandering, are present.

The diagnosis of AD has been largely one of exclusion, made only after other causes of dementia, including the following, are ruled out: hypothyroidism and other metabolic causes; vascular problems such as strokes; vitamin deficiencies, including B_{12}; hypercalcemia; normal-pressure hydrocephalus; psychiatric difficulties such as depression and schizophrenia; head trauma; structural brain lesions (tumors, injuries, or blood clots); Parkinson's disease; malingering and factitious disorder; dehydration and other causes of delirium; brain infections (brought on by HIV, encephalitis, meningitis, syphilis, and other causes); and the chronic effects of various substances, including alcohol and other medication (Whitehouse & George, 2008). A variety of laboratory tests and scans (magnetic resonance imaging, positron emission tomography, computed tomography) are given to rule out the pathologies listed previously.

Scales, such as the Global Deterioration Scale (Reisberg, Ferris, De-Leon, & Crook, 1982) and other measures of instrumental ADLs, are utilized to assess degree of cognitive and functional impairment and monitor changes (Hooyman & Kiyak, 2008; Segal-Gidan, 2013). Assessment scales are reviewed in detail for their practical use in clinical practice by Sheehan (2012), who stresses that useful scales are based on objective, rather than subjective, information and may incorporate the domains of cognition, function, behavior, quality of life, depression, caregiver burden, and severity levels. One quick and practical dementia screening tool uses only eight items to assess for dementia and outperforms longer and more traditional scales (Chen, Leung, & Chen, 2011).

This scale combines three-item recall, attention and calculation questions, a clock-drawing task, and instrumental ADL items and is a simple but sufficient tool suggested for use in the screening of early dementia, especially in primary care settings. The existence of screening tools that accurately predict the development of dementia is more challenging. In a recent review of 751 papers concerning the prediction of dementia, only four screening tools could be recommended for their test accuracy, coverage of relevant cognitive domains, predictive ability, and feasibility, and only the Addenbrooke's Cognitive Examination [ACE-R] was cautiously recommended as a potentially ideal tool (Lischka, Mendelsohn, Overend, & Forbes, 2012). The reviewers emphasize that no existing tool adequately addresses all domains and can be considered excellent in its ability to predict dementia. Exhibit 7.1 summarizes existing criteria for the clinical diagnosis of "probable Alzheimer's disease."

Described as a "clinical quandary," in which physicians tend to give the public the impression of greater certitude than realistically exists, a

EXHIBIT 7.1 Criteria for a Probable Clinical Diagnosis of Alzheimer's Disease

- Dementia established by clinical examination and documented by a standardized test of cognitive functioning (e.g., the Mini-Mental State Examination [MMSE], Blessed Dementia Test) and confirmed by neuropsychological tests
- Deficits in two or more areas of cognition (language, memory, perception)
- Progressive worsening of memory and other cognitive functions
- No disturbance of consciousness
- Onset generally between ages 40 and 90
- Absence of other systemic disorder or brain disease

Factors Supporting a Diagnosis of Probable Alzheimer's Disease

- Progressive deterioration of specific cognitive functions such as language (aphasia), motor skills (apraxia), and perceptions (agnosia)
- Impaired ADLs and altered patterns of behavior
- Family history of similar disorders, particularly if confirmed by neurological testing
- The following laboratory results:
  1. Normal cerebrospinal fluid (lumbar puncture)
  2. Normal electroencephalogram (EEG)
  3. Evidence of cerebral atrophy on computed tomography (CT), with progression documented by serial observation

Other Clinical Features Leading to a Diagnosis of Probable Alzheimer's After Excluding Other Causes of Dementia

- Plateaus in the course or progression of the illness
- Associated symptoms, including depression, insomnia, and emotional/physical outbursts
- Other neurological abnormalities, especially in advanced disease, including increased muscle tone and a shuffling gait, seizures in advanced disease, and CT normal for age

Features That Make a Diagnosis of Alzheimer's Uncertain or Unlikely

- Sudden onset
- Such early symptoms as seizures, gait problems, and loss of vision and coordination

Note: Criteria as established by the National Institute of Neurological and Communicative Disorders and Stroke in collaboration with the Alzheimer's Disease and Related Disorders Association.
Source: McKhann, Drachman, Folstein, and Katzman (1984).

definitive diagnosis can only be made in a postmortem examination. Even then, a conclusion is uncertain. For many patients there is an overlap between vascular problems and the plaques and tangles of Alzheimer's; brain pathology occurs in all of us as we age. Most important, there is no simple correlation between the appearance of the characteristic brain pathologies of Alzheimer's and the behavioral symptoms of dementia. So confusing and uncertain is this diagnosis that prominent neuroscientists are referring to the field as an empire, financed by pharmaceutical companies, that has fostered massive fear about a disease that is difficult to diagnose or effectively treat and impossible to cure. Whitehouse and George (2008), for example, are pushing back against the stigma and fear of the Alzheimer's label, advocating for a reframing of the symptoms as brain aging, a controversial and provocative stance. These authors are calling for a commitment to what is known about prevention and to the psychosocial needs of elders and a realistic acknowledgment that a complex interplay of environment, lifestyle, personality, genetics, and neurochemistry—little understood and different for each person—plays a part in how dementia is experienced by any one individual. There is a popular saying among medical professionals, family members, and caregivers: "If you've seen one case of Alzheimer's, you've seen one case of Alzheimer's!"

There is still no reliable indicator of when brain aging, which we all face, slips from the normal aging process into the dreaded disease of Alzheimer's. Brain aging is thought by some to begin in one's 20s; others argue for the decline of memory as beginning after age 40. Some researchers feel that we would all get Alzheimer's if we lived long enough, as what is certain is that brain aging is inevitable. On the other hand, newer discoveries about brain plasticity, as well as the ability of the brain to create new connections that were heretofore considered impossible, are undermining older theories of the brain, which have been based on the premise of localization in function (Doidge, 2007). Elders who show normal age-related declines in cognitive functioning, without significant evidence of memory or other cognitive impairment that is greater than would be expected in the normal course of aging, should not be diagnosed with dementia.

KEY POINTS

1. AD is the most prevalent dementia among elders and will present increasing social and medical challenges as the worldwide aging population increases.
2. The normal versus abnormal aging of the brain is complex and debatable; there is no specific point at which normal aging slips into AD.
3. Certainty about the presence of AD is present only on autopsy; the diagnosis remains one of the exclusions despite recent advances in brain research.

CURRENT THINKING ABOUT THE ETIOLOGY AND COURSE OF AD

The prevailing view is that Alzheimer's is a progressive, degenerative brain disease ending in death. The brain cells affected by Alzheimer's die and cannot regenerate. Shrinkage and atrophy occur in certain regions of the brain;

neurotransmitters, notably acetylcholine, decrease; and there are fewer synaptic connections that enable us to learn, create, and retain new memories.

Competing Theories of Etiology

Competing theories of Alzheimer's etiology exist: BAPtists believe that beta-amyloid protein (BAP) plaques initiate the cell death seen in Alzheimer's, whereas TAUists believe that tau protein tangles (TAU) are responsible. Plaques and tangles in the cortex and hippocampus have been observed in the autopsies of persons with Alzheimer's. BAPtists, or adherents of the amyloid cascade hypothesis, believe that BAP plaques, composed of a core of BAP surrounded by degenerating nerve cell processes, precipitate the formation of tau tangles, which lead to neuronal death, resulting gradually in Alzheimer's. Researchers following this theory are pursuing human trials with gamma-secretase inhibitors, attempting to short circuit the enzyme processes that lead to the tau tangles; but because gamma-secretase enzymes are involved in necessary processes in the body, such as the differentiation of stem cells in bone marrow, the attempt to inhibit these enzymes in animal trials has resulted in toxic effects. Neurofibrillary tangles are composed of abnormal structural proteins inside the nerve cell. The role of amyloid is uncertain. Some scientists believe that amyloid is the main perpetrator of Alzheimer's, whereas others think that amyloid buildup is simply a sign of other processes, perhaps even a self-repair process, in which the brain is trying to heal itself. The role of plaques and tangles thus remains controversial, both as to causation and as to which protein is more to blame—beta-amyloid or tau; hence, the division between the BAPtists and the TAUists in the scientific community (Whitehouse & George, 2008).

Heredity plays some role in the formation of plaques and tangles, as described previously. Studies have discovered genetic mutations on chromosome 21, which increase the formation of beta-amyloid in the brain and, when transmitted from parent to child, are said to create a genetic inevitability of developing AD if one lives long enough. Other mutations on chromosomes 1 and 14 cause a strong genetic form of AD that has a 50% probability of being inherited from a parent. Mutations on chromosomes 1, 14, and 21 are very rare, however, and are related to early-onset AD. Late-onset AD has been linked to a gene mapped to chromosome 19, which controls the production of apolipoprotein E (ApoE). ApoE has three gene variants—E2, E3, and E4—and helps to transport cholesterol. Individuals who inherit two copies of E4, one from each parent, are considered at highest risk for developing AD, but these genes increase susceptibility only and do not cause the disease by themselves (Whitehouse & George, 2008).

Critics of the amyloid cascade hypothesis argue that the toxicity of amyloid has been inconsistently demonstrated, that how beta-amyloid kills neurons is poorly understood, and that amyloid could actually be linked to the brain's attempts to repair itself. That amyloid deposits may result from a reparative process is supported by findings indicating that many aged individuals show no cognitive decline in the presence of high numbers of BAPs. BAPs may simply indicate where neuronal death has occurred; BAP accumulates in all brains and in up to one third of clinically normal elders. Some brains may be resistant to BAP and others may reveal a great deal of BAP but no signs of dementia. It remains unclear whether changing the metabolism of BAP will benefit patients or do harm (Whitehouse & George, 2008).

TAUists adhere to the theory that AD is caused by the intercellular formation of tangles rather than the intracellular BAP plaques. These tangles are said to occur when the tau protein, which functions to support neuronal structure and regulate nutrient transport, undergoes a chemical change, becomes stickier, and binds with other tau proteins to form tangles that clog neuronal axons and dendrites. As a result, communication between neurons falters, and cells eventually die of malnutrition. TAUists believe that BAP plaques result from the formation of tau tangles rather than vice versa.

Critics of the TAUists and the BAPtists argue that despite the fact that the correlation between amyloid plaques and cognitive function is weak and amyloid is unproven as the lone perpetrator of AD, these researchers have dominated funding sources, blocking biological and psychosocial research exploring the critical issues of quality of life, prevention, and the needs of caregivers. AD, they believe, is a general label that obscures the many genetic, environmental, and behavioral factors involved in brain aging (Whitehouse & George, 2008). This view is supported by the well-known longitudinal nuns study, in which many normally functioning elderly nuns of the School Sisters of Notre Dame religious order were found on autopsy to have high concentrations of plaques and tangles, whereas others with the symptoms of AD had smaller concentrations. These 678 nuns had identical lifestyles, and their differences in cognitive function in old age were attributed primarily to their educational levels and intellectual and physical activities throughout their lives rather than to the composition of their brains at autopsy (Hooyman & Kiyak, 2008).

Related to the lack of causal clarity regarding plaques, tangles, and AD, other causal theories have emerged. The antioxidant hypothesis asserts that free radicals, weakly bonded atoms with at least one unpaired electron, accumulate in the brain, causing nerve damage and cell death, altering protein DNA, and causing mutations. The production of these molecules is known to be accelerated by infections, tobacco, herbicides, solar radiation, and pollutants. Normally the body stabilizes free radicals; but if the diet does not contain antioxidants or free radical production is excessive, cell damage can result. Free radical damage is thought to accelerate the progression of cancer and cardiovascular disease as well as age-related degenerative diseases like AD. Recommendations for a diet rich in fruits and vegetables and for certain vitamin supplements are linked to this theory; however, clinical trials of antioxidants have been disappointing, and the theory does not account for the extent of multisystem damage in AD (Whitehouse & George, 2008).

Because senile plaques are often associated with inflammatory processes, some researchers believe that AD is a consequence of brain inflammation, causing abnormal brain metabolism. Traumatic head injuries or infections, even those that predate Alzheimer's symptoms by years, are thought to set off abnormal metabolites and reactive immune system proteins, which may modify BAPs and result in the characteristic plaques of AD. A combination of the ApoE4 gene with head injury has been shown to increase the risk of dementia 10-fold. Some studies have indicated that nonsteroidal anti-inflammatory drugs (NSAIDs) might be helpful to brain health, but serious side effects of gastrointestinal bleeding have prevented replication of early studies (Whitehouse & George, 2008).

Other researchers are exploring the theory that excitatory cell death, a process by which cells die through excess stimulation by excitatory amino acid neurotransmitters, may cause AD. This process has been demonstrated in laboratory experiments with isolated nerve cells, but its relationship to a disease process is unproven. The infectious disease hypothesis links the evidence of viral and other infections in the brains of AD patients to Alzheimer's symptoms, but these studies have not been replicated. Many AD patients present with a complicated combination of vascular and degenerative processes that obscure a single picture of causation; strokes, small clots, or any factor that reduces the brain's oxygen supply potentiates symptoms observed in AD. Most recently, links between diabetes and Alzheimer's have been proposed. Epidemiological studies have indicated that Alzheimer's patients had co-occurring diabetes more often than not, and that high blood pressure and prediabetic conditions were correlated with poor scores on cognitive tests. Researchers speculate that there may be a link with glucose metabolism and consequent vascular damage and suggest that antidiabetic drugs might be beneficial in the treatment of AD.

The role of estrogen in AD has been investigated, with disappointing results; the recent findings indicate that estrogen replacement therapy (ERT) in women neither prevented nor effectively treated AD and had no impact on the development of MCI; in addition, twice as many women using combined estrogen and progestin in one study actually developed dementia (Shumaker et al., 2003). The simplest explanation may be that AD has many etiologies with similar clinical and pathological features, and that even relative homogeneity of its symptomatic features may be more apparent than real (Amaducci & Lippi, 1992).

Historically, there has been no consistently agreed on biological marker of AD, behavioral manifestations vary widely, and the individual components of the pathology of AD occur to some extent in all of us in the process of aging. A recent article in the *Archives of Neurology* (Meyer et al., 2010), however, has claimed otherwise. Using a mixed modeling approach to identify biological markers of AD, without reference to clinical information or observation, researchers from the AD Neuroimaging Initiative found that a combination of low beta amyloid 1–42, high tau protein, and elevated phosphorylated tau 181 in the cerebrospinal fluid consistently identified individuals with AD at a rate of 90% in three independent data sets. These biological markers were also present in 72% of elders with MCI and, surprisingly, in 36% of normal elders with no signs of cognitive impairment. The researchers interpret the latter to mean that AD is active and detectable earlier than previously envisioned and recommend that future studies follow up normal elders for a period of 10 years in order to determine whether the markers accurately predicted the eventual emergence of AD in elders with normal cognitive functioning. The article has generated discussion regarding whether the analysis of cerebrospinal fluid for these markers should become a routine component of assessment and care for persons with signs of cognitive impairment and suspected AD. Critics have quickly pointed to the numerous drug companies that financed the research and the fact that the main findings predict the development of AD in persons already showing cognitive decline (Stevenson, 2010). The latter have expressed concern that the research will generate the use of cerebrospinal fluid tests followed by massive prescriptions for relatively ineffective AD medications in normal elders, with disappointing results, as the ability to prevent and treat AD remains to be discovered.

As this complicated discussion demonstrates, the search for a biological marker for AD continues unabated. The neurons in our brains fire throughout our lives, but how brain function is preserved or lost remains obscure. Recent cutting-edge research, however, may offer a breakthrough in understanding some of this complexity and lead to promising areas of research and future intervention. Lu et al. (2014) report in the scientific journal *Nature* that the induction of repressor element 1-silencing transcription factor (REST) is a universal feature of normal aging in human cortical and hippocampal neurons, but that REST is lost or much lower in persons with MCI and AD. REST is important because it represses genes that promote cell death and the pathological neural changes of AD. In the mouse brain, REST is protective against oxidative stress and amyloid b-protein toxicity of AD; furthermore, deletion of REST from the mouse brain leads to age-related neurodegeneration. In normal aging, REST is induced by cell signaling, but in AD, REST is lost from the nucleus and appears together with pathologically misfolded proteins. REST levels in aging closely correlate with the preservation of cognitive function as well as with longevity. Thus, the authors conclude that "the activation state of REST distinguishes neuroprotection from neurodegeneration in the ageing brain" (p. 448). These researchers hope that their findings will lead to promising areas of research and intervention.

A diagnosis of AD is terrifying for the recipients and their loved ones and scientifically uncertain as to accuracy. It can have demoralizing effects that stigmatize and isolate those who receive the label. This state of affairs requires the clinician working with the Alzheimer's patient and his or her loved ones to think carefully about the effect of such a diagnosis on the client, to avoid portraying certainty—either of false hope for a cure or the prospect of a meaningless future—and to facilitate the ongoing quality of life and full humanity of the AD patient.

KEY POINTS

1. Multiple theories of the etiology of AD compete for research money and scientific validity.
2. Recent research has demonstrated the presence of possible biological markers for AD, and this may lead to future interventions.
3. Early-onset AD is genetically based, whereas late-onset AD appears to be less so.
4. Conveying the diagnosis to patients and family members is a critical process in which hope and possibility should be emphasized along with decline and eventual mortality.

The Course of AD

The progressive course of AD is usually described in three major stages. In the *early stage*, loss of recent memory begins to affect the individual's performance. Mood and personality changes are noticed by family and friends; the individual exhibits less personal initiative and increasingly avoids others. Chores previously performed easily become more difficult to execute, and the individual becomes more confused. In the *middle stage*, memory loss and confusion escalate. The individual has more difficulty recognizing friends and family and may make the same statements repetitively. Word-finding problems increase, as well as difficulties with writing, reading, understanding numbers, and engaging in logical thinking. Muscle jerking or twitching may occur. The individual may wander away from home and needs increasing supervision in order to be kept safe. She or he may become suspicious and irritable, and have difficulty with self-care, such as toileting or bathing. In the *late stage*, the person does not recognize family members or lifelong friends, is unable to distinguish or use familiar objects such as eating utensils, and becomes incontinent (unable to control bladder or bowel). Difficulty with communication increases until the individual becomes mute, unable to speak or respond verbally to others. Difficulty with swallowing follows, and ultimately these individuals can no longer feed themselves or maintain their weight. Self-care, in general, becomes impossible, and the individual is totally dependent on others for care (Gray & Zide, 2008).

Co-Occurring Disorders and Differential Diagnosis: Depression and Delirium

Old age is associated with ever-increasing diagnostic complexity, as the incidence of chronic disease combines with the natural aging process and the social context to present complicated challenges for the professional. Depression and delirium are critical diagnostic issues in differential diagnosis and will be discussed in turn.

Depression is the most common psychological complaint of older adults. Reported symptoms may include weight or appetite loss, disturbed sleep, lethargy or agitation, loss of interest in activities, pervasive feelings of sadness and worthlessness, and thoughts of suicide. Depressive symptoms are made worse in the presence of chronic health problems, functional impairments, and/or medication side effects. Depressed individuals often have problems with memory and concentration and do not function at their optimal intellectual levels. Especially in an elder, it may be difficult to sort out depressive symptoms from evidence of dementia. In general, elders with depression, rather than dementia, show more abrupt declines in cognitive functioning, whereas those with dementia show a more gradual decline. Elders who have suffered losses or have had to cope with other chronic illnesses may be depressed in reaction to these stressors. Other elders may have been chronically depressed, perhaps diagnosed with persistent depressive disorder (dysthymia), and their condition may have worsened due to the increased life challenges of aging. The abuse of alcohol and prescription drugs to cope with depressive symptoms is considered a silent epidemic in that substance abuse is known to affect up to 17% of older adults (Arbore, 2007).

Careful assessment of past and present functioning, by spending quality time with the elder and his family members and making sure that a thorough medical evaluation occurs, is necessary in order to sort out the timing and course of symptoms. Depression can and does coexist with AD, and suicide is a real concomitant risk, with the highest completion rates in older persons in general and older White males in particular.

It is challenging to face old age, with its attendant decline in functioning and accumulated losses. When, in addition, an elder is given a diagnosis of AD, the impact is enormous. This is especially so when an elder who has been diagnosed with AD, or is frail and needing care for other reasons, suffers the loss of dignity and individuality that may ensue after placement in a nursing home. Institutionalization can be so demoralizing to an elder that Thomas (2004) describes nursing homes as riddled with loneliness, helplessness, and boredom, which he describes as the true plagues of old age in an institution. Viewed this way, the traditional diagnosis and treatment of AD in an elder, with accompanying placement in an elder facility, can cause or exacerbate depression, because learned helplessness and isolation are well-known causes of depressive conditions (Peterson, Maier, &, Seligman, 1993). The stigma of institutionalization, with attendant loss of individuality and personal agency, has been documented in many settings (Goffman, 1961).

Delirium presents another critical differential diagnostic issue in assessing for AD. Although dementia and delirium both exhibit memory impairment, delirium is distinguished by its rapid onset, fluctuating course, and disturbance in consciousness; it is coded in terms of its etiology—usually substance abuse, medication, or a medical condition (APA, 2000). Delirium may be superimposed on dementia. Dementia may precede and coexist with delirium. Although a few tools exist for detecting delirium superimposed on dementia, more research is needed in this area, using larger samples and more clearly defined indicators of both conditions (Morandi et al., 2012). Numerous research articles debate the merits of scales for assessing delirium and recommend improved interdisciplinary communication (Adamis et al., 2013; Davis et al., 2012; Detweiler et al., 2014; Tahr, 2012). Elders must be monitored carefully for interactive effects of medication as these may go unexamined. Delirium is often a medical emergency, and it is critical that mental health professionals understand the signs of delirium and help the client obtain prompt medical attention. The following are signs of delirium:

- Abrupt changes in behavior
- Fluctuations in behavior through the day
- Alertness and overall symptom severity is worse at night and when first awake
- Inability to focus attention on a task
- Problems with short-term memory
- Hallucinations
- Speech that makes no sense or is irrational
- Disturbance in sleep patterns (Hooyman & Kiyak, 2008)

The diagnosis of AD is complicated, and the etiology is still being researched and debated, Differential diagnosis is rarely an either–or process, as delirium and depression can coincide with AD, other dementias, and other medical conditions. As in all of the challenges elders face, mental and physical issues overlap and must always be considered in their complexity, with the humanity of the whole person kept in the forefront.

CASE STUDY 1

Thomas DeBaggio and May Sarton

Rarely can an elder person's diagnosis be explained or understood in terms of one particular *DSM-5* label, and never should the label overtake appreciation for the individuality of the elder, his or her personal history and identity, and unique subjective experience. Consider, for example, the accounts of AD and depression described by the two elders in the following insert. Thomas DeBaggio is depressed about having AD, and May Sarton describes an intense struggle with depression related to loss of function and mental confusion resulting from several strokes:

> My brain skitters from place to place, unable to alight on a single site that will provide me with succor or balance. I am easily overwhelmed now.... There is a dullness in my brain now to allow me to stare into silence without an idea or thought breaking the stillness. It is hard to live in a grown-up body and have the mind of a child. Nobody should have to know what this is like.... My world has become tentative and I have difficulty naming things ... my mind has become a handicap.... This may be the last Christmas of which I am conscious. You begin to think about what the disease takes from your life. It makes you think of simple everyday things becoming difficult and then impossible. Here I am alone, barking at death. Some days I feel I have fallen down a deep well of anxiety. (DeBaggio, 2002, pp. 96–108)

In the passage quoted here, Thomas DeBaggio, a person diagnosed with AD, offers us a rare glimpse into the lived reality of dementia in a way that is difficult for us to appreciate when, as human service and health care professionals, we are faced with a bewildering array of symptoms, pressed for time, confronting often conflicting needs and perspectives of family members, in the contexts of often inadequate resources and the medicalization of aging. The writer reminds us that a unique human being exists behind the diagnosis of AD—one who remains connected to and appreciates the daily kindness of friends, the warmth of a pet cat, and the beauty of nature as best he can.

May Sarton describes an intense struggle with depression, related to the loss of function and mental confusion resulting from several strokes:

> I am afraid because I am so depressed; it does not lift, and there is little I seem able to do to change it although I am certainly trying. Last night ... I was tired, and when I came up to get undressed, I got caught in my shirt. I cannot button things, so I try always not to unbutton a shirt, but put it on and off over my head. In pulling it over my head, one sleeve got mixed up in the rest of it and I could not find the button to undo it ... it was frightening.... I really

> did not know what to do.... Finally it did [come over the head], and by then I was very tired and simply wanted to go to bed and to sleep. There is part of me that only wants ... to lie down, if possible with the cat, and if possible go to sleep, for sleep is the way out of depression.... I do not want to live to be ninety. (Sarton, 1996, pp. 260–262)

Both of these elders had been highly productive individuals: Sarton as a published poet, novelist, and memoirist and DeBaggio as the owner of a well-respected, successful community business.

1. How are these two elders alike and different? Can you sort out the symptoms of AD, stroke, and depression in the two accounts?
2. What kind of understanding did these memoir accounts offer that a reading of the DSM symptoms does not? How would you apply this to clinical diagnosis and treatment?

While attempting to sort out the complexities of differential diagnosis when we are face to face with elder clients, we must remember the complex and fascinating person we are encountering. We address this issue further in the latter part of this chapter in applying the Diversity/Resiliency Formulation to case examples.

KEY POINTS

1. Critical co-occurring disorders with AD include delirium and depression.
2. Delirium should be considered a medical emergency; referral to a physician is always necessary.
3. Depression is ubiquitous in elders with dementia and should be treated. Suicide is an important risk factor.
4. The person behind the label, with her unique history, abilities, and strengths, must be seen and prized; a hopeful emphasis on the capabilities that still remain must be communicated, along with the realities of decline.

EVIDENCE-INFORMED PRACTICE

Because AD is often complicated by other chronic medical conditions and depression—creating complex challenges for the patient, family members, and community—evidence-informed practice of necessity includes psychopharmacological and psychosocial interventions. Attending to the needs of family members and to the environment of the patient is as important as caring for the AD patient's medical needs and symptoms. The following sections summarize current interventions in a variety of these areas.

Psychopharmacology

Although vast sums of money have been spent in the research, development, and marketing of drugs to treat AD, the overall results have been disappointing.

At best, donepezil (Aricept) slows the decline of memory loss by about 5% and only in the early to moderate stages of AD. For example, a patient for whom donepezil is prescribed may score an average of 1 to 2 points higher in cognitive capacity on the MMSE after taking the drug, but this change is rarely observable in the ability to function. Only one patient in four experiences improvement noticeable to family and practitioner. Among those who do not evidence improvement, half will show no decline over the first 6 to 9 months; after 40 weeks of treatment, most responders will have reverted to the level of disability noted when donepezil was started (Kennedy, 2000). Along with donepezil, two newer drugs, rivastigmine (Exelon) and galantamine (Razadyne), act to prevent the breakdown of acetylcholine; they also slow the decline in cognitive ability and the decline in ADLs (Feldman, 2002; Raskind, Peskind, Truyen, Kershaw, & Damaraju, 2004; Seltzer, 2006). Memantine (Namenda), another newer drug, lowers glutamate levels and is designed to treat moderate to severe stages of AD (Reisberg et al., 2003; Tariot et al., 2004). None of these pharmaceutical agents, however, has produced impressive effects; the impact on AD symptoms has been very modest, and no drug has been able to stop or reverse the formation of plaques and tangles in the brain. Moreover, the side effects are disturbing; they include liver disease, peptic ulcers, diarrhea, severe chronic obstructive pulmonary disease (COPD), and bradycardia (Hooyman & Kiyak, 2008; Whitehouse & George, 2008).

Interest remains widespread in the possible benefits of anti-inflammatory drugs, such as aspirin and ibuprofen. However, physicians are cautioned against prescribing them for the purpose of preventing cognitive decline owing to the risk of gastrointestinal bleeding and liver damage (Kennedy, 2000; Whitehouse & George, 2008). Ginkgo biloba and ginseng are over-the-counter herbs available in health food stores about which there has been considerable public interest, but these herbs are not FDA regulated and can pose dangers to the consumer, as the amount of herb present may vary widely and other ingredients that are unknown may possibly be mixed in (Hooyman & Kiyak, 2008; Kennedy, 2000; Whitehouse & George, 2008). In reviewing the state of the art, Whitehouse and George urge caution and a balanced approach to the treating physician, avoiding the creation of false hope in the context of hyperbolic claims in the media and at the same time responding positively to patients and family members who want to try drug treatment.

Managing the Environment and Supporting Behavioral Functioning

Maintaining a safe, stable, and supportive environment; enhancing individual competence; slowing the rate of deterioration; and preventing nursing home placement for as long as possible are considered to be important goals related to the well-being of elders with AD, who generally want to remain in their own homes. Recommendations include maintaining consistent lighting, removing glare, keeping a regular schedule, and encouraging moderate but not overwhelming activity and stimulation. Confused elders with AD benefit from written schedules of activities and directions for cooking, bathing, and taking medications. Deterioration in ADLs can sometimes be slowed if grooming

EXHIBIT 7.2 Caring for AD Patients at Each Stage of the Disease

Stages 1–3 (Mild Dementia)

- Create an area in the home where the patient's critical items (keys, glasses, wallet, etc.) are consistently placed and can always be found.
- Monitor the patient's driving for signs of problems.
- Encourage regular physical and social activity.
- Encourage the patient to concentrate and focus when placing objects in specific locations.

Stages 4–5 (Moderate Dementia)

- Make changes in the home environment to ensure safety and autonomy but maintain familiarity (constant light levels, reduced glare).
- Label important doors and other areas (e.g., bedroom, bathroom, kitchen drawers, location of clothing in bedroom, exits to safe areas such as yard or garden).
- Prominently display photos of friends and family important to the patient, labeled clearly with names.

Stages 6–7 (Advanced Dementia)

- Visit long-term-care facilities and/or in-home care options that fit the patient's needs.
- Simplify daily routines but encourage physical activity and contact with nature and visitors.
- Maintain personal contact through photos, touch, favorite music, and other experiences long familiar to the patient.

Source: Adapted from Hooyman and Kiyak (2008).

supplies are visible and there is a familiar sequence of their use. Familiar and productive activities—such as gardening, setting the table, folding laundry, singing, and even dancing—promote well-being and a sense of purpose. Similarly, photos and mementos that are visible and available are comforting and maintain the elder's awareness of identity through time. For elders who wander, it is helpful to lock exterior doors and/or to maintain a secure outdoor area available for the enjoyment of nature. A sensitive response to agitation, irritability, pacing, restlessness, and similar behaviors is important, as these are generally no longer considered a normal outcome of AD but are thought to be triggered by fear, fatigue, environmental changes, undiagnosed or poorly controlled medical conditions, or adverse reactions to medications. These changes should always be evaluated by a physician (Hooyman & Kiyak, 2008). Exhibit 7.2 presents suggestions for caregivers related to stages of AD.

Other lifestyle interventions with AD patients have focused on exercise, reminiscence, music, dance, and similar activities. Teri et al. (2003) have reported on the encouraging effects of 3 months of exercise training for AD patients combined with behavioral management education for their caregivers. Participants were significantly less depressed, had fewer days of restricted activity, and were less likely, over a 2-year period, to have been placed in nursing homes than AD patients who received only routine medical care.

KEY POINTS

1. **Evidence-informed practice embraces the complex medical, psychosocial, and spiritual needs of Alzheimer's patients and their families.**

2. Medical interventions alone, comprising psychopharmacology, have been disappointing at best.
3. Attention to the construction of environments that provide adequate safety and stimulation along with individualized care and support for family members are an increasing focus in the field.

EQUITY AND DIVERSITY ISSUES

Barriers to the effective diagnosis and treatment of AD exist in many forms and on many levels. They are embedded in the larger contexts of our cultural fear of dying, medical and other professional cultures, ageism and the devaluing of elders in general, and in the socioeconomic and cultural disparities that affect access to care. These areas are elaborated on in the following sections.

Psychological and Sociological Barriers: The Denial of Death

We have a great tendency to avoid sensitive, comprehensive contact with our elders because we fear our own death; elders remind us that we are all "terminal" in the end, as the quotation in the following case study illustrates.

CASE STUDY 2

AD and Denial of Death

> None of us seems psychologically able to cope with the thought of our own state of death, with the idea of a permanent unconsciousness in which there is neither void nor vacuum—in which there is simply nothing. It seems so different from the nothing that preceded life. As with every other looming terror and temptation, we seek ways to deny the power of death and the icy hold in which it grips human thought.... In recent generations we have added something new: we have created the method of modern dying. Modern dying takes place in the modern hospital, where it can be hidden, cleansed of its organic blight, and finally packaged for modern burial. We can now deny the power not only of death but of nature itself. We hide our faces from its face. (Nuland, 1993, p. xv)

(Author's note: The prolific and beloved author of this quote himself died in spring 2014.)

1. How do you think individuals with AD uniquely confront us with our mortality?
2. What do you think allows some people to remain lovingly connected and attentive to an Alzheimer's patient? What prevents others from doing so?
3. How can you apply your answers to questions 1 and 2 to clinical practice, education, and training?

The human tendency to avoid the reality of one's personal death is described in modern novels, nonfiction memoirs, and biographies (Didion, 2005; Jameson, 2009; Terkel, 2002; Yalom, 2008). Denial may sometimes serve us well. But when awareness seems unbearable, it can have serious consequences in the way we meet the challenges of AD. Gillick (2006), the Harvard Medical School professor and practicing physician/author of *The Denial of Aging*, describes the discrepancies between the way elders wish to spend their final years and the institutionalized way they actually die, asserting that "if we assume that AD will be cured and disability abolished in the near term, we will have no incentive to develop long-term-care facilities that focus on enabling residents to lead satisfying lives despite their disabilities" (Gillick, 2006, pp. 6–7). The denial of the realities of aging and dying leads to the pernicious combination of underdiagnosis (by avoiding prevention, education, and screening tests, which are proven to be useful) and overtreatment of elders (by intervening medically when comfort and support in the context of a loving community would be more helpful).

AGEISM

Sociological studies repeatedly demonstrate that older persons are viewed as undesirable, unattractive, deteriorating, curmudgeon-like, and useless; beliefs that elders are typically forgetful, irritable old codgers are endorsed by both majority and many minority communities in the United States (Hooyman & Kiyak, 2008). In this context, persons with AD may be increasingly viewed as threatening to the dominant cultural preoccupation with remaining young, healthy, and productive; these elders are thus at greater risk of being placed out of sight in an institution or in their own homes; they are also in danger, at a minimum, of losing whatever individual autonomy and identity they have left (Gray & Zide, 2008).

PROFESSIONAL ROLES

Invisible, with fewer sources of social capital in the society at large, elders are similarly devalued in the professions with the expertise and ethical mandate to care for them. Geriatric medicine is considered the least prestigious and certainly not the most revenue-generating specialty, and medical schools are struggling with how to attract students to focus on the care of elders. Some medical schools are requiring students interested in becoming geriatricians to spend time as patients in a nursing home. Medical training is so focused on learning the signs and symptoms of disease that physicians struggle to remember the humanity of the patient—a perspective critical at all ages but particularly so with elders who are facing the end of life, a developmental stage for which there is no ultimate cure. Pauline Chen (2007), a physician, reflects on Harvard's New Pathway program, an experiment in medical education that stresses case-based learning, which facilitates the collaborative relationship with the patient. During her training, Chen was deeply affected by the words of cardiologist Hacib Aoun:

> The process of becoming a doctor is so protracted and arduous that it is easy to forget along the way the initial reasons and ideals for wanting to become a doctor, especially because the current medical curriculum is disease-oriented, not patient-oriented ... let me suggest that the fewer the therapeutic options available, the greater your involvement with the patient should be. (Chen, 2007, p. 133)

In other words, the patient should not be abandoned merely because the condition is terminal.

Personal involvement and taking the time to listen are not prized commodities in current medical care; nor are they well reimbursed. Physicians are financially rewarded for high-volume patient care, for relying heavily on psychopharmacology, and for performing specialized medical tests, but not for interaction with families, for exploring the patient's personal strengths and interests, or for facilitating a caring community.

Siegel (2004) provides numerous examples of ageism in psychiatric diagnosis, illustrating how old age, as an important developmental stage in the life cycle, is not a mental illness but is seen as such. A pernicious combination of invisibility and hypervisibility characterizes ageism in the mental health professions as well as in society in general.

> Invisibility may lead to underdiagnosing the symptoms that bring old people into mental health offices, and this can result in the withholding of necessary services, while hypervisibility can lead to overdiagnosing, overmedicating, and even institutionalizing people who may not need it, resulting in further deterioration. The aged poor are subject to class prejudice as well as age bias and are even more likely to be ignored and over diagnosed. When institutionalized due to over diagnosis, they are often subjected to the worst possible treatment in poorly funded, understaffed institutions. Even experienced and well-meaning clinicians may find themselves caught between (these) two mistakes ... especially if [they] do not consistently examine their own biases. (Siegel, 2004, p. 90)

Mellor and Ivry (2002) describe the challenges faced by the social work profession in recruiting and training professionals for gerontological social work, the fastest-growing area of specialization within the profession. It is estimated that 70,000 social workers will be needed in the next 15 years to care for the expanding elder population; but between 1996 and 2001, the percentage of students specializing in aging dropped by 16%. At the same time, few stipends are available to students wanting to enter the field, and the social work role is undervalued in facilities that serve elders. Medicare requires social workers in skilled nursing facilities, but the position labeled "social worker" ironically does not require specific social work training. Moreover, working with elders is the path least valued by graduate students in social work; and those who enter this specialization at the undergraduate level lack upward mobility owing to the lack of jobs. The profession is attempting to interest more students in work with elders, with an emphasis on infusing more course content into the human behavior curricula of professional schools. The person-in-environment philosophy of social work is perhaps best suited to an adequate response to society's elders, whose welfare is so closely linked with the circles of loving care that ideally should surround them (Karls & Wandrei, 1994). The social work profession is actively exploring needed changes in social work education in order to train the practitioners who are so urgently needed (Brandel, 2011).

Nurses' aides or certified nurse assistants (CNAs) are notoriously underpaid and undervalued, earning the minimum wage or only slightly more. Skilled nursing facilities and home health care organizations are well known for their high employee turnover rates and for the burnout of their workers. These entry-level jobs are often filled by individuals whose own personal lives are troubled by the challenges of poverty. Caring for the employees closest to the elders is considered of paramount importance to adequate caring for the elders—a challenge addressed by the culture-change movement described further on in this chapter. In short, the status of geriatric practitioners in medicine and allied health professions mirrors the devaluation of elders in the society at large. AD patients and their families too often remain as invisible and undervalued to the professionals and institutional personnel who care for them as to the larger society (Hooyman & Kiyak, 2008; Novak, 2009).

MODERNIZATION AND SOCIAL REWARD

Industrial societies—emphasizing competition, individual achievement, and specialization—have made elders' skills more and more obsolete. Without the social bargaining power of specialized higher education and technological prowess, elders have trouble competing. Even in Asian countries where Confucian ethics have stressed respect for elders, communal responsibility is giving way to the fast pace of societal change in an acquisitive society (Kim, 2008; Korean National Commission for UNESCO, 2008). Where developing countries are rushing to catch up to their more prosperous neighbors, elders are often lost in the shuffle, without the protective safety net of social welfare programs that exist in Western Europe and the United States. At times these elders are actively scapegoated, judge to be witches and put to trial, or accused of other offenses against society; many have no pensions and no money for food or medication. Elders with AD and other forms of dementia are especially vulnerable to exploitation and abuse. Population shifts across the globe will intensify these challenges in elder care. Mexico's median age will increase from 23 to 34 by 2030, whereas Italy and Japan will have the "oldest" populations within 30 years, with median ages of 52 and 50, respectively. HelpAge International (www.helpage.org) is a global organization whose mission it is to highlight these issues and to promote the welfare of elders across the globe (Hooyman & Kiyak, 2008).

INSTITUTIONAL AND COMMUNITY BARRIERS

The paradigm of personal distance between staff member and resident and the loss of individuality are embedded in the hospital-like structure of care in traditional nursing homes. Nursing stations are situated in the middle of long corridors. Call buttons are heard going off as residents in their rooms signal for help, usually for going to the bathroom. It is not unusual to see several residents lined up in wheelchairs in the hall waiting for transportation to a meal and/or silently watching television in a sitting area. There is little in evidence of the individuality of the residents, few inviting tidbits of information or photographs that would invite a visitor or staff person to be curious about the unique history of the elder whose diaper she is changing or to whom she is giving medication or feeding. Most nursing home physicians rotate among several institutions, checking vital signs and writing prescriptions. Physicians may often make rounds early in the morning before residents are even awake, making little or no conversation with them and rarely, if ever, having any contact with family members. Social workers, trained to foster communication and facilitate interaction between persons and their environment, spend too much of their time attempting to keep up with paperwork to attend to the emotional needs of the elders. Activity and physical therapists have traditionally focused on group activities that do little to stimulate the genuine individual interests and abilities of a resident. The depressing impact of being placed in an institution, with its attendant loss of individuation, can be so profound that residents can turn away from life, stop eating, and give up on living. In this context, dementia and depression can so overlap and potentiate one another that the residents may become lost in a haze of institutional isolation, their uniqueness forgotten.

Elders living at home, where most elders prefer to be, theoretically should be free from the negative effects of institutionalization described previously. More elders reside in their own homes than in elder-care facilities; however, elders living on their own or being cared for in their own homes are extremely vulnerable to neglect and abuse. Most abuse occurs at the hands of a person known to the elder. Isolation, hunger, and lack of protection and support often render these elders vulnerable to depression and to harm, due to the lack of adequate medical care and early diagnosis of dementias, depression, or other challenges of aging. In a society with less face-to-face contact in small caring neighborhoods, conditions that might signal an elder's decline into dementia or depression can go unnoticed, sometimes with disastrous results, as when an elder who still drives becomes confused and unwittingly becomes involved in a fatal a car accident (McInnis-Dittrich, 2002; Quinn & Tomita, 1997).

In the context of loss of function, role, health, and important friends—which is the challenge of all elders facing the end of life—the importance of taking into account the elder's life story, culture, sources of meaning, and internal and external strengths becomes ever more central to effective diagnosis. Elders tend to be stereotyped, remaining perhaps more "invisible" in their uniqueness and complexity than any other group. In the last developmental stage of life, older persons are taking stock, looking back over their life's course. They are working on the psychological challenge of experiencing themselves as having lived a purposeful, meaningful life versus a life filled with regret. Aware of a foreshortened future, their need to be seen is acute, and it is imperative that the mental health professional look beyond the age and the diagnosis to the person with a unique life history. "They look at me, and all they see is a grumpy old man—they don't even see me as a person," said one hospital patient in response to being treated impatiently by an overworked nurse's aide (J. Mathers, personal communication, April 10, 2007).

DISPARITIES RELATED TO ACCESS TO CARE

Poverty, gender, race and ethnicity severely affect access to quality care financed by long-term insurance and to the ability to pay privately for home-based medical care, safety alterations to the home, and technological advances in care. Women and many ethnic groups are overrepresented in the population of elders below the poverty level. Cutler (2006) reports that 76% of older Whites had saved for later life, as compared with 43% of African Americans. Although women comprise 60% of the older population, they make up 70% of the older population in poverty (International Longevity Center & AARP, 2003). In 2006, the poverty rate for older men was 57% that of older women (Administration on Aging, 2007). African American and Hispanic American men over age 65 have median incomes representing only 66% of those of Whites, and women in each ethnic group have significantly lower income than males (Wu, 2006). Older Mexican immigrants who had lived in the United States the longest had the highest incomes in their ethnic group, but less health care coverage (Wong, 2002). African Americans have a higher percentage of elders over age 65 than any other minority group (Lewis & Ausberry, 1996) and may be at greater risk for AD (Fillenbaum, Heyman, Huber, & Woodbury, 1998; Tang, Stern, Marder, Bell, & Gurland, 1998). Numerous health care disparities have been reported for African Americans, including greater difficulty communicating with their physicians and less likelihood of having adequate or any health insurance (Cooper, 2002). Simply being African American or Hispanic qualifies as a risk factor for AD, along with exposure to environmental toxins and low educational and occupational status (Corcoran & Walsh, 2006). As a result of their greater poverty and low socioeconomic status, members of minority groups of color in the United States are subject to the interaction of several risk factors for AD.

Elders are the fastest growing immigrant group in the United States. Between 1990 and 2000, the number of foreign-born people over age 65 increased from 2.7 million to 4.3 million; their ranks will swell to 16 million by 2050. Considered the most isolated people in America, these elders are subject to a myriad of psychological problems as a result of language barriers and a lack of social connections (Brown, 2009), thus heightening their nonbiological risks of AD and depression. It has been reported that some subgroups of Asian Pacific Islander Americans may view memory problems as a normal part of the aging process (Braun, Takamura, Forman, Sasaki, & Meininger, 1995), but the same symptoms may also be viewed as bringing shame and stigma to the family (Elliott, DiMinno, Lam, & Tu, 1996; Phillips, 1993). A similar sense of embarrassment has been reported in Mexican American families (Gallagher-Thompson, Talamantes, Ramirez, & Valverde, 1996). Chinese families may view memory problems as normal consequences of aging and thus bring their relative to a physician only late in the disease process; on the other hand, they may view dementia as mental illness, because its symptoms may mimic mental disorders like schizophrenia. Mental illness is considered very shameful and stigmatizing, and if an elder with AD is viewed as mentally ill, caregivers may hide the elder from public view and avoid seeking help. Chinese families may further differ among themselves as to the appropriateness of help-seeking behavior, with some members seeking the help of traditional Chinese healers, whereas others adhere to Western biomedical care patterns (Kleinman, 1986; Lee, 1982; Phillips, 1993).

In summary, gender roles, differences in the amount and quality of education, poverty, access to medical care, immigrant status, and cultural attitudes may influence both the risk of developing symptoms of AD and access to adequate diagnosis and treatment (Gray & Zide, 2006, 2008). The previous sections have illustrated the myriad ways in which elders are rendered invisible and stripped of their individual identities—in the structure of care, in the training of those who work with them, and in the increasing complexity of modern fast-paced societies that prize youth, individual achievement, specialization, beauty, and vigor, while devaluing communal responsibility and the quieter contributions of elders.

The weaknesses of the *DSM* become especially glaring with respect to old age and to AD in particular in the tendency to ignore the patient's context. The environment—the context of care—is crucial to those vulnerable members of society at both ends of the life cycle, infancy/childhood on the one hand and old age on the other. When our elders are less visible and prized, they are less attended to, less listened to, and more vulnerable to being viewed as a social category rather than as individuals. This can lead to daily errors of diagnosis, which are compounded by a traditionally limited use of the *DSM*, with its focus on individual pathology at the expense of the environment and the individual's internal and external sources of strength and support. We view the following as characteristic of the challenges facing mental health professionals, in the face of these inequities and barriers, when attempting to assess for dementia in general and AD in particular:

1. Diagnosing dementia when the elder is depressed, lonely, or isolated.
2. Diagnosing the elder as depressed when the elder has AD or another form of dementia.
3. Ignoring co-occurring dementia and depression in favor of either diagnosis presented previously.

4. Viewing elders as incapable of change and growth, thus making either dementia or depression worse. Related to this, communicating about rather than with the elder.
5. Ignoring side effects of medical illness, medication, or substance use as causes of symptoms.
6. Failing to attend to the social and cultural contexts of the elder, either in or outside of an institution, owing to the parallel process of demoralization of elders and of those who care for them.

KEY POINTS

1. Multiple barriers and inequities affect the diagnosis and response to AD; these include differential access to care, cultural differences, traditional professional roles and institutional practices, ageism, and the psychological tendency to avoid and deny the realities of death and dying.
2. Equity and diversity issues cloud the process of accurate differential diagnosis.
3. In the context of inequity, the isolation and depression of elders with AD are deepened.

Despite the enormous challenges these equity issues present, exciting and transformative interventions are arising, leading to an atmosphere of increased hope with respect to a more humane response to the care of elders with AD. Some of these strength-based developments are described in the next section.

STRENGTH-BASED CONTRIBUTIONS TO DIAGNOSIS AND TREATMENT

As the global aging population is increasing exponentially, the desires and needs of elders in general and of those with AD in particular are beginning to receive more critical attention. During the 1990s, new models of continuing care, guided by a philosophy of retaining the individual dignity of the elder with AD and attempting to avoid the identity stripping, which occurs with institutionalization, began to arrive on the scene. Because individuals with advanced dementias comprise the majority of nursing home residents, our citizens aged 85 and older represent the fastest-growing segment of the population, and AD is by far the most common form of dementia among elders, we have chosen to highlight those residential models that are dedicated to the empowerment of the residents.

Special Care Units

Special care units (SCUs), designed for residents with dementia, are maintained by some nursing homes and assisted living facilities. These SCUs are often referred to, ironically, as memory units and are designed with the stimulation, comfort, and safety of the AD resident in mind. Special features may include architecture and interior decorating that remind the residents of their past; musical events featuring selections from the residents' youth; gardens and outdoor walking areas that are accessible but locked, so that residents can be protected from wandering; and staff trained in dementia care. The use of restraints, either physical or pharmacological, is avoided in favor of individualized attention to what is causing the behavior. SCUs are not licensed separately from other nursing or assisted living facilities, however, and the quality of care may be more apparent than real. *The Best Friends Approach to Alzheimer's Care* is the guiding philosophy for many of these organizations (Bell & Troxel, 2003). The practical and wise suggestions of the authors are applicable in any setting where the Alzheimer's patient lives, and those who subscribe to the model are guided by the "Alzheimer's Disease Bill of Rights" displayed in Exhibit 7.3.

The Culture-Change Movement

The hospital medical model, characterized by hierarchical lines of authority, with power residing in the hands of administrators and physicians, has traditionally defined the way care has been delivered in nursing homes. The emphasis in these institutions is on efficiency and the routine of care, delivered on schedule and in a similar manner to all the residents. This management structure is being challenged by more individualized, homelike models of care, such as the Eden Alternative, Green Houses and Small Houses, the Pioneer Network, and other components of what is called the "culture-change" movement in nursing homes (Hooyman & Kiyak, 2008). The goal of these facilities is to surround the elder with loving care and to empower residents and those closest to them to participate as fully in life as they are able.

One of the best-known examples of the culture-change movement is the Eden Alternative, founded by William Thomas, MD, and explained in his books (Thomas, 1996, 2004) and on his webpage (www.edenalt.com). Founded by Dr. Thomas after an upsetting and life-changing experience as a physician

EXHIBIT 7.3 An Alzheimer's Disease Bill of Rights

- To be informed of one's diagnosis
- To have appropriate, ongoing medical care
- To be productive in work and play for as long as possible
- To be treated like an adult, not like a child
- To have one's expressed feelings taken seriously
- To be free from psychotropic medications if possible
- To live in a safe, structured, predictable environment
- To enjoy meaningful activities that fill each day
- To be outdoors on a regular basis
- To have physical contact, including hugging, caressing, and hand-holding
- To be with individuals who know one's life story, including cultural and religious traditions
- To be looked after by individuals who are well trained in dementia care

Source: Bell and Troxel (2003).

encountering the loneliness of an elder in a nursing home, the Eden Alternative is dedicated to eliminating what Dr. Thomas considers to be the core plagues of loneliness, helplessness, and boredom in institutions for elders.

Using the deeply spiritual metaphor of the Garden of Eden, the goal of the Eden Alternative is to promote garden-like, beautiful, thriving, and secure communities where the elder residents are surrounded with love and their caretakers are equally prized. Constructing a common language of care and respect, the Eden founders are aiming at nothing less than transforming the culture of elder care by helping long-term-care organizations to revolutionize their environments in order to create a warm climate of trust, hope, and the lively presence of plants, animals, children, and activity. Training manuals have been developed; educational programs and ongoing consultation relationships have been created. Organizations that wish to become known as Eden facilities must subscribe to the 10 Eden Principles shown in Exhibit 7.4 and agree to an ongoing reciprocal relationship of consultation and support.

Although most accounts of "Edenized" facilities are anecdotal, preliminary studies have reported overall improvements in the quality of care (Schmidt & Beatty, 2005). Lower levels of boredom and helplessness (Bergman-Evans, 2004), increased staff morale, and lower staff turnover have also been noted. The reader is referred to the Eden website for videos and written reports of recent evaluations, along with personal reflections of staff, residents, and family members at Eden facilities (www.edenalt.com).

EXHIBIT 7.4 The 10 Eden Principles

1. The three plagues of loneliness, helplessness, and boredom account for the bulk of suffering among our elders.
2. An elder-centered community commits to create a human habitat where life revolves around close and continuing contact with plants, animals, and children. It is these relationships that provide the young and old alike with a pathway to a life worth living.
3. Loving companionship is the antidote to loneliness. Elders deserve easy access to human and animal companionship.
4. An elder-centered community creates opportunities to give as well as receive care. This is the antidote to helplessness.
5. An elder-centered community imbues daily life with variety and spontaneity by creating an environment in which unexpected and unpredictable interactions and happenings can take place. This is the antidote to boredom.
6. Meaningless activity corrodes the human spirit. The opportunity to do things that we find meaningful is essential to human health.
7. Medical treatment should be the servant of genuine human caring—never its master.
8. An elder-centered community honors its elders by de-emphasizing top–down bureaucratic authority, seeking instead to place the maximum possible decision-making authority into the hands of the elders or those closest to them.
9. Creating an elder-centered community is a never-ending process. Human growth must never be separated from human life.
10. Wise leadership is the lifeblood of any struggle against the three plagues. For it, there can be no substitute.

Source: www.edenalt.com

Aging-Friendly Design

Architects are acknowledging and focusing on the graying of the population. Aging-friendly design is an architectural concept that considers the specific needs of elders in the design of buildings, as described further on in this chapter and in a professional California journal devoted to the needs of elders. Buildings are constructed to promote the continuance of previously meaningful activities and relationships; to compensate for age-related disabilities that limit the capacity for physical, psychological, social, cultural, and spiritual fulfillment; to offer opportunities for connection and meaningful interpersonal relationships; to make meaningful contributions to the well-being of others; and to provide opportunities for challenging, enlivening, growth-producing experiences (Schlarch, 2009).

These architectural concepts have been applied to the design of small residences for eight to 10 individuals, with private rooms surrounding a living and dining space. Because these are usually licensed as skilled nursing facilities, elders with AD are being cared for in such homes, known as Green or Small Houses. These facilities are staffed by universal workers who are cross-trained to perform as nurses' aides as well as in dietary, therapeutic, and other support services. A democratic style of problem solving turns over much of the elder care to the staff closest to the residents, whereas residents and their families are actively encouraged to be involved in decision making. This may involve, for example, sharing recipes, planning an outing, or celebrating staff or resident birthdays. As they are able, residents may serve on hiring committees. Those with AD or other kinds of dementia are not transferred to "memory units" or otherwise segregated from less impaired persons; they are allowed to remain where they are until they die.

Anecdotal reports from these programs are very positive; administrators report extremely low staff turnover, greatly increased job satisfaction, and a virtual cessation of complaints to state licensing boards and regulatory agencies. A paradigm shift from a hierarchical to a democratic organizational structure that encourages resiliency in both staff and elders has been assessed as improving the quality of life for these elders (Angelelli, 2006; Angelelli & Higbie, 2005; Bergman-Evans, 2004; Boyd, 2003; Day, Carreon, & Stump, 2000; Fagan, 2004; Grant, 2006; Lustbader & Williams, 2006; Rabig, Thomas, Kane, Cutler, & McAlilly, 2006; Yeatts, Cready, Ray, DeWitt, & Queen, 2004).

Although the culture change movement is relatively recent and the outcome research is similarly tentative and new, the emphasis on the psychosocial environment of the AD patient in order to combat the hopelessness and dread associated with the Alzheimer's diagnosis is congruent with what is recommended by Whitehouse and George (2008), who have been involved in the medical research and treatment of AD for many years. These experts report having completely altered their approach to persons diagnosed with AD and their family members, de-emphasizing the use of medication and conveying both hope and the promise of a purposeful meaningful existence in contact with the human community, both in and outside of institutions. AD patients are encouraged to involve themselves in volunteer work, remain active participants in the life of their communities, and stay in regular contact with family and friends; family members are counseled to focus on what the elder can do as opposed to the elder's deficits. They further argue that the aging of the human brain remains less understood than the claims of pharmaceutical companies would imply and that the psychosocial needs of elders, as well as issues of prevention, should receive the bulk of society's attention and financial resources.

Aging in Place at Home

Although the long-term-care alternatives described previously are offering more humane, individualized care to elders with and without AD, most elders prefer to remain at home as long as possible (AARP, 2006a, 2006b, 2006c). Adult day-care centers and community senior centers can offer respite to family caregivers. In-home health services, home-delivered meals, alterations to the physical property to ensure the safety of impaired elders, safety response systems, and home monitoring of medical conditions via telehealth systems (Hooyman & Kiyak, 2008) are all enhancing the possibility that persons with AD can remain in their own homes. The Safe Return program, offered by the Alzheimer's Association, is a nationwide program in which caregivers and AD patients can enroll, so that the AD patient can be located if he or she wanders from home. In addition, many physicians are now defining themselves as "home-care physicians," offering home visits to frail elderly patients (Kehoe, 2008). Eden Alternative and Green House facilities strive to avoid the distressing transfers to and from hospitals and institutions licensed for differing levels of care by identifying medical problems early and thus preventing the need for hospital care and by responding flexibly to the inevitable decline of their residents by surrounding them with support and a family-like environment to the moment of death.

Strength-Based Clinical and Psychosocial Approaches

Narrative therapy methods have recently been adapted to clinical social work with couples in which one member has AD. The Couples Life Story Approach (Scherrer, Ingersoll-Dayton, & Spencer, 2014) is one example. Social workers visited couples approximately once a week in their homes for 5 weeks, helping them to narrate the story of their lives, emphasizing the construction of meaning and focusing on strengths. Mementoes, such as photos, are collected as part of this process, and life stories are gathered into a Life Story Book. Challenges noted in the description of several case examples include constructing a narrative from disparate stories, developing a mutual story meaningful to both members of the couple, telling the story of a couple whose relationship was of short duration, incorporating others in the story, including difficult life moments, and ending the story. The couples reported the process to be pleasurable, which is notable, in that the loss of autobiographical memory can be devastating to both partners. This research sample, however, was reported to be White, relatively highly educated, mostly heterosexual, and not suffering financial hardship. A hopeful and promising account, this research needs replication with more diverse samples. Notably, the researchers emphasize the purpose of working with couples, not individuals. As authors, recognizing the reality that many elders are lonely and without partners, we recommend adapting this approach for use with individual elders, both in their own homes and in institutions.

The use of music in working with Alzheimer's and other dementias is expanding across the globe and has become extensive enough to warrant a meta-analysis (Ueda, Suzukamo, Sato, & Izumi, 2013). These researchers examined several databases and selected 20 studies for review. Interventions using music are very varied and may include singing songs, playing the piano or hand bells, reminiscing while listening to music, movement or dance, clapping to one's favorite songs, or playing instruments. Music therapy, they discovered, has moderate effects on anxiety and small effects on behavioral symptoms and depression. Over a 3-month period, the effects on reducing anxiety were larger. There was insufficient evidence to support beneficial effects on cognitive function or ADLs. Music therapy seemed to be a more effective treatment for behavioral and psychological symptoms than other nonpharmacological interventions. The authors note that although pharmacological interventions were more powerful in controlling disturbing behaviors, these come with adverse side effects. The authors strongly recommend the use of music therapy before pharmacological intervention in the management of psychological and behavioral symptoms. Limitations of the study included the inability to describe what particular types of musical interventions were most effective and for which patients, but this is a promising area for future research.

A group of French researchers reviewed the use of music therapy with Alzheimer's' patients in France (Guetin et al., 2013). These researchers support psychosocial and nonpharmacological interventions that target quality of life, language, cognition, sensory stimulation, and motor activity, including speech therapy, psychosocial support, counselling, art therapy, occupational therapy, and others, and note that the French National Health Authority (HAS) has adopted a standard that these interventions must be tried first in order to prevent the use of antipsychotic drugs and other psychotropic drugs in elders. Music therapists, they note, usually combine active and receptive therapies. Musical stimuli have been demonstrated to activate neural pathways associated with emotional behavior, and listening to and producing music activates brain areas involved in cognitive, sensorimotor, and emotional processing. Music is important psychologically, as it links to important life events, facilitates social relationships, personal expression and communication, and can be tailored to an individual's personal history. At advanced stages of AD, music enables nonverbal communication, and has been shown to enhance the recall of autobiographical memory, reduce agitation, and reduce depressive symptoms. The authors recommend the integration of music therapy into multidisciplinary support interventions for people with AD, as well as for their family members, in both institutional and home settings. Studies, however, have not been rigorously controlled using randomized trials in a variety of settings.

Simmons-Stern et al. (2012) explored the use of music to enhance memory in persons with AD by making the content of song lyrics relevant to the daily life of an older adult. The use of musical mnemonics helped improve memory for general content information in both healthy older adults and patients with

AD. Lyrics addressed such activities as brushing and flossing teeth, buttoning clothing, and remembering the location of keys!

Researchers in the Netherlands tested the contribution of live music performance to quality of life in nursing home residents as nine professional singers, selected for their sensitivity and ability to make nonverbal contact, gave 45-minute performances in nursing homes and, occasionally in individual residents' rooms (van der Vleuten, Visser, & Meeuwesen, 2012). Costumes and poetry were used, along with other stimulating objects, such as plastic animals and special lighting, and residents were invited to dance at the conclusion of the performance. Although the residents were primarily spectators, results indicated that the performances had a positive impact on human contact, care relationships, and emotions, especially for those with mild dementia. The researchers strongly recommend that nursing homes make more extensive use of intimate live musical performances.

Can AD Be Delayed or Rendered Less Disabling by Promoting Resiliency?

A direction of very recent research focuses on the relationship among personality traits, resilience, and early behavioral and psychological symptoms of individuals in the early stages of AD. One prospective autopsy study examined whether personality traits were associated with resilience to clinical dementia in individuals whose autopsies showed the characteristic neuritic plaques and neurofibrillary tangles of Alzheimer's (Terracciano et al., 2013). The authors note that neuropathology is found in 30% of cognitively normal individuals, defined as resilient to the development of clinical dementia, as evidenced by the symptoms of AD. In this longitudinal study, broad and specific aspects of personality were assessed up to 28 years before the onset of dementia and up to 30 years before death in a cohort evaluated at autopsy for AD. Higher baseline scores on vulnerability to stress, anxiety, and depression (aspects of neuroticism), along with lower scores on order and competence (defined as conscientiousness) were significantly correlated with clinical symptoms of AD. Neuroticism and low agreeableness were also associated with advanced stages of neurofibrillary tangles, but in general, controlling for the extent of plaques and tangles did not correlate with personality traits or the risk of clinical dementia. The authors conclude that "a resilient personality profile is associated with lower risk or delay of clinical dementia, even in persons with AD neuropathology" (Terracciano et al. 2013, p. 1045). It is probable that emotionally stable individuals manage stress more effectively and more conscientious individuals exercise more and smoke less, but these associations are inconsistently demonstrated. Personality traits might also influence the individual's ability to follow through on recommended treatments. Other researchers have concluded that personality traits are not associated with behavioral and clinical symptoms in persons with early AD, but that personality and behavioral changes occur early in the course of AD, and their recognition might prove important in early detection and intervention (Pocnet, Rossier, Antonietti, & von Gunten, 2012). The previously cited research on the REST factor linked the failure of the brain's stress response syndrome to the development of the neuropathology of AD (Lu et al., 2014). Future related research may focus on the physiological and neurological correlates of lifestyle changes, such as exercise, meditation, or social support, that enable individuals to reduce psychological stress. If this line of research is pursued, the promotion of personal resiliency might become a core intervention related to AD.

Other intriguing findings point to the future possibility of delaying the onset or course of AD with diet. A recent *USA Today* article (Weintraub, 2014) reported on the identification, in a *Nature Medicine* article, of 10 fats seen in the blood of people who developed AD 2 years later in a test with 90% accuracy in distinguishing healthy brains from those with AD. Blood samples from 525 people age 70 and over were studied over time, and the blood of 50 who did not develop AD was compared with 50 who did, resulting in the identification of 10 fats that distinguished them. The worth of preventive activities, such as exercise, eating a Mediterranean diet, and being socially active was suggested as important for future research. These habits have been linked to lower rates of AD.

Recommendations of a Recent Summit Meeting

Recognizing that AD is a growing public health crisis, the Marian S. Ware Alzheimer Program at the University of Pennsylvania convened a summit meeting, "State of the Science Conference on the Advancement of Alzheimer's Diagnosis, Treatment, and Care," on June 21 to 22, 2012 (Naylor et al., 2012). Four work groups address core goals and made a variety of recommendations. Emphasis was placed on the need for integrated care, shifting resources and care delivery to the community and home. It was recommended that multidisciplinary professionals provided "one-stop shopping" that incorporates both medical and social interventions in one facility. Patients, family members, and advocacy groups should be actively encouraged to participate in the decision-making process. The search for biomarkers of AD should continue, along with the development of drugs and nonmedical interventions that have the promise of reducing the incidence and progression of AD. Responding humanely and adequately should be a priority in all segments of society, both nationally and internationally. The need to identify individuals at high risk for AD was emphasized in the summit meeting's recommendations. Traditionally, AD has been a disease defined during life by clinical signs and symptoms, and at death by the presence of neurological changes. In the future, AD will be defined in terms of the risks of developing symptoms and treated by reducing these risks and improving quality of life.

KEY POINTS

1. The culture of elder care is beginning to change.
2. Characteristics of this transformative movement include the empowerment of elders and of those who care for them; changing from a hierarchical to a democratic model of decision making in elder institutions; individualizing care; surrounding the elder with stimulation, security, and loving kindness; altering the architecture of care facilities to support these philosophical values.

3. A variety of community-based roles and programs are emerging to enable elders to age in place, either at home or in a community facility.
4. Narrative and music-based approaches show promise.
5. Research findings on the relationship between personality traits and resilience to AD are mixed. This area deserves further attention with respect to whether attention to managing stress and developing healthy lifestyle habits might reduce or delay the onset of AD.
6. AD is a growing public health crisis, which will require changes in national policy, law, and the development of effective integrated, multidisciplinary care.

CASE STUDY 3

An Alzheimer's Patient's Thoughts on Diagnosis

This Alzheimer's patient has the following to say concerning labels and communication in the diagnostic process:

> There is far too much emphasis on the label, the name, and the symptoms generally associated with the disease, and too little emphasis on the individuals who actually have the disease. The fact is, most experts spend more time talking to and listening to caregivers than they do talking to and listening to those of us with dementia. Perhaps too much time is spent trying to answer and question each other, when what I really need is to feel like I am being heard. (Taylor, 2007, pp. 30–31)

1. With respect to AD, reflect on your experience with the ways the Alzheimer's patient is rendered invisible in the diagnostic and treatment-planning process.
2. Create a scenario in which you role-play interacting directly with the Alzheimer's patient concerning the disease, thus facilitating his empowerment in the planning process.
3. With the societal and professional contexts described previously, we now turn our attention to the diagnosis of a Southeast Asian elder, contrasting a traditional approach to *DSM-5* diagnosis with the addition of the proposed Diversity/Resiliency Formulation.

CASE STUDY WITH AND WITHOUT THE DIVERSITY/RESILIENCY FORMULATION

Alzheimer's Disease

Noa Ying Vang is a 70-year-old Hmong widower, living at home with his adult son, age 53, and his daughter-in-law. Two grandchildren, ages 29 and 25, are married and living nearby; Mr. Vang is the great-grandfather of four great-grandchildren. Mr. Vang's wife, who had cooked and babysat for the grandchildren during their growing-up years, died 2 years ago of complications of diabetes. In his youth, Mr. Vang was an important man in his village in Laos. He actively supported the Americans during the Vietnam War, escaped across the Mekong River to Thailand, and left a Thai refugee camp for America in 1986. He has been a respected elder in his clan. Mr. Vang spends most of his days at home watching TV; he is bewildered and concerned about the behavior of teenagers in the neighborhood and afraid to go outside much because of gang activity. His son and daughter-in-law are worried about him because he is spending more and more time sleeping, has lost contact with the few friends he used to socialize with, and has stopped showing an interest in his grandchildren's or great-grandchildren's lives. He is alone in the house much of the time while his son and daughter-in-law are working. When questioned about how he spent his day, Mr. Vang forgets. He also has trouble remembering whether or what he has eaten.

Mr. Vang used to ride a bike in the neighborhood, but his fear of crime keeps him from going to the local Hmong grocery store as he used to do. He is also unsteady on his feet and, even more so, on his bike. On more than one occasion, he has been found outside by neighbors, a few blocks away from home, seemingly lost and appearing disheveled. Indeed, Noa Ying Vang, formerly a meticulous man, seems to have lost interest in his appearance and often does not bother to get dressed during the day. Much of the time, when not watching TV, Mr. Vang is silent; in fact, he has become increasingly mute during the past few years. When he does speak, he often stops in midsentence, struggling for words, and then gives up. His grandchildren do not speak Hmong, and his son and daughter-in-law prefer to speak English, especially around their children. Sometimes Mr. Vang cries silently to himself; he has at times stated that he might as well be dead. He is easily frustrated and lashes out at his son and sometimes at his daughter-in-law if his food is not prepared on time, even as he shows less and less interest in eating. Mr. Vang often wakes up at night, wandering around the small home, sometimes calling out in an agitated voice to his son for help; occasionally he calls to his deceased wife. He is increasingly demanding and accuses his son of leaving him for days, although his son has only left to go to work as usual. Mr. Vang is on medication for hypertension.

Diagnosing Noa Ying Vang, Using *DSM-5*

Concerned about his father's condition and safety, his son takes him to the family physician, who does not speak Hmong. Mr. Vang's son, as well as a Hmong interpreter, assist with the assessment of Mr. Vang's condition. The physician orders standardized tests in order to rule out disease processes that might explain his patient's symptoms. His mental status is examined via the clinical interview with both Mr. Vang and his son, as he is unable to respond to assessment instruments, such as the Mini-Mental State Examination or the Clock Test. There is no evidence of stroke, Parkinson's disease, tumor, vitamin deficiencies, substance abuse, hypothyroidism, or other glandular abnormalities. Mr. Vang's wandering behavior, difficulty with word finding, personality changes, paranoia, and problems with memory, as well as the results of the MRI lead his physician to the conclusion of probable mid-stage AD. In addition, Mr. Vang has symptoms of depression and bereavement. His working *DSM-5* diagnosis might be as follows:

> 331.0 (G30.9) AD (NOTE: This is the code for AD with behavioral disturbance)
> 294.11 (F02.81) Major neurocognitive disorder due to AD

Depending on an assessment of Mr. Vang's depressive symptoms, an additional mood disorder diagnosis might be consider for Vang, as follows:

> R/O 293.83 Major Depressive Disorder Due to AD
> This diagnosis would be given if an assessment of the timing of Mr. Vang's depressive symptoms were not a sustained reaction to his wife's death, but either preceded and/or accompanied his gradual decline from his previous active functioning, along with the insidious onset of symptoms of Alzheimer's.
> 296.2 3 Major Depressive Disorder, Single Episode, Severe Without Psychotic Features
> This diagnosis might be given if the clinician assesses the depression to predate or exist independent of AD, perhaps due to bereavement.

Based on the diagnosis of probable AD and significant mood symptoms, the physician might explain the diagnosis to Mr. Vang's son, provide psychoeducational reading material about dementia to the family, and prescribe standard Alzheimer's medications for AD as well as an antidepressant. In addition, a referral might be made to a geriatrician. In order to assess the home environment for safety and assist the family with caring for Mr. Vang at home, a referral to a home health agency would be made. Mr. Vang's son would be informed about what to expect in the future, with the expectation that placement in a nursing home would probably be necessary when Mr. Vang would require 24-hour nursing care, as the family would not be financially able to provide this at home. Mr. Vang's son would be informed about the existence of community Alzheimer's support groups, although it is doubtful that they would be available in the Hmong language or designed with the Hmong culture in mind.

Diagnosing Noa Ying Vang: Contributions of the Diversity/Resiliency Formulation

Attending to Mr. Vang's sources of resiliency and strength, the physician (or other health care professional) speaks directly to Mr. Vang, filling in with information provided by his son when Mr. Vang does not answer. He inquires about Mr. Vang's past history in Laos, his years in the United States, his family, his past interests, and the loss of his wife. He expresses great respect for Mr. Vang's honored position in his cultural group and for his military service in Laos. He also inquires about specific Hmong cultural health practices, such as shamanism, and encourages consultation with a shaman if this is Mr. Vang's usual practice. Mr. Vang is asked about his favorite TV programs and music, his family members, and his special interests and talents. The medical professional learns that

Mr. Vang used to play the *Qeej*, known in English as the red pipe, a traditional Hmong musical instrument. He has also helped out in a neighborhood community garden and enjoyed playing catch with his great-grandson. Mr. Vang used to get together at a nearby community center with a group of older Hmong men. His children and grandchildren value their cultural and spiritual traditions and are comfortable with both Hmong shamanism and American Roman Catholic religious practices. The Diversity/Resiliency Formulation follows.

In outline form:

> *Intrapersonal*: History of military leadership in Laos, musical and plays the *Qeej*, family patriarch
> *Interpersonal*: Supportive extended family and history of active involvement in play with great-grandchildren, active in group of older Hmong men until recently
> *Cultural*: Identifies with Hmong culture; speaks Hmong predominantly
> *Community*: Has participated in an informal men's group and community garden
> *Spiritual*: Shamanism; Hmong spiritual practices; some family attendance at Roman Catholic community church

In paragraph form:

Mr. Vang is a Hmong elder who emigrated to the United States 25 years ago. He was a military leader in Laos, is the patriarch of his family, and has played the red pipe (*Qeej*), a traditional Hmong instrument. Mr. Vang previously participated in an informal Hmong men's group and helped out in a community garden. He and his family members identify with the Hmong spiritual practice of shamanism and also occasionally attend a neighborhood Roman Catholic Church, where they feel welcomed. Until recently, Mr. Vang has especially enjoyed playing with his great-grandchildren and riding his bike.

If the clinician were to respond only to the *DSM-5* diagnoses, Mr. Vang's full humanity would immediately begin to disappear, especially when he is given the label, "Alzheimer's." Responding to the information gained as a result of inquiry into his cultural identification and sources of resiliency and support, however, a plan is made to include members of Mr. Vang's extended family and a Hmong shaman in his next medical office visit, in order to discuss the diagnosis and its implications and to welcome Hmong healing rituals if appropriate. With encouragement, Mr. Vang's grandson plans to accompany him to the community garden, and a small garden is begun in the backyard, where Mr. Vang can participate in planting and weeding without having to talk. The gardening activity is embarked on tentatively, however, as Mr. Vang used to garden with his wife, carrying out the cultural male role (the harder labor of digging and putting sticks into the ground) while his wife did the planting, weeding, and harvesting). It would be important for the medical professional to realize that engagement in this activity might trigger memories of sadness about activities he performed while his wife was at his side, but it is worth a try!

Similar caution would be exercised in encouraging Mr. Vang to visit a nearby Hmong community center, where a group of Hmong men are engaged in making the traditional *Qeej* out of bamboo. In Hmong culture, this instrument is used for entertainment and funeral purposes. Members of the culture who know how to play this instrument are deeply and passionately connected to the culture and to the spiritual world. When this instrument is played during a funeral, for example, the Hmong elder is using the instrument to sing a song accompanying and guiding the spirit of the deceased person back to the ancestral spiritual world. The activity of making this instrument in the company of fellow elders might be comforting and familiar to Mr. Vang; he would not be required to engage in conversation but would be accepted as an honored member of his culture, still able to make a genuine contribution to his community. On the other hand, this activity might also trigger deep sadness about the loss of his wife. Even so, there would be a chance to make an emotional connection with him.

Mr. Vang's great-grandchildren are brought over to visit; they bring storybooks on tape to which they can listen while sitting on Mr. Vang's lap without requiring their great-grandfather to read. Mr. Vang begins to receive regular visits from a community volunteer who speaks his language. The issue of spirituality is addressed very carefully with this family, as there may be a conflict between the Roman Catholic religious practice of the younger generations and the shamanism practiced by Mr. Vang. It would be important to express honor and respect for Mr. Vang's deep spirituality as his care changes and to reinforce respect for his spirituality among his extended family.

The loss of a spouse is an extremely important issue in the Hmong culture; married couples mate for life. As a result, the role of grief in Mr. Vang's diagnosis is important to understand. His loss should be honored and attended to by medical professionals, and he should be encouraged to talk about both the loss of his wife and his honored position in the Hmong culture in order to clarify as accurately as possible the role of bereavement and/or depression in his diagnosis.

When Mr. Vang can no longer be maintained at home, he will be referred to a small group home for Hmong elders, a facility that subscribes to a culture-change model of care, as described earlier. Mr. Vang will be allowed to age in place there, and his extended family will remain actively involved in his life. The emphasis in responding to Mr. Vang is on what he can still do and on his uniqueness as an individual, with the goals of enhancing his personal value and purpose in living. For example, the residents of the group home maintain a garden, and Mr. Vang will be encouraged to join in this activity. Throughout the diagnostic and follow-up progress, careful attention would need to be paid to adequate family communication and family dynamics. The establishment of a trusting and mutually respectful relationship with Mr. Vang and his family members would be of paramount importance in this process. Family members may not understand Mr. Vang's diagnosis, use different terms to discuss aging and mental health issues, and be baffled by the medical terms used to describe Mr. Vang's condition. As a result, the accuracy of his diagnosis would be affected. To facilitate accuracy of communication and mutual understanding, the "teach back" method to enhance medical literacy would be used (Schillinger et al., 2003). This means that the medical professional would ask the patient (in this case Mr. Vang and/or his relative) to describe what he has heard from the doctor and how he will explain this to other family members when he gets home.

Although the progression of AD would continue, the quality of Mr. Vang's life and of the support provided to him would be enhanced by attention to these diversity and resiliency issues. With the use of the Diversity/Resiliency Formulation, Mr. Vang emerges as an interesting, multidimensional human being with a unique personal history rich in culture and meaning. Rendering him more visible in this way has led to more relevant, compassionate, humane interventions (Cher Teng Yang, personal communication, October 27, 2009).

SUMMARY

Elders are the fastest-growing segment of the global population. Up to 50% of elders will have symptoms of AD by age 85. Although millions of dollars have been spent searching for the causes, the etiology remains complicated and obscure, and drugs to treat AD have at best limited utility. What has been too often lost is the individuality and the humanity of the person with AD, as few comparative resources have been devoted to psychosocial, psychoeducational, spiritual, cultural, and community interventions that facilitate our elders' ability to lead a life of meaning and purpose, surrounded by loving support, for as long as they are able. Using the Diversity/Resiliency Formulation as a standard part of the diagnostic and intervention process focuses a spotlight on the areas most neglected in responding to elders with dementia and facilitates an attitude of engagement that acknowledges strength and personal identity. This respectful, strength-based stance helps to mitigate the overwhelming tendency to focus exclusively on the pathology of this dreaded disease and, in doing so, to draw back from the personhood of elders with Alzheimer's, thus contributing to their isolation.

In his essay *Disabling Enablers*, Richard Taylor (2007), an Alzheimer's patient, makes a passionate plea for an approach to AD patients that focuses on the person behind the label:

> The professionals become cheerleaders for caregivers, and sympathetic observers of me. The professionals are well-intentioned, but it is quicker and easier to "fix" caregivers than it is to listen to, understand, and even attempt to "fix" me.... Where can I find the books on how to live with my disease? ... Why not spend a bit more time and effort talking with people who have the disease? Why not see us as a source of answers to our problems, rather than as a source of problems to which our caregivers need answers? We, too, want to be proactive when dealing with our symptoms, not just reactive to our problems. Professionals, encourage caregivers to talk to us about their problems, and encourage them to listen to us about our problems. Cut down on the visits to you, and increase the time we spend around the kitchen table trying to solve our issues, not just theirs. By their very nature, the symptoms we label as AD

create as many or more psychological problems as they reflect physiological problems. At least for a while, there isn't much that can be done about what is happening with the chemistry between my ears, so why not spend more time working on what is happening to the chemistry between my spouse and me? Between mothers and daughters? Within families? Among friends? For me, this is the neglected battle front of AD. (Taylor, 2007, pp. 67–68)

DISCUSSION QUESTIONS AND ACTIVITIES

1. Imagine being told that you have AD. Write a paragraph about what you feel. Then imagine yourself telling your friends and family about the diagnosis. How do you imagine yourself coping with the disease? How would you want other people to relate to you and care for you? What would you want your physician and other health care professionals to know about you in addition to your Alzheimer's symptoms? Why?
2. Visit culture-change nursing homes and Green Houses in your area; if this is impossible, visit them on the Internet and watch their videos.
3. Read *Alzheimer's From the Inside Out* (Taylor, 2007) and *The Best Friend's Approach to Alzheimer's Care* (Bell & Troxel, 2003). Volunteer at a nursing home with dementia residents once a week for the course of a semester; visiting the same resident each time. Apply the insights from these books to the relationship you develop with the elders you visit.
4. If you work in a setting where you encounter persons with Alzheimer's, practice adding the Diversity/Resiliency Formulation to your assessment and diagnostic activities. Reflect in writing on how this has affected your work. Present your experiences in classes you teach, in which you are a student, or in your workplace.
5. Form a study/support group with other students or professionals. Study humane approaches to Alzheimer's patients and their families. Consider as a group how to incorporate individualized resiliency perspectives and diversity competence into work with Alzheimer's patients and their families in facilities in your community. What prevention and psychosocial needs related to Alzheimer's could be responded to more effectively?
6. Regardless of whether you are a physician, psychologist, social worker, nurse, or educator, think critically about your professional role as it applies to your attention to elders with AD and their families. List three ways in which your role may distance you from persons with AD and three ways you would consider altering your professional behavior to reduce or eliminate the distance.
7. Discuss in a small group or write an essay concerning the following premise: When our elders are less visible and prized, they are less attended to, less listened to, and more vulnerable to being responded to as a social category rather than as individuals.

WEB RESOURCES

www.aahsa.org
www.aarp.org
www.adta.org
www.alz.co.uk
www.alz.org/Resources/Diversity
www.alz.org
www.alzfdn.org
www.alzheimers.org
www.alzsforum.org
www.aoa.gov/prof/aoaprog/caregiver/carefam/taking_care_of_others/wecare.asp
www.arttherapy.org
www.asaging.org
www.caregiver.org
www.caremanager.org
www.commonwealthfund.org
www.edenalt.com
www.elderabusecenter.org
www.eldercare.gov
www.geron.org
www.helpage.org
www.mayoclinic.com/health/alzheimers/AZ99999
www.musictherapy.org
www.nahc.org
www.ncbi.nlm.nih.gov/pubmed
www.niapublications.org/agepages/longterm.asp
www.nfcacares.org
www.nlm.nih.gov/medlineplus/alzheimersdisease.html
www.nscic.org
www.n4a.org
www.Research.Alzforum.org
www.respitelocator.org/index.htm

REFERENCES

AARP. (2006a). *Across the states: Profiles of long-term care and independent living*. Washington, DC: AARP Public Policy Institute.

AARP. (2006b). *Fixing to stay: A survey on housing and home modification issues*. Washington, DC: AARP Public Policy Institute.

AARP. (2006c). *The state of 50+ America 2006*. Washington, DC: AARP Public Policy Institute.

Adamis, D., Slor, C. J., Leonard, M., Witlox, J., de Jonghe, J. F., Macdonald, A. J., … Meagher, D. (2013). Reliability of delirium rating scale (DRS) and delirium rating scale-revised-98 (DRS-R-98) using variance-based multivariate modelling. *Journal of Psychiatric Research, 47*(7), 966–971.

Administration on Aging. (2007). *A profile of older Americans: 2007*. Retrieved from www.agingcarefl.org/aging/AOA-2007profile.pdf

Amaducci, L., & Lippi, A. (1992). Pro and con for heterogeneity of Alzheimer's Disease: A view from an epidemiologist. In F. Boller, F. Forette, Z. Khachaturian, M. Poncet, & Y. Christen (Eds.), *Heterogeneity of Alzheimer's Disease* (pp. 74–80). New York, NY: Springer-Verlag.

American Psychiatric Association. (2000). *Diagnostic and statistical manual of mental disorders* (4th ed., text revision). Washington, DC: Author.

American Psychiatric Association. (2013). *Diagnostic and statistical manual of mental disorders (5th ed.) Arlington, VA: American Psychiatric Press.*

Angelelli, J. (2006). Promising models for transforming long term care. *The Gerontologist, 46*, 429–430.

Angelelli, J., & Higbie, I. (2005). Unfolding the culture change map and locating ourselves together. *Journal of Social Work in Long-Term Care, 3*, 121–135.

Arbore, P. E. D. (2007, May 5). *Recognizing obstacles in making connection: Identifying and responding to substance abuse and mental health issues in older adults*. Training presentation. American Society on Aging to National Association of Social Workers.

Bajenaru, O., Tiu, C., Antochi, F., & Roceanu, A. (2012). Neurocognitive disorders in *DSM-5* project–Personal comments. *Journal of the Neurological Sciences, 322*(1–2), 17–19.

Bell, V., & Troxel, D. (2003). *The best friends approach to Alzheimer's care*. Baltimore, MD: Health Professions Press.

Bergman-Evans, B. (2004). Beyond the basics: Effects of the Eden Alternative model on quality of life issues. *Journal of Gerontological Nursing, 30*, 27–34.

Boyd, C. (2003). The Providence Mt. St. Vincent Experience. *Journal of Social Work in Long Term Care, 2*, 245–268.

Brandel, J. R. (Ed.). (2011). *Theory and practice in clinical social work* (2nd ed.). Thousand Oaks, CA: Sage.

Braun, K. L., Takamura, J. C., Forman, S. M., Sasaki, P. A., & Meininger, L. (1995). Developing and testing outreach materials on Alzheimer's disease for Asian and Pacific Islander Americans. *The Gerontologist, 35*(1), 122–126.

Brown, P. L. (2009, August 31). Invisible immigrants, old and left with nobody to talk to. *The New York Times*, p. 1.

Chen, C. Y., Leung, K. K., & Chen, C. Y. (2011). A quick dementia screening tool for primary care physicians. *Archives of Gerontology and Geriatrics, 53*(1), 100–103.

Chen, P. W. (2007). *Final exam: A surgeon's reflections on mortality*. New York, NY: Vintage Books/ Random House.

Cooper, L. (2002, May). Testimony on hearing on racial disparities in health care, U.S. House Government Reform Subcommittee on Criminal Justice, Drug Policy, and Human Resources, U.S. House of Representatives, U.S. Government Publishing. Retrieved from www.gpo.gov.

Corcoran, J., &. Walsh, J. (2006). *Clinical assessment and diagnosis in social work practice*. New York, NY: Oxford University Press.

Corr, C., Nabe, C., & Corr, D. (2009). *Death and dying: Life and living* (6th ed.). Belmont, CA: Wadsworth Cengage Learning.

Cutler, S. J. (2006). Technological change and aging. In R. H. Binstock & L. K. Beorge (Eds.), *Handbook of aging and the social sciences* (6th ed., pp. 257–276). Burlington, MA: Academic Press.

Davis, D., Muniz Terrera G., Keage H., Rahkonen T., Oinas M., Matthews F. E., … Brayne C. (2012). Delirium is a strong risk factor for dementia in the oldest-old: A population-based cohort study. *Brain: A Journal of Neurology*. *135*, 2809–2816.

Day, K., Carreon, D., & Stump, C. (2000). The therapeutic design of environments for people with dementia: A review of the empirical research. *The Gerontologist, 40*, 397–406.

DeBaggio, T. (2002). *Losing my mind: An intimate look at life with Alzheimer's*. New York, NY: The Free Press, Simon & Schuster.

Detweiler, M., Kenneth A., Bader G., Sullivan K., Murphy P. F., Halling M., … Detweiler J. G. (2014). Can improved intra- and inter-team communication reduce missed delirium? *Psychiatric Quarterly, 85*(2), 211–224. doi:10.1007/s11126-013-9284-0.

Didion, J. (2005). *The year of magical thinking*. New York, NY: Alfred A. Knopf.

Doidge, N. (2007). *The brain that changes itself*. New York, NY: Penguin Books.

Elliott, K. S., DiMinno, M., Lam, D., & Tu, A. M. (1996). Working with Chinese families in the context of dementia. In G. Yeo & D. Gallagher-Thompson (Eds.), *Ethnicity and the dementias* (pp. 89–109). Washington, DC: Taylor and Francis.

Fagan, R. M. (2004). Culture change in long term care: Creating true independence for elders. *Maximizing Human Potential, 11*, 1–6.

Feldman, H. H. (2002). Treated Alzheimer's disease with cholinesterase inhibitors: What have we learned so far? *International Psychogeriatrics, 14*(Suppl.), 3–5.

Fillenbaum, G. G., Heyman, A., Huber, M. S., & Woodbury, M. A. (1998). The prevalence and 3-year incidence of dementia in older black and white community residents. *Journal of Clinical Epidemiology, 51*(7), 587–595.

Fos, P., & Clark, M. (2008). *Human aging* (2nd ed.). New York, NY: Pearson, Allyn & Bacon.

Frances, A. (2013). *Saving normal: An insider's revolt against out-of-control psychiatric diagnosis, DSM-5, big pharma, and the medicalization of ordinary life*. New York, NY: Harper-Collins.

Gallagher-Thompson, D., Talamantes, M., Ramirez, R., & Valverde, I. (1996). Service delivery issues and recommendations for working with Mexican American family caregivers. In G. Yeo & D. Gallagher-Thompson (Eds.), *Ethnicity and the dementias* (pp. 137–152). Washington, DC: Taylor and Francis.

Gillick, M. R. (2006). *The denial of aging: Perpetual youth, eternal life, and other dangerous fantasies*. Cambridge, MA: Harvard University Press.

Goffman, E. (1961). *Asylums: Essays on the social situation of mental patients and other inmates*. Garden City, NJ: Random House.

Grant, L. (2006). *Culture change in for-profit nursing homes*. The Commonwealth Fund. Retrieved from www.cmwf.org/spotlights/spotlights_show.htm?doc

Gravenstein, S. T., Franklin, J., & Davidson, H. E. (Eds.). (2003). *A pocket guide to dementia and associated behavioral symptoms* (3rd ed.). Norfolk, VA: Insight Therapeutics.

Gray, S. W., & Zide, M. R. (2006). *Psychopathology: A competency-based treatment model for social workers*. Belmont, CA: Thomson, Brooks/Cole.

Gray, S. W., & Zide, M. R. (2008). *Psychopathology: A competency-based assessment model for social workers* (2nd ed.). Belmont, CA: Thomson, Brooks/Cole.

Guetin, S., Charras, K., Berard, A., Arbus, C., Berthelon, P., Blanc, F., ... Leger, J. M. (2013). An overview of the use of music therapy in the context of Alzheimer's disease: A report of a French expert group. *Dementia, 12*(5), 619–634.

Hebert, L. E., Scherr, P. A., Bienias, J. L., Bennett, D. A., & Evans, D. A. (2003). Alzheimer's disease in the U.S. population: Prevalence estimates using the 2000 census. *Archives of Neurology, 60*, 1119–1122.

Hooyman, R., & Kiyak, H. (2008). *Social gerontology: A multidisciplinary perspective* (8th ed.). New York, NY: Pearson, Allyn & Bacon.

International Longevity Center and AARP. (2003). *Unjust desserts: Financial realities of older women*. New York, NY: ILC and AARP. Retrieved from www.ilcusa.org/_lib/pdf/unjust desserts.pdf

Jameson, K. R. (2009). *Nothing was the same*. New York, NY: Alfred Knopf/Borzoi Books.

Karls, J. M., & Wandrei, K. E. (Eds.). (1994). *Person-in-environment system: The PIE classification system for social functioning problems*. Washington, DC: National Association of Social Workers Press.

Kehoe, S. M. (2008). *"Listen to me, I am still somebody": Understanding the Alzheimer's disease sufferer*. Boca Raton, FL: Universal Publishers.

Kennedy, G. (2000). *Geriatric mental health care: A treatment guide for health professionals*. New York, NY: Guilford Press.

Kim, K. (2008). *Social change in Korea*. Seoul: Korea Herald; Jimoondan Publisher.

Kleinman, A. (1986). *Social origins of distress and disease: Depression, neurasthenia, and pain in modern China*. New Haven, CT: Yale University Press.

Korean National Commission for UNESCO. (2008). Later life in flux: The reality and meaning of getting old. *Korea Journal, 48*(4).

Lee, E. (1982). A social systems approach to assessment and treatment for Chinese American families. In M. McGoldrick, J. K. Pearve, & J. Giordano (Eds.), *Ethnicity and family therapy* (pp. 527–551). New York, NY: Guilford Press.

Lewis, I. D., & Ausberry, M. S. C. (1996). African American families: Management of demented elders. In G. Yeo & D. Gallagher-Thompson (Eds.), *Ethnicity and the dementias* (pp. 167–174). Washington, DC: Taylor and Francis.

Lischka, A. R., Mendelsohn, M., Overend, T., & Forbes, D. (2012). A systematic review of screening tools for predicting the development of dementia. *Canadian Journal on Aging, 31*(3). 295–311.

Lu, T., Aron, L., Zullo, J., Pan, Y., Kim, H., Chen, Y., … Yankner, B. A. (2014). REST and stress resistance in ageing and Alzheimer's disease. *Nature, 507*, 448–454.

Lustbader, W., & Williams, C. C. (2006). Culture change in long-term care. In B. Berkman & S. D'Ambruoso (Eds.), *Handbook of social work in health and aging* (pp. 57–58). New York, NY: Oxford University Press.

Mclnnis-Dittrich, K. (2002). *Social work with elders: A biopsychosocial approach to assessment and intervention*. Boston, MA: Allyn and Bacon.

McKhann, G., Drachman, D., Folstein, M., & Katzman, R. (1984). Clinical diagnosis of Alzheimer's disease. Report of the NINCDS- ADRDA Work Group, Department of Health and Human Services Task Force on Alzheimer's disease. *Neurology, 34*, 939–944.

Mellor, J. J., & Ivry, J. (Eds.). (2002). *Advancing gerontological social work education*. New York, NY: Haworth Press.

Meyer, G. D., Shapiro, F., Vanderstichele, H., Venmechelen, E., Engelborghs, S., DeDeyn, P. P., … Trojanowski J. Q.; Alzheimer's disease Neuroimaging Initiative. (2010). Diagnosis-independent Alzheimer's disease biomarker signature in cognitively normal elderly people. *Archives of Neurology, 67*(8), 949–956.

Morandi, A., McCurley, J., Vasilevskis, E. E., Fick, D. M., Bellelli, G., Lee, P., … MacLullich, A. (2012). Tools to detect delirium superimposed on dementia: A systematic review. *Journal of the American Geriatrics Society, 60*(11), 2005–2013.

Moyer, V. A. (2014). Screening for cognitive impairment for old adults: U.S. Preventive Services Task Force recommendation statement. *Annals of Internal Medicine, 160*(11), 791–797. doi:10.7326/M14-0496

Naylor, M. D., Karlawish, J. H., Arnold, S. E., Khachaturian, A. S., Khachaturian, Z. S., Lee, V. M., … Trojanowski, J. Q. (2012). Advancing Alzheimer's disease diagnosis, treatment, and care: Recommendations from the Ware Invitational Summit. *Alzheimer's and Dementia, 8*(5), 445–452.

Novak, M. (2009). *Issues in aging* (2nd ed.). Boston, MA: Allyn & Bacon.

Nuland, S. (1993). *How we die*. New York, NY: Random House.

Peterson, C., Maier, S., & Seligman, M. E. D. (1993). *Learned helplessness: A theory for the age of personal control*. New York, NY: Oxford University Press.

Phillips, M. R. (1993). Strategies used by Chinese families coping with schizophrenia. In D. David & S. Harrell (Eds.), *Chinese families in the post-Mao era* (pp. 277–306). Berkeley, CA: University of California Press.

Pocnet, C., Rossier, J., Antonietti, J. P., & von Gunten, A. (2013). Personality traits and behavioral and psychological symptoms in patients at an early stage of Alzheimer's disease. *International Journal of Geriatric Psychiatry, 28*, 276–283.

Quinn, M. J., & Tomita, K. T. (1997). *Elder abuse and neglect: Causes, diagnosis, and intervention*. New York, NY: Springer Publishing Company.

Rabig, J., Thomas, W., Kane, R. A., Cutler, L. J., & McAlilly, S. (2006). Radical redesign of nursing homes: Applying the GreenHouse concept in Jupelo, Mississippi. *The Gerontologist, 46*, 533–539.

Raskind, M. A., Peskind, E. R., Truyen, L., Kershaw, P., & Damaraju, C. V. (2004). The cognitive benefits of galantamine are sustained for at least 36 months. *Archives of Neurology, 61*, 252–256.

Reisberg, B., Doody, R., Stofffler, A., Schmitt, F., Ferris, S., & Mobius, H. J. (2003). Memantine in moderate-to-severe Alzheimer's disease. *New England Journal of Medicine, 348*, 1333–1341.

Reisberg, B., Ferris, S. H., De-Leon, M. J., & Crook, T. (1982). The Global Deterioration Scale for assessment of primary degenerative dementia. *American Journal of Psychiatry, 139*, 1136–1139.

Reisberg, B., & Sartorius, N. (2007). Diagnostic criteria in dementia: A comparison of current criteria, research challenges, and implications for *DSM-V* and *ICD-11*. In T. Sunderland, D. Jeste, O. Baiyewu, P. Sirovatka, & D. Regier (Eds.), *Diagnostic issues in dementia: Advancing the research agenda for DSM-V* (pp. 27–50). Arlington, VA: American Psychiatric Association.

Sarton, M. (1996). *At eighty-two: A journal*. New York, NY: W.W. Norton.

Scherrer, K. S., Ingersoll-Dayton, B., & Spencer, B. (2014). Constructing couples' stories: Narrative practice insights from a dyadic dementia intervention. *Clinical Social Work Journal, 42*, 90–100.

Schillinger, D., Piette, J., Grumbach, K., Wang, F., Wilson, C., Daher, C., ... Bindman, A. B. (2003). Closing the loop: Physician communication with diabetic patients who have low health literacy. *Archives of Internal Medicine, 163*, 83–90.

Schlarch, A. (2009). Design for an aging California. *Architecture California; The Journal of the American Institute of Architects, California Council, Architect in the Community Issue, 2*, 12–13.

Schmidt, K., & Beatty, S. (2005). Quality Improvement: The pursuit of excellence. *Quality Management in Health Care, 14*, 196–198.

Segal-Gidan (2013). Cognitive screening tools. *Clinician Reviews, 23*(1), 13–18.

Seltzer, B. (2006). Cholinesterase inhibitors in the clinical management of Alzheimer's disease: Importance of early and persistent treatment. *Journal of International Medical Research, 34*, 339–347.

Sheehan, B. (2012). Assessment scales in dementia. *Therapeutic Advances in Neurological Disorders, 5*, 349–358.

Shinn, H. (2009, July 30). Korea needs to move toward cohesive society: Social and economic indicators by OECD, NSO reveal troublesome trends for Seoul. *The Korea Herald*, p. 4.

Shumaker, S. A. M, Legault, C., Rapp, S. R., Thal, L., Wallace, R. D., Ocken, J. C., ... Wactawski-Wende, J.; WHIMS Investigators. (2003). Estrogen plus progestin and the incidence of dementia and mild cognitive impairment in post menopausal women. *Journal of the American Medical Association, 139*, 2651–2662.

Siegel, R. J. (2004). Ageism in psychiatric diagnosis. In P. Cakplan & L Cosgrove (Eds.), *Bias in psychiatric diagnosis* (pp. 89–98). New York, NY: Jason Aronson.

Simmons-Stern, N. R., Deason, R. G., Brandler, B. J., Frustace, B. S., O'Connor, M. K., Ally, B. A., & Budson, A. E. (2012). Music-based memory enhancement in Alzheimer's disease: Promise and limitations. *Neuropsychologica, 50*(14), 3295–3303.

Stevenson, H. (2010). Alzheimer's can now be diagnosed 10 years before symptoms. Who benefits? *Journal of the American Medical Association*. Retrieved from http://gaia-health.com/article251/000284-alzheimers-can-now-be-diagnosed-10-years-before-symptoms-html

Tang, M. X., Stern, Y., Marder, K., Bell, K., & Gurland, B. (1998). The APOE-epsilon 4 allele and the risk of Alzheimer's disease among African American, Whites, and Hispanics. *Journal of the American Medical Association, 279*(10), 751–755.

Tariot, P. N., Farlow, M. R., Grossberg, G. T., Graham, S. M., McDonald, S., & Gergel, I.; Memantine Study Group. (2004). Memantine treatment in patients with moderate to severe Alzheimer's disease already receiving donepezil. *Journal of the American Medical Association, 291*, 317–324.

Taylor, R. (2007). *Alzheimer's from the inside out*. Baltimore, MD: Health Professions Press.

Terracciano, A., Iacono, D., O'Brien, R. J., Troncoso, J. C., An, Y, Sutin, A. R., ... Resnick, S. (2013). Personality and resilience to Alzheimer's disease neuropathology: A prospective autopsy study. *Neurobiology of Aging, 34*(4), 1045–1050.

Teri, L., Gibbons, L. E., McCurry, S. M., Logsdon, R. G., Buchner, D. M., Barlow, W. E., ... Larson, E. B. (2003). Exercise plus behavioral management in patients with Alzheimer's disease. *Journal of the American Medical Association, 290*, 2015–2022.

Terkel, S. (2002). *Will the circle be unbroken? Reflections on death, rebirth, and hunger for a faith*. New York, NY: Ballantine Books.

Thomas, W. (1996). *A life worth living: How someone you love can still enjoy life in a nursing home: The Eden Alternative in action*. Acton, MA: Vander Wyk & Burnham.

Thomas, W. (2004). *What are old people for? How elders will save the world*. Acton, MA: Vander Wyk & Burnham.

Ueda, T., Suzukamo, Y., Sato, M., & Izumi, S. (2013). Effects of music therapy on behavioral and psychological symptoms of dementia: A systematic review and meta-analysis. *Aging Research Reviews, 12*(2), 628–641.

Van der Vleuten, M., Visser, A., & Meeuwesen, L. (2012). The contribution of intimate live music performances to the quality of life for persons with dementia. *Patient Education and Counseling, 89*(3), 484–488.

Whitehouse, P., & George, M. (2008). *The myth of Alzheimers: What you aren't being told about today's most dreaded diagnosis*. New York, NY: St. Martin's Press.

Wong, R. (2002). *Migration and socioeconomic conditions of older adults*. Demos: Carta Demografica sobre Mexico (DEMOS) [A demographic letter concerning Mexico], 14. Retrieved from www.ssc.upenn.edu/mbas/Papers/3.pdf

Wu, K. (2006). *Income and poverty of older Americans in 2004*. Retrieved from www.census.gov/hhes/www/poverty/histpov/histpov3.html

Yalom, I. (2008). *Staring at the sun: Overcoming the terror of death*. San Francisco, CA: Jossey-Bass.

Yeatts, D. E., Cready, C., Ray, B., DeWitt, A., & Queen, C. (2004). Self-managed work teams in nursing homes: Implementing and empowering nurse aide teams. *The Gerontologist*, 44, 256–261.

EIGHT

Schizophrenia and the Diversity/ Resiliency Formulation

Somewhere in the illness, whose limits she could not yet define, lay a hidden strength. It was there and working; it had sounded in the glimmer of relief when the fact of the sickness was made plain, and most of all in the "suicide attempt," the cry for help, and the statement ... that the game was over and the disguising ended.

—JOANNE GREENBERG, *I Never Promised You a Rose Garden*

A diagnosis of schizophrenia is terrifying and demoralizing to both the client and family members and has, until very recently, been associated with dread and despair, the anticipation of a lifetime of chronic struggle, and a bewildering journey through the quagmire of psychiatric institutions and treatments. In this chapter we have chosen to focus on schizophrenia while noting the additional psychotic disorders in the *Diagnostic and Statistical Manual of Mental Disorders*, 5th edition (*DSM®-5*; American Psychiatric Association [APA], 2013) for the purpose of honing in on issues of diversity and resiliency. We will briefly summarize, but not expand on, other disorders in the *DSM-5* chapter, "Schizophrenia Spectrum and Other Psychotic Disorders" (APA, 2013).

Schizophrenia is a psychotic disorder with neurobiological and genetic vulnerabilities, it can become a progressive, debilitating, lifelong condition, and is known to affect 1% of the population (Rice, 1999). It represents a complex combination of symptoms that continue to challenge our understanding of its parameters, onset and course, and has a wide range of recovery outcomes. A challenge remains to find effective treatment outcomes. It is viewed as a thought disorder and is characterized by negative and positive symptoms.

The distinction and clarification of the subtypes and positive and negative symptoms identified by Andreasen (1982) constitute a watershed point in the elucidation of schizophrenia and in research on onset, manifestation of symptoms, course, and functioning of the individual in relation to neurotransmitters and brain regions. *Positive symptoms* refer to delusions, hallucinations, and disorganized thinking and speech. *Positive* symptoms also refer to abnormal behaviors such as agitation and catatonia, inappropriate affect, and disorganized behavior (Shahrokh & Hales, 2003). *Negative symptoms* include a loss of fluency, spontaneity, and content in speech (APA, 2013; Beck, Rector, Stolar, & Grant, 2009; Klingberg et al., 2011), an inability to sustain attention, lack of initiative, restricted affect, and difficulty in interpersonal interaction (Andreasen, 1982; Andreasen, Arndt, Alliger, Miller, & Flaum, 1995). Negative symptoms that are most commonly associated with schizophrenia are reduced emotional expression, a decrease in self-initiated activities, and decreased capacity to experience pleasure. Negative symptoms are thought of a behaviors that most individuals, who do not have schizophrenia, do have. Similarly, positive behaviors are considered behaviors that most people, who do not have schizophrenia, do not have.

Palmer, Dawes, and Heaton's (2009) review of the literature proposes that the relationship between "severity of cognitive deficits and psychopathologic symptoms is consistent in showing a significant but modest association between severity of cognitive deficits and negative symptoms, but there is no discernible association between cognitive deficits and positive symptoms" (p. 368). Without treatment and support, limitations arising from these difficulties can disrupt an individual's efforts to pursue education, a career, employment, self-care, and interpersonal relationships. Consequences of these behaviors—such as difficulty maintaining employment or experiencing pleasure (i.e., anhedonia) and social isolation—are associated with diminished functioning in attention, memory, and flexible, resilient thinking (Beck et al., 2009).

The cognitive impairments associated with schizophrenia affect prefrontal cortex processes such as executive functions and working memory, for example, interfering with recall and attention (Silver, Feldman, Bilker, & Gur, 2003; Weikert et al., 2000). Working memory deals with the storage and integration of concepts that are the basis of reasoning and judgment. Executive functions are significant for daily functioning and are the basis of "planning, abstraction, cognitive set-shifting, motivation, and self-regulation" (Frangou, 2006, p. 64). Prefrontal cortex functions are important in being able to go back and forth between tasks or mental sets, for example, with color and shape, or in shifting goals, skills that are learned from experience. There is some evidence that the cognitive impairments, such as language, memory, attention, and reasoning, are twice as severe for those diagnosed with schizophrenia compared to individuals without the diagnosis (Heinrichs, 2005).

Psychotic symptoms include perceptional distortion in the form of hallucinations, that is, sensory experiences (e.g., tactile, audio, olfactory, visual) in the absence of external stimulation; ideational disturbances, meaning delusions, and thinking disorder; and behavior that refers to odd postures, movements, and rituals (Walker, Kestler, Bollini, & Hochman, 2004; Walker & Tessner, 2008). Although there are other disorders that have psychotic features, the severity of the symptoms of schizophrenia, particularly at onset, bring about disturbances in cognitive, affective, and social functioning and a lack of connection with reality that is more serious than in the other psychotic disorders. It is significant that a psychotic episode can be followed by recovery or result in schizophrenia and a lifelong pattern of ongoing and intermittent symptoms.

It is well known that the variability in symptom profiles at onset and/or the constellation of symptoms makes it difficult to ascertain exactly what the parameters of the illness are. Theory of mind (Premack & Woodruff, 1978) suggests that an individual's ability to have insight and awareness into his feelings and thoughts underlies the capacity to deduce or recognize others' feelings and thoughts and captures one aspect of the nature of the impairments associated with schizophrenia. The remarkable finding that outcomes following a first episode of psychosis are highly varied and do not necessarily result in progressive deterioration has gained increasing attention. Kelleher and Cannon (2014) suggest that there is evidence in recent research that psychotic symptoms are commonly found with many nonpsychotic disorders and that the distinction between psychosis and neurosis is not as clear as once thought.

Research in the last few decades has also focused increased attention to the early course of the illness, in relation to both the preonset, known as the *prodrome*, and postonset behaviors. It is hoped that learning more about what precedes the initial onset can increase the potential for early detection of symptoms prior to the development of potentially more devastating presentations of psychosis. It is hoped that earlier diagnosis and treatment can prevent or mediate the development of chronicity. The recovery model, which has recently gained traction in practice with severe mental illness, offers a shift in philosophical attention from control of symptoms to positive coping and well-being, and is described later on in this chapter.

Historical Perspective on Schizophrenia

As early as the 1880s, John Hughlings Jackson proposed a framework for understanding schizophrenia that continues to influence current thinking. His major proposals held that severe mental illness originates in the cortical brain regions and that symptoms can be construed as an exaggeration or absence of behaviors considered to be "normal." He held further that the symptoms of severe mental illness have biological origins (Beck et al., 2009). Kraepelin (1896) thought of schizophrenia as a category of illness that he called dementia praecox, and gave particular attention to the deterioration of the individual's personality and thoughts. He considered the condition as irreversible, with little or no chance for remission. By the early 20th century, Bleuler (1911/1950) conceived of schizophrenia as a group of disorders. He also proposed that it represented a splitting of psychic functions and identified four "As", linked to symptoms, which are: (a) Associational disturbances in thinking and language, (b) Autism, meaning idiosyncratic and unusual functioning, (c) Ambivalence, referring to reduced discriminatory ability, and (d) Affect disturbance, referring to restricted affect or emotional dysregulation (Kellerman, 2009).

Increased knowledge of brain functioning in relation to schizophrenia led Crow (1980) to propose two subtypes of schizophrenia. Type I is characterized by the sudden onset of positive symptoms, the hallucinations and delusions, responds well to psychotropic medication, and stabilizes over time. Type II, in contrast, is distinguished by the presence of negative symptoms; flat affect, apathy, and difficult concentrating), responds poorly to medication, and has a less favorable long-term prognosis. Crow further hypothesized that a neurotransmitter (i.e., dopamine) is involved in Type I, and that different brain regions are involved in Type II. Subsequent research has identified other neurotransmitters, such as glutamine, as having a role in schizophrenia.

DIAGNOSTIC CRITERIA FOR PSYCHOTIC DISORDERS: CHANGES FROM *DSM-IV-TR* TO *DSM-5*

The *DSM-5* chapter on "Schizophrenia Spectrum and Other Psychotic Disorders" includes several major changes related to the definition of schizophrenia, identification of criteria for catatonia, and elimination of two disorders (i.e., folie a deux and psychotic disorder, NOS—not otherwise specified). The *DSM-5* "Schizophrenia Spectrum" chapter includes schizophrenia and other psychotic disorders that share symptoms in five areas that include delusions, hallucinations, disorganized thinking, abnormal motor behavior and negative symptoms. All diagnoses require impairment of functioning in important life areas.

Several important changes were made to the Schizophrenia diagnosis in *DSM-5*. The subtypes (e.g., Paranoid, disorganized, Catatonic, Undifferentiated, and Residual) were eliminated as separate Diagnoses but retained as descriptive specifiers (delusions, hallucinations, disorganized speech, grossly disorganized or catatonic behavior, and negative symptoms). The decision to eliminate the subtypes was based on their lack of relevance in effective diagnosis and clinical effectiveness. Not only has there been poor reliability with the application of the subtypes, but in line with that, there is the associated issue of what constitutes best practices with the identified symptoms. There are also specifiers on episode (e.g., first, state of remission, multiple episodes), presence of catatonia, and current level of severity. The *DSM-IV-TR* requirement of hearing two voices talking to each other is deleted. Criterion A in the *DSM-5* now requires only two symptoms (e.g., delusions, hallucinations, disorganized speech, one of which must be a *positive* symptom (i.e., delusions, hallucinations, or disorganized speech; APA, 2013). Tandon et al. (2013) suggest that there is increased clarification of the relationship between schizophrenia and catatonia. The addition of a specifier on current severity (5-point scale from not present to present and severe) is intended to contribute a dimensional approach to diagnosis by capturing more of the variety of symptoms and severity observed in individuals with psychotic disorders.

Other criteria include major impairment in work, interpersonal relations, self-care, and symptom duration of at least 6 months. Differential diagnosis is required in relation to schizoaffective, depressive, or bipolar disorder with psychotic features. Other disorders to exclude are effects of substance use or another medical condition. Finally, Criteria F points to examination of a history of autism spectrum disorder or onset in childhood of communication disorder.

The major change in the *DSM-5* Schizoaffective Disorder criteria is the requirement of an uninterrupted period of illness during which there is a major mood disorder, depressive or manic, concurrent with Criteria A of schizophrenia (APA 2013). This diagnosis can be made during or after the psychotic behavior. DSM-5 also now requires that mood episode symptoms be present for most of the time in both the active and residual phases of the illness. Delusions and hallucinations must be present for 2 or more weeks without mood episode symptoms during the illness; this distinguishes schizoaffective disorder from a depressive or bipolar disorder with psychotic features. Important considerations in differential diagnosis relate to determining whether the symptoms are caused by substance use or another medical condition. An additional specifier, bipolar or depressive type, clarifies whether there is a manic or major depressive episode present, respectively. Two other specifiers describe episode features (e.g., first episode, currently in acute episode) and current severity.

Schizotypal Personality Disorder is characterized by psychotic symptoms identified previously and thus listed in the *DSM-5* chapter that addresses psychoses, but is addressed fully later in the manual in the Personality Disorder section. Delusional Disorder is a psychotic disorder in which delusions are the prominent symptoms. In the *DSM-IV-TR*, delusional content was nonbizarre; that is, the false belief could be comprehensive to a person without a psychotic disorder (for example, the fixed but false belief that one's spouse is cheating on him when it is not happening). In the *DSM-5*, the requirement that the delusional content be nonbizarre has been eliminated, that is, the nature of the delusion may be bizarre and incomprehensible to the average nonpsychotic person.

Brief Psychotic Disorder criteria are retained in *DSM-5*; the psychotic symptoms are usually triggered by extreme stress and remit after 1 month. Specifiers can clarify the nature of the stressor, whether the symptoms occurred postpartum, and whether catatonia is present. It is very important for the clinician to assess for the possibility that the psychotic symptoms are an idiom of distress that is culturally normative, or an accepted mode of expression within the person's cultural context. For example, the *DSM-5* "Cultural Concepts of Distress" (APA 2013, p. 758) identifies "ataque de nervios" as a syndrome among individuals of Latino American descent, characterized by symptoms of intense emotional upset, including acute anxiety, anger, or grief ... and is associated with disability ... and acute distress. Schizophreniform Disorder criteria remain identical to schizophrenia, except for duration (1–6 months).

DSM-5 Criteria A requires the presence of delusions or hallucinations for Substance/Medication-Induced Psychotic Disorder. Criteria require evidence of both symptoms after substance use, and the capacity of the substance to produce said symptoms. Other criteria address differential diagnosis with a psychotic disorder that is not triggered by substance use, behavior that does not occur exclusively during a delirium, and a significant level of impairment in functioning in major areas of one's life (e.g., social, occupational). There is a coding note regarding *ICD-9-CM* and *ICD-10-CM* codes to identify specific substances. In addition there are two specifiers, one for onset features (i.e., during intoxication, during withdrawal), and current severity.

Criteria for Psychotic Disorder Due to Another Medical Condition address identifying prominent hallucinations or delusions caused by evidence of another medical condition or mental disorder. The psychotic symptoms cannot occur exclusively during the course of a delirium, and must cause significant distress in important areas of one's life such as social, occupational (APA, 2013).

Catatonia Associated With Another Mental Disorder (Catatonia specifier) is a new disorder category in the DSM-5. Catatonia is no longer seen as an independent type of disorder and, in facts, occurs in relation to several disorders. The range of disorders associated with catatonia include neurodevelopmental, psychotic behavior, bipolar, depression or a medical disorder. Regardless of context, *DSM-5* requires that three of 12 possible symptoms, be present (e.g., stupor, catalepsy, mutism, negativism, posturing). New in the *DSM-5*, is that catatonia can be diagnosed in several ways. It can be a specifier for another disorder, a separate diagnosis in relation to a medical disorder, or other specified diagnosis. Catatonia has a broad range of varied symptoms whose diversity contributes to lack of clinical understanding and potentially compromised treatment that fails to protect the individual from self-harm (APA, 2013). Catatonia can be *due to another medical condition* (which must be verified and distinguished from delirium) or *unspecified*, its relation to another underlying mental disorder or medical condition is unclear or when full criteria for catatonia are not met.

Other specified Schizophrenia Spectrum and Other Psychotic Disorder and Unspecified Schizophrenia Spectrum and Other Psychotic Disorder represent two classifications that apply to situations in which symptoms cause sufficient distress to cause impairment in functioning in social, occupational, and other areas; however, criteria are not met for a diagnosis of another psychotic disorder.

It is noteworthy that there was considerable prior discussion among the authors of the *DSM-5* about including a new prodrome diagnostic category called *psychosis risk syndrome*, which was ultimately not included in the *DSM-5*. This recommendation generated vigorous debate about whether the potential benefits would outweigh the possible stigmatizing consequences of being labeled as vulnerable to a major mental illness.

SCHIZOPHRENIA: CURRENT THINKING ABOUT THE ETIOLOGY AND COURSE

Schizophrenia is recognized as resulting from neurobiological and environmental stressors. There is now greater clarity about the neurobiological functions that are instrumental in producing positive symptoms in particular. What remains less clear are the genetic triggers, the nature of stressors, and their stress–diathesis interaction. The greatest evidence for vulnerability to the development of schizophrenia is found in genetic linkage, with a risk of about 13% in instances where a parent has been diagnosed with this disease (Gottesman & Shields, 1982). Glatt's (2008) review of 40 family studies concluded that individuals are at "elevated risk" when schizophrenia is present among relatives and that those with first-degree schizophrenic relatives are at more than twice the risk compared with those who are more distant (p. 60). However, empirical evidence has not clarified the particular genes, mechanisms, triggers, and other genetic factors that result in the onset of symptoms (Heinrichs, 2005). Although the role of genetics has gained in research focus, other explanations of etiology—including viruses, migration, winter births, urbanicity, compromised access to oxygen in childbirth, feline parasite—to some degree remain the focus of discussion and inquiry (Schwab & Wildenauer, 2008; Tandon, Keshavan, & Nasrallah, 2008). Still, the role of psychosocial stressors looms large in triggering onset and recurrent episodes. Central to this discussion are the roles of socioeconomic factors in the lives of individuals, the vulnerability that low-income status can introduce, and the necessity for clinical practice and policy to address these stress factors in a more systematic way. The psychosocial costs endured by target populations as a result of lack of access to individualized and timely services is a significant issue.

Research has identified several aspects of brain functioning associated with the development of schizophrenia. Various brain functions implicated in having a role include the limbic system, which affects emotion and motivation; the frontal cortex, which influences higher level executive functions; and temporal lobe functions, which influence sensation, perception, and memory (Bogerts, 1993). The dopamine hypothesis proposes a dysfunction in neurotransmitters related to dopamine and serotonin reuptake (Kaplan & Saddock, 1998). This hypothesis is the foundation for many of the antipsychotic drugs on the market today. Historically, prior to the growth of empirical work on schizophrenia, an interpersonal hypothesis engendered much attention based on the concept of double-bind interaction between parent and child, specifically the mother–child relationship. Double-bind theory holds that contradictory messages between verbal and nonverbal communication, in which one message negates the other, leaves the child confused as to what message to respond to and that this communication pattern lays the foundation for the development of schizophrenia symptoms (Bateson, 1972). This perspective has generated much controversy in relation to the inferred status of the schizophrenigenic mother in this interactional explanatory model and has been discredited over time.

Since the mid-1990s, it has become evident that the parameters of the disorder are not altogether clear. Researchers are unsure, in fact, whether schizophrenia represents one disease, several diseases, or perhaps a spectrum of disorders that could have different etiologies (Kirkpatrick, Buchanan, Ross, & Carpenter, 2001). Buckley, Miller, Lehre, and Castle (2009) assert that "clinical heterogeneity is indisputable" and that it is puzzling that "virtually no two patients present with the same constellation of symptoms" (p. 383). A major concern is the possibility of misdiagnosis of symptoms that actually are related to trauma and/or overwhelming stressors and the implications of this for treatment and long-term outcomes.

During the mid-1990s the focus of clinical and academic research shifted from the search for etiology to learning more about the early stages of schizophrenia and the symptoms that precede its onset. This change in emphasis supports the idea that a first psychotic episode need not necessarily determine a lifelong pattern of impaired functioning and has brought intense attention to characteristics that precede the first psychotic episode. Considerations related to the etiology, prodrome, and course of illness are addressed in the following sections.

Unequivocally, the jury is still out regarding the status of knowledge about what causes schizophrenia; we have yet to attain a thorough understanding of the roles of stress, various brain regions, and neurotransmitters and/or of the interaction between genetic and environmental factors (Tandon et al., 2008). Heinrichs's (2005) summary of findings on stress, distress, and treatment illuminates several areas of ongoing learning. These include the lack of clarity regarding whether "chronic stress and distress are byproducts of schizophrenia or precede it and contribute to [its] onset" (p. 237). Heinrichs suggests that alterations in the brain resulting from psychotropic medication, as in the growth of receptors in response to receptor blocking medication, need to be understood in relation to their role in cognitive functioning. Although there is evidence that gene variants can increase the risk, it is still unclear what mechanisms mediate the development of vulnerability (Tandon et al., 2009).

The momentous significance placed on effective diagnosis and treatment at the point of onset of symptoms, places even more importance on the reduction of societal stigma in relation to mental illness and on the implementation of consumer-focused interventions. Such interventions engage the consumer in decision making, and utilize relevant supports (e.g., medical, therapy, social support, peer support, employment) in the service of the consumer engagement in the community. The consumer-driven movement will be discussed later in the chapter when we address strength-based interventions.

Genetic, Brain Region, Neurotransmitter Hypotheses

Advances in understanding schizophrenia in relation to psychosis and brain functions, brain regions, and neurotransmitters have clarified the role of several neurotransmitters such as dopamine and glutamate, the involvement of several regions of the brain, and the growing observation that schizophrenia "involves brain-wide disruption of connectivity, explaining why so many areas and functions are involved" (Zalesky et al., 2011). For example, the striatum system is implicated in psychosis, and specific brain regions and structural differences (i.e., size) in right- and left-brain hemispheres (e.g., frontal, occipital, and temporal cortices) have been linked to schizophrenia-like symptoms (Flor-Henry, 1983; Rao, Arasappa, Reddy, Venkatasubramanian, & Gangadhar, 2010).

Course of Illness

Schizophrenia is the most prevalent of the psychotic disorders and affects approximately 1% of the population. Typically, the initial onset is in adolescence and early adulthood (Addington et al., 2007); schizophrenia can result in the development of lifelong symptoms as well as leading to higher mortality rates and suicide (Auquier, Lancon, Rouillon, Lader, & Holmes, 2007).

The onset of psychosis in schizophrenia is preceded by what is called a nonspecific prodromal phase, which refers to the period prior to the onset of positive psychotic symptoms, during which there are behavioral changes indicative of a decline in capacity to function, social withdrawal, and an increase in the development of subtle symptoms. In the acute or active phase, serious symptoms, which are most often positive symptoms, such as hallucinations and delusions, are clearly present. In the final residual phase, behaviors that were present in the prodromal phase reappear at a later point in the progression of the disorder (J. Johnson, Srinivasan, & Xiong, 2009; Pratt, Gill, Barrett, & Roberts, 2007).

Although there is tremendous heterogeneity in the profile of the initial symptoms, there is still a clear pattern in the long-term progression of the disease, which consists of ongoing negative symptoms interspersed with periods of positive symptoms. Limitations arising from apathy, difficulty focusing, and attention can disrupt efforts to pursue educational goals, a career, employment, or an avocation. This is particularly momentous in light of findings that a significant number individuals formerly diagnosed with schizophrenia do in fact live in recovery in the years following their psychotic episodes (Harding, Brooks, Ashikaga, Strauss, & Breier, 1987).

Co-Occurring Disorders and Conditions

There is unequivocal agreement about various antecedent biopsychosocial conditions, factors, and life events that combine to produce symptoms associated with schizophrenia. Schizophrenia often co-occurs with depression, anxiety, and substance abuse during any point in the course of the illness. These co-occurring disorders further aggravate symptoms—for example, anxiety attacks or paranoia become worse as an effect of substance abuse (Green, Canuso, Brenner, & Wijcik, 2003). Assessment of cognition, depression, and mania is underscored as essential to explore with all of the schizophrenia spectrum and other psychotic disorders (APA, 2013).

The greatest increase seen in comorbidity is with disorders such as panic disorder, posttraumatic stress disorder, obsessive-compulsive disorder (OCD), generalized anxiety disorder, and social anxiety disorder (Pokos & Castle, 2006). The high rate of comorbidity with depression and anxiety can further undermine the individual's capacity for self-care and the ability to work and function within his or her social network. Buckley et al. (2009) point to research showing that comorbidity with depressive symptoms is associated with a worse outcome, including being more at risk for psychotic relapse and more chronic symptoms (D. A. Johnson, 1988; Mandel, Severe, Schooler, Gelenberg, & Mieske, 1982). There is some recognition that the depression associated with schizophrenia could actually result from possible trauma and/or reaction to the psychotic episode (Buckley et al., 2009).

Posttraumatic stress disorder (PTSD) and traumatic stress have been identified as co-occurring with schizophrenia; however, there is lack of clarity about whether the psychosis could also incite trauma or if prior trauma could create a vulnerability to a psychotic episode (Morgan & Fisher, 2007; Strakowski, Keck, McElroy, Lonczak, & West, 1995). The large number of individuals diagnosed with schizophrenia who also have a history of PTSD suggests that clinicians might mistakenly misattribute PTSD symptoms, such as flashbacks, to psychosis. Individuals with "schizophrenia may be at increased risk for exposure to trauma, due to illness, related features, environmental influences, and/or comorbid substance use" (Buckley et al., 2009, p. 385).

In their review of studies on the prevalence of OCD and schizophrenia, Buckley et al. (2009) found that the neurotransmitters dopamine and serotonin are also involved in the pathophysiology of schizophrenia and OCD. Significantly, it is possible that second-generation antipsychotics (SGAs) may aggravate or create obsessive-compulsive symptoms in individuals diagnosed with schizophrenia (Ertugrul, Yagcioglu, Eni, & Yazici, 2005; Lykouras, Alevizos, Michalopoulou, & Rabavilas, 2003; Mahendran, Liew, & Subramaniam, 2007;

Tranulis et al., 2005). Buckley et al. (2009) suggest that "schizophrenia and OCD may represent a 'schizo-obsessive' subtype of schizophrenia, with differences in psychopathology, course of illness, and response to treatment," whereas co-occurring depression is not a subgroup of schizophrenia (p. 386).

The high incidence of substance use associated with schizophrenia highlights the importance of assessing for the presence of substance use and either including this in the treatment goals or making a referral for such services at another agency (Buckley et al., 2009). There is evidence that factors associated with substance abuse for individuals with schizophrenia include depression, psychosis, academic and employment difficulties, and court involvement, as well as mania, traumatic stress, and lack of self-care (Schwartz, Hilscher, & Hayhow, 2007).

In summary, research has explored factors associated with poor prognosis, the relationship between schizophrenia and co-occurring disorders, and the role of stress and trauma in causing or being caused by schizophrenia. There is high comorbidity of schizophrenia with substance abuse, anxiety disorders, depression, and PTSD. There is some indication that poorer outcomes are associated with depression.

Risk and Protective Factors

Suicide rates are higher than those in the general population for individuals diagnosed with schizophrenia, particularly with younger individuals (O'Hare, 2005). Also, there is some indication that a personality disorder, such as paranoid or borderline, might create an increased vulnerability to this disorder (APA, 2013). Genetic risk factors, poverty, trauma, and other devastating life events, such as overwhelming loss, can have a role in the development of schizophrenia.

Expressed emotion (EE) research documents how persons with schizophrenia whose families are high in criticism, hostility, and/or emotional overinvolvement are more at risk for relapse than are individuals whose families are low in these characteristics (Hooley, 2007). Ramirez, Garcia, Chang, Young, Lopez, and Jenkins (2006) observe that the EE findings and evidence that family support is associated with adherence to medication (Fenton, Byler, & Heinsese, 1997) suggest the importance of investigating both supportive and conflictual aspects of family ties. Diversity and cultural differences bear greater attention in relation to EE research—for example, with evidence of cultural variability of EE and the role of culture in shaping the expression of criticism and emotional overinvolvement (Jenkins, 1991; 1992; Lopez et al., 2009). The study by Lopez et al. (2004) of key relatives and family members with schizophrenia found that for Mexican Americans, family warmth is a protective factor, whereas for European Americans, family criticism is a risk factor. The authors suggest that if family ties are valued but warmth is lacking, this can then become a stressor; or if independence is valued by the family, criticism can be experienced as stressful. In addition, the reality that many of the Mexican American families in this research sample belonged to low-income groups suggests the formative role of the socioeconomic and cultural context in determining what is important for families and what types of interactions might be stressful.

A long-standing theme in the schizophrenia literature from a biopsychosocial perspective is the need to have a greater appreciation of the role that socioeconomic hardships and limitations can play in increasing an individual's vulnerability to the onset of symptoms. For example, schizophrenia has long been known to occur more frequently in highly stressful urbanized, industrial settings and less in rural settings. The stress-process model (Pearlin, Menaghan, Lieberman, & Mullan, 1981; Turner, 1981) posits that compromised coping resources—such as social support, self-efficacy, and problem-solving skills—can place individuals at risk for the development of symptoms.

EVIDENCE-INFORMED PRACTICE

Several disparate streams of research, practice, and philosophy characterize the current professional approach to research and interventions with schizophrenia. These approaches include psychopharmacological treatment, particularly to stabilize initial psychotic episodes; ongoing attention to the clinical implications of the stress–vulnerability–coping model (described further on in this chapter) of severe mental illness; and concerted efforts to understand the initial stages of onset of schizophrenia. Each of these advances has significant support because of the surge in research and knowledge about brain function and its implications for short- and long-term treatment of schizophrenia, as well as long-standing recognition of the interactive role of biological (e.g., brain functions, genetics) and environmental factors in producing psychosis and other symptoms associated with schizophrenia.

Evidence-based and evidence-informed practice with schizophrenia includes both psychopharmacological treatment and psychosocial interventions directed to both the person with schizophrenia—in the form of integrated services involving environmental and peer support—as well as to the family unit. Assertive community treatment (ACT), supported housing and employment, social skills training, cognitive behavioral therapy (CBT), family services (psychoeducation, and alcohol and substance abuse interventions), in conjunction with psychopharmacological treatment, are the most effective measures for avoiding relapse (Hogan, 2010). The goal is to have these interventions support an individual's choices regarding learning to live with the illness and the ability to sustain a long-term commitment to recovery.

Treatment, service delivery, and systems of care for individuals with severe mental illness began in the 19th century with the asylum as a well-intentioned setting that would provide an environment to facilitate the stabilization of symptoms. The fate of asylums in becoming warehouses that worsened conditions via isolation from the residents' communities and socialized the residents into a passive patient role, rather than providing help and effective treatment, is now legendary. Nonetheless, it is interesting to note, from a historical perspective, that initially the idea was an advancement beyond the lack of humane treatment at that time.

Stress–Vulnerability–Coping Model

The stress–vulnerability–coping view of severe mental illness, also called the diathesis–stress model, emphasizes the formative role of the interaction between genetic and biological vulnerabilities and the environment in the development of mental illness. A basic assumption is that a genetic or biological predisposition is not sufficient in itself for an individual to develop severe mental illness; that is, it holds that development of the disorder is contingent on the experience of sufficient stress to precipitate an onset of symptoms. This distinction is significant in view of earlier beliefs that mere genetic lineage could sufficiently alarm someone and result in fears of marriage or having a family. The recognition that severe mental illness is highly likely to be the outcome of the combination of biopsychosocial factors indicates that rigorous and comprehensive interventions directed at providing psychosocial supports may reduce the heightened vulnerability to severe mental illness for those with a genetic or biological predisposition to such a disease.

The programs and interventions that have been found to be effective include psychosocial treatment, peer support, family interventions, social skills training, vocational rehabilitation, illness self-management, supported housing, and cognitive behavioral training that addresses neurocognitive impairments associated with schizophrenia (Mueser & Jeste, 2008; Twamley, Jeste, & Bellack, 2003). Silverstein and Wilkniss (2004) argue that there is increasing hope that the potential for cognitive recovery is real; however, more research is needed, for example, to identify the unique activities that promote recovery. More theory is also needed to guide future research, as well as more information that will increase our understanding of the affective and motivational aspects of learning.

Psychopharmacology

Prior to 1954 lobotomies were thought to be the best practice for individuals with schizophrenia and other severe mental illness! Since then, the use of medications introduced the "golden age" of treatment for schizophrenia. These antipsychotics, known as neuroleptic medications, or typical antipsychotics, are potent D2 dopamine receptor blockers (Roth, 2003). The most common of these are chlorpromazine (Thorazine) and haloperidol (Haldol). Although the typical antipsychotics were initially hailed as a major breakthrough in managing psychotic symptoms, the extrapyramidal side effects were disconcerting and are viewed as having a role in nonadherence, relapse, and future hospitalizations. Some of the side effects include parkinsonism (tremors); dystonia (altered muscle tone associated with central nervous system dysfunction and odd movements or postures); akathisia (e.g., restlessness, fidgeting, difficulty sitting or standing); tardive dyskinesia, an irreversible neurological condition characterized by involuntary mouth and tongue movements as well as erratic arm, leg, and body movements (Byrden, Carrey, & Kutcher, 2001; Hertz, 2008; McClellan & Werry, 2001). Although these medications did reduce the positive symptoms (i.e., hallucinations, delusions, disorganized thinking) characteristic of schizophrenia, the side effects of movement disturbances, fatigue, and lethargy did not assist in alleviating the negative symptoms of schizophrenia or significantly improve the quality of life of its sufferers. Persons with schizophrenia all too often continued to suffer lifelong disabilities and a pattern of frequent rehospitalizations.

The second generation of antipsychotics, introduced in the 1990s, known as atypical antipsychotics, block dopamine and serotonin receptors (Shahrokh & Hales, 2003). They include clozapine (Clozaril), risperidone (Risperdal), aripiprazole (Abilify), quetiapine (Seroquel), and olanzapine (Zyprexa, Zydis); these have, with limited success, been more effective in improving cognition (Keefe et al., 2003). The Clinical Antipsychotic Trials of Intervention Effectiveness (CATIE) project is a randomized controlled trial of approximately 1,600 individuals diagnosed with schizophrenia; its purpose is to investigate the long-term effectiveness and tolerability of the individual atypical antipsychotics (i.e., perphenazine, fluphenazine, decanoate, clozapine, olanzapine, quetiapine, risperidone, ziprasidone, and aripiprazole; Keefe et al., 2007). Atypical antipsychotics are known to have several potential side effects, such as sexual dysfunction, that merit serious consideration in treatment planning.

The newer, second-generation atypical antipsychotics are touted for posing less risk of the development of extrapyramidal symptoms. These newer medications are also viewed as more effective with negative symptoms that are often difficult to treat, such as social withdrawal, lack of motivation, and restricted affect (Byrden et al., 2001; McClellan & Werry, 2001; Shahrokh & Hales, 2003). Increasingly, weight gain associated with atypical antipsychotics has gained greater attention over extrapyramidal and tardive dyskinesia as the overriding adverse effect (Werneke, Taylor, & Sanders, 2013). Weight gain and obesity place individuals at risk for disorders such as type II diabetes, metabolic syndrome, and heart disease (Werneke et al., 2013; Panariello, De Luca, & Bartolomeis, 2011).

A major concern in the administration of medications is that adherence to antipsychotic medication regimens is low. Often individuals either forget to take their medications or take them inconsistently. Gray, White, Schulz, and Abderhalden (2010) investigated the need for clinicians to understand how consumers view the process of treatment, including their understanding of the illness, their awareness of why the medication is being prescribed, their attitude toward taking medication, their experience of and ability to cope with side effects, and their feelings about their interactions with their clinicians. The researchers found that engagement, dealing with resistance, actively eliciting information from the consumer as part of the provision of information, and highlighting inconsistencies in consumers' attitudes toward their medication and illness were effective techniques to enhance adherence.

Similarly, adherence to the medication regimen can be improved through effective communication with family members and caretakers. The research of Perlick et al. (2010), involving the burden of care of caregivers dealing with schizophrenic family members and review of effectiveness of first-generation antipsychotics and SGAs, concluded that it would be valuable to educate family members on how "different antipsychotics are equally beneficial" (p. 122).

Psychosocial Interventions

Psychosocial interventions encompass services that are delivered by professionals, often in the context of integrated service delivery programs that are community based and run by both professionals and consumers who subscribe to the recovery model and incorporate peer support. The following discussion presents best-practice models for individuals with schizophrenia.

Family services and psychoeducation have proven to be highly effective in reducing relapses and rehospitalizations and in enhancing coping and problem-solving skills (Barrowclough & Tarrier, 1998). Working with the families of individuals with serious mental illness is essential in order to help them in several areas, including adapting to the course of the illness and dealing with a multitude of institutions that, along with mental health and/or substance abuse agencies, can include social services, medical treatment, the Social Security Administration, and the court system. The shift to community treatment has placed greater responsibility on the family in caregiving, and research shows that approximately three out of four people with a psychiatric disability remain in contact with their families (Lehman, Steinwachs, & PORT Co-Investigators, 1998; Manderscheid & Sonnenschein, 1997). Hoenig and Hamilton (1966) proposed two types of burden experienced by families: objective burden, the concrete financial costs and necessary daily adjustments; and subjective burden, each family member's personal experience of stress (Corrigan, Mueser, Bond, Drake, & Solomon, 2008). Baronet's (1999) review of 28 studies on caregiver burden found that at least half of the caregivers were parents, about a quarter were spouses, and that the objective burdens they faced included a wide array of consequences arising from daily maintenance tasks that included transportation, financial management, domestic tasks, monitoring the family member, restrictions of time, and financial liability. The review of Corrigan et al. (2008) of the burden research highlights how negative symptoms can be more demanding for families than positive symptoms. Perceptions that the family member can control his or her behavior are related to subjective greater burden; but, significantly, the ability to cope with and adapt to the realities of the disorder is related to a sense of well-being on the part of parents. This positive finding suggests the importance of attending to the "the strength of [family members'—i.e., their] ... psychological resources" (p. 237). The subjective element of burden found across cultures is addressed in the section titled "Equity and Diversity Issues," in the context of cultural differences that emerge in the literature on the burden of care.

A review of the tasks involved for both the individual with schizophrenia and the family members focuses on living with the illness, understanding what symptoms mean and how medications work, coping with the side effects of drugs, and managing the course of the illness. The concern and worry that families have for the well-being of their family member with schizophrenia and their lack of knowledge about possible outcomes can potentially lead them to have less faith in the ability of their relative with schizophrenia to achieve his or her personal dreams. The family member with schizophrenia, however, still cherishes his dreams and this deserves recognition and realistic assistance (Stein, Mann, & Hunt, 2007). Support for families can also address concerns of siblings who must deal with the predictable limitations experienced by aging parents and the inescapable decision making about future caregiving for their family member (Smith, Greenberg, & Seltzer, 2007). Research demonstrates that psychoeducation for families is effective when it supports families in discussing their problems and perceived needs, helps them find ways of coping, and clarifies their expectations of the services they are receiving (North et al., 1998). An important lesson to be learned from these studies is that support for family members and caregivers must address what is possible as well as what is difficult and limiting.

Illness management and recovery: Recovery is both a process and an outcome. In the past, individuals with severe mental illness were viewed as relegated to a life of psychiatric impairment and debilitation. Evidence has shown that is not reality. Programs, such as Fountain House in New York and The Village, in Long Beach, California, where consumers are involved in every part of the organization in leadership, training, and mentoring roles, are leading the way with practice models that empower their members toward recovery and overall well-being. Family and consumer organizations, such as the National Alliance on Mental Illness (NAMI) also provide essential perspectives to advocate for social policy on behalf of persons with mental illness. These organizations "speak truth to power" in educating mental health professionals about the real-life experiences of consumers as they try to navigate the complex and often maddening worlds of mental health treatment.

ACT is an "effective evidenced-based service delivery model for providing comprehensive community-based treatment and support to persons with a severe and persistent mental illness" (Test, 2009, p. 869). An interdisciplionary team uses an outreach approach, on a 24/7 basis, with an emphasis on integrated community-based services, rehabilitation, and individualized support services. A key element is that services are provided on site where the consumer needs them, which can be in the home, at work, at a recreation locale, or in any setting chosen by the consumer. Test's review of guidelines for the ACT teams illustrates how conventional mental health services are not set up to meet the unique and demanding needs of this population in relation to housing, employment, community integration, social relationships, education, management of their symptoms, and the stressors related to these factors as well as to validate and support their right to a decent quality of life.

Supported employment and supported housing are two very essential resources that bring hope to individuals' lives and provide an essential foundation for the long-term management of mental illness. Supported housing programs aim to provide suitable, permanent residences as well as needed services, such as case management, both in the consumer's home and in community settings such as group homes. In principle, various housing options are provided via rent subsidies, which aim to meet the individualized needs of the consumer. The ability to have one's own home, which reflects one's individual interests and preferences, is an essential cornerstone for the maintenance of a life where one can focus one's energies on identified goals and the struggles potentially encountered in the process of achieving them. Not to have this element of stability leads to ongoing coping with distractions and forces the use of personal energy to negotiate basic needs.

Supported employment is an individualized psychiatric rehabilitation approach to securing and keeping employment; it embodies an immediate activation of job-seeking activities and represents a supportive approach to the work setting. Staff members monitor work demands, consumer preferences and capabilities, and mental health services (Kukla & Bond, 2009). This evidence-based practice model emphasizes that assisting individuals to secure employment is a fundamental treatment-planning feature (Becker & Bond, 2002; Becker & Drake, 2003). Its application to mental health practice in the 1980s was an incisive shift from earlier intervention options that were dominated by group homes, day treatment centers, and sheltered workshops. The sheltered workshops in particular, although well intentioned, are now viewed as having further isolated, marginalized, and potentially stigmatized individuals with severe mental illness. There is empirical support for the positive effectiveness of these assisted employment models in other aspects of consumers' lives (Corrigan et al., 2008), including the improved ability to manage symptoms and an enhanced sense of self (Bond, 2004). Despite what some might fear, employment, when supplemented with support, has not added undue stress to the lives of persons with schizophrenia (Becker, Smith, Tanzman, Drake, & Tremblay, 2001).

Supported education programs provide services to assist individuals with severe mental illness to access higher education and to complete their degrees. The concept is grounded in the notion of inclusion in higher education as opposed to isolated day treatment programs. The Americans with Disabilities Act (1990) provides for accommodation, skills training, and supports.

Social skills training for individuals with severe mental illness is effective in assisting them to gain the skills necessary for interacting with others. This lessens social isolation and helps to secure and maintain employment whenever possible. These interventions are specifically intended to "help people improve their communication skills, express their emotions, and increase their effectiveness in social situations" (Gingerich, 2009, p. 666). The effectiveness resides partly in the method, which emphasizes learning skills in stages, using a problem-solving approach and role plays, and in the consumer-driven design, which allows for clients to identify the skills they wish to develop. Skill categories include significant areas of interpersonal activities and self-care such as conversation, friendship and dating, managing conflict, and medication management. The skills developed in these domains include learning verbally and nonverbally to express positive emotions, to make requests, to listen actively to others, and to communicate and express distressed feelings in such a way that others will hear their communication (Gingerich, 2009).

CBT approaches challenge habitual, irrational beliefs and promote the learning and practice of new behaviors, offering significant hope to those with severe mental illness who can utilize the interventions. This approach explores and works with the negative, disempowering beliefs about one's abilities, expectations about pleasure, and interpersonal capacities. Beck et al. (2009) highlight the importance of keeping a perspective on the multiple goals that require attention, including social and functional changes; these investigators stress that it is possible for individuals to "maintain 100% delusional convictions but still make changes to [how they act] on the belief [that they can] improve quality of life" (p. 199). Remarkably, this means that individuals can maintain employment despite the existence of paranoid delusions about the workplace.

Assisted outpatient treatment and mental health courts are gaining traction in discussions of community-based treatment. Both are court-involved supports for treatment. Assisted outpatient treatment (AOT) refers to court-ordered treatment (e.g., medication) as a basis for remaining an outpatient and living in the community. Mental health courts provide alternate routes for individuals who meet specific criteria (e.g., nonviolent crimes, felony), are court involved, and have a mental disorder. Established by local mandate, there is variability in criteria and functions. Several relevant issues for treatment efficacy are raised in relation to the AOT, which represents a community alternative to incarceration. Considerable discussion focuses on the merits of the AOT in particular in relation to outcomes, costs, and possible coercion (Munetz, Ritter, Teller, & Bonfine, 2014; Ray, Kubiak, Comartin, & Tillander, 2015; Swanson, et al., 2013).

EQUITY AND DIVERSITY ISSUES

A new feature in the *DSM-5* is the caveat that with psychotic disorders it is essential to clarify the cultural context, and to explore for cultural norms, as some behaviors may be normative idioms of expression in particular cultural groups. Moreover, there is a heightened need for attention to the diagnostic process in instances in which the clinician does not share the same cultural background as the client.

Internationally, the number of cases of schizophrenia within any time period and the number of cases that arise within a specific population are similar (APA, 2000), and the rates across all ethnic groups (e.g., White, Latino American, African American, Asian, Native American) in the United States have been found to be similar (U.S. Department of Health and Human Services, 2001). There are, however, several significant risk factors associated with schizophrenia. Diversity and equity issues associated with schizophrenia point to remarkable differences. Cultures differ in how often and why they regard behavior as severe mental illness. Development of a severe mental disorder is affected by ethnicity, gender, and age as well as by whether one lives is a developing versus developed society or a rural or urban setting. There is evidence that gender differences exist in relation to incidence, genetic transmission, and brain abnormalities that have implications for risk and structural brain changes (Goldstein & Walder, 2006). Males are more likely than females to be diagnosed with schizophrenia (O'Hare, 2005) and tend to have more severe schizophrenia with more cognitive impairment (Heinrichs, 2005). Birth in an urban center is associated with higher rates than birth in a rural area, and African Americans are diagnosed at higher rates, suggested to be three times higher, than White Americans (Bresnahan et al., 2007). Individuals diagnosed with schizophrenia have shorter lives (Brown, 1997), with about one third of the deaths attributed to suicide (Auquier et al., 2007).

African American males are more likely to be diagnosed with a psychotic disorder than are White males, even though their level of functioning in the context of the disease is higher in comparison to other groups (Minksy, Vega, Miskimen, Gara, & Escobar, 2003). African Americans are also overrepresented among individuals diagnosed with serious mental illness who do not have access to treatment (Wang, Demler, & Kessler, 2002). Snowden's (2003) review of research on the experience of African American males in mental health systems highlights their greater presence in inpatient and psychiatric emergency treatment as well as greater likelihood to "receive injectable antipsychotics" (p. 240). Understanding more clearly the dynamics that lead to the overdiagnosis of schizophrenia for people of color can only occur within a context of more rigorous methodology that distinguishes schizophrenia spectrum diagnoses as well as demographic variables that acknowledge diverse levels of acculturation and intersectionality (Vespia, 2009).

The *burden-of-care concept* has been refined to include objective effects related to the mentally ill family member's behavioral status as well as the subjective experience of burden by the caregiver related to feelings of distress, such as physical, psychological, social, and financial difficulties associated with the caregiving role (Chou, 2000; Rungreangkulkij & Gilliss, 2000; Schene, 1990). The study by Chien, Chan, and Morrissey (2007) involving Chinese individuals in Hong Kong regional clinics found that elders were the primary caregivers, possibly because they were culturally viewed as most prepared, and reported high levels of burden. This finding encourages careful assessment of acculturation levels of Chinese consumer's families for the purpose of exploring implications for practice, for example, supporting respite services and/or the family finding ways to share tasks.

EMPOWERING, RESILIENCY-BASED DIAGNOSIS AND INTERVENTIONS

The strength-based approaches to the diagnosis and treatment of schizophrenia have been summed up most effectively in the recovery model, mentioned previously. This model is unique in that it does not discard evidence-informed approaches and includes the contributions of medicine, psychopharmacology, and psychosocial interventions. What is uniquely empowering, however, is the configuration of evidence-based approaches in the context of consumer-driven programs. The voice of the consumer is present in the design and implementation of programming.

Recovery Model

The recovery model paradigm views individuals with severe mental illness as going through a life-changing situation that is coped with, rather than a process that leads to a life organized by impairment (Substance Abuse and Mental Health Services Administration [SAMHSA], 2011).

The recovery model represents a shift that, although begun in the 1970s, did not achieve widespread recognition within the mental health profession until the early 1990s. Recovery model-based approaches value the individual's lived experience as the basis for the development of hope, managing one's mental illness and identification of goals. The focus is away from an exclusive concern with symptom reduction and onto managing and living with illness. Deegan (1996) suggests the goal is to develop our unique humanity, rather than to fit in or become normal. Consumers participate in taking responsibility for identifying their needs and goals and for collaborating with others in the process of meeting them. Recovery-focused programs have come to the fore as the best practice for individuals with severe mental illness. These programs promote a process in which healing can take place within the context of consumer-driven services, family involvement, and a culturally relevant, seamless system of care, providing services in the least restrictive environment, along with peer support and a wellness orientation. A community mental health and rehabilitation emphasis supports the provision of services where the consumers live, with the goal of reintegration of the consumer into the community.

Corrigan and Ralph (2005) propose three key concepts that underlie implementation of the recovery model in a range of contexts, from clinical diagnostic processes to integrated service delivery programs. Essential in all recovery model-oriented practice are the notions that recovery is a naturally occurring or normative phenomenon, that individuals can recover when they have access to suitable treatment and supports, and that the presence of hope for improvement drives the initiative for change and the slow but sure process of identifying meaningful options. A key aspect of this approach is an emphasis on consumers living with and managing their illness rather than an exclusive focus on "symptom reduction" and, more important, on developing and maintaining meaning and purpose in living.

The Vermont Longitudinal Research Study on Mental Illness (Harding, Brooks, et al., 1987) found that approximately 65% of individuals formerly diagnosed with schizophrenia were in recovery, based on the Global Assessment Scale of the *DSM* (GAF); the World Health Organization in Boston and Washington found that about 45% did not relapse (Harding, Zubin, & Straus, 1987). The recovery model approach suggests that these successes are attributable in large part to the individual's learning to live with the disorder and to manage the symptoms. Stories about living in recovery describe "accepting their illness and incorporating it into a newly defined sense of self" that enables and promotes having hope in one's life and achieving valued goals (Davidson, 2003, p. 44). This is very different from interventions that approach treatment from a perspective of achieving a cure and/or symptom management.

The recovery model approach illuminates diversity issues regarding consumer and stakeholder advocacy. There is an increased demand from consumers for client involvement in the diagnostic and treatment processes, for family participation, and individualized and culturally relevant services. Many of the advocacy initiatives have focused on the role of stigma in the lives of consumers and strategies for its reduction. Replacement of the term *schizophrenia* is a long-standing wish, owing to the negative consequences for the individual and on his or her interactions in society (Ono et al., 1999). One advocacy group, the Campaign for the Abolition of the Schizophrenia Label

(CASL; www.runciman.dk/CASL_Schiz.pdf), suggests elimination of this label, to be replaced with "dopamine dysregulation disorder," in an effort of reduce/eliminate the negative stereotyping associated with the term *schizophrenia*. CASL views the label as damaging, in that it is all too often associated with bizarre behavior that includes dangerousness, severe functional impairment, and a chronic lifelong condition. Person-first language promotes supporting integrity by distinguishing the person from the condition and minimizes labeling (American Psychological Association, 2010). Stigma occurs on a personal level, where individual self-esteem is affected by the target status, and on a societal level that maintains the existence of negative stereotypes; each level must be addressed (Corrigan et al., 2008).

The recovery model approach has added significant and remarkable contributions to perspectives on severe mental illness that move away from the medical model view of schizophrenia as a progressive, chronic, and incapacitating illness. The concept of recovery is viewed as a process and not an outcome, meaning that the qualities associated with recovery have more to do with "people who are concerned about their psychological wellbeing, struggling with their symptoms, and attempting their life goals" (Corrigan & Ralph, 2005, p. 5) rather than about being symptom free.

Also, in line with President George W. Bush's New Freedom Commission on Mental Health (2003), recovery-oriented approaches to severe mental illness aim to reduce and eliminate stigma via societal and institutional interventions that promote the development of environments conducive to full participation in society. Corrigan (2004) proposes that the ability of stigma to create ambivalence about seeking treatment suggests that professionals need to engage in the development of antistigma initiatives that can enhance access to services and greater consumer participation in their treatment. Chien, Yeung, and Chan's (2014) research with Hong Kong patients found that a family's EE and caregiving burden can increase a family member's perceived stigma; this highlights the importance of clinicians recognizing the significant role of family for those in recovery. Sartorius (2002) expresses concern about the role of psychiatrists in creating iatrogenic stigma by insensitive use of labels or utilizing medication with side effects that can contribute to identifying the person as mentally ill. Corrigan (2013) distinguishes between *public* stigma, that is, behaviors that are evoked toward others who are targets of a negative social belief, and *self-stigma*, which addresses the harmful effects on one's behavior of internalizing a negative social valuation of oneself (e.g., low self-esteem and low self-efficacy). Persons with schizophrenia learn to identify with their label, equating their essential personhood with their disease. The implications of these two types of stigma necessitate greater investigation and understanding for the purpose of enhancing the engagement of individuals in needed treatment and increasing their access to services.

With a strong rehabilitation emphasis, the recovery model supports the development of initiatives, interventions, treatments, and programming that facilitate inclusivity, participation, and collaboration on the part of the consumer with the treatment clinician and treatment team and aim for genuine participation in the community at large. This is in line with the systems concept of equifinality, which means that sought-after goals can be achieved in a variety of equally effective ways and there is no one correct way to achieve one's goals.

As a mental health approach, the recovery model is consumer driven and embodies interventions that include integrated service delivery, peer support, family focus, cultural relevance, and inclusivity at all levels of the diagnostic process, formulation, interventions, and program development. As a social movement, the recovery model represents ideals of advocacy, social justice, and equity in the provision of resources and services for those diagnosed with severe mental illness; it creates a context for consumer empowerment and participation in regaining their lives following the devastating effects of symptoms associated with onset of a psychosis such as schizophrenia. The passage in 2004 of Proposition 63, known as the Mental Health Services Act, in California, is one example of a successful consumer-driven legislative initiative.

The Substance Abuse and Mental Health Services Administration emphasizes wellness via a self-directed life and proposes four dimensions that support recovery: health, home, purpose, and community. These dimensions promote interventions that focus on several recovery processes. These include promoting hope and client self-direction; individualized, person-centered, respectful, strength-based practice; encouragement for individual empowerment to take responsibility and make decisions; recognition that recovery encompasses a person's entire life (e.g., self-care); awareness that recovery occurs in many different ways based on an individual's strengths, culture, and goals; and necessitates support from peers and allies. In addition there is recognition of the vital role of networks and relationships within a multisystemic perspective (i.e., individual, family, community), and culturally based and trauma-informed practice (SAMHSA, 2012).

In contrast to earlier perceptions that schizophrenia was incurable and that diagnosis augured progressive restrictions that interfered with a meaningful life, recovery and integration into community life is now viewed as viable when the essential conditions are provided (Lieberman & Kopelowicz, 2005). Such goals can be achieved when several aims are kept at the forefront of treatment planning. Early detection, administration of appropriate levels and types of medication, closely monitored community follow-up with comprehensive monitoring of medication effects, and clear identification of the changing landscape of stressors and their management by the consumer are key elements of effective community-based treatment. Moreover, efforts to stabilize consumers within a context of medication and recovery model strategies and treatment interventions can have the significant benefit of limiting needless engagement with programs that do not identify as recovery-based programs or provide individualized treatment that reflects consumer-driven, family-focused, culturally relevant services. Effective programs include active outreach alongside clinical treatment in the early course of the illness, case-management services, and the involvement of family members and relevant support systems in the treatment. Chronic stages are treated with "well-coordinated and continuous biobehavioral treatments" germane to the phase of illness (Lieberman & Kopelowicz, 2005, p. 101). The shift from a focus on etiology to biopsychosocial management of the early course of the illness is momentous in that it promotes wellness and recovery in place of a lifelong decline in functioning.

The following discussion, congruent with recovery model principles, identifies several models of practice that have advanced practice beyond the notion of the expert professional administering interventions on an individual and have promoted consumer agency in the diagnostic, formulation, treatment, and recovery process. All services based on recovery model principles are characterized by the key values of consumer-driven services, family focus, individualized services, and the provision of services in settings where the participants live.

The Village Integrated Services Agency in Long Beach, California (www.mhavillage.org) is a recovery model–based integrated services delivery program with a focus on facilitating consumers' managing and living with their symptoms, gaining independence, and achieving their personal goals within a context of peer support. The mission is (a) to assist people with mental illnesses, recognize their strengths and power to recover and achieve full participation in community life; and (b) to encourage system-wide adoption of the practice and promotion of recovery and well-being. The program is organized around 14 principles and values, including the role of hope; the wholeness of the individual; self-determination and personal responsibility; collaboration; respectfulness; and the role of community, education, and employment. This program exemplifies a paradigm shift that emphasizes the provision of an environment that is affirming, validating, and welcoming.

Fountain House (www.fountainhouse.org) came into being in the early 1940s in New York City. Based on the principle of a supportive community and characterized by the belief that individuals with mental illness have much to offer in helping others with mental illnesses, Fountain House represents a holistic approach to recovery. The mission statement reflects a commitment to support recovery from mental illness by making opportunities available that facilitate recovery, such as work, learning, contribution of one's talents, and participating in the Fountain House community. The vision to assist individuals in achieving their full potential includes efforts to eliminate the stigma that is often associated with mental illness. The programs include education, employment, housing, and wellness interventions on a variety of topics that range from physical health care and exercise to stress management.

It is worth noting that in line with a recovery model focus on living with one's disorder, there are a number of innovative treatment approaches that support the individual's efforts to achieve personal goals and independent living. Some of these include the use of "service" animals to assist in supporting the individual's management of his or her behavior—for example, in remaining calm when feeling distressed (Wisdom, Saedi, & Green, 2009), and weight management, which integrates physical health concerns by providing nutritional counseling to offset the weight gain associated with the second-generation antipsychotic medications (Hogan, 2010).

CASE STUDY WITH AND WITHOUT THE DIVERSITY/RESILIENCY FORMULATION

Schizophrenia

Douglas A.'s onset of schizophrenia occurred as he was approaching his senior year in college as a management systems major at a local university in Seattle. He lived at home the first year and eventually moved into his own apartment near campus. By his third year of study, the family noticed that he was calling less and they were not seeing him as often. They assumed that he was busy with the demands of studying and perhaps had begun to form new friendships and had a more active social life. Douglas initially put all of his energy into his studies, had very little contact with classmates, and spent long hours in the computer lab, often being the last one to leave and then staying up most of the night doing computer assignments or playing video games. Although a few student friends invited him to gatherings and one of the professors showed interest in Douglas because he was such a bright student, Douglas was so painfully uncomfortable socially that he was not responsive to such gestures. Over time, he became increasingly withdrawn and isolated. The little social contact he had was with other students and new friends, who all were socially isolated and mainly involved with their interest in computers, social media games, and their studies. Although social contact was not very consistent, and he was ambivalent about his friendships, nevertheless these were the only meaningful contacts that he had. At some point Douglas began to develop delusions related to some of the violent language in the social media and believed that his brother and sister were going to harm him in some way.

Slowly, he began to develop paranoid ideas that he was being followed or watched both by cult members and by school administrators. He was sleeping less, missing classes, not eating well, and spending all of his time alone in the lab or in his apartment. His first hospitalization occurred on the day that he stormed into the dean's office in an angry, agitated state, speaking loudly with paranoid ideation, claiming that the school was spying on him and other students were following him and videotaping him in his apartment. Douglas's family members had no idea of his decline and were stunned to find out what had occurred.

James, his older brother, received the phone call from the university informing him that his brother was in the campus infirmary and required immediate attention. James had not seen his brother recently; his parents were on vacation on the East Coast; and Eva, Douglas's older sister, was married and lived out of state. Upon arriving at the infirmary, James was informed of what had occurred and that his brother had been medicated. When James saw his brother, he was astonished to learn that Douglas was both mentally ill and on medication. He was particularly shaken by his brother's appearance, because he could not differentiate how much of his behavior was due to his mental illness or the heavy medication. Douglas appeared dazed, remote, grimacing, subdued, and did not even seem to recognize James. James was alarmed and shocked, not knowing previously about his brother's condition and overwhelmed at the degree of his brother's distressed appearance and obvious lack of well-being. Because James valued the family's closeness and always intervened when conflicts seemed to threaten family cohesion, the confusion around the nature of the mental illness and his inability to help his brother at this point were very upsetting, to the point of feeling traumatic. Douglas was sufficiently agitated that he was placed on a 72-hour hold in a psychiatric inpatient facility, and this hospitalization was subsequently extended for an additional 2 weeks. Once the family found out about Douglas's hospitalization, everyone came together to support his treatment and discharge. The hospital staff communicated with the parents; however, the parents were not involved in the discharge planning and, more significant, were at a loss as to what to do in the event that, once Douglas returned home, he did not adhere to his medication treatment plan.

Assessment of Douglas' situation revealed that he was spending so much time sitting in school labs and at home at the computer that he had developed bedsores. His delusions included paranoid beliefs about being watched; he also believed that his father had molested him and both of his siblings. He was convinced that his brother James was going to harm him and had special powers. These allegations were puzzling to James and Eva, his sister, in that they had no experience with their father that could be construed as sexually abusive.

The onset of Douglas's mental illness came at a time when James and Eva were focused on developing their careers and busy with their personal and family lives. It came at a time when James was busy developing a new company, which required a substantial amount of his time and energy. He was also preparing for his upcoming marriage and was absorbed in demands associated with his occupational as well as his private life. As a result, Douglas's caregiving and meetings with mental health staff were dealt with mainly by his parents.

Douglas's mother recalled that he had always been a sensitive child, as evidenced on one occasion on a bus when he was startled and frightened by some of the passengers until she calmed him down. In his youth he was seen as quiet, smart, introverted, and socially withdrawn. The few friends that he had were generally younger, and he spent most of his time playing music on his guitar or, like many in his generation, playing video games. As Douglas was the youngest of three children, his older siblings had moved out by the time he reached adolescence; thus his teen years were spent alone with his parents. Although family life was basically organized around work and family activities, Eva always felt that her father's drinking was problematic. Mr. A. worked at a local bank, and Mrs. A. was a homemaker who focused on raising the children. Both parents were second-generation children of Canadian and Russian immigrants and grew up with strong beliefs in family, hard work, religion, and managing on your own when difficulties surfaced. The strong family values and the context of living in a family-oriented suburb left the mother feeling major responsibility for the well-being of the children; she was particularly concerned that she had not done enough for Douglas. She was puzzled by how this could happen, what had caused his illness, and worried if she was the cause. The family's social life was limited to immediate extended family, which for Mrs. A. meant talking with her sisters, from whom she received much support. Mr. A., on the other hand, had never tended to be reflective or forthcoming about his feelings, did not share his feelings about his son's predicament, and was perceived by the family as denying that Douglas had any "real" problem. Often, Mr. A. would question Douglas sarcastically about when was he going to start a family or suggest how he should look for a job.

Initially, after the onset of his schizophrenia, Douglas went through a period of living with his parents; however, he did not adhere to his medication regimen and would become increasingly agitated, loud, and paranoid. By the end of the first year he had begun to talk to himself often, hear "cult voices" talking to each other about him, and display bizarre physical movements. On one occasion, at a local neighborhood store, he doused himself with gasoline and lit a match to ignite himself; fortunately a witness intervened and helped to get him home. Nights were often tormenting to the family, with Douglas shouting, laughing, and thrashing about in his bedroom. He was never violent; still his agitated state and threats of self-injury were alarming, and his family members felt traumatized by seeing him go through obvious torment. Douglas's initial diagnosis was psychotic disorder; but by the end of the first year, he was diagnosed with schizophrenia. For several years, he was in and out of the hospital, where he would stabilize and then return to the community to live with his parents, only to have the cycle start all over again.

Eventually, after one of the hospitalizations, the medication appeared to stabilize him for longer periods and he was able to move into a group home. There was some contact between Douglas's case manager and his parents every month or 2, and although some day treatment activities were available, Douglas never utilized those services. Ten years later, he remains in the group home, is unemployed, receives Social Security payments, and visits his parents every weekend. Although he sporadically continues his academic studies in the belief that he will secure his degree and have a career, Douglas remains socially isolated except for the little contact he has with other group home residents and with his parents.

James is conflicted about how much he could have done for his brother and feels guilty about the constraints, related to his own needs, that made it difficult for him to do more. Douglas has such overwhelming difficulties that James fears that Douglas's recovery and higher functioning could enable him to have the means to fatally harm himself. The parents are concerned about the credit cards Douglas was given; although the debt he has accrued has not been substantial, they ponder whether they should pay off his debt for him and worry that the debt could get larger. Eva worries about what would happen if Douglas were to somehow father a child and about who will care for Douglas after his parents reach old age, can no longer care for him, and ultimately die. She would like to visit more, but the distance makes this difficult. It was especially difficult for Eva at first, when Douglas needed so much attention and everyone's pitching in was so important. Initially, Eva even found herself upset with James because his wife got pregnant after the onset of Douglas' psychosis. This left her feeling that she was the only one who could offer support to her parents. Both James and Eva were "doers" and wanted to do more. They felt that there were not enough answers about what had happened to their brother and did not feel satisfied with the process their parents were going through with the mental health staff. They see their brother as a shadow of his former self. There is no history of schizophrenia in the family. Eva and James wonder if Douglas's condition was related to exposure to toxins, a virus, a consequence of congenital factors at childbirth, or related to his use of hallucinogens.

DSM-5 Diagnostic Impression Without Diversity/Resiliency Formulation

Diagnosis:

295.90 (F20.9) Schizophrenia

Specifiers:

- Multiple episodes, in acute episode
- With catatonia; stupor, mutism, grimacing
- [Identification of severity level is not required for diagnosis]

Douglas had a typical onset of schizophrenia in young adulthood. Paranoid symptoms were prominent sources of his impaired relationship with reality. The co-occurring use of hallucinogens, combined with his social isolation and dependency on relationships with friends who shared his social media interests, may have precipitated and worsened his psychosis. Douglas displays an apparent vulnerability to major mental illness, as evidenced by his mother's description of his sensitivity as a child and by his prodromal symptoms of increased eccentricity and social withdrawal. The course of his illness—managed with medication, hospitalization, support from government disability programs, and residence in a group home—illustrates the increasing chronicity characteristic of schizophrenia. Although Douglas has had several relapses due to problems with medication compliance, his condition has also become more stable, probably because of the continued support of his family. The obvious emotional pain, stress, guilt, anxiety, and confusion that Douglas's condition causes his family are common responses. Learning that one's child or sibling has schizophrenia is often a devastating and extremely demoralizing experience. The traditional treatment response to Douglas, based primarily in the medical model and relying heavily on the control of his symptoms through medication, has been successful in keeping him out of the hospital and restoring some measure of physical and mental stability to his life. Douglas's future is uncertain, but the possibility of successful college completion and the attainment of occupational success looks remote.

Adding Diversity/Resiliency Formulation Information to Douglas's Diagnosis

The degree of isolation and lack of contact with friends and family prior to the onset of symptoms intensified the rapid decline of Douglas's functioning. Had he been in contact with family or with service providers, the onset might not have been as intense. It is not clear how quickly he progressed from relatively benign behaviors, such as being socially withdrawn, to the development of delusional ideation, which eventually led to his agitated outburst in the dean's office. However, it does seem obvious that Douglas was a vulnerable young man. Given the separation of Douglas from his family at college and their lack of awareness of the seriousness of his problems, it is likely that his descent into full-blown psychosis could not have been prevented.

Intrapersonal: Above average intelligence; strong motivation to complete his studies, develop a career, and become independent; musical interest and ability (played trombone in his high school band); computer savvy and interested in video games
Interpersonal: Likeability, other students and a professor sought his company; availability and willingness of parents to provide care; intentions by siblings to be available to help their younger brother; parents who remained together despite noted problems
Community: Family known in the community; father's connection to local community's private and public sector
Spiritual: Interest in spirituality, significance and meaning of having a career
Cultural: Curiosity about family's religious life and connections and family's heritage from their national origins and regional culture

Comments on Diversity/Resiliency Formulation Information

The psychological and physical state that Douglas exhibited when he was sent to the infirmary was alarming and raised concern about his safety and identification of treatment interventions that would stabilize him. Although the hospitalization was vitally important and may have saved his life, the type and dosage of medications that Douglas received at the onset bear further exploration. As is often the case, it is uncertain to what extent drug use potentiated his symptoms; an emphasis on restoring rest, healthy eating, regular exercise, and supportive therapy might have allowed for the use of less disabling medication and helped to clarify the confusion inherent in co-occurring substance abuse and schizophrenia. Douglas's diagnosis, assessment, and treatment focused on the management of his symptoms via a traditional medical focus on pathological processes. Although his family members appear to have received some basic education about schizophrenia, and community resources were utilized to help Douglas qualify for disability and arrange a satisfactory living situation for him, the resolution of this case without the active use of the Diversity/Resiliency Formulation is focused on survival and on coping with illness rather than on the development of hope and the opportunity for future achievement and meaningful relationships with others.

If Douglas had had access to mental health professionals committed to his own and his family's strengths from the outset, interventions would have stressed positive potential for the future, emphasized specific roles his siblings and parents could play in his recovery, and mobilized friends to help Douglas remain socially connected. Active referrals could have been made to the local chapter of the National Alliance for the Mentally Ill, and hospital staff could, with Douglas's permission, have involved campus disability services to help him continue college coursework while in the hospital, especially in the area of computer science, which is his strength. An awareness of Douglas's interest in music could lead to encouraging him to play his trombone in the community orchestra and/or with a small group of former friends. Douglas could be assigned a mentor to work with him on building social skills. Most important, Douglas could be introduced to the local consumer group composed of persons with major mental illnesses. This could provide him with the beginnings of a social life at a level of contact he could tolerate and introduce him to job coaches and self-help groups for coping with mental illness. Participation in a consumer-driven program, based on a recovery model philosophy, would offer Douglas as well as his family and the mental health professionals who work with him role models of hope and achievement to combat the stigma and demoralization that accompany a diagnosis of schizophrenia. In short, the entire diagnostic and treatment process should balance opportunity for positive achievement with the identification and management of pathology. Given the time pressure and stress characterizing much of psychiatric care, it is difficult to focus on strengths unless one is forced to do so by the diagnostic protocol. The addition of the Diversity/Resiliency Formulation to the process would have facilitated the assessment of what was possible in addition to the attention to what had gone wrong.

SUMMARY

Gaining greater understanding about the nature of schizophrenia and other psychotic disorders requires the development of more effective strategies for treatment at the onset and with long-term chronic conditions. This necessitates improved resources and commitment by mental health professionals. A challenge remains regarding understanding schizophrenia in that its parameters have changed over time. There is much heterogeneity in the etiopathology (i.e., cause of the disorder), symptoms, and progression (Tandon et al., 2009). There is greater attention on the prodromal phase of psychotic disorders, with the aims of prevention and effective treatment. Evidence-based practice points to a combination of psychopharmacological and psychosocial interventions. Once thought to be a life-long downward spiral of impairment, schizophrenia is no longer viewed exclusively in that light. The recovery model has introduced and supports progressive practices that place the individual first and emphasizes creating visions of how that individual wants to live fully beyond effective coping with his or her symptoms. The recovery model approach, based on hope and lived experience, emphasizes the centrality of the individual's desires and initiative in relation to treatment planning.

DISCUSSION QUESTIONS AND ACTIVITIES

The following are intended for work in small groups.

1. The consumer movement has introduced many changes in clinical practice with populations suffering from serious mental illness. Respond to each of the challenges identified here:
   a. You are a licensed clinical supervisor in a setting that includes peer support (i.e., consumers) as part of the service and you have several

seasoned clinicians who are confused by their recovery model-oriented role in working collaboratively on clinical teams with peer support specialists. For example, some staff feel that their clinical expertise is not valued in the new practice paradigm. How would you approach your staff in learning to partner and collaborate with the peer support staff on teams?

   b. What skills do you feel clinicians must exercise as they engage with peer support in the process of staff meetings, case assessment, and intervention planning? For example, the experience many consumers have had with mental health professionals may leave them distrustful or feeling patronized.

   c. As a supervisor or administrator, what activity or activities would you like to initiate with your staff in order to help them understand stigma, promote its elimination, and normalize concepts of wellness and recovery?

2. Several competing perspectives coexist in clinical settings providing services to those with severe mental illness.

   a. Define the assumptions and principles of the approaches of the medical model and the recovery model. What are the strengths and limitations of the medical model? What advantages does the recovery model introduce in practice with individuals suffering from serious mental illness and their families?

   b. Medical settings often utilize diagnostic and treatment terminology inherent in the dominant practice paradigm (e.g., medicine), which focuses on symptoms of pathology. What are the implications of using the term *patient* versus the term *client* or the term *consumer* when referring to the person with schizophrenia? Which do you prefer, and why?

   c. To engage consumers in the diagnostic process while bringing to bear your clinical expertise is a challenging practice. How would you approach this? What would you say to the consumer to start the discussion about his diagnosis, and what would you do to involve him in the exploration of symptoms, coping skills, and treatment planning and future goals?

   d. A Diversity/Resiliency Formulation–based diagnosis requires several activities that begin with gathering information and end in the identification of a diagnosis and/or the development of a formulation. How would you approach identifying a specific diagnosis for consumers to reflect on and discuss? How would you elicit their perspective on what diagnostic category they feel best matches their symptoms and experiences?

3. Discuss the following in small groups: You have been designated as the licensed clinician who will initiate several activities in your public mental health department. How will you address the following?

   a. The agency would like to initiate community-based stakeholder forums for the purpose of identifying mental health needs within various populations in the region. How will you identify participant stakeholders? How would you publicize the forums and encourage attendance? Where would you hold these meetings? What types of incentives for participation might you include and publicize?

b. As a clinical supervisor, you will take the lead in developing a community-based day activity center for individuals with serious mental illness who live in the community. What features will the program have? Who will run it and what kind of training will they receive? What activities will be included and why?

4. You are a licensed mental health clinician who is colocated in the emergency room of a hospital. In the middle of an assessment with a young man who was referred to you by a physician because he was incoherent, you realize that he is delusional and hallucinating. It is not clear whether he is under the influence of a substance of abuse or whether these symptoms are related to a general medical condition.
   a. Where would you start as you begin to explore his current behavior?
   b. How would you explore his mental status? What would you look for in his presentation?
   c. What considerations would you take into account in determining whether an involuntary 72-hour assessment is needed? What steps would you take to initiate the 72-hour hold once you realized it was necessary?
5. Many mental health practice areas require clinician development of specialized knowledge. What are your thoughts on the following?
   a. What type of minimum baseline knowledge on medication and its effects do you feel will assure your effectiveness as a mental health clinician?
   b. What kinds of skills and interventions are needed in working with consumers and their families with the goals of their empowerment vis-à-vis being informed about the course of their disorder, medications and their side effects, and managing stressors as they arise?
6. Open discussion of mental health teams in staffing cases is essential.
   a. What perspectives can the variety of mental health professionals who work collaboratively on teams bring to their interaction and dialogue that will enhance mutual team effort and effectiveness? Specifically, what perspectives can reduce the all-too-frequent presence of professional hierarchy on mental health teams?
   b. How do codes of ethics and the role and purpose of various professions affect team functioning? How might professionals from different backgrounds (e.g., psychiatry, social work, psychology, marriage and family therapy, counseling) work with the variety of ethical principles that drive each professional and/or the professional role that defines each profession in the context of the team or colocation efforts?

WEB RESOURCES

Fountain House, NYC: www.fountainhouse.org
Mental Health America: www.mentalhealthamerica.net/annualconference
National Association of Peer Specialists: www.naops.org

Recovery to Practice: www.dsgonline.com/rtp/resources.html
Substance Abuse and Mental Health Services Administration: http://mentalhealth/samhsa.gov/cmhs/CommunitySupport/toolkits/employment/default.aspx
The Village, Long Beach, CA: www.mhala.org/mha-village.htm

REFERENCES

Addington, J., Cadenhead, K. S., Cannon, T. D., Cornblatt, B., McGlashan, T. H., Perkins, D. O., … Heinssen, R. (2007). North American Prodromal Longitudinal Study: A collaborative multisite approach to prodromal schizophrenia research. *Schizophrenia Bulletin, 33*(3), 665–672.

American Psychiatric Association. (2000). *Diagnostic and statistical manual of mental disorders, DSM-IC-TR.* (4th ed., text rev.). Washington, DC: Author.

American Psychiatric Association. (2013). *Diagnostic and statistical manual of mental disorders* (5th ed.). Arlington, VA: American Psychiatric Press.

American Psychological Association (2010). *Publication manual of the American Psychological Association* (6th ed.). Washington, DC: Author.

Andreasen, N. C. (1982). Negative symptoms in schizophrenia: Definition and reliability. *Archives of General Psychiatry, 39*, 784–788.

Andreasen, N. C., Arndt, S., Alliger, R., Miller, D., & Flaum, M. (1995). Symptoms of schizophrenia: Methods, meanings, and mechanisms. *Archives of General Psychiatry, 52*(5), 341–351.

Auquier, P., Lancon, C., Rouillon, F., Lader, M., & Holmes, C. (2007). Mortality in schizophrenia. *Pharmacoepidemiology and Drug Safety, 16*(12), 1308–1312.

Baronet, A. M. (1999). Factors associated with caregiver burden in mental illness: A critical review of the research literature. *Clinical Psychology Review, 19*, 819–841.

Barrowclough, C., & Tarrier, N. (1998). Social functioning and family interventions. In K. T. Mueser & N. Tarrier (Eds.), *Handbook of social functioning in schizophrenia* (pp. 327–341). Boston, MA: Allyn & Bacon.

Bateson, G. (1972). *Steps to an ecology of mind.* New York, NY: Ballantine Books.

Beck, A. T., Rector, N. A., Stolar, N., & Grant, P. (2009). *Schizophrenia: Cognitive theory, research & therapy.* New York, NY: Guilford Press.

Becker, D. R., & Bond, G. R. (Eds.). (2002). *Supported employment implementation resource kit.* Rockville, MD: Center for Mental Health Services, Substance Abuse and Mental Health Services Administration.

Becker, D. R., & Drake, R. E. (2003). *A working life for people with severe mental illness.* New York, NY: Oxford University Press.

Becker, D. R., Smith, J., Tanzman, B., Drake, R. E., & Tremblay, T. (2001). Fidelity of supported employment programs and employment outcomes. *Psychiatric Services, 52*, 834–836.

Bleuler, E. (1950). *Dementia praecox or the group of schizophrenias* (J. Zinkin, Trans.). New York, NY: International Universities Press. (Original work published 1911)

Bogerts, B. (1993). Recent advances in the neuropathology of schizophrenia. *Schizophrenia Bulletin, 19*, 431–445.

Bond, G. R. (2004). Supported employment: Evidence for an evidence-based practice. *Psychiatric Rehabilitation Journal, 27*, 345–359.

Bresnahan, M., Begg, M. D., Brown, A., Schaefer, C., Sohler, N., & Insel, B. (2007). Race and risk of schizophrenia in a U.S. birth cohort: Another example of health disparity? *International Journal of Epidemiology, 36*, 751–758.

Brown, S. (1997). Excess mortality of schizophrenia: A meta-analysis. *British Journal of Psychiatry, 171*, 502–508.

Buckley, P., Miller, B., Lehrer, D., & Castle, D. (2009). Psychiatric comorbidities and schizophrenia. *Schizophrenia Bulletin, 35*(2), 383–402.

Byrden, K. E., Carrey, N. J., & Kutcher, S. P. (2001). Update and recommendations for the use of antipsychotics in early-onset psychosis. *Journal of Child and Adolescent Psychopharmacology, 11*(2), 113–130.

Chien, W. T., Chan, S. W., & Morrissey, J. (2007). The perceived burden among Chinese family caregivers of people with schizophrenia. *Journal of Clinical Nursing, 16*(6), 1151–1161.

Chien, W. T., Yeung, F. K. K., & Chan, A. H. L. (2014). Perceived stigma of patients with severe mental illness in Hong Kong: Relationships with patients' psychosocial conditions and attitudes of family caregivers and health professionals. *Administrative and Policy in Mental Health, 41*, 237–251.

Chou, K. R. (2000). Caregiver burden: A concept analysis. *Journal of Paediatric Nursing, 15*, 398–407.

Corrigan, P. W. (2004). How stigma interferes with mental health care. *American Psychologist, 59*(7), 614–625.

Corrigan, P. W. (Ed.) (2013). *The stigma of disease and disability: Understanding causes and overcoming injustices*. Washington, DC: American Psychological Association.

Corrigan, P. W., Mueser, K. T., Bond, G. R., Drake, R. E., & Solomon, P. (2008). *Principles and practice of psychiatric rehabilitation*. New York, NY: Guilford Press.

Corrigan, P. W., & Ralph, R. O. (Eds.). (2005). *Recovery in mental illness*. Washington, DC: American Psychological Association.

Crow, T. (1980). Molecular pathology of schizophrenia: More than one disease process? *British Medical Journal, 280*, 66–68.

Davidson, L. (2003). *Living outside mental illness: Qualitative studies in schizophrenia*. New York, NY: New York University Press.

Deegan, P. (1996). Recovery as a journey of the heart. *Psychiatric Rehabilitation Journal, 19*(3), 91–97.

Ertugrul, A., Yagcioglu, A. E., Eni, N., & Yazici, C. M. (2005). Obsessive-compulsive symptoms in clozapine-treated schizophrenic patients. *Psychiatry and Clinical Neurosciences, 59*(2), 219–222.

Evans, R. (2010, March 18). *Schizophrenia: cognitive theory, research and therapy*, by Beck, A. T., Neil, A. R., Stolar, N., & Grant, P (Review). Retrieved from www.miwatch.org/2010/03/aaron_beck_schizophrenia_cogni.html

Fenton, W. S., Byler, C., & Heinsese, R. (1997). Determinants of medication compliance in schizophrenia: Empirical and clinical findings. *Schizophrenia Bulletin, 23*, 637–651.

Flor-Henry, P. (1983). *Cerebral basis of psychopathology*. Bristol, UK: Wright PSG.

Frangou, S. (2006). Early onset schizophrenia: Cognitive and clinical characteristics. In T. Sharma & P. Harvey (Eds.), *The early course of schizophrenia* (pp. 59–69). New York, NY: Oxford University Press.

Gingerich, S. (2009). Guidelines for social skills training for persons with mental illness. In R. Roberts (Ed.), *Social workers' desk reference* (pp. 666–671). New York, NY: Oxford University Press.

Glatt, S. J. (2008). Genetics. In K. T. Mueser & D. V. Jeste (Eds.), *Clinical handbook of schizophrenia* (pp. 55–64). New York, NY: Guilford Press.

Goldstein, J. M., & Walder, D. J. (2006). Sex differences in schizophrenia: The case for developmental origins and etiological implications. In T. Sharma & P. Harvey (Eds.), *The early course of schizophrenia* (pp. 147–173). New York, NY: Oxford University Press.

Gottesman, I. I., & Shields, J. (1982). *Schizophrenia: The epigenetic puzzle*. New York, NY: Cambridge University Press.

Gray, R., White, J., Schulz, M., & Abderhalden, C. (2010). Enhancing medication adherence in people with schizophrenia: An international programme of research. *International Journal of Mental Health Nursing, 19*, 36–44.

Green, A. I., Canuso, C., Brenner, M. J., & Wijcik, J. D. (2003). Detection and management of comorbidity in schizophrenia. *Psychiatric Clinics of North America, 26*, 115–139.

Greenberg, J. (1964). *I never promised you a rose garden*. New York, NY: Penguin.

Harding, C. M., Brooks, G. W., Ashikaga, T., Strauss, J. S., & Breier, A. (1987). The Vermont longitudinal study of persons with severe mental illness, I: Methodology, study sample, and overall status 32 years later. *American Journal of Psychiatry, 144*, 718–726.

Harding, C. M., Zubin, J., & Strauss, J. S. (1987). Chronicity in schizophrenia: Fact, partial fact, or artifact? *Hospital and Community Psychiatry, 38*(5), 477–486.

Heinrichs, R. W. (2005). The primacy of cognition in schizophrenia. *American Psychologist, 60*(3), 229–242.

Hertz, P. (2008). The psychoses with a special emphasis on schizophrenia. In J. Berzoff, L. M. Flanagan, & P. Hertz (Eds.), *Inside out and outside in* (pp. 281–310). Lanham, MD: Jason Aronson.

Hoenig, J., & Hamilton, M. (1966). The schizophrenic patient in the community and his effect on the household. *International Journal of Social Psychiatry, 12*, 165–176.

Hogan, M. (2010). Updated schizophrenia PORT treatment recommendations: A commentary. *Schizophrenia Bulletin, 36*(1), 104–106.

Hooley, J. (2007). Expressed emotion and relapse of psychopathology. *Annual Review of Clinical Psychology, 3*, 329–352.

Jenkins, J. H. (1991). Anthropology, expressed emotion, and schizophrenia. *Ethos, 19*, 387–431.

Jenkins, J. H. (1992). Too close for comfort: Schizophrenia and emotional overinvolvement among Mexicano families. In A. D. Gaines (Ed.), *Ethnopsychiatry: The cultural construction of professional and folk psychiatries* (pp. 203–221). Albany, NY: State University of New York Press.

Johnson, D. A. (1988). The significance of depression in the prediction of relapse in chronic schizophrenia. *British Journal of Psychiatry, 152*, 320–323.

Johnson, J., Srinivasan, M., & Xiong, G. (2009). Psychotic disorders. In R. McCarron, G. Xiong, & J. A. Bourgeois (Eds.), *Lippencott's primary care psychiatry* (pp. 80–102). Philadelphia, PA: Wolters Kluwer/Lippincott Williams & Wilkins.

Kaplan, H. I., & Saddock, B. J. (1998). *Synopsis of psychiatry*. Baltimore, MD: Williams and Wilkins.

Keefe, R. S. E., Bilder, R. M., Davis, S. M., Harvey, P. D., Palmer, B. W., Gold, J. M., ... Lieberman, J. A.; CATIE Investigators; Neurocognitive Working Group. (2007). Neurocognitve effects of antipsychotic medications in patients with chronic schizophrenia in the CATIE trial. *Archives of General Psychiatry, 64*(6), 633–647.

Keefe, R. S. E., Mohs, R. C., Bilder, R. M., Harvey, P. D., Green, M. F., Meltzer, H., ... Sano, M. (2003). Neurocognitive assessment in the Clinical Antipsychotic Trials of Intervention Effectiveness (CATIE) Project schizophrenia trial: Development, methodology, and rationale. *Schizophrenia Bulletin, 29*(1), 45–55.

Kelleher, I. & Cannon, M. (2014). Whither the psychosis-neurosis borderline. *Schizophrenia Bulletin, 40*(2), 266–268.

Kellerman, H. (2009). *Dictionary of psychopathology*. New York, NY: Columbia University Press.

Kirkpatrick, B., Buchanan, R. W., Ross, D. E., & Carpenter, W. T. (2001). A separate disease within the syndrome of schizophrenia. *Archives of General Psychiatry, 58*, 165–171.

Klingberg, S., Wolwer, W., Engel, C., Wittorf, A., Herrlich, J., Meisner, C., ... Wiedemann, G. (2011). Negative symptoms of schizophrenia as primary target of cognitive behavioral therapy: Results of the Randomized Clinical TONES study. *Schizophrenia Bulletin, 37*, S98–S110. doi:10.1093/schbul/sbr073

Kraepelin, E. (1896). *Dementia praecox and paraphrenia* (R. M. Barclay, Trans.). Chicago, IL: Medical Books.

Kukla, M., & Bond, G. R. (2009). Supported employment approaches. In A. R. Roberts (Ed.), *Social worker's desk reference* (pp. 704–711). New York, NY: Oxford University Press.

Lehman, A. F., Steinwachs, D. M., & PORT Co-Investigators. (1998). Patterns of usual care for schizophrenia: Initial results from the Schizophrenia Patient Outcomes Research Team (PORT). *Schizophrenia Bulletin, 24*, 11–20.

Lieberman, R. P., & Kopelowicz, A. (2005). Recovery from schizophrenia: A criterion based definition. In R. O. Ralph & P. W. Corrigan (Eds.), Recovery in mental illness (pp. 101–129). Washington, DC: American Psychological Association.

Lopez, S. R., Hipke, K. N., Polo, J. A., Jenkins, J. H., Karno, M., Vaughn, C., & Snyder, K. S. (2004). Ethnicity, expressed emotion, attributions, and course of schizophrenia: Family warmth matters. *Journal of Abnormal Psychology, 113*, 428–430.

Lopez, S. R., Ramirez Garcia, J. I., Ullman, J. B., Kopelowicz, A., Jenkins, J., Breitborde, N.J., & Placencia, P. (2009). Cultural variability in the manifestation of expressed emotion. *Family Process, 48*(2), 179–194.

Lykouras, L., Alevizos, B., Michalopoulou, P., & Rabavilas, A. (2003). Obsessive-compulsive symptoms induced by atypical antipsychotics. A review of the reported cases. *Progress in Neuro-psychopharmacological & Biological Psychiatry*, *27*(3), 333–346.

Mahendran, R., Liew, E., & Subramaniam, M. (2007). De novo emergence of obsessive-compulsive symptoms with atypical antipsychotics in Asian patients with schizophrenia or schizoaffective disorder: A retrospective, cross-sectional study. *Journal of Clinical Psychiatry*, *68*, 542–545.

Mandel, M. R., Severe, J. B., Schooler, N. R., Gelenberg, A. J., & Mieske, M. (1982). Development and prediction of postpsychotic depression in neuroleptic treated schizophrenics. *Archives of General Psychiatry*, *39*, 137–203.

Manderscheid, R., & Sonnenschein, M. (1997). *Mental health America, 1996*. Washington, DC: Substance Abuse and Mental Health Services Administration, U.S. Department of Health and Human Services.

McClellan, J. M., & Werry, J. S. (2001). Practice parameter for the assessment and treatment of children and adolescents with schizophrenia. *Journal of the American Academy of Child Adolescent Psychiatry*, *40*(7), 4S–23S.

Minksy, S., Vega, W., Miskimen, T., Gara, M., & Escobar, J. (2003). Diagnostic patterns in Latino, African American, and European American psychiatric patients. *Archives of General Psychiatry*, *60*(6), 637–644.

Morgan, C., & Fisher, H. (2007). Environment and schizophrenia: Childhood trauma—A critical review. *Schizophrenia Bulletin*, *33*, 3–10.

Mueser, K. T., & Jeste, D. V. (Eds.). (2008). *Clinical handbook of schizophrenia*. New York, NY: Guilford Press.

Munetz, M.R., Ritter, C., Teller, J. L., & Bonfine, N. (2014). Mental health court and assisted outpatient treatment: Perceived coercion, procedural justice, and program impact. *Psychiatric Services*, *65*(3), 352–358.

New Freedom Commission on Mental Health. (2003). *Achieving the promise: Transforming mental health care in America. Final report* (DHHS Pub. No. SMA-03–3832). www.mentalhealthcommission.gov

North, C. S., Pollio, D. E., Sachar, B., Hong, B., Isennberg, K., & Bufe, G. (1998). The family as caregiver: A group psychoeducation model for schizophrenia. *American Journal of Orthopsychiatry*, *68*(1), 39–46.

O'Hare, T. (2005). *Evidenced-based practices for social workers*. Chicago, IL: Lyceum Books.

Ono, Y., Satsumi, Y., Kim, Y., Iwadate, T., Moriyama, K., Nakane, Y., ... Yoshimura, K. (1999). Schizophrenia: Is it time to replace the term? *Psychiatry and Clinical Neurosciences*, *53*, 335–341.

Palmer, B. W., Dawes, S. E., & Heaton, R. K. (2009). What do we know about neuropsychological aspects of schizophrenia? *Neuropsychological Review*, *19*, 365–384.

Panariello, F., De Luca, V., & de Bartolomeis, A. (2011). Weight gain, schizophrenia and antipsychotics: New findings from animal model and pharmacogenomics studies. *Schizophrenia Research and Treatment*, *2011*, 1–16.

Pearlin, L., Menaghan, E. G., Lieberman, M. A., & Mullan, J. T. (1981). The stress process. *Journal of Health and Social Behavior*, *22*, 337–356.

Perlick, D. A., Rosenheck, R. A., Kaczynski, R., Swartz, M. S., Canive, J. M., & Lieberman, J. A. (2010). Impact of antipsychotic medication on family burden in schizophrenia: Longitudinal results of CATIE trial. *Schizophrenia Research*, *116*, 118–125.

Pokos, V., & Castle, D. J. (2006). Prevalence of comorbid anxiety disorders in schizophrenia spectrum disorders: A literature review. *Current Psychiatry Reviews*, *2*, 285–307.

Pratt, C. W., Gill, K. J., Barrett, N. M., & Roberts, J. (2007). *Psychiatric rehabilitation* (2nd ed.). Burlington, MA: Elsevier Academic Press.

Premack, D., & Woodruff, G. (1978). Does the chimpanzee had a theory of mind? *Behavioral and Brain Sciences*, *4*, 515–526.

Ramirez Garcia, J. I., Chang, C. L., Young, J. S., Lopez, S., & Jenkins, J. (2006). Family support predicts psychiatric medication usage among Mexican American individuals with schizophrenia. *Social Psychiatry and Psychiatric Epidemiology*, *41*, 624–631.

Rao, N. P., Arasappa, R., Reddy, N. N., Venkatasubramanian, G., & Gangadhar, B. N. (2010). Antithetical asymmetry in schizophrenia and bipolar disorder: A line bisection study. *Bipolar Disorders*, *12*(3), 221–229.

Ray, B., Kubiak, S. P., Comartin, E. R., & Tillander, E. (2015). Mental health court outcomes by offense type at admission. *Administration and Policy in Mental Health and Mental Health Services Research*, *42*(3), 323–331.

Rice, D. (1999). The economic impact of schizophrenia. *Journal of Clinical Psychiatry*, *60*(Suppl. 1), 4–6.

Roth, R. L. (2003). Biologic mechanisms of psychosis and antipsychotic drug actions: From dopamine excess to dopamine stabilization. *Advanced Studies in Medicine*, *3*(8C), S776–S781.

Rungreangkulkij, S., & Gilliss, C. L. (2000). Conceptual approaches to studying family caregiving for persons with severe mental illness. *Journal of Family Nursing*, *6*, 341–366.

Sartorius, H. N. (2002). Iatrogenic stigma of mental illness. *British Medical Journal*, *324*(7352), 1470–1471.

Schene, A. H. (1990). Objective and subjective dimensions of family burden: Towards an integrative framework for research. *Social Psychiatry & Psychiatric Epidemiology*, *25*, 289–297.

Schwab, S. G., & Wildenauer, D. B. (2008). Research on causes for schizophrenia: Are we close? *Schizophrenia Bulletin*, *102*, 29–30.

Schwartz, R. C., Hilscher, R. L., & Hayhow, P. (2007). Substance abuse and psychosocial impairment among clients with schizophrenia. *American Journal of Orthopsychiatry*, *77*(4), 610–615.

Shahrokh, N. C., & Hales, R. E. (Eds.). (2003). *American psychiatric glossary*. Arlington, VA: American Psychiatric Press.

Silver, H., Feldman, P., Bilker, W., & Gur, R. C. (2003). Working memory deficits as a core neuropsychological dysfunction in schizophrenia. *American Journal of Psychiatry*, *160*(10), 1809–1816.

Silverstein, S. M., & Wilkniss, S. M. (2004). At issues: The future of cognitive rehabilitation of schizophrenia. *Schizophrenia Bulletin*, *30*(4), 679–692.

Smith, M. J., Greenberg, J. S., & Seltzer, M. M. (2007). Siblings of adults with schizophrenia: Expectations about future caregiving roles. *American Journal of Orthopsychiatry*, *77*(1), 29–37.

Snowden, L. (2003). Bias in mental health assessment and intervention: Theory and evidence. *American Journal of Public Health*, *93*(2), 239–243.

Stein, C. H., Mann, L. M., & Hunt, M. G. (2007). Ever onward: The personal strivings of young adults coping with serious mental illness and the hopes of their parents. *American Journal of Orthopsychiatry*, *77*(1), 104–112.

Strakowski, S. M., Keck, P. E., Jr., McElroy, S. L., Lonczak, H. S., & West, S. A. (1995). Chronology of comorbid and principal syndromes in first-episode psychosis. *Comprehensive Psychiatry*, *36*, 106–112.

Substance Abuse and Mental Health Services Administration (SAMHSA). (2011). *The evidence: Supported education. A promising practice.* Retrieved from http://SAMHSA.gov

Substance Abuse and Mental Health Services Administration (SAMHSA). (2012). *SAMHSA's working definition of recovery*. Retrieved from http://blog.samhsa.gov/2012/03/23/definition-of-recovery-updated/#.U7XQ7bGGc8U

Swanson, J. W., Van Dorn, R. A., Swartz, M. S., Robbins, P. C., Steadman, H. J., Mcguire, T., & Monahan, J. (2013). *American Journal of Psychiatry*, *170*(12), 1423–1432.

Tandon, R., Gaebel, W., Barch, D. M., Bustillo, J., Gur, R., Heckers, S., ... Carpenter, W. (2013). Definition and description of schizophrenia in the *DSM-5*. *Schizophrenia Research*, *150*(1), 3–10.

Tandon, R., Keshavan, M., & Nasrallah, H. (2008). Schizophrenia, "Just the Facts": What we know in 2008 Part 1: Overview. *Schizophrenia Research*, 100, 4–19.

Test, M. (2009). Guidelines for assertive community treatment teams. In A. R. Roberts (Ed.), *Social workers' desk reference* (pp. 869–871). New York, NY: Oxford University Press.

Tranulis, C., Potvin, S., Gourgue, M., Leblanc, G., Mancini-Marie, A., & Stip, E. (2005). The paradox of quetiapine in obsessive-compulsive disorder. *CNS Spectrums*, *10*(5), 356–361.

Turner, R. J. (1981). Social support as a contingency in psychological well being. *Journal of Health and Social Behavior*, 22, 357–367.

Twamley, E. W., Jeste, D. V., & Bellack, A. S. (2003). A review of cognitive training in schizophrenia. *Schizophrenia Bulletin*, *29*(2), 359–382.

U.S. Department of Health and Human Services. (2001). *Mental health: Culture, race, and ethnicity—A supplement to Mental health: A report of the Surgeon General*. Washington, DC: Author.

Vespia, K. M. (2009). Culture and psychotic disorders. In S. Eshun & R. A. R. Gurung (Eds.), *Culture and mental health* (pp. 245–272). Malden, MA: Blackwell Wiley.

Walker, E., Kestler, L., Bollini, A., & Hochman, K. (2004). Schizophrenia: Etiology and course. *Annual Review of Psychology*, *55*, 401–430.

Walker, E., & Tessner, K. (2008). Schizophrenia. *Perspectives on Psychological Science*, *3*, 30–37.

Wang, P. S., Demler, O., & Kessler, R. C. (2002). Adequacy of treatment for serious mental illness in the United States. *American Journal of Public Health*, *92*(1), 92–98.

Weikert, T. W., Goldberg, T. E., Gold, J. M., Bigelow, L. B., Egan, M. F., & Weinberger, D. R. (2000). Cognitive impairments in patients with schizophrenia displaying preserved and compromised intellect. *Archives of General Psychiatry*, *57*, 907–913.

Werneke, U., Taylor, D., & Sanders, T. A. (2013). Behavioral interventions for antipsychotic induced appetite changes. *Current Psychiatry Reports*, *15*, 347–356.

Wisdom, J. P., Saedi, G. A., & Green, C. A. (2009). Another breed of "service" animals: STARS study findings about pet ownership and recovery from serious mental illness. *American Journal of Orthopsychiatry*, *79*(3), 430–436.

Zalesky, A., Fornito, A., Seal, M., Cocchi, L., Westin, C., Bullimore, E., Egan, G. & Pantelis, C. (2011). Disrupted axonal fiber connectivity in schizophrenia. *Biological Psychiatry*, *69*(1), 80–89.

NINE

Co-Occurring Disorders and the Diversity/Resiliency Formulation

This appetite to choose death by pleasure if it is available to choose—this appetite of your people unable to choose appetites, this is the death. What you call the death, the collapsing: this will be the formality only.

—David Foster Wallace, *Infinite Jest*

The complexity of human beings is our recurring theme in this book as we address the needs of those whom we serve. These needs are as complicated and unique as the individuals themselves, embedded as they are in contexts that are sources of both stress and resiliency. Perhaps nowhere is this complexity as challenging as when substance use is combined with one or more mental disorders, known as *co-occurring disorders*. The Substance Abuse and Mental Health Services Administration (SAMHSA) reports that approximately 8.9 million adults have co-occurring disorders, only 7.8% receive treatment for both conditions and 55.8% do not receive treatment (SAMHSA, 2010a). Evidence points to a need for greater attention to the development of best practices to serve this population. Goldner, Lusted, Roerecke, Rehm, and Fisher's (2014) meta-analysis of clinical data found that higher rates of anxiety and depression disorders were associated with nonmedical opioid use. Progress in the monitoring of individuals with co-occurring disorders was found to have positive treatment outcomes in relation to substance use and recovery rates (Goodman, McKay, & DePhilippis, 2013). Fortunately, the cost of treatment and stigma associated with substance use treatment can be overcome via affordable integrated treatment of the co-occurring disorders (Mojtabai, Chen, Kaufmann, & Crum, 2014).

Even though the evidence demonstrates better outcomes with combined treatment of co-occurring disorders, most services are for either substance use or mental health issues, but not both (McGovern, Lambert-Harris, Gotham, Claus, & Xie, 2014). Accurate diagnosis with adolescents with co-occurring disorders is particularly challenging. This can elude the clinician when the client's behavior presents a bewildering array of symptoms that appear at various times to be evidence of substance use, conduct disorder, the effects of trauma or depression, bipolar disorder, or a psychotic disorder. As illustrated in the clinical vignette that concludes the chapter, it is not unusual for young patients with psychiatric disorders to be diagnosed with a variety of mental health and substance use labels and simultaneously be prescribed several different medications from various clinicians. A *behavioral health* approach integrates both substance use and mental health disorders. The *DSM®-IV-TR* (*Diagnostic and Statistical Manual of Mental Disorders*, 4th ed., text revision; American Psychiatric Association [APA], 2000) and *DSM-5* (APA, 2013) each have chapters on "Substance Abuse Disorders and Substance-Related and Addictive Disorders," respectively; however, an integrated co-occurring approach to treatment that is inclusive of both substance and mental disorders is not addressed in the *DSM-5*.

Philosophies of assessment and treatment are changing in reaction to the frustration of practitioners, the availability of funding, or the inflexible commitment of staff to a particular theory of practice. Given the limited scope of our book, it is impossible to do justice to the subject of substance use in itself, or to comprehensively discuss the context and effective practice of co-occurring disorders. We will summarize the issues in recent research and view them through the lens of the Diversity/Resiliency Formulation (DRF).

Substance use refers to the consumption of psychoactive drugs, secured through both legal and illegal means, that influence and alter cognition, mood, and ultimately behavior (McNeece & Barbanell, 2005). McNeece and Barbanell propose that the consumption of legal and illegal stimulants is best described as substance rather than drug use. It is useful to cluster substances into CNS (central nervous system) depressants (i.e., alcohol, cannabis), and stimulants (caffeine, cocaine, amphetamines, methamphetamines, and amphetamine-like substances). Opiates (i.e., opioids) are similar to CNS depressants but with less motor and intellectual impairment; these include heroine, morphine, codeine, and synthetic morphine-like substances. As mind-altering substances, hallucinogens alter perceptions, thoughts, and feelings. Lysergic acid diethylamide (LSD), mescaline, and psilocybin-based mushrooms are the most often used hallucinogens; however, gasoline, benzene, and trichloroethylene can have effects similar to CNS depressants and hallucinogens when inhaled (Drugtext, 2001, as cited in McNeece & Barbanell, 2005).

In 2007, illicit substance users included 19.9 million Americans age 12 and over, with marijuana as the most commonly used (14.4 million), followed by cocaine (2.4 million), hallucinogens (1.0 million), and methamphetamine (529,000); another 6.9 million individuals used prescription-type psychotherapeutic drugs for nonmedical purposes (SAMHSA, Office of Applied Studies, 2008). Regarding alcohol use, more than half of the American population (51.1%, or 126.8 million) is reported as current drinkers. Binge drinking was identified for 23.3% (57.8 million) and heavy drinking for 6.9% (17 million). Notably, adults between the ages of 18 and 25 showed a binge-drinking[1] rate of

1 National Survey on Drug Use and Health defines as drinking five or more drinks on the same occasion (i.e., at the same time or within a couple of hours of each other) on at least 1 day in the past 30 days; heavy alcohol use is defined as drinking five or more drinks on the same occasion on each of 5 or more days in the past 30 days; all heavy alcohol users are defined as binge alcohol users (Substance Abuse and Mental Health Services Administration, 2006).

41.8%; heavy drinking was at 14.7%. The rate of current drinking for youths aged 12 to 17 was 15.9% (SAMHSA, 2008). In 2000, youths who reported alcohol or illicit drug use were more likely than youths who did not use substances to be at risk for suicide, and only 36% of youths at risk for suicide received mental health treatment (National Household Survey on Drug Abuse, 2002). In 2008, some 6.3% of drug-related emergency department visits made by adults between the ages of 18 and 24 involved suicide attempts; almost three out of five visits for drug-related suicide attempts were made by females (Drug Abuse Warning Network, 2010).

There is some indication that youths who indulge in heavy alcohol use are more likely to have participated in delinquent behavior (SAMHSA, 2005) and that youths who report alcohol or illicit drug use are at higher risk for suicide (SAMHSA, 2002). An increase, however, was seen with a doubling of the rate of admissions to substance abuse treatment for individuals aged 50 or older between 1992 and 2008 (SAMHSA, 2010b).

Key Points

1. Co-occurring disorders, consisting of substance use and another mental disorder, are widespread, complicated, and difficult to treat; this can result in a confused presentation and confusing response to the client seeking help.
2. Substance use involves the ingestion of legal or illegal substances that alter mood, cognition, and eventually behavior.
3. Substance use remains a prevalent and pervasive problem in American society.
4. Substance use increases the risk for depression, suicide, and delinquency; it co-occurs with many mental disorders.
5. Substance use occurs at all ages, and the rate of substance use for older persons is increasing.

DSM-5 DIAGNOSTIC CRITERIA

"Substance-Related and Addictive Disorders" in the *DSM-5* is organized into Substance Use and Induced Disorders and Non-Substance-Related Disorders, the latter of which contains one disorder (i.e., Gambling). The chapter contains 10 classes of substances that include (a) alcohol; (b) caffeine; (c) cannabis; (d) hallucinogens (separate from phencyclidine or arylcyclohexylamines and other hallucinogens); (e) inhalants; (f) opioids; (g) sedatives, hypnotics, and anxiolytics; (h) stimulants (amphetamine-type substances, cocaine, and other stimulants); (i) tobacco; and (j)other or unknown substances (APA, 2013). In addition, Substance/Medication-Induced Mental Disorders is identified in this chapter; however, criteria and other information are located in the relevant *DSM* chapter, such as "Depressive Disorders" or "Neurocognitive Disorders." The *DSM-5* approach to substance and addictive disorders focuses on the role of the brain-reward system in reinforcing behaviors and the capacity of substances to activate the reward system at the expense of neglecting one's day-to-day activities and responsibilities. It is often said that when there is substance use the dominant relationship is with the substance. The emphasis on the brain-reward system in understanding addiction is the basis for inclusion of a gambling disorder in the *DSM-5*, premised on the effects gambling has on behavior that is similar to substance use.

In the *DSM-5*, Substance Use Disorder replaces the former categories of Substance Abuse and Dependence in the *DSM-IV-TR*. Criteria for substance use disorders consist of four patterns of maladaptive behaviors: impaired control, social impairment, risky use, and tolerance/withdrawal. In addition there are criteria for intoxication, withdrawal, substance/medication-induced disorders, and unspecified substance-induced disorders (APA, 2013). The change in terminology from dependence to a pattern of use, which can include addiction, is in part based on the limited clinical utility of dependence in the diagnostic process. Dependence, in and of itself, has been recognized as normal and not pathological, especially with respect to pain medication necessary in medical treatment. Minor changes from the *DSM-IV-TR* include removal of legal problems as a criterion and addition of craving as a new criterion. The *DSM-5* now requires presence of two or more criteria, rather than the one required in the *DSM-IV-TR*. Caffeine and cannabis withdrawal are new additions, as is tobacco use. Severity criteria for different substances identify mild, moderate, or severe indicators. Several other changes include removal of polysubstance use and inclusion for some substances of a specifier on remission. This specifier calls for identifying 3 but less than 12 months without meeting criteria (except for craving) and 12 months as an indicator of sustained remission. Specifiers have been added regarding provision of a stable environment for treatment as well as long-term treatment support.

The essential characteristics of substance use disorders are the cognitive, behavioral, and physiological symptoms. There is greater attention to the neurological and physical (i.e., CNS) changes that occur with substance use and how these changes can endure beyond the detox stage.

Welsh, Cargiulo, Gandhi, Liberto, and Weintraub (2004) point out that the progressive changes in the *DSM* toward a greater focus on substance-related impairment in functioning have not gone far enough. For example, the *DSM* requirement of identifying an agonist treatment specifier for opioid use (e.g., methadone, buprenorphine) but not for alcohol (e.g., naltrexone) is unbalanced. Stigmatization of opioid use is perpetuated by equating agonist therapy for opioid use as substance use rather than remission. From a clearly strength-based perspective, Welsh et al. (2004) propose that diagnostic qualifiers "should be based on the patient's behavior and not on the treatment" (p. 87). Interestingly, the *DSM-5* added a treatment specifier for nicotine.

A review of the *DSM-5* diagnostic categories shows that to a large degree criteria and specifiers are shared across disorders. Shared criteria for use disorders include: increasing amount of consumption, persistent desire for the substance, significant amount of time in securing the substance, craving, recurrent use that interferes with key responsibilities, continued use despite negative effects of substance use, reduced involvement in key activities, substance use in hazardous situations, continued use in the face of knowledge of negative effects, changes in tolerance, and withdrawal effects. Specifiers address whether the person is in early remission or sustained remission, or in a controlled environment. Indicators are provided for a specifier on how to determine current severity.

Substance/Medication Induced Mental Disorders are distinguished from the substance use disorders in which cognitive, behavioral, and physiological symptoms have a role in continuing use. Substance/medication-induced mental health disorders are viewed as potentially severe but most often temporary, in that persistent CNS changes can develop in response to the effects of substance use, medication, or toxins. Several common features of these disorders are identified, such as evidence of development of the disorder within a month of intoxication and capacity of the substance to produce the identified symptoms.

Alcohol-Related Disorders include alcohol use, intoxication, withdrawal, other alcohol-induced disorders, and unspecified alcohol-related disorder. Diagnostic criteria are identified for all except for Other Alcohol-Induced Disorders and Unspecified-Related Disorder. Alcohol use and alcohol withdrawal include specifiers that address whether one is in remission or in a controlled environment, and perceptual disturbances, respectively.

Caffeine-Related Disorders include caffeine intoxication, withdrawal, other caffeine-induced, and unspecified-related disorder. Caffeine intoxication and withdrawal each have identified criteria.

Cannabis-Related Disorders include use, intoxication, and withdrawal. Cannabis withdrawal criteria address the cessation quality (e.g., prolonged), and behavioral symptoms that include: (a) irritability, anger, aggression; (b) nervousness or anxiety; (c) sleep difficulty; (d) decreased appetite or weight loss; (e) restlessness; (f) depressed mood; and (g) one of the following—abdominal pain, shakiness, seating, fever, chills, or headache (APA, 2013). Presence of significant distress and differential diagnosis are also criteria.

Hallucinogen-Related Disorders include a larger range of disorders compared with other substance use disorders. Phencyclidines and phencyclidine-like substances (e.g., PCP, "angel dust") are distinguished from other hallucinogens; they were developed in the 1950s as dissociative anesthetics and later became street drugs (APA, 2013), They can have brief or longer effects, depending on the individual, and can lead to a persistent psychotic episode similar to schizophrenia. Differential diagnosis is particularly needed because these drugs are often additives to other substances. Specifiers call for state of remission, if in a controlled environment, and current severity. Other Hallucinogen Use Disorder shares criteria with Phencyclidine Use Disorder, however, these criteria relate to a hallucinogen. Specifiers call for identification of the hallucinogen, state of remission, if in a controlled environment, and current severity. Phencyclidine Intoxication and Other Hallucinogen Intoxication share criteria regarding recent use, problematic behavior, presentation of specific symptoms, and differential diagnosis. Hallucinogen Persisting Perception Disorder has several criteria related to onset and symptoms.

Inhalant-Related Disorders include use, intoxication, other inhalant-induced disorders, and unspecified inhalant-related disorders. Inhalant use disorder shares criteria with other disorders, including specifiers on state of remission, if in a controlled environment, and identification of current severity. *Inhalant intoxication disorder* has several criteria that address intended or unintended exposure, problem behaviors, identification of symptoms, and differential diagnosis. Other Inhalant-Induced Disorders refer to inhalant-induced disorders that are found with other disorders in other chapters of the *DSM* with the same phenomenology. Unspecified Inhalant Disorder refers to severe symptoms that cause distress and impair functioning in social, occupational, or other important areas of an individual's life, however, criteria are not met. Opioid-Related Disorders refer to "compulsive, prolonged self-administration of opioid substances that are used for no legitimate medical purpose or, if another medical condition is present that requires opioid treatment, that are used in doses greatly in excess of the amount needed for that medical condition" (APA, 2013, p. 542). This category of substance use is receiving increased attention due to the misuse of prescription medications by consumers.

"Sedative-, Hypnotic-, or Anxiolytic-Related Disorders" include Sedative-, Hypnotic-, or Anxiolytic Use Disorder and Sedative-, Hypnotic-, or Anxiolytic Withdrawal, have criteria and specifiers that address state of remission and if in a controlled environment, and perceptual disturbance, respectively.

"Stimulant-Related Disorders" include Stimulant Use Disorder that has criteria regarding pattern of behavior leading to impairment, and specifiers related to state of remission and level of severity. Stimulant Intoxication has criteria related to type of substance, presence of problematic behavior, symptoms, and differential diagnosis; specifiers relate to specific intoxicant, and presence or absence of perceptual disturbances. Stimulant Withdrawal has criteria related to cessation/use reduction, mood, and a specifier on the specific substance.

Tobacco-Related Disorders include Tobacco Use Disorder, which has criteria related to identification of behaviors associated with a problematic pattern of use (i.e., impairment). There are specifiers related to state of remission, if on maintenance therapy or in a controlled environment, and level of severity and Tobacco Withdrawal, Other Tobacco-Induced Disorders are discussed in other DSM chapters (i.e., "Sleep-Wake Disorders and Substance/Medication-Induced Sleep Disorder"). Unspecified Tobacco-Related Disorder refers to severity of symptoms that cause distress and impair functioning in social, occupational, or other important areas of an individual's life, however, criteria are not met. Other (or Unknown) Substance Use Disorder is a diagnostic category with criteria related to problem behavior associated with use of a substance that does not fall into other DSM substance categories, and behaviors associated with usage, tolerance, and withdrawal behaviors. Other (or Unknown) Substance Intoxication reflects the broadening of the DSM-5 to expand the range of problematic substances. The criteria relate to identification of substance, not identified in the DSM, problematic behavior, and differential diagnosis. Other (or Unknown) Substance Withdrawal has several criteria related to cessation/use reduction, and differential diagnosis. Other (or Unknown) Substance-Induced Disorders are found with other disorders in other chapters of the DSM with the same phenomenology.

Unspecified Other (or Unknown) Substance-Related Disorder refers to severity of symptoms that cause distress and impair functioning in social, occupational, or other important areas of an individual's life, however, criteria are not met.

Nonsubstance-Related Disorders, a new category, includes a new disorder, Gambling Disorder. The criteria relate to problematic gambling behavior, differential diagnosis, and specifiers that address whether the behavior is episodic or persistent, status of remission, and level of severity. The *DSM-5* points out that individuals with this disorder often have poor health, and that some medical conditions, such as angina, are more frequently found with this population. There is some discussion that other types of nonsubstance addiction behavior (e.g., social media) bears more investigation, and as yet there is insufficient evidence as a basis for inclusion in the *DSM*.

KEY POINTS

1. Diagnostic categories involving substance use contain the terms *use*, *intoxication*, and *withdrawal*. In addition there are now additional categories of other and unspecified use disorders.
2. There is greater attention in the *DSM* to changes in the brain resulting from substance use.
3. All Substance-Use Disorders involve impairment in functioning.
4. Substance intoxication and withdrawal may be life threatening and require immediate medical intervention.
5. Substance use may induce many other disorders, including dementia, delirium, anxiety, psychosis, and depression.
6. It is important to avoid stigmatizing individuals as substance users who are dependent on prescribed medication to control pain or other symptoms; for this reason the term *dependence* has been removed as a criterion.
7. Gambling Disorder has been added due to its addictive pattern of behavior with deleterious results for functioning.

Based on evidence from clinical trials (Anton et al., 2006; Crits-Christoph et al., 1999; O'Malley et al., 2007), the Substance-Related Disorder work group recommended three procedures to be utilized as measures of substance use and of changes in severity in substance use disorder during extended periods of time. These include "(a) self-report of frequency of use; (b) when possible, similar reports from a closely involved observer; and (c) tests for substance or substance related biological products in ... samples of urine, blood, saliva, breath, or hair" (see www.dsm5.org/ProposedRevisions/Pages). The increased *DSM-5* emphasis on level of impairment aims to improve the effectiveness of diagnostics and treatment planning; this introduction of dimensional approaches to the diagnosis of alcohol-related disorders is welcomed (Hasin, Liu, Alderson, & Grant, 2006) for several reasons. The intent to "unpack" more aspects and related behaviors of key symptoms will increase insight into the nature of these disorders. The use of dimensional assessment can be invaluable in the diagnosis of individuals using gateway substances that can result in the use of other, more serious substances that place the individual at greater risk for addiction.

Consistent with our emphasis on co-occurring disorders, the vignette presented for discussion embodies the development of both a substance abuse and mental disorder. The story of this young woman, whose difficulties began in adolescence, illuminates the vicissitudes of coping with both disorders, the challenges in coping for both the individual and her family, and perhaps most important, the capacity for resilience in the most dire of circumstances.

CURRENT THINKING ABOUT THE ETIOLOGY AND COURSE OF SUBSTANCE-USE AND MENTAL HEALTH DISORDERS; COMORBIDITY

Societally, substance use, when it reaches the level of a disorder, is viewed as a maladaptive, learned behavior (i.e., habit), disease, or moral defect that is attributable to genetics, culture, or possession. The learned behavior perspective focuses on the environment that promotes the learning, the disease perspective views substance use as a progressive disorder that undermines any control of substance use, and the moral defect perspective views substance use as a choice. McNeece and Barbanell (2005) emphasize the importance of clinicians having knowledge of the various etiological perspectives and their implications for individualized and effective treatment.

Straussner (2004) emphasizes that the risk for addiction to various substances is highly variable, with some substances being more addictive than others. Jellinek's (1952) work on alcoholism and drug addiction identifies a "progressive deterioration of the individual's social, physical, and mental status" (p. 4). The disease concept of addiction, as defined by the professional community, promotes the medicalization of treatment, with an emphasis on medical interventions. The term *chemical dependency* originated in the 1970s based on clinical observation that individuals who abused alcohol were also dependent on other substances. In the 1980s, clinical practice was challenged by recognition of the increased use of both alcohol and illegal drugs (Straussner, 2004).

The jury is out regarding the identification of any one etiological factor that explains the development of addiction (McNeece & Barbanell, 2005; Straussner, 2004). However, there are several overlapping explanatory perspectives in three major categories: biological, psychological, and sociocultural. Endorsement of a perspective has implications for related treatment interventions. Regrettably, the view of addiction as a moral problem continues despite its bias toward a treatment focus on moral vulnerability and its role in the persistence of stigma.

Biological theories represent neurobiological and genetic explanations of addiction. The neurological approach emphasizes changes in brain neurotransmitter functions and the effects of dopamine on parts of the brain that regulate pleasure, contributing to the addiction process. Although there is substantial research based on twin studies (Goodwin, 1984) that points to strong genetic influence, the view remains that the evidence is associational rather than causal (McNeece & DiNitto, 2005).

Directly related to the question of genetic predisposition is the experience of historically, socially, and economically marginalized populations who are at high risk for substance use, such as alcoholism. The level of substance use leads to the societal view of some groups, such as First Nation Peoples (Native Americans), as having a "vulnerability" to addiction and abuse. Such discussion might address the high rates of alcoholism in First Nation communities in relation to the role of social learning, intergenerational family processes, and biological effects of substance use (e.g., alterations in metabolic reactions and brain functioning). However, a culturally relevant approach, by necessity, must be grounded in recognition of the magnitude and scope of historical oppression that First Nation Peoples have experienced in the United States. The historical use of alcohol as a strategy to appropriate resources from these communities, unequivocally has been damaging and is associated with violence, suicide, and sexual abuse (Bachman, 1992; Weaver, 2011). The historical and sociopolitical context of the experience of the Irish as immigrants to the American Northeast would suggest that their social status might have a role in understanding the alcoholism stereotype associated with that group as well. The rates of drinking patterns in Europe associated with the highest health risks are identified in Northern and Eastern Europe (WHO, 2004).

There are several psychological theories that propose explanations for substance use related to learning as an etiology. These theories address factors related to cognitions and behavior, learning, and psychodynamic and personality factors. This diverse set of theories is based on assumptions about the effects of cognition (e.g., effects of the "rewarding" effect of intoxication, on behavior, reinforcement of behavior, coping with unacceptable sexual and aggressive drives, and the long-term enduring effects of formative life experiences). The approaches related to these perspectives (e.g., cognitive behavioral, use of learning theory in interventions, psychodynamic therapy) can be applied in individual, family, and group treatment modalities.

Sociocultural factors span family, environment, and cultural aspects of an individual's life. Family factors address lived experience within the family and social support system that could provoke substance use (e.g., abuse, coercion) and the intergenerational transmission of behaviors. An environmental context that offers access to substances creates vulnerability. This is even more significant for youth, when access includes the ready availability of gateway drugs whose consumption leads to the use of additional substances (Wagner & Anthony, 2002). Cultural identifications and community context have a role in defining substances, their effects, behaviors related to substance use, and how the use of the substance is experienced (Goode, 1972 as cited in McNeece & DiNitto, 2005). A contemporary example of the role of community in defining substances of abuse (i.e., that present potentially hazardous consequences) is the current controversy across the United States to legalize marijuana, with a small proportion of the population holding the belief that cannabis is not a potentially risky and hazardous substance.

There is general agreement that "substance abuse and dependence result from a combination of biochemical, genetic, familial, environmental and cultural factors, as well as from personality dynamics" (Straussner, 2004, p. 13). The diversity of possible factors suggests the importance of comprehensive assessments and multisystem treatment planning that includes individual, family, and group interventions as well as community prevention and response efforts.

KEY POINTS

1. Substance abuse has been viewed as a habit, a disease, and a moral defect caused by culture, possession, heredity, and intergenerationally transmitted familial behavior patterns.
2. Etiological factors overlap and include biological, genetic, psychological, and sociocultural perspectives, and accurate assessment must take this into account.
3. Neurological research implicates the dopamine system in the brain as related to the pleasure seeking involved in substance use.
4. Environmental contexts, such as teen cultures, can be extremely important in reinforcing experimentation with gateway drugs, which lead to further and varied drug and alcohol use.
5. The complexity of substance use disorders implies that effective treatment must involve individuals, families, communities, and cultures.

Co-Occurring Disorders

The increase in co-occurring substance abuse and mental health disorders has created a demand for improved and relevant services for individuals who are challenged by coping with both types of disorders. Approximately 33 million Americans seek health care services for a co-occurring mental health disorder and substance use such as alcohol, prescription medications, or illegal drugs (Institute of Medicine [IOM], 2006). Some 20% of adolescents who received treatment for emotional problems in 2001 to 2003 also received treatment for substance abuse difficulties (Kessler, Berglund, Demier, Jin, & Walters, 2005). In 2002, some 5 million adults aged 18 or older who had a severe mental illness [SMI]) used an illicit drug; individuals with an SMI were more than twice as likely to use an illicit drug (17.1%), compared with those who did not (6.9%) have an SMI (Epstein, Barker, Vorburger, & Murtha, 2004). Males, age 18 and older, with substance abuse admissions in 2005 and with co-occurring disorders were more likely to report daily use of substances. Sixty two percent of male admissions with co-occurring disorders reported more than one substance of abuse, compared with 52% of male admissions without co-occurring disorders; male admissions with co-occurring disorders were more likely than those without co-occurring disorders to report five or more prior episodes of substance abuse treatment (Drug and Alcohol Services Information System, 2007). Moreover, 72% of male and female jail inmates were found to have a co-occurring disorder (Abram & Teplin, 1991). Major depression and alcohol use have been linked for men and women (Substance Abuse and Mental Health Services Administration, 2006); mood disorders have been linked with alcohol abuse and major depressive disorder and drug dependence for women (Goldstein, 2009).

Co-occurring disorders in adolescence and young adulthood are particularly challenging for an effective diagnosis due to the long-term consequences of the diagnosis and treatment. The complex assortment of presenting symptoms of amphetamine use, for example, can be similar to those of bipolar disorder. The diagnosis of co-occurring disorders is also complicated in relation to mental disorders that can develop following withdrawal, or withdrawal from substances. The prevalence of co-occurring disorders is troubling and deserves serious attention, due to their long-term consequences, particularly for adolescents, when early intervention is so essential.

Wallace and Muroff's (2002) review of the literature suggests that the "equal exposure and vulnerability" hypothesis (that race differences are not significant in understanding risk for substance use among adolescents) does not hold. In fact, the experiences of racial groups differ. More African Americans are exposed to economic and academic performance risk factors, whereas ethnic Whites are more exposed to risk factors related to sensation seeking and peer pressure. This highlights how the socioeconomic stress, which adversely impacts African Americans and other at-risk cultural minorities, compounds the vulnerability to co-occurring substance abuse and mental disorders, and this is worsened by problems of lack of access by persons of color to state-of-the-art treatment.

Among adults, depression most often occurs with either an anxiety disorder and alcoholism, and often in the context of isolation and violence (National Research Council and Institute of Medicine, 2009). It is significant that in 2002, more than half of the adults with a co-occurring disorder (i.e., SMI), approximately 2 million, did not receive substance abuse or mental health treatment (National Survey on Drug Use and Health, 2004). Services continue to lack the individualized and relevant treatments for effective interventions for persons with co-occurring disorders, in part due to the continuation of separate care systems for substance use and mental disorders (IOM, 2006).

KEY POINTS

1. Substance abuse co-occurs with depression, schizophrenia, bipolar disorders, anxiety, and a multitude of other mental disorders.
2. A great proportion of individuals with substance abuse disorders do not receive treatment for their co-occurring mental disorders, and vice versa.
3. Separate care systems, historically the design of treatment programs, make this reality worse.
4. Race and culture affect the motivation for substance use, the complications of co-occurring disorders, and access to effective treatment.

EVIDENCE-INFORMED PRACTICE

Most substance use programs place a heavy emphasis on abstinence; if a client cannot sustain abstinence, services are limited or withdrawn. The extremely frequent incidence of the co-occurrence of substance use and mental health disorders suggests the importance of striving for the development of service delivery programs that have a co-occurring focus. The literature is rich with examples of treatments such as group work, peer, and professionally led self-management skills and medication (Beatie, Battersby, & Pols, 2013; Ralevski, Gianoli, McCarthy, & Petrakis, 2014; Rosenblum et al., 2014); the aim is simultaneous attention to the complexities of both disorders. In the service of maintaining a focus in this chapter on strength-based recovery models and co-occurring treatment, the following discussion addresses approaches and interventions relevant to that intervention strategy.

Stages-of-Change Model

The stages-of-change model for substance abuse treatment addresses the issue of an individual's resistance to treatment by identifying a framework that assists in matching the focus of interventions to the client's level of commitment to change a specific behavior (i.e., substance use). Prochaska and DiClemente (1982, 1992, 2005) developed a model involving five stages of change that include precontemplation, contemplation, preparation, action, maintenance/relapse/recycling. This framework is valuable for practice with clients at their individual levels of capacity to take responsibility for their actions, awareness of obstacles, understanding of the consequences of their behavior, their readiness to work on their issues, and recognition that recovery includes relapse (Prochaska, Norcross, & DiClemente, 1994). It is premised on the understanding that change is a process and that individuals fluctuate between going forward and regressing, all as a part of the change process. The efficacy of this model has led to its adaptation to changing other health-related behaviors, such as quitting smoking. This model allows the practitioner to engage the substance abusing individual at a point before or during the change process from a position of unconditional acceptance, a recognition of human potential, and an effort to reduce harm and strengthen motivation.

Pharmacological Treatment

Treatment of substance abuse can include medications directed at blocking the craving that leads to the substance use. Agonist therapy includes methadone programs and opioid substitutes. Buprenorphine has been used with opioids (Johnson et al., 2000, as cited in IOM, 2006); naltrexone (sold as ReVia) and acamprosate are prescribed in dealing with alcohol use (Kranzler & Van Kirk, 2001) as is disulfiram (Antabuse). Straussner (2004) suggests that the effectiveness of this treatment is questionable; however, agonist therapies have utility when they complement other treatments.

Psychosocial Interventions

Psychosocial interventions such as cognitive behavioral therapy (CBT), contingency management, and motivational interviewing (MI), have been shown to be highly efficacious. The cognitive behavioral approach focuses on the development of new behaviors by practicing adaptive behaviors in response to hypothetical situations and practicing between sessions (Foreyt & Goodrick, 2001). The principles of contingency management, most often utilized in abstinence-focused treatment, emphasize the reinforcement of behaviors that demonstrate attempts at making progress, such as adherence to testing by providing or withholding reward (Callaghan & Jones, 2010). Contingency management rewards the smallest of behaviors (e.g., completion of urine testing) in the service of remaining engaged with clients as they slowly implement positive changes at a pace that is manageable for them. It makes use of various rewards—such as cash, vouchers, or even methadone treatment—that can be administered at home (Iguchi et al., 1996). This approach has been found to be successful for individuals with a cocaine addiction, helping them to stay in treatment and to improve social outcomes, such as gaining employment and engaging in less substance use (Higgins et al., 2003).

Psychoeducation for individuals and their families is recognized as an effective intervention that provides knowledge on the course of disorders, their symptoms, strategies for coping with co-occurring disorders, and effective treatment approaches. Gingerich and Mueser (2005) point out that psychoeducation "alone is not associated with improved outcomes defined as reduced relapses and rehospitalizations" (p. 398) and that it is most useful to assist in making informed decisions. Psychoeducation can also provide information on medications, such as their side effects and usefulness.

Group work encompasses several approaches with differences based on purpose, structure, function, and process (Yalom, 2005). The purpose is determined by the consumer needs and interpersonal/psychological capacity; structure regards logistical needs such as setting, length of activity, and number of members; function relates to processes that will be utilized to build group cohesion such as rules or norms; and process addresses expectations about the nature of the interaction, which can range from interpersonal, behavioral change, support group, or task group. Group interventions are valuable in providing opportunities to build interpersonal skills and, depending on the group activity, can also build self-esteem. Group activity focused on tasks—such as cooking, music, art, or program decision making—can provide opportunities for relational connection as well as the development of various interpersonal skills.

Harm Reduction

Harm reduction is an approach, not characterized by any one intervention, and emphasizes prevention. It has the benefit of working with problem behavior to reduce harm and suffering of the individual and society by making risky behaviors less risky. Rather than focus exclusively on abstinence, the approach aims to minimize potential harm, such as with "homelessness, contracting HIV/AIDS, injection abscesses, legal consequences, or whatever is a concern to the person" and includes services such as needle exchange programs (Davis, 2008, p. 312). Marlatt (1998) proposes that harm reduction is an approach of choice because risky behaviors will never be eliminated on a societal level; therefore, a public health-based approach with a focus on reducing stigma is preferable to a moralistic judgment-based approach, and access to services that do not require abstinence are effective at engaging clients. Roberts, Bewley-Taylor, and Trace (2006, in Davis, 2008) suggest that on an international level reduction of rates of death and disease, crime costs, and environmental damage are far more meaningful than reduction of use rates. Harm reduction contrasts significantly with the law enforcement zero tolerance approach espoused by the George H. W. Bush administration that aimed to eliminate illegal drugs (McNeece & DiNitto, 2005). It is a misconception to view the harm reduction approach as condoning substance use; the aim is to reduce risky behavior. As opposed to zero tolerance, the focus is on change in relation to a continuum from safer use, to managed use, to abstinence. Psychotherapy interventions that are integrated into this approach include behavior therapy, CBT, dialectical behavioral therapy (DBT), and MI.

Motivational Interviewing

MI emphasizes resolving ambivalence for the purpose of changing behavior by evoking intrinsic motivation. This engagement and treatment approach is characterized by four principles: expressing empathy, developing discrepancy, rolling with the resistance, and supporting self-efficacy. The assumptions that underlie this approach are the importance of taking the client's perspective, heightening awareness about differences between one's goals and values and one's behavior, going with the client's resistance rather than contesting it, and communicating belief in a person's capacity to follow through successfully on identified activities (Miller & Rollnick, 2002).

Co-Occurring Treatment Approach

Recognition of the significant amount of co-occurring substance use and mental disorders, along with the lack of available, relevant treatment, has led to increased attention to the need to develop service delivery programs for the treatment of co-occurring disorders. Comprehensive continuous integrated systems of care for individuals with co-occurring disorders (CCISC), developed by Minkoff (2001), is an approach that aims to provide integrated services for consumers with SMI and substance abuse disorders, who are frequently difficult to engage, by utilizing a multisystems perspective. The approach incorporates principles, practice guidelines, and clinical standards that encompass clinician protocols as well as organizational policy. The principles include the following assumptions: (a) co-occurring disorders are an expectation, not an exception; (b) effective interventions are empathic and convey hope within an integrated approach (i.e., substance use and mental disorder) and continuous relationship; (c) treatment is individualized, particularly in relation to severity of both disorders; (d) interventions need to address the client's phase of treatment and phase of change in relation to each disorder; (e) mental health and substance abuse professionals should have expertise in both types of disorders; (f) treatment should proceed within a long-term perspective that promotes continuity with practitioners; (g) admission to treatment should be based on the consumer's motivation and readiness with any constellation of co-occurring disorders; (h) service delivery should aim to reach the most isolated individuals, such as the homeless; and (i) budget and administration of the organization should support the system's mission as reflected in these principles (Minkoff, 2001).

It is noteworthy that the Comprehensive Continuous Integrated System of Care (CCISC) challenges clinicians and staff to demonstrate welcoming behavior from the first contact with the consumer and throughout treatment. Historically, individuals with co-occurring disorders, formally called dual diagnoses, experienced barriers in services. Neither mental health nor substance professionals addressed the totality of the individual's challenges in coping with both disorders; psychiatric programs typically refused to accept patients with substance abuse disorders, and vice versa. Key features of the CCISC include clinical treatment of co-occurring disorders as primary disorders, the use of both the disease and recovery model with parallel phases of treatment, and treatment by professionals with expertise in both substance abuse and mental health (Minkoff, 2001).

Systemic change that incorporates quality and outcome measures, practice guidelines for "assessment, treatment, and rehabilitation, and psychopharmacology" for clinicians (e.g., including the identification of stage of change and not prohibiting the use of medication to address the co-occurring mental disorder due to the consumer's use of substances), identification of competencies, and development of training curricula are all necessary components of an effective response to co-occurring disorders (Minkoff, 2001). Significantly, this approach emphasizes providing consumers with what they need, when and where they need it. Professionals who treat co-occurring disorders practice within their respective substance abuse and mental health settings with the intention of providing integrated services rather than remaining in their separate domains of conceptualization and treatment. Minkoff and Cline (2004) identify 12 steps for CCISC implementation, which are invaluable courses of action for the systemic changes that must occur at an organizational level in order for front-line clinicians to achieve effectiveness with co-occurring–disordered consumers.

Sowers and Rohland (2004) propose a Level of Care Utilization System for Psychiatric and Addiction Services (LOCUS), which offers guidelines for continuity in treatment and recovery services for co-occurring disorders. The guidelines are invaluable for identifying an integrative, comprehensive framework for addressing both substance use and disorders. Moreover, the guidelines enhance effective assessment and treatment by operationalizing outcomes that can guide implementation of services.

KEY POINTS

1. Strength-based intervention models integrate substance abuse treatment with treatment for co-occurring disorders and employ a variety of strategies, including individual counseling, family and group work, and psychoeducation.
2. Effective responses, such as harm reduction and MI strategies, match individual readiness with the level of interventions.

3. Integrated treatment models emphasize a welcoming attitude toward persons with co-occurring disorders, regardless of the complexity of co-occurring conditions, and a removal of procedural and attitudinal barriers to access.
4. Effective responses to co-occurring disorders value giving the consumers of treatment what they need wherever the need it, calling for increased flexibility and creativity in engaging clients.

EQUITY AND DIVERSITY ISSUES

Equity assures quality, individualized services. Diversity concerns highlight culturally relevant practice within a social justice perspective. Examples of research that addresses both equity and diversity dealt with appreciation of conceptions of illness such as anxiety and depression for elder Mexican Americans and implementation of culturally based substance use models of care with indigenous Native Americans and Alaskans (Croff, Rieckmann, & Spence, 2013; Letamendi et al., 2013). Culturally relevant practice is based on the awareness of culturally based substance practices. For example, some substances that produce mild intoxications are culturally identified resources; when chewed, betel nut creates mild euphoria; and kava promotes sedation, weight loss, and mild forms of hepatitis. The increased use of over-the-counter and prescription drugs in the United States raises questions regarding the ubiquity and normalization of substance use in dominant American culture as well as in subcultures based on ethnicity, class, and/or religion.

Evidence indicates that the rates of substance dependence and abuse increased between 2002 and 2006 by 5.7% for women, 10% for Latinos, 9.4% for Whites, and 8.5% for Blacks (Department of Health and Human Services, 2008). In 2007, rates of substance dependence or abuse were associated with level of education. Among adults 18 years of age and older who had a 4-year higher education degree, the rate was 7.5% compared with those who did not graduate from college (9.8%) or had some college (10.3%). In 2007, rates of substance dependence or abuse were also associated with employment status; unemployed adults showed higher rates (20.0%) compared with the full-time employed (10.1%) or part-time employed (10.6%). The striking differences in findings raise questions about what these profiles mean in each category in the context of a recent economically stressful historic period. It is noteworthy that recent reports by the National Institute on Drug Abuse (NIDA, 2010) suggest little change in rates of substance use within a context of a huge stressor, as seen in the post 2006 economic downturn. However, NIDA findings point to increased nonmedical use of prescription drugs by 12th graders. All too often the complex of factors that place individuals at risk for co-occurring disorders (e.g., intersectionality of class, gender, ethnicity) or the costs incurred by individuals, their families, and communities are not sufficiently understood. For example, self-efficacy, motivation for sobriety, and physical health (Kelly & Greene, 2014; Tripp, Skidmore, Cui, & Tate, 2013) have been associated with positive outcomes and are reminders of the necessity of thorough assessments and individualized treatment.

Various issues surface in relation to substance use within different populations. Vinton and Wambach (2005) propose that there is some indication that at least 10% of persons of age 65 and over abuse alcohol and are more likely than other age groups to deny that they have a problem. Rondero Hernandez and Mendoza's (2011) research on the effects of shame on Latina substance abusers highlights their resiliency in response to interventions that focus on assisting them to (a) recognize shame and its triggers and expectations that fuel the shame; (b) develop skill in securing empathy and support; and (c) learn to express their feelings, particularly in relation to asking for what they need.

STRENGTH-BASED CONTRIBUTIONS TO DIAGNOSIS AND TREATMENT

The co-occurring focus on the combined treatment of substance abuse and mental health issues is fundamentally a strength-based approach that includes elements of the recovery model, as discussed in Chapter 8 in this text. By integrating the importance of a welcoming stance on the part of the clinician and working from the identified motivational aspects within the client's behavioral repertoire, clients can experience the type of person-centered interaction that facilitates their engagement in treatment. Specifically, the strength-based features of a co-occurring focus of treatment involve viewing individuals in their contextual totality and realistically addressing the importance of coping with both types of disorders. This necessitates sustaining continuity in mental health treatment as the individual periodically cycles back and forth through recovery and relapse. The client's long-term commitment to treatment, along with the long-term commitment of treating professionals to the client, must be strengthened so that these commitments can override the situational decline into substance use and/or relapse into mental illness.

Strength-based clinical interaction is characterized by various elements. The terminology utilized in practice is but one facet of a constellation of factors that combine to demonstrate a client-centered, strength-based approach. Use of the term *adherence*, which conveys decision making by the consumer, in place of the term *compliance*, which suggests obedience to directions imposed by an external authority, is a small but meaningful shift from a medical model approach.

Continued debate about the application of the disease model to understanding substance abuse, based on the assumption of lack of control, suggests the need for mindful consideration by clinicians about the implications of the concepts that are chosen to drive practice. Although use of the term *disease* initially was a positive change in 1950s from a view of addiction as a moral weakness, the concept implies acceptance of the medical model and the belief in the primacy of predisposing biological risk factors, such as defects in neurotransmitter functioning, deficiencies in enzymes, and arousal dysregulation (Brown, 1995; Wallace, 2003), as exclusive explanations of co-occurring disorders. On the other hand, 12-step programs, such as Alcoholics Anonymous, Narcotics Anonymous, Alanon, and Alateen, have undoubtedly saved many lives and arguably continue to be the mainstay of effective empowerment of substance abusers through the fellowship of the group, despite the program's essential belief in a disease model of causation. Although Alcoholics Anonymous does not engage in research or formal professional affiliations, this global fellowship fundamentally facilitates the empowerment of its members who choose to follow the 12 steps of the program, adhering to its model of abstinence, explained in the *Big Book*, now its third edition, and first published in 1937 (Alcoholics Anonymous World Services, 2001).

KEY POINTS

1. Alcohol and substance use affect all socioeconomic groups throughout society.
2. The understanding of etiology according to the medical/disease model can be used to stigmatize and shame or conversely to empower those with substance disorders through psychoeducation and referral to 12-step programs.
3. Hidden co-occurring depression and substance abuse includes persons who abuse prescription drugs and the rising rate of alcohol and substance abuse among elders. These realities cry out for interventions that address the shame and stigma that inhibits access to care.
4. Socioeconomic status (SES) factors present a variable pattern in the incidence of co-occurring disorders, but economic pressures make things worse, contributing to more alcohol and drug abuse and greater co-occurring anxiety and depression.
5. Effective strength-based to co-occurring disorders require culturally competent integrative models that simultaneously address both substance use and mental disorders.

DSM-5 DISCUSSION

CASE STUDY WITH AND WITHOUT THE DIVERSITY/RESILIENCY FORMULATION

Co-Occurring Disorder

Ariel is a 25-year-old European Latino female whose father, Leon, age 57, is Puerto Rican and whose mother, Anne Marie, age 55, is ethnic White. Ariel has one brother, Sam, who is 2 years older than she. She was diagnosed in adolescence with schizophrenia, paranoid type, and later with bipolar II disorder, depressed. The onset of paranoid and psychotic symptoms occurred following a transition into a new high school setting, at the age of 16, from a private to a public school in a large city in the eastern United States. Ariel's childhood was primarily stable with the family living in the same home throughout her growing-up years. Her father completed community college and owns a hardware store. Her mother completed high school, has taken community college classes, and is employed as a hair stylist. From the time she was 5, Ariel's family life was characterized by her father's long hours at work and her mother's employment, which meant growing up with babysitters as a latchkey child. Her parents' marriage was stormy. Hearing her parents argue with raised voices was very upsetting to her and led her to isolate herself in her bedroom. On one occasion, during a middle-school field trip, the school bus was hit by a car on the highway, leaving a few students injured. Ariel was uninjured but was very distressed by the event, because she was friends with the students who were hurt.

The period before her shift from private to public school was fraught with stress owing to the effects of bullying activity by older girls, its negative impact on her ability to concentrate on her work, and the consequent need for academic assistance with math and science classes. Ariel found it frustrating that although her parents made efforts to tutor her, she did not experience this as helpful. Shortly before the transfer to public school, tensions with her private school peers intensified; they began to harass her both on and off campus. As Ariel's academic difficulties worsened, she increasingly worried about not doing well and became withdrawn from the few friends she had. The only bright spot in her memory of these years was her participation in the private school choir, led by an inspiring and supportive teacher. Music class was a refuge for Ariel, where she felt welcomed and confident. The significant social and academic stresses Ariel continued to experience at the private school coincided with her parent's need, for economic reasons, to move her to a public school. Although she was relieved to get away from the bullying, she was dismayed about having to part with her beloved music teacher and start all over again in a new school setting.

The shift to the public school brought its own difficulties with respect to Ariel's making new friends and finding her place in the new setting. To make matters worse, this change coincided with Ariel's need to adjust to a changing body image and cope with the onset of menstruation. The interpersonal challenges of meeting new students and teachers eventually affected her grades, which continued to decline. Ariel began to spend time with friends she met through her brother, going to parties, and staying out late in increased defiance of her parents' attempts to control her. For the first time she started to use street drugs, such as marijuana, amphetamines, and LSD. Eventually, Ariel was rarely present at school. She was sleeping all day, which further isolated her from other students. In an attempt to assist her in completing her junior year, Ariel was transferred to a special program for at-risk students, but this intervention did not succeed. Ariel's world came to consist of social gatherings with a mixture of students who were still in school and others who had dropped out; drug use was a routine and predictable part of their activity.

Ariel's brother, Sam, who had been diagnosed with attention-deficit hyperactivity disorder (ADHD) in the fifth grade, was instrumental in introducing her to drugs, both by providing them to her and bringing her into his circle of friends who used street drugs. One of them, Geoff, age 19, became Ariel's boyfriend. She gained weight during this period and began using cocaine, in part at the suggestion of a girlfriend who recommended the drug as a way to control weight. Ariel often had auditory and visual hallucinations and was convinced someone was "after her." After using cocaine for 4 or 5 months, she dropped out of school completely and began working full time. Ariel describes using cocaine each morning as a way to deal with the tiredness that she constantly felt. She describes "being awake but feeling like she was asleep with dreams from her unconscious coming into her awareness in waking life" in a frightening way.

Most of these waking "dreams" had nightmarish content dealing with someone "coming after me" or someone trying to "hurt me."

Eventually Anne Marie became sufficiently distressed about her daughter's condition that she drove her to a hospital for an assessment, whereupon Ariel was initially hospitalized for 72 hours. She was diagnosed with co-occurring disorders, including schizophrenia, paranoid type; amphetamine abuse; and cocaine dependence. Ariel was subsequently hospitalized for 4 months with treatment focused on stabilizing her on psychotropic medication. Her parents attempted to participate in treatment meetings to discuss Ariel's diagnosis and progress, but they did not feel welcomed by the hospital staff. At one point the parents were asked to leave a treatment-planning meeting with the explanation that the planning process did not require their involvement. They were informed that Ariel's substance abuse and possible trauma may both have played a role in the hallucinations, delusions, and paranoia that she experienced and that the substance abuse was the dominant factor in the development of her symptoms.

Ariel's treatment was basically determined by the health care (psychiatrist, social worker, rehabilitation, and nursing) staff. Her parents found it difficult to balance medical appointments with the obligations of their jobs and felt that their voices were not welcomed or heard by the service providers. The parents felt at a loss regarding what Ariel's symptoms meant or what they ought to do. They had little support from extended family or friends as they tried to find the needed resources for treatment. Remarkably, while hospitalized, Ariel continued with her academic studies and her interest in music. She corresponded occasionally with her former choir teacher and enjoyed listening to CDs of choral music. It was terrifying, however, for her to be surrounded by others who were suicidal and displayed physically agitated behavior. In addition, Ariel's medication had negative effects, often leaving her feeling physically ill or very tired. When she refused to take her medications orally, Ariel received injections. She was particularly troubled by the fact that she understood that she was taking part in a clinical trial, but she did not know what this meant. Ariel attempted to talk with the psychiatrists about the medication, but she did not feel that they listened to her. She also found their attitudes at times to be patronizing and demeaning.

On discharge, Ariel lived in a board-and-care home for 6 months, where services were limited to caregiving; counseling was not available. Following the board-and-care arrangement, she moved home; however, this period was fraught with threatening, stalking behavior by her boyfriend, Geoff, which included, on one occasion, his striking her and her car with a bat. Geoff's stalking continued on and off for 6 years. He sometimes hid in the bushes on her property with a gun. Ariel was terrified of him and had said that she was afraid that he wanted to kill her; but because of her drug use and bipolar diagnoses, she felt that her fears were dismissed as symptoms of paranoia. Geoff's history as a self-mutilator ("cutter"), along with episodes of holding a gun to his head and threatening to kill himself, had left Ariel fearful of any contact with him. The effects of his history of molestation by an uncle and his parents' divorce when he was a 5-year-old were never dealt with and were undoubtedly a factor in Geoff's increasingly harmful, frightening behavior. The stress of dealing with his violent disposition provoked and intensified feelings of generalized paranoia in Ariel.

The uneasiness brought on by this situation led Ariel to go back and forth between living at home and staying with friends. As a result, her difficulties increased. She had less contact with her family and missed them, yet she was unable to adhere to their expectations, leading to even more alienation between them. The inability of either Ariel or her parents to cope with her problems eventually led to her being placed on a conservatorship, creating even more conflict between Ariel and her parents. The effects of her substance use and psychological state also caused deterioration in her friendships. Eventually Ariel was hospitalized again in a rehabilitation center for adolescents, where she received a diagnosis of bipolar II disorder, depressed. The staff made little to no effort to involve the parents or explain the medication and symptoms to them. This second hospitalization coincided with Geoff's moving out of state and losing contact with Ariel. The primary purpose of the second hospitalization was to detoxify Ariel from cocaine use and address her depression.

Throughout the period of hospitalizations, Ariel never felt suicidal. The family does not have a history of suicide, schizophrenia, or bipolar disorder. Despite the hospitalizations, she completed community college and transferred to a 4-year college, where she is currently studying to be a music teacher. In time, she discovered that her former boyfriend had committed suicide. As difficult as it was to receive this news and to relive her past memories of Geoff, Ariel felt relief at not having to fear his possible intrusion into her life again. With the stability of college courses, a focus on her interest in music, the help of the student counseling service at her university, and regular attendance at Narcotics Anonymous meetings on campus, Ariel has increasingly been able to recognize her needs and to examine her relationships in the context of those needs. Although she struggles with self-doubt, loneliness, and feelings of distance from and ambivalence toward her parents, she is motivated and determined to complete school and pursue her chosen career. She recognizes the effects of a drug culture and how it has undermined her capacity to be close to others, because in reality substances had become her primary relationship to the exclusion of all others.

Case Commentary *DSM-5* Diagnosis With and Without the Addition of the Diversity/Resiliency Formulation

Ariel's diagnosis, which changed in subsequent hospitalizations, was:

Diagnosis: Schizophrenia, with Catatonia
305.70 Amphetamine Type Substance,
305.60 Cocaine Dependence

As illustrated earlier in this chapter, co-occurring substance abuse and other psychiatric disorders present a confusing diagnostic picture, and the proliferation of diagnoses over time is not uncommon. The presence of possible trauma in her history was alluded to by Ariel and is included previously, but it is unknown to what extent the school bus accident in her childhood created lingering posttraumatic effects. It may be that the atmosphere of strife between her parents over time was a more important source of anxiety and insecurity, leaving her more vulnerable to bullying at school and self-doubt about her academic abilities. The intensity of her depression, exacerbated by drug use, along with the prolonged effects of victimization by both her school peers and her boyfriend, her increased isolation from prosocial school peers, and the loss of her music teacher combined to fill Ariel with paranoid anxiety, expressed to the psychiatric hospital staff as the belief that "someone wants to kill me" and "people are out to get me." However, Ariel had exhibited no prodromal signs or negative symptoms of schizophrenia, and her paranoia proved to be based on a great deal of reality as well as secondary to substance abuse; also, Ariel had no family history of bipolar disorder or schizophrenia. Ariel's family history, and the more recent effects of stalking by her boyfriend, suggested the possibility of posttraumatic stress disorder.

Ariel is in a better place today, probably because she was never truly bipolar or schizophrenic. She possesses strengths that involve musical ability and personal determination and was removed from her drug-using environment by her hospitalization. On the other hand, her experiences in psychiatric and aftercare facilities leave a lot to be desired. From the outset, Ariel's description of her paranoid symptoms, based in real experiences of bullying peers and an abusive boyfriend, were discounted and mislabeled as evidence—first of schizophrenia and later of a bipolar disorder. The effects of growing up in the context of her parents' stormy marriage and a frightening school environment, along with the possible long-term impact of the school bus incident, were not explored in a treatment setting that was focused on giving her medications for an inaccurate diagnosis. To make matters worse, the medications themselves blunted Ariel's ability to use the strengths she did have with respect to her interest in music and her desire to maintain the few prosocial friendships she had. Further, the experience with psychiatric personnel was a negative one for both Ariel and her parents, whose estrangement from Ariel and her treatment was deepened by their being excluded—or their perception that they were being excluded—from her treatment. It seems that Ariel's treating professionals did convey that substance abuse was of overriding importance in her symptoms, but the medical decisions regarding psychopharmacology remain a mystery to Ariel and her parents to this day. The treatment, in fact, deepened the rift and mutual antagonism between Ariel and her parents—a lost opportunity for family healing. Ariel came to feel that her parents had abandoned her to psychiatric bureaucracies. Ariel's hospitalizations may well have kept her alive by removing her access to street drugs and thus containing her behavior for a time, but the exclusive focus on medications not only ignored important environmental contexts but also made her problems worse by robbing her of energy and focus and medicating her for diagnoses that were inaccurate. Ariel was a victim of the prevailing tendency of psychiatry, especially with respect to acting-out, drug-using teenagers, to control and medicate.

Adding Diversity/Resiliency Formulation Information to Ariel's Diagnosis

To begin with, we believe that had diversity and resiliency content been a core consideration in Ariel's diagnosis, Ariel's own account of her anxieties would have been taken seriously and their bases in reality more accurately understood. Rather than viewing her parents as an impediment to her treatment, they would have been viewed as core sources of attachment in her life and invited to participate fully, along with Ariel and with her agreement, in all decisions about her diagnosis and treatment. With a more careful family history and sensitive attention to Ariel's story, her diagnosis would most likely have been limited to the categories of drug dependence and abuse, along with depression, mixed with anxiety, possibly related to past and ongoing trauma. Medications for schizophrenia and/or bipolar disorder would not have been prescribed; instead, she might have been given antianxiety agents temporarily, which would have helped to restore normal sleep and eating patterns. A primary emphasis on healthy coping behaviors, family involvement, and restoration of Ariel's vocational goals would also have been helpful. The following is Ariel's Diversity/Resiliency Formulation (DRF) in outline form.

Intrapersonal: Above average intelligence; musical interest and ability; desire for prosocial friendships; personality traits of persistence and motivation for college
Interpersonal: Attachment to former music teacher; former neighborhood and school friends; willingness of family to participate in family counseling; parental valuing of education and positive work ethic
Community: Lifelong residence in the same community; parental occupational connections to local community college and businesses
Spiritual: Intermittent attendance at a local community church
Cultural: Curiosity about her mother's Danish ancestry and father's Puerto Rican heritage, but never explored

Comments on the Diversity/Resiliency Formulation

Despite the strengths noted on the DRF, Ariel would probably still have needed hospitalization. There were many complex issues involved that included parental marital discord, problems with peer group (victim of bullying), drug-using peer culture, academic problems, past traumatic experience (school bus accident). However, attention to her sources of resiliency and strength, noted in the DRF, may have had a significant impact on the attitude of the psychiatric staff toward her parents and toward Ariel herself. Arguably, at the time of her admission, Ariel's parents were exhausted and angry with her, probably struggling with guilt and shame, doubting their abilities as parents, and possibly blaming her for their own marital problems. If the hospital environment had drawn a protective and educational circle around her parents as well as around Ariel, empathizing with the worry and strain of having a daughter with long-standing and frightening drug and peer problems and reaching out to her family as sources of support rather than as irritating impediments to be managed, her diagnosis might have been more accurate from the start and related interventions would have focused intensively and immediately on her involvement in Narcotics Anonymous, special tutoring, family counseling, and relapse prevention. The use of antipsychotic drugs would have been avoided, and Ariel would instead have been offered classes in self-defense, meditation, journal writing, and substance abuse recovery and been encouraged to seek out her former music teacher for personal mentoring and support. She also would have been introduced to sports activities, such as swimming, jogging, tennis, and soccer, for the purpose of exploring forms of physical exercise that she could build into her life. Using the concepts of multisystemic family therapy, active and intense follow-up with the family would have been offered, including crisis phone counseling, a 12-step sponsor, and a circle of neighborhood friends who would commit to specific behaviors in support of Ariel's recovery. Ariel and her parents would have been active participants all along the way in the process of diagnosis and treatment planning. With intensive attention to environmental strengths, Ariel's subsequent drug abuse, rehospitalization, and stay in an aftercare facility might have been prevented, and she could have experienced a less lengthy derailment in her academic career.

Because the formation of identity is the defining developmental challenge of adolescence, Ariel might also have been encouraged to get to know her own cultural history by exploring her parents' sense of their cultural roots and the unique characteristics of Danish and Puerto Rican ethnic identity. In so doing, she might have come to see her parents as interesting characters in their own right rather than simply as being critical and rejecting of her. Further inquiry about the family's spiritual identification might also have encouraged them to become more involved in their local church if this were deemed to be a potentially important source of support. In addition, school personnel, such as social workers and counselors, would have been invited to be a part of treatment planning in order to provide a supportive environment for Ariel after she was discharged from the hospital.

Obviously the crisis nature of Ariel's initial hospitalization did not allow for an exhaustive exploration of these resiliency sources at the outset. However, an attitude that took into consideration Ariel's sources of resiliency as well as her sources of stress and pathology would have conveyed more hope and the possibility of conflict resolution to her family, contributed to a more accurate initial diagnostic impression, and perhaps have prevented the arduous course of relapse and recovery that ensued. For too much of the diagnostic and treatment process, Ariel was a casualty of the psychiatric profession's current single-minded focus on medication, aimed at signs (in this case inaccurately interpreted) of pathology and dismissive of the unique complexity of the whole person and her context.

SUMMARY

Substance use disorders take their toll on individuals, their families, and society in relation to the level of functional impairment, short- and long-term physiological effects, and the consequences for education, employment, and interpersonal activities. Both illicit and legal bases of addiction are now included in the *DSM*, and the combination of criteria and specifiers will enhance the diagnostic process and thereby support improved treatment and intervention planning. Recognition of the co-occurrence of substance abuse and mental health disorders and newly developed approaches have advanced and improved practice goals and objectives within a multisystem framework. It is increasingly recognized that, in order to respond effectively to individuals with substance abuse and co-occurring disorders, change on the clinical practice and organizational levels will be required. The disease model of substance use remains one of the main underlying assumptions of causation and a foundation for 12-step programs. When 12-step and other substance use models, such as harm reduction, are embraced in conjunction with a recovery model approach, there is a potential for creative, empowering, integrative responses to interventions with co-occurring disorders. Increased knowledge of biological functions, such as the importance of the dopamine system in brain functioning, in part underscores the persistence of the disease model perspective, which has had a significant role in the perpetuation of stigma. The new challenge is now to take the best of what has been discovered in empirical research and in best practices with consumers and their families toward the promotion of increased functioning within a supportive and integrated service delivery system.

DISCUSSION QUESTIONS AND ACTIVITIES

1. Individualized treatment and the removal of stigma must be implemented in the treatment of individuals with co-occurring disorders. Some mental health treatment programs decline to treat such clients for fear that this population would influence other agency consumers toward substance use. How would you approach this as a clinician? As an agency policy maker?
2. Strength-based values that underlie the Comprehensive CCISC for individuals with co-occurring disorders presume that clinicians' interactions will communicate and demonstrate welcoming behavior. How do you intend to do that?
3. CCISC interventions include educating the consumer about the value of adhering to psychiatric medication and simultaneously participating in substance abuse programs, such as a 12-step program. What barriers do you imagine you might encounter with the consumer? How do you expect that you might address them?
4. The CCISC is based on systems change in that positive outcomes cannot be accomplished by individual clinician effort alone but rather require systemic policy and programming. What skills and supports do you feel you need to utilize or develop in order to engage in and support organizational change toward the goal of integrated service delivery?
5. Addiction is explained by three broad perspectives: biological, psychological, and sociocultural.
   a. Which of the three do you find most compelling?
   b. What is your rationale?

   c. What is it about this perspective, in your view, that gets at the core of issues involving assessment and prioritization?

6. Individuals' perspectives about substance use are influenced by behaviors and practices (e.g., addiction, substance use) that they were exposed to (or not exposed to) in their formative years in their homes and neighborhoods.
   a. How would you identify your experience with substances in your youth? Exposure in the home, in the neighborhood, or no exposure?
   b. These formative experiences can lead to subjective responses in which we may overestimate or underestimate the seriousness of the use or the intentions of the client. What is your impression of the effects of your experience on your perceptions of substance users?
7. Simultaneous intervention with co-occurring substance abuse and mental health disorders is now the treatment of choice. In light of your educational and practice experiences, consider the following:
   a. What knowledge and skills do you have that prepare you for this intervention approach?
   b. What knowledge and skills do you need to enhance and/or develop to work effectively in a co-occurring treatment setting?
   c. What resources would you need to learn more about a co-occurring practice approach?
8. Imagine that you are a physician, social worker, nurse, or psychologist in a mental health setting, such as an outpatient clinic or psychiatric hospital. Clients are often brought to this setting with a confusing set of symptoms that may or may not clearly represent a diagnosis of substance abuse, SMI, or both. You are concerned that with the pressures of time and dwindling resources, these clients are too often not adequately assessed or responded to in a comprehensive manner and as a result may be inadequately assessed and treated (e.g., over- or undermedicated), and not fully understood with respect to the complicated contexts of their lives.
   a. How might you use the perspectives of the DRF in the service of more accurate diagnosis and effective treatment?
   b. How would you advocate for a response to family, community, cultural, or other environmental factors in the patient's situation that you believe are critical to the onset and continuation of his or her co-occurring disorder (i.e., substance abuse and mental disorder)?
   c. Prepare a hypothetical PowerPoint presentation regarding these issues to the medical staff, the interdisciplinary team, the hospital administration, or other relevant decision-making body.
9. Attend at least two Alcoholics Anonymous, Narcotics Anonymous, Alanon, or Alateen meetings in different socioeconomic areas of your community. What do you notice about the atmosphere and content of the meeting? Reflect in writing on your experience. To deepen this experience, talk to a 12-step sponsor affiliated with the group and listen to his or her story of addiction, recovery, and experiences as a mentor to others.

10. Think about the culture of your profession (e.g., a teacher of higher education, a physician, nurse, minister, social worker, or psychologist) and its implicit attitudes toward co-occurring substance abuse and a mental disorder. If you had a problem with alcohol, drugs, and depression, would you feel safe in disclosing this to a colleague and asking for help? What would it take for you to do so? How would you respond to such a disclosure made by a colleague?

WEB RESOURCES

http://drugabuse.gov/nidahome.html
http://oas.samhsa.gov
www.aa.org
www.al-anon.alateen.org
www.asam.org
www.draonline.org
www.ihra.net/files/2010/08/10/Briefing_What_is_HR_English.pdf
www.mha.org
www.na.org
www.nasmhpd.org
www.nasmhpd.org
www.psych.org

REFERENCES

Abram, K. M., & Teplin, L. A. (1991). Co-occurring disorders among mentally ill jail detainees. *American Psychologist, 46*(10), 1036–1045.

Alcoholics Anonymous World Services. (2001). *Alcoholics anonymous: The big book* (3rd ed.). New York, NY: Author.

American Psychiatric Association. (2000). *Diagnostic and statistical manual of mental disorders* (4th ed., text rev.). Washington, DC: Author.

American Psychiatric Association. (2010). *Cocaine-use disorder*. Retrieved from www.dsm5.org/ProposedRevisions/Pages/proposedrevision.aspx?rid=455#/

American Psychiatric Association. (2013). *Diagnostic and statistical manual of mental disorders* (5th ed.). Arlington, VA: American Psychiatric Press.

Anton, R. F., O'Malley, S. S., Ciraulo, D. A., Cisler, R. A., Couper, D., Donovan, D. M., … Gastfriend, D. R. (2006). Combined pharmacotherapies and behavioral interventions for alcohol dependence. *Journal of the American Medical Association, 295*, 2003–2017.

Bachman, R. (1992). *Death and violence on the reservation*. New York, NY: Auburn House.

Beattie, J., Battersby, M. W., & Pols, R. G. (2013). The acceptability and outcomes of a peer-and health-professional-led Stanford self-management program for Vietnam veterans with alcohol misuse and their partners. *Psychiatric Rehabilitation Journal, 39*, 386–391.

Brown, S. (1995). Introduction. In S. Brown & I. D. Yalom (Eds.), *Treating alcoholism* (pp. 3–25). San Francisco, CA: Jossey-Bass.

Callaghan, P., & Jones, D. (2010). Psychological interventions. In P. Phillips, O. McKeown, & T. Sandford (Eds.), *Dual diagnosis: Practice in context* (pp. 67–75). Chichester, UK: Wiley-Blackwell.

Crits-Christoph, P., Siqueland, L., Blaine, J., Frank, A., Luborsky, L., Onken, L. S., Muenz, L. R., … Beck A. T. (1999). Psychosocial treatments for cocaine dependence: National Institute on Drug Abuse Collaborative Cocaine Treatment Study. *Archives of General Psychiatry, 56*, 493–502.

Croff, R. L., Rieckmann, T. R., & Spence, J. D. (2013). Provider and state perspectives on implementing cultural based models of care for American Indian and Alaska native patients with substance use disorders. *Journal of Behavioral Health Services & Research*, *41*, 64–79.

Davis, D. R. (2008). Harm reduction. In T. D. Mizrahi & L. E. Davis (Eds.), *Encyclopedia of social work* (20th ed., Vol. 2: D-I, pp. 312–314). Washington, DC: NASW Press & Oxford University Press.

Department of Health and Human Services. (2008, September). *Results from the 2007 National Survey on drug use and health: National findings*. Retrieved from www.oas.samhsa.gov/nsduh/2k7nsduh/2k7results.cfm/

Drug Abuse Warning Network. (2010, May 25). *Emergency department visits for drug related suicide attempts by young adults aged 18 to 24: 2008. The DAWN Report*. Retrieved from http://dawninfo.samhsa.gov/files/SpecTopics/DAWN2010_SR002.html/

Epstein, J., Barker, P., Vorburger, M., & Murtha, C. (2004). *Serious mental illness and its co-occurrence with substance use disorders, 2002* (DHHS Publication No. SMA 04–3905, Analytic Series A-24). Rockville, MD: Substance Abuse and Mental Health Services Administration, Office of Applied Studies.

Foreyt, J., & Goodrick, G. (2001). Cognitive behavioral therapy. In W. N. Craighead (Ed.), *The Corsini encyclopedia of psychology and behavioral science* (Vol. 1, pp. 308–312). New York, NY: John Wiley & Sons.

Gingerich, S., & Mueser, K. T. (2005). Illness management and recovery. In R. E. Drake, M. R. Merrens, & D. W. Lynde (Eds.), *Evidence-based mental health practice* (pp. 395–424). New York, NY: W. W. Norton.

Goldner, E. M., Lusted, A., Roerecke, M., Rehm, J., & Fischer, B. (2014). Prevalence of Axis-1 psychiatric disorder and symptomology among non-medical prescription opioid users in substance use treatment: Systematic review and meta-analyses. *Addictive Behaviors*, *39*, 520–531.

Goldstein, R. B. (2009). Comorbidity of substance use disorders with independent mood and anxiety disorders in women. Results from the National epidemiologic survey on alcohol and related conditions. In K. T. Brady, S. Back, & S. F. Greenfield (Eds.), *Women and addiction: A comprehensive handbook* (pp. 173–192). New York, NY: Guilford Press.

Goodman, J. D., McKay, J. R., & DePhilippis, D. (2013). Progress monitoring in mental health and addiction treatment: A means of improving care. *Professional Psychology: Research and Practice*, *44*(4), 231–246.

Goodwin, D. W. (1984). Studies of familial alcoholism: A review. *Journal of Clinical Psychiatry*, *45*(2), 14–17.

Hasin, D. S., Liu, X., Alderson, D., & Grant, B. (2006). *DSM-IV* alcohol dependence: A categorical or dimensional phenotype? *Psychological Medicine*, *36*, 1695–1705.

Higgins, S. T., Sigmon, S. C., Wong, C. J., Heil, S. H., Badger, G. J., Donham, R., ... Antony, S. (2003). Community reinforcement therapy for cocaine-dependent outpatients. *Archives of General Psychiatry*, *60*, 1043–1052.

Iguchi, M. Y., Lamb, R. J., Belding, M. A., Platt, J. J., Husband, S. D., & Morral, A. R. (1996). Contingent reinforcement of group participation versus abstinence in a methadone maintenance program. *Experimental and Clinical Psychopharmacology*, *4*, 315–321.

Institute of Medicine. (2006). *Improving the quality of health care for mental and substance-use conditions: Quality chasm series* (Committee on Crossing the Quality Chasm: Adaptation to Mental Health and Addictive Disorders). Washington, DC: National Academy Press.

Jellinek, E. M. (1952). Phases of alcohol addiction. *Quarterly Journal of Studies on Alcohol*, *13*, 673–684.

Kelly, J. F., & Green, M. C. (2014). Where there's a will there's a way: A longitudinal investigation of the interplay between recovery motivation and self-efficacy in predicting treatment outcome. *Psychology of Addictive Behaviors*, *28*(3), 928–934. doi:10.1037/a0034727

Kessler, R. C., Berglund, P., Demier, O., Jin, R., & Walters, E. (2005). Lifetime prevalence and age of onset distributions of *DSM-IV* disorders in the National Comorbidity Survey Replication. *Archives of General Psychiatry*, *62*(6), 593–602.

Kranzler, H. R., & Van Kirk, J. (2001). Efficacy of naltrexone and acamprostate for alcoholism treatment: A meta-analysis. *Alcoholism: Clinical and Experimental Research*, *25*, 1335–1341.

Letamendi, A. M., Ayers, C. R., Ruberg, J. L., Singley, D. B., Wilson, J., Chavira, D., ... Wetherell, J. L. (2013). Illness conceptualizations among older rural Mexican-Americans with anxiety and depression. *Journal of Cross Cultural Gerontology*, *28*, 421–433.

Marlatt, G. A. (1998). *Harm reduction: Pragmatic strategies for managing high-risk behaviors*. New York, NY: Guilford Press.

McGovern, M. P., Lambert-Harris, C., Gotham, H. J., Claus, R. E., & Xie, H. (2014). Dual diagnosis capability in mental health and addiction treatment services. An assessment of programs across multiple state systems. *Administration in Policy and Mental Health*, *41*, 205–214.

McNeece, C. A., & Barbanell, L. D. (2005). Definitions and epidemiology of substance use, abuse, and disorders. In C. A. McNeece & D. M. DiNitto (Eds.), *Chemical dependency: A systems approach* (3rd ed., pp. 3–24). Boston, MA: Allyn & Bacon.

McNeece, C. A., & DiNitto, D. M. (2005). *Chemical dependency: A systems approach* (3rd ed.). Boston, MA: Allyn & Bacon.

Miller, W. R., & Rollnick, S. (2002). *Motivational interviewing* (2nd ed.). New York, NY: Guilford Press.

Minkoff, K. (2001). Best practices: Developing standards of care for individuals with co-occurring psychiatric and substance use disorders. *Psychiatric Services*, *52*, 597–599.

Minkoff, K., & Cline, C. A. (2004). Changing the world: The design and implementation of comprehensive continuous integrated systems of care for individuals with co-occurring disorders. *Psychiatric Clinics of North America*, *27*(4), 727–743.

Mojtabai, R., Chen, L., Kaufmann, C. N., & Crum, R. M. (2014). Comparing barriers to mental health treatment and substance use disorder treatment among individuals with co-morbid major depression and substance use disorders. *Journal of Substance Abuse Treatment*, *46*, 268–273.

National Household Survey on Drug Abuse. (2002, July 12). *Substance use and the risk of suicide among youths. The NHSDA Report*. Retrieved from www.oas.samhsa.gov/2k2/suicide/suicide.htm

National Institute on Drug Abuse. (2010, January). *NIDA InfoFacts: Nationwide trends*. Retrieved from http://drugabuse.gov/pdf/infofacts/NationalTrends10.pdf/

National Research Council and Institute of Medicine. (2009). *Depression in parents, parenting and children: Opportunities to improve identification, treatment and prevention efforts*. Washington, DC: The National Academies Press. Retrieved from www.nap.edu/catalog,php?record_id=12565

National Survey on Drug Use and Health. (2004, June 23). *Adults with co-occurring serious mental illness and a substance use disorder. The NSDUH Report*. Retrieved from www.oas.samhsa.gov/2k4/coOccurring/co-Occurring.htm/

Prochaska, J. O., & DiClemente, C. C. (1982). Transtheoretical therapy: Toward a more integrative model of change. *Psychotherapy: Theory, Research and Practice*, *19*, 276–288.

Prochaska, J. O., & DiClemente, C. C. (1992). Stages of change in the modification of problem behaviors. In M. Hersen, R. M. Eisler, & P. M. Miller (Eds.), *Progress in behavior modification* (vol. 28, pp. 183–218). Sycamore, IL: Sycamore.

Prochaska, J. O., & DiClemente, C. C. (2005). The transtheoretical approach. In J. C. Norcross & M. R. Goldfriend (Eds.), *Handbook of psychotherapy integration* (2nd ed., pp. 147–171). New York, NY: Oxford University Press.

Prochaska, J. O., Norcross, J. C., & DiClemente, C. C. (1994). *Changing for good: The revolutionary program that explains the six stages of change and teaches you how to free yourself from bad habits*. New York, NY: W. Morrow.

Ralevski, E., Gianoli, M. O., McCarthy, E., & Petrakis, I. (2014). Quality of life in veterans with alcohol dependence and co-occurring mental illness. *Addictive Behaviors*, *39*, 386–391.

Rondero Hernandez, V., & Mendoza, C. T. (2011). Shame resilience: A strategy for empowering women to treatment for substance abuse. *Journal of Social Work Practice in the Addictions*, *11*(4), 375–393.

Rosenblum, A., Matusow, H., Fong, C., Vogel, H., Uttaro, T., Moore, T., ... Magura, S. (2014). Efficacy of dual focus mutual aid for persons with mental illness and substance misuse. *Drug and Alcohol Dependence*, *135*, 78–87.

Sowers, W. E., & Rohland, B. (2004). American association of community psychiatrists' principles for managing transitions in behavioral health services. *Psychiatric Services*, *55*, 1271–1275.

Straussner, S. L. A. (2004). An overview. In S. L. A. Straussner (Ed.), *Clinical work with substance abusing clients* (2nd ed., pp. 3–35). New York, NY: Guilford Press.

Substance Abuse and Mental Health Services Administration. (2006). *Results from the 2005 National Survey on Drug Use and Health: National Findings (Office of Applied Studies, NSDUH Series H-30, DHHS Publi cation No. SMA 06-4194)*. Rockville, MD: Author.

Substance Abuse and Mental Health Services Administration. (2002, July 12). *The NHSDA Report: Substance use and the risk of suicide among youths*. Rockville, MD: Author.

Substance Abuse and Mental Health Services Administration. (2005, April 1). *The NSDUH Report: Alcohol use and delinquent behaviors among youths*. Rockville, MD: Author.

Substance Abuse and Mental Health Services Administration. (2010a). *Results from the 2009 National Survey on Drug Use and Health: Mental health findings*. Office of Applied Studies (NSDUH Series H-39, No. SMA 10-4609). Retrieved from http://oas.samhsa.gov/NSDUH/2k9NSDUH/MH/2K9MHResults.pdf

Substance Abuse and Mental Health Services Administration. (2010b, August 5). *The TEDS Report: Sociodemographic characteristics of substance abuse treatment admissions aged 50 or older: 1992–2008*. Rockville, MD: Author.

Substance Abuse and Mental Health Services Administration, Office of Applied Studies. (2008). *Results from the 2007 National Survey on drug use and health: National findings* (NSDUH Series H-34, DHHS, Publication No. SMA 08–4343).

Tripp, J. C., Skidmore, J. R., Cui, R., & Tate, S. R. (2013). Impact of physical health on treatment for co-occurring depression and substance dependence. *Journal of Dual Diagnosis*, *9*(3), 239–248.

Vinton, L., & Wambach, K. G. (2005). Alcohol and drug use among elderly people. In C. A. McNeece & D. M. DiNitto (Eds.), *Chemical dependency: A systems approach* (3rd ed., pp. 484–502). Boston, MA: Allyn and Bacon.

Wagner, F. A., & Anthony, J. C. (2002). Into the world of illegal drug use: Exposure opportunity and other mechanisms linking the use of alcohol, tobacco, marijuana, and cocaine. *American Journal of Epidemiology*, *155*, 918–925.

Wallace, J. (2003). Theory of 12-step-oriented treatment. In F. Rotgers, J. Morgenstern, & S. T. Walters (Eds.), *Treating substance abuse* (2nd ed., pp. 9–30). New York, NY: Guilford Press.

Wallace, J. M., & Muroff, J. R. (2002). Preventing substance abuse among African American children and youth: Race differences in risk factor exposure and vulnerability. *Journal of Primary Prevention*, *22*(3), 235–261.

Weaver, H. N. (2011). Cultural competence with First Nations peoples. In D. Lum (Ed.), *Culturally competent practice: A framework for understanding diverse groups and justice issues* (4th ed., pp. 223–247). Belmont, CA: Brooks/Cole Cengage Learning.

Welsh, C. J., Cargiulo, T., Gandhi, D. H., Liberto, J., & Weintraub, E. (2004). The role of diagnostic symptoms in the continued stigmatization of patients with opioid dependence. *Psychiatric Services*, *55*, 86–87.

World Health Organization. (2004). WHO global status report on alcohol and health. Geneva: Author. Retrieved from www.who.int/substance_abuse/publications/global_alcohol_report/en/

Yalom, I. (2005). *The theory and practice of group psychotherapy* (5th ed.). New York, NY: Basic Books.

TEN

Future Directions

The introduction of a new edition of the *Diagnostic and Statistical Manual of Mental Disorders* (*DSM*®; American Psychiatric Association [APA], 2013) in May 2013 added state-of-the-art research findings that have expanded our knowledge about the course of mental disorders, placed the disorders in the context of life-span development, and moved away from a categorical conceptualization toward a dimensional understanding of mental illness. The *DSM-5* has recognized complexity in introducing cross-cutting measures that assess symptoms occurring across disorders and in offering an alternative way of conceptualizing personality disorders. Clinicians are encouraged to stay abreast of emerging research by utilizing web links that promise to be updated on a regular basis. Global communication and international research are facilitated by making it clear that the *DSM* and the World Health Organizations, International Classification of Diseases (ICD)codes are identical. These innovations may prove to be beneficial in enhancing international collaboration and keeping mental health personnel current about scientific progress with respect to mental illness.

On the other hand, the elimination of the multiaxial structure that had been in place through *DSM-III* (APA, 1980) and *DSM-IV* (APA, 1994) pushed the domains of information that assessed patient contexts into the background, increasing the risk that these contexts could largely disappear from view in the process of diagnosis. The proposed alternative conceptualization of personality disorders was not adopted, and the categorical description of these disorders remained in the body of the *DSM-5*, despite considerable research suggesting the greater validity and reliability of a dimensional approach. Suggestions in the multidisciplinary research literature for alterations in the diagnostic structure to incorporate contextual factors, including sources of strength and resiliency, the focus of this text, were largely ignored. These contextual factors, often relevant to the quality of the patient–clinician relationship, were sacrificed in the service of making the *DSM-5* more like the medical diagnostic structure so that psychiatry could appear more "scientific" and thus gain more prestige within medicine. In doing away with the multiaxial system of former *DSM* editions, the authors of the *DSM-5* have increased the risk of reducing the patient to a list of pathological symptoms located inside the patient. The patient's disease can be too easily summed up by one label, ignoring in the process those unique strengths and stresses that facilitate encountering him as a whole person.

To make matters worse, the addition of new diagnoses, such as Temper Dysregulation Disorder, Gambling Disorder, and the categories of Mild Cognitive Disorder, risk medicalizing normal human problems, leaving the field of psychiatry open to charges of undue influence by and collusion with the pharmaceutical industry, which profits from the proliferation of mental illness diagnoses. Thus, the *DSM-5* reinforces a reductionist view of the patient, who can be summed up in terms of a single pathological label, while increasing the possibility that many normal persons struggling with the challenges of being human will receive a mental disorder diagnosis.

Substantial discussion in the empirical and conceptual literature supports the idea that ethnographic and narrative approaches are uniquely conducive to creating the kind of clinician–client interaction that promotes communication, regardless of the client's ability to articulate symptoms clearly or rationally. This text identifies clinical approaches that can enhance the *DSM* diagnostic process by attending to the individual's diverse contexts, including culture, and to both internal and external sources of resiliency. We believe that systematic attention to diversity factors and sources of resiliency have become even more important in the wake of the publication of *DSM-5* and that the voices of interdisciplinary mental health professions, consumers, and their families, in addition to those of medicine, are necessary to facilitate this strength-based focus.

COMPETING PERSPECTIVES

Competing assumptions continue to drive discussions about what kinds of new knowledge and protocols are meaningful in generating effective diagnosis that is relevant to treatment. A major difference in perspectives concerns the relative importance of the social environment versus biological bases for vulnerability to the development of mental disorders. Two long-standing, disparate viewpoints put forth diverse positions on the concept of the person–environment interaction.

The Biopsychosocial Model

The advocates for a biopsychosocial model of mental illness argue that mental disorders are by their very nature complex and embedded in psychosocial, cultural, and community issues with multiple etiologies, outside of as well as within the client. The role of psychological and social factors, such as identity (e.g., ethnic, social), group affiliation(s), spiritual/religious associations, and socioeconomic status are formative in how individuals perceive their lived experience. These factors influence how patients interpret the meaning of their symptoms, the ordinary challenges of living, and their struggles with mental illness. In validating the worldview of the client, the biopsychosocial model promotes delving into healing processes embedded in the client's cultural perspective, even though these cultural beliefs may appear to be premised on the paranormal without a logical basis (Sue & Sue, 2008).

Advocates of this perspective often highlight the iatrogenic effects of medications, the lack of attention to psychosocial factors in research, the undue influence of the psychopharmacology industry on research and treatment, and the reality that clear biological markers of mental disorders cannot yet be identified (Frances, 2013). Although there is wide acknowledgment, for example, of advances in drug treatment, the side of effects of psychoactive drugs can reduce the patient's quality of life and contribute to his feeling stigmatized. A narrow view of psychopharmacology as the gold standard of treatment can serve to blind both practitioners and the society at large to health-promoting behaviors and social support that may be most critical to recovery. In our emphasis on factors of diversity and resiliency and in our proposed formulation for adding these factors to the diagnostic process, we have in the preceding chapters advocated for the biopsychosocial perspective as essential to assessment and argued against a strictly biologically based model of mental illness.

The Neurobiological Model

The alternate perspective focuses on separating "true" mental illness, conceived as biologically based, from human suffering, which is caused by a myriad of factors, including poverty, discrimination, family discord, and social and economic distress. The advocates for an emphasis on the biological basis of mental disorders promote the search for positivist, empirical data gathered through implementation of the scientific method as a means to understand physiological causation, assumed to be based in genetics and brain biology. These theorists and researchers believe that the focus on complex psychosocial components of mental illness does not lend itself to the scientific method, hampers research into the biological bases of behavior, and facilitates an atmosphere in which clinical practice is divorced from research. They further warn that a biopsychosocial approach may ultimately harm patients and their families by medicalizing problems of living that are not true illnesses, often institutionalizing racial, gender, ethnic, and class bias in the bargain (Kutchins & Kirk, 1997). For example, the human reaction of grief to significant loss is expressed in a variety of ways in relation to behaviors, rituals, and practices in different cultures. Lack of understanding or recognition of the cultural variations could be misperceived as mental illness.

The failure to separate out true mental disorders, understood as brain diseases, from human suffering in response to many psychological, economic, and sociological factors may have contributed to an abandonment of the seriously mentally ill, in the form of changing social policy that leaves this population vulnerable to homelessness and all kinds of victimization. In his most recent book, *American Psychosis* (2014), E. Fuller Torrey eloquently traces the abandonment of the mentally ill in American society through mental health policies that have destroyed the state hospital systems and failed to replace them with community treatment programs, destroying any semblance of continuity of care for the most psychiatrically vulnerable among us. From a social justice point of view, the most vulnerable among us deserve the bulk of our attention and resources.

Acknowledgment of the shameful condition of the seriously mentally ill would seem to support a primary focus on the neurobiological model, the allocation of resources to biological research, the development of more effective drugs, and a greater understanding of the genetics and neurobiology of mental illness. From our perspective, however, it is a grave mistake to frame the issue in terms of either/or competing perspectives. Even with the best psychopharmacology available, persons suffering from severe mental illness need the supportive context of a safe environment and the opportunity to participate in the human community to comply with the medical treatment of their biologically based illness. A more fruitful stance, we believe, is to embrace both perspectives.

Commonalities

On the surface, these contrasting neurobiological versus biopsychosocial perspectives are often described in polarizing language that oversimplifies each viewpoint. They appear more in opposition than they really are or may need to be. Proponents of both perspectives are increasingly concerned about understanding antecedent conditions that lead to the development of mental disorders for the purpose of early detection and diagnosis; both advocate for the provision of effective treatment that will stabilize the disorder and minimize later deterioration. Proponents of each perspective, for example, would support recovery models in response to serious mental illnesses and other effective programs that enhance compliance with medication regimens and reduce relapse. All research methodologies are embedded in the researchers' value assumptions; these assumptions determine the focus of inquiry. Because researchers must compete for funding to support their inquiry, the relative power of these two perspectives affects what is funded for research and how resources for increasing the knowledge base of mental disorders are allocated.

Torrey (2014) points out that few clinics or practitioners treat the seriously mentally ill, who are now found and treated more in the correctional system than in mental health institutions. Persons with schizophrenia are more likely to be poor and to lack mental health insurance coverage. Insurance reimbursement structures reward mental health clinicians not for treating those who suffer from schizophrenia but for treating the "worried well," who suffer from psychosocial disorders that can meet criteria for mental illness; the latter are more likely to have health insurance and to keep their appointments. In contrast, Medicare and Medicaid programs have spawned the burgeoning nursing home and board and care for-profit industries, where the seriously mentally ill are warehoused with little to no treatment in dehumanizing environments (Torrey, 2014). Dr. Thomas R. Insel, the current director of the National Institute of Mental Health (NIMH) is a strong proponent of the biological model described previously. Nevertheless, Dr. Insel supports some psychosocial research related to effective new services for people with schizophrenia, criticizes the *DSM-5* as "at best a dictionary, lacking scientific validity," and questions whether some individuals with a long-term history of psychosis might "do better off medication" (Insel, 2014).

The Affordable Care Act (HHS.gov/HealthCare), enacted in 2010 and implemented in October 2012, will offer opportunities to address these dilemmas. New multidisciplinary care clinics are beginning to offer integrated medical, co-occurring mental health, and substance abuse assessment. Current discussions support increased collaboration among mental health disciplines and a greater focus on prevention of medical and mental illness. Primary care physicians, it is hoped, will work within a system that gives them immediate and ongoing access to behavioral health specialists who work with them on an ongoing basis in the context of a multidisciplinary team. These proposed structures acknowledge the complexity and interactive effects of co-occurring medical, mental health, and substance use disorders, along with the awareness of psychosocial environments and their effects on functioning.

Although it is not clear yet how all of this will unfold, we can conjecture that there will be several notable implications for both primary care providers and behavioral health professionals. This formative shift in service delivery will enhance the colocation of primary care and behavioral health professionals so that there will be increased attention to the integration of physical health, mental health, and substance abuse treatment concerns. This will increase the opportunities for primary health and behavioral health professionals to learn about psychological disorders that are associated with particular physical disorders, such as the high rate of depression associated with diabetes. The shift and expansion of health service delivery to become more inclusive will sharpen the need to integrate a recovery model perspective (focused on coping effectively with mental illness) alongside the medical model approach (focused on signs and symptoms of pathology) in diagnostic and treatment-planning discussions that strive to provide best practice services from competing perspectives. Such an integrated focus assumes an active, reciprocal partnership between clients, family members, and professionals, as opposed to viewing the patient as a passive recipient of the diagnostic label and ensuing treatment. Even if the Affordable Care Act succeeds in generating more integrative care, however, the plight of the seriously mentally ill remains unsolved in the context of their abandonment in social policy. It is easier to engage in artificially polarizing debate about biological versus psychosocial causation than to find the political will to address these issues effectively.

CHALLENGES AND PROBLEM AREAS

Building on the multitude of issues regarding *DSM* limitations that have been raised in the literature and presented in the preceding chapters, the following represent some of our strongest concerns.

- The *DSM-5* continues to have significant weaknesses in its failure to address in a substantial way the vital client contexts of diversity and resiliency. As a result, these contexts are ignored or minimized in the diagnostic process, despite the fact that these factors help link diagnosis to treatment planning and predict successful treatment outcomes. The institutionalized racism, cultural biases, and the marginalization of culture, evident in former versions of the *DSM* (Kutchins & Kirk, 1997), were not taken seriously by the authors of the *DSM-5*. Problems with reliability and validity of *DSM* diagnostic labels continue, along with the proliferation of mental illness diagnoses in the *DSM-5*. The medicalization of ordinary human suffering may be exacerbated while the environmental contexts of the seriously mentally ill continue to be minimized or ignored.

- The development of a *DSM* focused on symptoms and decided on in committees composed predominantly of psychiatrists has resulted in a questionable alliance between the pharmaceutical industry and medicine. An outcome of this dynamic is that the training of psychiatrists has largely been limited to the prescribing of psychoactive medications for symptom reduction. Engagement and intervention skills, which address the complex causes of mental and emotional problems through interactive, relationship processes, have largely been sacrificed in the training of psychiatrists (Carlat, 2010). The client has too often been reduced to an assortment of symptoms, for which a label is sought to find the right medication. This then changes the definition of psychiatric practice to the prescription of psychotropic drugs to wider and wider segments of society, including young children. The exclusive focus on psychopharmacology has been emphasized to the point that psychiatry has come to be defined as a profession in crisis (Carlat, 2010).
- Mental health professionals—such as nurses, counselors, psychologists, and clinical social workers—who are trained to provide psychotherapy but have less power and prestige than psychiatrists are largely left out of the diagnostic decision-making process despite their greater in-depth understanding of the consumers of mental health services as unique whole persons living in an ecological matrix of interacting internal and external contexts.
- Despite a stated commitment to do so, peer support specialists were not consulted in the development of the *DSM-5* and are also invisible in the diagnostic assessment process.
- The number of mental disorders defined in the *DSM* has proliferated over the years, with the result that the current diagnostic nomenclature arguably medicalizes and pathologizes existential problems in human living (Gambrill, 2005).
- Despite the predominance of biological psychiatry in research institutes, the abandonment of the patients whose diseases they research continues unabated. The most seriously mentally ill do not have ready access to affordable treatment or to a continuity of care in a responsive community.

Accessibility and Social Justice

Whether a civil, humane society has the responsibility for responding to human suffering without having to label that suffering as a mental disorder to fund an effective response remains a dilemma yet to be solved. The dilemma goes beyond the profession of psychiatry to a question concerning the kind of society we desire to achieve. Kutchins and Kirk (1997) suggest that narrowing the scope of diagnoses to those with strong evidence for internally caused mental disorders and a refusal to impose disease labels that poorly fit personal and social problems would lead to the development of an effort "to assist troubled children, adults, and families without labeling so many of them as mentally ill" (p. 264). At the same time, effectively responding beyond research studies to the serious mentally ill is just as, and perhaps more, important.

In the arena of social policy, we have yet to summon the will to respond effectively to the complex conundrum of multiply determined mental disorders, some of which are more biologically based than others. Despite these well-known problems with the structure of the *DSM*, clinicians need a more effective diagnostic protocol and access to its ongoing development. Such a system would enable sorting through the complex presentations of clients and facilitate arriving at conclusions that lead to effective interventions, in the process enhancing communication between clients and practitioners.

With all its limitations, the *DSM* is an important tool that deserves constructive criticism and relevant change for the sake of those who look to us for assistance. The emphasis on access to web-based information on current research and evidence-based treatments, promised by the authors of the *DSM-5*, could facilitate the process of increased accessibility, but this would require that all of the mental health professions, along with consumers of treatment and their families, are able to utilize this source and engage in the dialogue.

PROPOSALS FOR CHANGE AND FUTURE DIRECTIONS

In thinking through the challenges involved in understanding the complex causes of both medically determined mental illness and social problems in living, we conclude with the following recommendations to mental health practitioners, educators, researchers, policy makers, and administrators:

1. *Integrate our Diversity/Resiliency Formulation systematically into the diagnostic and treatment-planning process, regardless of whether it is an official part of the DSM structure, and in future DSM revisions, incorporate it as an official part of the structure.*

In Chapters 1 and 2, we reviewed traditional definitions of diagnosis and assessment, noting that the term *diagnosis* is generally restricted to the criteria (taxonomy) of pathological symptoms, presumed to describe a disease process that determines the presence or absence of a disorder in binary format; it is either present or not. The addition of the Diversity/Resiliency Formulation enhances the *DSM* as a diagnostic taxonomy system by adding elements that are necessary to the traditional process of medical diagnosis. It is pertinent that the *DSM* has historically acknowledged the necessity of examining behavior in context with the introduction of Axis IV, which identified external stressors, and Axis V, which rated the general level of functioning. The use of these axes helped clinicians produce formulations that addressed the stressors relevant to the challenges faced by the individual given a mental health diagnosis. These stressful client contexts receded into the background with the elimination of the multiaxial system in *DSM-5*, and addressing them will rely on training that emphasizes the use of the V/Z Codes. Our proposed Diversity/Resiliency Formulation can counterbalance the essential pathology-based data derived from *DSM-5* diagnosis by helping to construct a more accurate diagnostic profile of the wholeness and humanity of our patients.

The Western bifurcation of mental and physical health and illness is inherently problematic in that many non-Western traditions do not share the distinction. An individual's beliefs that have a role in perceptions and meaning making must be explored in the process of determining what is normal or pathological within different cultural contexts. The clarification of the *DSM-5*'s merger with the *ICD* global system of physical and mental diagnoses may facilitate dialogue across paradigm differences in the way mental and physical health and illness are viewed.

We strongly believe that the addition of the Diversity/Resiliency Formulation strengthens the comprehensiveness and thus the accuracy of the *DSM* without sacrificing the search for scientific verification of the biological bases of mental disorders. We are persuaded that its use is relevant to both sides of what we might term the biology–ecological controversy described earlier.

Our application of the Diversity/Resiliency Formulation to patients with Alzheimer's disease demonstrated how culturally competent attention to the strengths that remain in the patient, along with the use of current philosophies of care, can lead the practitioner to an awareness of and participation in elder care that preserves the full humanity of the Alzheimer's patient. Adding the formulation to the diagnosis of an individual with schizophrenia can enlarge the clinician's diagnostic lens to include the awareness of strength-based consumer-driven models such as the recovery movement. This more comprehensive assessment, we believe, will facilitate medication compliance and reduce the noxious effects of expressed emotion on optimal treatment response. We have shown how limited diagnostic understanding, focused mainly on the control of disruptive behavior, has led to poor long-term outcomes for children and adolescents with oppositional defiant and conduct disorders. The addition of the Diversity/Resiliency Formulation could lead the clinician to assess and make extensive use of school, family, and community supports that have been demonstrated to enhance protective factors; in this process, the role of symptom reduction via medication is a minor one at best.

With respect to mood disorders, the Diversity/Resiliency Formulation would require the diagnostician to inquire into how moods are understood and expressed in diverse cultures, to involve the client's family and community in the diagnostic process, and to assess for protective factors, such as exercise and meditation, that are known to enhance recovery. Perhaps most important, using our Diversity/Resiliency Formulation lens to diagnose and respond effectively to substance abuse is critical to our clients. The roles of gender, race, national origin, and culture in the use and abuse of symptoms permeate and define the pattern of substance abuse, dependence, and addiction that so often co-occur with other mental disorders. The failure to understand the positive aspects of culture and other contexts in the lives of drug or alcohol abusers could literally have life-and-death outcomes for our patients and/or their family and community members.

In short, individuals who suffer from mental disorders are more than the sum of their symptoms. They do not exist in a vacuum. They are unique individuals with lived experience in the contexts of culture, family, and community, members of visible and not so visible cultures, and possessors of particular talents and abilities. All of these sources often represent surprising wellsprings of resilience.

2. *Continue to support research into the biological and genetic bases of mental disorders.*

A growing body of research regarding the role of neurotransmitters, genetic heritability, and the symmetry of brain regions supports neurobiological etiologies of mental disorders. These developments have assisted in understanding (a) the neurobiological underpinnings of attachment disorders; (b) developmental trauma, schizophrenia, and mood disorders; (c) the links among temperament, stress response, and brain function and many disruptive behavioral disorders; (d) the stress response and its role in anxiety; and (e) the genetic susceptibility to substance abuse and dependency. Recent progress has been made in the search for biological markers of Alzheimer's disease and bipolar disorder. The recognition of the biological bases of mental disorders has been important for some in reducing the social stigma associated with mental illness. Although genetic predispositions have been identified via extensive research, there is widespread recognition that there is yet much to learn about the complex interaction between environment and vulnerability based on biological factors such as genetics. Much remains to be learned regarding what factors and triggers combine to produce mental disorders in some individuals and not in others with similar profiles. Despite the ongoing science of neurobiological psychiatry, the challenge will remain to assess sources of support that enable science to be applied effectively to promote compliance with biological treatments and prevent relapse. Our proposed Diversity/Resiliency Formulation will enhance, not compete with, the findings of neurobiological psychiatry.

3. *Increase funding for research related to the diverse psychosocial contexts of mental illness.*

The diverse environmental contexts of mental health and illness have yet to be explored more systematically in research that yields vital new information regarding early detection, prevention, and effective psychopharmacology. Review of the literature on etiology and evidence-informed diagnosis and treatment consistently demonstrates that the development and duration of mental illness needs to be understood in relation to multiple biopsychosocial factors and socioeconomic status. Mental disorders cannot be responded to effectively without a stress–diathesis orientation that includes a full appreciation for the client's diverse personal, cultural, and community contexts. The current structure of the *DSM* ignores and/or minimizes the role of client culture by relegating this core aspect of identity to Section III of the manual, thus reinforcing the tendency of overextended professionals to gloss over cultural factors. The need to understand the role of culture in the experience of mental disorders and the course and duration of the illness has emerged as vital by virtue of a small but growing body of incisive research (Alegria et al., 2004; Lopez et al., 2009; Yamada & Brekke, 2008). A central theme in this literature is the dominant Western cultural bias that permeates much research and identification of criteria, particularly in the *DSM* (Carlat, 2010; Kutchins & Kirk, 1997).

4. *Attend in the assessment process to diversity factors, rather than to a narrower view of culture as synonymous with ethnicity, and incorporate this focus at the center of the diagnostic process.*

The cultural context has a formative role in eliciting diagnostic data. To ignore it is to lose valuable and significant information whose very solicitation engenders credibility in the clinician and content that is essential to truly understanding what is going on with the client, which is after all our key task. Culture affects every aspect of living, the meaning given to existence, the language used to describe human experience, one's relationship to oneself and others, and one's sense of family and community. The term *culture* as it is commonly understood and talked about is often viewed as synonymous with *ethnicity* or even *race*. In diagnosing the role of culture in a patient's mental disorder or emotional problems, clinicians' understanding of culture must encompass and recognize covert, often unacknowledged diverse identifies, such as those related to one's workplace, occupation, profession, political affiliation, gender, geographic area, social class, and spirituality or religion.

The intersectionality of these factors is particularly important to explore as we aim to understand the impact of various aspects of social identity on the client's sense of self-worth, personal meaning, and life purpose. The combination of diverse identifications in the life of an individual creates a true challenge for clinicians who aim to provide "individualized" services. For example, a White low-income fundamentalist female may differ in important aspects from an African American middle-income fundamentalist female, and a second-generation Hmong male may different in important attitudes and practices from a first-generation Hmong male. The intersections of race, class, gender, age, generational status, religion, and occupation present endless combinations of social identity that are very important for clinicians to understand. The unacknowledged cultures of the various mental health professions themselves, as well as the cultural and class identities of their practitioners, are part and parcel of these intersections, impacting the nature of the client–clinician relationship in a multitude of ways. Diversity considerations are as varied as the complexity of human experience, and attempts to understand a client from this perspective invites creative engagement and respect for the personhood of those we hope to understand and help. To the extent we are able, as mental health professionals, to encounter and even celebrate this complexity, we avoid the trap of equating the personhood of the patient with a diagnostic label based on symptoms of pathology.

In *DSM-5*, the Cultural Formulation, placed in Section III, is given too little prominence, and its structure focuses exclusively on ethnic/racial identification in the context of how this might interfere with the diagnostic and treatment process. Adding the concepts of diversity and resiliency to the equation gives a truer picture of both stresses and sources of resiliency and strength and goes beyond a simple focus on ethnicity to an appreciation of intersectionality. The Diversity/Resiliency Formulation helps the clinician to encounter the whole person from a position of self-awareness, humility, and mutuality.

5. *Increase carefully designed research into protective as well as risk factors for mental illness.*

The fact that many mental disorders are known to have a strong biological basis does not reduce the importance of exploring client contextual factors that promote resiliency (e.g., personal strengths and a responsive community). Not everyone with the same biological predisposition to schizophrenia or bipolar disorder, for example, will develop these mental illnesses, which supports the validity of a stress–diathesis model of illness. Attending to the biology of the illness and to environmental sources of stress addresses only part of the equation and undermines a true encounter with the whole patient in interaction with his or her world. Contextual sources of support that are often overlooked are those that undergird patient strengths and resiliency. It is also recognized that comprehensive multimodal responses that integrate client culture and make use of multiple sources of support are often short- and long-term interventions with lasting positive effectiveness (Cheung & Leung, 2008; Cohen, Tran, & Rhee, 2007; Saleeby, 2002; Smith, 2004). Outcome studies support the view that the extratherapeutic factors of client characteristics and the quality of the patient–therapist relationship most robustly influence treatment outcome (Hubble, Duncan, & Miller, 1999). Creation of a therapeutic relationship and conducting a thorough diagnosis can only be achieved through systematic attention to these positive resources of resiliency as well as to the symptoms of pathology.

A research agenda for protective factors would highlight the growing fields of positive psychology, resiliency, recovery, and wellness and legitimize the use of interventions, such as mindfulness, meditation, tai chi, and diet and exercise programs, which are beginning to demonstrate effective outcomes for many varied mental disorders. In Chapter 3, on mood disorders, for example, we discussed the powerful impact and role of activation of the endorphin system in creating a sense of well-being and the implications for addiction. Clinical and social psychological research has generated positivity ratios (Fredrickson, 2009), well-being and optimism scales (Lopez & Snyder, 2003) self-efficacy, and locus-of-control measures (Bandura, 1997). These contributions to the understanding of mental and emotional illness and to the provision of a sustainable sense of well-being are rarely acknowledged in the medically driven diagnostic world.

6. *To accomplish these proposals, utilize more mixed methodology research.*

Qualitative, exploratory data can identify unique and subtle distinctions in the experiential world of the client that quantitative methodology is unable to capture. Qualitative, contextual information can be gathered in conjunction with quantitative data. Qualitative data can illuminate the significance and meaning of specific symptoms to the client and facilitate meaningful interactions with professionals and others involved in the treatment planning and implementation. Narrative and ethnographic approaches to the study of mental illness can provide valuable information about the phenomenology of individuals diagnosed with mental disorders. These methods can focus on processes, such as engaging with mental health professionals, participating in peer support activities, defining symptoms, receiving a mental disorder label, relating to family and community in the context of that label, attempting to adhere to treatment plans, and coping with a changing sense of self and life purpose.

Being the recipient of a mental disorder label directly or indirectly affects feelings about the ability to continue one's life with hope, meaning, and purpose. Qualitative research would regard the client, along with his or her cultural community, as a fully human partner in the diagnostic and treatment process. Challenges involved in outreach and prevention, barriers to effective treatment, factors related to relapse, protective and risk factors could be better understood and, in turn, promote the design of effective treatment interventions.

Quantitative research could compare and analyze outcomes related to diagnosis and treatment for large samples of patient populations who are responded to by utilizing, versus not utilizing, information in our proposed Diversity-Resiliency Formulation. The relative value of this information could be compared in terms of age, gender, ethnicity, culture, and socioeconomic status. Although development of scales to measure dimensions assessed via the proposed formulation would greatly enhance this process and facilitate its use by clinicians, those currently in existence (Lopez & Snyder, 2003) utilizing the constructs of resiliency, self-efficacy, and positive psychology, could be put to immediate use as evaluative measures.

7. *Communication across professions and schools of thought, as well as with consumers and family members, is needed to define and implement relevant research agendas and to promote effective mental health policy.*

The *DSM-5* task force made an effort in the direction of open communication within the mental health community and its stakeholders by inviting commentary via its web page (www.dsm5.org). The *DSM*'s stated intent was to promote a taxonomy that transcends theory and etiology, is descriptive in nature, and conducive to dialogue among professionals. The promise of the *DSM* also included assisting clients and their families to understand the mental disorders and to facilitate their empowerment as partners in the treatment process. This had the potential to contribute to the lessening of stigma against the mentally ill. This promise was ultimately not realized in the development of the *DSM-5*. Decision-making committees and the power structure of the *DSM* task forces largely excluded the interdisciplinary mental health community and the experiences of the clients themselves from the decision-making process, leading to adaptations of the diagnostic taxonomy. This situation has resulted in the complete dominance of the medical profession, along with the undue influence of pharmaceutical companies, in the classification of and research into mental disorders. Scientific integrity can only be enhanced by a commitment to inclusiveness.

In principle, the *DSM* Work Group/Task Forces should have included all professionals as well as consumer advocates and the patients themselves. Not to include such representation risks ignoring the perspective invoked by examination of the psychosocial, cultural, and spiritual contexts of the clients' lives. This renders the client perspective and the perspective of less powerful mental health professional as less important. The recovery model (Corrigan, Mueser, Bond, Drake, & Solomon, 2008; Davidson, 2003; Linhorst, 2006; Ralph & Corrigan, 2005), which is arguably now state of the art for working with clients with severe mental illness, has relevance for diagnostic formulation and practice with all disorders due to its focus on empowerment, effective coping, health promoting behaviors, and community involvement. Foremost, the idea that consumers participate in all activities that bear on their lives, as witnessed in an advocacy mantra, "nothing about us without us," highlights the necessity of clinicians to develop skill in working collaboratively with consumers. This model challenges us to bring patients and their family members "to the table" as we seek to define their disorder in our official taxonomy.

We further recommend that every ongoing and future *DSM* Task Force reflect, as much as possible, the increasing diversity that characterizes our nation and the world. We believe that these changes could not only promote more authentic scientific inquiry and a more relevant diagnostic system, but could also ameliorate the iatrogenic effects that occur as a result of unnecessary misinterpretation and pathologizing of the ordinary, normal range of human behavior. A more effective diagnostic process will increase rather than diminish hope in the face of the often demoralizing and bewildering challenge of mental illness.

8. *Incorporate the addition of the Diversity/Resiliency Formulation into the education and training of primary care physicians, psychiatrists, and all interdisciplinary professionals who treat mental illness.*

The Diversity/Resiliency Formulation incorporates a dimension of diagnosis that, we believe, must not be left to chance or to informal strategies. Rather, the use of the formulation should be integral to medical training, as well as to the training of all mental health professionals, particularly allied health professionals. In this way, it could be utilized from the first contact with the consumer, regardless of the clinician's background. Persons struggling with uncomfortable mental and emotional symptoms most frequently talk first with their primary care physician or spiritual or religious confidante rather than with a mental health professional. This may be particularly true of individuals from more traditional cultures, whether they are religious, class based, or ethnic. Encouraging respectful attention to the strengths and diverse identities of clients by physicians, nurse practitioners, or spiritual counselors enhances successful engagement with a client, increasing the possibility of building a positive working relationship, and gaining useful information necessary for accurate diagnosis. In addition, many mentally ill persons are primarily seen in correctional settings (Torrey, 2014); we recommend that correctional personnel also be trained in the use of the Diversity/Resiliency Formulation.

Interdisciplinary training must integrate a professional perspective that emphasizes clinical preparation in the context of organizational procedures and policies that support clinical teamwork and diversity-relevant practice with individuals. On a microlevel, the training spectrum should include individual self-awareness regarding the biases that one brings into interactions with clients. Likewise, it is important to understand the role of institutional procedures on practice and how they affect practice effectiveness. Pedagogy in medical and mental health education could incorporate these perspectives into the educational process by including personal memoirs (Fontaine & Fontaine, 2006; Hagener, 2005; Kaysen, 1993; Shawn, 2007; Zailckas, 2005), journals, documentaries, and in-person presentations by clients and family members who have experienced mental and emotional problems. We have so often heard from our students that these personal encounters, in personal or written form, have been the educational experiences they have valued the most.

There are a multitude of challenges that limit interdisciplinary exchange among mental health professionals, for example, the territoriality derived from professional interests, resource considerations that limit the interdisciplinary composition of teams, and/or a hierarchy that privileges psychiatry over other mental health professions. Over time, we believe that interdisciplinary training in the use of the Diversity/Resiliency Formulation is more likely to facilitate a more constructive and comprehensive approach to the client's mental and emotional diagnoses and problems in living and to better collaboration among diverse treating professionals. The formulation has the potential to strengthen the practitioner–client relationship, elicit honest information about the effects of medication and responses to therapeutic intervention, reduce the likelihood of relapse, and promote the engagement of the real world of the client toward recovery. To do any less is to dishonor our clients.

CONCLUDING REMARKS

We anticipate the argument that medicine necessarily focuses on signs and symptoms of illness, leading to an understanding of etiology and a correct diagnosis, followed by the application of a treatment protocol logically related to the diagnosis. Attending to strengths, internal and external sources of resiliency, and diversity factors, it may be argued, is and should remain the province of the allied health professions of social work, nursing, rehabilitation counseling, psychology and pastoral counseling, and is ancillary to the diagnostic process, which focuses on disease located in the patient. As authors and mental health professionals, we recognize the need for careful assessment of signs (e.g., measureable physiological indicators) and symptoms (e.g., observable or reported behaviors) of pathology and for a rigorous diagnostic classification of symptoms. However, because mental illness has repeatedly been demonstrated to be thoroughly linked to the socioeconomic, cultural, family, and community contexts of the client, accurate diagnosis is impossible while ignoring these components. These contexts, which contain sources of strength as well as pathology, are recognized and honored through our proposed Diversity/Resiliency Formulation, with the result that the mental health patient is encountered realistically and respectfully as a whole person. We believe that this perspective offers a corrective to the all too frequent overreliance on the singular use of medication, for conditions that may or may not be biologically based, at the expense of including interventions that make use of the client's sources of support and are demonstrated to be effective. The components of the proposed formulation are also vital to a comprehensive, effective response to mental and emotional suffering that may not meet the criteria of current or future biologically based mental disorders, and are relevant to the assessment process involved in the diagnosis of all medical disorders.

Exploring protective factors and resiliency in the lives of clients, regardless of whether or not they have a mental disorder with a clear biological basis, would necessitate asking ourselves as professionals and members of society questions such as the following: What is a mentally healthy community? What is a caring society? What is the role of social support in emotional and mental well-being? What is meant by happiness, and what is its relationship to being a responsible citizen? What choices must we make in responding to mental disorders? Do we finance the treatment only of mental disorders with a known biological basis? If so, do we respond with effective social policies and a range of treatment facilities in a psychosocial context that promotes true recovery? The addition of the Diversity/Resiliency Formulation would legitimize the core importance of these questions and offer fruitful guidelines for expanded research agendas. Such a focus underscores the need for a public health perspective and agenda for mental health and illness, for social policy and programs that place primary importance on prevention. It is a focus imbedded in values of social justice. Many prominent researchers and mental health leaders have called for an analysis of mental health as well as illness dimensions and an exploration of social policy that promotes mental health and prevents mental illness (Bandura, 1995; Gambrill, 2005; Keyes & Haidt, 2002; Linley & Joseph, 2004). Prevention is not a frill or an extra but is central to an effective response to many mental disorders. This was demonstrated, for example, in our summary of effective responses to conduct and oppositional defiant disorders in Chapter 5.

Mental and emotional suffering takes its toll on everyone in a myriad of ways. An effective diagnostic process includes thoughtful and vigorous exploration of these sources of pathology in multiple domains as well as probing into the social and ethnic cultural contexts and internal and external sources of resiliency that have a role in creating strong family bonds and community well-being.

Rigorous research is needed in further clarification of the role of genetic and biological factors in leading to mental disorders. The status of the *DSM* as the gold standard taxonomy of mental disorders presumes that having "cut nature at its joints," the distinctions among disorders are real. This charge represents the quintessential challenge in mental health practice, that in fact the diagnostic guide directs accurate diagnostic processing and that the clinician exercises diagnostic acumen in the implementation of the taxonomy. This suggests that the diagnostic system must embrace as accurately and fully as possible both the biological and psychosocial components of the disorder in ways that facilitate an excellent working relationship with the client and connect to accurate and reliable diagnosis and effective treatment. Ongoing advancement and improvement of the *DSM* must be based on unequivocal separation of research from special interests, such as pharmaceutical lobbies, on a recognition of the complex realities of mental and emotional disorders, and on the courage to embrace inclusivity in the development of the diagnostic taxonomy.

Astute comprehension of the dynamic biopsychosocial, diverse existential worlds of the client involves exploration of sources of support, resiliency, and strength. To be entrusted with the concerns of individuals struggling either with diagnosed mental illness or the challenges of daily living is a remarkable responsibility and an honor. We owe it to our present and future clients, to our students and future professionals, to embrace the depth and scope of mental disorders, and to create a climate of hope and support for recovery. We hope that this multidisciplinary text has contributed to the furthering of humane, comprehensive responses to mental and emotional suffering and to the training of compassionate professionals.

REFERENCES

Alegria, M., Takeuchi, D., Canino, G., Duan, N., Shrouot, P., Meng, X., & Gong, F. (2004). Considering context, place and culture: The National Latino and Asian American Study. *International Journal of Methods in Psychiatric Research*, *13*(4), 208–220.

American Psychiatric Association. (1980). *Diagnostic and statistical manual of mental disorders* (3rd ed.). Washington, DC: Author.

American Psychiatric Association. (1994). *Diagnostic and statistical manual of mental disorders* (4th ed.). Washington, DC: Author.

American Psychiatric Association. (2013). *Diagnostic and statistical manual of mental disorders* (5th ed.). Arlington, VA: American Psychiatric Press.

Bandura, A. (Ed.). (1995). *Self-efficacy in changing societies.* Cambridge, UK: Cambridge University Press.

Bandura, A. (1997). *Self-efficacy: The exercise of control.* New York, NY: W. H. Freeman.

Carlat, D. (2010). *Unhinged: The trouble with psychiatry—A doctor's revelations about a profession in crisis.* New York, NY: The Free Press.

Cheung, M., & Leung, P. (2008). *Multicultural practice and evaluation.* Denver, CO: Love Publishing Company.

Cohen, A., Tran, T. V., & Rhee, S. Y. (2007). *Multicultural approaches in caring for children, youth, and their families.* Boston, MA: Allyn & Bacon.

Corrigan, P. W., Mueser, K. T., Bond, G. R., Drake, R. E., & Solomon, P. (2008). *Principles and practice of psychiatric rehabilitation.* New York, NY: Guilford Press.

Davidson, L. (2003). *Living outside mental illness: Qualitative studies in schizophrenia.* New York, NY: New York University Press.

Fontaine, C., & Fontaine, M. (2006). *Comeback: A mother and daughter's journey through hell and back.* New York, NY: HarperCollins.

Frances, A. (2014). *Saving normal: An insider's revolt against out-of-control psychiatric diagnosis, big pharma, and the medicationalization of ordinary life.* New York, NY: Harper Collins.

Fredrickson, B. L. (2009). *Positivity.* New York, NY: Random House.
Gambrill, E. (2005). *Critical thinking in clinical practice: Improving the quality of judgments and decisions.* Hoboken, NJ: John Wiley & Sons.
Hagener, N. (2005). *The dance of defiance.* Scottsdale, AZ: Shamrock Books.
Hubble, M. A., Duncan, B. L., & Miller, S. D. (1999). *The heart and soul of change.* Washington, DC: American Psychological Association.
Insel, T. (2014, February 4). Blazing trails in brain science. *The New York Times*, pp. D1–D3.
Kaysen, S. (1993). *Girl, interrupted.* New York, NY: Random House.
Keyes, C.L.M., & Haidt, J. (2002). *Flourishing: Positive psychology and the life well-lived.* Washington, DC: American Psychological Association.
Kutchins, H., & Kirk, S. A. (1997). *Making us crazy. DSM: The psychiatric bible and the creation of mental disorders.* New York, NY: The Free Press.
Linhorst, D. M. (2006). *Empowering people with severe mental illness: A practical guide.* New York, NY: Oxford University Press.
Linley, P. A., & Joseph, S. (Eds.). (2004). *Positive psychology in practice.* Hoboken, NJ: John Wiley & Sons.
Lopez, S., Ramirez Garcia, J. I., Ullman, J. B., Kopelowicz, A., Jenkins, J., Breitborde, N.J.K., & Placencia, P. (2009). Cultural variability in the manifestation of expressed emotion. *Family Process, 48*(2), 179–194.
Lopez, S. J., & Snyder, C. R. (2003). *Positive psychological assessment: A handbook of models and measures.* Washington, DC: American Psychological Association.
Ralph, R. O., & Corrigan, P. W. (Eds.). (2005). *Recovery in mental illness.* Washington, DC: American Psychological Association.
Saleeby, D. (2002). *The strengths perspective in social work practice* (3rd ed.). Boston, MA: Allyn & Bacon.
Shawn, A. (2007). *Wish I could be there: Notes from a phobic life.* London, UK: Penguin Books
Smith, T. B. (2004). *Practicing multiculturalism: Affirming diversity in counseling and psychology.* Boston, MA: Allyn & Bacon.
Sue, D. W., & Sue, D. (2008). *Counseling the culturally diverse: Theory and practice* (5th ed.). Hoboken, NJ: John Wiley & Sons.
Torrey, E. F. (2014). *American psychosis: How the federal government destroyed the mental illness treatment system.* New York, NY: Oxford University Press.
Yamada, A. M., & Brekke, J. S. (2008). Addressing mental health disparities through clinical competence not just cultural competence: The need for assessment of sociocultural issues in the delivery of evidence-based psychosocial rehabilitation services. *Clinical Psychology Review, 28*, 1386–1399.
Zailckas, K. (2005). *Smashed: Story of a drunken girlhood.* London, UK: Penguin Books.

Index

CPSIA information can be obtained
at www.ICGtesting.com
Printed in the USA
LVOW04s2334110917
548301LV00007B/47/P

9 780826 126627